ı, less than twenty years after the US Navy's 'Black Ships' under
ıodore Perry first displayed the might of the industrialized
ro an isolated and still largely feudal Japan, the administration
new Meiji Emperor sent a high-ranking delegation to the USA
ʾurope, to negotiate treaties and trading agreements and to
ıgate how Japan might modernize its political and economic
ıtions.

ɪ by Foreign Minister Prince Iwakura Tomomi, the 'embassy' of
ʾıcians, courtiers and officials set out for San Francisco on the
ıc mail steamer *America*, and thence on the Union Pacific
ʾoad to Washington and a meeting with President Ulysses
rant. It also travelled to Chicago and New York, to Philadelphia
Boston, observing the infrastructure, industries and institutions
ıat it soon recognized as a new land of boundless enterprise and
ırtunity.

fʾer fully eight months in the USA the embassy turned its
ıtions to the Old World, where it spent a further year examining
ʾɪh manufacturing industry, German armaments and French
ıre; meeting crowned heads and chancellors, including Queen
ʾɪria and Otto von Bismarck; and observing men and manners
ı Liverpool to Vienna, from St. Petersburg to Marseilles. It sailed
tʊ ɪome, via the recently opened Suez Canal, in July 1873.

ʾhe Iwakura Embassy helped change the course of Japanese history,
for the official report of this unprecedented epic journey, compiled by
Prince Iwakura's personal secretary, the young Confucian scholar
Kume Kunitake, was to play a key role in Japan's transformation into
a modern industrial nation. The report was translated into English in
five large volumes in 2002. This carefully prepared abridgement
makes it accessible to a wider range of scholars and students, and to all
who are interested in the remarkable rise of modern Japan.

D1612957

# JAPAN RISING

*The Iwakura Embassy to the USA*
*and Europe 1871–1873*

COMPILED BY

KUME KUNITAKE

EDITED BY

CHUSHICHI TSUZUKI

AND

R. JULES YOUNG

WITH AN INTRODUCTION BY

IAN NISH

CAMBRIDGE
UNIVERSITY PRESS

CAMBRIDGE UNIVERSITY PRESS
Cambridge, New York, Melbourne, Madrid, Cape Town, Singapore, São Paulo, Delhi

Cambridge University Press
The Edinburgh Building, Cambridge CB2 8RU, UK

Published in the United States of America by Cambridge University Press, New York

www.cambridge.org
Information on this title: www.cambridge.org/9780521735162

First published 2009

Printed in the United Kingdom at the University Press, Cambridge

*A catalogue record for this publication is available from the British Library*

Library of Congress Cataloguing in Publication data
Kume, Kunitake, 1839–1931.
[Tokumei Zenken Taishi Bei-Ō kairan jikki. English. Selections]
Japan rising : the Iwakura embassy to the USA and Europe 1871–1873 /
Kume Kunitake ... [et al.].
p. cm.
Includes bibliographical references and index.
ISBN 978-0-521-51385-2 (hardback)
1. Europe–Description and travel. 2. United States–Description and travel.
3. Iwakura Shisetsudan (Japan) 4. Kume, Kunitake, 1839–1931.
5. Japan–Foreign relations–Europe. 6. Europe–Foreign relations–Japan.
7. Japan–Foreign relations–United States. 8. United States–Foreign relations–Japan.
9. Japan–Foreign relations–1868–1912. I. Kume, Kunitake, 1839–1931. II. Title.
D919.K9513 2009
914.04′287–dc22 2009000066

ISBN 978-0-521-51385-2 hardback
ISBN 978-0-521-73516-2 paperback

# Contents

# *Introduction*

This is an introduction to the journey of the Iwakura Embassy which was sent out by the Japanese government in 1871. It was an ambitious journey round the globe and lasted for nineteen months. The chronicler of the Mission, Kume Kunitake, skilfully indicates both the wonderment of the visitors at what they saw and the hard-working intensity of their programmes. On the other side, it shows the open-heartedness of the countries visited whose citizens were ready to show off their wares and share their technology with their unfamiliar visitors from Japan.

Kume Kunitake (1839–1931) was chosen by Prince Iwakura as his secretary for the journey. Kume, a young Confucian scholar from a samurai background, was born in the domain of Saga in the island of Kyushu, not far from Nagasaki. That port was the access-point for foreign traders, whether from China, Korea or the Netherlands, in the days of Japan's seclusion from the rest of the world. Through his father's bureaucratic connections with trade, Kume would presumably have become acquainted with some of the ways of the non-Japanese world. His experiences by the age of thirty-two were such that he was neither bewildered nor star-struck by what he discovered as the Embassy travelled round the world's capitals and met the world's leaders. On the contrary he makes shrewd observations throughout. It was Kume's task to take notes and, on his return to Japan, to edit them for publication.

## THE RELUCTANT OPENING OF JAPAN

To understand the motives for the Iwakura Embassy one needs to examine the main issue which worried the Japanese at the time, that of the unfairness of the treaties which they had been forced to sign by foreign countries which wanted Japan to end its isolation and start trading with them.

Foreign interest in Japan began with the visit of Commodore Matthew Perry of the US East India squadron on 8 July 1853 to Uraga, a small port at the entrance to Tokyo Bay. Perry's 'Black Ships' were symbols of technological progress which scared the Japanese. But Perry had instructions to present gifts and not to open fire. Japan was then governed by the shogun based at Edo (Tokyo), the representative of a warrior family which had kept Japan under strict control since the start of the seventeenth century. The shogun's representative accepted the letter which Perry conveyed from President Millard Fillimore and circulated it among the leadership. By this bold step Perry succeeded in breaking the seclusion which had encompassed Japan for over two hundred years. As a precaution against future foreign encroachments, the shogun authorized the building of ocean-going craft and lifted the ban on Japanese going abroad.

A year later Perry returned to Japanese waters, this time with a squadron of nine vessels, including the *Powhatan*, a steamship of 2400 tons. He called for a response to Fillimore's letter and presented the draft of a treaty. Impressed by the opulence and resources of the Americans, the Japanese concluded the US–Japan Treaty of Peace and Amity on 31 March 1854. The main provision was for the small ports of Shimoda and Hakodate to be opened, largely as harbours of refuge, but no mention was made of trade.

Within six months, the fears of the Japanese about further foreign intrusions were confirmed. The British Far East squadron under Admiral Sir James Stirling visited Tokyo Bay, demanding a treaty of a different type. Britain, which was pursuing Russian ships in East Asian waters as one aspect of the Crimean War of 1854, asked for access to Japanese ports for the repair of its naval vessels. The shogunate concluded treaties with Britain which opened the more important ports of Nagasaki and Hakodate.

The United States appointed Townsend Harris as consul at Shimoda. He succeeded in concluding on board the *Powhatan* on 29 July 1858 the US–Japan Treaty of Amity and Commerce which opened five ports for international trade. These were Hakodate, Kanagawa (Yokohama), Nagasaki and (to be opened later) Hyogo (Kobe) and Niigata. The most important of these was Yokohama, which offered a good deep-water anchorage. Harris had succeeded in persuading Japan reluctantly to adopt a free-trade policy, only excluding transactions in opium.

The Dutch, Russian, British and French governments then sent their representatives to negotiate treaties with Japan. Within a month the first three had concluded treaties, adopting many of Harris's terms and incorporating 'most favoured nation' provisions. The French followed suit in October. But the shogunal government, which had agreed to open the country, ran into domestic opposition, especially from the emperor's court in Kyoto. Attacks took place on foreigners in the new treaty ports and on Japanese and others associated with them, notably Hendrik Heusken, the secretary and interpreter to Townsend Harris, who was killed in a night-time brawl. The shogun, unable to suppress anti-foreign violence, appealed to London and Washington to postpone the opening of the two ports and cities as specified in the 1858 treaties.

It was laid down in Harris's treaty that the ratifications should be exchanged in Washington. To that end the Japanese sent a mission to the United States in March 1860. Harris was enthusiastic about the idea and thought that it would be good for the Japanese to learn about his country. But the delegation which sailed on the *Powhatan* to San Francisco and travelled on by Panama to Washington showed no great curiosity beyond the specific task of ratification. In this respect its attitude differed markedly from that of the Iwakura Mission a decade later. It complied meekly with the programme set out by the State Department.

Because of its Civil War (1861–5) and the relatively small number of American merchants on the China coast, the United States was less well placed than Britain to take advantage of these treaties. British merchants rushed to Japan from the Chinese ports, but it was at a price. Life in Japan was not easy for foreigners and could be positively dangerous. Japanese were generally hostile to these foreign contacts, and the samurai of the Choshu and Satsuma clans were especially implicated in attacks on foreign merchants and diplomats.

This led the British government to authorize its ships to retaliate by bombarding Kagoshima, the capital of the Satsuma clan (1863). In retaliation for attacks on American and French ships off Shimonoseki, the port of the Choshu clan, the Western powers took punitive action there the following year and staged a further bombardment. The clans on the receiving end of these assaults now changed their attitude. From being hostile to foreigners and seclusionist, they showed a desire to catch up with the West and were ready to send their ambitious young samurai overseas to learn foreign skills. By the end of the decade there were many young Japanese studying abroad.

CHANGE OF GOVERNMENT, 1868

The clans on the periphery of the country took up arms against the Tokugawa shogun, the supreme authority of the day, and a civil war

ensued in 1867–8. The Tokugawa family was defeated and handed over
power to a coalition of rebellious clans who took over in Edo. The
emperor who had for centuries lived in seclusion in Kyoto was invited to
become head of state; and Mutsuhito, the youngster who was later to be
given the reign-title of Meiji, moved his capital to Edo which was now
renamed Tokyo. This tumultuous change of government after centuries
of tranquillity was described as 'the Meiji Restoration', implying that it
was an attempt to restore imperial rule in place of that by the shogun.
This outcome was not directly caused by outside powers forcing the
Tokugawa to stand down, but it was certainly influenced by the difficulties the ruling family had faced in handling pressure from foreign
governments. In the new government representatives of the rebellious
Choshu and Satsuma clans predominated. Paradoxically these clans
which had earlier opposed the treaties opening Japan now came out in
favour of investigating and imitating the rest of the world in order that
the new united country should be able to stand up against the West.

On the domestic front the government made fundamental social
changes, abolishing the clans, ending feudalism and bringing an end to
the role of the samurai. It centralized the administration. Feudal lords,
court nobles and government officials were pledged to support the
Charter Oath which in five articles set out the programme of modernization. The Restoration government felt confident that its new progressive
measures to abolish feudalism would be welcomed in Western countries.
As early as February 1868 the head of the Board of Foreign Affairs called
together the diplomatic corps at the port of Kobe and informed them of
the restoration of rule by the emperor. Foreign governments duly recognized the new administration.

The new government thought that the treaties of 1858 were humiliating
and 'unequal' and blamed the Tokugawa rulers for their weakness in
agreeing to them. It further emphasized its desire to renegotiate the
unequal clauses of the old treaties or to devise entirely new foreign
treaties. In the case of the United States, the existing treaty was due to
expire on 1 July 1872 after fourteen years.

The idea had been maturing that an exploratory embassy from the new
government to its treaty partners would be necessary. On 29 August 1871
Prince Iwakura Tomomi (1825–83), the aristocrat and former court official who had come to accept the need for opening up Japan to trade, was
appointed foreign minister. He announced that he would head a special
mission to observe Western countries at first hand and exchange views on
treaty revision before starting to negotiate with the United States and the

nations of Europe. The Embassy set off on 23 December, carrying letters from the Emperor Meiji to heads of state which constituted the mission's credentials. Iwakura was clearly charged with the task of discussing substantive issues regarding treaty negotiations; but the authority he had to sign documents that would form the basis of formalized treaties was more ambiguous. This ambiguity led to many complications for the Mission, especially in the United States.

### COMPOSITION OF THE DELEGATION

The members of the Iwakura Mission were young but they all had government experience. Although Kume in his report refers to these members as 'we' and tends to omit mention of individuals by name, these were significant statesmen and strong-minded individualists. Prince Iwakura originated from the emperor's court and was a government minister. He was accompanied as vice-ambassadors by Kido Koin (Takayoshi) (1833–77) and Okubo Toshimichi, minister of finance (1830–78), who represented the Restoration government, being the most prominent politicians from Choshu and Satsuma respectively. They were assisted by deputy ambassadors: Yamaguchi Naoyoshi of the Hizen clan (1842–94), assistant vice minister of foreign affairs, and Ito Hirobumi of Choshu (1841–1909) who came from the Ministry of Public Works. The most Westernized of his senior colleagues, Ito had already spent time in London and visited Washington for six months in 1870 in his capacity as a finance official, and admitted receiving 'most valuable assistance from the Treasury Department'. By virtue of the time he had spent overseas, he was able to speak passable English and was the deputy ambassador often called upon to deliver the formal addresses at receptions.

In addition there were some 45 clerks and commissioners, who were charged with writing specialized reports. There were also junior officials and students who temporarily put aside their quest for education and were expected to run errands for the dignitaries. This made up the full complement of 108 people who left Japan's shores. It was a balanced delegation of progressive forces within the Restoration government. Apart from Iwakura, they were young men, the average age being 32. Though they already had some experience of high office, they were not always in agreement over policy, and they squabbled among themselves throughout their travels.

When they reached the United States, the visitors had access to Japan's skeletal diplomatic staff there. The Japanese minister in Washington was

Mori Arinori (1847–89) of Satsuma. He had been trained in London for two years and gone to the United States in 1867 for study. Since his appointment, Mori had developed good contacts with the State Department and within Washington society. Though he was not a member of the delegation, he acted occasionally as interpreter and had the overall responsibility for arranging for the comfort of the visitors. His knowledge of the country put him in a strong position to argue over the course of action the ambassadors should pursue and his views were to have an important bearing on their deliberations. To assist the ambassadors, Mori was also able to assemble in Washington students who had found their way independently to the United States. Iwakura's own son was one of those already there.

It was remarkable that in a country like Japan which had recently come through civil war and 'restoration', so many important leaders could be spared for such a lengthy journey. At the point of departure, of course, it could not be foreseen that the Embassy would encounter such considerable delays as occurred in the United States and Britain. But the sheer size of the group was amazing, and created considerable administrative problems. It goes without saying that there were acute jealousies between those who were able to join the deputation and those who were left behind in Tokyo. Before the party left, there was a compact between them whereby the Embassy would not make any commitments without consulting the home government, and the Tokyo government would not take any major steps in their absence. These undertakings were not scrupulously observed, leading to bitter feelings when the party eventually returned to Japan in 1873.

The Mission had three comprehensive aims: to visit countries with which Japan had entered into treaties and raise its profile there; to inspect institutions in advanced countries which would be helpful for Japan's modernization; and to begin soundings for the revision of the treaties and present the Japanese standpoint. Before departure Iwakura said positively that he would not renegotiate the treaties while he was abroad. But it was still a primary task to ventilate the issue and try to convince opinion abroad in favour of a revision of the 'unequal treaties' which the Meiji government had inherited from its predecessors.

One historical question is why the delegates went to the United States first against the advice of a respected foreign adviser, Dr Guido Verbeck, who suggested that they should start their study in Europe. They presumably thought that the United States would be a more favourable and liberal starting-point and were perhaps suspicious of Britain after her aggressive inroads into China. In the case of the United States, moreover, there was an advancing frontier which had reached California, a neighbour on the coastline of the Pacific Ocean and one that was linked from 1869 by the trans-continental railroad to its eastern seaboard.


ACROSS THE AMERICAN CONTINENT

On the morning of 15 January the US-owned Pacific mail steamer *America* arrived at San Francisco with its 108 Japanese passengers. Of these, 50 constituted the members of the Embassy, while the remainder consisted of 5 young ladies of rank, 53 young gentlemen of noble families, and domestics. They were accompanied by the Hon. Charles E. DeLong, American minister to Japan. Mrs. DeLong had custody of the young ladies, who were much the same age as her own daughters and were on their way to college. W.S. Rice of the American legation at Edo attended as interpreter, though a few of the members of the ambassadors' staff could speak tolerable English.

Kume sets out the Mission's itinerary in diary fashion. It includes a day-by-day account of the weather with (as the hot weather approached) details of temperatures. It is best to leave the text to speak for itself, but certain general points should be stressed. Japan was a non-industrial country with a small-scale agriculture. The delegates were astonished at the agricultural states they passed through. But they were equally amazed at the smoke rising from chimneys of factories in the urban centres they visited. They unquestionably suffered from culture shock, not least sartorially. One observer recounts an example of their adaptability:

Members of the Embassy appeared at the reception [in Washington in March] in complete court costume, of satin purple underskirts and rich black overskirts reaching to the knees, each one carrying a long sword at his silken girdle. This was their last appearance in what to our eyes appeared a grotesque costume . . . Not one member during their long sojourn in the Western hemisphere of 18 months, ever appeared afterwards in public, with what we would call feminine garments made of silks and satins . . . At state ceremonies they dressed in a mixed European court costume, while in public they appeared in broad cloth coats and trowsers [sic], wearing chimney-pot hats and boots with elastics [which] did not improve their appearance in dignity or elegance. (Mossman, p. 433)

While this account may be exaggerated, the writer reports that the delegates were nonetheless distinguished in manner and gravity. Moreover they had within a day changed to 'attire suitable to a visiting diplomatic delegation'. Only the head of the Mission, Prince Iwakura, continued generally to wear the ground-length kimono appropriate for a courtier. The contrasting styles were an indication of their thinking: they were quick to adjust their mode of dress to conform to international conventions but they were also proud that Iwakura should continue to wear traditional Japanese clothes.

The Mission traversed the whole American continent by rail, a major source of interest for the new Meiji government. As soon as the Restoration government came to power, it had decided to build railways. As a pioneering venture it had started building the eighteen-mile Shimbashi (Tokyo) to Yokohama line in 1870 with the help of British engineers, to be opened for traffic in 1872. But major problems emerged – natural obstacles, the lack of finance and the scarcity of managerial skills. The ambassadors had, therefore, a practical interest in all aspects of American railroads: port facilities, tunnels, bridges and how the railways coped with gradients. They suffered for their experience. The Union Pacific Railroad on which they embarked in February could not cope with the heavy snowfalls on the Rocky Mountains and beyond, which stopped all traffic. The ambassadors were snowed up at Salt Lake City for eighteen days, visiting the famous Mormon Tabernacle and meeting Brigham Young. Despite the snow and the floods that followed, Kume reports enthusiastically about the overall rail experience:

Thanks to the admirable engineering achievement of the Central Pacific Railroad Company, we were able to cross much of this vast territory in a train, comfortably relaxing or sleeping. (Kume, p. 32)

After passing through Chicago and Pittsburgh, the delegation arrived in the capital at the end of February. On 4 March ten of its principal members were presented to President Ulysses Grant by Minister DeLong. In his address Iwakura promised to 'consult with your government on all international questions, directing our efforts to promote and develop wide commercial relations', while the president replied that 'it will be a pleasure for us to enter upon that consultation upon international questions in which you say you are authorized to engage' (Mossman, p. 433).

It was then that the Mission learnt from Minister Mori that, after the many exchanges of views he had had, there was a distinct possibility that the State Department might be responsive to the idea of revising the 1858 treaty without delay. Clearly the delegates had run into an unforeseen problem in that they had not received a specific mandate to negotiate

before leaving Japan and had not brought adequate powers of accredi-
tation. The crucial decision was made that two of the senior members,
Okubo and Ito, should return to Japan in order to procure the necessary
documents. They left Washington on 20 March for their daunting
journey of 3000 miles by land and 5000 miles by sea.

Meanwhile the remainder of the delegation held intermittent discussions with various government departments and institutions and undertook sightseeing trips in the Washington area. As summer set in, they
embarked at the invitation of the US government on what Kume calls
'The Journey Through the Northern States'. On 10 June they set off for
upstate New York, calling at West Point, Albany, Rochester, Syracuse and
on to Niagara. It was of course educational for Iwakura and his party and
compensated for the delay and the intolerable heat. On their return to
Washington on 22 June they found that diplomatic business was almost
at a standstill. An element of frustration set in. Kume records mournfully
that 'We did little worth recording. All we could do during the day was try
to keep cool by taking carriage rides to see various sights' (Kume, p. 88).

Such a lengthy stay for the enormous retinue was a burden for the
Americans, but Congress had made an appropriation of $50,000 for
entertaining the Japanese, so part of the Embassy's expenses was paid by its
hosts. American leaders clearly saw great potential in the members of the
delegation who were likely to be the leaders of Japan in the next generation.

Okubo and Ito did not return from Japan until 20 July. They brought
better credentials but were given instructions not to conclude a new treaty
with the United States alone but to propose convening an international
conference on the subject. The Embassy went to the State Department
the same afternoon only to discover that Secretary of State Hamilton Fish
would not agree to negotiations alongside other powers, especially if they
were to be held in Europe. Fish, like some of the Japanese delegates, was
bitterly disappointed that this aspect of their discussions had come to
nothing. But some delegates like Kido thought that the prospect of an
immediate settlement of the treaty issue had always been wishful thinking
on the part of the Japanese. The failure on this one point during their
American stay arose from a lack of clarity in Japanese thinking. It was
something that the Mission did not pursue during the rest of its world
tour: its members ventilated the issue but merely explored the views of the
countries they were visiting.

Two days later Iwakura went to the White House and announced that
his party would soon be leaving the country. After short visits to Baltimore,
Philadelphia and New York, on 6 August the ambassadors left from

Boston for Liverpool. They had prolonged their stay in the United States beyond all expectations. They had been industrious: there were few cities of importance that they had not visited and few public offices or national institutions that they had not inspected. But it was disappointing that the main delegation had to spend so long marking time. If treaty revision had made little progress, there were consolations in the detailed understanding it acquired about American educational methods and institutions.


FOUR MONTHS IN BRITAIN

Because of their protracted stay in the United States, their schedule for Britain was greatly delayed. Eventually the Mission reached Liverpool on 17 August in the middle of the holiday season. It had travelled from a pioneering society moving rapidly towards industrialization to a country which had already experienced an industrial revolution and its dire consequences. No sooner had Kume reached the south bank of the Mersey than he records:

[T]he smoke of coal fires billowed up in dense clouds [over Liverpool] to a height of two or three hundred feet, permanently darkening the blue sky. Our escorts pointed to this and said, 'The people of the city have to breathe in the midst of that black haze.' So great is the city's prosperity. (Kume, p. 139)

Between September and early November the delegates, either individually or in groups, visited twenty British cities and travelled over 2000 miles. By this time they tended to break up into smaller units and pursue their individual interests and assignments. The main body moved from London to visit industrial centres like Manchester and Glasgow with hectic daily rounds. When they reached Edinburgh, they were so exhausted by the daily round of inspecting factories and offices that their escort urged them to visit the Scottish Highlands and relax. Kume reported:

The view of the flat English landscape and of the Scottish lowlands was one of unrelieved monotony. The hills of Edinburgh were pretty enough, but there was more than this to the beauties of the Scottish landscape. (Kume, p. 166)

Duly revived by his holiday, Iwakura proceeded to industrial centres like Newcastle, Sheffield and Birmingham before returning to London. He met Foreign Secretary Lord Granville on 22 November and again five days later, making it clear that Japan's ultimate objective was to negotiate certain modifications to the existing treaties in order to bring them into line with the political transformations that had taken place in Japan since 1868. He also asked for the British troops stationed in Yokohama to be withdrawn. For his part, Granville complained about the lack of religious toleration in Japan and the inability of foreigners to go upcountry. There was cordiality in the exchanges but not amity. The delegation, which had waited long for Queen Victoria's return from Balmoral, eventually had an audience with her at Windsor Castle on 5 December and presented a letter from the Emperor Meiji.

CONTINENTAL EUROPE

The Embassy arrived in Calais from Dover on 16 December at the start of its tour of Europe. Rather than deal with its visit to continental Europe country by country, let us examine in particular the general map of their travels and try to analyse what aspects interested them. The timing of their arrival in France over the Christmas period was not ideal. The initial focus of their activities was on Paris; and the visitors took part in talks with officials on treaty revision and on religious freedom for Japanese Christians. This was followed by shorter visits to Belgium and Holland, which naturally had a special link with Japan because of the existence of a Dutch settlement at Deshima in Kyushu island over the previous centuries.

The Embassy allocated three weeks for its initial stay in Germany but it in fact returned to tour the north and south of the country later in its schedule. The delegates' stay included influential interviews with Otto von Bismarck who gave them a memorable speech which was transcribed by one of the commissioners and reproduced in full in Kume's report (Kume, pp. 306–7). The impact of the German Chancellor certainly had a considerable effect on the thinking of politicians of the Meiji period on military, constitutional and other matters. By late spring the domestic situation in Japan was causing the government that remained there some alarm. It was sufficient for them to call for the return of the deputy leaders, first Okubo and then Kido. The latter, the intellectual of the Embassy, did not want to miss visiting Russia and delayed his departure accordingly.

The main party continued its circuit to Russia, which was only allocated two weeks because it was not thought to have much relevance to the problems of the emergent Japan. After this Iwakura led his members to Sweden, while Kido's group travelled round Austria-Hungary, Italy,

Switzerland and France at a leisurely pace before arriving at Marseilles to board the ship for home. Iwakura with Kume went to Italy and Austria-Hungary where they paid several visits to the Vienna Universal Exposition. This was the first exhibition in which Japan had taken part, albeit in a modest way, and was to have a great influence on its attitudes towards exhibitions later in the century. Kume expresses pride in the Japanese artifacts on view.

The full Mission received instructions to return to Japan on 9 June so it could not complete its coverage of Europe by visiting Spain and Portugal. After spending a few weeks in Switzerland and southern France, it joined its ship on 20 July at Marseilles.

As representatives of a new nation born out of a civil war, the Japanese were anxious to visit countries with similar experiences. While in the United States they had seen changes brought about by the civil war of 1861–5, they were the witnesses of more dramatic changes in Europe. As Kume observed, they arrived in Paris in 'France's hour of deepest misfortune' (Kume, p. 227). It was its defeat by Prussia which brought about the fall of the empire of Napoleon III. When President Thiers received his guests, he was beset by the problem of pushing through a republican constitution which would address the concerns of the Paris Commune and the urgent issue of raising the indemnity payable to Germany in order to secure the evacuation of German troops from French soil. Meanwhile Prussia used her victory over France to declare the foundation of the German Empire in 1871. This German unification brought together the various divergent principalities which made up the German Confederation. But, if German unification had been the result of a short, sharp shock, that of Italy had been created slowly over the previous decade. It reached its culmination when the Papal territories, the last link in the chain, were brought within the fold of a new Italy and Rome became the new national capital. These radical changes were very relevant to Japan where the problems of creating a nation out of a congeries of clans and the centralization of government in a new national capital at Tokyo were very much in the minds of Iwakura's delegates. Although European countries approached these issues differently, the members of the Iwakura team took pains to study their common problems.

The Japanese were able to achieve their object of observing European societies with a view to using 'the new knowledge' for their own purposes because the governments were ready to show off their wares. But let us remember that the subjects for inspection were not entirely self-selected. The Japanese were, at one level, open to the suggestions of the foreign advisers who were attached to their suites and, at another, to those of the governments which were hosting their visits, and those in the local area who offered them the hospitality of their municipalities and country houses.

The general impression given by the ambassadors and their underlings was that they were collecting information on virtually any subject. But let us consider the subjects on which they concentrated.

## Industry and Trade

Clearly factory visits were a first priority for the Japanese, who wanted to know how the new industries worked. Those visited included iron and steel plants, textile mills (cotton, wool and silk), carpets and glass. They took part in inspections of more specialized factories like the Naumann factory in Germany which supplied Japan's demand for banknotes and Swedish match manufacturers.

One of the delegation's other aspirations was to expand Japan's trade with the rest of the world. The existing trade between Europe and Japan had traditionally been limited to the Dutch and had recently been opened up by Britain and France. Now that Japan was open for commerce, the opportunity was fast approaching for all European countries to develop markets in the east. All European leaders from Prince Bismarck downwards were interested in the prospects of trade with Japan and anxious to cultivate Japanese traders. Kume remarks: '[T]he attention we have hitherto devoted to London and Paris must now be shared with Berlin and Vienna' (Kume, p. 300).

## Military–Naval

The visitors were assumed to have military interests and were taken round battlefields, especially those connected with the Franco-Prussian war. They also visited ordnance factories, arsenals, shipyards, fleet depots and port facilities generally. Its members who came on the whole from military backgrounds were welcomed on board battleships and introduced to up-to-date military–naval technology. They asked to see military academies and barracks and attended countless military parades. They met international armament producers like Sir William Armstrong at Elswick near Newcastle and Alfred Krupp in Essen, the hub of the Ruhr.

As a seafaring nation, Japan was anxious to install modern facilities which would prevent accidents. In Britain the Commissioners of the Northern Lighthouses arranged for visits to their lighthouses off the east coast; and arrangements for the building of further lighthouses were made.

*Transportation*

Japan was about to launch a programme of railway building. Much as the emissaries enjoyed travelling around by rail, they were primarily interested in the lessons to be learnt from Europe's rail experience. Their country with its mountains and fast-flowing rivers was an inherently difficult terrain for railway-building and they were interested in the technology of tunnels and bridges as employed in European countries. Some members of the party also expressed a wish to travel on the London underground whose Metropolitan line had not long opened. The success of the Embassy depended greatly on innovations in transport, whether by steamship or by rail.

*Royalty*

The Japanese visitors met the crowned heads of Europe and the leading world statesmen in the course of their journey. One Japanese newspaper was impressed by their celebrity and wrote:

Kings and Queens opened their palaces to them, nobles and corporations feted them, the populace followed and ran after them . . . Had they been royal princes visiting nations where every door flies open before exalted rank, they could not have been met with more warmth, more interest or with a greater readiness to serve them. (*Japan Mail*, Feb. 1874)

They were received hospitably by every royal house and were awarded honours. Their purpose in observing courts was to discover the relationship which existed between European monarchs and their subjects. This was very relevant to the position of the new Japanese emperor, who had only been on the political scene for three years. But the dignitaries were treated with respect wherever they went and also studied the constitutions of republican states like the United States, France and Switzerland.

*Institutions*

Turning to the cultural front, the Embassy had a wide remit to visit hospitals, universities and schools (including charity schools and girls' colleges). Occasionally they attended theatres, though their appreciation was limited because their knowledge of foreign languages was often inadequate. They were frequently to be found at museums and exhibitions.

On the related issue of religion, the Embassy could not escape the wrath of foreign statesmen who championed the cause of the Christian churches in Japan. The Restoration government whose representatives they were was rather vulnerable on this subject. It had persisted with the imprisonment of Christians at Urakami in Nagasaki domain. The US government and virtually all the European governments were, therefore, quick to raise officially with the visitors the need for Christian missionaries and converts to be protected under the new enlightened regime. These representations were successful and the outcome was that the Tokyo government announced in March 1873 that the prohibition of Christianity would come to an end, that signs banning it would be removed and that a policy of tolerance towards Christian believers would be observed. The 3000 Catholics imprisoned at Urakami were released and returned to their villages. This shows the influence wielded by the commissioners, even when abroad.

Kume, expressing a personal view, was far from convinced. He is critical in his observations on Christianity. His comments on the Christian churches and Christian statuary which he found in the United States are less than complimentary. When he moves to Britain, he observes that 'the intensity of religious observance dropped a degree, but when we moved from Britain to France, it dropped one or two degrees more. Indeed, nowhere on the continent of Europe did we see anything to compare with the strength of religious practice in America and Britain' (Kume, p. 223). His perceptive conclusion is that 'those brought up on the political morality of East Asia cannot imagine the influence which religion exerts [in the world]' (Kume, p. 280).

On its return journey the party travelled through the Suez Canal. They paused at Aden and the port of Galle in Sri Lanka (then British Ceylon). After they were forced to pass by Singapore because of an outbreak of typhoid, they did manage to visit hotels in Saigon, Hong Kong and Shanghai. This afforded them the opportunity to see colonialism and the spread of the great European empires at first hand.

By 13 September 1873 when the main body reached Yokohama, most of the other delegates had already returned. They found Japan in a dangerous state and not very welcoming. They made it clear that they favoured the cause of reform but found that Japan had to establish peace and stability before they could deal with the implementation of the findings reached during their travels. Kido, the deputy leader of the group, prepared an important memorandum in October advocating constitutional government, perhaps the single most significant outcome of the Mission. But reforms took time, and the leaders were determined not to rush them. In any case, Kido, who returned home as a sick man, retired from politics in 1874 and died three years later. His colleague, Okubo, died at the hands of an assassin in 1878. Prince Iwakura, who survived an attempt on his life in 1874, died in 1883. It was, therefore, the youngest of the leaders, Ito Hirobumi, who became an imperial councillor and steered through the developments in Japanese politics and industrialization for the rest of the century. Ito had had a large hand in the preparation of the Mission and was able through his public-works connections to make significant appointments of foreign nationals to posts in Japan. After four decades of public service, his life eventually ended in assassination in 1909 by a Korean. Japan itself remained a dangerous place to be a politician.

KUME ASSEMBLES THE EVIDENCE

After the return of the mission, Kume was charged with writing its official report, which was entitled *Tokumei zenken taishi Bei-Ō kairan jikki* (literally, 'the true version of the tour of the special embassy to the United States and Europe'). This was eventually published in 1878 in five volumes. Four reprints were issued up to 1883, and it is estimated that the overall total of copies sold was 3500. In his reports each country is given a 'survey' and each major city which was visited by the Embassy is described in a 'record'. There are at the end four chapters with general observations. The author also notes with regret that he was only able to include one or two things out of every thousand on which he had taken notes. While it was an official publication, it does contain many reflections which must have come from the pen and thinking of Kume himself and could not be attributed to the leaders he served.

Kume clearly bore in mind that his readers were generally ignorant of the rest of the world but knew enough to be intrigued by it. His chapters include a geography and history lesson for each country. While the text is, at one level, simplistic, there are passages which show remarkable shrewdness and penetrating insights. First, an insight from the United States where the Embassy visited first and stayed for over half a year:

Such people [Europeans] opened up and pioneered this land of freedom and have nurtured their spirit of enterprise here. Although they say that this country has relied on new creativity, new development and new immigrants, in reality America is a land of people who, in Europe, felt the urge for independence and self-government most strongly. (Kume, p. 104)

Then some insights on the comparative league-table of countries in Europe as Kume viewed them:

In both England and France, for example, civilisation flourishes and industry and commerce prosper together. However, when one looks at the products of Belgium and Switzerland, the achievements of their peoples in attaining independence and accumulating wealth would impress even the largest nation. Prussia is a large country and Saxony a small one, but the latter is by no means inferior to the former in the industrial arts. Conversely, Russia is a large country, but it cannot stand alongside these nations. (Kume, pp. 429–30)

Kume's report had an impact on a Meiji Japan which was ambitious for change. The lessons he drew came not from any one country but from the cumulative impression of the countries which the Embassy had visited. These formed the database for the remarkable grassroots transformation that took place in Japan as the reign of the Emperor Meiji progressed. Apart from Kume's work, but associated with it, were the many specialized reports compiled by the junior officials who accompanied the Mission. It seems to have targeted certain countries on its itinerary as special areas for study, e.g. Britain for information on the industrial revolution, and Germany for military information. In the United States it would appear that the officials were particularly trying to understand its forms of government, local, state and national, and its educational methods. They painstakingly studied the basic laws of the American constitution with the help of Japanese scholars already at US universities and paid many visits to legislatures. These comparative studies, ranging over the northern hemisphere, were to lead in time to far-reaching constitutional amendments and to the introduction of universal education which was vital to nation-building in Japan.

Kume was discriminating and not averse to criticizing what he saw. He was full of gratitude for foreign hospitality the Mission had received and appreciative of the privilege of observing and studying foreign societies at close quarters. But on occasions Kume is less than impressed. As we have seen earlier, he reports unfavourably on Western religion. Another specific case was on a visit to West Point in the United States which had refused to accept Japanese cadets on security grounds in contrast to Annapolis Naval College where they were readily admitted. On attending manoeuvres there, he writes:

We often observed large and small cannon in target practice, but compared with Japanese soldiers American gunners rarely hit the targets, giving us the impression that their gunnery skills were rather backward. In nimbleness of fingers and speed of reaction, the Japanese are superior to the Americans and the Europeans. (Kume, p. 78)

There was an essential ambiguity about the Embassy itself. On the one hand, the Japanese leaders of the time were fearful and suspicious over the imperialist ambitions of the West. On the other, they admired the West and wanted to learn from it. So their fundamental object was to study the West in order to resist the West. Let us remember that the Iwakura Mission was proud of the progress which the Restoration government had made in the three years it had been in power. But they were also open-minded and full of curiosity about improvements that could be made for their greater security.

Kume himself merits a final word. His report was an outstanding piece of work, containing shrewd analysis and compelling observations. This was recognized by the Japanese government; and he was appointed to various official posts connected with compiling Japan's national history. The oversight of this important task passed in 1888 from the cabinet office to Tokyo Imperial University where Kume became a professor lecturing in *kokushi* (national history). But in 1892 he published a controversial article about the role of Shinto which displeased conservative scholars of the day. His views became notorious; and he was forced to resign from the prestigious state university. By a paradox Kume, who had been the chronicler of new Western values, became a casualty of older Eastern values. He later joined what became Waseda University, a private college, where he taught into his 80s. He died in 1931 at the age of 91, more than half a century after the publication of the monumental study which made his name.

FURTHER READING

W.G. Beasley, *Japan Encounters the Barbarian: Japanese Travellers in America and Europe*, New Haven: Yale University Press, 1995
Sidney Devere Brown and Akiko Hirota (trans.), *The Diary of Takayoshi Kido*, vol. 2, '1871–1874', Tokyo: Tokyo University Press, 1985
Sydney Checkland, *The Elgins, 1766–1917*, Aberdeen: Aberdeen University Press, 1988
Martin Colcutt, 'Education for a New Japan: Kume Kunitake's Observations on Education in 1872 America' in Collcutt, Kato and Toby (eds.), *Japan and Its Worlds*, Tokyo: International House Press, 2007, pp. 187–208
Gordon Daniels, *Sir Harry Parkes, British Representative in Japan, 1865–83*, Folkestone: Japan Library, 1996
Toru Haga (ed.), *Iwakura shisetsudan no hikaku bunkashiteki kenkyu*, Kyoto: Shibunkaku, 2003
Shigekazu Kondo, 'Kume Kunitake as a Historiographer' in Ian Nish (ed.), *The Iwakura Mission in America and Europe: A New Assessment*, Folkestone: Japan Library, 1998

Charles Lanman, *The Japanese in America*, New York: University Publishing, 1872

William McOmie, *The Opening of Japan, 1853–5*, Folkestone: Global Oriental, 2006

Marlene Mayo, 'The Western Education of Kume Kunitake, 1871–6' in *Monumenta Nipponica*, 28(1973), 3–68

Hiroshi Mitani, *Escape from Impasse: The Decision to Open Japan*, Tokyo: International House Press, 2006

Masao Miyoshi, *As We Saw Them: The First Japanese Embassy to the United States (1860)*, Berkeley: University of California Press, 1979

Samuel Mossman, *New Japan: The Land of the Rising Sun*, London: John Murray, 1873

Ian Nish, 'The Iwakura Mission: The Issue of Treaty Revision' in Japan Society, *Proceedings* (London), 122(1993), 52–64

Akira Tanaka, *Iwakura shisetsudan no rekishiteki kenkyū*, Tokyo: Iwanami-shoten, 2002

# Note on the text

The original account of the Iwakura Embassy, compiled by Kume Kunitake, was published in Japanese in five volumes in 1878 under the title *Tokumei zenken taishi Bei-Ō kairan jikki*. A complete English translation, also in five volumes, was published by The Japan Documents in 2002, edited by Graham Healey and Chushichi Tsuzuki, entitled *The Iwakura Embassy 1871–73: A True Account of the Ambassador Extraordinary and Plenipotentiary's Journey of Observation through the United States of America and Europe*. The English translation was made by Andrew Cobbing, Martin Collcutt, Graham Healey, P. F. Kornicki, Eugene Soviak and Chushichi Tsuzuki.

This one-volume abridgement of the English translation was prepared by Chushichi Tsuzuki with the assistance of R. Jules Young. A new introduction to the abridged text has been written by Ian Nish.

Cambridge University Press is glad to take this opportunity to acknowledge the contribution of Sumio Saito, the founder of The Japan Documents project, whose vision and commitment have been instrumental in the publication of both the complete English translation and this new popular abridgement.

VOLUME I

# The United States of America

# *Preface*

These volumes contain the record of the daily activities of the Embassy which left Japan on December 23rd, 1871, and returned on September 13th, 1873 – about one year and nine months later. It was led by Iwakura Tomomi, Ambassador Extraordinary and Plenipotentiary to Europe and the United States.

The Embassy first crossed the Pacific Ocean and traversed America, then sailed across the Atlantic and travelled around England and Scotland. After that, it crossed over to Europe to visit France, Belgium, Holland, Prussia, Russia, Denmark and Sweden, subsequently passing through Germany to Italy, Austria and Switzerland. From there it went to southern France, and from the Mediterranean it sailed through the Arabian Sea into the Indian Ocean and the China Sea and so back to Tokyo. Thus, the Embassy visited most of the major cities and towns in the continents of America and Europe.

During the journey through the West, the secretaries collected all the official documents and also kept a diary of formal functions and meetings with foreign dignitaries. The councillors, who had been dispatched by various government ministries, gathered information and made numerous detailed reports pertaining to the politics, education, military affairs and commerce of each country, and these were later compiled into several large volumes. In addition to the official business of the ambassador, this book records all the facts and the actual situation observed in each region. Thus, it is called a 'True Account' of a 'Journey of Observation'. It omits discussion of social events, diplomatic exchanges and political meetings – the main objective of the Embassy – because these are covered in other books and reports.

Dispatching an ambassador is a remarkable privilege. It is the most important and respected type of delegation, and for Japan to be able to take advantage of this is truly an unparalleled achievement. We must consider ourselves fortunate to have enjoyed such an exceptional

3

opportunity in these times. The Meiji Restoration [1868] has brought about an unprecedented political transformation in Japan. Three elements were essential to this transformation: 1. Curtailing shogunal power and restoring direct rule by the emperor; 2. Amalgamating the varied administrations of the feudal domains to make a unified polity; 3. Reversing the country's isolationist policy and deciding on the degree to which it should be opened. Any one of these reforms would have been difficult to accomplish; to attempt all three at once, in a hazardous period of rapid change, was to attempt a miracle almost beyond human capability.

When we consider what has come about, we realise that everything was related to changes in world affairs. The seclusion laws had to be removed, come what may. With the country's opening, we needed a united government. Having unified the government, the power of the shogunate had to be restrained. Even the German Confederation and the Italian Papacy have not been immune to the tide of world events; numerous reforms there, tentative at first, were later successfully implemented. Japan's reform movement is no different, and the principles of our domestic politics have already been established. In order to lay the foundation for diplomatic exchanges with other countries, we have availed ourselves of this exceptional opportunity to dispatch an embassy abroad. From now on, those who hold the reins of power must recognise the aims and intentions of the reform movement and maintain its momentum. The general populace should also be made aware of its importance so that they cannot but encourage its progress.

In all the countries we visited, the ambassador presented his credentials. It was our duty to establish diplomatic relations on our government's behalf. It was also our responsibility to observe and report on local customs on behalf of the Japanese people. Therefore, each day we were fully occupied and had scant time for rest. We covered great distances in the heat and cold, travelling to remote areas to visit farms and ranches. In the cities we observed the operation of industries and commerce. Whenever time permitted we met and talked with specialists in various fields. Our journey could not be compared to that of wandering literati or religious pilgrims, who are free to move as they please. In the West it is believed that government is an assembly of the people, so an embassy dispatched by a government is regarded as representing the people.

The fact that officials in each country treated the Embassy with great hospitality indicated their cordial feelings towards our people. By showing us what their countries had to offer in achievements and productivity, they demonstrated friendship and sought favour from us as representatives of Japan. Ambassador Iwakura realised this and urged us to spare no effort in conveying where we went and what we saw to our countrymen at home.

Among the many interesting places we visited, some were made accessible to us through the kindness of that country's rulers. On occasion we were the official guests of the government (as on our tour of the northern states of America). At other times we were invited by reception committees (as on our inspection tours in England and Scotland; half of this 'True Account' is made up of such visits). We were also received by the ordinary citizens of cities, towns and villages (especially in America and Britain). We were invited by factory owners to visit their factories; we accepted invitations from noblemen, prominent figures and commoners.

When we arrived at a destination, we would hasten to an hotel to unpack and immediately set out on a tour of observation. We spent days on trains with screaming wheels and screeching whistles, careering through billowing clouds of smoke amid belching flames and the smell of iron. Soot and smoke caked our bodies and flew into our eyes. When darkness fell and we reached our hotel rooms, we scarcely had time to wipe off the dirt before it was time for the next banquet. We had to be dignified at table. We wore out our eyes and our ears at theatres. No sooner did we go to bed at night than it was time to wake up, with representatives from the next factory awaiting us. As a result, many marvellous sights and unfamiliar sounds filled our days. Day by day, our bodies and nerves grew exhausted, and we became weary of splendid dinners. We wished, just once, to enjoy the simple pleasures of drinking plain water and lying with our heads pillowed on our bent elbows, but to do so would have damaged our relations with other countries.

As I edit these volumes, I recall the wonderful sights and sounds we saw and heard on our travels to some of the most distant parts of the earth. With the passage of time, those memories now seem like images of splendid mountains engraved in my heart. Our travels are already fading into a fleeting dream, and our hardships are like wounds which have already healed. My thoughts and feelings at this time may only be appreciated by those who have experienced a similar lengthy journey.

This edition takes the form of a journal. Rather than embellishing the narrative with anecdotes and hearsay, I have tried to report exactly what we saw when we were seeing it. Because of this, an account of a factory visit, for example, may end abruptly and a description of an old palace begin. Or, when I am describing the beauty of a landscape, the reader may suddenly encounter statistics for production and trade. If the narrative seems disjointed in places, that is because it is essentially a record of events as they occurred.

In Western arts, sciences and technology, theory and practice are distinct from each other. Theory lies in so-called general rules; practice involves working with actual machinery in different fields. Neither should be favoured above the other; nor should one be neglected at the expense of the other. The main purpose of this 'True Account' lies in explaining the practical and reaffirming the theoretical. If errors have crept into my descriptions of the technological processes, readers should be able to correct them by the application of theory.

Since returning to Japan, I have constantly revised my work by referring to books on physics, chemistry, mechanics and related subjects, statistics, official reports, history, geography, politics and law. Furthermore, I made summaries of the official reports submitted by the various councillors. In the cities I recorded our conversations with doctors and scholars and have added relevant comments. In many sections I have reconstructed from memory, or patched together, what I was told.

The world is moving as rapidly as a turning wheel. The affairs of mankind rise and fall like waves in the open sea. My pen never left my hand from the day we set sail in December 1871 until our return in September 1873. I then spent several months preparing these volumes, and later expanded and revised each of them several times. Three years have now elapsed, and many developments have occurred in the world at large. Hardly a week goes by without some changes in commerce, law or international relations. I describe thriving silk industries in England and France, but since then they have declined in value every year. Moreover, changes in the price of tea from the British colony of Assam in India have had a major effect on Japan. Nevertheless, if the countries we visited remain at peace and their civilisations advance, I expect them to flourish still further in the next five years.

*January 1876*                                              Kume Kunitake
                                            *Private Secretary to the Ambassador*

# CHAPTER I

# The Voyage Across the Pacific

December 21st, 1871. Winter solstice.
Ambassador Extraordinary and Plenipotentiary to Europe and the United
States Iwakura Tomomi and Vice-Ambassadors Kido Takayoshi, Ōkubo
Toshimichi, Itō Hirobumi and Yamaguchi Naoyoshi, with a retinue of
councillors and officials from various ministries, totalling forty-eight in
all, left Tokyo for Yokohama, where they stayed at several inns.

December 22nd. Fine.
On this day relatives and friends who lived in the capital came to attend
farewell parties before the long voyage. At six in the evening a dinner was
given at the Yokohama Court House for the consuls and ministers representing various foreign countries.

December 23rd. Fine; rain at night.
The recent fine weather has continued and the cold is not unduly severe.
At dawn this morning the frost was especially heavy, and the sun rising
over Japan seemed extremely bright. At eight o'clock everyone gathered in
the Prefectural Office. We left there at ten and went by carriage to the
harbour, where we boarded steam-launches.

At that moment a nineteen-gun salute was fired from the shore battery
in honour of the Embassy. That was followed by a fifteen-gun salute to
mark the return to the United States of the American minister in Japan,
Mr. [Charles E.] DeLong. Smoke from the cannon drifted over the bay
and the echoes of the salvos resounded over the waves, with the rever-
berations continuing for some time.

All the members of the Embassy and the students who were going to
study in America and Europe – making a total of fifty-four peers, former
samurai and commoners, and including five girl students – embarked on
the mail-boat. As each found his or her assigned cabin and attended to
unpacking the luggage, for a time there was considerable confusion. At

noon a cannon was fired to signal our departure; the anchors were raised and the paddle-wheels began to turn. Sailors on the decks of the many foreign warships in Yokohama Bay all manned the rigging and doffed their caps in salute as we passed. We were followed for several miles by a crowd of well-wishers in a flotilla of small boats.

Our ship was called the *America*. Reputed to be the most elegant vessel in the Pacific Mail Steamship Company fleet, the *America* was 363 feet long, 57 feet wide and 23 feet deep, with 8 feet above the deck. The steam-power was said to be 1,500 horsepower. (This seemed to refer to the actual horsepower, but it seems much too weak for the tonnage, so we probably misheard.) Its displacement was 4,554 tons. There were 30 first-class cabins and 16 second-class ones – 46 in all. The vessel could carry 92 passengers. Under Captain Doane were 24 officers and 79 sailors and stewards, making a complement of 103. The ship was powered by a balance-wheel steam-engine driving external paddle-wheels.

That day we moved out of Yokohama Bay and sailed along the Bōsō Peninsula and through the waters off Sagami and Izu. We could see snow on the slopes of Mt. Fuji, which, with the ranges of Hakone-Ashigara, glittered in the evening sun. The scenery was magnificent and we all looked back nostalgically, feeling sad to be leaving the landscape of Japan behind.

December 24th. Morning fine; strong wind.
From this morning we entered the sea-lanes of the Pacific Ocean. At noon our position was latitude 33°38′ N. Our longitude (this is measured from the Greenwich Observatory in London) was 142°38′ E. We had travelled 210 nautical miles from Yokohama. Such information was posted daily in the saloon for the benefit of the passengers. Crossing an ocean, there is little to see all day. You realise the ship is advancing only by the sound of the paddle-wheels. All you can hear are the rumble of the engines and the churning of the paddle-wheels as the ship lumbers forward. We enjoyed looking at the daily notices to learn how many degrees of longitude the ship had crossed and changing our watches each day. This was far more enjoyable than arriving at an inn after a day's journey.

We crossed the Pacific in a total of twenty-two days, covering 4,853 nautical miles. We did not see so much as the silhouette of a single island, so there was really nothing much to record. Although we steamed south to latitude 30°, there is little difference in temperature at sea, unlike on land. However, it was often a little warmer than in Japan. At the time of our crossing, the weather in the Pacific Ocean was rather like the rainy season in Japan. Rain began to fall on the night of our departure. White clouds gathered and for more than ten days it rained most of the time. Although it was the time of the full moon, the fact that we could hardly ever see it intensified our feelings of loneliness. When the wind rose, the waves towered upwards; the rolling of the ship was severe and it made one very dizzy. However, when the wind dropped, the ocean was as smooth as water in a dish.

The twenty-first day of the eleventh month by the lunar calendar was New Year's Day, 1872, by the Western calendar. On the previous evening everybody gathered in the saloon. All kinds of liquors were set out on silver trays, including champagne, brandy, and a concoction of other alcoholic drinks called 'punch'. While drinking this, people chatted until midnight. This is similar to the Japanese custom of staying up until midnight to welcome the New Year.

On the seventeenth day of the twelfth month by the Japanese lunar calendar a thanksgiving ceremony called '*Daijōe*' [Great Enthronement Festival] was held in the Imperial Palace. Although we were in the midst of an ocean voyage, we distributed champagne around the ship in order to make a toast to wish Emperor Meiji a long life. Ambassador Iwakura wore formal court robes. He greeted the Western passengers and explained the ceremony. Mr. DeLong, the American minister, translated his speech into English, whereupon all the passengers stood and raised their glasses. Speeches are given to express sentiments at formal occasions and dinners, and they are especially frequent in America and Britain. During the voyage, members of the Embassy started giving speeches from this day on.

# CHAPTER 2

# A Survey of the United States of America

When Columbus of Spain discovered the continent of America it was the Meiō era [1492–1501] in Japan. As is well known, the land he discovered was not the one which later became the United States of North America.

A representative government was established in Virginia in 1619 (with a governor sent from England to represent the Crown). This was the age of Queen Elizabeth I [James I] in England, where disputes over religion had erupted. Among Protestant believers there was a group called the 'Independents', who pleaded for the right of religious freedom. They were not satisfied with the English style of Protestantism, and in 1620 the Pilgrim Fathers – William Bradford and Edward Winslow among them – boarded a boat and sailed to America. Making landfall at Cape Cod, they pledged themselves to Heaven and established a colony in what is now the state of Massachusetts. This marked the opening of the continent of America. Subsequently, the Englishman William Penn founded the state of Pennsylvania, and Henry Hudson founded the state of New York. In addition, Danes and Frenchmen opened up various areas of wilderness. Eventually, these became British possessions and the English kings dispatched governors to oversee them. Provincial governments were established with the king's authority to rule each colony.

Because the British were eager to extract as much of the wealth of this country as they could, illegal taxes were imposed. Leading advocates of people's rights such as Patrick Henry and Samuel Adams voiced bitter criticism of these impositions and refused to submit to them. Although the British recognised the force of their arguments, they were reluctant to relinquish the profits from the colonies and passed a law imposing a heavy tax on tea. Superficially, the British appeared to make concessions to the colonists, but in reality they monopolised the taxes levied. The American colonists resented these policies to an increasing degree. They formed a national party which started a rebellion in 1774 to challenge British rule and in 1776 asserted their independence. A republican confederation of thirteen states was established, and [George] Washington was appointed commander-in-chief. A militia of citizen-soldiers was raised and the colonists fought the British for eight years.

Most Americans loathed royal authority as if it were a viper. The famous Patrick Henry and many others declared that a presidency was merely kingship under another name, but they finally agreed to the idea of federalism, saying that their apprehensions would be allayed if Washington would accept the presidency. From these debates the present government of the United States came into being in 1789.

Thus it is that all the people of this country grow up breathing the air of democracy. They respect each other as equals without discrimination. In their dealings with other people, they mix easily and without formality; they are sincere and friendly. They go about their affairs calmly and without being constrained by others. They are truly free citizens of the world.

The defects in the American character are that the people make light of public authority, resulting in laws having little effect and individuals asserting their own rights. Officials accept bribes and factionalism is rampant within the established parties. Yet Americans have long been accustomed to this style of government and have created a thoroughly democratic polity. They would not wish to return to the peace of monarchical rule. Nevertheless, when such an attitude spreads to foreign countries, it can divide ruler from subjects, and once established institutions are overthrown, the foundations of the nation are shaken and disturbed. France was the first to suffer such troubles, and later Spain was subjected to similar evils. For this reason countries in Europe established constitutional governments and preserved national unity and peace.

America was originally a federation of thirteen states with a population of less than 5,000,000. In the last ninety-six years, the work of opening up and colonising the land has advanced rapidly. Today thirty-seven states have been established and America has become a great nation of some 39,000,000 people. The United States is a new country, only two or three hundred years old. It covers an area equivalent to the whole of Europe, and we can observe the hard work and diligence of its people in promoting the country's development and wealth, and the wise and far-sighted effects of the policies of state and municipal governments. Many crops are grown throughout the land, and profit is obtained by harvesting them, their value being further enhanced by efficient distribution. Water transportation is of the greatest importance in collecting and distributing products effectively.

The people of America are bursting with vitality, and because of their energy new machines are constantly being invented. The ingenuity of these machines, of which the people of this country are justly proud, is said to be the greatest in the world. When we examined machines made here, their operation was speedy and their design astonishingly innovative; many of them gladden the heart. When we travelled through the countries of Europe and examined hundreds of machines, we saw many clever devices. When we enquired about their origin, on several occasions we were told that they were invented in the United States. However, the one defect they have in common is that they are rather rough-and-ready in construction. Compared with German precision, British quality or French elegance, they must inevitably be called 'unrefined' and rather crude. The peoples of Europe take pride in European culture and readily dismiss Americans as uncultured bumpkins. However, herein lies the very meaning and purpose of America, for Americans deride 'culture' as merely another word for superficial veneer with no practical use.

This country was first opened up by England and France, and later by Holland and Denmark. The population increased seven-fold within a century, mainly due to immigration. In the fifty-one years between 1820 and 1870, foreign immigrants increased by 7,500,000, and the majority of these were British, followed by Germans.

From the beginnings of colonisation, many black slaves were shipped from Africa and forced to work in the fields. As a result, the many black people make up one-seventh of the population. In the central regions there are 'Indians', and in the west Chinese (Ch'ing people) are used as labourers. The population is so diverse that it is hardly an exaggeration to say that every race is represented in America.

The pioneers who developed the country were wealthy merchants, aristocrats, and people with strong religious beliefs. They invested enormous amounts of capital and employed the poor people who flooded in after them. For this reason white people dominated the country's leadership. The most numerous were the British, and since the country was established on the basis of their educational tradition, English is the common language and British institutions are widespread. Britain is still regarded as 'the mother country'. In some states German is spoken, and French is widely used in Louisiana in the South. In the south-west, in New Mexico and Arizona territories, many people speak Spanish. There are also numerous towns and villages where other languages and dialects are heard.

Because America is so huge, with abundant land which is only sparsely populated, the work of building the country was achieved through pioneer settlements. So desperate were the people to increase the population that they turned to any and every means at hand, even raising bastard children and orphans. As a result, a distinction between good stock and bad ensued. On the whole, immigrants have been drawn from the worst elements – the ignorant, idle, or obstinate masses – in various countries. In addition, the illegitimate offspring of common-law unions are looked after, and it must be said that their general character is extremely bad. Murders and robberies are rife. The hovels in which these people live are so dirty and unsanitary that legal efforts to educate and protect them need to be strengthened.

Protestantism is the national religion. At the same time, there are many Roman Catholics, Greek Orthodox Catholics and Jews, and California has some Buddhist temples. Although freedom of religion has been a common policy in most European countries in recent years, America is the only Western country with Buddhist temples. Americans, in general, are very devout in their religious beliefs. In Europe it is Britain whose people are the most religious, but when you travel from America to Britain, you feel that the British are not really so fervent. People who come from Britain to America learn that British piety is still superficial. Most commerce ceases from Saturday afternoon, and on Sundays almost all American shops remain closed. I feel that this helps maintain the customs and character of this country.

CHAPTER 3

# A Record of San Francisco, 1

January 15th, 1872. Fine.

At first light this morning the sea fog was so thick that we could not distinguish objects which were only a foot away from us. The entire deck of the *America* was shrouded in mist. The captain therefore ordered the ship to heave to in the ocean for a while to await the dawn. As the sun rose and the mists began to lift, we could distinguish the mountains of California ahead. They emerged more clearly as the sun rose higher. The *America* advanced slowly. Directly to the east, two mountains ridges parted to reveal a great natural gateway. Through it we could see steamships passing to and fro with smoke rising from their funnels, making a truly beautiful sight. This was the celebrated Golden Gate.

In our twenty-two-day voyage across the Pacific Ocean this was the first land we had glimpsed east of Japan. Words are inadequate to express our pleasure as we gazed upon this golden gateway, where sea and sky meet directly to the west and coastal mountains rise on both sides.

Today the *America* steamed into the bay flying the flag of Japan emblazoned with the red sun. The citizens of San Francisco had learnt of the Embassy's visit from newspaper reports, and the news of our actual arrival was telegraphed from the Golden Gate to City Hall and to our consul. As a result, when we passed Alcatraz Island we were greeted with a fifteen-gun salute from the battery on its cliffs.

We berthed at the wharf shortly after ten o'clock. Mr. [Charles Wolcott] Brooks of the Japanese consulate in San Francisco had arranged our hotel accommodation. The councillors, Mr. Williams and Mr. Phelps, as well as officials representing Japan who are resident here, all came to the wharf to meet the ship. The Grand Hotel had sent porters to attend to our luggage. In no time we had disembarked, climbed into horse-drawn carriages and been conveyed to the Grand Hotel on Montgomery Street, where we arrived at eleven o'clock.

The Grand Hotel is a five-storeyed building spanning two blocks on both sides of a street leading off Montgomery Street. The two wings of the hotel are joined by an overhead bridge. With its ornate construction, it is not the kind of large building one often sees in this city. The dining-room is more than 700 square feet in area, ample enough to accommodate three hundred diners at once. Because it had been built only recently, the upholstery of the armchairs and couches in the public rooms was still fresh and their silk had lost none of its sheen. The first floor was covered with marble and so highly polished that our feet slipped on it. The hotel is equipped with such amenities as bath-houses, barbers and billiard-rooms. On the first floor, as well as the offices there are rooms rented out as shops to merchants selling wine and liquor, fruit, medicine, tobacco and fabric for clothing. They make their living from the guests staying in the hotel.

From the second floor to the top floor are the guest rooms, almost three hundred of them. In the suites, the largest room is the sitting-room. In France it would be called a '*salon*'. There is a sleeping room ('bedroom'), a bathing room ('bathroom') and a lavatory ('water-closet'). Everything a guest could want is provided. Large mirrors resemble pools of water; the carpets are like fields of flowers. Gas chandeliers hang from the ceiling. In the daytime the iridescent crystal glitters with the seven colours of the spectrum and the gilt of the chandelier sparkles where the light strikes it. At night, when one turns on a tap to light the gas, the crystal drops radiate the colours of the rainbow as light is refracted through them.

Lace curtains on the windows give the impression of looking at flowers through a mist. The smaller rooms are about the size of an eight-tatami-mat room in Japan. The beds have mattresses with metal springs underneath, but the mattresses are soft and the springs do not touch the body directly. There are wardrobes and chests of drawers in which to place one's clothes, and a basin where one can wash one's face. When one turns on the faucet, clean water comes gushing out. An electric bell allows one to call the maid-servants. A light touch of a button with a fingertip makes a bell ring a hundred paces away. A desk is provided for reading and writing. And one can inspect one's appearance in the mirrors placed in the rooms. Soap, hand-towels, matches, a spittoon, a stove, a water-pitcher, a chamber-pot and other small amenities are provided in each room.

Since most Western hotels have similar facilities, it will not be necessary to describe them all in such detail. Readers may imagine what the others are like.

January 16th. Fine.

At eleven o'clock in the morning the mayor [William Alvord] came to welcome Ambassador Iwakura, accompanied by local navy and army officers. Then the consuls of the various countries represented in San Francisco came to pay their respects. After lunch the resident Japanese officials arrived, and at three o'clock a delegation of wealthy businessmen visited the ambassador.

At ten that night, on the paved street below the hotel rooms occupied by the Embassy, the band of the San Francisco artillery regiment gave a concert. The citizens gathered and cheered, celebrating our safe arrival. Ambassador Iwakura made a speech from the balcony, which Mr. DeLong translated into English. After that, he said a few words on his own behalf. The crowd cheered and clapped for quite some time. Western people are ever eager to promote trade and like to extend a warm welcome to foreign visitors. Such gatherings, which are part and parcel of American customs, are unusual in Japan. The concert ended at midnight and the crowds dispersed.


January 18th. Fine.

Guides from the city took us to the following factories. The Kimball Carriage Factory in Bryant Street, the largest such factory in the state, produces some 500 large and 1,200 small carriages each year. One hundred and fifty workers are employed here every day. The Mission Woolen Mill specialises in weaving blankets and carpets. The factory utilises 1,200,000 pounds of wool a year, worth $1,000,000. There were 100 white workers, 240 Chinese, and 2 Japanese. The mill gave us a collation of wine and fruit.

On the way back to our hotel we stopped at Woodward's Gardens in the southern part of the city, each of us paying twenty-five cents to enter. This combined a zoological and a botanical garden, and a museum and an art gallery. At its centre was a stone fountain. On a hillside there was a large stage where dances and other entertainments were performed. The gardens were said to be very popular, especially on Sundays.

Customs and character in the East and West are very different; indeed, at times they seem to be direct opposites. Westerners enjoy social activities and public events; Eastern peoples tend to avoid them. This is not only a relic of Japan's policy of national isolation. Eastern people are also indifferent to wealth and do not regard commerce as a primary concern. Westerners like to go out and enjoy themselves socially, and even in the smallest towns they establish public gardens. Eastern people, on the other hand, prefer to stay indoors to relax, creating gardens within their own houses. Does not this contrast in character between Eastern and Western people derive, perhaps, from different attitudes fostered by the great contrast in the fertility of their lands? Westerners stress practical science and the rationality of material things, whereas Eastern people emphasise the science of the abstract and non-material. The disparity between the wealth of the peoples of the East and West is, I feel, the result of their different natures.

January 20th. Cloudy.
In the morning, Kido, Ōkubo and Yamaguchi, the three vice-ambassadors, went to inspect Booth and Company of San Francisco, a manufacturer of mining machinery, mainly water-pumps.

In the afternoon three large groups of California militia held a parade for us in front of the hotel. We reviewed the parade together with their officers from a wooden stand which had been erected at the Montgomery Street intersection. As each unit marched past, the commanding officer raised his sword in salute. More than twenty thousand spectators had come to watch, and the streets were so densely packed with hat-covered heads that there was no room to insert even a needle.

Although the American military system does not rely on a large standing army, citizens in town and country alike usually receive military training and practice. Should there be an emergency, an alarm is sounded and they immediately take up their guns and are ready to do battle. This reminds us of the fire-brigades in Japan. Among the troops parading today was one cadet company made up of fourteen- to fifteen-year-old boys, students from the military academy in Oakland. There are military academies in various states which are licensed by the government. Boys from wealthy families enter at their own expense and study military subjects; those who complete the curriculum are selected to be officers.

January 21st. Fine.
At the invitation of both D. O. Mills, president of the Bank of California, and William C. Ralston, we boarded a train at the Southern Pacific Company depot at a quarter to nine in the morning and rode south-west for seventeen miles to San Bruno, where Mr. Mills has his estate. Several carriages came to the station to meet us. Ambassador Iwakura had excused himself because he was not feeling well. The gardens of the estate are extensive and contain many unusual trees, rare and exotic plants and beautiful flowers, which scented the air with their fragrance.

From there we went to the village of Belmont, twenty-seven miles from San Francisco, where Mr. Ralston had his estate. We were invited to his house and he showed us around it and the gardens.

There are many expensive estates like this five or ten miles outside the city. Their wooded gardens are quiet and peaceful, and one can enjoy strolling about and breathing the fresh air. The houses themselves are very tasteful and completely different from the buildings in the city. Most Americans conduct business in corporations or shops in the city, working in these buildings like government employees going to their offices. The people engaged in small and medium-sized businesses live their entire lives in the bustling heart of the city, toiling there until their death. Those who have made some money, however, build retreats in outlying districts and live there, going daily to their businesses in the city by train or by carriage. This is common practice across the United States and Europe.

January 22nd. Cloudy.
At nine o'clock in the morning, at the invitation of the Central Pacific Railroad Company, we went with Minister DeLong to the passenger wharf for Oakland, where we boarded the steamship *El Capitán* and were ferried across to the long pier at Oakland, known as 'the Long Bridge'.

This pier projects a mile into the bay from the Oakland shore. When the ferry-boats from San Francisco to Oakland first started, it was promised that they would reach Oakland as fast as the trains. However, the trains were always faster and the ferry-boats were always late. Besides, the bay is shallow here and it was very costly to dredge the channel. After much discussion, this long wooden pier was constructed in the bay. At the head of the pier, rising above the water, is a large building which serves as the station for passengers to transfer to the train. When the steamer arrived at the station we thought we had landed on an island. Then, boarding the train, everybody was astonished that the railroad ran along the pier. Racing forward with the whistle screeching, we seemed to be soaring over the bay.

San Francisco and Oakland face each other across the bay and are linked by ferry-boats which shuttle to and fro every hour without a break. The *El Capitán* ferry-boat has no fixed prow or stern; the prow on the outward voyage becomes the stern on the return voyage. The ferry approaches the dock via a channel which is just the width of the vessel. When the ferry reaches the dock, a ramp is lowered, and since the ferry deck and the dock are on the same level, one cannot detect the join. Arriving passengers leave the ferry from the bow. Those boarding for the return voyage enter from the side. Whether one is arriving or departing, there is no confusion at all. Only when the paddle-wheels turn and the waters churn do you know that you are at sea. And only when the whistle blows and the train wheels clatter do you realise that you are on land. Although San Francisco has only recently developed as a city, already such complex constructions as this ferry system exist. From this account readers can perhaps imagine the vitality of the great cities of America and Europe.

Today, at the Central Pacific Railroad Company depot, we were shown a train that consisted of newly built [Kimball] carriages. The Embassy was invited to celebrate the start of its operation. On the train a kitchen was provided to serve lunch. Passing through Oakland, we travelled thirty-five miles to the north, then south along the eastern shore of San Francisco Bay, and at noon arrived at Milpitas, the station for the town of San Jose. The members of the Embassy and others alighted and walked around the nearby gardens. After a brief tour we returned to the train.

San Jose is a large town south of San Francisco and is the site of the State Superior Court, which judges cases for the Southern District of California. The town centre was crowded with people.

January 23rd. Fine.
At ten o'clock in the morning we visited the Denman School for girls. The school is housed in a four-storeyed building. Inside were fourteen classrooms, with one teacher for every 28 students. The total number of students was 820. The school was built in 1864, and it taught the usual subjects for a grammar school: reading, writing, arithmetic, geography, science, general history, singing and needlework. On this day a teacher played the piano and the girls sang the first verse of Schubert's 'Rose Song'.

Singing is taught every day in elementary schools. Through singing, students praise the divine, and this fills the heart with harmonious feelings. With a piano accompaniment, the children are taught to dance with rhythm and timing. Both boys and girls learn singing, which stimulates and attunes the emotions. Subsequently, whenever we visited elementary schools, the children sang for us. Since this was customary, I will not mention it each time.

After this, we went to Lincoln Elementary School. This, too, was a grammar school, the largest boys' school in the city. Occupying a four-storeyed building, the school was built in 1865, and its twenty-one classrooms could each accommodate a maximum of fifty-six students.

Here one teacher was assigned to each room, and there were altogether twenty-one teachers. Among them was a male teacher who had been appointed the head-teacher. On this day we visited the first-grade classroom. Minister DeLong asked the children about the geography of Japan. They all knew the answers and not one made a mistake.

Besides these two schools there were forty elementary schools and two middle schools (one each for boys and girls) in the city of San Francisco. The number of school-children under fifteen years old was 19,885. When you compare this to the total number of boys and girls, it appears that eight out of eleven children attended school.

At one o'clock we went to the Telegraph Office, where we sent a telegraph to Secretary of State [Hamilton] Fish, as well as to Professor Morse, the father of the telegraph machine, and to the mayor of Chicago. This line was especially made available by the federal government – at a cost of $6,000 to the federal treasury – to allow our Embassy to communicate easily with Washington and Chicago.

At eight o'clock this evening a banquet hosted by the citizens of San Francisco was given in the hotel dining-room. With more than three hundred guests, it was a splendid occasion. Wreaths made with green leaves interspersed with flowers decorated the windows and walls. The crossed flags of the Rising Sun of Japan and the Stars and Stripes of the thirty-seven United States were hung in several places. The whole Embassy, Mayor Alvord of San Francisco, Governor Booth of California, and officers of the army and navy all sat at a raised table at the head of the room. A band played during the banquet. The food was elegantly presented and very delicious. At the close of the dinner fifteen dignitaries gave speeches. The banquet ended at midnight.

In this city there are many wealthy citizens who are active in society. When a party is planned, the organisers estimate the per-person expense, print the invitations and tickets and send them out. Those who wish to attend pay for their ticket. The hotels arrange banquets for every size of budget and collect the tickets from the guests. Their profit depends upon the number of tickets sold. In this land of trade, paying for such entertainment is common and hardly differs from commerce.

# CHAPTER 4

# A Record of San Francisco, 2

January 26th, 1872. Fine.

We received a telegraph saying that heavy snows in the Rocky Mountains had made the Union Pacific Railroad tracks impassable, and we therefore postponed our departure. Several groups of students accompanying us, who had proceeded ahead, had run into blizzards and deep snowdrifts. The track was closed and the trains were halted for seventeen days. Because of the remoteness of the mountains, food was scarce and the passengers barely managed to avoid starvation by sharing bread, cheese and potatoes. After much effort the line was re-opened and we could proceed. Normally there is not much snow in the Rocky Mountains, and people say that such a heavy snowstorm occurs only once every ten years or more.

This afternoon, from ten minutes to one, there were horse races at the Agricultural Gardens, and the Embassy received a special invitation to the day's opening events. This park is in the southern part of the city and is surrounded by white sand-dunes and vacant land. The race-track was made by clearing the land and compacting the earth. Inside the grounds, wide lawns had been laid around a circular track; three circuits of the track made about one mile. Near the entrance, viewing-stands had been erected and men and women crowded into these. A few couples came riding up together. Some horse-loving women drove their own carriages and arrived whipping their horses. In front of the stands there was a tremendous whinnying of horses and rattling of carriages. When the races began, people placed bets by buying tickets. It was very clear that Western men and women love horses.

In this type of horse racing the jockeys do not ride astride the horses but compete on lightweight, two-wheeled buggies [sulkies]. The starting gate was at the head of the track, with a tape stretched across to mark the barrier. Before the race started, four or five sulkies came onto the track and made a leisurely circuit of the track to allow the horses to warm up. Then, slowly, they lined up, and when they were all under the tape, a bell was rung to signal the start. The horse that crossed the finishing line first, after racing two or three times around the track, won the race.

On the way back we drove our carriages along the beach and visited Cliff House, which, as the name suggests, is perched atop high cliffs. It is less than one mile west of the Agricultural Gardens and overlooks a beach which is exposed to the waves of the Pacific Ocean. Just beneath Cliff House are the Seal Rocks, where countless seals and sea-lions are always relaxing or playing on the rocky ledges in the ocean. With white gulls wheeling around the rocks and great breakers curling skywards, it was a magnificent sight. The whole scene of the sea, with the Golden Gate to the north, could easily have been one found in an ink painting.

January 27th. Fine.
At eleven o'clock in the morning, at the invitation of Mr. [Alfred A.] Cohen [head of the Central Pacific Railroad Company], we boarded the ferry *El Capitán* and crossed over to Oakland, where he lived. On this day most of the senior members of our Embassy were sick, so only Vice-Ambassador Kido went. Oakland lies just across the bay from San Francisco. Facing the mouth of the Golden Gate and backed by a range of hills, it enjoys some of the most notable scenery in San Francisco Bay. Mr. Cohen's house in Oakland was serene and elegant. The landscaping of the gardens and orchards was in extremely good taste. Here Mr. Cohen gave a small party, and we talked and passed some time before returning to San Francisco.

January 29th. Fine.
We visited a winery [Landsberger's in Oakland] which produces 232,000 bottles annually. Champagne costs $7 to $10 per case; wine, $2.50 to $3 per case. The bottles are imported from Paris at a cost of 1 3/4 cents each. The corks are imported from Spain and Portugal, with five corks costing 2 cents. The winery employs twenty-four workers each day.

Wine bottles are made of crude glass. Even copper and iron slag can easily be used to make glass, so it would be quite possible to make the bottles in America. Why, then, do they import them from such a far-away place as France? French wine is a well-known product whose fame has spread and is acknowledged throughout the world. French wines are given names according to their regions of origin, such as 'Bordeaux' or 'Champagne', and in making and bottling wine Americans pretentiously borrow French names. Probably this is because the market is still poorly developed. In the practice of trade, reputation (that is, credibility among customers) is so highly valued that even millions of dollars in capital cannot compensate for its loss. A good business works to enhance its name year after year. The reason for foregoing short-term profits is to use the reputation or the name to add value. Bad business practices, on the contrary, sacrifice reputation and grasp at small immediate profits. If you compare results over a few years, there may seem to be no difference, but in the long run the difference in profit is like that between Heaven and Earth. This frequently happens. If a wine has a name which is well-known, it will easily generate enough extra money to pay for the bottles. This principle is worth noting.

Although Japan has only recently begun intercourse and commerce with foreign countries, many items made in Japan are regarded as unusual and attractive by Europeans and Americans. Nevertheless, Japan does not profit from exports for the following three basic reasons: 1. The volume of exported goods is so small that it does not satisfy overseas demand; 2. Shipping is unreliable, and we have not yet established a regular presence and role in foreign markets; 3. Aiming only for short-term profits, we do not build any reputation or fame; worse, we even squander any recognition we may have won.

The example of the corks proves that spreading one's reputation and promoting demand throughout the world creates profit and results in the volume of trade increasing tremendously. Corks are made from the bark of a tree (cork-trees were growing in the flower-beds in Woodward's Gardens) and are exported from Spain and Portugal. In Algeria, in Africa, planting French cork-trees on about 350,000 acres of land yielded a profit of 10,000,000 francs a year. If cork-trees and corks can yield such profits, how large a business it must be!

Today, those of us who specialise in education were dispatched to Oakland, where officials showed them several schools. Oakland is a famous educational centre in the western United States and has districts with elementary schools, several higher schools (or universities), a military academy and a school for the deaf and blind. The elementary schools are co-educational and children from the area come to study there, bringing their lunches and books with them. At lunch-time, tables with pitchers of water are set out in a room below the assembly hall. This is where the students have their lunch. The boys and girls generally bring buttered bread and salt-meat sandwiches and they drink water, which is easily drawn from taps. Other kinds of drinks are always omitted from Western meals. The custom is for lunch, especially, to be very simple, for adults as well as for school-children.

Oakland Military School is a private school built by a benefactor and licensed by the federal government. More than one hundred cadets were enrolled, all of whom were the sons of wealthy families from San Francisco and nearby towns who came daily to study and drill. Tuition is much more expensive than at other local schools. The academy provides students with such items as small-arms, leather powder-pouches and musical instruments, and they practise marching in the large parade-ground. On the day we visited, they demonstrated their drills, marching in lines.

Schools for the blind and deaf are public schools supported by the government of every state. The one in Oakland is housed in an imposing stone edifice, four storeys high, set in the foothills. There were fifty or sixty deaf students, both boys and girls, divided into upper and lower classes. The lower level was an elementary school, which included children five or six years old. They were able to communicate by making different shapes with their fingers, using signs as a substitute for speech. They also communicated by writing on the blackboard. One child of about six years old was thoroughly accomplished in sign language and several times engaged in a sign discussion with his teacher.

With regard to blind students, there were twenty boys and just seven girls. Because of the difficulty of coming to school, most were boarders. In the case of blind people, the 'seeing' nerves are concentrated in the tips of their fingers. Hence they use raised letters [Braille] and their fingers serve as eyes. They are given textbooks which they read by touch. The Braille alphabet uses nine raised dots in various combinations for the twenty-six letters of the alphabet. These are stamped on thick paper. The students also use two special machines to help them write. One is like a brass chessboard, which they place on top of a piece of paper. Using a blunt needle instead of a brush, they push down in the squares to form raised letters on the back. With the other machine, which is used to write letters to friends, horizontal lines are marked on a rectangular plate and a piece of cloth is stretched over it. This is placed under the paper and serves the same purpose as ruled lines. A finger of the left hand is placed at the beginning of the line, and a pencil is grasped in the right hand; every time a letter is made, the left hand is advanced one space and the right hand moves ahead of it to write the next letter. This is a recent invention in America.

In order to do arithmetic, a machine similar to the brass plate for reading and writing is used. The block on which raised numbers are written corresponds to our abacus with its rows of beads. With their fingers the students search for the raised numbers and, following the rules of arithmetic, arrange them on the lined, abacus-like block. Depending on the problem, they rearrange the numbers to do addition, subtraction, multiplication and division. Using this machine the advanced male students were able to solve difficult problems even in geometry. To teach geography, raised maps of the world and of various individual countries are arranged on a wooden board so that students can learn their shapes by touch.

January 30th. Fine.
In the morning we went to a leather factory where horse harnesses are made. From there we went to the Pacific Mail Steamship Company's wharves to observe the freight warehouses.

The development of San Francisco has taken place only over the last thirty years. Learning from urban development elsewhere, the streets have been laid out in a neat checker-board pattern, with wide, straight thoroughfares. Main avenues are forty yards wide, normal streets thirty yards, and even the narrower streets are broad enough for two carriages to pass side by side. A broad avenue cuts diagonally across the grid. This is Market Street, the liveliest street in the city. Montgomery Street, the most prosperous, is lined with hotels on both sides. The Grand Hotel can accommodate five hundred guests; the Occidental Hotel is a seven-storeyed building towering straight up into the sky; Lick House is a secondary guest-house. In addition, there are shops and office buildings which are five or six storeys high. Although the streets are wide, one feels as though one is passing through a narrow gorge of tall buildings. Carriage wheels rattle and rumble noisily, like thunder rolling nearby or waves breaking in the distance. The gaslights shine brilliantly, lining the streets like constellations of stars which have fallen to the earth.

The maintenance of the streets in San Francisco is still inadequate. The soil is merely tamped down to harden it sufficiently to take the wheels of carriages. When the air is dry, the carriage wheels churn up clouds of blinding dust which irritate the eyes. And the nuisance is even greater with the mud which follows rain. Streets paved with stone are rare, and even in the busy shopping district many roads consist of wooden blocks laid in the earth. The cut faces are placed close against one another to make the surface of the street, just as paving stones are laid. Shaking is greatly reduced when carriage wheels run over this surface, but the disadvantage is that it must be repaired frequently.

City life offers many conveniences, such as pipes laid underground to supply gas and water, and for sewage disposal. These pipes are connected to each house in every town as branches of the main system. Rooms are all lit by lamps, and there is no need to haul water because pure water is provided from a tap in every house. Such conveniences are more common in new towns than in older cities because they are more advanced. Thus, although the port of San Francisco is flourishing, adequate plumbing is still in short supply. Since the city is built on a peninsula jutting into the ocean, no water supply is available from the mountains and water must be pumped from Mountain Lake, three miles to the west, and brought to the city in pipes.

The rapid growth of San Francisco in size and prosperity is staggering. When you look at population figures, until 1845 San Francisco was a small village with only 150 people. One can imagine the conditions at that time: the native people fished in the ocean or bay and farmed the land; the plains were wide and the mountains rugged; and practically no boats sailed to Mexico. However, when gold was discovered in 1848, prospectors flocked here, and by 1850 San Francisco was a thriving town of 5,000. In 1862 it had grown into a city of 57,000; and in 1870 it was a great metropolis of 150,000. There is no other example in the world of this kind of startling growth. The reasons are clear: California, Nevada and the surrounding states are rich in gold, silver and mineral ores; together they are reputed to be the greatest producer of these in the world. All this profitable trade is conducted through San Francisco.

There are other reasons for the city's vitality. First, it enjoys a mild climate with no extremes of winter or summer weather. This land of California and the British territory of Victoria Island (an Australian state) are both new states and are said to be like paradises, tempting travellers to immigrate there. Second, the land is fertile and beautiful as far as the eye can see, even for a thousand miles. Whether you raise cattle or grow fruit-trees or cultivate crops, no resource is lacking. It is natural that people from all over the world should flock here like pigeons. Third, the state of California includes three climatic zones: cool, temperate and semi-tropical. The mountains of California are heavily wooded, and its valleys so broad that they could easily swallow all the islands of Japan. The two large rivers, the Sacramento and the San Joaquin, are useful for transportation. If the population continues to expand, these rivers will reduce the problem of transporting products to and from San Francisco. These three factors contribute to the profitable economy of the interior as well as San Francisco.

Fourth, trade with China and Japan opened up at the same time as the discovery of gold, and all vessels have to visit this port on the Pacific.

Fifth, trading ships from Europe and America and the East ply between San Francisco and the Isthmus of Panama. Thus, San Francisco is a port constantly visited by trading ships sailing between Europe and America and the Orient. Sixth, the building of the railroad over the Rocky Mountains has improved transport between land and sea and created a short-cut between the Pacific and Atlantic oceans. These latter three reasons have a large influence on world trade and are of vital significance for the present and future prosperity of Japan.

In addition, because California is rich in gold and silver, its development knows no bounds. Commercial theory tells us that if you have one active trading centre, there is always a counterpart city responding to it and stimulating it. London flourishes with Paris; London and Paris together flourish with New York and Philadelphia. In this way, considering their locations, the cities which could co-operate with San Francisco would be Yokohama in Japan and Shanghai and Hong Kong in China.

Thus, our countrymen should consider what we can do to encourage competition and contribute to mutual prosperity. Profits are only obtained from natural resources through the application of human effort. Today's wealth results from yesterday's labour. It is not difficult for what is a small village today to become a large city in the future. In the final analysis, it depends on long-term planning and foresight. Ill-planned, haphazard actions will never produce lasting profit. This lesson is evident through the reading of history. If one studies local or regional history it is possible to predict the future clearly on the basis of past experience.

CHAPTER 5

# The Railroad Journey in the
# State of California

California is a large state on the Pacific coast of North America and
includes a semi-tropical and a temperate zone. Originally it was a possession of Mexico, but Mexico was forced to relinquish control of much
of it as a result of uprisings and conflict with the United States.

The indigenous population consisted of Mexicans and Indians. Later,
waves of immigrants from Europe increased year by year, and in 1860 the
population reached 280,000. Since then it has grown rapidly, and the
figure for 1870 was 590,247. The bulk of the population, however, is
concentrated in the counties around San Francisco Bay, while districts to
the north and south remain sparsely populated and largely undeveloped.

The rapid growth of San Francisco is due to gold-mining, and the
Chinese have therefore given it the name 'Gold Mountain', but not
because any gold-mines are found in San Francisco itself. From the very
opening of the city the Chinese arrived to dig for gold and found
employment there; as a result, many amassed fortunes and returned to
China. Soon the Chinese were competing to come here, and because of
this situation the city earned the name 'Gold Mountain'. In 1870, there
were 49,310 Chinese living in San Francisco in a crowded part of the city
known as 'China Town'. They have also dispersed into surrounding
counties, where they are employed as farm labourers to cultivate grain
and plant vegetables and fruit-trees, or as factory workers. Coming
mainly from the cities of Canton and Fukien, the Chinese are not afraid
of hard work and are willing to endure hardships. In five or six years,
despite meagre wages, they will scrimp and save a considerable amount of
money. With this, some will buy land and houses and settle in California,
while others return to China and build houses there.

Whenever Pacific Mail steamers come or go, there are always three or
four hundred Chinese people in steerage. The Chinese are frugal and
conservative by nature and are reluctant to change their customs.
Although long resident in California, they keep their queues and wear

28

Chinese robes. The goods they need are all ordered and brought from China. They eat rice and wear Chinese sandals. They avoid American products such as the hides of cows and sheep. The number of Chinese who save all their money and return to their country is always large; it is estimated that more than $10,000,000 a year is taken to China from America. Because of this competition, American workers have complained that their jobs are being taken from them and that Chinese immigration should be forbidden. However, it is said that little can be done about this.

The influx of millions of Chinese is not limited to California; they are also to be found in South America, Australia and in the islands of the South Seas. Everywhere they settle they either engage in trade or are employed as labourers. It is the same in Japan's newly opened ports, where many Chinese have gathered to make a living. This migration is simply due to the great demand for cheap labour in colonies.

Basically, there are two types of immigrants to newly developing lands. The first consists of wealthy, upper-class people with large amounts of capital. Because they cannot invest their capital effectively in their own countries, where there are few opportunities to profit from manufacturing and protective laws are numerous, they emigrate to start enterprises in developing lands. The second type of immigrants is comprised of migrant workers with no capital. As upper-class people acquire houses, land, factories, farms and machinery for their enterprises, they also require labour. Since hiring local workers is often expensive, poor people come from all over the world to take employment as labourers.

The employment of cheap, indentured labour is an urgent problem in newly developing lands. The seriousness of this issue should be clear from the fact that the northern and southern states fought a bloody civil war for six years over slavery, and this should provide food for thought. In the West, every edict and law is directed towards protecting people's life and property. Thus, no measure, even when clearly justified by circumstances, can be adopted lightly. This is how wealth and power have been preserved in the West.

Because cattle-raising does not suit the character of the Chinese, it is mainly Indians, Americans and European immigrants who are employed on ranches. There are now 7,241 Indians registered in San Francisco. California is famous for cattle-raising. Ranchers also brought stud stallions from Arabia for breeding, and their thoroughbreds are not inferior to those of England. When horses are imported from other countries, the stud line is said to deteriorate in three generations. Therefore, after the third generation the horses are re-bred with stock from the original country. This is also done with plant and vegetable seeds. Because the land is vast and grass is rich and plentiful, cows, sheep, poultry and pigs tend to revert to the wild, but no matter how many hundreds of animals are released to roam, they have no trouble finding food.

January 31st, 1872. Cloudy; light rain.
We set out from the Grand Hotel at seven o'clock in the morning and took the steamship across the bay to the terminal at the head of the long wharf in Oakland, where we boarded a train of the California Pacific Railroad.

In America there are trains which run during the night as well as in the day, and they have carriages called 'sleeping-cars'. Upper-class passengers ride in these cars. On either side of a central corridor in the carriages are six compartments, each accommodating two passengers, making twenty-four people in every car. The central corridor serves as a passageway. At one end of each carriage is a large space, or parlour, where a stove is kept burning. There are also hand-basins for washing one's face, water-pitchers and a water-closet. During the day a table is placed in the middle of each compartment. The two passengers sit on long, upholstered seats facing each other across this table. It is very comfortable, and the table can be used for reading or writing on. At night the seats are joined together to become a bed. When an overhead latch is released, a bunk drops to become another bed, thus making two beds, an upper one and a lower one. Bedding and pillows are provided and passengers can draw a curtain beside each bed and sleep. The ceilings of the carriages are decorated with floral designs in gilt and oil-paint. It is all quite opulent. Glass lamps in wall-brackets provide illumination at night. The construction of these carriages is very carefully planned.

In Europe they do not have such carriages, not because Europeans would find them uncomfortable but for a different reason. In Europe's monarchical countries, with their class-conscious societies, there are distinct upper and lower classes. Rich and poor do not like to mingle, and both classes tend to avoid situations in which they might have to share sitting or sleeping arrangements. Thus, even if such carriages were built, upper-class people would not like them and would reject them as primitive.

The whole mission, including officials, students and Mr. DeLong and his family, numbering more than a hundred people, set out in five especially commissioned Pullman carriages. At half past six that evening we reached the depot for the city of Sacramento, where we alighted and were taken to rooms in the Orleans Hotel. Although Sacramento is the capital city of California, it did not seem a very prosperous town.

February 1st. Cloudy.

At noon we went to the State Capitol in Sacramento by carriage. At the time of our visit it was being re-built and had almost been completed. The Capitol is a large, imposing building standing on a raised foundation. There was a huge dome at the centre of the building, and it was 150 feet from the ground to the tip of the flag-pole on the top. It truly seemed to be pointing to the navel of the distant heavens.

Inside the building was a spiral staircase for visitors to climb to a balcony near the top of the dome. If one walked around this, one could see in all directions, with Sacramento lying like a grid at one's feet and the Sacramento River winding from the north in the distance. To the east, south and west, the Central Valley plain stretched as far as the horizon, and here and there swamps and marshes glittered like mirrors scattered about the landscape.

The chambers of the upper and lower houses are located in the left and right wings of the Capitol. Both chambers are pleasantly bright, large rooms some thirty feet in height. The lower house can accommodate eighty or ninety representatives, with room to spare. Two chandeliers, their crystal droplets glittering, hang from chains. The floors are covered with floral carpets, evoking eternal spring. In front of the seats is a raised dais for the speaker's podium, and a long table used by the secretaries is set up there. Each representative sits at his own desk, facing the dais. Surrounding the room on three sides are seats for observers. On the upper level is a three-sided gallery where the citizens of California, both men and women, can come and listen to the debates. The lay-out resembles a theatre. In the outer hallways are stalls where fruit, toys, prints, newspapers and other items are sold. In general, the organisation of state governments and that of the federal government are much the same. The upper house consists of delegates from each city and county, and the lower house consists of members who represent the citizenry. On this day the members of the Embassy were invited onto the dais. Mr. DeLong and the speaker of the assembly, as well as some others, sat beside them and made speeches.

At dusk we returned to see the Capitol illuminated. When we arrived it was already dark inside the chambers. At the right moment, more than one hundred electric lamps were turned on and the building was bathed in light which was as bright as day.

That night we were invited to a banquet hosted by the city at the hotel. With the Embassy known to be passing through Sacramento, wealthy people from the city had raised $1,500 in order to entertain us for three days. However, because we still had a long journey ahead of us, we thanked them, made our apologies and excused ourselves. The party was extremely lively, continuing until twenty minutes to midnight.

February 2nd. Rain and snow.
At three o'clock this morning we boarded the train. From Sacramento, the single-track railroad stretched ahead of us, and we crossed the Sierra Nevada, passed through the desert wilderness of Utah Territory and headed towards the Rocky Mountains. This transcontinental railroad was completed only a few years ago. Thanks to the admirable engineering achievement of the Central Pacific Railroad Company, we were able to cross much of this vast territory in a train, comfortably relaxing or sleeping.

At a quarter past nine we approached the very steep section of track known as Cape Horn. The railroad wound upwards alongside the canyon walls, high above the steep banks of the American River. In places, elevated bridges supported the rails between two mountains. The mountains were piled up, one on top of another, and before long we had climbed another 600 feet to reach the foot of the rocky bluff of Cape Horn, which is famed for its views.

How can I describe the scenery at Cape Horn? Behind, grandly aloof, towered steep, craggy walls dotted with pine-trees. Below, the valley was so deep that the roar of the river at the bottom of it was faint. Far below, at the foot of the valley, was a tiny village near the river, which meandered like a winding sash. We could see people the size of peas and inch-high horses moving along a thread-like road. The train stopped here for a while to allow us to admire the scenery. Cape Horn lies 3,000 feet above sea-level. Above and ahead of us it was snowing, which unfortunately interfered with the view.

At ten minutes past ten in the morning we passed Gold Run village. We began to see the sluice-boxes used for hydraulic mining. Streams of water are fed from the mountain valleys into these wooden flumes, which are set up to sieve out the gold-dust. We ran into a sudden flurry of hail, which fell from dark clouds and flecked the ground with white. At Dutch Flat, to our right we saw several hundred shacks in the valley. Each one belonged to someone engaged in gold-prospecting. When we reached Alta, our train was halted for several hours because a rock slide had fallen onto the track ahead.

Here, too, we could see the sluice-boxes for sieving gold-bearing sand from hydraulic mining. The sluices run down from the upper part of the valley on a seven- or eight-degree incline. Miners spray great spouts of water against the mountain walls in two-hundred-foot sections to wash out the ore-bearing gravel and channel it into these sluices, where it settles for a while. Then the water pressure and gravity of the downward flow carry it fifty to sixty feet up and over another mountain ridge, driving the flow down into a lower valley ahead. Here, too, sluice-boxes are set up to trap the water. Various devices are used in the sluices for sieving the sand containing the gold. In principle, a filter containing quicksilver is set in the bottom of the sluice. When the water carrying mineral ores runs down, because gold is heavy and gold and mercury have an affinity, the gold-dust adheres to the mercury and settles at the bottom of the sluice. The gold is then separated from the mercury and the mercury flows back into the filter in the sluice to be re-used.

A train made its way back down the tracks towards us, and we were informed that the boulders had been cleared from the rails ahead. At half past one the brakes were released. After climbing steeply for five miles we reached Shady Run. This was already 4,430 feet high, and from there the incline was even steeper. The number of locomotives was increased, with three coupled in line being needed to haul the carriages. The high peaks of Shady Run and China Ranch closed in around the train. Tall trees shrouded in clouds seemed to reach the skies, and peak upon peak shone like polished gems. Wind-whipped snow flurries whirled around us, and mottled patches of snow lay scattered among the pine-trees. Mountains rose in tiers above the steep track. Inside the train, the carriage windows had two layers of glass to keep out the cold and there were stoves to heat the compartments. Traversing the steep mountains on comfortably upholstered couches, we gazed out over a silver world lashed by spring winds. Our only regret was that the double-glass panes, while they held the frigid air at bay, kept fogging up because of the contrast in temperature inside and outside the carriages. This caused our breaths to condense on the glass and obscure the view.

From here the train began to pass through what are called 'snow-sheds'. These are strong roofs built over the track to keep it clear of snow. They are constructed of tall timbers, each a foot square, with boards nailed across them to make solid buttresses semi-octagonal in shape. The overlapping boards on the roofs form a pattern resembling that on a turtle-shell. The snow-sheds run for two to three miles and in some places up to fifteen or sixteen miles. When our train passed through one of these sheds, the carriage interiors grew dark, just as when passing through a tunnel. Only occasionally could we see, through the gaps between the timbers, flashes of light reflected from the snow beside the sheds.

Five miles above Shady Run we came out of the [West Boulder] tunnel. The snow-sheds continued, and as we roared through them the carriages became dark, then light, then dark again. This went on for an hour and a half before we entered a snow-shed twenty miles long and the sunlight was suddenly extinguished. Because it is not easy to transport coal up into these mountains, locomotives burn logs as fuel. Mounds of logs were stacked for thousands of yards beside the snow-sheds. The track became very steep and the train struggled forward so slowly that in five hours we covered only forty-eight miles. Climbing nearly 3,000 feet, at half past six in the evening we reached Summit.

At 7,017 feet above sea-level, Summit is the highest point on the railroad across the Sierra Nevada. Mountain crests surged in all directions like great waves seeming to break against the sky. Just where a tunnel had been blasted into the bowels of the mountains there was a station with a large cottage. The people here were expecting us and had prepared a hot meal. Because of the breakdown we had not had an opportunity to eat lunch, so we took lunch and dinner at the same time. Up here in the High Sierra, the snow was six or seven feet deep and the train depot was half-buried in a drift. When we got out of the train the cold seared our skin. At this point a snow-plough locomotive was attached to the train to help clear the snow ahead. This has a grill made of hard wood in the front. Advancing once more, we entered a tunnel, roaring into the blackness of night again. Peacefully asleep in our carriages, we were oblivious to the steepness of the incline as we descended.

CHAPTER 6

# The Railroad Journey in the State of Nevada and Utah Territory

February 3rd, 1872. Fine.

From Summit, we descended 1,700 feet within a distance of eleven miles. When the train pulled into Truckee Station, we heard the sounds of a river rushing beside the track. From here we entered the state of Nevada.

The track wove back and forth between the left and right banks of the Humboldt River as it proceeded eastwards. After two hours we reached the village of Humboldt, where we stopped for twenty minutes to have breakfast. This region is now known as the Humboldt Wilderness; originally it was called 'the American Desert'. Dry desert with sagebrush stretched as far as the horizon. The river meandered across the arid landscape in broken streams. No trees grew on the hillsides, no springs welled up in the canyons and no houses were visible in any direction.

This is an area inhabited by American Indians. From the train windows we sometimes caught sight of their winter dwellings, which are dugouts among the rough sagebrush, with roofs thatched with bundles of grass in the shape of a small dome. Wondering what such a house was like inside, we asked somebody who is familiar with Indian customs. He told us that it is spherical, with half the sphere above the ground and half below it. Having journeyed through a realm of civilisation and enlightenment, we were now crossing a very ancient, uncivilised wilderness.

All the land around here was the territory of the native Indians. In recent years, however, white Americans have pushed them out and deprived them of their land, angering the indigenous inhabitants, whose desire for revenge is implacable. When the railroad was first constructed, the Indians banded together and tore up the rails or rolled boulders onto the tracks in a constant effort to halt the trains. They even shot quiverfuls of poisoned arrows at the railroad passengers.

Although all native Americans are generally called 'Indians', they do not comprise a single tribe. Those who live around here are among the most impoverished and debased. They wear their hair long, hanging

35

down their necks, and as adornment paint their faces yellow with the sap of trees and plants. Their features display the bone structure often seen among our own base people and outcasts. Their colour is a darkish yellow. Their noses are wide, their lips thick and rough, and their cheek-bones high. They wear tattered robes, some of which were probably begged from the nearby houses of white settlers. From their motley clothes it is difficult to tell much about their tribal customs or traditional way of life. Some Indians carry fire-wood on their shoulders to sell to settlers, while others sell beads to passers-by on the streets. Each tribe speaks its own language.

February 4th. Cloudy.
Last night we entered Utah Territory, just before we reached Lucin Station. We were still crossing the American Desert, which is 4,500 feet above sea-level.

At half past seven this morning we reached Ogden Station, where we had breakfast. Ogden has a population of nearly 3,000. Eastwards lie the foothills of the Wasatch Mountains, and to the west is the swampy land which borders the lake. At times we could see brilliant flashes of sunlight reflected on the lake. The marsh close to the shore is made up of silt from the Weber River. There were no signs of cultivation. On higher ground, however, there were many places where fences had been erected to enclose and pasture cattle. On the hills and mountains some trees were visible. Ogden had many houses, most of them small cabins. Around the town, in every direction, the land was beginning to be opened up and settled, but 80 to 90 per cent remained uncultivated. The Central Pacific Railroad Company track terminates at this station and connects with the Union Pacific Railroad Company track. Because of the deep snowdrifts in the Rocky Mountains, the track ahead was buried. We were told that the company had dispatched several thousand workers to try to clear the snow, but the track was not yet open. We therefore transferred to a train belonging to the Utah Central Railroad Company and headed south to Salt Lake City.

The Great Salt Lake is like a small sea. A large desert basin east of the Sierra Nevada and west of the Rocky Mountains is surrounded by mountains on all sides, and since there are no outlets to allow the lake water to drain into the sea, the overflow from one lake runs into another. The lake is 2,100 square miles in area and roughly rectangular in shape. Mountain ridges extend into promontories and four large islands and four small ones are scattered over the lake. If one gazes across the lake at its widest point, the water seems to merge with the boundless blue sky.

The mountains around the lake are rocky and jagged; the reddish-yellow soil, arid and bare of vegetation, is bone-dry. The striated rocks, with strangely cleft faces, are reflected in the lake, creating an impressive picture. Despite this, the scene is raw and primitive. The surrounding desert wilderness is barren and open, and impressive for its stark emptiness.

Because the lake contains thick veins of rock-salt, its waters are extremely briny and no fish live in it. It is said to be even saltier than the Dead Sea. The salt content of even the saltiest sea-water is only 3 parts per 100, but the Great Salt Lake is said to be 25 parts per 100.

Salt Lake City has prospered in recent years thanks to the profits derived from mining. The city is laid out on the flat plains of the lake shore. To the west is desert, while to the east the red-rock peaks of the Wasatch Mountains in the outer ranges of the Rocky Mountains run north for miles.

The streets in Salt Lake City are 100 feet across at their widest and are laid out in a regular grid pattern. Trees resembling oaks have been planted on both sides of the streets and divide the footpaths from the carriage-ways. Because the streets are unpaved, whenever it rains or snows one's boots sink into a quagmire. Sand is spread on the footpaths to make it easier to walk. There was no gas company in the city yet, so only oil-lamps at the corners of major intersections illuminated the streets at night. Most of the residential houses are built of timber. It is said that when a man of the Mormon sect takes a new wife, a window is added to his house.

We arrived at Salt Lake City in the afternoon and found rooms at the Townsend House.

February 5th. Snow, then clear; the morning temperature was 34°.
Because we had hurriedly put up at a remote inn on the edge of town yesterday evening, half the Embassy members did not have time to arrange for proper accommodation. Trudging back and forth between the station and the hotel through the snow early this morning was very tiresome.

In the afternoon we went to some hot-springs on the eastern edge of the city, a mile from the centre at the foot of the mountains. The temperature of the briny springs felt comfortable to the skin. A wooden bath-house had been erected over the springs, and the pools of hot water were about four and a half feet deep. The bathing area was divided into sections, and each person paid a fee of 25 cents to bathe there.

February 6th. Cloudy and cold; temperature 28°; rain at night.
Today we visited Utah Territorial Legislature [Salt Lake City Hall]. A
'territory' is land which is being opened up for development by the
federal government and has not yet been designated as a state.

The United States has grown as a nation by uniting the states, one by
one. Every state maintains its own constitution, and the citizens of each
state elect a governor and set up a state government. With its own
legislature, each state maintains its autonomy and assumes the features of
a genuine independent state within the federal union. In relations with
foreign countries, however, the United States deals with them federally, as
a single nation. Thus, the federal government derives its power from the
states; the states are not created by the federal government. Territories
which were not yet states when the federal union was created are
administered under the supervision of the federal government, including
Congress and the president. The government selects one person to serve
as governor of the territory. Under him the citizens elect representatives.
That is about the extent of political representation. Territories cannot
send congressmen to Washington; they may send one representative, but
he only has the authority to speak on matters relating to the territory.

Today, at City Hall, we met the governor of Utah Territory, the mayor
of Salt Lake City and more than one hundred other officials. Speeches
were made in the legislative chamber. From there we went to the residence of Mr. [William] Jennings, the wealthiest citizen in the territory,
who provided wine and food for our refreshment.

On our way back to the hotel we visited the Mormon Tabernacle, the
great temple of the Mormon sect. It is built with stone pillars and has a
vast timber roof in the shape of an oval dome 250 feet long and 150 feet
wide. The interior is very spacious; it is free of pillars and can seat 12,000
people. There is a pipe-organ in the front and galleries around the other
three walls. Beside the Tabernacle the ground has been dug and stones
laid in order to build a huge hall. The foundations are almost complete
and in scale it is even larger than the Tabernacle.

There are said to be no more than 200,000 Mormon believers in all,
and yet they have built their great Tabernacle in this rural city in the
midst of a mountainous wilderness. It can easily be deduced from this
that Western people who are religious believers give generously to build
their temples.

The Mormon sect is a kind of heterodoxy derived from Christianity
and is rejected by most Western people as a false teaching. According to
Mormon beliefs, if a man does not have at least seven wives he cannot

enter Heaven. This sect was founded by Joseph Smith [1805–44], who was born in the state of Vermont. He claimed he encountered a divine apparition in a grove of trees and, on God's instructions, found a volume of teachings in a stone hut. After he started to proclaim these teachings, he was murdered. Smith had a nephew called Brigham Young, from New York State. At the age of thirty-two, Young lost his wife and from then on devoted himself to study. He was later sent to Britain where he mastered the inner secrets of Mormon prophecies. When he returned to America and spread these teachings, he was expelled from New York. Together with 143 followers, he hid in these mountains, eventually establishing this city and making it prosper. That was in 1847, twenty-three years ago. Mr. Young, seventy-one years old this year, is hale and hearty and has sixteen wives and forty-eight children. He has accumulated a tremendous fortune.

The Mormon religion has also spread into the neighbouring territories of Nevada and New Mexico. The number of believers has reached 200,000 and the sect is growing rapidly. It is also spreading into California, but the American people all detest it. This year the House of Representatives, in an effort to outlaw the spread of Mormon proselytising, summoned its missionaries before Congress to explain their activities. The Mormons sought to justify themselves, but the meeting ended in a setback; and they were forbidden in future to preach except to their own believers. Young was placed under house-arrest, and the authorities posted guards around his house to prevent him escaping.

CHAPTER 7

# *The Rocky Mountain Railroad*

New Year's Day (February 9th, 1872). Cloudy, with mixed rain and snow; the temperature outside fell to 46°.

As we were still in Salt Lake City, champagne was served to all to usher in the [lunar] New Year. At night we invited the city officials and Mr. and Mrs. DeLong to a New Year's party at the hotel. Speeches were made and hosts and guests all joined in a festive celebration which continued until after one o'clock.

February 11th. Cloudy and cold; the temperature outside fell to 36°.

From two o'clock in the afternoon we went to the Mormon Tabernacle and listened to a sermon. The service began with the breaking of what looked like a rice cake. After that, organ music was played in the rear hall, and the congregation sang hymns and said prayers. A minister ascended the pulpit and preached a sermon drawn from the New Testament on the theme of the brotherhood of all nations. The style of the service, like that of other Protestant denominations, was simple and clear.

February 12th. Fine.

This night the mayor of Salt Lake City, Mr. D. H. Wells, and city officials and merchants hosted a banquet at the hotel. The dining-room was decorated with the crossed flags of our two countries and a portrait of Washington. The food was varied, sumptuous and delicious. A band played continuously throughout the evening. Women as well as men attended, and after dinner there were many speeches, followed by ballroom dancing. After midnight the party disintegrated completely and sank into disorderliness. It did not break up until three o'clock in the morning. The social customs in this remote mountain area were, we thought, somewhat less than refined.

40

February 15th. Fine.

The prosperity of Salt Lake City is based on the profits derived from mining. Although Salt Lake City is located in a mountain wilderness seven hundred miles from the Pacific Ocean, it is as rich as Nevada in its silver veins, and its wealth lies in its deposits of silver. Six years ago a silver-mine was opened on the outskirts of the city. Vice-Ambassador Ōkubo wanted to visit it today, but because the road was blocked with snow, he could not realise his wish.

The Pacific Plain, for the most part unproductive desert, stretches endlessly to where horizon and sky meet. The mountains are bare, and the desert plains red in colour. Dust fills the air, making the sunlight appear yellow. The land in this region is not conducive to farming or cattle-raising. In the soil, however, veins of precious gold have been discovered. We have been told that even though there is much gold in South America, the people there still suffer from starvation. This is not surprising, for land containing precious metals is always barren.

February 21st. Fine.

In the morning we learned by telegraph that, because the snowdrifts on the Rocky Mountain plateau had started to melt, the rivers had over-flowed and the railroad track had been washed away in places. Our departure was, therefore, delayed again. Because of the deep snow in the Rocky Mountains, we had already been confined to this remote western town for seventeen days! We had seen everything which might possibly be interesting and the bright moon was now full. Even if we had wanted to amuse ourselves night and day, there were only four or five desolate streets in this isolated town. Our spirits grew gloomier by the day.

February 22nd. Cloudy.

Today, after receiving a report that the track ahead had been repaired and re-opened, we set out from the hotel at ten minutes to ten in the morning and arrived at Ogden just after noon. After a few hours two dining-cars were coupled to our train and food was loaded on as well. We left Ogden at half past four in the afternoon.

The day was cloudy, but it was not yet dusk when suddenly the interior of the carriages became as dark as night. Astonished, we looked out of the windows and saw that we were passing through a very narrow ravine with rock walls rising on both sides. This gorge is a natural tunnel known as Devil's Gate.

Although we were still on the desert plains of Utah, the dust had now settled because of the rain. As we travelled along the narrow track through the Wasatch Mountains, we saw clumps of trees here and there, which provided patches of greenery. Although the colour of the landscape was no longer the burnt red of Utah, as we penetrated deeper into the mountains the remoteness and isolation grew increasingly pronounced. We did not hear the cry of a single bird, perhaps because it was the depths of winter. All we could hear was the wind in the pines above the track and the roar of the Weber River in the ravine below.

After sixteen miles we passed Echo, a village with a population of about 600. From Echo the gradient became steeper, and at times we entered tunnels or ran through canyons in which the walls rose sheer. In twenty-five miles we climbed 1,300 feet out of Echo Canyon to a village called Wasatch, another spectacularly scenic area. The sun had set and it was nearly dark. When the whirling snow cleared, a cold moon shone, looking as if it had been washed clean. The sharp angles of the mountain peaks were etched against the clear dark sky, gleaming in the moonlight as if reflected off the shining blade of a sword. The canyon walls on both sides were so steep that no grass or trees grew there, but the beauty of the rocky landscape was enhanced by the snowfall. As the train approached the rocky walls, they seemed to close in over us. We were so busy looking to left and right that we forgot our weariness.

After advancing nine miles from Wasatch village and descending forty-five feet, we reached Evanston. Up to Evanston we had been travelling across Utah. After that we entered Wyoming Territory.

February 23rd. Fine.
At half past nine in the morning we received a telegraph saying that the Green River Bridge had been repaired. The driver released the brakes of the locomotive and we steamed ahead into Wyoming Territory.

From Utah Territory in the west through Wyoming lies the largest stretch of wilderness in the United States. Even with the train racing at full speed we did not reach a major population centre until we had travelled for a full four days. Withered prairie grass and thick scrub stretched away endlessly. Here and there we saw native Indians or their pit-dwellings. Only every ten miles or so did we see small hamlets consisting of two or three houses beside the track. Beyond the railway, rugged peaks continued for a thousand miles. There was not the shadow of a single bird. Although one may tire of hearing about the vastness of the

United States, when one experiences it, it is even more astonishing than one could believe.

The area we travelled through had been buried beneath snow for a month. By the time we passed, however, most of the snow had melted, leaving only a few lingering traces. At night we raised our sleepy heads, surprised by the cold light reflected on the windows of the carriage. We saw that we were still rolling across a deserted plain, but in order to keep the track open, the snow had been piled high on both sides, creating icy dunes which glittered in the bright moonlight. We felt as if we were riding through some gigantic jewel. When I looked at the time-table I saw that we had reached Creston and were travelling at 7,000 feet above sea-level.

February 24th. Very fine.
The sun was rising as we passed through Laramie. Looking out of the window to see where we were, I spied twenty or thirty houses. They all looked substantial and Laramie had the appearance of being an established settlement. From here we passed through more snow-sheds and then the incline of the track rose sharply until Sherman Summit, where we had breakfast on the train.

Sherman is at the highest point of the Rocky Mountain railroad, about 8,240 feet above sea-level. Although high in the mountains, it lies on a broad plateau, where gently rolling hills make the landscape look no different from low-lying plains. The yellowish-black soil was covered with sparse grass, and to the left of the railway track were scattered mounds of flattish rocks. A small grove of stunted pine-trees growing crookedly among the rocks made an extremely elegant and tasteful scene. Since leaving Salt Lake City we had travelled only over plains of withered grass and sagebrush. The unexpected sight of wind-shaped pine-trees with their green needles in this high place was strangely moving. In the distance, forty or fifty miles away, we saw the blue mountains which we were told make up the Medicine Bow Range. The weather was fine every day now, and all the snow had melted away. Not even on the high peaks were any patches to be seen. The sky was a brilliant indigo blue.

From Sherman Summit the track descended gently through the village of Sherman. From this point on we were descending the eastern slope of the Rocky Mountains, but the downward incline was so slight that we hardly noticed it. This gentle slope led onto the famous plains of Cheyenne, where short, dried grass stretched into the distance. No mountains were visible, and there was nothing to look at all day. This barren, empty plain spreads over a thousand miles, with no inhabitants or trees to be seen.

In the afternoon we reached Sidney, a village with a population of a little over 600. In this region there is a United States Army garrison of more than 200 infantry and cavalry to defend it against the Indians.

At nine o'clock at night we crossed the North Platte River [in Nebraska]. The twin forks of the Platte River, which rise in the Medicine Bow Range high in the Rocky Mountains, cross the prairie north and south of the railroad and meet at North Platte village to form the Platte River, which flows into the Missouri River near Omaha. The Platte is more than 1,000 feet wide, its waters clear and the current gentle. Icicles still hung down, and the shallow pools among the sand-bars were all frozen. The railway track ran straight across the river on a bridge which lacked any wooden cross planks; the rails were simply fixed directly onto the bridge in a very rough-and-ready fashion. To cross the bridge, the locomotive slowed down and inched forward. Dusk gave way to darkness and the waning light reflected dimly off the clumps of prairie grass; a biting wind cut across the river and the moon looked as if it was frozen. Along the river-banks some Indians had lit fires. The scene truly deserved to be captured in a painting.

February 25th. Fine.
Dawn broke as we were passing Columbus. From the train windows all we could see was the vast deserted prairie. Here and there, however, were cultivated fields and pastures, and in the distance we could distinguish the shadowy outline of woodlands. This scenery was already different from the parched plains and prairie of the previous days.

At eleven o'clock we reached Omaha. From Ogden to Omaha is 1,032 miles. Even with the train travelling at full speed it had taken us three days to cross these plains. The empty landscape weighed on our hearts. We asked what roads and trails travellers had used five or six years ago, before the railroad was built, and the reply was that people did not travel much. To provide a postal service to the territories of Utah, Nevada and California, 'pony-express' relay stages were set up, with horses always at the ready. The riders changed horses frequently as they crossed and re-crossed the continent. Indians often ambushed them, so the riders carried pistols for their protection. Men had to ride back and forth across the continent regardless of the risks because the postal service was essential to trade and commerce. We could see how much work had gone into making this harsh territory their own, ready for settlement. There are many other examples of such pioneering efforts.

That morning our train steamed into Omaha along the west bank of the Missouri River. Omaha is the eastern terminus of the Union Pacific Railroad track. From here we were to cross the Missouri River, but we stopped for a while at the river-bank. A grain storage depot had been built here, criss-crossed with railroad tracks. It must have been filled with maize, or Indian corn, as we could see the husks scattered about.

We noticed a line of railway-carriages approaching from the new bridge across the Missouri River. The carriages looked rough and rickety, and we were told that they were 'immigrant carriages', transporting immigrants to various settlements within the state. The fare was said to be less than one-third the usual amount. The convenience of the railways and the profits from Indian corn have transformed this prairie wilderness into a flourishing and fertile land. This is the characteristic face of American development.

On the basis of what we had seen as we traversed the American continent, we could readily imagine the course of its future development. It was only when we approached Omaha, after travelling across the plains from the Rocky Mountains, that we regained the sense of being in the realm of human habitation. Not surprisingly, the streets of Omaha still seemed rather quiet. Forty years earlier, when the present large city of Chicago had barely existed, the territories making up the states east of Omaha must have been in the condition that the Rocky Mountains are today. Chicago, however, is now a flourishing, smoke-belching metropolis; the Mississippi Valley basin is filling with people; and Omaha is a city. How lively will the streets of Omaha be in another forty years? And will towns not be seen springing up all over the virgin prairie as the immigrant carriages roll in?

Having passed through a land such as this, we are increasingly convinced that the great treasure of the world lies not in material things such as money but in the force of human energy. In cities such as San Francisco, Chicago and St. Louis, wealthy merchants and prosperous farmers compete with one another and count their fortunes in millions of dollars. In the past, the fertile lands from California to Nebraska were left as desert and prairie. This was not due to a lack of funds but to a shortage of physical energy, or manpower, the driving force of change. Machinery and livestock can be found in all the states and territories, but much has not yet been developed because of the shortage of population. Although railways were constructed and trains provided for transporting settlers, and all things managed in such a way as to accumulate manpower, human beings cannot be created by kneading clay into a human shape. Immigrants were therefore encouraged to come from many countries until the number of them from both Europe and other parts of America has recently reached around 400,000 annually.

When we look at our own country of Japan, its 'great treasure' of population is about the same in number as America's, but our country is one hundred times older. Its size is less than three-hundredths that of America, but there are profits lying fallow in its fields and unexploited treasures in its mountains. Why is it then that the Japanese of both the upper and lower classes remain poor and miserable? It is because uneducated people are hard to employ, untrained people are useless and enterprise without organisation is ineffective. Even though manpower is abundant in Japan, if we want to show how productive our population can be, it is not enough to sit back and indulge in wishful thinking.

American gentlemen are all deeply religious and build a lot of elementary schools. They put all their effort into basic education, regarding higher education as something to be tackled later. Let us consider their reasons. Vagrants and labourers are stubborn and ignorant, and consequently it is necessary to inculcate a respect for God in them to improve their character. They are taught the necessary essentials of language, arithmetic and science in order to make a living. They are given rules and tasks, are strictly supervised – with honesty rewarded and unreliability punished – and they are directed in their work. In this way, the people will be united in their thinking, the means to create wealth will be fostered and the nation will gain in strength.

The East, however, does just the opposite. Look at how the upper classes study, for example. If they are not indulging in empty speculation, they devote their time to literature, which is trivial and fleeting. They dismiss the most important matter of making a living as mundane, of little or no consequence. Middle-class people either hoard their wealth or gamble it away. They do not have the steadfastness of purpose necessary to build a family fortune or engage in business. As a result, people of the lower orders have barely sufficient food and clothing. They struggle merely to exist from day to day. Human though they are, they are not accorded any respect as human beings.

CHAPTER 8

# *The Chicago Railroad*

February 25th, 1872.

Our train stopped on the west bank of the Missouri River and we waited several hours while our luggage was transferred into cars belonging to the Chicago Railroad. Then the train began to proceed slowly over the still-unfinished bridge to the other side of the river.

The rich, moist loam of the Mississippi and Missouri basin is very suitable for growing Indian corn, the common grain grown in the most fertile regions of these states. Corn is said to have first been the staple crop of the native Indians of this area, hence the name 'Indian corn', and the practice then spread around the world. Corn is very nourishing, but the kernels are hard and difficult to digest and, according to physicians who have conducted experiments, can take as many as five hours to digest. However, if eaten with other, more digestible grains and meat, it is good for the stomach. Enormous quantities of corn are exported to Britain, especially from the states of the Mississippi River basin.

February 26th. Fine.

At three o'clock in the morning we passed Burlington, where we crossed a long bridge over the Mississippi. The river marks the boundary between the states of Iowa and Illinois, and we were now entering Illinois.

The Mississippi is a mighty river which flows through the underbelly of the United States. Although we crossed the upper Mississippi, the river was already 1,800 feet wide. Here, an iron railroad bridge has been constructed across it, which was a tremendous engineering achievement. The grand scale of the construction is known around the world.

As the interior of the United States has been opened up and developed, the frequency with which the Mississippi overflows its banks has steadily increased. This is because as the states in the Mississippi River valley develop, the number of vessels using the river has risen annually. In order to ease navigation and promote transportation, channels were cut clear through many of the river's bends. As a result formerly sluggish sections flow much more rapidly, and this has made the current both rougher and faster. In addition, levees have been built and they are reinforced every year to prevent the river from overflowing its banks. These have enabled the flood plain on both sides of the river to be developed. Reservoirs have been built to control the water, and irrigation ditches lead water from the furrowed fields back into the river. In addition, because grass and trees grow luxuriantly on the flood plain, this has led to a decrease in evaporation. All this extra water now pours into the Mississippi, making its currents stronger and rendering river transportation more difficult.

In the West we did not see any paddy-fields. The emphasis is on draining water away from dikes and furrows in the fields in what might be called a 'ditch and drain method'. Even so, damage to fields from river water occurs in the manner described above. In Japan farmers put great effort into making and maintaining irrigated paddy-fields. This is the method of agriculture used in ancient China. Paddy-fields are always under water. When it rains, all the rain water runs into the rivers. Moreover, when it rains, all the sluices to the paddy-fields are closed to protect them. Thus, rivers flood and the damage is widespread. When the rain stops and the waters subside, all the sluice gates are opened, with the result that river water inundates the fields and river transportation becomes impossible. Moreover, farmers cultivating paddy-fields often extend them to the river-banks. The rivers are reduced and inevitably there are many natural disasters from flooding. When there are no ditches or channels for the water, the roads are affected, and this interferes with transportation.

From now on, those studying the benefits of water-power must look into the Western method of dry-field agriculture, recognising the differences with our wet-field agriculture. Depending on the suitability of the land for wet or dry farming, we should use American methods of controlling great rivers and apply them to Japanese rivers. It could help to eliminate our problems with water disasters.

Our train pulled into the station in Chicago at half past two that afternoon. With the vastness of the station building, the complexity of the railroad tracks, and the constant traffic of passenger and freight trains, we experienced the vitality of a great metropolis for the first time since San Francisco. Most of the stations up to now had been rather insignificant places.

We transferred to horse-drawn carriages and were taken to the Tremont House and Grand Central hotels. The mayor of the city and

General Sheridan of the United States Army, among others, came to our hotels to welcome us. They requested that we stay for three days in order to see the city fully.

February 27th. Fine.
North-east of Chicago is the shore of the vast Lake Michigan, its waters still and clear. Looking north across the expanse of water, the lake seemed to merge with the sky. This is one of the five Great Lakes. As mentioned earlier, transportation in the northern part of the United States relies heavily on the waterways provided by its lakes and rivers. Chicago is the southern centre for transportation on the lakes.

Most of the products of the Mississippi River valley and the northern states pour into this city. Year by year it grows more prosperous. The streets are lined with the shops of wealthy merchants. Thousands of rich people live in Chicago, and their collective capital almost exceeds the wealth of New York City.

On the night of October 9th last year, a fire started which quickly roared into a huge conflagration. Over twenty thousand buildings in the most flourishing sections were reduced to ashes. The fire continued to burn for more than two whole days, and the loss of property was estimated at $500,000,000. People who were caught in this disaster and lost their houses, family treasures and businesses wandered the streets homeless and starving. It is said to have been the worst fire since the city was founded.

This morning our guides from the city government arrived, and at ten o'clock we boarded carriages for a tour of the city. We passed through the area in the north-west which had been devastated in the fire. Exposed foundations and broken walls thrust bare and jagged into the sky. Within the walls of the burnt-out houses were piles of broken tiles and charred stones and timbers mixed with earth, and ash and dust rose into the air as if some heat still remained. Labourers were carrying the charred debris out in carts and piling it beside the roads. Although there was no wind, the ash continued to rise into the air. The suffering citizens had built temporary shelters and huddled around them: it was almost unbearable to observe their misery. From every state in the union, and from Europe as well, people have donated relief funds, which have now amounted to $5,000,000. Today, through our ambassador, the Embassy donated $5,000. Already four months have passed since the disaster, and houses were gradually being re-built. Although some had already been completed, our guides told us it would take at least three years to restore the city to its former condition.

Our carriages then rattled over an iron drawbridge, the construction of which displayed advanced engineering techniques, to reach Lake Michigan. On the shore of the lake stands a pumping station which provides the city with clean water. Due to the wind and waves, the water by the shore is sometimes covered with debris. Therefore, three miles out from shore, a water collection station has been built, and the Lake Michigan Tunnel was dug under the lake-bed to the pumping-house on shore. When they started laying the pipes, one group of workers dug the tunnel from the lake, while another group dug outwards from the shore, following measurements made by the city's hydraulic engineers. When the two groups met at the centre, there was a discrepancy of only one inch. Cylindrical in shape and lined with tiles, the tunnel is a great conduit running eighty feet below the lake-bed. The pumps in use at first were rather small, and because the city was growing so rapidly, the water-supply was not sufficient. Recently, new and more powerful pumps have been installed. Some Chicagoans boastfully claim that their water pumping and water distribution facilities are unrivalled in the world. They are not exaggerating.

On the shore of the lake, a fire-extinguisher recently invented in this city was on display. We were given a demonstration of this device, called the Babcock Extinguisher. Chemicals are mixed with water in two copper drums which contain 150 gallons. Each container is attached to a rubber hose twenty or thirty feet long, with a heavy brass nozzle fitted at the end. The firemen grasp these hoses to direct the jets of water.

On the day of our tour, firemen piled up oil-soaked barrels of tar in a wooden shanty on the sandy shore of the lake. When they set fire to them, the flames leapt up immediately, engulfing the whole hut and shooting out of the gaps between the wooden boards. At the height of the conflagration, when the hut was burning furiously, the firemen outside aimed the hose nozzles and sent streams of water and chemicals gushing out to extinguish the flames. Within a few seconds, the flames had abated and white smoke billowed up. The firemen then dragged the hoses into the shed and extinguished the remaining flames. With only 150 gallons of liquid they were able to save the hut and the barrels.

Western cities possess very advanced fire-prevention equipment. First of all, they have underground water-pipes and fire hydrants throughout the cities. When the pipes are opened, water shoots twenty or thirty feet into the air. This alone would be sufficient to extinguish a small fire. However, available water supplies are often inadequate when fighting a fire, and for this reason fire-brigades have started using this chemical-and-water method.

We continued our drive through the city and reached a very prosperous district where as many as one hundred telegraph wires converged, then radiated out in all directions like a spider's web. This was the Chicago Board of Trade (like the British Royal Exchange), an assembly of merchants which sets the values of commodities and stocks. As we entered, many merchants were gathering in the hall. The president of the board ascended a platform and delivered a speech, introducing us to the audience. The traders, who had swarmed in like an army of ants, cheered us.

At ten minutes past nine that night we boarded a train at Chicago East Station and set off. Once again we passed through gentle rolling landscape dotted with woodland, and during the night we crossed the state of Indiana.

# CHAPTER 9

# The Railroad Journey from Chicago to Washington, D.C.

February 28th, 1872. Fine.
Early this morning we crossed the border into Ohio. The two states of Indiana and Ohio, together with Missouri and Illinois, are in the northern part of the Mississippi River valley and they are all among the most developed and settled of the large states.

At half past four we arrived at Pittsburgh, the great city of western Pennsylvania. The station was teeming with travellers, as numerous as swarming bees. The hotel by the station, where we had dinner, was magnificent; the dining-room on the top floor could seat several hundred people. All the floors of the building were of white stone and were so similar that even though we were at the very top of the building we felt as if we were at ground level. At half past five in the evening we boarded the train again and left Pittsburgh.

The United States of America originally started its development from the Atlantic Plain. After independence, settlers soon pushed through the Mississippi River valley, and every thirty years or so a great wave rolled farther and farther west. From the time we disembarked in San Francisco harbour until we reached Pennsylvania, we witnessed the panorama of the pioneering development of America unfolding before us.

In Sacramento, California, we had asked a representative of the state government about the procedures for the allocation and registration of land claims in the state. He told us that land located near a railroad or trans-portation centre is generally sold for $1.50 per acre. Land farther away from the railroad and less conveniently situated is $1.00 per acre. Remote land is given away for nothing to those who are willing to settle and develop it.

Later, at the Salt Lake City territorial government offices, we learned that a Land Claims Bureau had been established to oversee the acquisition of wilderness and unsettled land for development. Land near roads or on river-banks, considered suitable for development, is surveyed and divided into lots. Large lots known as 'townships', similar to Japan's 'large wards', are first marked out in six-mile squares. These are further sub-divided by grid-lines into thirty-six blocks, each a mile square called a 'section', which corresponds to our 'small wards'. Each block is again sub-divided into halves, quarters and eighths, and these are sold at a dollar an acre. All land is re-surveyed every ten years, and if there is no evidence of any improvement or production being undertaken, it is re-possessed by the Land Claims Bureau.

Land is sold under the name of the governor of the territory, and a certificate of sale is issued. When the buyer has received his certificate, he determines the boundaries of the plot and puts up fences, which one sees everywhere on the plains. Land may be extremely cheap, but erecting fences costs a great deal of money. After that is done, the landowners will hire help to develop the land. Because the hired hands who work the land and raise livestock demand high wages, farmers must have some savings or a family fortune, and they must know what they are doing. The only way to make a profit is to lower costs by reducing the number of employees and by using farm machinery.

The current population of the United States is much the same as that of Japan. However, in size the United States is dozens of times larger. It is truly astonishing how much of this land is under cultivation. As we crossed from one state into another and saw extensive areas being cultivated, it made Japanese farmers seem indolent by comparison. Some Westerner gave the example of an Arab who made his emaciated horses till the land with a shoddy plough; in ten hours he turned only 160 square yards of rough land or about three-quarters of an acre of cultivated land. A farmer here, using a well-made plough and driving a healthy team, is three times more productive, cultivating about 2.5 acres in ten hours. When steam traction-engines are used, the output is ten times greater. Japanese farmers are nowhere near this level of productivity.

During the 1850s, when the Mississippi River valley was being opened up, word reached British people of the fertile land and easy transportation by river and canal. Immigrants flocked to the area and competed for farmland. Like fish from a small pond swimming into a great ocean, they attempted to cultivate large tracts of land but often lost much of the harvest because they could not reap the crops in time. Then Mr. [Cyrus Hall] McCormick invented a wheat-harvesting machine, and another man invented a grass-mowing machine. Before that, the harvesting machine invented by Mr. Patrick Bell of Scotland had already been abandoned in Britain, but this, together with the other two machines, is now valued around the world.

American agriculture operates on a huge scale, and American farmers do not bother with intensive farming. Rather, they rely on machines to cultivate the vast plains, and plant seed by scattering it [instead of planting it in furrows as in Europe]. When you consider the extent of the area under cultivation, the yield is relatively small.

Ten years ago, at the start of the Civil War, farm workers were drafted into the armies. This reduced the number working, but cultivation and development continued to proceed apace thanks to mechanisation. The benefits of mechanisation are evident, but farming cannot depend entirely on machines, however important they may be.

February 29th. Cloudy in the morning; snow from midday.
At first light, as we were passing through the fields and woodlands of Pennsylvania, we saw a great city emerging on our left, the rays of the early morning sun striking the rooftops. Smoke and vapour rose in clouds above the city, and tall chimneys soared skywards. We saw a river spanned by many iron bridges, with houses lining the banks. When we asked the name of this beautiful metropolis, we were told it was the famous city of Philadelphia.

At eleven o'clock we reached Baltimore Station. Among the cities to the south of Philadelphia, none surpasses Baltimore. The city hall, court house, custom house and exchange are all imposing edifices, and the shops were bustling with customers.

The railroad cut through the centre of the city, where the streets were laid out in a grid-like fashion. Out of consideration for pedestrians, the railroad cars were uncoupled and each one was pulled by six horses. A driver sat in front of each carriage, blowing a horn in warning. After driving among the slate-roofed houses, we eventually reached the southern station, where we stopped for a while.

At about the time we left Baltimore, rain gave way to steadily falling snow, and by the time we reached Washington the ground was covered with several inches of it. At three o'clock that afternoon we arrived at the station, which is near the Capitol. Mori Arinori, the resident Japanese minister in Washington, and General [William] Myers of the United States Army, the official in charge of the reception committee, came to the station to welcome us. We boarded carriages and drove to our accommodation at the Arlington Hotel on Vermont Avenue.

CHAPTER 10

# A Survey of the District of Columbia

The city of Washington is the capital of the union of thirty-seven states and forms an independent region known as the District of Columbia.

In upholding their pledge of confederation, the present thirty-seven states confer among themselves, obey federal laws and regulations, collect and transmit taxes, nominate and elect a joint chief executive, and support a single national government. The federal government is thus the locus of the Constitution and of the laws of the land. It governs the land and the people of all the states. There is no absolute need for the central government to possess land or people of its own. However, for the government to have to reside on a temporary basis in one of the states would be inappropriate. Having agreed upon a federal government, the states eventually decided to allot land on which to locate their government. The District of Columbia was created after the government had been established, just as West Point was founded after the system of military academies had been set up.

Before the government was settled in the District of Columbia [in 1790], there was no established capital. After the original thirteen colonies rejected British rule and established an independent confederation, there were long and bitter debates [over the rights of the states versus the claims of the central government and over the location of a capital]. Moreover, unlike today, none of the states wanted to grant the federal government the power to impose taxes. Even the representatives in Congress were short of money and sometimes had to contribute their own private funds or cover emergencies with ad hoc levies. The representatives had discussed political matters without having the proper authority, and the government was accommodated in a series of temporary capitals.

The population of the District of Columbia is 131,700, of which the population of Washington City [excluding Georgetown] is 109,199. When the British colonised the two states of Maryland and Virginia, many people had slaves, so in both states there are large numbers of black people. Of the total population of the District of Columbia, 44,000 are black people.

As the seat of the federal government, Washington is crowded with official visitors. Bureaucrats, generals, senators and congressmen from all over the country, as well as foreign diplomats, are constantly coming and going, all travelling at public expense and staying there temporarily. Despite the large population, the prices of goods are the highest in the nation because the city has no sources of production but only stores selling clothing, food, utensils and furniture. Many large hotels are mixed in among the public buildings, and the city is magnificent in both appearance and scale, but it is not a commercial centre and commerce seemed to be rather depressed.

The city stands on gently rolling land. The brilliant white Capitol building, towering above the city on its central hilltop, is the great landmark and symbol of the city. The Capitol lies at the centre of the city streets, which are laid out around it like the lines on a *go* board. Cutting diagonally through these are wide streets called 'avenues'. Four great avenues – Pennsylvania, Delaware, New Jersey and Maryland – converge on the Capitol.

The careful attention devoted to the paving and maintenance of the streets is a fine custom in industrialised countries and worthy of con-templation. In Washington, D.C., Pennsylvania Avenue is especially beautiful. It is 160 feet wide and has a central carriage-way. To the left and right of this are pathways for pedestrians, each more than 20 feet wide and paved with brick. At 30- or 40-foot intervals American poplars have been planted along the edges of these. During the spring and summer the avenue runs under a canopy of leaves providing green shade. The leafy streets off Pennsylvania Avenue gradually give way to cobble-stone paving, and in the quieter sections the paving becomes earth, which turns to dust when the weather is hot and mud when it rains.

Western cities spare no expense in paving and maintaining their roads. People do not carry loads themselves, nor do they use pack-horses, yet they can apply several dozen times the power of Japanese people to haul loads. A single horse can exert enough force to pull up to thirty tons. This may seem astonishing and incredible, but it is really quite simple. Wheels are very well made and roads are well surfaced. A load of one ton can be carried by twenty people or seven pack-horses. However, if it is hauled on well-made wheels, one healthy horse will be sufficient. If it is moved on rails, only eight pounds of pulling power is necessary.

Carriages called 'street-cars' or 'omnibuses' run on iron rails laid in the streets of many American cities; the large avenues of Washington, D.C., all have these rails. The routes are fixed and the street-cars stop at designated points to allow passengers to get on and off. Some of them are quite large, others are smaller. The larger ones resemble train carriages, and they are pulled by several horses and can carry up to fifty people. The smaller ones are pulled by a single horse and carry twenty-seven or twenty-eight people. Other street-cars are used for transporting freight and baggage; these are generally drawn by one horse.

The interiors of the large street-cars are spacious and comfortable, with benches on each side for the passengers to sit. When the cars are crowded, some passengers stand between the benches and hold onto leather straps for support. Platforms mounted at the front and rear of each car have guard rails to prevent people falling off. There are steps on both sides of the platforms, and passengers ride according to the class. The conductor stands on the platform. A cord runs through each car with a bell attached to it, and when passengers want to alight or to let someone board, the cord is pulled to signal the driver to halt the car. The frequency of cars varies somewhat, depending on the number of passengers along the route. Some run every five minutes, some every ten minutes and some at fifteen-minute intervals. Cars run day and night and try to be on time. The fare is three cents, five cents or, at most, seven cents for three or four miles.

Large hotels are scattered about the city, including the Arlington Hotel, in which the Embassy stayed. Not many of the theatres, squares, or gardens call for any special mention, but the cemetery in Georgetown is very pleasant. Department stores carrying a variety of goods are found only on two or three avenues. Most of the other streets contain the residences of officials or the homes of academics. When we had time to spare, we relaxed under shady trees and read, or went sightseeing by carriage to all parts of the city.

# CHAPTER II

# A Record of Washington, D.C., 1

February 29th, 1872. Snow.

When we arrived at the Arlington Hotel we learned that Mrs. Grant, the wife of the president, had sent a magnificent bouquet of fresh flowers for Ambassador Iwakura. The bouquet was reported to have cost $300; such a gift represents great tribute in the West.

March 4th. Fine.

At noon we were granted the honour of a formal state reception, at which we presented our credentials to President Grant. The president's official residence is located very close to Arlington Hotel, merely one square (a public garden) away to the west. It is known as the White House, and presidents live here from the day of their inauguration until the end of their term of office.

The grounds of the White House are an extremely neat and beautiful area in the capital. The laws of the United States are very relaxed, especially so in Washington. Even foreign visitors are permitted easy access to the White House and allowed to go sightseeing freely, unhindered by guards. Americans smile rather scornfully about European palaces and other sites where soldiers guard the premises and forbid entry to the common people. They think this a very antiquated, undemocratic custom.

March 6th. Fine.

At ten o'clock in the morning, accompanied by the commissioners, we were taken to the Capitol by carriage. (It is also called the Congress, or the national assembly.) This is the seat of government of the entire United States, and the Capitol building which houses it is the most splendid in Washington. The entire building is of stone and its total cost was $12,500,000. The main entrance is to the west. The north wing contains the upper house, or the Senate. The south contains the lower house, or the House of Representatives.

In the House of Representatives that day an exchange of speeches, or a debate, was in progress. The Speaker of the lower house, Mr. [James G.] Blaine, sat on the raised platform at the front. The Embassy members and various officials stood around that rostrum. Behind us sat all the representatives listening to the debate, as they do every day. All the seats in the galleries, running around three sides of the hall, were occupied by men and women wishing to observe the proceedings. First, the chairman made a speech of welcome, to which Ambassador Iwakura responded. One of the senators, General [Nathaniel P.] Banks, then read the translation of the ambassador's speech in English and added a few words. When the ceremony was over, we all left the lower house to visit some of the Capitol chambers.

Congress is the supreme government of the United States. The president is the chief executive, the vice-president is leader of the legislature [in the Senate], and the chief justice heads the judiciary. This is the framework of the federal government of the United States, which differs quite markedly from the governments of monarchies. (In a monarchy, both judicial and executive power are exercised by the monarch, who is assisted by a prime minister. Parliament only exercises legislative power.)

When the thirteen colonies rejected British rule, they established a confederation in which the representatives of the states debated issues and made decisions. With the war won and independence declared, statesmen-scholars such as Jefferson, Hamilton, Franklin and others drafted a constitution establishing a federal republic. Under this Constitution they established Congress as the national assembly and decreed that a president should be elected by the populace. Two representatives from each state were to be selected to serve as senators in an upper house. Representatives were to be elected from among the people of each state to serve in a lower house. The latter were called 'Congressmen'. When these proposals were debated in the states, many delegates voiced fierce opposition to them. Some claimed that a president is merely a king; others argued that raising armies and levying taxes should be left to the individual states. Still others declared that the confederation was adequate just as it was. Public debate seethed for almost a year before the turmoil was resolved through the moral influence of George Washington.

Because the Constitution was hammered out in this way, over long months of searching argument, it embodied the finest principles and touched the hearts of the people. Indeed, it has been venerated as though it embodied heavenly precepts. Today, ninety-six years later, even though thirty-seven states are now included in the Union, none dares to violate it. Nonetheless, assertions of autonomy by some states, as well as efforts to restrict the powers of the president and bitter debates among the citizens, have increased over the years.

The citizens of European monarchies, hearing of such wars of words among the American people in peacetime, tend to smile, thankful that they do not live in a republic. Of course, no man-made constitution will be perfect, and if power is given to the people, the power of the government will be reduced. The more one promotes liberty, the laxer the laws will become. It is a natural principle that if you gain something in one direction, you lose something in another. However, the American people have been nurtured on this kind of government and now, after a century, even children feel it would be shameful to serve a king. Because this is the wisdom of their experience, they see no fault in their democratic system, only perfection. Because they think their system is the best in the world, they encourage everyone to adopt a similar one. Even in brief conversations they manage to convey this opinion with unshakeable conviction. Theirs is the very soul of a republican people.

At night we were invited to the National Theatre. The crossed flags of Japan and America were displayed throughout the building.

March 11th. Cloudy.
The Embassy met Secretary of State Fish at the State Department. From there we went to the Japanese legation.

March 12th. Snow in the morning; fine in the afternoon.
At half past eight in the evening, having received an invitation to a banquet from President Grant, we set out by carriage for the White House. We were led to the Blue Room, where we were presented to the president and leading civil and military officers, who were all accompanied by their wives. At dinner everyone was extremely cordial. We chatted across the tables and enjoyed ourselves immensely. The banquet ended at eleven o'clock. In the West, the host observes great courtesy and elaborate decorum when holding such functions, which enhance the importance of the gathering. It is always considered proper etiquette for the main guests to attend with their wives.

March 14th. Snow.
We went again to the State Department for a second meeting.

Five [American] Indians visited us at our hotel today. They had asked for an interview with the Embassy, and Vice-Ambassador Itō talked with them. They left after a short meeting.

At night at the hotel we gave a reception for many government officials and wealthy Washington merchants. Several large rooms of the hotel were gaily decorated for the occasion. The ambassador and other members of the Embassy, including the councillors, wore 'dress coats'. We formed a line to receive our guests, who all came arm-in-arm with their wives. Some brought their children, too. They advanced along the line in an orderly manner, shaking hands with each of us, before making their way to the seats. After this, everyone engaged in spirited conversation. More than a thousand people attended. The rooms had lavish displays of flowers and greenery. Drinks and food were laid out in the great dining-room so that people could serve themselves as they pleased. A band played while people enjoyed the food and the conversation. The party ended at eleven o'clock.

March 20th. Fine; cold winds.
At six o'clock this morning Vice-Ambassador Ōkubo left Washington for Japan, travelling by way of New York.

March 21st.
At eight o'clock at night Vice-Ambassador Itō left for Japan.

March 25th. Cloudy.
At ten o'clock in the morning, guided by General Myers, the army quartermaster who had been assigned to attend us, we visited a Soldiers' Home located two miles south of the city, where veterans of the war are looked after. Built high on a pleasant hill, well away from the city smoke and chosen for this very reason, the home enjoys a superb view over the whole of Washington. The building is constructed of marble and is as magnificent as any other public building in the city. Above the doors an inscription in gilt letters reads: 'Let Us Reward Those Brave Men Who Have Defended the Country.' The Soldiers' Home cared for 273 veterans of the Civil War, including those injured or maimed who have no one to look after them. They do not have to work and pass the time gardening, growing flowers, relaxing and enjoying a tranquil life.

At half past twelve we visited a college for black students. The recent conflict between the North and the South erupted during the debate over the emancipation of black people from their manacles of slavery, which flared into a great war. Blood flowed for four years until eventually the issue was settled and for the first time black people gained the freedom enjoyed by other Americans. However, because they had been made to labour like horses and oxen they were regarded as ignorant and uncultured. Even today there is still a tendency for white people to feel shame about associating with them. For this reason, public schools have been established so that black children can receive the same education as white children, even though their schools are separate.

Although the city is divided into four large school districts, there are only two superintendents. One of these, Mr. [George F.] Cook, is a black man who supervises the schools for black students. Under him are several inspectors who manage the education taxes, donations and reserve funds. They take in black children and teach them to read and write. There are as many as four thousand students in all. In this school the children memorise Greek and Latin expressions and quite a few students go on to college. Besides Greek and Latin, some study science, chemistry and mechanics.

At the time of American independence there were 500,000 black slaves (one-sixth of the total population). When the Constitution was being drafted, it was recognised that slavery was inhuman, but the practice was too deeply entrenched to be suddenly abolished. It was therefore restricted by introducing an import tax on slaves, to be levied until 1808. Around 1790, an American named [Eli] Whitney had invented the cotton-gin, a machine which could separate cotton fibres from the seeds. This encouraged cotton-production in the southern states. Plantations made ever greater use of slaves for planting and picking cotton. English industrialists used steam-driven looms to increase cloth manufacture and made greater profits. Thus, even after 1808 it was impossible to stop the slave-trade in the cotton-producing states. From then on there was a bitter debate within the country on whether to continue to permit slavery and the slave-trade. This debate became more acrimonious with every passing year.

In 1820, when recognition of Missouri as a state was being debated in Congress, anti-slavery delegates threatened to withhold statehood unless slavery was abolished in Missouri. Slavery supporters opposed abolition, and a fierce debate continued until a compromise was reached, whereby slavery was to be prohibited north of latitude 36°30′ N. This was the beginning of the rift between North and South.

The survival of slavery affected cotton production in the southern states, and the profits from cotton made millions of people in both America and Britain prosperous. Plantation owners and industrialists were anxious to protect their profits and thus tightened the bonds of slavery, arguing that slaves were 'base people' provided for labour and were hereditarily inferior as human beings, and that the treatment meted out to them was justifiable.

Faced with such determination, the abolitionists looked into their hearts and fought harder. In the presidential election of 1860 they supported Mr. Lincoln, whom they admired. As soon as he was elected, even before he engaged in any emancipation activity, South Carolina began to advocate secession from the Union and other states quickly followed suit. They elected Jefferson Davis as their president and General [Robert E.] Lee as their commander-in-chief. This sparked the terrible four-year war between the North and South.

Eventually the South was defeated, and in 1865, after much debate, the Constitution was amended to abolish slavery. Slaves were emancipated and for the first time were recognised as human beings. This, however, did not bring greater contact between the races. Because black people were regarded as ignorant savages, white people did not want to mix with them. The separation between white and black people is as distinct as that between clear and muddy water.

Some black people achieved freedom early on, other outstanding black people were elected to the House of Representatives and still others have accumulated great wealth. Clearly, the colour of one's skin has nothing to do with intelligence. People with insight have recognised that education is the key to improvement, and they have poured their energies into establishing schools. It is not inconceivable that, within a decade or two, talented black people will rise and white people who do not study and work hard will fall by the wayside.

# CHAPTER 12

# A Record of Washington, D.C., 2

April 2nd, 1872.

In the afternoon, with General Myers again as our guide, we visited the Patent Office. It is a bureau of the Department of the Interior. Depending on the originality and importance of the invention, various degrees of recognition are accorded. Some people are simply granted a licence of patent, while others are awarded a medal of honour. Even though a new invention may not be good enough to win a medal, it is still an honour to have it put on display.

The Patent Office is an imposing building of brilliant white stone across from the United States Post Office. There are several dozen large rooms, each divided into sections where newly invented machines and models are exhibited. Americans boast that they lead the world as inventors of machinery. Their inventions include the steamship, the telegraph, the warship with an armoured steel hull, apparatus for academic research and science, as well as for household use, crafts of all kinds, fine arts and small objects such as toys and snuffboxes. Everything with some novel application is registered and a model of it displayed. There was such a bewildering array of inventions that merely asking their names was exhausting. Many of the machines were so cleverly contrived that even if one watched their movements, in eight or nine cases out of ten it was hard to grasp the secret of their mechanisms. Last year America granted 13,360 patents for new inventions, which gives some idea of their staggering numbers.

Because inventions are so numerous in America, even if one visited the Patent Office every day for several months it would be impossible to absorb the workings of all the large and small machines and models exhibited. And if one were to enquire about each of them, even if one spent a lifetime one would not have enough time to listen to all the explanations. Americans like to brag that they have no peer in the realm

of machines. They think their most important technological developments are, first, steamships and, second, the electric telegraph.

April 3rd. Cloudy.
At ten o'clock this morning we went to the Printing Office. This is a four-
storey building located in the vicinity of the Capitol, with mechanical
typesetting, stereotyping and printing presses filling the composing room
on the top floor. They are all operated by steam-power. The largest
presses cost as much as $25,000 each, and even the small ones cost at least
$2,000. Printed documents are sent downstairs to the bindery, where they
are folded, stacked, stitched into signatures and given covers, and gold is
applied to the edges of the pages. All the work is done by men and
women specialised in each stage.

   In the United States, since Washington was established, books have
been much cheaper than in other countries because people understood
the enormous benefits of printing to civilisation and because they competed to make printed materials inexpensive and readily available. The
results are evident throughout the country, with improved general
learning and scholarship. The funds expended on printing and newspaper
production in the District of Columbia alone is more than $800,000.

April 16th. Fine; strong wind.
As this was the day commemorating the emancipation of slaves, the black
citizens of Washington marched in procession through the city carrying
guns and waving banners, with bands playing and women riding in
carriages. All converged on the White House, and a 101-gun salute was
fired. With all the celebrations, the capital was very lively. On one banner
borne by the marchers was a depiction of President Lincoln on the
occasion of the Emancipation Proclamation.

April 17th. Fine; strong wind.
Vice-Ambassador Yamaguchi went to the Smithsonian Institution in
response to an invitation. This school and research institute is one of
several established in different countries by a wealthy Englishman, James
Smithson. Having no children to whom he could leave his fortune, he
wanted to educate the young people of the world. The Smithsonian
occupies a large area of the city and is set in a garden with hundreds of
trees and fine lawns with paths laid out among them. It is as elegant as
a park and has a school in the centre. The architecture is impressive.

Inside there is a glass conservatory where plants and trees are cultivated. The building, full of all kinds of machines and artefacts, serves as Washington's pre-eminent educational institution.

April 20th. Light cloud.
From eight o'clock in the morning the city entertained us with a cruise on the Potomac River. After relaxing a while at the admiral's residence, we boarded the government steamer USS *Tallapoosa* at the wharf, and more than one hundred citizens, male and female, accompanied us on the vessel.

At the mouth of the river were the gun emplacements around Alexandria, Virginia. Since the Civil War ended, the defences of the capital have been strengthened even further. Within forty miles there are countless batteries armed with formidable cannon – in some places as many as fifty guns and usually no fewer than ten.

As we sailed southwards, the mountains of Virginia were reflected in the river. After eighteen miles, we reached Mt. Vernon, where wooden pilings driven into the river-bed made a projecting jetty. When the vessel moored, we disembarked and strolled along a carefully tended path up the hillside of thick woods. At the top we came to a mausoleum, the tomb of the famous George Washington. Even the most badly behaved of children admire his character. Men and women of the neighbourhood collect money for the maintenance of the tomb. Above it stands a brick building surrounded by a fence, which contains the tombstones of Washington and his wife. Western tombstones are quite varied. Many wealthy and respected citizens have a stone slab carved in the shape of a coffin set above the ground. The tomb of the Washingtons is made of white marble with carved inscriptions. The entrance is closed off by an iron gate, and visitors pay their respects outside the railings. In front of the mausoleum stands a pair of white marble pillars, each twenty feet tall. The tomb is set among rolling hills, with trees, paths, and well-tended lawns. Most of the trees are cherries, which happened to be in bloom. It was a spectacular sight.

Washington's residence stands on the hill behind the tomb. It has been left just as it was during his lifetime, and is carefully maintained and preserved. In front of the house is a tree-filled garden.

April 23rd. Fine.
This evening we went to the National Observatory in Georgetown, a grand, elegant building overlooking the Potomac River. The observatory director, Mr. [Benjamin F.] Sands, welcomed us and guided us around the three-storey building.

On the top floor stood a huge telescope [the Equatorial], more than ten feet long, made in Berlin (Prussia) and bought in 1842 at a cost of $18,000. The telescope is set on a rotating mechanism and the surrounding windows can be opened on all four sides. The telescope is first adjusted and aimed at the moon or a particular star or planet. Then, rotating by clockwork machinery, it follows the movements of the moon and stars, which can therefore be kept in view for a long time. That night we observed Mercury, Jupiter and its four moons, and the orb of our own moon.

April 24th. Fine.
At eleven o'clock in the morning, with General Myers as our guide, we visited the Department of the Treasury. Treasury Secretary [George S.] Boutwell welcomed us and had the chief clerk guide us around the tax office, the accounting office and the vaults. All the four walls of the vaults are double-lined with iron plate and specie is kept inside. Although currently $100,000,000 is said to be stored in the vaults, this amount occupies only one-tenth of the space inside.

On the floor above are the presses for printing paper money. The paper is made in Philadelphia and sent to Washington to be printed. Workers wet the paper, clean it and spread it on copperplates. After the notes are printed, they are passed from person to person in succession as they are counted, straightened, cut and stamped with the Treasury seal. It takes more than ten operations to complete the whole process, with each procedure supervised by inspectors who examine the notes carefully before sending them on. In each section the inspectors check the desks where workers sit, and careful attention is paid to anyone who enters or leaves. If they were not so careful, there might be irregularities, as it would not be difficult to commit a crime here.

To print serial numbers on each note, cog-wheels with ten teeth are positioned to print units of tens, hundreds and thousands. The numbers on each wheel move in sequence. When a note is printed, a machine moves it away and the wheel advances by one digit. The notes are then stamped with the seal of the mint. The workers who count the notes use wet sponges kept in dishes to dampen their fingertips as they work. In all, eight hundred workers are employed here daily, most of them women.

# CHAPTER 13

# A Record of Washington, D.C., 3

April 30th, 1872. Fine.

At eleven o'clock in the morning, escorted by General Myers, we visited the United States Post Office. First we visited the Dead Letter Office, the repository for mail which cannot be delivered. Letters and parcels with illegible or mistaken names or addresses are brought here and opened in order to return them to the senders. If the sender cannot be determined, they are sent to the paper-making department and destroyed. If a letter contains money, the contents and date are recorded in a ledger. Until a few years ago people were required to pay a handling charge to retrieve mail. More than fifty men and women work here, opening and re-directing more than ten thousand letters which are sent here daily.

We were next shown the sorting and delivery department, where postal workers sort all the letters posted in the city's mail-boxes. On both sides of the tables the workers were sorting them by city, district and street address, and cancelling the postage stamps. Letters which seem too heavy are weighed and the addresses checked before they are sent on for delivery. Several hundred people, divided into various sections, work in the sorting department. The department gave us a book on postal regulations to help us understand the system.

The development and organisation of a postal system is vital to any country intent upon economic growth. Before railroads came into existence, mail was delivered by stage-coach to each city under the direction of the postal bureau. The development of railroads made mail delivery much easier. Postal rates were set quite low, and as a result of the greater ease of transportation the number of people sending letters rose year by year. America is so vast, however, that until recently postal charges were insufficient to cover the cost of delivery, forcing the government to underwrite some of the expenses. Theft of the mails is severely punishable by federal law.

Despite the efficiency of the postal system, it is not suitable for the transportation of gold and silver, or for sending commodities. Thirty or forty years ago, an American company started an express delivery system which was so successful that it is used throughout Europe. Now this system has spread, like a spider's web, throughout the entire United States. It has brought great convenience and profit, and is indispensable to commerce, where the waste of a single day can result in financial disaster.

When one buys anything in a European or American city, as soon as the price is settled the clerk requests the address where the item is to be delivered. When we asked clerks to have the parcels sent to Japan, they always complied, asking whether they should be delivered to Yokohama or Nagasaki. Having ascertained whether delivery is to be by steamship or sailing-ship, they calculate the freight charges and dispatch the goods. We send details of the purchase by mail or telegraph to inform people in Japan about the shipment. Even though it may take a number of days, the items will be delivered to one's home. When Japanese people think of the West, they imagine some distant galaxy. When Western merchants view the world, however, they see it as a single city. With this attitude, they cannot fail to prosper.

From the Post Office we went to the Bureau of Agriculture (known as the Agricultural Hall). It is headed by a director of agriculture, who is appointed by the president and confirmed by the Senate. Under him are eight departments or bureaux: namely, Entomology, Analysis, Seed Cultivation, Seed Storage, Library, Plants, Publishing, and Farm and Garden Equipment. Each has three officials: a bureau chief and two deputies.

The Entomology Department has an agricultural museum. Taxidermists (using the technique of drying skins) make models of animals or insects for display or storage. Everything relating to cattle and pasture animals, down to insect carapaces, is dried or preserved in alcohol. Birds, animals, insects and moths are divided into those which damage plants and those which benefit them. Eagles, for instance, catch fieldmice, and swallows and sparrows eat harmful insects, thus providing natural protection to the fields. Because some creatures multiply, metamorphose, or hide themselves and do harm, this department conducts research into ways to be rid of them. In the case of useful creatures such as honey-bees or silkworms, it is important to find better methods of raising them. These matters all come under the purview of the Entomology Department, which studies these creatures and has specialists on hand to respond to visitors' questions.

In the Analysis Department, the scientists analyse all kinds of agricultural products, including grains, meat and vegetables; the composition of manure and fertiliser; and the constituents in fermented liquids. When there are practical or theoretical innovations relating to agriculture, they test the seeds here. A meteorological section has also been set up to observe changes in climate and weather, while a mechanical section conducts tests on, for example, agricultural machines or thermometers.

In the Seed Storage Department, hundreds of varieties of seeds are gathered from both the United States and foreign countries and distributed on the basis of requests from the various states. The Publishing Department produces detailed monthly and annual reports on planting and harvesting conditions and other agricultural topics. The Plants Department collects and stores samples of plants. The Library collects all kinds of books, both domestic and foreign, and maps and reports relating to agriculture, which are catalogued and made available to visitors.

In its effort to improve agriculture, the bureau provides both theoretical and practical support. Between planting and harvesting, it conducts tests on the effects of climate and soil conditions; once the crops are harvested, it transports them, establishes a market value and releases them to the people as necessary. This is the ultimate contribution of the Bureau of Agriculture. Those who publish its reports note variations in planting and harvesting, observe market conditions, as well as increases in supply and demand and fluctuations in prices. They gather information for the reports, maps and charts by visiting various states and engaging in active correspondence. A secretary in the Publishing Division is responsible for co-ordinating all the reports. Although many industries flourish in America, the greatest profits are derived from agriculture. The encouragement of agriculture is, therefore, particularly important and is given close attention throughout the country. To most of the people in America, promoting agriculture means opening up and developing the land rather than increasing yields. When yields are compared, one acre in a European country produces the equivalent of three acres in America.

The United States of America has been settled and developed by Europeans. Men and women eager to forge new lives for themselves and their families and with an independence of spirit emigrated to America to exploit this land so full of opportunities. This was the driving impulse behind the opening up of America. The country possesses the prime requirements for agriculture: good climate and a vast amount of land. Further investigation reveals that wise leaders displayed striking originality in emphasising practical learning in the arts and sciences. This independent spirit is not a characteristic unique to those living in America, nor is it simply something present in the air there; rather, it has been brought over by the flood of European immigrants.

In fact, the immigrants included absconders, scoundrels, criminals and other riff-raff, many of whom were fleeing from the law in Europe. At the same time, there were also some who had family fortunes or superior education. Finding their own country too restrictive and its politics too repressive, they came to America to exploit the land and to indulge their yearning for freedom. These people educated the less-cultured immigrants, gave them a sense of community and directed their energies toward opening up the land. The enormous success of this is evident everywhere. Thus, it is clear that America is a country which was pioneered by independent-minded Europeans. The republican form of government and the benefits of it enjoyed by the people are based upon this freedom of spirit and the absence of constraints.

Having reached America, we rode across it by rail and saw immense plains, both those cultivated and those awaiting cultivation. Despite travelling for seven days and seven nights, we saw only a small part of the country. This made us wonder whether it would not be possible for America alone to produce more than enough to feed the entire world.

May 4th. Fine; cold wind.
At half past seven in the morning, accompanied by Secretary of the Navy [George M.] Robeson and Secretary of State Fish, the whole Embassy set out from the railroad station beside the Capitol. We travelled thirty-six miles north-east to Annapolis, the capital of Maryland.

To the south-east Annapolis overlooks Chesapeake Bay. Because of this favourable location, it was chosen as the site for the United States Naval Academy, which in scale and facilities is reputedly the finest in the West. The academy is extensive and is set among shade trees, spreading lawns and verdant gardens, which refresh the spirit. Part of the park is a parade-ground. Here the naval cadets formed up, marched and demonstrated their drills. This was followed by another drill by the artillery cadets. Several iron-clad warships were moored at the head of the bay and the cadets were learning to sail them.

Luncheon was served to several hundred men and women in one of the halls of the academy. This was a buffet lunch, at which everyone ate and drank standing in groups and talking in a relaxed manner. The food was very elegant, the drinks most refreshing and the small hall was crowded. When the meal ended, the cadets and their ladies danced. About an hour and a half later we set out to return to Washington and reached there at half past five.

In America, women are not forbidden from entering government buildings. Indeed, at both the navy and the army academies, women gathered to watch the drills. When the cadets finish their training exercises, the men and women go arm-in-arm to the dance-floor, where they dance in close embrace and thoroughly enjoy themselves. This is a custom of republican political systems. From the earliest days of intercourse between the East and the West, the two have not really understood each other since they have totally different outlooks, with the customs and character of the one the opposite of those of the other in every respect, down to the smallest detail. Since our Embassy embarked on the American ship in Yokohama, we have been journeying through a realm of foreign customs. And just as our behaviour is surprising to the Americans, their customs seem baffling to us.

Among these differing customs, by far the strangest was the social relations between men and women. In conjugal and family relations in Japan, a wife is dutiful to her mother- and father-in-law, and children show respect to their parents. In America, however, it is the custom for the husband to serve his wife. This may involve carrying her lantern or shoes, offering her delicacies, dusting off her garments, helping her when she boards or alights from a carriage, pushing her chair forward when she sits, or carrying articles for her when she is walking. If the husband senses even the slightest displeasure from his wife, he demonstrates his love and respect by bowing and apologising. If the apology is not accepted, he may be sent out of the room and cannot even eat. When men and women are travelling in the same carriage, the men stand immediately to offer their seats to the women, who take them without hesitation. While women are present, men are circumspect in their behaviour, speaking softly and avoiding cursing and argument. At dinner, only when the women have risen from their chairs and left the room do the men then relax. If these rules of behaviour were to be transplanted and replace our own forms of filial duty towards our parents, that would represent a great improvement.

Although respect for women is the norm throughout the West, America and Britain are extreme in this regard. This custom is most marked in Britain, a country ruled by a queen. As a republic, America responds with noisy debates over equal rights for men and women. There is a woman doctor in Washington who walks around in men's clothes, including top hat and trousers, but women of proper upbringing all scorn her. The duties of men and women are naturally different. It is also clear that women should not be given the task of defending the nation. In the Eastern view, women should manage the home and not work outside it. The differences between men and women are based on natural principles: thoughtful people cannot but take these principles seriously.

May 23rd. Fine.
We visited the parade-ground of the volunteer city militia to watch the drills. White and black troops drilled in separate units. When the drills ended, they marched to the White House before dispersing.

May 30th. Cloudy, fine, rain, all mixed.
At eleven o'clock this morning we attended a memorial service in the Arlington Hills for those killed in the Civil War. Arlington Cemetery is located on the other side of the Potomac River, in the state of Virginia. When we looked around, we saw the fields covered with row upon row of white wooden grave markers. Our guides explained that the reason the Confederate troops fought so tenaciously was due to the inspiration of General Lee. If Lee had not taken up the Confederacy cause, this past war would never have taken so many lives. The North–South Civil War was fought to a bitter conclusion in the Arlington Hills.

Men and women came from far and near to attend the memorial service today. First, a thirty-seven gun salute was fired. President Grant and the navy and army chiefs-of-staff took their places on the dais, priests and ministers gave sermons, and poets recited elegies. General Banks made a speech and a band played at intervals in the programme. After that, pastors led boys and girls from an orphanage to the tomb containing the remains of unknown soldiers. There, a memorial service was conducted and hymns were sung. The entire event was extremely solemn, sad and moving.

CHAPTER 14

# The Journey Through the Northern States, 1

June 10th, 1872. Light cloud; moderately hot with occasional showers. At twenty-five past nine last night, at the invitation of the United States government and with General Myers as our guide, we set out from the station to the north of the Capitol to visit some famous sights of the northern states. Travelling in a train equipped with two sleeping cars, we were accompanied by the wife and daughter of Senator General Banks, the daughter of General Myers and our minister, Mori Arinori, as well as a number of secretaries. It was already night when the train departed, and there was nothing to see on the way but fireflies in the trees and flitting over the grass. We soon went to sleep.

We arrived at Jersey City Station at a quarter to seven in the morning. Located on the shore of the Hudson River directly opposite New York, this is a flourishing city with a population of more than 80,000. Shops and houses are densely packed together, and the station is particularly noisy and crowded. Here we transferred to horse-drawn carriages and were soon driving upstream beside the Hudson estuary.

Ferries steam back and forth day and night, carrying passengers from the New Jersey shore across the Hudson to New York City. An astonishing number of people and horses are said to cross the river daily. On both banks of the river large ferry stations have been built, with piers extending into the river. When a boat pulls in, its deck is level with the pier, allowing carriages to drive straight on or off the boat with the passengers still on board. We had expected to wait in our carriages at the ferry station before transferring to the boat. However, when the boat left the pier, we suddenly found ourselves surrounded by the chop of waves. We then realised, for the first time, that our carriages were already on the boat. We barely had time to register our surprise before we arrived at the New York City wharf where, with wheels squealing, our carriages were driven off the ferry. Before we had overcome our astonishment, we were transferred from ship to shore and we were rolling along the streets of New York City. Trains were also hurtling along in both directions on an elevated railroad supported on iron pillars more than twenty feet above the street. The carriages emerged onto the grand avenue of Broadway with a tremendous clatter. The shops and houses were tightly packed together and the scene was full of bustle. Accommodation had been reserved for us at the St. Nicholas Hotel on Broadway. It was still only seven o'clock in the morning.

Broadway is the busiest street in New York City, overflowing with carriages, horses and people on the cobblestone surface. The horse-drawn omnibuses shuttling up and down are small and do not run on rails. They arrive at frequent intervals, one after the other, so that even if one is missed, another is immediately behind; you do not have to wait even a minute. This is the most crowded street in the world. In our hotel rooms overlooking Broadway, the din was at times as loud as a hundred thunderclaps, or a gale blowing at full force through a forest of pine-trees. All day long our ears were filled with squealing and rattling, and the noise was such that we could hardly carry on a conversation.

At ten o'clock in the morning we boarded carriages and drove south down Broadway to the tip of Manhattan, to a district known as the Battery. In front of us, on Long Island, was Brooklyn. Above us the smoke rising from Manhattan mingled with that of Brooklyn. On our left, beyond the mist over the river, we could see the tiled roofs of Jersey City. The sea-water was a vivid blue, and on it great ships seemed to float like fallen leaves. Rocks had been piled up in the bay and stones had been laid on them to create a park. There was a gazebo from which to view the river, and the bay was less than five feet away. The waves were gentle and the view extensive.

We turned our carriages around and drove from the Battery up the wide avenue in front of City Hall. We were now in upper Broadway, the liveliest and most dynamic area in the city. It resembled the eight crossroads of central Tokyo. City Hall, large commercial buildings, the Telegraph Office, major newspapers and other enterprises are housed in clusters of tall buildings. The whole avenue is paved with round cobblestones. The neighbourhood sidewalks attract traders and are lined with booths, which make every day there seem like a festival. From very early in the morning until just before noon there is a fruit and vegetable market, with produce sold by auction. Small farmers, merchants and domestic servants crowd around, eager to make bids. The auctioneer climbs up onto a high podium to conduct the sale. It was reminiscent of the wholesale dealers in the large cities or river-bank markets in Japan. Once the price is settled and the sale completed, a chit is given as proof of the price agreed.

We then drove along the wharves and piers on the East River. There are fifty-five piers along the river, all lined with commercial shipping. We could see five or six small vessels moored at a single pier, while larger ships were berthed two to a wharf. Along the dock a multitude of goods was being unloaded. Horses hauled produce out, and men loaded all kinds of fruit and vegetables onto drays. Pineapples, bananas, pears, oranges and apples were piled high everywhere, some in hemp sacks, others in boxes, forming mountains of merchandise. Buyers and sellers, both men and women, had set up booths among the piles, and draymen bustled around them. Here on display was the commercial vitality of this famous city, in all its boisterous cacophony.

At three o'clock in the afternoon we went by carriage to tour Central Park. In New York, where land is extremely expensive, this park can only be described as a golden nugget set in the city's heart. The park is two and a half miles from north to south, and half a mile from east to west. It was bought at great expense with public funds to create a place of recreation. When planning Central Park, landscape artists were invited to compete in designing hills, peaks and rocky escarpments.

From the hotel we drove uptown, heading north along a straight avenue. When the street ended, we crossed into the park by a bridge over a small pond. Because the park was still unfinished, rocks and timbers were heaped up in a jumble along the banks. Here we began to experience the true beauty of Central Park. We passed an expanse of lawn with trees planted in an orderly pattern. A road ran down the middle of the park as straight as an arrow, vanishing into the distance. With lush grass at our feet and green trees above our heads, everything was thoroughly refreshing and beautiful.

From there we drove through hills with wooded ridges. Rounding one hill, a lake came into view, with a peninsula jutting out into it. The lake narrowed to a wasp's waist in places, but then widened before narrowing again. We passed a spit of land crowned with trees and a gazebo on a hilltop. The rocks and stones displayed fantastical shapes; trees presented varied and unusual forms. Some were planted with regularity as if a ruler had been used, while others were in a tangled and haphazard state. Gazing at a luxuriant stand of trees shrouded in blue haze on a hilltop on the far shore of the lake, we wondered if we were not in some mountain fastness or mysterious valley.

June 11th. Fine; slightly cool.

We left the hotel at eight o'clock this morning, boarded the steamer *Chauncey Vibbard* at the pier at the mouth of the East River, rounded the tip of the Battery and sailed up the Hudson River. After we had pro-ceeded upstream for forty-eight miles, the river became shallower and we approached the promontory of West Point, on which stands the United States Military Academy. We arrived there at noon.

At four o'clock in the afternoon we visited the academy. Schools in the West have recesses during the summer and winter after conducting examinations or exercises. Since West Point was about to recess, various officials had gathered to examine the cadets on what they had studied. Family members, too, both men and women, had come to watch the exercises and to attend the ceremony in which their sons would be promoted, so the inns were very crowded. When the cadets are promoted, they can stand shoulder-to-shoulder in honour with their fathers and brothers. Those who fail are shamed before their relatives, but, on the other hand, this may serve as a spur to them.

This afternoon we watched the cadets doing infantry drill. Six com-panies made up one battalion. The cadets demonstrated basic drills, including marching in slow and quick time, falling in, dispersing and rallying. They must master these drill sequences before they can become officers, and their drill was extremely professional. A thousand or more spectators, including women, were either sitting or standing in the shade of the trees in front of the academy. We were offered benches, from where we watched in the company of the secretary of war and Colonel Thomas H. Ruger. When the manoeuvres were completed, a simple buffet was served in an official residence of the academy. Some visitors also attended the reception. The secretary of war and other officers served the guests themselves. In contrast to the Naval Academy graduation ceremony, at West Point the men and women gathered in different rooms and it was less crowded and chaotic. By the time the reception was over it was close to six o'clock.

From there we went to the south of the drill ground to inspect several large cannon, among them some captured during the Mexican War. There was also a newly invented American gun called a 'Gatling gun', which fires from multiple barrels. The muzzles resemble a honeycomb, and when a crank is turned, the barrels rotate and the cartridges drop from above the firing mechanism into the revolving barrels to be fired. As many as two or three hundred rounds can be fired every six or seven seconds. This kind of gun is said to have felled many soldiers during the Civil War.

June 12th. A beautiful day; rather hot.

At half past seven in the morning we again went to the academy to watch the cadets drill and to visit the dormitories and classrooms. The Naval Academy [at Annapolis] is now accepting Japanese students to study in America, but the army ministry, claiming it has to protect vital information, has been unwilling to permit foreigners to enter. The two differ on this point because army affairs include many confidential matters. After being served wine, we returned to our hotel at noon.

At half past five in the afternoon we observed the examination manoeuvres by troops of light artillery. Six cannon were each drawn by two-horse teams, with artillery cadets riding on the horses and the limbers. They fired as soon as they reached battle positions. Once they had finished firing, they re-mounted and rode on, firing from various directions – sometimes in a horizontal line, sometimes in a line at right angles, sometimes in order, sometimes in reverse order, in the best style of rapid manoeuvres.

At the start of today's manoeuvres, threatening clouds began to pile up, and about midway a strong wind sprang up. Trees groaned and bent in the gale, and grass and shrubs whirled about madly, causing spectators to abandon their viewing places and run for cover. The artillery cadets, however, held firm and did not break rank as they calmly followed their commander's orders. In a matter of moments rain pelted down so hard as if to smash the gun-carriages, and it poured out of the gutters. The cannon, however, continued to roar on the drill ground, their wheels still turning. The rain did not stop until the exercises were over. This was the first time we had encountered such a severe summer storm since we set out on our journey to the West. Thunder crashed and lightning flashed repeatedly; the turbulent air whipped up whitecaps on the Hudson; and the scudding clouds obscured the mountain peaks. Looking out from the windows at the rapidly-changing scene, we were impressed by the mysterious force of nature.

At half past eight live shells were used. The targets were lanterns set along the foot of the mountains across the river 1,400 feet away from an embankment inside the academy grounds. Because it was already dark and the wind still somewhat strong, few gunners hit their targets. We often observed large and small cannon in target practice, but compared with Japanese soldiers American gunners rarely hit the targets, giving us the impression that their gunnery skills were rather backward. In nimbleness of fingers and speed of reaction, the Japanese are superior to the Americans and the Europeans.

# CHAPTER 15

# The Journey Through the Northern States, 2

June 13th, 1872. Fine; slightly cooler than yesterday.

At ten o'clock in the morning we bade Colonel Ruger farewell and crossed the Hudson by ferry from the West Point Academy pier. Looking back, we could see the rocky palisades towering above the river and a ribbon of road winding along the side of the mountains. The tiers of hills were deep and wooded, looking like a green folding screen, and the river scenery was extremely lush and beautiful. At this point the Hudson is quite shallow, and we could see weeds swaying beneath the surface. On the opposite shore we disembarked at Garrison Station, where we waited thirty minutes for our train.

At eleven o'clock the 'Columbia', a train especially provided for the Embassy by the New York Central Railroad Company, pulled in. The interior of the car was decorated with the crossed flags of the United States and Japan, eleven pairs of them, and the conductors and dining-car attendants all wore small Japanese flags in their lapels. A meal had been prepared for us in the dining-car.

We headed north, travelling beside the Hudson River. After following the river for 120 miles, we reached the city of Albany. Upon crossing a long bridge, we lost sight of the river among the buildings and beheld instead a vista of chimneys, some tall, others short. Here we stopped a while.

Leaving Albany, our train immediately crossed a bridge to the west bank of the Hudson, and we were soon speeding through the rich farm country of western New York State. Wherever we passed we saw fertile land. There was the occasional hill, but in general the landscape was flat. Everywhere we looked, from plains to hillsides, there was not one area which had not been settled and developed as farmland, with cattle and sheep grazing on the lush grass. Pastures were numerous, cultivated fields comparatively scarce. Here and there we saw orchards among the pastures, and shrubs growing along canal banks. We came to the shore of a large lake

79

which stretched endlessly into the distance. Although we followed the shoreline, we were never able to obtain a view of the entire lake.

Beside the railroad to our left we could see gently flowing water. This was the Great [Erie] Canal which runs from Lake Erie to the Hudson River, a distance of 300 miles. It passes through the cities of Buffalo, Rochester and Syracuse and connects with the transportation network of the northern Mississippi farther south. It is a vital waterway and one of the best-known canals in the world.

We passed Syracuse at half past seven in the evening, when darkness fell and obscured the scenery. At twenty minutes to midnight we reached Niagara, where we stayed at the International Hotel, a large, newly built hotel.

June 14th. Light cloud; occasional sunshine.

At eleven o'clock we set out in carriages to view the Niagara Falls. Within the territory of the United States are three of the greatest natural wonders of the world: the Mississippi River, for its volume of flowing water; the five Great Lakes, for their volume of fresh water; and Niagara Falls, for its volume of cascading water. This last is the greatest falls in the world because of the width of the falling water, which is like an ocean, too vast to be encompassed in a single view. The waters tumble down, splashing and scattering in all directions, and are a magnificent sight. In winter, they freeze into columns of ice and in mid-summer they generate a chill storm, making the most sublime sceneries. Most people who come to this country, even if they are not looking for curiosities or seeking marvels, make a special effort to see the Niagara Falls.

The area above the falls where the Niagara River divides into two is known as Goat Island. The Niagara Falls is created by water rushing down from the left and right of Goat Island and pouring into the gorge. The lower river, which flows into Lake Ontario, is known as the Niagara Gorge. Goat Island is located at the very centre of the falls, and the great cascade between it and Canada is called the Horseshoe Falls, or the Canadian Falls. The water descending [on the Canadian side] forms the front and is the main stream. The torrent roaring down between Goat Island and the village of Niagara is known as the American Falls.

We had our first view of the full power of the Niagara River when our carriages emerged from the back of the hotel. We crossed a long bridge beneath which the river surged in rapids, the boulders on the river-bed causing the waters to swirl and churn in a roaring tumult. Rushing under the bridge, the rapids suddenly slowed to make a deep, swirling pool, and then the water cascaded over the falls like scattering jewels and flying snowflakes. Such was the upper stream above the American Falls.

Crossing over the bridge we reached Goat Island, which is uninhabited although there is an old hut there. The trees were as dark as in a dense forest, and mouldering leaves lay mixed with the grass. The track was not well maintained, but it was adequate for our carriages to pass. Turning right, the carriages halted, and when we walked down the trail towards the gorge we emerged directly above the American Falls. Rising mist enshrouded us, and cold clammy air wet our clothing.

When we had gazed our fill at the American Falls, our carriages turned right and took us around Goat Island. We soon came to a viewing hut from which we could descend to the bottom of the gorge by means of a staircase. Inside the hut, men and women who had come to view the falls donned oilskins, which they tied tightly, then put on sou'-westers before descending into the gorge. They wished to experience the rare sensation of going behind the falls. This, too, is a breathtaking view.

Leaving our carriages, we walked along the track beside the gorge. After twenty or thirty steps over a wooden bridge we reached a precarious little platform giving access to the viewing tower. A circular staircase leads to the topmost balcony of this viewing stand, which overlooks the Horseshoe Falls.

Turning around and leaving Goat Island, we drove through the village of Niagara down to the great whirlpool basin in the Niagara gorge, about a mile and a half below the falls. The river swirls in the form of the interlocking symbols of yin and yang, and there seems to be no way out. At the edge of the water, where the river churns against the cliff face, rocks have broken away and piled up. Such is the famous scenery of the Whirlpool Gorge.

The current in this cauldron is so rapid that the river throws up gravel and sand from the bed. A water-wheel has been installed on one of the banks to capture the energy of the racing water. A thick rope attached to the central axle of the wheel runs up to a building on the cliff 180 feet above. As the water-wheel turns, its power is used to hoist and lower inclined cars, in which seven or eight people sit, up and down the cliff face.

Two bridges are suspended between the falls and the whirlpool's cauldron. One of them is above the river in the upper gorge. The other bridge is about 600 feet downstream from the falls and is suspended from only two steel cables. From nearby it looks as if long ropes are stretched 200 feet above a sheer cliff. Looking down from the bridge, the river races down the gorge tossing white spume. It flows under the bridge into a deep pool of emerald green. Looking around, we saw that the rock faces on both sides leant inwards as if about to break away. The seven carriages of the Embassy rolled onto this bridge. At the middle the bridge seemed very narrow, and high above the deep gorge it felt unsteady, as if we were floating in the sky. When the bridge shook, we were all terrified. In the past, a fearless European acrobat calling himself 'Napoleon' or something similar [probably Blondin] walked a tightrope over this gorge with unrivalled skill. This tightrope artist is still active and we saw him doing his daring tightrope walks in New York City.

When we had seen the sights at Niagara, we crossed the second suspension bridge to the Canadian side, where a road ran above the gorge. Here people have opened stores and built a town.

This evening we invited the former president, [Millard] Fillmore, to dinner and entertained him at the hotel. During the Kaei era [1848–54] he was the president who sent Commodore Perry to Japan for the first time. Fillmore was still very hearty and robust at the age of seventy-three.

CHAPTER 16

# The Journey Through the Northern States, 3

June 15th, 1872. Fine.
At half past seven in the morning we left our hotel at Niagara and returned by the same route we had taken to come. The shore of Lake Ontario was predominantly flat, broken by an occasional hill.

After passing Syracuse we reached the village of Saratoga and took rooms at the Grand Union House. Saratoga is a summer resort where people go to escape the heat. It became famous because of the number of tourists who visit every summer, but it has no other industry. The size of Saratoga's hotels is quite astonishing. The Union House is the biggest, offering as many as one thousand rooms. The building surrounds a large, tree-filled garden where guests can stroll in the mornings and evenings. The dining-room seats two thousand people, and meeting rooms and the ball-room are all extremely grand. After dinner, guests gather in the ball-room and dance to the accompaniment of a piano. Although the Union House is not particularly elegant in appearance, for sheer size it is unmatched among the hotels which we have seen. The Grand Hotel in Paris is only half the size. The presence of several medicinal springs has attracted numerous visitors to this resort, and the profits of the springs have allowed such enormous hotels to be built.

June 16th. Fine.
At eleven o'clock in the morning we went by carriage to Saratoga Lake to enjoy the cool breeze. It turned out to be a small lake, little more than a pool, and its water was not very clear. Peaks and mountains opened up around it, but they were not especially spectacular. Beyond the lake were tall trees and dark woods. The clumps of grass and bushes seemed carelessly tended, making for an indifferent landscape. When we stopped to rest at a restaurant overlooking the lake, the host, a Mr. Moon, served us wine and potato chips, which are thin slivers of potatoes deep-fried in oil and are said to be a delicacy of the area.

We then turned around and drove to a medicinal spring. There are several in the area, each one different in character. The water at this one tasted like seltzer water, salty and astringent, with a slight odour. Elsewhere in Saratoga are springs whose waters are rich in magnesium and iron. Mineral springs are medically beneficial for the human body and, like hot-springs in Japan, can cure illnesses. It is these springs which have made Saratoga one of America's leading tourist resorts.

June 17th. Fine.
At nine o'clock in the morning we left the Grand Union House in Saratoga and boarded a train for Boston. At the north-east border of New York State we entered a mountain range and sheer peaks gradually reared up beside the tracks. As we headed towards the Massachusetts–Vermont border, the landscape became ever steeper and the mountains larger. The railroad cut through imposing scenery of rocky gorges. The mountains are intricately convoluted, thickly wooded and rich in minerals. Our impression of America as a land of grassy knolls and fields began to change.

At eleven o'clock we passed a village (probably on the border with Vermont). There were quarries where marble was mined with hydraulic power. It is said that Massachusetts marble, popular for buildings in the United States, comes from around here. We also saw piles of a material used for roof tiles; this stone, or slate, has tightly compressed layers. Workers must split it into thin slabs according to the layers. Once the pieces are cut to size, they are placed on roofs like tiles. Slate is very hard and has a smooth, polished surface, making it impervious to wind and water. It comes in a reddish-brown or blue-black colour. It is cut into squares or hexagons and laid on roofs in fish-scale, tortoise-shell, or circular patterns. A mixture of colours is used for decorative effect. In America and Europe, people in the middle and upper classes usually roof their houses with slate as it is a durable, high-quality material.

Arriving in Boston at the Fitchburg Railroad depot at eight o'clock in the evening, we boarded carriages and were taken to the Revere House.

June 18th. Fine.
At ten o'clock this morning we set out on a tour of Boston by carriage, first visiting a pleasure-garden north of the river. This park is called Common Park, and it covers about twenty-five acres. A pleasant path winds through dense trees around a marshy pond with stone bridges. Fountains threw out cold gems of splashing water in umbrella-shaped

showers. Bronze and stone sculptures flanked side paths which ran between flower-beds. The paths had been strewn with gravel, which made them as white as snow.

From two o'clock in the afternoon we attended a concert at the World's Peace Jubilee and International Musical Festival. People flocked to these concerts in celebration of peace around the world, making the event a great success. A decade ago America was embroiled in internal strife for four years, when the southern and northern states fought each other bitterly. The soul of the nation became spattered with blood in what has come to be known as the Civil War. This ended in 1865 and people were able to enjoy peace again. In Europe, war between France and Prussia ended in a peace agreement [in 1871]. Now the world is at peace, with not a speck of dust stirring. The Jubilee concert was planned in recognition of this momentous peace.

The concert began at three o'clock, when the musicians started tuning their instruments. As they played and the sounds of the organ and other instruments mounted to a crescendo, even the clouds above seemed to be brought to a halt. With more than 10,000 vocalists singing with one voice, all was in harmony.

Next, a lady in make-up and wearing a glittering costume ascended the platform. When she faced the auditorium and bowed, the whole audience clapped and cheered. As the orchestra played, she began her song. Sometimes her serene voice resonated throughout the hall; at other times her notes held a gentle echo. During a particularly melodious passage, it was as if graceful cranes were flying overhead; then all at once the song turned soft and smooth, as if nightingales were cavorting among flowers. The audience all clapped and stamped their feet, and the applause seemed never-ending. Western singing makes the human voice as harmonious as a musical instrument. Therein lies the art.

Next, the orchestra played a piece especially composed for this occasion which combined cannon fire with the music of the instruments as it rose to a crescendo. The musicians, including several hundred in the per-cussion section of the orchestra, were seated around the conductor, who stood on a podium. The cannon had been set up outside the hall, with electric wires leading from the string section to the firing mechanism of the cannon. At the appointed moment, during a quiet passage, the cannon fired two or three times, their roar replacing the sound of the large drums. Truly, the booming cannon fire provided the perfect climax. Moreover, an electrical gadget informed each nearby church when the climax was approaching and the church bells rang out in unison, adding their 'voices', too. This piece of music is especially grandiose and is intended to astonish listeners.

Today the band of the British Grenadier Guards, resplendent in their bearskins and crimson uniforms, took part in the concert. The chorus was accompanied by this band, which gave the finest possible rendition of English music. The applause was endless and the audience demanded encores. One piece played later was about an American captured in the War of Independence, whose patriotism never wavered. The American audience, upon hearing this, could not stop applauding. They clapped and stamped their feet, demanding encore after encore, and it was some time before the hall settled down again.

June 19th. Fine.
Accompanied by the city officials, we sailed from the pier called Long Wharf on the steamship *Mahoning* and cruised around Boston harbour. We boarded the ship at nine o'clock. Mr. Russell, the collector of taxes, and the members of the entertainment committee all brought their families with them, making a total of fifty to sixty men and women. From the bay we could see the outline of the city in the distance. Columns of smoke rising from the chimneys indicated the city's vitality. When we reached the battery of cannon at the mouth of the bay, we were honoured with a fifteen-gun salute, and at the lighthouse platform we took our time viewing the harbour. As we did so, many thoughts came to mind. When America declared its independence from Britain, Boston was the first port to fight in the war. With Charlestown taking the lead, there were many bitter battles around here. In American history there is a lot to remember and reflect upon both in the past and the present. We returned to the wharf at noon.

At two o'clock we again went to the World's Peace Jubilee concert. After the concert, we went up in a balloon from the shore in front of the Jubilee Hall. We rose more than three thousand feet before we descended. We were told that these balloons were made by a New York company and represent the most advanced scientific knowledge of the day.

June 20th. Fine; the temperature rose to 87°.
We left Boston at nine o'clock. The entertainment committee accompanied us to the railway station where they made their farewells. We boarded the train and set out for New York, reaching Springfield at noon. There we went by carriage to a small-arms factory [the Federal Arsenal]. The factory was established by the federal government to manufacture

guns for the army. The water of the Connecticut River is harnessed to drive the water-wheels to work the machinery. Inside the grounds a reservoir had been dug for storing water, and a long mound ran on one side of it above the water surface. On the opposite bank was a long brick shed, with solidly-built cubicles for the purpose of testing the rifles. The front of the shed faced the mound, which was the target. After loading a double charge in the rifles, thirty or forty of them were connected by an electric wire. They were all fired at once by a man inside the shed. Afterwards the armourers went to examine the results. This was a demonstration for our benefit, and not one of the guns had burst.

We then toured the small-arms factory, which was very extensive. The metal parts for the weapons are manufactured in a long, four-storey building. We also watched men carving the wooden stocks for the guns. The work was divided among the workers, who were all engaged in specialised tasks. On this occasion three hundred men were producing about 100 guns a day. During the Civil War three thousand workers had been employed to produce 1,000 guns a day. These guns, known as 'Springfields', were loaded from the breech. Remington rifles were made by a New York company, but because they had many advantages for military use they were also made in this factory. From here we went to the armoury, where 90,000 rifles were stored in ranks like trees in a forest. These formed only a part of the store. We were told that 1,200,000 guns are kept in armouries around the country.

At seven o'clock in the evening we boarded the train and reached New York at midnight.

CHAPTER 17

# A Record of Washington, D.C.: Epilogue

June 22nd, 1872. Fine.

It was mid-summer when we returned to Washington, and the heat steadily increased. Congress (which had risen before we left for our northern trip) was still in recess. The president and the cabinet officers had left the city, and politicians and other celebrities had all gone in search of cooler climes. With the city's residents dispersed to various parts of the country, half of the businesses in Washington were closed (since commerce in the capital is heavily dependent on government officials). The streets and avenues were deserted, and the only people strolling in the parks were poor white and black people. It seemed a completely different city from the one we had seen earlier, before our tour of the northern states. Because Mr. Fish, the secretary of state, had also gone to Boston and then to his summer home near West Point to escape the heat, diplomatic business was almost at a standstill. All we could do during the day was try to keep cool by taking carriage rides to see various sights. We did little worth recording.

Because the purpose of gathering senators and congressmen in Washington is to bring together representatives who understand conditions in the various states, politicians spend half the year in Washington and the other half in their own districts. Thus, they gain experience in administration and at the same time become familiar with the affairs of the people. It is essential for them to be able to deal effectively with both. If elected representatives spent the whole year in the legislature in Washington, their value as local representatives would diminish. If they spent too much time in their own districts, they would have no time to attend to government matters, which would then see no progress. Under this system, the three months of summer always become a period of recess. As most people in Europe and America take a holiday in the summer, popular custom coincides with the government's recess from official duties.

July 3rd. Fine; scorching heat; temperature rising to 101°; thunderstorm in the evening.
Day after day the heat here has been extreme and that in New York City even worse, reaching 104° on some days. Fifty-four people have died from heat-stroke in New York. Here in Washington six people have died, and many cattle and horses have also perished.

July 4th. Temperature a little cooler, 90°; heavy rain at night.
Today is Independence Day, so the citizens had a day off work. Concerts were held in various places during the day, and fireworks illuminated the night skies. New York and Philadelphia were said to be particularly lively.

July 5th. Fine; temperature similar to the previous day.
Although our stay in the District of Columbia was prolonged, we did not travel anywhere south of Washington. After returning from our tour of the northern states, it was the full heat of mid-summer – not the best time of year to tour the South.

July 9th. Fine; temperature 82°.
We heard that Secretary of State Fish returned from Boston to his summer home at West Point and has been taken ill. To visit him we took a nine o'clock night train to West Point.

July 10th. Fine; temperature 84°.
We visited the secretary of state at his summer home at Garrison, on the bank of the Hudson opposite West Point, and there conversed for several hours. At two o'clock lunch was provided, and we left at five.

July 11th. Temperature 85°.
Last night we left West Point, travelled down to New York City and stayed at the St. Nicholas Hotel. This evening we set off on the nine o'clock night train and returned to Washington.

July 12th. Rain.
We arrived in Washington at dawn.

July 14th. Light cloud.
We received a telegraph informing us that the steamer carrying Vice-Ambassador Ōkubo and Vice-Ambassador Itō had arrived in San Francisco.

July 22nd. Fine.
At six o'clock in the morning Vice-Ambassador Itō and Vice-Ambassador Ōkubo, with Terashima, the deputy foreign minister, arrived in Washington. At three o'clock this afternoon a meeting was held at the State Department.

July 24th. Fine.
At noon Ambassador Iwakura, Vice-Ambassador Itō and other members of the Embassy visited the White House and were received by President Grant. The ambassador announced that we would soon be leaving the United States. They both gave short speeches and the ceremony ended. We returned to the hotel at half past one. Ambassador Iwakura visited Fish's residence.

July 25th. Fine.
We visited various embassies and consulates to announce our departure and make our farewells. At seven o'clock we invited the heads and deputies of the various ministries and our entertainment secretary, General Myers, to the hotel for a farewell party, which lasted until midnight.

July 27th. Fine.
We left Washington by train.
　　The United States is a federal republic made up of thirty-seven states. Germany has united twenty-five states under a monarch. To foreign countries, each appears as a unified nation. Internally, however, each country retains some features of feudalism. In the United States, the politics of each state reflects its individual interests, and the most important issues affecting the lives of the citizens are in the hands of the state government. The federal government sees to it that the Constitution is observed. The city of Washington in the United States can be compared to the city of Frankfurt in Germany. Just as one cannot hope to know the whole of Germany from Frankfurt alone, familiarity with Washington is insufficient to understand the different states.
　　We are told that when the Civil War broke out, the European countries promised to observe neutrality. In secret, however, they encouraged the Southern Confederacy and sold weapons to it. They favoured secession and the destruction of the Union, plotted to interfere in the border states and engaged in all kinds of secret stratagems. The Confederate cruiser *Alabama* was dispatched from Britain to aid the South. When the ship was sunk by a Northern warship, the incident sparked

a heated dispute between America and Britain. While we were in Washington, the two countries were on the verge of declaring war over this issue until other nations came to the rescue and defused the situation. After we left Washington, a settlement was still being negotiated.

While we were in Washington, the United States was in the throes of a presidential election. Therefore, we were able to observe political candidates gathering in conventions and holding primary elections. In the current election campaign, when there could be a change of administration, the views of the opposition parties came to the fore. The Democratic and Liberal parties had banded together and given their endorsement to the Democrat [Horace] Greeley. Mr. Greeley was, for many years, the president and publisher of a New York newspaper [*New York Tribune*] and enjoyed a sterling reputation as an honest gentleman. He was very knowledgeable and accomplished in political, academic and practical affairs, and he expounded his views through his newspaper. He was well respected throughout the United States. He espoused democratic ideals, and thus held out the hope of greater freedom in America. Although over seventy years old at the time [actually, sixty-one], he was determined to realise his ambition to become president. Wealthy and talented supporters joined his ranks and advertised his accomplishments in various fields. In his speeches he used every means possible to explain his ideas, and many among the nation's politicians gave him their vociferous support.

Mr. Grant had the support of the military establishment; Mr. Greeley had the support of the intelligentsia. Both had zealous backers, right and left, and heated debates were held in cities, towns and villages across the country. Merchants forgot their calculations; women stayed their sewing needles in mid-stitch. Everybody lauded his or her particular candidate. People in Europe described this as a 'war in peacetime'.

At the convention [of the newly-formed Liberal-Republican party] in Cincinnati at the end of the fourth month, the majority voted to nominate Mr. Greeley. At this stage political gossip suggested that Grant's re-election was rather doubtful.

Another convention was held in Philadelphia, and while both parties waited for the result with bated breath the majority of delegates emerged in favour of Grant. When the chairman asked those who supported the re-nomination of President Grant to stand, most of them jumped up, and it was almost as though the floor itself was rising. The news was quickly telegraphed to Washington.

All these events were occurring while we were travelling in the north and staying in Washington. In every city during this time conventions and meetings were held by both parties and filled buildings everywhere. People placed placards written in large letters to announce the meeting-place of this party or that, or they hung banners in busy streets where people passed, or printed photographs of the two candidates, in various poses, for sale in the shops. The excitement was extraordinary. Everywhere we went there was talk of nothing but the election.

Later in Boston we read in the newspapers that a certain close friend of Mr. Sumner, an erstwhile supporter of Greeley, changed his views and wrote a letter to Sumner attacking him for his outspoken support of Greeley. Sumner retreated, and others also distanced themselves from Greeley. Enthusiasm for Greeley evaporated. Later, when the people had voted to re-elect Grant, Mr. Sumner departed for Europe and Horace Greeley died suddenly of a broken heart. This reveals how Westerners are willing to throw their whole heart into the pursuit of their convictions, and if they do not realise them, they are even willing to sacrifice their lives. Without such extreme virtue and endurance, it is hard to expect success in this world.

# CHAPTER 18

# A Record of Philadelphia

July 27th, 1872. Fine.
Today we packed our luggage and left Washington, D.C., on the noon train. After travelling north through Baltimore, we passed to the west of Philadelphia at seven in the evening.

We had accepted an invitation from Mr. Jay Cooke, a wealthy Philadelphia banker. When we reached a small village station some ten miles north of Philadelphia, we were met by carriages of the Cooke family and taken to his country estate. In recent years Mr. Cooke has come to be highly regarded for his enormous wealth and benevolence. On the evening we arrived, he was away on business and had not yet returned. His younger brother welcomed and entertained us.

July 28th. Fine.
Mr. Cooke returned this morning. He had travelled fifteen miles into the mountains the previous day to inspect some mines and had mistaken the departure time of the return train. He apologised for being late. Today we also enjoyed a banquet with his whole family in the grand dining-room. The family welcomed us wholeheartedly at each meal, doing everything possible to entertain us.

July 29th. Fine.
The Philadelphia municipal government had urged us to visit the city and we could not refuse such hospitality, so at nine o'clock in the morning we said goodbye to the Cooke family and left by train for Philadelphia, where we took rooms at the Continental Hotel. Wealthy merchants and citizens of Philadelphia welcomed us warmly, begging us to stay a few days. We declined, however, telling them we were anxious to proceed with our journey. Whereupon they immediately ordered carriages and showed us some of the major sights.

Philadelphia is particularly famed for the manufacture of iron and steel, due to the fact that Pennsylvania produces the best coal and iron-ore.

The city's success in iron production has also stimulated the spinning industry, so cotton and woollen mills are flourishing there. Of all the states, those best-known for spinning and weaving are Pennsylvania, Massachusetts and Rhode Island; all three states produce cottons, woollens and linen.

Philadelphia is also justly famous for its culture and education. The library on the fifth block of Chestnut Street was set up by the famous scholar [Benjamin] Franklin in 1731. This, the Philadelphia Library, and the Loganian Library altogether contain 180,000 volumes. The Mercantile Library has 30,000 books, as well as newspapers for merchants, who can sit there and read them at their leisure. The libraries in this city used to be the foremost in the United States, but they have yielded pride of place to the libraries in New York City.

At nine o'clock this morning we went by carriage to the United States Mint on Chestnut Street, where three kinds of American coins are produced. We were shown the general method of making silver coins, whereby silver ingots are rolled into thin sheets, blanks are cut out with circular punches, the edges milled and the designs impressed. Each procedure is carried out in a separate room, and the coins are carried from one room to the next in an orderly manner. Each stage of the process is carefully monitored, security is strict and the rooms are locked to prevent anything untoward occurring. However, through the windows we could see the city streets and people walking by, and I wondered whether this might breed evil thoughts in the minds of the workers at the mint.

The minted coins are counted by a machine which drops them into cloth bags. These machines are very ingenious. Each has a weighing scale, a flat tray with rows of indented holes. When the coins are tossed onto the trays and the trays are shaken, the coins drop into the holes. Then a spring is released which tilts the tray, and the coins not in the holes slide into a box underneath. The tray then tips over and the coins pour into a funnel, which is wide at the mouth and narrow at the bottom. A cloth bag attached to the bottom of the funnel catches the coins as they fall.

This evening the city arranged a reception for us, which was held in a mansion in a park and attended by over seventy people. An orchestra played during the banquet, and speeches were made at the end; it was a most enjoyable occasion. By the time it ended it was nearly midnight. Then there was a ball and we did not return to our hotel until three o'clock in the morning.

America and Britain are like siblings who share the same language and customs. When one meets Americans for the first time, they are very friendly and open; even casual acquaintances and passers-by on the street behave like old friends. With time, however, these feelings inevitably turn to dislike. The British, in contrast, are at first very aloof and dignified (as befits the subjects in an imperial monarchy), but they gradually thaw and after two or three meetings they open up their hearts and become less reserved.

Visiting a large city far from home, where the language, customs and religion are unfamiliar, and spending only a day or two there makes it extremely difficult to judge the character of the people. However, since the people are permeated with the nation's spirit, if one pays the slightest attention, their character will reveal itself naturally, even to a mere passer-by.

July 30th. Fine.
At ten o'clock in the morning we went by carriage to Independence Hall, where the first national Congress was held. The building is on Chestnut Street, at the fifth block. Before America gained independence, this hall served as the meeting place for representatives of the thirteen colonies, and it was here that a national (revolutionary) government was established. The famous Declaration of Independence was drafted in and promulgated from this hall, and we were told that the original document is still kept here.

Independence Hall is built of plain brick, but the craftsman's spirit is evident in the restrained use of decoration and the building shows character, elegance and good taste. Moreover, because this is a famous monument dating from the time of independence, visitors come in great numbers to see it. In the hall stands a large bell. Before the War of Independence, the people of Pennsylvania were suffering under Britain's tyrannical rule and rang this bell with its mournful note over and over again until it cracked. The bell has been preserved with the crack still in it. In the hall, portraits of the heroes of those days, such as General Washington, hang on the walls; the desk at which the Declaration of Independence was drafted is also said to be here.

From Independence Hall we went to inspect the [Baldwin] locomotive works. In it were gigantic steam-driven wheels which supply the power to cut iron and steel plates, drill holes and rivet metal plates together. We next visited a workshop where men were producing fittings for locomotives, making screws and polishing brass plates. We rested a while in the room for design and drawing. The ink which is used for drawing comes from Japan, and we were told that ink from Europe or China is not suitable so they have to import Japanese ink.

After the locomotive works we visited a prison, a well-known Philadelphia institution. Most countries in Europe at that time had adopted the system we saw here, beginning with Britain and France. A long, high stone wall marks the outer perimeter. The front of the prison is secured by a fortress-like gate-house with enormous iron doors. The prison itself is located in the centre of the compound and consists of stone buildings two storeys high and several hundred feet long. There are seven wings in all, which radiate from one central hub, rather like the rays around the sun. A large room at the centre serves as the watch-tower, from where guards can easily oversee the seven wings. Each cell-block has a long corridor, with cells along either side. One criminal is housed in each cell.

Inmates are kept hard at work weaving straw mats, stitching shoes and cutting corks. The tasks are set according to the skills of the inmates, and necessary tools such as knives, hammers and chisels are allowed. Within the cells are gas-lamps, and each cell is equipped with a bed, a desk and a chamber-pot. The size of a cell is about nine feet by six feet. The open spaces between the buildings are exercise areas where the prisoners are allowed to walk once a day.

At half past five that afternoon we left our hotel, boarded the train at Market Street Station and journeyed north to New York.

Our stay in Philadelphia lasted only two days. Although we observed as much as we could, we were only able to visit five or six places, so the record of our stay there is rather short.

CHAPTER 19

# A Record of New York City

July 31st, 1872. Fine.

Accompanied by guides provided by the New York City government, we visited the Astor Library, where the director gave us catalogues.

From there we went to the Bible Society. This society was established with donations collected from those who wanted to spread the Bible's teachings throughout the world. At that time the book had already been translated into thirty languages. The society sells Bibles in many countries, and we were each given a Chinese translation. Not only does everyone in America own a copy of the Bible, which is kept in each home, but if people go away on a journey of a few weeks, they feel obliged to take it with them. It is especially revered by women. If the owner is wealthy, the book may be lavishly bound and decorated with gold and jewels, and some spare no expense in adorning their Bible, but there are also very plain versions which poor people can afford. Editions in Braille are also available for blind people. A copy of the book is always kept in the reception-rooms of commercial establishments and in hotel rooms; and each inmate in prisons or patient in hospitals is given a Bible and encouraged to study it. The Bible Society publishes the books very cheaply, selling them for less than the cost of the paper.

Next we visited the Young Men's Christian Association. This is a gathering place for young men and women to study the Christian way, promoting good and instilling respect for the Bible's teachings. This building is very much like a school, and it even has a gymnasium with equipment for all kinds of physical exercise. There was nothing else worthy of notice. In towns and cities across the United States there are 308 such associations, which encourage good behaviour and moral conduct.

The Bible is the sacred book of the West and the basis of the people's morality. It is veneration of God which drives people to work hard. Good behaviour is the basic element in maintaining order in society and gives rise to the enrichment and strengthening of a country. It is like oxygen: though without substance, it flows into hapless lands and bestows brightness; it is without taste but imparts a strong flavour. Thus, when Western people talk about a nation and its character, they always discuss religion. When a foreigner comes to their country, they always ask what religion he observes and what god he worships. When they meet someone who professes no faith, they think of him as a lost soul or a heathen from the wilderness. They become wary of him and sever all social relations. They tend to think that a person who does not have a religion will not respect the law.

The various countries of the West each have their own civilisations and compete with one another. When we read the Old and New Testaments, which Christians respect, some parts contain unbelievable tales of voices from Heaven or relate the resurrection of a crucified criminal. Thus, the Bible can easily be dismissed as the ramblings of a lunatic. We were suspicious of the tears of those who prayed before a man condemned to death for heresy, whom they acclaim as the son of a celestial king. Every city in the West has images of this dead man being taken down from a cross, with streaks of blood running down his body. These images are hung on the walls and placed in the corners of rooms, giving the impression that one is passing through a cemetery or lodging at a place of execution. Is this not a strange custom? Yet Westerners think it strange that people in the East have not accepted Christianity, and even rational people well versed in world affairs urged us to display these images. What is their intention? Western people are sincere in worshipping God and practising morality. They are hard-working and strive to co-operate with one another. The root of this co-operation is to be found in religion, so it cannot be explained simply in terms of form and theory. We must enquire about the actual practice of it.

In the East, Confucianism is a system of ethical principles, and Buddhism is a religion. These two teachings provide the essential guidelines for governing a nation and have permeated the hearts of the people there. When it comes to beliefs and practices, who can say which is deeper: Christianity or the doctrines of the East? The Four Books and Six Teachings of the sages have been known in Japan for two thousand years. However, those who are able to read and understand them are merely a few of the well-educated. Others have picked up bits and pieces and have spread the concepts of loyalty, filial piety, benevolence and righteousness to the populace through government and the law. Even if we were to ask Confucian scholars about the essence of the teachings on ethics, it would be hard to receive a satisfactory explanation of the finer points.

Unlike Confucian scholars, Buddhist monks in general have observed their precepts and obeyed the rules. Yet only two or three monks out of a hundred are able to give basic explanations of a few sutras. The Buddhist faithful merely chant the sacred name of Amida Buddha over and over again. There are many strange aspects in Christ's teachings, and it would scarcely need an intelligent scholar to defeat the arguments advanced by Christians and render them silent. However, when we compare the sincerity of their practice to ours, we cannot but feel ashamed.

We next visited a hospital for handicapped children, and from there we went to the new railway terminal. In America, where buildings tend to be simple and functional, railroad depots are often crude constructions, no more than long wooden sheds to keep out the rain. This new station building, however, is grand and spacious, elegant and beautiful. From the Grand Central Terminal we went to Mr. Stewart's store on Broadway.

The large stores of wealthy merchants are all located along this avenue. Traffic on this street is heavy and business is brisk. Mr. Stewart's store, which occupies an entire block in this bustling area, is a five-storey building constructed mainly of iron. Rows of big windows give it a light and airy appearance. There is an empty space inside with a glass roof enclosed by four walls, which is used as the office. In various departments the store displays cloth, carpets, tapestries, gold embroidery, clothing, bedding, upholstered chairs, sofas and so forth. It was built at a cost of $5,000,000. However, the fortunes of the Stewart family do not depend on the store alone. The Stewarts have provided a magnificent building filled with merchandise in order to stimulate the New York City economy. However, when the annual profit was calculated, we were told that it was extremely small, barely covering costs.

After that we visited the *Tribune* newspaper. America is a country where many newspapers are published, and New York, especially, is a city in which newspapers are widely read. In America and in Europe, where parliamentary policies and trade are carried out on a large scale, newspapers are extremely popular and influential. Newspapers are more popular in America than in other countries, and there are 1,845 publishers, which sell 20,545,845 copies of their newspapers annually. This means that half the citizens of the country read at least one newspaper each.

Newspapers are regarded as important in Europe and America because they monitor the policies of national, state, county and village governments; they are conducive to learning and scholarship; they provide reports on trade, thereby building and strengthening the country's economy; and they encourage good habits and moral behaviour. Without leaving home one can learn about conditions all across the country; from one's house one can obtain a grasp of world affairs. Thus, newspapers truly encourage the spread of culture and are indispensable. The value of a newspaper depends on the editor's qualities and learning; the might of an editor's pen exceeds that of a million foot-soldiers. Educated people accept this, so that journalists often have greater influence than politicians.

From the *Tribune* we went to the main office of the Telegraph Company, and as a test we communicated with Cleveland (over a thousand miles from New York) and Washington. Responses from both came instantly. The replies offered greetings and hopes for the safety, peace and tranquillity of the Embassy.

The telegraph was established twenty-eight years ago, when Samuel F. B. Morse of New York strung a line beside the railroad between Washington and Baltimore, a distance of thirty-six miles. About that time in Europe, too, people were trying to send messages using electricity. There were several systems similar to that of Morse, so it is not absolutely certain which country actually invented the telegraph. However, it is not unreasonable for Americans to take pride in it and claim it as their invention. Although several different kinds of telegraph were invented in various countries at around the same time, Morse's equipment was superior. Now nearly nine countries out of ten have adopted his system, with France bestowing a prestigious award on Mr. Morse.

The invention of the telegraph has brought extraordinary benefits to people, and in every part of the United States new lines have been hurriedly set up. Because the lines soon became congested, it was decided to create zones and establish central agencies to control them and reduce interference. Despite this, the inconveniences persisted, so eventually a headquarters for the telegraph companies was established in New York City. This is the company we visited. Its telegraph lines link almost all the eastern states of the United States. The total length of lines up to last year was 56,000 miles, and there were 4,200 telegraph offices.

August 1st. Fine.
At four o'clock in the afternoon we left the hotel and took the steamer to Rhode Island from the Fall River Depot. Boarding the ferry *Providence*, we left the port and sailed past Brooklyn and up the East River. There were two islands in the river. Because of the clean air, they have built a hospital and a prison on one of them. Prostitutes who become pregnant come here to give birth, and their children are raised at the hospital. The same rules are imposed here as in a children's hospital. Because America

is so enormous and its population so small, every effort is made to encourage a rise in population, even to the extent of raising illegitimate children. America and Russia are the most advanced in providing such well-equipped hospitals. Men of discernment argue, however, that rather than opening the flood-gates of immorality to increase the population, it would be better to have a smaller population and encourage correct morals, customs and education. This approach better accords with the aims of civil life and is indeed a sound argument.

One noteworthy fact about New York Bay is the profitability of its oyster cultivation. Oysters flourish in tropical and semi-tropical bays. Those grown in Ceylon and in the Mediterranean Sea are gigantic. They grow here and in other bays, too, and vary in size depending on the area. In certain places in America and Europe oysters are raised for profit. While we were in Washington, oysters were served at every large function. The most productive oyster-beds are said to be in New York Bay. Oysters are the most delicious of all shellfish. Their flesh is tender, they are good for the digestion and very nourishing. Western people prize them highly and, consequently, they are expensive and regarded as a delicacy.

CHAPTER 20

# A Record of Boston

August 2nd, 1872. Light cloud.

At half past five this morning our steamer arrived at the harbour of Providence in the state of Rhode Island. From here we travelled north by train, arriving at eight o'clock in the morning in Boston, where we took rooms at an old inn [Revere House]. City Hall stands in the centre of the city, but its architecture is not particularly imposing. Boston is an old city. When the colonists rejected British rule, Boston had a population of 2,000 and took the lead in the fight for independence.

At four in the afternoon the city hosted a banquet in our hotel which was attended by 180 people. After dinner there were speeches, and the party ended at ten o'clock. It was the most elaborate dinner we had attended since we left San Francisco.

August 3rd. Cloudy.

At nine o'clock in the morning we set out by train for Lawrence, to the north of Boston, to inspect its cotton mills. American cotton is the finest in the world. The crops are large, and the fibres of the cotton are long and lustrous. Cotton is concentrated in the southern states, while spinning and weaving flourish in the north.

The city of Lawrence, with a population of 28,921, is north of Boston. Thanks to water-power from the Merrimack River, cotton-spinning and weaving mills were built here, and the prosperity of Lawrence soon came to depend on these mills.

There were three mill buildings, each of them a massive four-storey red-brick construction. A water-wheel was turning at the first building; beside it stood a huge warehouse where bales of cotton were stored. As the cotton moves through the three buildings, the bales of raw cotton are turned into bolts of printed cloth. The whole process is most astonishing.

From Lawrence we went to Lowell, where we visited several woollen mills. Water from the Merrimack River is harnessed to drive the machinery. Here the factories were even larger than the one in Lawrence. They spin cotton to make printed cloth, and they also weave woollen yarn into carpets. The machinery used for washing and bleaching the wool and for making the yarn is basically the same as in the manufacture of cotton cloth. The machinery for weaving patterned carpets, however, is extremely intricate, and the Jacquard apparatus is used to control the movements of the warp-threads. This device was invented by Jacquard, a Frenchman from Lyons, in about 1800.

August 4th. Fine.
At eleven o'clock in the morning we set out by carriage beyond the high point at Beacon Street to visit the reservoir, a gourd-shaped lake some two hundred acres in area, surrounded by solid stone embankments.

On the way back, we saw two rays of light in the sky to the north. That evening the northern sky was cloudy and tempestuous, and the light, which shone mysteriously from within dark mists, was like the rays of the setting sun breaking through the clouds. It was yellowish with a pale red tinge, and vague in outline rather than clearly defined. Our guide pointed at it and said, 'Those are the Northern Lights.' In Europe these often appear in the frigid zone above latitude 75° N, where there are several months of continuous darkness in winter. When you reach the latitude of London, however, the lights are rarely seen.

August 5th. Fine.
Upon the request of the citizens of Boston, the vice-ambassadors and Embassy members divided into two groups. One party, led by Vice-Ambassadors Kido and Itō, with members of the entertainment committee – in all more than ten people – went to the town of Hudson [Marlborough], where a luncheon was held in the townhall, to which more than two hundred guests, both men and women, were invited. Beginning with the mayor, several people gave speeches. It was a very lively event. From there we went to a boot and shoe factory and a clothing factory.

The second party, led by Vice-Ambassadors Ōkubo and Yamaguchi, went to Providence, Rhode Island. There, too, a luncheon was provided, with more than three hundred guests, and speeches were made. It was most convivial. After lunch they visited a factory producing gold and silver utensils.

Commodore Perry, who led the mission to Japan, came from this state. It is for this reason, people say, that the people of Rhode Island are the most friendly toward Japan. They did entertain us most warmly.

August 6th. Fine.

At half past nine in the morning we packed our luggage and left the hotel. Boarding a steamer, we sailed out of the harbour. The people of Boston came to the harbour and lined the piers to see us off. At the mouth of the bay we transferred to the Cunard Line mail-boat *Olympus*. As we moved off, salutes were fired from the batteries at the mouth of the bay. Citizens boarded seven tugs and cutters to see us off, and one hundred or more men and women came out to the base of the outer lighthouse where the *Olympus* anchored for a while. A meal was served on board, and the speaker of the lower house of the city assembly, Mr. Rice, sat at the head table. It was a parting lunch at which we exchanged speeches and farewells.

American people treat foreigners like family or friends, and are very warm and welcoming. For five days since our arrival in Boston, especially, not only the city itself but also the surrounding towns had been extremely generous in entertaining us. At the time of our departure, their representatives came to the mouth of the bay to give us a farewell feast and see us off. This was sufficient to allow people like us from Eastern countries to reflect on our own past, making us uncomfortable and embarrassed. Ah, at this time of enlightenment, waking up from the dream of isolation and bathing in the harmony of world-wide relations, all the people in Japan cannot fail to engrave this on their hearts.

From our arrival in San Francisco until our departure from Boston, we traversed the breadth of America, and I would like to summarise what we witnessed. This whole country has adopted European culture but is filled with its own spirit of independence. Funds for promoting industry have flooded into this land and have multiplied greatly. Although America is comparable to the whole of Europe in size, much of Europe is cold and barren, and the regions flourishing there represent only one-third the extent of those prospering in America. Kings, aristocrats, wealthy merchants and large companies have monopolised Europe's lands and assets and have shaped the countries to their own purposes. There was little left for late-comers to develop independently. Such people opened up and pioneered this land of freedom and have nurtured their spirit of enterprise here. Although they say that this country has relied on new creativity, new development and new immigrants, in reality America is a land of people who, in Europe, felt the urge for independence and self-government most strongly. America is the country where such people have gathered and where they are now the leaders. The land is huge and rich, and because manufactured goods and agricultural produce are abundant, a tolerant country with a thriving economy has been established. Though many aspects are still rough-hewn, all their efforts have been successful. It must be said that this is what makes America truly America.

VOLUME II

# Britain

# CHAPTER 21

# A Survey of Britain

The country of Britain, which lies in the north-west corner of Europe, comprises two large islands and 5,500 small islands. It is separated from the continent of Europe by a strait called the English Channel, on the other side of which lies Calais, in France. The sea-route across the Channel is no more than twenty-two miles at its narrowest point.

The area of the United Kingdom as a whole is 121,362 square miles, and according to statistics for 1871 its total population was 31,817,108. Its form, location, size and population are very similar to those of Japan. For this reason, the people of Britain are in the habit of referring to Japan as 'the Britain of the East'. From the point of view of economic power, however, the disparity is immense. Lands belonging to this country are spread across the five continents. In Asia its possessions include most of India, and in the South Seas the Australian continent and New Zealand. In North America, all the vast territory to the north of the United States is British, and Britain also has numerous possessions in South America, including Panama, Guiana and the Antilles Islands. As well as these, in the Mediterranean Britain rules Gibraltar, at the south-west corner of Spain, and the island of Malta, to the south of Italy. It leases Aden, at the mouth of the Red Sea, and Singapore, at the tip of Malacca. It also governs the island of Hong Kong, in southern China, and seven territories on the coast of Africa. In short, many strategically important places on the shores of the world's oceans are British possessions, almost all the world's sea-lanes are under Britain's control, and along the sea-ways Britain has established commercial bases and naval stations. The British boast that the sun never sets on their empire. (The Spanish said the same thing about their own empire when it was at its height.)

The weather in Britain is very inconstant. Through autumn and winter until about the beginning of the year it is overcast and gloomy, and sunlight is very rarely seen. Even in London it is not considered unusual to see the sun for only three days in a month. In Scotland there is ceaseless rain and snow and the gloom is almost permanent. Sometimes a whole month at a time is passed under lamplight. When summer arrives it is extremely bright and sunny, but the heat is not oppressive. This country, which lies at the edge of the temperate zone, is described as very humid, but compared with Japan the air is as dry as that of America. The proof of this is that wet cloth will dry indoors even on cold and rainy days, and articles made of iron do not rust. There are also frequent fogs. Even on fine days it often happens that a thick fog suddenly descends, reducing visibility to almost nothing, and lamps are lit to provide illumination indoors. Rain does not come in prolonged downpours or sudden cloudbursts. When the temperature falls a little, the sky becomes overcast for days on end and a constant drizzle sets in. Something which is particularly striking is that in London and the other big cities, buildings of white stone all become smoke-blackened with the passage of time because of the soot which is present in the fogs in this country. Since large-scale manufacturing is carried on throughout Britain and the country burns 100,000,000 tons of coal annually, it is hardly surprising that fogs should be full of the resulting soot.

Britain's wealth is essentially founded on the exploitation of mineral resources. The national production of coal and iron is the greatest in the world. Its people have, by exploiting these two resources, developed steam-powered machinery, steamships and railways. Britain has harnessed the power of steam, has thereby multiplied its power to produce, has come to monopolise the profit to be derived from textiles and sea transport, and has thus become the country which bestrides the world. As a result, the huge scale of the metals-manufacturing industry in Britain was such as to astonish our party.

Such is the size of Britain's trade that it is described as the great market of the world. The location of the country, which lies between Europe, America and Africa, completely surrounded by the sea, means that there are no natural obstacles to the conduct of trade. In addition, Britain has very many large ports and good harbours. The historical reasons why Britain's trade has flourished are many and various but may perhaps be summed up as follows. Because the land is of poor quality and is therefore difficult to wrest a living from, the people of Britain can only expect to secure a livelihood by depending on trade with other countries, and as a result the British have devoted themselves from early times to seaborne commerce. In addition, due to the influence of the Danes and Norsemen, they were accustomed to seafaring and were thus able to exploit their domestic mineral resources and livestock by carrying them to other countries to exchange for goods they needed. The success of these ventures meant that they accumulated wealth and thus attained their present prosperous condition. This is why iron and coal are predominant among the country's trade goods and why it depends on imports from abroad even for animal feed. Britain transforms its iron and coal into the power of machines and steam and uses these, along with water- and wind-power, to manufacture goods. Thus, cotton from America, hemp from the East Indies and raw sugar from the West Indies come into this country and are turned into textiles and refined sugar, which are then supplied to the rest of the world. These are the principal items of Britain's trade. All its other revenue also derives from the transformation of iron and coal.

Goods imported into Britain from abroad fall into two categories: first, food-stuffs for its people; second, raw materials for the goods they manufacture. If the coming and going of ships to and from the country's ports ceased for even a single day, the people would grow pale with hunger. The world trade in cotton, wool, hemp and iron goods depends on the state of the British market. All commodities such as raw cotton first find their way to Britain and are then re-exported to Europe. This one country monopolises the profits from dealing as a middleman in the produce of nature.

Since 1850 Britain has enjoyed domestic prosperity and peace, and trade and manufactures have increased year by year. Consequently, both livestock and arable farming have also flourished. Nevertheless, Britain's imports of food-stuffs have gradually increased. Grain exported from Russia, America, India and Australia goes mainly to the British market and next to France. This grain is not used only to feed people and livestock. This increase in imports is partly because there has been an increase in the amount which is subjected to manufacturing processes and then re-exported. (For example, starch is used in textile-manufacture and grain is used for brewing.) So products which derive from the natural resources of Britain's overseas possessions which are sent to the home country account for one-third of the total value of its imports of food and raw materials. From India come cotton, wool, raw silk, hemp, cane-sugar, indigo, tea, rice, spices and timber. From the West Indies come sugar, tobacco, coffee, cotton, hides and rubber. From Australia are sent gold, copper and wool; and from British North America grain, timber, hides and fish. Among these, the greatest profits are derived from India. An American has criticised this state of affairs, saying that the British live like ants in their little islands, owning fields in India, where they squeeze the fat from the people while growing fatter themselves. They extract profits from their colonies just as one extracts juice from a lemon: they squeeze with all their strength until not a drop is left, and only then do they stop.

Britain and America, to put it briefly, are like parent and child. The language and culture are fundamentally very similar, but while the Americans are impetuous and do things in a rough-and-ready fashion, the British are cautious and pay great attention to detail. Because goods of British manufacture are all of solid construction, are extremely durable, and exhibit skilled craftsmanship, they are highly regarded throughout the world. Someone has expressed the following judgement on them. If you examine an article of British make and one of French make together, the article made by the Frenchman is both beautiful – so you will never weary of admiring it – and cheap, about half the cost of the British article. However, when you take into account the fact that when used it soon wears out, while the article of British manufacture lasts for an exceptionally long time before it is no longer serviceable, it would make good sense to buy the British article even if the price were still higher. This is Britain's strong point. Yet in elegance and delicacy, even their best efforts cannot match those of France. The fact that the bravery of the British, too, is calm and considered rather than rash and hot-headed is the reason why they are constantly victorious.

This is an overall picture of Britain's domestic prosperity. Such an account may leave the reader with the impression that the whole country is an earthly paradise and that all classes of the people are prosperous and contented. Be that as it may, comfort is the fruit of hardships undergone, and wealth is a flower which hard work has caused to bloom. That Britain has been able to become the wealthiest country in the world is because its people's industriousness exceeds that of other nations. The people who live in Britain are unable to be idle even for a moment. We heard it said that the Spaniard makes an occupation of sleeping all day, but that the Englishman's foot never rests on the ground for more than a moment. In Spain, therefore, simply taking a shorter siesta is enough to gain one a reputation for hard work; but in London just walking at an ordinary pace gives the impression that one is an idler. As a result, many people simply run out of energy, and the numbers of the poor are probably greater than in almost any other country.

The population of England is 23,000,000, and the number of destitute persons is over 1,000,000. The people of town and country alike all work hard for their living. They keep the accounts of their family businesses very carefully. On Saturday evenings, husband and wife compare their books and do the week's calculations. They discuss the smallest matters and let nothing slip by. They fill the pages of their daily account books with tiny figures, and when they present their sales ledger to their money-lender, he polishes his spectacles, examines the accounts line by line and compares them with his own books. If there is the slightest discrepancy, he disputes the figures and will not agree to a loan. This life of unremitting work resembles that of the humblest labourer in Japan. The passers-by in the streets swarm together like ants and scatter again like bees, doing business on the run. If one asks how much those who have no craft or trade earn in a day, one finds that they can be hired for only a shilling or two. Beggars congregate at crossroads carrying brooms and brushes with which they sweep the street in front of people and clean their shoes. The number of prostitutes in London exceeds 100,000. Child thieves loiter in streets where there are few passers-by. One child approaches the chosen victim from the front and knocks his hat down over his eyes, while another snatches his wallet from behind and runs off. The bustling cities are full of gangs of ruffians, and within a few paces one's gold watch and chain will have disappeared. In ill-frequented country districts there are footpads armed with pistols and carrying poison [acid or chloroform?] in their pockets who waylay travellers. In trains, gamblers pass through the carriages looking for people up from the country to flatter and deceive. An unending succession of poor men and women throw themselves into London's rivers and canals. There are thieves' kitchens where all kinds of malefactors gather to gamble and smoke opium, ready for any kind of evil-doing.

The fact is that the vast profits which are reaped year by year are all garnered by the rich. There is a comprehensive system of laws to protect them, so that those who lose their fortunes are few, and there are not many who start up businesses all at once or suddenly go bankrupt. We were told that the number of people who owned land in England had grown smaller every year, so that there were now no more than 20,000. And in Ireland, we were told, apart from 1,000 aristocratic families, there were only 8,412 landowners. It can be seen from this fact alone that the rich get richer by the day, while the poor struggle throughout their lives simply to feed themselves. Such is the unequal distribution of wealth among the people of this country. Many therefore risk much and travel far to seek their fortunes elsewhere. As many as 120,000 British people go to America each year. If those who go to Canada and Australia are included, the number rises to nearly 300,000. Most of the settlers in America are immigrants from Britain and Germany. The great number of migrants is a sign of the difficulty of making a living in those countries.

The strength of religious conviction of the British is equal to that of the Americans. The religion most widely practised throughout Britain is Protestant Christianity, which is therefore the national religion. Roman Catholicism is also practised, but by no more than two-ninths of the population. There are also followers of the Jewish faith. The number of different sects which each religion has is very large. In England, the chief one is Episcopalianism. It is called the Church of England, and its liturgy and other practices are very similar to those of Roman Catholicism. Presbyterianism is the chief religion in Scotland, where it is called the Church of Scotland. In Ireland, Roman Catholicism alone is practised. The number of such sects is not less than forty.

In the West, religion underpins culture and is of vital importance in encouraging industriousness. Whether a people have religious faith or not bears no small influence on their manners and morals. British politicians regard it as particularly important, and in Britain no one of any class would dare to fail to attend church services. Throughout the towns shops are shut from Saturday night, and on Sunday, the day of rest, hardly any business is done. Even those who are away from their homes invariably go to church. In Scotland this custom is particularly strict, and even a traveller on the road who omitted to attend a place of worship would be shunned.

The Christianity of Europe and America, the Islam of western Asia and the Buddhism of the East are all alike in having a single origin but many different sects. A people's religious adherence always brings gains as well as losses. The benefits which priests and nuns bring to a country go ineluctably together with the abuses which they are responsible for. And as human knowledge increases, we find many aspects of religion laughable. However, for guiding people's consciences, for turning their characters towards good and inducing them to put aside worldly desires, for teaching them that there are things which ought to be done and things which ought not to be done, for these things we cannot but rely on the support of religion. It is those with little knowledge who talk about the evils of religion. In recent years in Europe, the study of natural philosophy and moral philosophy has been pursued in an attempt to do away with the abuses of religion and preserve its benefits alone. Broadly speaking, this rationalist philosophy is merely a recapitulation of the Christian scriptures. The French hold religion in low regard, while the British and Americans value it highly. On reflection, it seems that at the moment religion is still indispensable. Since it already exists, to value it is wiser than to despise it.

CHAPTER 22

# A Survey of London

August 16th, 1872. Cloudy; rain.
At one o'clock in the afternoon we passed the Fastnet Light on the coast
of Ireland, and at two arrived off the port of Queenstown [now Cobh]. It
was so named because the present queen landed there when she toured
Ireland twenty years ago. The harbour was a small bay encircled by hills.
Today it was raining and there was a heavy swell. We did not enter the
harbour, therefore, but hove to at the mouth of the bay to allow some of
the passengers to go ashore by boat. We then got under way again. After
nightfall we sailed through St. George's Channel, which lies between
Ireland and England.

August 17th. Fine; light breeze.
During the morning we sailed along the coast of the region called Wales.
Wales is described as a mountainous area of Britain. Ranges of hills sweep
down to the sea, and some high peaks could be seen among them. Today,
the wind having died down, the sea was like a millpond. All the way to
Liverpool nothing lay ahead but the smooth and boundless sea, with not a
glimpse of a single hill on the horizon.

Our official host, General [George Gardiner] Alexander, and the
interpreter, Mr. [William George] Aston, had come to Liverpool to
welcome us on behalf of the British government and were awaiting us
aboard a small steamboat anchored in the estuary of the river Mersey.
Also on board were some of the Embassy's officials who had travelled
directly from Japan. We therefore transferred to the tender, which then
headed for the port.

Liverpool is the principal port for trade with the Americas and its
waterfront is magnificent. An unbroken line of huge docks, enclosed by
stone walls and filled with forests of masts, stretches for six miles along
the northern foreshore. Carriages sent by the mayor were waiting for us at
the quayside. There was an ant-like throng of people at the dock, and it

was only with some difficulty that the police managed to open a path to enable our carriages to make their way through the jostling crowd. We were entertained to lunch at the North Western Hotel, which was adjacent to a railway station in the city centre, and then boarded our train.

The land alongside the railway was all low-lying. We could not make out any hills, even in the far distance. On the bed of the track was a layer of clean sand, and the grass on the embankments on either side was neatly trimmed, like hair – it was as though the whole line had been swept and mopped. The local people had divided the land neatly into fields and cultivated it thoroughly and meticulously. To the eye, this landscape was a great improvement on the rough and ready American railroads and those parts of the endless open plains alongside them which were tilled.

As we proceeded we found that, while there were stations in the larger towns, the railway passed by the smaller towns and villages through cuttings. In the meantime darkness fell. At twenty past eleven we arrived at Euston Station in London. We alighted from the train and went by carriage to the Buckingham Palace Hotel, where we took rooms.

The population of London in 1872 was 3,251,804. This area of land lies on the two banks of the river Thames, sixty miles upstream from its mouth. Two-thirds lie on the north side of the river and one-third is on the south. All the prosperous districts of London are north of the river; on the south side are many factories. The Thames is a highway for London's trade and is more than a thousand feet wide. The bridge farthest downstream is called London Bridge. Merchant vessels come upriver as far as this point. The stretch of river immediately below London Bridge forms the Port of London. On the north bank by the bridge stands the Custom House, a large, imposing building of white stone. Steamships from Belgium, Holland, Germany, Denmark and Sweden arrive here constantly. Downriver from the Custom House lies a continuous line of docks called London Docks. Here are warehouses for tobacco, chinaware, liquor and other goods, and they are at all times filled with mountains of piled-up barrels and stacked crates.

Downstream from the London Docks there is a tunnel under the river which makes it easier to go back and forth between the north and south banks. It was built in 1843 using a device invented by a man called Brunel and is a celebrated structure. It is about twenty-seven feet high and about twelve feet wide and is entirely lined with brick. It allowed people to pass backwards and forwards beneath the river: ships sailed above and pedestrians walked below. It is one of the marvels of London. One entered and left the tunnel by flights of stone steps, so horse-drawn vehicles could not go through. The width of the river is well over two hundred yards. The tunnel was illuminated by gas-lamps. In recent years, apparently, it had not been much used because of poor ventilation, but it was this tunnel which launched the great enterprise of driving roads beneath bodies of water. Recently it had been taken on by a railway company, which, we were told, intended to link it to the underground railway traversing the city.

Upstream from the London Docks thirteen bridges cross the river. Four carry railway lines and do not permit people or horses to cross. Nine carry horse-drawn traffic and pedestrians. They were all constructed to the highest standards and the cost of them was enormous.

The most prosperous districts of the city lie between Westminster Bridge and London Bridge. Massive stone embankments have been built on both sides of this stretch of the river, with extremely wide roads running along them. There are no houses on the riverside, but gas-lamps have been installed to provide light at night. They run alongside the river like a necklace of stars. On moonlit evenings and snowy nights they make an extremely beautiful sight.

A railway also runs underground alongside the river. Starting from near the Mansion House in the City, it follows the river as far as Vauxhall Bridge, from where it goes round the western edge of the city and to the north. It encircles a third of London, running for the most part through tunnels excavated under built-up areas. The tunnels, being made of brick or stone and arched in section, are as strong as a solid block of stone buried in the earth. Anyone sitting or lying in a house in one of the streets beneath which the railway runs hears a constant rumbling all day, like thunder under the ground.

The streets throughout London are paved with close-laid stones, resembling tiles. In the sixteenth century, when the city had a population of no more than 150,000, the streets were very narrow. Since no method of disposing of sewage was provided, as the population increased epidemics frequently occurred, which were the cause of much distress. Even now, the area of about four square miles which extends from the Tower of London through the City to the vicinity of Waterloo Bridge has extremely cramped streets, with no squares or gardens. Many efforts have been made during the last century to open up the district, but because the value of the land is so high no more has been done than the widening of one or two streets. Consequently, the crush of vehicles and pedestrians is especially great, and the pandemonium of the scene only serves to increase the impression of prosperity.

Omnibuses run along the main thoroughfares. British omnibuses are very different in design from American street-cars. American street-cars run on rails, so the body of the car is mounted on bogeys with small wheels, like railway rolling-stock. British omnibuses run on the road itself, so they have large wheels outside the body of the vehicle. The roof of the bus is surrounded with an iron balustrade and an iron staircase runs up the side of the vehicle, enabling passengers to sit either inside or on top. In some cases, a single bus can carry as many as sixty people. They are usually drawn by two powerful cart-horses. The fare, which varies according to the distance travelled, is collected after the passenger has boarded, a ticket being issued in exchange. However, tickets are often dispensed with.

Cabs also stand in the streets awaiting passengers. Some are drawn by two horses, some by one. We saw them everywhere we went. The fare is determined by calculating the length of time it will take to reach the destination, which depends on how far away it is. The cab fare is sixpence a mile. A printed list of rules is displayed inside the vehicle.

If people are pressed for time, and the journey is one which would take a long time by cab, they go by the underground railway. The first-class fare is sixpence, second-class fourpence, third-class threepence. For these sums one can travel in a circle round the whole city, arriving at one's destination in just a few minutes: a circular route becomes the quicker way.

When assessing their own character, the British say that their feet never rest for long on the ground. The British also have an adage, 'Time is money.' These facts are enough to tell one that the people all work hard at their occupations and are very diligent. There is a saying in Europe about the British, Americans, French and Germans. If each is set a task and given six hours to do it in, the American will finish his work in four hours and fill the remaining time by taking a leisurely stroll; the Frenchman will finish in four hours and spend the spare time drinking, singing and dancing; the Englishman will finish the job in five hours and spend the sixth hour working at another task; and the German will not be able to finish the task in six hours but will go on working through the night. It has to be said that this story sums up well the characteristics of the four nationalities.

London is divided into six districts. The eastern district is the City of London. It is London's most prosperous business district. The population, which numbers something over 160,000, has certain privileges. There are gates across the streets where the City adjoins other districts and the Lord Mayor keeps the keys. Even the monarch dare not enter without getting the Lord Mayor's leave to open the gates.

The City sprang up along the north bank beyond the Custom House, past London Bridge to a point upriver of Blackfriars Bridge. The City is paramount among the six great London districts, and contains the Mansion House (the townhall), the Bank and the Royal Exchange. 'The Bank' means the Bank of England: there are many other great banks in the City. The 'Royal Exchange' is the building where merchants gather to determine the prices of commodities by offering competing bids, and to conclude commercial contracts. These are all large buildings of white stone. They are handsome and imposing structures and are the great sights of the City.

At the northern end of London Bridge stands a column two hundred feet high. A fire broke out here in 1666 and turned into a conflagration which destroyed most of the City. This monument was erected afterwards to commemorate the fact (like Ekōin temple in Tokyo). Twenty-two thousand vehicles, on average, cross London Bridge each day. The carriage-way of the road across the bridge, leading to the Mansion House, is jammed with carts and carriages, the horses head to head and the carriages wheel to wheel, with no gaps between them. The pavements on either side are constantly thronged with hurrying men and women. At intersections where it is necessary to step off the pavements in order to cross the roadway, policemen are posted to control the traffic, so as to assist children and old people who are daunted by the horses and vehicles. Because of the continuous stream of vehicles it is often necessary to wait for several minutes before being able to cross.

St. Paul's Cathedral on Ludgate Hill is the largest church in London. The height of the dome is 370 feet, and its diameter 145 feet. It is a copy of St. Peter's in Rome (the principal church of the Catholic religion). It is possible to survey the greater part of the city from the top. The area to the east was the ancient town called Londinium in Roman times, some remains of which still survive.

The western district is called Westminster. This, too, is a 'city' with special privileges. Its area is four times that of the City of London, and its population is over 500,000. In this district there are many attractive areas where the streets are broad and well laid out, with gardens among them. At the end of Westminster Bridge over the Thames stands Parliament. Beside it stands Westminster Abbey. This is the ancestral church of the British monarchy and many kings and queens are interred there. It is a building of the utmost magnificence. The coronations of monarchs and the weddings of members of the royal family are conducted here.

In London's wealthiest districts, the price of land is extraordinarily high – in some cases equal to the number of shillings which would be needed to cover it. Very many plots of land command such prices. Throughout the city, therefore, buildings seek to make the most economical use of the land they occupy. Basements are dug below them to a depth of six feet or more, and above ground the buildings rise to a height of several storeys – sometimes as many as eight or nine. The upper storeys – the seventh, eighth and ninth – are where the poorest classes live: they are like the back-streets of Tokyo. The people who live on the middle floors are of a slightly higher class than this – craftsmen, tradesmen-shopkeepers, the employees of merchant houses and the like. The ground floors house shops selling goods of all kinds. This is the norm for western cities: London is simply the supreme example.

# CHAPTER 23

# A Record of London, 1

August 19th, 1872. Fine.

At one o'clock in the afternoon we visited the residence of Lord Granville, the foreign secretary, to report to him the nature of our mission and to request an audience with the queen. At the time the queen was on holiday at her castle [Balmoral] in Scotland. Since there was no precedent in the history of the country for her to return to Buckingham Palace from holiday for the express purpose of seeing foreign ambassadors, it was agreed that we would await Her Majesty's return.

As Lord Granville had invited us to dinner at seven o'clock that evening, we occupied the afternoon with a visit to the South Kensington [later, Victoria and Albert] Museum. This museum, the building of which was begun in 1856, houses a permanent exhibition. Much excitement was aroused among the British people by the Great Exhibition held in Hyde Park in 1851. The Hyde Park exhibition revealed that although British products were able to hold their own against those of other countries in quality of workmanship, they were inferior in design. Plans were therefore made to establish this institution, with the object of encouraging and stimulating improvements in design and decoration. Profits remaining in the hands of the royal commission for the exhibition were allocated to this purpose, and Parliament supplemented this with a sum equivalent to half that given by the commissioners.

The first room in the museum was devoted to ornamental arts and crafts. It contained an exhibition of Indian products, all of the most intricate workmanship and the greatest delicacy. These were items of clothing and costly personal adornments chased with gold and silver and inlaid with precious stones. Figures of an Indian nobleman and his wife, especially carved for the purpose, had been dressed in the clothes to show the styles of the garments and how they were worn. On examining these figures we saw that the woman, as well as bangles on her wrists, had rings not only in her ears, at her bosom and on her fingers, but also in her nose.

Her whole person was robed in brocades and embroidered fabrics decorated with precious stones. The materials were dazzling.

We came next to galleries on right and left. Here were displayed in separate sections examples of the ceramics, jewellery, gold and silver ware, textiles, needlework and other crafts of many different countries, including examples of articles of high quality and of objects for daily use. In one section, items of clothing decoration, toys, books, writing materials and scientific apparatus were on show. In the case of pieces of equipment whose workings needed to be demonstrated before their use could be understood, the manufacturers provided attendants to operate them. Despite this museum not being established long, it had already become one of the half-dozen or so most popular of the city's great sights. The number of visitors in 1872 was 50,000.

European countries at the present day stand at the pinnacle of civilisation. They are immensely rich and powerful, their trade is on a huge scale, they excel in arts and manufactures, and their peoples live pleasant lives and are extremely happy. It is natural to assume that all this is the product, achieved over many centuries, of the high value which Europe places on commerce, and that it is peculiar to this continent. However, the truth is otherwise. It is since 1800 that Europe has attained its present wealth; and it is only in the last forty years that it has achieved the truly remarkable level of prosperity we now see. While the countries of Europe were harrowed by the Napoleonic Wars early in this century, Britain alone remained in safety, aloof from the turmoil. It began to acquire its overseas territories and to lay the foundations of its national prosperity about the year 1800. The establishment of steamship lines and railways in the 1830s utterly transformed the trade of Europe.

It was no more than thirty-four years ago that the people of Britain first realised this, and the government, under the pressure of popular demand, began discussing proposals to establish a system of education to develop the manufacturing arts. At that time, no European country except France had such arrangements. The will to stimulate industry grew ever stronger among the British people, and eventually, as a result of the efforts of the queen's consort, Prince Albert, the Great Exhibition was held in Hyde Park in 1851. Of the manufactured goods sent to the exhibition by the countries of Europe, those of one country, France, won a reputation which wholly outshone the others. Most of the British exhibits were aesthetically inferior machine-made items. Refinement of taste and quality were found, surprisingly, in the products of Belgium and Switzerland, which had been thought of as small countries of little consequence, and

British goods were no longer held in high regard. Seeing this, the British became aware for the first time of the reason for the poor design of their products. After much reflection, they put behind them the undesirable practice of copying the French and began to seek instead their own country's individual style.

The view taken of British goods at the next international exhibition, held in France in 1855, was very different, and from then on the number of industrial products imported from France began to decline. This change was due entirely to the exhibitions, and it is for this reason that the South Kensington Museum has had such a great influence on the minds of people throughout the country, and why it continues even now to grow ever bigger. As a result of the advances made by Britain, France also abandoned its complacency and began to exert greater efforts, mounting industrial exhibitions and setting up art galleries in order to promote its own industrial arts. Since then, a variety of institutions have been established in other countries, too, with the same objective.

In Europe, agriculture was said to be the least developed industry. It had throughout history been the occupation of serfs and peasants and had not begun to attract the interest of the gentry until about a hundred years ago. It was only in the 1830s that associations for the scientific study and promotion of agriculture began to be formed in European countries, and it was only in the last twenty years or so that they began to produce an effect. It was formerly the agriculture of France and Germany which was admired by the great countries of Europe, but in the last ten years Britain, too, has made great advances and has now gained the reputation of being at the forefront in agricultural progress. We learnt, in short, that European agriculture, industry and commerce had all reached their present flourishing condition in the space of a few years. The vast difference between the appearance of Europe now and that of the Europe of forty years ago can be imagined.

August 20th. Fine.
At the invitation of the British minister to Japan, Sir Harry Parkes, we took a train from Victoria Station to travel fifty miles south through the counties of Surrey and Sussex to the town of Brighton. The countryside we passed on the way was all one rolling landscape of rich farmland.

Brighton's prosperity is founded on the discovery by a certain doctor that the breathing of pure sea-air and the astringent effect of sea-bathing on the skin are beneficial to the health. Not long ago this was a small, isolated shrimp-fishing village. However, at the suggestion of their doctors, two or three invalids came here to take the cure and it was found to be effective. Gradually word spread in London and people flocked to this part of the coast. The town grew richer year by year, until eventually the prince of Wales, later King George IV, himself came here to seek amusement and to escape the heat. It then rapidly became a large town, and the coast became so crowded with houses that those who disliked the noise and bustle but wished to take the cure now went to other places farther along the coast. We went to Brighton at the suggestion of our official host, who had told us that many members of the London aristocracy and gentry went there at this time of year to seek relief from the heat.

When the train reached Brighton Station, we were met by the mayor and proceeded to inspect the museum next-door. We then went to a school where a lecture on geography was in progress, the subject being Tokyo. When it was over, the lecturer vacated his seat and invited Sir Harry Parkes to say something about Japan as it is now. Sir Harry went up onto the platform and spoke about some of the differences and similarities between China and Japan. Sir John Bowring, the distinguished governor of Hong Kong, was also present at the meeting.

We were entertained to lunch at the mayor's house. Afterwards we returned to London by train, arriving in the early evening.

August 26th. Fine.
At three o'clock in the afternoon, accompanied by Sir Harry Parkes and General Alexander, we left Victoria Station by train for Blandford Forum. Their Imperial Highnesses Prince and Princess Fushimi were also in the party. We stayed the night at Blandford Forum and the next day watched a great march past of the army.

In the early evening [of August 27th] we travelled to Portsmouth, a great port in Hampshire. It is famous as the place where the headquarters of the British fleet is located. The harbour fortifications and the docks themselves were of the stoutest construction.

August 28th. Fine.
At one o'clock we visited Admiral Mundy's official residence, where we were invited to lunch. We were then taken aboard a ship [HMS *Excellent*]. This was an obsolete ship, permanently moored to be used for training. Aboard her, seamen were instructed in small-arms, taught swordsmanship and given physical training. When their gunnery training was completed, they shot at targets set up on a sandy beach. The ship was equipped with machinery which caused it to roll while they were firing, so as to improve their skill in sighting guns in heavy seas.

We went next to a shipyard. It was being extended at the time, and four docks were still under construction. Twenty-four miles of railway had been laid along the shore to transport the blocks of artificial stone. In one of the docks was an iron-clad ship of a new type. It was in fact a turret-ship, with two circular gun-turrets which were designed to revolve. The whole vessel was clad in armour-plate eight to ten inches thick. Four big guns were to be mounted in the revolving turrets, which were rotated by machinery. If the ship had to attack an enemy in a given quarter, all the guns could be brought to bear in that direction, fire and turn about, thus obviating damage to the guns from overheating and allowing the enemy ship no time to take evasive action. Full consideration had been given to every eventuality. The ship had little free-board, so only the gun-turrets would be exposed to enemy fire, and it had a very shallow draught so it was not prevented from sailing at speed even in shallow waters. This iron-clad turret warship was the jewel in the British navy's crown. Not a single one among the iron-clads of the world's great powers would be a match for it. Britain invests much of its power in its navy and builds such ships as this in its quest for ever greater improvement. If there were to be a mightier ship than this one, how formidable would be those who had it under their command!

August 29th. Fine.
In the afternoon we went aboard the *Victory*, which is moored perman-ently at the dockside and manned by sailors of the Royal Navy. Fur-thermore, because this is the ship on which the great British admiral Nelson died at the historic Battle of Trafalgar, off the coast of Spain, relics of him and many of his papers are preserved on board. Large numbers of people who have a love of history and a love of country – both men and women, and of all classes – come here to see his ship and to pay their respects to his courage in the face of death. The letters still kept on board the *Victory* were some which he had written by hand after he had lost his right arm. The handwriting was perfectly formed. His glorious spirit will undoubtedly live for a thousand years.

August 30th. Fine.
In the morning there was a military parade. No more than two thousand men took part. We were invited to lunch at the general's house and afterwards inspected the soldiers' quarters. At seven o'clock in the evening we left by train for London. We arrived at Victoria Station at half past ten and returned to our hotel.

August 31st.
At two o'clock in the afternoon we went to the zoological gardens in the
north-west part of Regent's Park. These gardens were opened in 1828
on the initiative of several members of the aristocracy, including Sir
Stamford Raffles, Sir Humphry Davy and Lord Auckland, who had
solicited funds from various aristocratic families and formed the
[zoological] society.

In the gardens, paths meandered among hills and woods and lakes. The
greenness of the trees and shrubs was offset by the brightness of the gravel
paths. The wooded hills were charming in appearance. At every step one
paused; at every turn one raised one's head. There was not enough time to
gaze at everything. In the midst of this landscape, enclosures had been
created with various different structures, and in them were kept birds and
animals which had been sought and trapped all over the world.

There were placid beasts such as the elephant and the camel, and
ferocious creatures such as bears, wolves and jackals. The woods quaked
at the roaring of lions, tigers and leopards; the air shivered at the
screeching of eagles, hawks and falcons. There was a lake where hippo-
potamuses splashed up water as they trotted along; there was a field where
ostriches kicked up dust as they ran. When the giraffe (a large animal
resembling a deer, but with a long neck) raised its head, it made its house
seem too small. A kangaroo (an animal with a pouch on its belly)
bounded along, flexing its legs and pushing itself off at each leap with its
tail. Inside the tropical house, where the humidity of spring was maintained by steam heat, parrots squawked and monkeys played. The air was
fragrant with the scent of flowers. Small, brightly coloured birds twittered
as they flitted about their cages. Their brilliant colours made them seem
as if they were flowers fluttering about at random. The birds of paradise
from South America, the beautiful birds of India and the South Seas – the
zoo would be embarrassed not to have a specimen of every one. Snakes
and other reptiles are not overlooked: they are kept, too. There were so
many things to see that we were oblivious to the fact that night was
falling.

There is not a great variety of birds and animals in the West, while in
tropical regions there are many exotic birds and curious animals. Most of
the unusual animals kept in these gardens come from South America,
Africa, India and the islands of the South Seas, and to buy them requires
the expenditure of a great deal of money. If they are not kept in conditions appropriate to their natures, then even if they do not die they will
waste away and will not be worth seeing. By that alone can be seen the

degree to which the care of animals has progressed as a science in this country. Members of the monkey family are born in the tropics. In a cold climate their lungs are affected and they die, so they must always be kept in a heated house.

We saw nothing in Europe to compare with the richness of this zoo.

# CHAPTER 24

# A Record of London, 2

September 3rd, 1872. Cloudy.

By gracious permission of the royal household, we were shown round Buckingham Palace, accompanied by Sir Harry Parkes and General Alexander. The building of the palace was begun in the reign of George IV and completed after the accession of the present queen. To front and rear, and to the left, there are extensive gardens, which lack any slopes or elevations but present a pleasing prospect when seen from the upper storeys of the building. The palace is built entirely of white stone. The columns, walls and beams are carved with the greatest skill. The walls inside are covered with gorgeous hangings, and everywhere there is the sumptuous glow of gold-leaf and the brilliant gleam of precious stones. Room after room is adorned with priceless objects and curios, and there is an endless collection of superb pictures whose beauty dazzles the eye. The person who showed us round, however, said that none of this could stand comparison with the magnificence of the Tuileries palace in Paris. We were not permitted to go into the queen's dressing-room and bedroom. She had departed for her holiday in Scotland leaving them in the state of disorder in which they had been while she was in residence, so her staff did not want strangers to see them.

September 4th. Fine.

In the afternoon we went to the Palace of Westminster, which houses the parliament of the United Kingdom. The construction of this palace was begun in 1840, after an earlier building on the site had burned down in 1834. There are high towers at either end. The one at the southern end is 80 feet square and 340 feet high. It is called the Victoria Tower. The one at the northern end, which is a clock tower capped with a spire in the form of a square pyramid, is 40 feet square and 320 feet high. Inside are hung huge bells, and on all four sides are installed the faces and hands of a clock. The mechanism is wound daily, and the bells chime automatically at set times. The ornamental stonework of the exterior walls is extremely fine.

Parliament is Britain's legislative assembly. The sovereign is, by right, the head of this body and also has the power to summon and dismiss its members. It is the general rule throughout Europe that legislative power is exercised by representatives of the people, chosen through public elections. It is in this respect that government in Europe differs most from government in China and Japan, where customs and usages are essentially those of an agricultural people. The Chinese and Japanese hold that the main end of government is the inculcation of morality and think that wealth is no concern of government. The attitude of extensive study is therefore absent from their law-making processes. As a result, they disregard almost entirely both civil rights and property rights. It seems that they are not simply indifferent to such rights but deliberately repress them, and regard acceptance of the wishes of those who hold the reins of government as a good model.

Chinese and Japanese theories of government and national security, therefore, have never devoted any attention to wealth. And because their governing classes and their common people have inhabited separate worlds, these countries have gradually declined into poverty and weakness. Because the cultures of the East and West are different, it is natural that their forms of government should also be different. In the modern world, however, a world interconnected by trade, in which ships constantly ply back and forth, if a country is to exercise its national rights fully and protect its interests, it is necessary that all the people, high and low, must give first priority to the creation of wealth in order to achieve economic prosperity and military strength. It is on these that a country's right to make and enforce its own laws rests.

Legislative assemblies are always divided into an upper and a lower house: no country has an assembly which consists of a single chamber. But the nature of the two houses varies from country to country. In the government of the United Kingdom, the upper house comprises peers and the lower house consists of representatives of the counties.

The members of the upper house, the House of Lords, include members of the royal family, peers and bishops. It is because the tradition of an 'aristocracy' in its original sense (government by the best citizens) still survives that British peers have hereditary legislative powers and sit in the upper house. This is said to be because, to the British, obedience to the law is a virtue more admirable than any other. It was the seizure of legislative power from the aristocracy by the lower house, the House of

Commons, which gave rise to the modern Parliament, but it was in fact the aristocracy which preserved the rights of Parliament through the period from King John – whom they forced to grant a charter which restored their rights – until the time when those rights were extended to the common people as well.

All the peoples of Europe, high and low, attach the very greatest importance to wealth, but those who have been born and brought up in the midst of riches and privilege, remote from the circumstances of the poor, know nothing of real productive work. There are very few indeed who are skilled in business or experienced in worldly affairs. Since it is these aristocrats who sit in the House of Lords, it is thus very rare that speeches of any great moment are made there on matters which affect the country's interests, and so the debates in the upper house are very mild-mannered and often devoted to frivolous topics. For this reason, there are those who argue for the abolition of the House of Lords, but such is the temper of the British that once a law has been made, they do not like to change it too readily.

The lower house is composed of representatives chosen in public elections in the counties from among those people who are self-sufficient: that is to say, men who own enough property to be able to maintain a household and are thus in a position to discharge satisfactorily the duties of a citizen. These are called 'electors'. Those who own insufficient property, those who pay only small amounts in tax, those who are not able to contribute to the poor relief fund or who receive poor relief, and those who have committed crimes are all denied the franchise. The particular prerogative which the lower house has in the legislative process is that it proposes tax bills. Tax bills are the laws which project expenditure and determine the income of the government. On them depend, for an entire year, both the objectives of the government and the weal or woe of the people. They may be said to be the whole foundation of legislative power.

The members of the lower house take their seats on left or right according to their party. The ministers' seats are on the right of the speaker, so the government party takes its seats on that side. On the left sits the opposition party. This division into parties is of long standing. At present it is the Conservative and Liberal parties (whose forerunners were the Tories and the Whigs) which carry most weight in national politics. The Conservatives are advocates of the preservation of existing institutions and the Liberals are advocates of reform. Reformers are divided into gradualists and radicals, but the radicals are not very numerous.

The Conservative Party does not necessarily favour unyielding adherence to old customs and practices. Its guiding principle is to preserve and perfect the achievements of the past. Most people who are well informed about history and experienced in public affairs are adherents of this view, and Britain's progress towards civilisation and enlightenment has been achieved by making advances under Liberal governments and consolidating them under Conservative governments, so that there has been all along a natural tendency towards improvement. This is the greatest benefit which political parties bring to the system of government.

The device which the monarchical system of Britain employs to maintain a balance between the legislative and executive powers (and the main respect in which it differs from the republican government of America) is that the chief minister, who is appointed by royal command to assist the monarch because he has the support of a political party, always has a seat in Parliament, where he engages in debate in order to win over the majority to his opinion. This principal minister is called the 'prime minister'. He always serves both as chief among the ministers of the crown and as president of an inner council of those ministers, at the same time undertaking the duties of First Lord of the Treasury. He attends meetings of the inner council of ministers and sometimes has meetings with other ministers as well. He is so busy that he frequently leaves his residence early in the morning and does not return till the small hours of the next day. It is therefore said that the prime minister of Britain, however exemplary his character and however outstanding his learning and wisdom, will not be able to carry out his responsibilities to the full unless he is also a man of great mental energy.

The selection of the prime minister is a royal prerogative. The whole complexion of the government of Britain is determined by the choice the monarch makes. By what method does the monarch choose her prime minister from among all the gentlemen of the country? The answer is that she selects the person whom the people of the country most favour. The sovereign does not exercise a personal choice, nor is the prime minister chosen by public election. He is, in brief, chosen from that party which has most supporters.

Among the assembled members of parliament, who number more than 650, are to be seen white-haired elders, polished gentlemen and young men of great promise. There are those whose speeches are full of flights of eloquence and those who expound their views in a precise and methodical manner. Some gaze at the ceiling, others stare at the floor; some sit in silence, others hum to themselves; some write, some read; there are even some who draw pictures. There are men of every kind, and they present a spectacle of splendid variety.

During the time our party was in Britain, the government's popularity fell very low and the prime minister, Mr. Gladstone, offered his resignation. Opinion in London was that Mr. Disraeli, of the Conservative Party, would become prime minister, but the queen did not accept Mr. Gladstone's resignation. The Liberal Party subsequently recovered its popularity.

The present queen is immensely popular among the British people, revered as a great monarch of a kind rarely seen since ancient times.

September 7th.
From Victoria Station we travelled by train twenty-one miles up the valley of the river Thames to Windsor Castle in Berkshire. This is the sovereign's usual residence. It is an ancient castle, begun in the time of William the Conqueror, the Norman ancestor of the present house, and has been the residence of successive generations of monarchs. The castle stands before a backdrop of low hills on the upper reaches of the Thames, which at this point is about three hundred feet wide. It is surrounded by a vast area of lush, delightful parkland. There are flower-gardens, green-houses and vegetable plots. There is even a plot which the prince of Wales is said to cultivate himself.

September 10th.
At nine o'clock in the morning we were escorted by General Alexander to a jetty at Westminster Bridge, where we boarded a small paddle-steamer (Sir Harry Parkes joined us on board) to travel eight miles downstream to Woolwich. This was a town where Britain's armaments were manufactured.

We went first to the museum. Inside, we saw guns and other objects captured in Russia and China. We toured other departments also. The huge scale on which manufacturing was undertaken in all these depart-ments would lead one to believe that Britain was beset by enemies on all sides. No arsenal in the whole of Europe exceeded this one in size. When the Embassy expressed admiration for its size and the volume of its production, General Wood, the commandant, responded by saying: 'The sole purpose of all these things is in the last analysis the spilling of human blood. How can they be for the good of a civilised world? I am utterly ashamed of them.'

We were given lunch in General Wood's dining-room while the band of the artillery played outside. We were most cordially entertained and returned to our hotel in the early evening.

September 12th. Fine.
There was to be a grand military review at Beacon Hill on this day. At the invitation of Sir Harry Parkes and General Alexander, we left our hotel at half past six in the morning and took a train from Waterloo Station, arriving at Grately Station at half past nine. Two cavalrymen were awaiting the arrival of our party and rode ahead of our carriages to Beacon Hill. This was almost eighty miles from London, but on this day great crowds of ladies and gentlemen had come out from London to see the march past. They filled the high ground overlooking the place where the review was to be held. This was a level area surrounded by rising slopes, eminently suitable to serve as a parade-ground. A place had been reserved for our party to watch from. It was in an area to which only families of the British aristocracy were admitted. A flag-pole had been erected beside this spot and a large flag was flying from it. At noon a twenty-one-gun salute was fired and the review began. Before this, the prince of Wales, together with the commander-in-chief (Prince George, duke of Cambridge, the queen's cousin), and generals as well as officers who had come from various countries to observe had drawn their horses up beneath the flag.

The soldiers then all formed up and marched past the prince of Wales. The precision with which the approximately 35,000 men – infantry, cavalry and artillery – kept ranks was beyond description. Finally, the 10,000 cavalry were divided into two and drawn up in battle array. Then, from a distance of about 650 yards, they galloped headlong towards each other, as though charging the enemy. When they reached a spot a few dozen yards in front of the prince, the commander-in-chief and the generals, a word of command was given and they pulled up their horses instantly, all in a perfect line. It was the grandest sight. The review over, we returned to our hotel by the way we had come.

Britain's geographical situation is such that the navy has always defended the nation against attack. The sole objective of maintaining an army, therefore, has been to supplement the navy. We were told that because domestic government is honest and just, the people are imbued with a spirit of obedience to the law, have acquired the habit of industriousness and achieve independence by co-operation with one another. The great majority, therefore, are happy and contented, so the standing army and auxiliary forces which Britain maintains are smaller in proportion to the country's population than those of any country in continental Europe. This is something which all the people take pride in.

CHAPTER 25

# A Record of London, 3

September 17th, 1872. Fine.
In the afternoon, accompanied by General Alexander, we visited one of
the city's primary schools in a district close to our hotel. The school had
been built to provide education for both boys and girls. It had over 150
pupils in all, mostly from seven or eight to thirteen or fourteen years
of age. The school taught English, reading, writing, religion, drawing,
British history, geography and music. Science would undoubtedly have
been taught as well, although we saw no science apparatus.

The girls were taught spinning, weaving and needlework. They used
their knowledge of arithmetic to make patterns and what they had learnt
of optics to arrange the yarns on their looms. Through weaving this and
braiding that, they learnt the principles of stretching and shrinkage. Such
tasks as arranging yarns on their warp beams in the right order to make
letters and patterns in the fabric called on their knowledge of both
mathematics and optics. In the West, the teaching of handicrafts always
includes simple basic instruction which begins, like this, with the
minutest theoretical principles. The more the pupils study, the deeper the
knowledge they acquire of such principles.

September 18th. Cloudy.
In the afternoon, accompanied by Sir Harry Parkes and General Alexander,
we visited the following places.

First, the Tower of London, the ancient castle of London. It was built
by the founder of the Norman house, King William the Conqueror, and
succeeding monarchs lived there. It therefore has a remarkable number of
ancient relics and historic associations. This castle stands on the bank of
the river between the Custom House and the London Docks. A moat
more than ten feet deep was dug and the castle built within it. Along the
river-bank runs a royal highway. The Tower is surrounded by luxuriant
trees. We went in through the main entrance and proceeded between

immense stone walls in which were set iron gates. Everything had a patina of age. We passed now and then through extremely dark places, very daunting to the spirit.

There were the remains here of an old prison and also the site of a scaffold where in earlier times a king of England had beheaded his wife. Within the Tower itself was the place where two princes had been killed and their corpses hidden. There were many relics of other acts of wanton cruelty committed in days gone by. Even now, simply looking at the traces of such things makes one's hair stand on end.

The upper part of the Tower was the jewel-house, where the monarch's jewelled crowns and ceremonial regalia were kept in an apartment comprising several rooms. Next to that was the armoury, with a huge array of old armour and weapons, each item labelled with its date. There was a breech-loading gun made three hundred years ago, which was a great rarity. There was a set of Japanese armour said to have been sent from Japan as a gift to King Charles II [James I]. There was also a collection of Japanese swords, but they were inferior pieces of the kind found in any antique shop and not worth looking at.

Next, the Telegraph Office, which was in the City. For forwarding incoming telegrams quickly to their destinations, there was a system of underground pneumatic pipelines. The telegram was put into a cylindrical container, which was then wrapped in flannel and packed tightly inside an iron tube, as a cartridge is put into a breech-loading rifle. This iron tube led to one of the underground pipelines. A steam-powered mechanism was then operated, air was compressed by a device mounted at the mouth of the tube and the capsule was sent flying along one of the underground pipelines to emerge almost instantly at an outlet above ground. These pipelines ran below ground to various strategic points (by which I mean such places as post offices, newspaper offices and the principal railway stations). The system was originally invented by a Prussian but had been adopted in Britain. There were now eighty-nine pipelines installed in London. While we were there several telegraphs were sent out from this office and several came in from other places. They arrived like bullets, hurtling out of the tubes with a bang.

Since the invention of the technology for sending messages by electro-telegraphy, the use of telegraph wires in the West can be regarded as as simple as ringing a bell in Japan. Connection by means of a single wire makes it possible to convey information from one side of a room to the other, or from one city to another, or even from one country to another. Telegraph wires therefore hang like spider's webs above the streets. All the interstices of the cosmos are filled with electricity: because it has no substance, there is nowhere it does not penetrate. It is so abundant that once man learnt how to use it, it was like harnessing the wind. It is kept in glass containers. Even a thunderstorm can be tamed. It is sent running along copper wires, covering a great distance in an instant. It is generated by friction; it is generated by chemical action. There is positive electricity; there is negative electricity. Ever since the fabric of his secret was unravelled, the God of Thunder has worked night and day for mankind, going about the streets and among the houses, dashing across the mountains and the seas. The tools which Heaven provides man for his use are truly wonderful!

Next, the General Post Office. Because there are so many post offices in Britain, and its overseas possessions are also large, two general post offices have been established, one to deal with domestic mail, the other with overseas mail. In Europe and America – in all countries, indeed, where trade prospers and literacy is widespread – the postal service is regarded as an undertaking of the first importance. It sets up and oversees post offices in every large town. It also prints postage-stamps and sells them throughout the country. The postage-stamps produced in Britain are roughly an inch long and three-quarters of an inch wide. Those of other countries may be slightly smaller or larger, but are of a similar size. Their colours and designs differ according to their value. They have gum on the back to make it easy to attach them to letters, and there are shops which sell stamps. The principle underlying this system is that by paying the value of the stamp before affixing it to a letter, the sender has paid the charge for delivery in advance. In the streets of towns and villages alike there are iron pillar-boxes for putting mail in. After letters are put into one of these boxes, a postman comes at a specified time, collects the letters and continues on his rounds. Even if a letter does not have a stamp it is still delivered to its destination, but a stamp twice the value of that required is affixed at the sorting office and that fee must then be paid by the recipient. This is a universal rule in all countries.

Europe's trade increases month by month and year by year, and the wakes of its ships criss-cross the world's oceans. Europeans rely on the postal services to enable them to follow their trades and professions and to communicate with friends and family. Furthermore, literacy is ever-increasing and people have many topics to discuss. If someone merely steps out of his own front door, walks a few hundred yards and returns, he is bound to hear one or two pieces of news or see one or two uncommon sights which are worth the telling. And how trivial are the things which people compose accounts of and set down in writing! When members of a family are apart for two or three days, they are certain to exchange letters several times. They even take the trouble to pass on the news that the family cat has had kittens!

In a country such as Britain, in particular, because its trade is on a larger scale than that of any other, the volume of mail is truly remarkable. In front of the General Post Office we saw an unending stream of postmen, one every five or six seconds, arriving from all directions with sacks of mail which they had collected from pillar-boxes and which they flung into receiving-boxes. The mail was first divided into categories, examined and weighed; then the addresses were read and the items were sorted according to destination, ready to be delivered to the addressees. Some would go as far as Hong Kong and Yokohama; others would travel only a few hundred yards. Envelopes large and small arrived all jumbled together. There was a separate window for sending money. Nothing compared with the bustle inside the Post Office.

September 19th. Fine.

At three o'clock in the afternoon, at the invitation of Sir Harry Parkes and General Alexander, we travelled by train to Sydenham to see the Crystal Palace, which was built entirely of glass. It was originally erected in Hyde Park in London in 1851 to serve as the pavilion for the display of exhibits at the Great Exhibition held that year. When the exhibition was over, it was moved to its present site so that its beauty should be preserved. Inside it, curiosities were on show and objects of interest displayed. Outside were green trees and fragrant grass, paths of white sand and pools of clear water. It would be difficult to encompass it all even if one spent a whole day here.

The palace had a wooden floor. Because the walls and roof did not obstruct the light it was as bright inside as out. The nave was over a thousand feet long: one strained one's eyes and still could not make out the end. On either side of the nave were courts and galleries. There were refreshment rooms, some selling tea, others alcohol. There were shops selling coloured pictures and all kinds of goods. There was a concert room and also a stage with seats for spectators ranged in front of it, providing room for a thousand people and more. In the gallery above, extending over several of the courts below, was a collection of oil-paintings for sale. They were of all sizes: some were finely executed, others merely daubs. In another part of the palace were courts displaying all the art of the ancient world: in one stood a model of a Spanish palace [the

Alhambra]; in another were models of ancient Greek temples; and in a third models of painted Egyptian temples and tombs. The more one wandered about the building looking at what was on show, the more wonderful it was.

Near the Crystal Palace was a firm which made gunpowder. As an entertainment for their leisure time, well-off people from London would commission this firm to make fireworks and have them set off in the gardens in front of the palace after dusk. There would sometimes be such a display every week, or even twice in a week. A display was given on the day we were there. Stars of the seven colours besprinkled the sky; light of the five colours stained the water. Golden serpents writhed in battle beside the lake. Wheels of fire revolved on stone plinths. The light of magnesium flares was as brilliant as the brightest moon. A set-piece revealed the figure of a giant. When filings of metals other than magnesium were ignited, giving light of many different colours, the pure sand and clear water of the gardens took on those hues. We had been entertained to dinner in the guest-house of the palace before watching the firework display, and it was already eleven o'clock when we left.

September 20th. Cloudy.
At one o'clock we visited Sir Harry Parkes's house [at Chislehurst], where we had lunch. Afterwards, Sir Harry accompanied us to the country house of the Lord Chamberlain [Baron Sydney of Chislehurst], where we were given tea.

September 27th. Rain.
At eleven in the morning we went to the British Museum. This is Britain's national museum, a vast building renowned throughout Europe for its size. Its hundreds of rooms are all filled with exhibits. All who aspire to learning or who wish to improve their professional skills, whether men or women and whatever branch of learning they are interested in, will derive some profit from a visit here. Its collections are so large that it was of course impossible to see them all in a few hours.

The library contained 750,000 volumes, shelved in a circular book-stack called the 'vault'. This surrounded an area of desks at which books, issued to users of the library in return for call-slips, could be read. This reading-room is a magnificent structure. The extraordinary engineering skill which it exhibits and its sheer size are astounding. Around its periphery are curved galleries where ancient, rare and foreign books are kept. Here are the writings left by the greatest sages and wisest men of all the ages: Sanskrit works from India, Buddhist scriptures written on pattra leaves, and ancient books from Greece, Rome, Egypt and Persia. Some have bloodstains on them; some have been retrieved from fires. Even remnants and damaged books have been collected and are preserved in glass cases. Japanese and Chinese books were in a separate room, and Chinese books were particularly numerous. The Japanese books were for the most part popular works of topography containing pictures of famous places, illustrated encyclopaedias, and dictionaries of everyday usage. There were no official records or government decrees.

When one looks at the objects displayed in its museums, the sequence of stages of a country's civilisation is immediately apparent to the eye and can be apprehended directly by the mind. No country has ever sprung into existence fully formed. The pattern in the nation's fabric is always woven in a certain order. The knowledge acquired by those who precede is passed on to those who succeed; the understanding achieved by earlier generations is handed down to later generations; and so we move forward by degrees. This is what is called 'progress'. Progress does not mean discarding what is old and contriving something which is entirely new. In the forming of a nation, therefore, customs and practices arise whose value is tested by constant use, so that when new knowledge appears it naturally does so from existing sources, and it is from these sources that it derives its value. Nothing is better than a museum for showing the stages by which these processes happen. 'Seeing but once is better than hearing a hundred times', said the ancients, and truly the sense of sight is more important than the sense of hearing in enabling people to absorb information.

Among the peoples of Europe, once a house has been built it is inherited by succeeding generations, who not only keep it in good repair but also improve it, so that it becomes increasingly beautiful. The people of China put a great deal of thought into building a house, but when it is finished they do not trouble to keep it in good repair, so it becomes dilapidated. Even so, they do not demolish it. We Japanese differ from both. We build a house quickly, giving little thought to the workmanship, and no sooner is the house finished than we knock it down and build again. Thus, we see little progress or improvement. How have we come to be like this? Perhaps it is because we are still insufficiently educated. We do not record the useful things which people have said and done and pass them on. We do not stimulate the sense of sight through museums. We do not introduce new things through exhibitions. To excuse ourselves by saying that we are of a different habit of mind is not an honest argument.

# CHAPTER 26

# A Record of Liverpool, 1

September 29th, 1872. Cloudy; in the evening a fog descended and there was thunder.

It had been arranged that, at the invitation of the British government, a party of nine members of the Embassy, escorted by Sir Harry Parkes and General Alexander, and accompanied by Mr. Aston as interpreter, would tour parts of England and Scotland. At four o'clock in the afternoon we left our hotel to go by carriage to Euston Station, where we boarded the special train the government had arranged for us and departed for Liverpool in the north-west. This was the same line by which we had travelled from Liverpool to London when we first arrived in Britain, but as it had been night on that occasion this was the first time we were able to observe the scenery along the way.

It was 201 miles from London to Liverpool by rail. The terrain was for the most part level, with no more than the occasional low hill. Everywhere the countryside was divided up like a chessboard, the boundaries being marked by trees planted at intervals along them. The gaps between the trees were filled by hedges, with ditches running alongside. The land within these boundaries formed fields, most of which were pasture where sheep and cattle grazed at liberty. There were also many fields of stubble, and only occasionally did we see fields of vegetables. There was not a single paddy-field. As to rivers, there were very few clear, fast-flowing ones. The turbid, sluggish streams which we came across from time to time were canals.

Britain lies above latitude 50° N, and in autumn and winter the hours of daylight are very short. This day was only a week after the autumn equinox, but the sun set at twenty past five and the stars were visible by six o'clock. At half past ten that night we arrived at the London and North Western Railway Company's station in Liverpool and took rooms at the North Western Hotel, adjacent to the station.

The city of Liverpool has prospered along with the ever-increasing prosperity of America, and an unbroken line of docks has been built along the northern foreshore. The arriving and departing ships all berth in these docks. Their masts resemble a forest of saplings; their shrouds are like nets hung out to dry in a fishing village. These, we were told, were the largest docks in the world.

When on one occasion we had a distant view of the city from the south bank of the Mersey, the smoke of coal fires billowed up in dense clouds to a height of two or three hundred feet, permanently darkening the blue sky. Our escorts pointed to this and said, 'The people of the city have to breathe in the midst of that black haze.' So great is the city's prosperity.

September 30th. Heavy cloud; light rain.

At half past one in the afternoon we left by carriage for the townhall. Having welcomed us, the mayor conducted us into a reception room where all the city officials were seated. Speeches were made and replied to in turn. In the council chamber itself, the mayor would take his seat in the front, the members of the council sitting in rows facing him, and when a council meeting was in progress members would stand in turn to present their views just as though they were making a speech of welcome or offering an after-dinner toast. This is the etiquette according to which debates are conducted in the West. After these formal addresses were concluded, we spent a little time looking round the rooms of the townhall before leaving.

We then proceeded to the exchange. This is the building in which merchants gather to determine the market-prices of goods and to make agreements to buy and sell. A commercial intermediary, who was chosen by election in the city and then commissioned by the government, acted as master of the exchange. He guaranteed, by means of a written record of undertakings given, the market values of promissory notes for goods (the principal import and export commodities), these having been settled by a process of bidding among the members of the exchange. Any merchants who wished to buy or sell in this locality would therefore assemble here to carry out their transactions in accordance with the prices which currently prevailed. Information and reports were gathered from every possible place. Telegraph wires converged here like the strands of a spider's web, and through them any increases or decreases in trade, large or small, were carefully observed, so that each day's rises and falls in market-prices could be ascertained. The prices of company shares, promissory notes and public bonds were also determined here.

Today, the ambassadorial party was invited to visit the trading floor, where the merchants of the city had congregated. The crowd all raised their hats and cheered us. The din was tremendous. We looked round the building's various rooms before leaving.

At seven in the evening the mayor gave a banquet at the townhall. The number of city officials and merchants who sat down to dinner in order of precedence was 160 in all. A band played and there was singing. After dinner, toasts were drunk to the queen, to Emperor Meiji, and to the Embassy. Speeches were made. The hospitality was of the warmest and the banquet itself sumptuous.


October 1st. Cloudy.

At eleven o'clock in the morning we set out by carriage to tour the docks. On the streets, on the ships, even inside the docks, the men and women of the city had gathered in great numbers to see us. At the behest of the townhall, police were on duty to line the route and maintain order. The policemen saluted as our party's carriages passed. The crowds of specta- tors also paid us the courtesy of raising their hats. Even people going about their business did so as they walked along. Their manners were impeccable. This was the first time we had seen the etiquette observed by the people of a monarchy.

The docks of Liverpool, which extend for six miles, cover an immense area. They are bounded on the city side by a straight brick wall about seven feet high, pierced at intervals by gates. We passed through one of these gates and found another road inside the boundary-wall. Rails were laid down the middle of it, along which an omnibus service ran. On the other side of this roadway were rows of sheds, in which cargo awaiting loading was held, and warehouses where goods were stored. Beyond those lay extensive quays and wharves onto which arriving ships discharged their cargoes. The docks were so extensive that it was impossible for us to see them all in one day.

We visited a dry dock, one of a group of three connecting docks. Three sides and the bottom of this dock were lined with massive blocks of limestone, the side walls curving inwards towards the bottom. It was seventeen feet deep. At the top, the dock would have been about forty yards by two hundred yards; at the bottom it was a little smaller. On the fourth side was a pair of gates. On the sides of the dock were installed mechanisms, one of which served to fill the dock with water and to drain it. When empty, the dock was a vast stone-lined basin; when filled, it was a deep pool of great size. Because the machinery used for filling and emptying the dock was installed beneath the dockside quays, we were unable to learn what form it took, but it probably consisted of a piston inside a cylinder. For the benefit of the ambassadorial party the intro-duction of water into the dock was demonstrated. In less than half an hour the basin was filled to a depth of two or three feet.

We drove past the long line of sheds on the cargo wharves to a mail-ship belonging to the Cunard Line which was employed on the Atlantic run. It was called the *Cuba*. It was over 350 feet in length and contained more than three hundred passenger cabins. A telegraph had been installed in the steering compartment and orders were transmitted to the steers-man, from the aft end of the ship rather than the bow, by means of a system of bell signals. This ship plied between Liverpool and Canada. Today, the company gave a luncheon for us on board. There were thirty or forty guests. After the meal, speeches were made.

# CHAPTER 27

# A Record of Liverpool, 2

October 2nd, 1872. Beautiful weather in the morning; showers in the early afternoon.

At half past ten in the morning we went by carriage to visit a museum. We then proceeded to the floating landing-stage, where we boarded a boat. As on the previous day, our route was lined by police, and a band played on the quayside while we boarded. We cast off and headed west down the river. After going two miles downstream we reached the forts situated at the harbour mouth. The fort on the dock on the right bank fired a seventeen-gun salute. The boat then turned round and made its way back upstream.

We then proceeded to Birkenhead, on the south bank of the Mersey, where we disembarked. There was a large shipyard here with a number of dry docks. At the point on the bank where we landed were three dry docks. In two of them new ships were being assembled, and in the third a ship was undergoing modification. The new vessels under construction were both iron steam-packets, intended for service in the Pacific. The vessel undergoing modification was also a mail-boat. Since it was not long enough for its new purpose, it had been cut in half at this yard and a new section had been inserted amidships to lengthen it by over twenty feet, thus increasing it to a suitable size.

We visited a room where models were kept. In shipbuilding, the shape of the hull is of the utmost importance, so pictures of vessels built in all the countries of the world are copied as soon as any information about them is obtained, and in some cases models are also made. There are people who design improved ships by refining these forms; there are people who change them by embellishing them further. New inventions are copied when building a new type. So when a ship of a new type has been built in another country, people are sent from all the shipyards to look at its design and to draw pictures of it to be shown as samples to people who order ships.

Building a ship is like building a great mansion; it is not something which can be done properly by a single carpenter. In organising a ship-yard, the various tasks are divided up and a certain part of the yard is allotted to each. The men employed to construct the ships' frameworks spend their whole working lives shaping iron components; the men employed to make propellers devote their whole working lives to forming propellers; there are men who spend their whole time cutting wood; there are men who do nothing but assemble iron components. To construct a single vessel, in other words, a work-force is gathered which consists of many men, each skilled in a single trade. Each spends his whole life working at the yard without acquiring any knowledge of the overall structure of the ships. This overall structure is determined in the drawing office. The men who work there are all extremely knowledgeable about ship design and master the principles of ship construction by studying models. But if they were to be asked about the industrial techniques actually employed in building the ships, they would not be able to answer.

The importance of designers to a manufacturing works is like the importance of the brain to the human body. They are the repository of all the basic principles of the industry. Because the building of a ship is such a huge undertaking, everyone must be confident that it is based on correct scientific principles. Indeed, this is true of all kinds of manufacturing. Building locomotives, making clocks or porcelain, manufacturing kit-chenware or textiles: all are the same in this respect. The more minutely the manufacturing process is divided into various stages and aspects, the higher the standard to which each phase of the process is carried out.

Most Japanese manufacturing is of poor quality because our manu-facturers know little about the fundamental principles embodied in the disciplines of physics, chemistry, mechanics and mensuration and are in the end reluctant to make plans and models because they are unwilling to stake the cost. It is invariably this sort of person who, when some project occurs to him, mulls it over speculatively until he has formed a rough idea of how to set about it, then immediately embarks on manufacturing in a rash attempt to see whether the product will be successful or not and inflicts ruin on his family when it fails. This is probably the reason why our industry is backward. It is probably also the reason why our science is undeveloped.

We then proceeded upstream to inspect some training-ships. There were four in all. The first [the *Conway*] took boys from good families and taught them the arts of seamanship. There were 129 cadets, all youths of fifteen years or more. These cadets paid fees of £10 a month for the training they received. The interior of the ship was fitted out with tables and benches where the boys were taught reading, writing and arithmetic. A large open space below decks, provided with hammocks, served as their sleeping quarters. Each boy had a chest in which to keep the kit he needed. As our party went aboard today, we were greeted with a tune played on a bosun's pipe, and when we left the ship the cadets manned the yards and gave us three cheers. At the foot of each mast large nets were rigged to catch any boy who might lose his footing and fall. Everything was in first-class order.

The second [the *Indefatigable*] was a ship which took in the sons and orphans of mariners to teach them the seafarer's trade. There were 170 trainees in all. Again we were piped aboard. As we left after looking over the ship, one of the instructors gave a command, at which the boys swarmed up the rigging and, when in place, doffed their hats and gave three cheers. In this ship the boys, who paid no fees, were taught seamanship by being made to perform tasks involved in the handling and maintenance of the vessel. Our reception on board this ship was very rough-and-ready.

The third [the *Akbar*] was a ship into which boys of bad character from poor families, such as those in the habit of stealing, were taken at the request of their relatives, with the aim of teaching them the seaman's trade so that they might earn their own living and thus become reformed characters. There were 160 or 170 trainees. We were piped aboard as before. On board this vessel a picture of the crucifixion and other religious artefacts were displayed. This ship was in the charge of teachers of the Roman Catholic Church. As we left, the boys manned the yards and cheered us as before.

The fourth ship [the *Clarence*] also took in delinquent boys for instruction. We were again piped aboard and cheered on our way. There were no pictures of Jesus on board this ship. It was in the charge of instructors of the Protestant faith. The number of boys was about the same. Some boys had stripes of yellow cloth sewn on their sleeves. Those who observed the rules and were of good conduct were periodically awarded one of these stripes. A test was held once every three months or so. After passing five or six such tests, a boy would be permitted to ply his trade on another ship. Those, on the other hand, who were untrustworthy and put no effort into their work were unable to leave the ship even after three years. While on board they were obliged to work for no wage. On the third and fourth ships, order and discipline were poor and the manning of the rigging was done in a very dilatory manner.

At eight o'clock in the evening a dinner was given for us by the merchants of the town. There were more than a hundred people present. When the dinner was over we went to a circus, where we saw a strong woman perform.

October 3rd. Rain in the morning; fine in the afternoon.
At ten to eleven in the morning we went to St. George's Hall, opposite our hotel. A path was kept open for us from the hotel to the hall by the police. Besides our party, more than a hundred men and women of the city entered the hall. The outer doors were then closed and we listened to a recital of music.

At ten to twelve we caught a train to travel forty-three miles to Crewe, a large town in south-east Cheshire which lies at the junction of six railway lines. There is a large works there, renowned throughout Europe, which manufactures rails and locomotives. This company owned 1,500 miles of railway track throughout Britain. Five thousand hands were employed daily in manufacturing. The works completed four locomotives each week, and it was the largest engine-works in Britain. Half the houses in the town were occupied by this company's workers who formed, in effect, a town of their own.

At ten to five we boarded a train back to Liverpool, arriving at our hotel at ten to six. The chairman of the company travelled in our carriage to be present at dinner in the evening. He was already over eighty years of age.

At seven o'clock in the evening we gave a dinner for the officials and leading merchants of the city at our hotel. The meal ended at nine.

# CHAPTER 28

# A Record of Manchester, 1

October 4th, 1872. Rain.

At nine o'clock in the morning we left Liverpool to travel east to Manchester. The railway line which joins these two cities, some thirty and a half miles in length, is the progenitor of all the world's railways. In 1825 Mr. Stephenson had proposed for the first time that iron rails should be laid on roads and carriages drawn along them using steam-power. After arguing this case in all quarters he eventually formed a company and obtained the permission of Parliament to proceed. Construction of the line was completed, and trains began to run on it in 1830.

The town of St. Helens is also in Lancashire, about twelve miles east of Liverpool. In 1869 a group of wealthy men from London and Manchester had formed a company and set up a factory there, at a cost of £100,000, to manufacture plate-glass. Today we broke our journey at St. Helens in order to inspect the factory. We were met by the chairman and other members of the firm, who showed us first the workshop where the ingredients of the glass were mixed. Here, steam-powered machinery was used to crush flint into coarse fragments. This material was then further pulverised, using a machine which consisted of three hard grindstones revolving in a huge iron pan. Below this machine, one bag of lime, two bags of pulverised flint and one bag of soda were mixed together. To this mixture were added small amounts of arsenic and charcoal. We were not told the exact amounts because the precise recipe was secret.

The second workshop we went to was huge. Brick furnaces up to about 30 feet wide had been built along each side. In the centre of this room stood a row of charcoal-burning furnaces, in which the materials mixed in the first workshop were melted. A particular technique is used in the building of these furnaces, but because they were so large we were unable to inspect all aspects of their construction. The furnaces used for making glass are re-built twice a year.

The iron table on which the glass was rolled would have been something over 10 feet in width and about 20 feet in length. The upper surface was perfectly flat. Two men, one on either side of the table, and each holding a long iron tool, then loosened the plate of glass by passing this tool between the underside of the glass and the surface of the table. When this had been done once or twice, the door of the annealing oven in front of the rolling table was opened and the plate of glass was thrust inside by men using long iron rods with hooks at the end. Long iron poles were then used to push the plate right to the back of the oven. The next plate of glass was then rolled. Two plates of glass were put into the annealing oven together, where, over a period of seventeen days, they gradually lost heat and solidified.

The third workshop, the polishing department, was divided into three sections. In the first section, the rough plate was ground with sand in order to render the surface flat. In the second section the same machine was used to smooth the glass with 'emery' (a form of alumina). This mineral was in the form of a dark grey or black powder, resembling pulverised coal. The purpose of this second stage of polishing was to render the surface of the glass smooth. In the last section, powdered stone called 'crocus' [colcothar] was used to polish the glass. This powder was a deep red and seemed to be an earth containing iron oxide.

The glass, which at the beginning had been cloudy, tinged with blue and lacking in transparency, had, after being ground, smoothed and polished, become as clear as the waters of a crystal spring. We were told that it was the object of this works to attain perfect transparency in the glass it manufactured.

We then boarded a train to continue our eastward journey, and before five o'clock in the evening arrived at Manchester Station. The mayor himself came to the station to meet us. We went by carriage to the Queen's Hotel, where we took rooms.

Manchester is the third-largest city in Britain. Canals have been built to join Manchester with the river Mersey, which flows through Liverpool, so ships are able to ply back and forth between the two cities. The land around is all flat and the rivers are dirty. In addition, there are frequent fogs and much rain. The sun is rarely seen during autumn and winter. There are many factories in this city. In cotton-spinning and -weaving in particular there is nowhere in Europe which rivals it in scale. The looms are all driven by steam-power, and throughout the city smoke from burning coal cloaks the sky and turns the air a yellowish-black. Eight or nine years before, during the American Civil War, cotton had become impossible to obtain from that country and many people were laid off by the factories in Manchester. The factory hands, both men and women, lost their livelihood and were brought to the brink of starvation. As merchants turned to India and the West Indies to obtain cotton, the world price of cotton went up and the distress which confronted this city was comparable to that suffered during the great famines in Japan when the harvest fails for several years in succession. The city corporation collected £30,000,000 to relieve the distress. In view of the effects which the abolition of slavery would have on cotton-growing, it can be imagined why many, both in America and in Britain, opposed it.

In the evening, we were taken to the theatre.

October 5th. Rain, clearing later; thick fog.
At ten in the morning, accompanied by the mayor, we went by carriage to a cotton-spinning mill. Including the basements, this mill was nine storeys high. A total of eight hundred hands were employed here, most of them women and children.

After this we went to Whitworth's iron and steel works. This works was founded in 1834 and had gradually grown to its present great size. The products manufactured at this foundry ranged from iron and steel and large items such as guns, shells, gun-carriages and limbers, to a wide variety of iron machinery and machine parts.

In the steel-casting workshop it was mainly gun-barrels which were cast. Because gun-barrels must withstand very violent explosive forces, the grain structure of the steel must be extremely fine. In recent years Westerners have tried in various ways to find techniques for manufacturing such steel. The technique used at this factory was that of subjecting the molten steel to immense pressure after it had been poured in order to eliminate sponginess. We were shown the casting of a gun.

We then went outside, where we saw a rifled steel gun with a bore of two inches charged with nine ounces of powder test-fired at an iron plate. The projectile passed through the iron plate at an angle and flew on. When we measured it, we found that the thickness of the plate it had pierced was three inches. We then briefly observed the manufacture of shells before proceeding to a building where guns were displayed.

In the afternoon, we left by carriage again to visit the assize court building. This housed the 'circuit courts', where itinerant judges of the superior courts heard cases. The whole structure was of granite, and although it was a single-storey building the ceilings were very high and the main entrance wide and very imposing. The windows were of stained glass, resembling those of a church: this was, after all, a building in which God was invoked and oaths were sworn. To left and right were the courts, the one on the right being used for civil cases and the one on the left for criminal cases.

We then proceeded to a prison [Strangeways], which stood next to the court building but was separate from it. The prison covered a large area and was surrounded by a brick wall more than twenty feet high. The turreted gateway housed a pair of massive gates; in one gate was a small door through which only one or two people at a time could enter or leave. Spikes three or four inches long were planted along the top of the wall. Immediately inside the gates were the offices of the prison staff. Here was a towering chimney more than two hundred feet high. It was built with a double skin, smoke being expelled by way of the inner flue and air by way of the annular flue. Thus, the vitiated air within the prison was removed and replaced by fresh, pure air.

The arrangement of the prison in the form of six wings radiating like spokes from a central hub was the same as that of the prison at Philadelphia. Indeed, this prison had been modelled on that one, the only differences being that the Philadelphia prison was built of stone and was two storeys high, while this one was built of brick and was four storeys high. One warder was stationed on each floor. There were in all one thousand cells. The hub at the centre served as the warders' station. There was a separate women's prison, its structure similar in all respects to the men's prison.

This was a convict prison, to which men were sent who had been tried and sentenced to a term of imprisonment with hard labour. While in prison they were given work to do. Every prisoner was confined in a separate cell, where he wove matting, stitched shoes, or did metalwork or carpentry. Each was assigned whatever work suited his capabilities, and each had a daily task to complete. Knives and edge tools were freely used in the prison. All the cells were about six by fifteen feet, and were furnished with a bed, a water jug and a gaslight. Everything, including the provision of a Bible in each cell, was just as it had been in Philadelphia.

The convicts' uniforms were of rough woollen cloth striped horizontally or vertically in yellow and black. Each prisoner received a daily payment for his labour, half the money being given to him and half being collected by the prison authorities to meet the cost of maintaining, feeding and clothing him. If the prisoner worked hard enough to exceed his daily quota, his pay increased proportionately, the additional sum being wholly his. Those who worked hard, therefore, were able to set money aside to be received as a lump sum on their discharge. By performing such labour, we were told, the prisoners also learnt the habit of hard work and a gradually increasing number of them, having reflected on how they were to make a living, set up their own businesses on release.

Those idlers who would not work hard enough to perform their daily quota were sent to the tread-wheel. The tread-wheel sheds, at the rear of the prison, housed four huge water-wheels, some dozens of feet wide, constructed from massive timbers. The wheels were sheltered under the shed roofs, and the sheds themselves were divided by partitions at intervals of about two feet. Part of a wheel was exposed at the rear of each of these compartments. Each prisoner was made to go into one of the compartments and step onto the wheel. The compartments had two levels, upper and lower. The wheels were heavy and turned sluggishly. After ten minutes, every man's back was dripping with sweat, which showed how great their exertions were. Each prisoner was kept at this hard labour for fifteen out of every twenty minutes and was allowed to rest for five. A warder standing watch rang a bell every five minutes. At this signal, those whose rest period was due stepped off the wheel and those who had been resting stepped back on. This was where convicts sentenced to penal servitude performed the hard labour which was part of their punishment. The water raised by the tread-wheels supplied the whole prison.

The warders who guarded the female prisoners were all women. The male and female prisoners were confined in separate parts of the prison, but the basement floor of the men's section and that of the women's section communicated, and it was possible to pass back and forth between them. They were separated by a heavy door. Women convicts wore white caps and cotton dresses. Among the women warders was one who must have been over sixty years of age. We were told that she had worked here as a warder for as long as thirty-three years. The number of criminals currently incarcerated there was 470 men and 196 women.

CHAPTER 29

# *A Record of Manchester, 2*

October 6th, 1872. Fine.
Today being Sunday, the people of the city closed their doors and commercial activity ceased almost completely. There are few places, even in Britain, where Sunday is so strictly observed as a day of rest. This is no doubt because there are so many factory workers here.

October 7th. Cloudy; rain.
In the morning we received a deputation from a temperance society and speeches were exchanged. Temperance societies are associations which advocate the prohibition of alcohol and tobacco. Among the various pleasures which people indulge in, the drinking of alcohol and smoking of tobacco are regarded, in Western culture, as unseemly habits. No woman, therefore, smokes in public, and it is also regarded as shameful for a woman to drink alcohol. Generally speaking, alcohol is drunk only at certain times and in accordance with strict customs. Smoking is permitted only in particular rooms: one is not allowed to smoke wherever one wishes.

In the West, the educated man, the gentleman, regards decorum, especially in language and in eating and drinking, as the beginning of propriety in all conduct. And his restraint in smoking and drinking has naturally influenced those below him, as the wind causes the grass to bend, so that ordinary people also now take the view that drunkenness is shameful and that one should exercise moderation in smoking. Smoking is forbidden in most railway-carriages and hotel rooms, but it is very hard to prevent people from indulging in smoking and drinking. According to the statistics of the countries of the West, millions of pounds are spent on them. The amount rises constantly and never falls. But people exercise restraint in public and indulge in these habits only in private. Thus, they support sound manners and morals and do not undermine them. They deal with the sexual appetite in the same way. In the East, men regard drunkenness as a mark of virility, women believe that smoking is seductive, and licentiousness is *à la mode*. But these are things which the civilised countries of the West abominate as unclean. It seems to me that the prevalence of these evil customs in the East tempts people to idleness, interferes with their pursuit of their occupations and is a great obstacle to the attainment of autonomy. These are things which we ought to be most ashamed of and ought above all to restrain.

We went to a cotton-spinning mill. This works employed 900 hands, more than half of them women and children. The cotton came mostly from America, but some was obtained from India. Cotton with a long staple and a high lustre is produced in America. The produce of other countries is invariably inferior. (The cotton grown in Japan is a variety with a short staple and is of poor quality.)

We then went to a cotton-weaving mill. There were six hundred looms in the mill. One woman was in charge of two looms, and each loom wove thirty-seven yards of cloth a day. The finished cloth was sent to another department, where a girl examined its surface and picked out any burls with iron tweezers. The cloth was then folded. The textiles manufactured at this mill were mostly striped cotton. It was of better quality than printed cotton, and the price was accordingly higher.

In the afternoon we went by carriage to an india-rubber factory. India-rubber gum is the substance commonly known in Japan by the abbreviated name '*gomu*'. It is also called 'gum elastic'. It is manufactured from the solidified latex of the india-rubber tree, which grows in Central and South America. This tree grows in the tropical regions and resembles the *yuzuriha* tree [*Daphniphyllum macropoda*] of Japan, but its growth is more luxuriant. The leaves are large and the stems thick, and both are very glossy. It is attractive in appearance, and many Westerners keep small rubber trees as decorative plants inside their homes. The coagulated milk obtained from this tree looks just like dried fat. It comes in pieces up to about eight or nine inches square and a little over an inch thick. The best latex is that which has set perfectly like this. The poorer quality is that which has set like pieces of rag. Since a method of manufacturing rubber was first invented in 1823 by Mr. Macintosh, the range of uses to which it is put has gradually widened, until now it is used for making tyres for traction engines, for making beds and chairs, for making tents, and even for making small boats. In the West it is a truly indispensable product, and it would be difficult to enumerate all the uses to which it is put.

At four o'clock a luncheon was given for us by the mayor at the townhall. Well over a hundred gentlemen sat down to the meal. There were the usual toasts. At eight o'clock we went to the theatre. This was a special performance for the Embassy. Everyone was presented with a programme printed on red and white silk, and the auditorium was decorated throughout with the crossed flags of the two countries.

October 8th. Fine.

At ten o'clock we went by carriage to a wholesale store selling textiles and fancy goods. This was Watts's warehouse, an emporium dealing in cotton textiles. The stock, displayed in different departments throughout the five floors, ranged from plain silks, figured silks, velvets, satins and damasks through cottons, chintzes, calicoes and men's and women's clothing, underwear and hats, to figured cotton fabrics, laces and artificial flowers. In each department several men and women were in attendance to serve customers. It was as though each department constituted a separate shop. The merchandise included both locally manufactured goods and those brought in from other cities. The lightest and most delicate fabrics were those obtained from Paris.

We then went to the police court. This was an entirely new building, and extremely handsome. The windows were of stained glass. All criminals who had been arrested by the police, or against whom a complaint had been lodged by a citizen, were first brought before this court for a committal hearing before being sent for trial in a higher court. In a large room, seating was provided for the participants in these hearings, including places for the witnesses and the jury. Compared with the assize court, which we had visited two days earlier, this court-room was very plain.

On this day, the court was in the process of hearing the case of a criminal who had stolen a watch and, together with his wife, had committed thefts at the railway station and elsewhere. The man had been arrested and brought before the court by a policeman. We sat beside the magistrates on the bench for a while to observe the proceedings. When the hearing started, the prisoner was made to stand up in his allotted place. He was not bound or shackled at any time, simply guarded by a policeman. The policeman bringing the charge went into the witness-box and took an oath, kissing a Bible. He then described the circumstances of the arrest and stated the grounds on which he had made it. Next, several witnesses he had brought went forward to the witness-stand in turn, took the oath in the same way and gave their individual evidence as to what they had seen and heard. As they did so, the magistrates, the clerks and the defending lawyers all took up their pens to write down what was said.

If any point in the evidence given was unclear, the magistrates or the lawyers would ask further questions, the magistrates if it was something which would be important in reaching a verdict, and the defending lawyers if it was something which had a bearing on the gravity of the crime. Otherwise, everyone in the packed court-room remained silent, simply listening to the testimony of the witnesses. We formed the impression that this was a simple and efficient procedure.

Next we visited the Owens College. This institution had been established twenty years before, and over three hundred students were currently enrolled. We went first to the staff room and talked informally to the teachers. We were then shown round the various lecture-rooms and listened for a while to a lecture on chemistry.

Afterwards we went to the Royal Exchange, an extremely imposing building. All such exchanges, in every European and American city, seem to be built according to the same plan. The Manchester exchange was an entirely new and very handsome building. The exchange was open for business on three days each week, when bids could be made for commodities and various kinds of securities. This was the place where all the city's commercial contracts were agreed. Some people, on hearing the prices, would depart with ashen faces, while others would go away wreathed in smiles. The vicinity of the exchange was always bustling; the streets around it were much busier than other streets. Because it was known that the ambassadorial party was to visit on this day, a particularly large crowd had gathered outside; even before we entered the building we had to make our way through a great press of people. Inside we found a vast interior and a huge throng of merchants: the whole room was packed. The mayor, the president of the chamber of commerce and the other gentlemen escorting us pushed through the crush, enabling our party to proceed, with some difficulty, to the dais. When we had mounted this we turned to the assembled throng and bowed. Those at the front raised their hats and cheered, while those at the back pressed forward. The crowd surged back and forth, and the din was tremendous. When the formalities were over, we inspected the galleries at the sides of the floor before leaving.

# CHAPTER 30

# A Record of Glasgow

October 9th, 1872. Rain in the morning; fine from midday.

In the morning we packed and at half past ten left our hotel in Manchester to take the eleven o'clock train north to Scotland. The morning was overcast, with a steady drizzle. The mayor and the president of the chamber of commerce accompanied us to the station by carriage to see us on our way. As the train left the station, the wheels set off dozens of detonators which had been placed on the track to offer us a farewell salute and wish us a good journey.

About an hour and a half after we had left Manchester, the sky suddenly cleared. Throughout our tour of Britain it was usually overcast and rainy while we were in cities, but when we went out into the countryside the weather was always fine. One reason may be that because of the density of the population, so much coal is burned in the cities that it generates clouds and fogs. In the case of Manchester, in particular, everyone we talked to who had visited the city said that it was almost always raining there.

At two in the afternoon, we began to pass the shore of a bay [Morecambe Bay]. From Manchester thus far, the land beside the railway had all been low-lying, with occasional patches of marshy ground. From time to time we saw stretches of a canal [Lancaster Canal] by the line. We were told that it was possible to travel by canal through the whole of Lancashire from Manchester and Liverpool to the county town, Lancaster. We now began to see pine-woods. In cold northern latitudes much effort is devoted to growing this tree on a large scale.

Far off across the bay we caught our first glimpse of ranges of mountains receding into the distance. It was now a fine, bright day, and for the first time there was a completely clear blue sky: it gave us a great sense of invigoration. The railway, having followed the curve of the bay, now turned away from the coast and began to climb into the mountains. To left and right were the undulating profiles of mountain ridges. The sides of the valley were bare rock, from which gushed babbling rivulets which tumbled down into a beck at the valley's foot, forming a clear stream flowing north.

This prospect of mountain ranges and sinuous streams had a particular attraction for us as it so much resembled the scenery of our own country. It was the first time since we had left on our journey to the West almost a year before that we had seen a landscape which embraced both mountains and sea. Looking into the distance we were captivated by the setting sun against the blue sky and the overlapping ranges of mountains, one behind another: it was a most inviting prospect.

Some time after half past eight we arrived at Bishopton Station. Lord Blantyre had sent people to meet us there with carriages to convey us to his house. Our party, eleven all told, arrived at Erskine House, Lord Blantyre's country-seat, at twenty to ten. The master of the house, Lord Blantyre himself, came to greet us at the door and show us to our separate rooms to change. Lord Blantyre had invited Admiral Sir James Hope to meet us, and formal introductions were made in the drawing room. We also shook hands and exchanged courtesies with our host's two daughters, who then took our arms and led us into the dining-room. The meal was magnificent. After dinner we sat talking, and it was not until after midnight that we retired.


October 10th. Cloudy.
At ten o'clock we left in Lord Blantyre's carriages for Bishopton Station. When our train arrived at Bridge Street Station in Glasgow, we were formally received by the Honourable Lord Provost, Sir James Lumsden (one of the city's businessmen) and Mr. W. West Watson. There was a huge crowd at the station. From here we left in carriages to visit some of the city's factories.

Because Glasgow lies so far north, the winters here are especially cold. There are frequent damp fogs and constant rain, and it is rare to see the sun. While we were there the weather was unusually good. There were, it is true, few days when the sun actually shone, but when for some days in succession there was no more than a thin veil of cloud, the people of the city said that the fine weather was a present brought by the Japanese ambassadors! Later, we were told by someone who had visited Glasgow in November that he saw the sun on no more than three out of the thirty days he was there, that rain and snow fell unceasingly, and that even on the days when it did not rain or snow there were such gloomy fogs that from breakfast to supper the lamps indoors were never extinguished.

We toured the city, arriving first at Messrs. Higginbotham's works, an iron foundry manufacturing all kinds of textile machinery. Next we visited the factory [Glasgow Locomotive Works] of Messrs. Dubs and Company, employing 1,500 hands. After that, we went to the Royal Exchange, the chamber of commerce and the Corporation Galleries.

A fundamental feature of the culture of countries of the East is that they promote agriculture and restrain commerce, and regard governance solely as a matter of civil administration. Nevertheless, the governance of populous cities must have different features. The West has attained its great wealth and power because it encourages commerce to flourish and thereby enables agriculture to thrive. Municipal government there is of a quite distinct kind. In the spheres of commerce and industry, there are different laws and separate courts; the central government includes a ministry of trade and industry; and those citizens who are engaged in trade and manufacture are separately registered. Industrial and commercial enterprises hold the possibility of vast profits, but they also carry the risk of huge losses. The inhabitants of cities derive their livelihoods from such risky projects, and their undertakings also have a direct effect on the rural population. This is why municipal government is so important. Every possible means must be employed to safeguard it.

As the landowner and the rich farmer have their tenants and labourers, so the industrialist has his factory hands and the merchant his clerks and shop-assistants. They are naturally divided, forming upper and lower classes. The way for government to safeguard their undertakings obliges the upper class to protect the lower class and safeguard its interests. Therefore, in every city a municipal corporation is established by electing members from among the upper class, whose duty it is to exercise authority, apply the laws and invoke the penalties prescribed. Officials appointed to the commercial exchange ensure that everyone's transactions, both buying and selling, are convenient, certain and expeditious. Below that, groups of people with a common purpose form corporations, either to conduct business ventures or give aid to the lower classes. When there are many such institutions, industry and commerce enjoy the benefits of stability. Contracts are therefore speedily agreed, goods are promptly delivered, and some of the resulting profits are used to buy the agricultural produce of rural areas, so the products of all parts of the country find their proper prices and everyone is encouraged to work hard.

On our tour of the cities of Britain, we saw first at Westminster the glory of a monarchy exemplified in the power and dignity of the sovereign. When we visited the City of London and other cities, we saw a republican form of government in operation, which sprang from the seed of a broad freedom to form corporate bodies. And when we travelled through the rural areas, where the power of the aristocracy and the rich was very great, we saw at work an autocracy of distinguished men. When we had earlier been told that the British had put these three types of government together into a single polity, we were sceptical, but when we actually travelled round the country and observed conditions for ourselves we felt that some kind of marvellous mechanism was indeed at work here. It was simply this: the practical consequence of the freedom of the upper and lower classes to form associations in which they depended on each other was that this practice came to be used in the organisation of commercial affairs and as a result became both the basis of government and its supreme safeguard.

October 11th. Fine.
At half past ten we caught a train from Bishopton Station to Greenock, twenty miles down the Clyde from Glasgow. The river grows very wide as it nears the sea, so big ships are able to come up this far.

We proceeded in carriages, accompanied by our hosts, to an engineering and shipbuilding works belonging to Mr. Caird. This firm was divided into three sections. The first was a yard where iron ship-components and boilers were fabricated and assembled. Three thousand five hundred hands were employed here. Twelve ships were under construction at the time, valued at £100,000 to £110,000 each. It was thirty years since Mr. Caird had set up this company, and up to the time of our visit, we were told, the company had built a total of 234 vessels and engines. Of all the shipyards in and around Glasgow, this was the leading one. The second section was a works making brass fitments for use in the interiors of the ships being built. The third section was a shop making painted wooden fittings to decorate ships' interiors. The hands employed here were mostly women.

Finally, we went on board the *City of Chester*, a steam-packet then under construction at the yard. It was intended for use as a mail-boat plying the Atlantic between Britain and America, and would be the largest packet-boat in the world.

October 12th. Fine.
At ten o'clock, accompanied by Lord Blantyre in person, we went by carriage to look round a nearby farm which he owned. In the fields stood a large barn for the storage of grain and a place where flour was ground by

means of a water-wheel. Twelve men and eight women were normally employed here to do the work of the farm. The staple food in the daily Western diet is bread, and there the grinding of wheat to make flour corresponds to the flailing of rice to remove the husk and produce white rice in Japan. It is an important agricultural process, and mills large and small are frequently seen. A prosperous farmer invariably has such a mill. Care must be taken to ensure that the grinding machinery rotates slowly. If it turns too fast, the resulting flour is coarse. In Japan, too, if the husking of rice is done too fast, the grains are not of even size. The principle is the same.

The farmland of Britain is all owned by the aristocracy or rich families. All others are tenants who rent their farms. In Scotland, besides Lord Blantyre's estate, all the land which we saw along the shores of Loch Tay belonged to Earl Campbell, and the land between Blair Atholl and Birnam was all the property of the duke of Atholl. When we inquired about their annual income from rents we were told that in both cases it would be about 1,000,000 yen. The estates of the duke of Devonshire and of Mr. Tollemache, which we saw later, after our return to England, were of similar size. We saw many other great houses built by rich men, set in wooded parks on the outskirts of villages and surrounded by hundreds of acres of farmland. The ordinary people live in dilapidated thatched cottages in the villages or among the fields. Usually they rent land and manage to scrape a living by hard work. Their houses, for the most part, have also been built by the landowners and are rented to them for a price. In urban areas there are ground landlords who rent out the land on which houses stand and landlords who let houses. There are many people who make their living by renting houses belonging to others and sub-letting rooms to transient lodgers.

In Britain, those who own land and houses are exclusively wealthy families who are thus able to feed and clothe themselves well without the necessity of working. People refer to them enviously as 'men of property'. The people who become members of Parliament are generally chosen from among them. The ordinary people own neither the smallest piece of land nor even their own dwellings but always live on someone else's property and subsist by means of their labour. In agriculture such people are called 'farm labourers', in manufacturing they are called 'factory hands' and in commerce they are called 'clerks' or 'shop-assistants'. These are all occupations of the lower orders. By-laws and industrial and commercial laws lay down rules of contract for employers and employees. The principal duty of government is to enforce these strictly. This is what they call the 'protection of property'.

In the West, people are not particularly looked down on because they rent land or a dwelling from someone else. They include people who are extremely well-off, and who would be entitled to vote. The deference accorded to land-owning families is very much like the esteem in which families of the former samurai class are held in Japan. Even the monarch cannot match the wealth of the very richest of them. So great is the gulf between rich and poor.

We had lunch, then packed our bags and at three o'clock took our leave of Lord Blantyre to go to Bishopton Station, where we took a train departing at four o'clock to travel east to Edinburgh. There we took rooms at the Royal Hotel.

# CHAPTER 31

# A Record of Edinburgh

Edinburgh was formerly the royal capital of the kingdom of Scotland. The city lies in a narrow valley between two ranges of hills. Over it loom the walls of a castle perched on a towering crag. There is just a single road by which the castle can be reached. For the rest, a precipitous cliff overhangs the valley and buttresses of bare rock jut into it. The city's shops and houses fill the remaining space. A forest of church spires points heavenwards. Whitewashed houses and gleaming buildings of pale stone line the hillsides, following the contours of the land. The railway station lies in the valley bottom. On the northern slope of the valley are the [Princes Street] gardens, in which stands a lofty tower [the Sir Walter Scott monument] designed in a Scottish style. Before the memorial to Prince Albert was erected in Hyde Park, in London, to commemorate the Great Exhibition, this was built as a trial. It is a magnificent structure, finer indeed than the memorial in Hyde Park. Immediately opposite it is the Royal Hotel. The land on the south side of the valley consists of high hills, on which the 'Old Town' of Edinburgh stands, its houses crowded together in narrow streets. The very extensive 'New Town' spreads out among the hills on the north side. The hilly nature of the terrain does not prevent the use of horse-drawn vehicles. There is a bridge across the valley, and the railway runs along the valley floor. The hills are very beautiful and picturesque. Of all the cities in Britain, Edinburgh has the coolest climate, so at the height of summer the monarch takes up residence here to escape the heat. The Scots compare it to Athens, sometimes calling it the 'New Athens'.

October 14th, 1872. Fine.
At ten o'clock in the morning we went on foot to the Parliament House, where the High Court sits. Among the paraphernalia kept there for use in trials were one or two curious items. There were wigs of white horse-hair which, we were told, judges once wore when sitting to hear cases. There

was also a black cap which judges wore when passing the death sentence, and the robes worn by judges on ceremonial occasions. These resembled the vestments of Catholic priests.

Next to the Parliament House was a school where we were shown an electric motor in operation. From here we went to the industrial museum and the university. The number of students entering and graduating from the university each year is two thousand. This city is celebrated for scholarship and the arts, and the university is its most renowned seat of learning.

From there we drove through the hills to the foot of Arthur's Seat. We left our carriages there and walked to the top. This hill is a famous beauty spot, as well as having many historical associations dating back to the earliest times. The summit commands a magnificent view, encompassing the whole city and taking in the sea beyond. The hill is 800 feet high and is completely treeless, being covered with fine grass.

We descended the hill and went to the Palace of Holyroodhouse. This is an ancient royal palace, built over five hundred years ago, and includes some portions which are even earlier. In the King's Suite was a large chamber in which hung portraits of the kings of Scotland up to King James VI (who became James I of England). We then inspected the royal bedchambers. They were furnished just as they had been in former times. Among the apartments we saw was the bedchamber of Mary, queen of Scots, who came to the throne in 1542. A secret staircase built inside the wall of the bedchamber led to the floor below. Beside her bed were arranged such articles as her needlework box and toilet accessories, just as in the past.

This queen was a ravishing beauty and the licentiousness of her conduct was extreme. She went first to France as bride to the Dauphin Francis, but when Francis died shortly after acceding to the throne, she was driven out by the French and returned to Scotland. She took as her husband David Rizzio, but soon tired of him and had him murdered by her lover. She admitted this lover secretly by way of the concealed staircase to her bedchamber, where they conducted their illicit liaison. Her debauchery stands out in the historical record. A rebellious faction sprang up within the country and stabbed her lover to death inside the palace. The room where his corpse was left was next to the bedchamber. Bloodstains still remain on the panelling and floorboards. Afterwards Mary was driven out of Scotland, too, and suffered a life of exile and great privation. She again took a lover, the English minister the duke of Bothwell, and suffered a series of misfortunes. Her heir was made King James VI of Scotland and eventually became king of England also.

At three o'clock in the afternoon we went by carriage to a factory where traction-engines were built. This machine, recently invented by a Mr. Thomson, was a steam-locomotive capable of travelling on ordinary roads without rails. Manufacture of this machine had begun three years previously. The intention was to send it to India and Australia to be used on plains where there are no railway tracks. We were told that one had recently been sent to China to be tried out near Peking.

When members of our party rode on one of these traction-engines in the yard of the factory, they found that it could change direction with complete freedom and that there was little jolting. The manufacturers urged that since this was an indispensable vehicle for use on continental plains and gently undulating terrain where there were no railways, it should be used in Japan, too. But Japan's topography is not continental. Not only is it one of the world's most mountainous countries, it is an unusual country in other respects also. There is much marshy land along its coasts, and its agriculture consists predominantly of the cultivation of rice in paddy-fields. There are, therefore, very few places where the traction-engine could be used.

October 15th. Cloudy.

At ten in the morning we went by carriage to an india-rubber factory in the south-west of the city which belonged to the Bartlett Company. Mr. Bartlett, an American, was head of the factory. Under him were five 'directors' (that is to say, the principal officers of the company) and sixty 'managers' (officers of the company).

We then drove ten miles or so south to the Valleyfield paper mill. The landscape on either side of the road consisted of fields embraced by green hills, with now and then a peak of particular beauty. The scenery was just like that which one would see in the region around Tokyo. The paper mill belonged to the firm of Mr. A. Cowan, one of the great names of the county. He had formerly been elected as a member of Parliament and had been well regarded in the House of Commons. After lunch, Mr. Cowan himself conducted us to the paper mill. A very fast-flowing river ran through the village, and the mill, which was very large, used a water-wheel to exploit it as a source of power. A steam-engine had also been installed.

On our way back to Edinburgh, we visited an ancient church founded in 1446 by Lord Rosslyn. Rosslyn Chapel was not particularly large, but the craftsmanship it embodied was magnificent in every respect. The front of the building was all of carved white marble. To the left of the chapel were the remains of the ancient castle of Lord Rosslyn. Its ruined walls still stood in thick woodland. In front of them was a dry moat, now overgrown with grass, with the remains of a drawbridge. On the right, the chapel overlooked a valley, the bottom of which was thickly wooded. We heard now and then the sound of water. Because it was the time of year when the leaves had taken on their autumn tints, the view was particularly pleasing. When we went down into the valley and made our way into the wood, we found a path running alongside a stream. On the other bank were towering rocks, the water cascading through them and flowing away with a roar. By this time dusk was falling. The rays of the setting sun pierced the clouds, and there was no breath of wind. Now and then we heard a leaf fall. We strolled about for a little while, then returned to our carriages and drove back to the north.

October 16th.

At eight o'clock we left by train for Granton, on the eastern outskirts of the city, where the Commissioners of the Northern Lighthouses had arranged for their steamship *Pharos* to be waiting for us. We went aboard straight away and the ship left the harbour at nine o'clock. The weather was gradually improving, and we had breakfast aboard as we began to steam eastwards. Forty miles to the east of Granton we came to the Bell Rock Lighthouse. This was a celebrated structure standing in the open sea, eleven miles from land. It had been built by a Mr. [Robert] Stevenson and was completed in 1811, after five years of work. Because the sea-bed at this point consisted of solid rock, the construction of the foundations presented particular difficulties.

The devotion to duty of the employees of the Northern Lighthouse Board who keep the lighthouses is well known throughout the country. Forty-five keepers are responsible for this light. Their roster requires each of them to be on duty at the lighthouse for six weeks out of every eight. They come ashore in turns for a two-week rest period. As the tide was unfavourable, we were unable to land, so we steamed away from Bell Rock and had lunch on board.

We then proceeded to the lighthouse on the Isle of May. This is a small island in the mouth of the firth. To the east it overlooks the vast expanse of the North Sea, lying at the farthest point from the land which encircles it on the other three sides. The construction of this lighthouse was also very fine. One of the commissioners indicated the light mounted on top of the lighthouse tower. It was, he told us, constructed from prisms of glass and was called a 'dioptric apparatus'. Concentric rings of triangular prisms surrounded the lamp burning at the centre of the apparatus, projecting the light to a distance of about fifty miles. The apparatus incorporated a mechanism for adjusting the focal distance. Such was its power that if the surface of the earth were flat, an observer would be able to discern the light 150 miles away.

We boarded the steamer again and got under way. We had dinner on board. The commissioners provided all three meals. Mr. Fordyce proposed a toast and the ambassador and Sir Harry Parkes replied. It was half past eight when we docked at Granton, and after nine by the time we got back to our hotel.

CHAPTER 32

# A Tour of the Highlands

Three regions of Europe are celebrated for the exceptional beauty of their mountain landscapes: the first is Switzerland, the second Italy, the third Scotland. Westerners enjoy walking and love mountain scenery. They are tireless in visiting distant places, even if the roads are winding and the hills steep. When the Scots find themselves in faraway places, it is said, they recall the mountain landscapes of their homeland and become heart-sick with longing. All peoples think of their homelands with affection, but this trait is particularly marked in the Scots. Perhaps this is because of the strength of the bonds with which the soul of the landscape binds them to it; or perhaps it is accounted for by the honest simplicity of spirit of this nation.

Since leaving London, day after day we had endured spatters of mud thrown up by carriage wheels and dust kicked up by horses' hooves when travelling by road, and thick smoke and acrid smells when travelling by rail. The view of the flat English landscape and of the Scottish lowlands was one of unrelieved monotony. The hills of Edinburgh were pretty enough, but there was more than this to the beauties of the Scottish landscape. Sir Harry Parkes had urged the ambassador to seek the mountains of the Highlands, so a party of seven of us left Edinburgh at eight o'clock on the morning of the seventeenth to travel north-west by train.

October 17th, 1872. Fine.
At half past one we arrived at Blair Atholl Station, where we alighted and went to the Atholl [Arms] Hotel to rest.

The village of Blair Atholl consisted of no more than five or six houses, all humble cottages, but the hotel was very handsome and clean. We were served venison, which is a local delicacy. We then went on foot to visit the grounds of the duke of Atholl's country-house [Blair Castle], opposite the hotel. At the entrance to the estate stood a pair of iron gates, chained shut, with a lodge built of stone beside them. We pulled the bell-wire and an elderly gate-keeper emerged to let us in. From the gates a straight, wide road, which must have been about 400 yards in length, led across a grassy expanse. Trees were planted on either side of it, their luxuriant branches intertwined overhead. The roadway was covered with fallen leaves, which rustled beneath our feet. At the end of the road we came to a hill covered in a thick carpet of soft green grass. In a valley to our right we could hear the sound of water, like the tinkling of jade ornaments.

Overlooking the valley stood the duke's house, built entirely of white stone. Beyond it, a number of pretty hills clothed in green trees rose from a river-bank. The rays of the setting sun fell on them and an evening mist was rising, giving the scene an air of profound tranquillity. The old gate-keeper led us across the soft grass to our right to show us a waterfall in the garden. The branches of the ancient trees were interlaced overhead and the wood was dark. The path rose and fell. We walked on, and when we emerged from the gardens we found ourselves at a double-arched bridge. Here the burns which ran down the valleys came together to form a broad river. Pine-trees had been planted along the banks and a semicircle of hills in the distance enclosed the scene. Scattered here and there were little hamlets. It was an extremely beautiful prospect. This was the farthest north we went on our tour of Scotland.

We then hired a carriage and, crossing the double-arched bridge, drove to the south-east. On the right-hand side a shallow stream ran beside the road, its pure water washing a sandy bottom. Salmon bred in large numbers in this stream. The road was in a good state and the surface was very smooth. The peoples of the West know how essential to their lives it is to keep roads in good repair. This was an out-of-the-way mountain region, yet the roads were maintained as well as this.

From this point on, the road took us deeper into the mountains. All the land roundabout was the private property of rich families. The owners built new roads, broad and level, on which vehicles could travel easily. They also turned a profit from sightseers. This was why there was always a gate, where a toll of one or two pence was collected, across any road which led to a place of scenic beauty or to a remote spot. One paid for the beautiful scenery – and it was cheap at the price.

After covering five miles of mountain road south-eastwards from Blair Atholl, we entered the ravine of Killiecrankie. Picturesque mountain peaks towered before us and at their foot ran a river. The leaves were already turning, fading from a vivid green to yellow and tawny.

We came to a stone bridge. Even though we were deep in the coun-tryside, this quaint bridge was clearly an ancient one. In the West the beauty of a landscape is often enhanced by a bridge. The water beneath the bridge was very dark and gave an impression of great depth. The golden leaves on either bank were reflected in its surface, as were the mountain peaks. The view above the bridge was also very beautiful. I used to think that water was always blue or green, but as we travelled in America and Europe, I found that in Britain the water was black, in Switzerland emerald green and in Sweden dark blue.

Our carriage was waiting for us beside the bridge. We got into it straight away and headed south. At every turn a scene of beauty presented itself; on all sides we saw magnificent mountains. The country-seats of rich men were visible, some looking down over the river, some turning their faces towards the mountains. We could hear the crowing of cocks and the barking of dogs; we saw rare birds roaming free.

After some miles we arrived at Pitlochry Station. By this time it was five o'clock, and the sun had set behind the Killiecrankie mountains. The dusk was thickening and we could see a sprinkling of stars overhead. The sky was clear, a panorama of mountains and rivers was spread out before us, and a cool breeze caressed the skin: this was a very different scene from the gloomy fogs of the cities. We had brushed away the dust of many days and suddenly felt clean. After we had waited for half an hour or so, our train arrived and we immediately boarded it. Travelling about ten miles to the south, we arrived at a station in the village of Dunkeld. Here we took rooms at the Birnam Hotel. That evening there were seven or eight other guests, both men and women, and we all sat down to dinner at the same table. The manners of the people of the Scottish Highlands are simple and unaffected, and their comportment is open and straightforward. Travelling in these mountain villages, we were able to forget for a while the formality required by our official positions and were able to appreciate the simple frankness of the people.

October 18th. Cloudy.
We rose at first light and had breakfast at eight o'clock. This morning we saw frost flowers on the eaves of the village houses. The red circle of the sun rising in the east was a pleasing sight and the air was crystal-clear. Suddenly, a thick mist began to boil up among the mountains, and by the time we had finished breakfast dark clouds covered the sky. At nine o'clock we hired a carriage in order to drive round the nearby villages. Having crossed the bridge of the river Tay, we came to another estate belonging to the duke of Atholl.

Later, we left this park, turned our carriage round, crossed the bridge over the Tay again and drove north. The country through which we now travelled was lonely moorland, with only an occasional house. To the north we could see the snow-clad peak of Ben Macdui. We were told that it was no more than 4,300 feet in height. (It was the second-highest peak in Scotland.) We came to another toll-gate. When we had paid the toll and passed through, we found ourselves in a wooded valley, the leaves of the trees tinted yellow. This was called the Rumbling Valley. We walked down a path through the woods, following the sound of water, to find ourselves looking down into a ravine. This was the Rumbling Falls. The attractiveness of these falls lay in the way the water was broken up into a myriad forms by the rocks. It was a scene to which no description could do justice.

After our visit to the Rumbling Falls, we turned our carriage round and went back to Dunkeld Station, where we boarded a train to travel sixteen miles west to Aberfeldy. Here we hired another carriage. To the south of the road were hills covered in rough vegetation. Occasionally we saw wandering deer: this area is famous for deer. We came to a gateway across the road, furnished with a pair of iron gates. This was the rear entrance to Earl Campbell's estate. The Campbells were once one of the most powerful clans in Scotland, masters of the whole of Argyll. The clan later divided into several branches, and its land was shared out among them, but they retain great influence.

Most of the people who live in the Highlands are of the Celtic race and speak the Gaelic language. Sir Harry Parkes and General Alexander laughed because neither was able to understand what the railway porters and the drivers of our carriages said.

At four o'clock we reached the village of Killin at the head of Loch Tay. In Scotland the days are very short in winter, and it was already nearly sunset. We therefore decided to stay here for the night. The hotel was small but again extremely clean. It overlooked a pool, on the other side of which stood an old castle of the clan Campbell [Finlarig Castle]. We decided to go across to it in a small rowing boat. There was a man of some distinction in the village, and he escorted us up a hill which was an old battlefield: in the religious wars of three hundred years ago, soldiers in the castle and soldiers on this hill had shot at each other. We crossed the pool and ascended to the ruins of the castle, which was surrounded by ancient trees and bushes, and the ground was covered with fallen leaves, so there was a sense of desolation. The castle was a small fortress which had been built 340 years before (in the reign of James V) and garrisoned by only fifty men. The castle was still owned by the Campbells, and one part of it was kept as a mausoleum. Around three walls of an inner vault were forty-five stone niches ready to receive coffins. There were only four children entombed here.

Our distinguished guide told us that his son was a merchant in Yokohama. He was delighted that the ambassadors should have come to this remote village and invited us to accompany him home. He conducted us to his house, which stood in extensive grounds, overlooking a pool. A wood fire was burning on the drawing-room hearth. His wife and daughter received us with handshakes. We spent half an hour talking. This being a remote mountain village, conversation was offered rather than alcoholic drinks or tea, and our hosts showed the warmth of their welcome by pulling chairs up to the fireside and putting more wood on the fire. The sun set and the room grew dark, so we took our leave and returned to the hotel.

October 19th. Cloudy; clearing after midday.
At six o'clock we had tea before leaving the hotel. It was still not fully light at this time. Our carriage drove at a good speed alongside the river, which flowed into the head of Loch Tay. The country alongside this mountain road grew ever wilder, and there was now no sign of cultivation. Ben Lawers was wreathed in cloud and we could not see the summit, but we were travelling among its outlying hills. The road grew somewhat steeper and we climbed gradually up the mountainside until we came to a railway station. A train was on the point of leaving, so we boarded immediately and the train departed towards the south. This railway line was a newly opened one, which made its way through the mountains towards the port of Oban in the west. The stations along the line were small and passengers were few. The station buildings were very simple in construction: inside a fenced area there would be a small wooden building of about sixteen or twenty square yards. This would be for the sale of tickets only. We laughed and said, 'We have seen the great Victoria Station in London, and now we have seen these little stations. The very largest and the very smallest of stations are both found in Britain. This really is a great country – everything is here.'

At half past eight we arrived at Callander, where we alighted. The village was well populated and was packed with shops and houses. We rested briefly at an hotel before departing westwards by carriage. The land all along the road was uncultivated. We passed by a number of ancient battlefields. The grass was withered, and the exhausted trees were shedding their leaves. Pheasants started from among the yellowed ferns; quail roamed in the dry bracken. The scene left an impression of melancholy, windless but cold.

After travelling some miles we left the waters of Loch Venachar behind us and entered a forest of yellow leaves. On our left was a mountain, the attractive shapes of its rocky crags visible above the trees. We saw a solitary figure walking along a path on the lower slopes of this mountain carrying something on his shoulders. It was an artist who had come, his canvases on his back, to paint the landscape. In the West, too, painters compete with one another in technique, but what is most admired is the painting of actual landscapes. Painters therefore come from all quarters to gather at famous beauty spots, where they take lodgings, choose places from which to observe the scenery and paint directly from nature. Such paintings fetch huge sums of money and become the objects of bidding by rich men and great merchants. This mountain landscape, we were told, was one of the most famous in Scotland. From this point on, the golden leaves stood between us and the sun, turning the light itself yellow. Our carriage went round a bend in the road, so that we were heading in a different direction, and all at once we saw mountain peaks reflected in the waters of a loch. This was the beauty spot known as the Trossachs. It gave us more pleasure than any other we had seen during our journey.

Loch Achray is very small, no larger than what one would call a pool. Overlooking the loch was a large, handsome building called the Trossachs Hotel. We went in and had breakfast. The proprietors of the hotel were two brothers who treated their guests with great cordiality, and they welcomed the arrival of the Japanese ambassador's party, with carriages waiting on the road and a steamboat moored on the loch. The brothers, moreover, offered to act personally as our guides. When we had finished breakfast, we got into a carriage, and, accompanied by the brothers, we set off. Leading us was another carriage which carried a man playing a Scottish musical instrument called the 'bagpipes'. This consists of a pair of trumpet-shaped flutes which the musician plays standing up. They have a clear, bright sound, pure and refined.

Leaving Loch Achray behind, the road once again entered a wood of yellow leaves. It was a bright, sunny day, the sky a clear blue. No sound of wind came from any quarter, only the soft sound of leaves falling. We felt that the farther we ventured into the Scottish mountain landscape, the more scenic it became. Emerging from the yellow woods, we found ourselves at a landing-place on the loch shore. A covered pier permitted passengers to board a steamer, and as soon as we had embarked the paddle-wheels began to turn. Ahead was an island; to left and right, and behind us, nothing but range upon range of mountains, every peak presenting a most picturesque appearance, each seeking to overtop the others, all alike in the strange beauty of their forms. The scenes which we saw during this tour reached the pinnacle of their beauty here. When the boat had passed the island the view before us changed once more: the loch, its tranquil surface reflecting the light, lay between ranges of mountains on either side. This loch was called Loch Katrine. Its water was extremely clear. On all sides were mountain peaks wreathed in mist. When we were near the end of the loch, we saw on one bank the mouth of the tunnel through which water is conveyed to Glasgow. The boat pulled alongside and we landed.

When we boarded the boat again we proceeded to Stronachlachar, near the head of the loch, where we disembarked. We then hired a carriage and drove west. The country was very hilly, but the carriage roads had been artfully constructed to wind their way round the slopes of the hills so as to keep inclines to a minimum and allow wheeled vehicles to proceed without difficulty. The landlord of the Trossachs Hotel had taken his leave of us on the loch shore and returned to the boat, but his younger brother accompanied us farther. When we had left the loch behind us and had climbed some way up the hillside, we looked down on the waters below. The steamboat, puffing smoke, was on the point of leaving; our carriage was about to enter the mountains. Those in the carriage and those on the boat gazed at one another from a distance, full of regret at parting, and waved their handkerchiefs in farewell. We went on our way, stopping our carriage frequently to look back once more at the scene. Thus, even in this secluded Scottish glen the warm affection of brother for brother did not easily fade away.

Loch Lomond, which is in Perthshire, is the largest of the lochs. It is twenty miles long, but less than a mile wide at its head, although it becomes much broader towards the foot, where it is four miles wide in places. There are many lovely mountains along its banks, and islands and promontories offered a variety of fine views. A steam-packet plied back and forth on the loch, carrying tourists. At many of the landing-stages tolls were collected.

We boarded a boat and sailed up the loch. When we reached the head of the loch, we went ashore for a while and strolled a few hundred yards. The rustic appearance of the lakeside villages was charming. We boarded the steamer again and returned down the lake. When we had gone six or seven miles, a wind rose and rain began to fall. It became uncomfortable to sit on deck, so we went into the saloon, which was very large and where there were about thirty passengers, both men and women. Several were artists carrying their canvases, but most were tourists who had come in search of beautiful scenery. We were told that this steam-packet service had been instituted on the loch for the purpose of carrying tourists.

At seven o'clock we landed at Balloch. With our arrival here, our tour came to an end. The local station had been notified that we would be coming, and we were welcomed by members of the railway company's staff. A special train had been arranged and was awaiting us at the landing-stage. As soon as we boarded, the train set off. We arrived back at our hotel in Edinburgh at about ten o'clock.

October 20th. Cloudy.
At eleven o'clock we attended a service at St. John's Episcopal Church, the largest Anglican church in Scotland. A famous cleric, Dean Ramsay, preached. The number of men and women who had gathered here to worship was six hundred in all.

At two o'clock in the afternoon we went to St. George's Church. This was the largest of the churches belonging to the Scottish Presbyterian Church. The Reverend Dr. Candlish, who had been minister of this church for thirty-three years, preached the sermon. The congregation numbered seven hundred men and women. The Americans and the British are very devout believers, and the Scots are the most devout of all. For this reason they lead honest and upright lives and are also well educated. The people of this country, therefore, unfailingly urge visitors, even those from distant lands, to accompany them to church on the day of worship.

# CHAPTER 33

# A Record of Newcastle, 1

October 21st, 1872. Rain.

At ten o'clock in the morning we left our hotel in Edinburgh to travel south to Newcastle. Detonators had been placed on the line to provide a farewell salute as we left the station. Several people from a firm of tweed-makers in Galashiels had come as far as the station at Edinburgh to meet us and travel back with us. It was raining during the journey, so we saw nothing along the way. At half past eleven we arrived at Galashiels Station, where we were met by the deacon [of the Manufacturers' Corporation]. We went straight to the tweed mill by carriage.

Galashiels is sixty miles south of Edinburgh by rail, close to Scotland's south-eastern border. It is a town of something over 10,000 inhabitants, who are very upright in character: we were told that the whole town had only five policemen. When we arrived at the station we found that men and women from all over the town had gathered in the street to see us. The little boys ran up to us, the little girls followed them, and as we moved away our carriages were surrounded, before and behind, by a jostling throng.

The tweed mill, which was very large, belonged to two brothers, Adam and Archibald [Cochrane]. Tweed is woven from wool. Wool is divided into seven basic grades, and it is the finest and softest grade which is used for weaving tweed. It has a yielding quality, like cotton. Most wool is imported from Australia. Sheep are reared on a large scale in Britain, too, and Scottish wool is particularly highly regarded, but most of the woollens woven in Britain are made with Australian wool. This is because not only is it of the finest quality but it is also low in price. The assertion by some Japanese that Europe has a climatic advantage in wool production because the finest and softest animal fleeces are those produced in cold countries is completely erroneous.

On leaving the factory we were entertained to lunch at the public hall. On the left-hand side of the room two musicians played, and rows of ladies looked on from a dais in front. Forty gentlemen sat down at table with us. After the meal there were speeches. It was past three o'clock when we caught our train.

Rain fell hard and ceaselessly. In twenty minutes we arrived at Melrose Station, where we alighted to look at Melrose Abbey. This was a famous church, founded in 1136. It had been destroyed in a war three hundred years ago and subsequently repaired, but had now fallen into a ruinous state. All that remained were the outer walls and parts of the roof. This church was considered to be the work of master builders. More recent architects had tried to reproduce the fineness of the stone-carving and the vaulting, but without success. Even now, many of the leading figures of the surrounding counties stipulate in their wills that they be buried at this church. There were graves both inside and outside the ruined building. One of the headstones was that of someone who had been buried as recently as 1869. After spending some time looking round the church interior, we departed. It was still raining heavily. On the hills behind the church the leaves were changing colour, and now and then there was a gentle breeze. The scene prompted melancholic and nostalgic thoughts.

We rested for a while at the Abbey Hotel, where some of the town's officials kindly provided us with refreshments. We waited here about an hour for our train, which left at around five o'clock, and we arrived at Newcastle Station at half past nine. The mayor and the president of the chamber of commerce met us at the station in their robes of office and invited us into the station waiting room for a ceremony of welcome. Speeches were made and replied to. They then conducted us to the Station Hotel, beside the station, where we took rooms.

October 22nd. Thin cloud.
At half past nine in the morning Sir William Armstrong came to our hotel to escort us personally to his company's ordnance factory. Sir William was a genial old gentleman well over six feet tall. He was a man of few words, and his appearance did not obviously bespeak intelligence. Wherever we went, the famous manufacturers we met were frequently men of this type.

We were taken to a shop containing steam-powered machines where there was a 1,000-horsepower steam-engine. None of the steam-engines which we had seen in all the places we had visited was as large as this one. Some of this power was used to drive the huge hammers, some to move ladles of molten iron, some to cut iron, and some to transport the finished metal products. Finished locomotive wheels and shafts were piled in great heaps inside and outside the workshop. Inside the shop were a great many furnaces for melting iron. When their doors were opened to lift out the crucibles, the wave of heat released was like that of the hottest day in summer. Besides guns, all kinds of iron and steel products were manufactured here, such as steam-engines, hydraulic machinery and a wide variety of new inventions. Gun-carriages were the most numerous.

At the rear of the factory was a firing range. Here a Gatling gun was demonstrated for us. This is a most destructive weapon, invented by an American and improved by Sir William Armstrong.

We were given lunch in a room at the factory, after which Sir William made a speech. Only three or four people joined us at table. We then left the factory and called briefly at one of Sir William's houses. Having been shown round the house, we left with Sir William for the Gosforth coal-mine.

Gosforth Colliery is only two miles from Newcastle. A vertical shaft had been sunk to a depth of four hundred yards. At the foot of this was a seam of coal six to nine feet thick. In quality, the coal was of the superior middle grade. Over the mouth of the shaft a tower-like framework had been erected, and beside it a large steam-driven pump had been installed which operated night and day to pump water out of the mine. To carry the miners and ponies down into the pit, a cage hanging from the top of the frame was raised and lowered by a steam-engine. The miners got in at one side and out at the other. The cage was constructed of iron. Six men rode in the upper compartment, and coal and equipment was carried in the lower compartment. The cage was suspended from thick hemp ropes. It took as long as five minutes to travel from the pit-head to the bottom of the shaft.

The number of miners working in the colliery varied, but there would normally be between 250 and 300. They worked in five-hour shifts, each miner working one shift a day, and were paid a wage of about eight shillings ($2) a shift. The mining of coal from this part of the colliery had begun about three years previously, and the workings now covered three square miles. Props had been put in and roadways made which intersected one another at right angles. The coal was brought out in wagons running on iron rails along the roadways. We saw a map of the mine which showed the roads laid out in orderly fashion, like those of some underground city.

Today we changed our clothes in the office and, together with Sir William Armstrong, descended to the bottom of the shaft, escorted by Mr. Crone, the engineer. Each of us carried a safety lamp, enclosed in glass, and a staff. When we reached the foot of the shaft, we could hear the trickle of water dripping from the pumps. All about us was utter blackness, and our small lamps only cast light a few paces ahead. We picked our way forward cautiously but stumbled over the rails and our progress was unsteady. Frequently there were pools of water on the roadway. Now and then we came to a crossroads where doors or curtains of heavy cloth were installed to keep the air in the mine from escaping. A gentle, steady breeze of fresh air blew towards us. The temperature was a constant 55°. After proceeding about a mile and a half into the workings, we arrived at the coal-face, where the seam was thin – no more than about five and a half feet. We made our way back to the foot of the shaft by riding on the wagons on the rails. There we inspected the stables, where twenty or so ponies were tethered. In the darkness of the mine we were unable to make out any details. Eventually we entered the cage again and were hoisted to the surface. We felt as though we had ascended out of Hell into Heaven. By this time night had already fallen.

# CHAPTER 34

# A Record of Newcastle, 2

October 23rd, 1872. Fine.

At ten o'clock we went by carriage to the Newcastle exchange, which was not a particularly imposing building. A group of businessmen had gathered to receive us, and raised their hats to us in a gesture of courtesy. They first invited us into the offices, then conducted us onto the floor of the exchange, where we were encircled by the merchants. The president of the chamber of commerce made a speech. When the ambassador had replied, the crowd of merchants stamped their feet, raised their hats and gave a tremendous cheer.

We then proceeded to the bank of the river Tyne, where a river-steamer was moored, and the heads and members of several manufacturing and commercial firms had come to receive us with the intention of showing us round a number of works along the river-banks.

We cast off and steamed upriver about 240 yards to where a new bridge was being built. The massive stone piers were still under construction and a steam-powered lifting machine had been set up to move the equipment and materials required. The river-bed had been excavated and huge metal cylinders had been set vertically in place. Their size was about that of a Japanese well. They narrowed towards the bottom and were as much as thirty or forty feet deep. The depth of the cylinders was enough to make anyone looking down into them tremble with fear. Six or seven great concrete columns like this went to make up one of the bridge supports, each of which was then clad externally with massive blocks of stone, forming a hexagonal pier. The river was eighteen feet deep at this point and would have been four or five hundred feet in width. For the whole bridge, six of these concrete and stone hexagonal piers were being built. They were to support round arches like our 'spectacle' bridge [in Nagasaki] for a stone bridge which was both solid and beautiful.

The building of a bridge is a great feat of engineering. In particular, it is no simple matter to plan the building of a stone bridge, because it is a work which will not perish. When planning it, Western engineers measure with great accuracy the average depth of the water, the difference in depth between high and low water, and the rate of flow. They can then determine the forces which the water will exert on the piers. In order to decide the right method for building the foundations, they survey the contours of the river bottom, test the strength of the mud and sand and ascertain the nature of the underlying rock. They then choose the stone, making sure that the structure will not be eroded by wind and water. They thus ensure that the bridge will be strong enough to support so-and-so many tens of thousands of tons in weight at one time. When they have done all this, we were told, they turn their attention to the appearance of the bridge, even going to the lengths of applying some decorative carving. The stone buildings and bridges which we saw in our travels round European cities were all magnificent structures.

We then steamed downriver to visit a number of factories. The south bank of the river was entirely lined with factories, the smoke from their towering chimneys discolouring the sky. It was a fine day, but we had hardly a glimpse of a clear sky. We went first to a factory of the Tharsis Company, a metal-extracting company which refined copper, at Hebburn Quay.

We then crossed to the other bank, near Hebburn Station. Here a ship was at work dredging the river bottom. We had already briefly seen a dredger in operation at Liverpool, but on this day we were able to make a detailed inspection. On either side of the vessel was an endless chain of iron buckets which descended one after another, picked up mud from the river-bed, then rose out of the water. When they reached the top they tipped upside-down, emptying their contents before descending again towards the surface of the river. At the point where the buckets released the mud, a string of small barges stood alongside to receive it. As soon as one was full it was instantly replaced by the next.

After lunch we disembarked and went to a factory at Hebburn. This was a works which imported bar lead from Greece and extracted the silver it contained, leaving pure lead. This was then rolled into sheets, from which white lead was made by oxidation, and red lead was obtained by raising the lead to a high temperature.

When we in Japan hear of the huge scale of manufacturing and research in the countries of the West and visualise these countries, we probably assume that everyone there must be fully conversant with all branches of science and technology. This is completely untrue. The people in charge of the various operations in a factory have a detailed knowledge only of their own specialisations. Having devoted themselves wholly to that one field, many have only a vague understanding of the most superficial aspects of other technologies. Even the head of a manufacturing firm is not necessarily an expert in chemistry, mechanics and physics. Whether in theoretical planning or practical execution, a particular person will be strong in one field of knowledge and weak in others. In order to begin a manufacturing venture, many outstanding people are brought together and each undertakes the work for which he is fitted by his skills. These various contributions are combined in the manufacture of a single article.

About four miles farther down the river Tyne we came to the town of South Shields, which stood on a headland on the south bank. The houses were all crammed closely together. On either side of the river at this point were many shipyards, giving the impression that shipbuilding was the principal industry of the town. The scale of activity was just as great as at Liverpool. We proceeded to the South Shields headland, which looked directly out onto the North Sea. Because it was exposed to the pounding of waves from the open sea, a breakwater had been built out from the headland to provide protection. Furthermore, a jetty had been constructed at the end of this mole in order to hold back silt from the mouth of the Tyne. Nearby was a quarry from which the limestone was hewn for the jetty.

The portion of this curved stone breakwater which had been completed already extended a mile into the sea. The breakwater rose more than twenty feet above the sea-bed. Several railway lines had been laid along it to facilitate the transport of materials. Beside the tracks ran a long iron pipe, at the shoreward end of which a steam-engine had been installed to pump air through it. A rubber hose led from the end of the pipe to the air inlet in the top of a diving-bell, enabling men inside the bell to work on the sea-bed. The bell was made of iron plates riveted together, and the upper part was hemispherical. Six windows in the sides admitted light. In the top of the bell was a hole into which a copper pipe, fitted to the end of the rubber hose, was firmly screwed, allowing the air inside the bell to be constantly replenished. Inside the bell were two benches, one on either side, for the men to sit on. After the men entered the bell, it was lowered to the sea-bed so they could work. When our party arrived at the headland the bell was already on the sea-bed. At a signal, it was raised, and when the two workmen emerged from it, they were not at all wet. In the West, these diving-bells are always used for underwater work. There are various types, but the basic principle is always the same.

In the estuary here there was a training-ship like those in Liverpool, to which youths of bad character were sent to be taught seamanship. The boys climbed up the masts, doffed their hats and cheered us.

We then crossed over to the opposite shore, where the Tynemouth Lighthouse stood. On this day, the rescue of people on a ship in distress was practised for us to see. A rocket with a rope attached was fired from the top of the hill opposite the breakwater. To the end of it was attached a thick cable, which in turn supported a set of ropes by means of which an iron tub shaped like a helmet was lowered from the hilltop. It was possible to put passengers or goods into this tub. A further arrangement of ropes made it possible to haul the tub in either direction, and another piece of equipment allowed a [bosun's] chair to travel back and forth. This apparatus could be attached to a stricken vessel to carry those aboard on shore and, if time permitted, cargo as well.

Today Sir Harry Parkes got into the chair and was carried across the bay. As he left the shore, a cheer went up from the people on this side, and when he reached the far shore we heard another cheer from the people there. By this time it was almost dark, so magnesium flares were lit on the hilltop, illuminating the whole bay. Then we saw the shadow of the tub on the water, and the indistinct form of Sir Harry coming back across the waves. The cheering from both sides of the bay never stopped. It was a remarkable scene.

When this spectacle was over, we walked through the streets of Tynemouth with the captain and other local people to the railway station. We were accompanied, before and behind, by a huge crowd of men and women of the town. We left the station at six o'clock. By the time we reached our hotel it was already seven o'clock.

CHAPTER 35

# A Record of Bradford

October 24th, 1872. Rainy; this is the season when frosts begin.

At ten o'clock in the morning we left Newcastle and travelled ninety miles south through County Durham to the western part of Yorkshire, arriving in Bradford at half past two in the afternoon. We were welcomed at the station by the mayor and went by carriage to the Victoria Hotel, where we took rooms. Both inside the station building and lining the street leading to the hotel was an uninterrupted throng of onlookers. Crowds turned out to see us in every other city we visited, both before and after, but this was the largest such reception we received. At many places in the streets bills had been posted announcing, 'Japanese Ambassadors Will Arrive On Thursday, Escorted By The Mayor.' When we arrived at the hotel, we found that lunch had been prepared for us at the mayor's behest. After the meal he came to make an address of welcome. His hospitality was boundless. In the evening he gave a dinner for us at the hotel.

October 25th. Cloudy.

At ten o'clock in the morning we travelled about three miles by train to the town of Saltaire. Until twenty years ago this had been open moorland, used only as pastureland for sheep and cattle, but since Sir Titus Salt had built a mill for weaving the wool of the animal called the 'alpaca', industrial and commercial enterprises had flocked there. It was now a considerable town with a population of 5,000.

The alpaca is a kind of sheep whose wool not only has a lustre to rival that of silk but also has a long staple. An enterprising person had obtained a quantity of this wool from South America with the idea that it could be used for spinning and weaving, but he met with no success. The wool was stored in a warehouse in Liverpool, and years passed without a single buyer being found for it. The owner proposed disposing of it in the sea but was prevented by the docks board; he made plans to burn it but was

182

prevented by the city council. He was spending money on warehouse rent to no purpose, and the wool was nothing but a burden to him.

For a long time Mr. Salt had also been pondering the right techniques for spinning and weaving this wool. Having eventually invented methods of doing so, he contracted with the owner to take all the wool. Word of this spread throughout Britain and Mr. Salt was relentlessly mocked, and was even ridiculed in the press. However, using machinery of his own design, Mr. Salt eventually managed to weave a fine cloth, and from then on the useless alpaca suddenly acquired value. His business prospered, and beside the river Aire he built a large mill which produced more cloth year by year. Thus, the pastures were transformed into a smoky town. The town was named 'Saltaire', and the streets were named after Mr. Salt's sons and daughters. Mr. Salt became immensely rich, and [in 1869] he received the honour of a baronetcy from the government. He was still alive, but on the day of our visit he was away from Bradford and we were unable to meet him.

Sir Titus had built a primary school and arranged for the children, both boys and girls, to work at the factory for half a day and attend school the rest of the day. By this excellent method, theoretical understanding and practical skills progressed in tandem. Moreover, not only did the children benefit by receiving a wage from the mill, but their work also benefited the enterprise. The British regard it as a point of honour to look after their workers and to do their utmost to succour the poor, and the provisions made by this factory-owner are to be admired. The subjects taught at the school were those normal in primary schools. They were skills which both boys and girls needed to know and did not extend to more advanced subjects.

In front of the school were almshouses. The workers no longer able to work because of old age were placed there to be cared for. There was also a hospital, which treated the sick, and a church, which the residents attended to hear sermons and thus improve their moral natures. At none of the factories we saw before or after were there such provisions as these. Every one of the five thousand inhabitants looked up to the Salt family. This way of organising towns where workers live is an important way of encouraging them to work hard.

Today we were given lunch in the board-room adjoining the mill offices. We then went to a park on the edge of the town. This, too, had been provided by Sir Titus as a gift to the workers. It occupied a sloping site on the banks of the Aire, backed by rolling hills, and presented a very fine prospect.

October 26th. Cloudy; rain.

At five to ten in the morning we boarded a train at the station near our hotel to travel eight miles to Halifax. The mayor, the town clerk and others met us at the station, accompanied by the president of the chamber of commerce and the heads of the wool-weaving company we were to visit. Such a crowd of townspeople had gathered, moreover, that the roadway was completely blocked. The cheers of the crowd rang through the streets, and it was only with difficulty that our carriages were able to make their way through. After about half a mile, we reached the Dean Clough wool mill of Messrs. John Crossley and Sons.

This mill, reputed to be the largest in Britain, wove blankets, carpets and rugs made of velvet and other materials. The carpets and rugs were of every kind, and the scale of production defies description. The mill comprised several multi-storeyed buildings, in all containing four hundred rooms. The company imported various types of wool, which was first sorted into grades, each grade being used for a particular purpose. The sorted wool was sent to the dyeing department to be dyed in a wide range of colours. It was then ready to be spun and woven.

The patterns – of birds, animals, grasses, trees, and beautiful designs and motifs of different shapes and colours – came from many countries and from various regions. Those new and fashionable among them were copied and sample weavings were made. Thus, there was an unceasing supply of different ideas and no lack of 'master designers' was felt. Having exhausted their own creativity, they learnt from every country of the world. In this way, their fund of knowledge became ever greater.

In Halifax we also visited a school built by Sir John Crossley. The school had 250 pupils, of whom 75 were following a middle school curriculum. When the ambassador's party arrived, the children assembled to sing for us, and when we left they gave us three cheers.

We then went to the townhall. An address was made and replied to, and we were given lunch in the reception room.

As the next day was Sunday, Sir Harry Parkes and General Alexander suggested that we should go to see something of the countryside nearby. Only three of us went: Vice-Ambassador Yamaguchi, Hayashi Tadasu and Kume Kunitake. We caught a train at four o'clock, and after twenty miles we alighted and took a carriage. The people of the village had all gathered to see us. The British have the reputation of being great overseas travellers and therefore of being most accustomed to intercourse with foreigners, but the proportion of them who have in fact been overseas and are familiar with foreign lands is no more than one or two in ten thousand, and particularly in country districts like this a foreigner is regarded as a great curiosity. After some miles, we arrived at the Bolton Bridge Hotel, where we took rooms.

This area was part of the duke of Devonshire's estates. The prince and princess of Wales (the princess is a member of the German royal house) had once stayed at this hotel when they came here for the shooting. The bedroom they had occupied was kept as the best room in the hotel. On this occasion it was given to the vice-ambassador.

In the West, royalty and aristocracy alike take great pleasure in shooting game. Even ladies are skilled in the use of guns. In the northern parts of Britain there is a bird called the 'grouse'. It resembles the pheasant but is somewhat smaller. Its claws are like those of the owl, and it nests among the moorland grass. This bird is hunted according to strict rules. Its cover is beaten to make it fly up into the air, and it is shot while on the wing; it is considered shameful to shoot a bird while it is on the ground. The prince of Wales and the duke of Devonshire were both first-class shots. During the shooting season, we were told, the bag would sometimes reach 7,000 birds in a month.

October 27th. Fine.
At ten o'clock in the morning we walked to Bolton Priory, an ancient church built seven hundred years ago. This was a sacred place and, with its ancient appearance and sombre air, inspired a sense of awe. The setting was beautiful: below it flowed the river Wharfe; hills rose at its back; it overlooked open country; and a waterfall tumbled down the hillside. We attended a service here, which lasted about two hours. Seven hundred years before, a nobleman and his wife lived near here; their only child tried to cross the river but fell into the water and was drowned. For the repose of the child's soul, his grief-stricken parents built a chapel farther down the river. That was the origin of Bolton Priory.

The whole valley and its river were the property of the duke of Devonshire. He had planted trees and laid out pathways in keeping with nature. Among the trees nearby lived the forester who oversaw the woodland. Beside his house he had established a plantation in which he grew saplings to plant along the river-banks farther upstream. Thus, no part of the countryside of Britain is left uncultivated, and with the passage of time the land-owning families create beautiful landscapes. The development of the land has reached a peak, and so great is the surplus wealth of the landowners that they have no hesitation in investing huge sums in railways, telegraphs and every other modern convenience.

CHAPTER 36

# *A Record of Sheffield*

October 28th, 1872. Cloudy.
At half past one in the afternoon we left Bradford and travelled by train forty-two miles south to Sheffield. While we were in Bradford, a leading citizen of Sheffield, Mr. George Wilson, had come personally to invite us to visit that city when we left Bradford, and had, moreover, promised to put us up at his own house. Mr. Wilson and his brother were at the station to meet us with their private carriages to bring us to their houses. Because there were not enough rooms at Mr. George Wilson's house, Vice-Ambassador Itō and the two secretaries stayed at the house of his younger brother, Mr. Alexander Wilson, but were brought each evening by carriage to the house of the elder Mr. Wilson to join the others for dinner. The Wilsons' hospitality was whole-hearted. The atmosphere was most friendly and relations extremely harmonious.

October 29th. Cloudy.
At nine o'clock in the morning we went by carriage to Messrs. Charles Cammell and Company's iron and steel works. This factory occupied an enormous tract of land from which a forest of chimneys, great and small, reached upwards. Smoke from burning coal spread across the heavens like spilt ink, making it look as though a great thunderstorm was about to burst upon us. Even from a distance it was a sight to unsettle the nerves. We never saw such a huge factory either before or after. (The only one we saw comparable to it was the Krupp works in Germany.) Until twenty-five years ago, this factory had been no more than a small works making and selling files. The items now manufactured were mainly very large iron and steel forgings. It was the first place to roll armour-plating for iron-clads. It also cast blocks for the barrels of artillery pieces and shafts for steam-engines, and rolled rails for the railways and many different kinds of iron wire and rod, as well as continuing to make files.

After this we proceeded to the shop where armour-plate for warships was forged. This operation was the largest of all those in the works. On the day of our visit, a wooden stand had been erected upon which our party was invited to sit to observe the operation. When the door of the furnace was opened, six or seven workmen, under the direction of a foreman, used hooks and chains to drag out a steel plate which had been heated in the furnace. It was sixteen feet long by four and a half feet wide, and more than one foot thick. The whole plate had been raised to a white heat and was spitting flames from its entire surface. At a distance of ten or twelve yards from the furnace door stood a huge rolling machine. To the front and rear of it were iron tables, on each of which was mounted an array of iron rollers. The red-hot slab was laid on one of these tables, and a gang of eighteen workmen, divided into two teams, left and right, used long pincers to push it between the rollers, which rotated with immense force and expelled it to the rear, where another gang of eighteen workmen turned it, sending it through to the front again. This action was repeated a dozen times, the slab being reduced at each pass until it was no more than nine inches thick. The foreman, after checking the thickness with a rule, then stopped the operation.

While the slab was being passed backwards and forwards between the rollers, workmen used pumps to spray it constantly with water and long brooms to sweep scale from the surface. The water turned instantly to clouds of steam; the broom-heads were reduced to ashes the moment they fell and touched the metal. The red-hot steel bathed the whole workshop in a crimson glow. After being forged, the slab was raised by a machine and laid aside, gradually turning purple, then black. Workmen were moving about among stacks of these plates. All Westerners, high and low, wear boots or shoes, so even if they walk on hot iron or sharp steel they run no risk of injury to their feet.

From here we went to the shop where malleable iron was manufactured by the Bessemer method. Members of the firm stood beside us and explained in detail the principles behind this. 'Steel' is pure iron with a carbon content of fifteen parts per thousand. The degree of heat applied is the secret of forging steel since iron changes its character according to the carbon content and the degree of oxidation. Thus, the most intense heat is needed to refine it. It is impossible to exploit all the uses steel is capable of unless these principles are thoroughly understood. We in the East do not understand them, so we have satisfied our needs simply by using what nature has provided.

Next we were given lunch in the conference room, with Mr. Cammell in the chair. In the centre of the room were the crossed flags of our two countries. About fifty people from the company were present. Both the table decorations and the food were of the very best. After lunch we went on a tour of the file-making shop.

October 30th. Cloudy.

At ten o'clock in the morning we left by carriage for Chatsworth House, the home of the duke of Devonshire, which lies on the upper reaches of the river Derwent, seven or eight miles west of the city. The road was winding and passed through hilly country. Little of the land we saw was cultivated, and from time to time we crossed rough moorland covered in coarse grass, all of which was withered and darkish grey. The weather was dismal and overcast with a biting wind, and we were bitterly cold. In the north of England, autumn comes early. The scenery was extremely pleasant, and the road was well maintained. Before long we saw deer roaming on the grass among scattered groves of trees and knew that we were approaching the duke's house.

The duke, [William] Cavendish, was the most famous, and the richest, of the Yorkshire aristocracy. He owns six estates in Yorkshire, and his total revenue exceeds £200,000 a year. Chatsworth House lies in a valley, with hills rising in front and behind. Along the middle of the valley flows the Derwent. To the south-west the view is exceptionally wide and sweeping: dark blue hills could be seen in the distance. This part of the country is outstandingly beautiful. The house is a lofty building, three storeys high, built entirely of gleaming white stone, its surface pristine, with little carving.

We went in through the carriage entrance and were met in the hall by a servant who led us into a room lined with shelves filled with books. This was the duke's sitting-room. When we entered, the duke rose to greet us with a handshake. He was most cordial and personally showed us round the house. When he opened one door we emerged into a large hall where there was a visitors' book which the duke invited the members of our party to sign.

We went into various rooms where *objets d'art* and curios were displayed. It is the custom in the West not to keep all one's possessions shut up in boxes but to display them, and it is regarded as an honour to show them to visitors. In every room all four walls were adorned from floor to ceiling with examples of the most exquisite craftsmanship. There were beautiful embroideries and delicate carvings, some of them gleaming with burnished gold-leaf. The walls were hung with brocades, damasks and French Gobelin tapestries. There were, of course, countless European antiques and curios, but we also noticed some from China, Japan, India and America.

In several rooms china from every country was displayed. Flower vases were placed on stands; smaller objects were arranged on shelves. The larger plates were hung on the walls like pictures. Among them were several examples of Old Imari ware, which has long been highly valued in Europe: one or two examples are always found in great houses. One even sees on display pieces which have been broken and repaired. Indeed, it seemed to us that works of the highest quality were all in Europe and would be hard to find in Japan.

The part of the house where the guest bedrooms were had portraits of earlier dukes and of foreign monarchs. Underfoot were brilliantly patterned carpets. The chairs were upholstered in brocade, and there were ornately carved tables. Wherever we went, there was nothing which failed to please the eye. We were told that even the queen of England's palaces would have to yield pride of place to this house. From here we went to the billiard room and then to the chapel.

Below ground, barrels of beer and wine were stored in cellars. There were some fine wines over a hundred years old. As wine continues to ferment slightly with the passage of years and the flavour constantly improves, it is the Western custom to value old wines especially; the price of some reaches scores of dollars per bottle. The spigot on one of the beer barrels was opened to draw a glass for each of us. We then went to the kitchens. There were four kinds of ranges: coal-burning, gas-burning, charcoal-burning and wood-burning, the different fuels being used for cooking different foods. The most commonplace foods were cooked on the coal-fired range, mostly beef and mutton. A rotating mechanism was mounted on the range, and the meat was roasted by being thrust through with an iron spit and turned in front of the fire.

Lunch was served in one of the dining-rooms. The duke's whole family joined us, including his mother and wife, and entertained us very pleasantly. We then went out into the grounds and walked around the flower gardens. Along one of the walks was an avenue of statuary. One of the statues was of Napoleon I by a celebrated sculptor, which was heroic in appearance and very lifelike. We went through a green-house to the stables, where all the horses were sleek and glossy and there were several riding horses, all worth thousands of pounds. They were impeccably groomed from their manes to their hooves, which gleamed like gems;

their coats shone as if oiled. After touring the stables we emerged again into the gardens.

From near the top of the hill down to its foot, the trees had been cleared to make way for an artificial cascade. A flight of stone steps had been built, and the water descended it step by step, like the plates of a suit of Japanese armour. On the way it would suddenly leap and scatter like the beaded tassels on a dancer's silken parasol, then converge again to tumble to the next step in a little waterfall. It is customary in the West to employ water as a means of pleasant diversion. As the science of hydrology has developed, the people of the West have not only exploited all the benefits of water for everyday use but have employed it in different forms to beautify the parks and gardens of their cities. Fountains are everywhere, and one often sees water given various unusual forms, but we had not previously seen anything to surpass the waterfall in these gardens. At the bottom of the cascade the water disappeared, running away underground with a loud rushing noise. After flowing more than a hundred paces below ground, it emerged again as dozens of fountains in the pool in front of the house. The force of these fountains was something which even the fountains of the Crystal Palace could not match.

At the other end of the grounds was another garden. Here was a large glass conservatory stocked with a huge variety of tropical plants, including banana-trees, oil-palms, date-palms, bamboos and rubber-trees. There were several smaller hothouses filled with flowers – too many for us to look at one by one. As time was growing short, we returned to the house and there took our leave of the duke. He accompanied us to the door, where we got into our carriages and left.

October 31st. Cloudy.
At ten o'clock in the morning we went by carriage to Rodgers's cutlery works. The items manufactured at this works included all kinds of small steel articles for use at the dining-table, the writing-desk and the dressing-table, from table-knives, pocket-knives, tweezers, scissors and surgical instruments to button-hooks and nail-files. They also made gold-plated steel pens. This was the most-renowned cutlery firm in the city.

The Vickers iron and steel works was a huge factory, comparable with Cammell's. In one large workshop, big guns were cast. We were told that the steel ingots for the guns made at Armstrong's works in Newcastle were sent there after being cast at this works. Axles and cylinders were also cast here. There were in all 670 furnaces. On the day we were there we were shown the process of casting a nine-inch gun. Some 120 crucibles, each containing about sixty pounds of molten steel, were withdrawn from the furnaces and carried to the mould, into which the steel was immediately poured. The whole workshop glowed red and the workmen's sweat fell from their bodies like rain. The heat generated in the workshop was tremendous.

We then went to the townhall. The mayor and council and members of the chamber of commerce were gathered in the council chamber. After an address had been presented and replied to, we left.

After that we visited a factory manufacturing silver-plated ware, that of James Dixon and Company. For the white-metal goods made at this factory, 'Britannia metal' was used. 'Britannia metal' means 'British metal'. It is a white metal of very inferior quality made by alloying tin and antimony. Tin is a soft white metal; antimony is a hard white metal. When the two are alloyed, the resulting metal is hard. Articles of various kinds were made from this metal by beating it into the shape of the component parts in moulds and soldering the pieces together. It was sometimes cast in moulds, the articles then being decorated by chasing. The main part of the company's production was table-ware, from tablespoons, tea-spoons and carving-knives to candlesticks, meat dishes, teapots, flower vases, salt-cellars, oil containers and other items. Since these are household necessities they are bought in great quantities. Time was pressing, so we did not stay long.

At half past five we attended the Cutlers' Feast. This was a great gathering held in the town every year at this time. Since the Japanese ambassadors happened by a lucky chance to be in Sheffield on this occasion, they were invited as guests of honour. In all, 221 people were present. A master of ceremonies placed the guests in their seats in order of precedence. He seated the ambassadors, members of the local aristocracy and other notable gentlemen at the high table, which was elevated on a dais at the front of the room. On a slightly lower level were seven more rows of tables, at which were seated businessmen from leading companies. In a gallery at the rear of the room a group of musicians – men and women – had been engaged to play during the meal. Prominent ladies of the city were seated in another gallery to the left, watching the proceedings. It was the most magnificent meal we had had since America. A dozen speeches were made, including those given by the Master Cutler and the ambassador. Others replied to the toasts. We were told that many famous and distinguished men were among those present. The banquet went on till midnight.

CHAPTER 37

# A Record of Staffordshire and Warwickshire

November 1st, 1872. Cloudy; a little rain.
At ten o'clock in the morning we left Mr. Wilson's house in Sheffield to catch a train at Midland Station. Mr. Wilson and his brother accompanied us to the station. From here we travelled across Derbyshire. The countryside was all flat, and after forty-four miles we arrived at Burton-on-Trent, a town in Staffordshire, where beer was brewed. We alighted here to visit one of the breweries.

The Allsopp family's brewery was a very large concern, occupying almost the whole town. They had arranged for a meal to be prepared and, after meeting us at the station, entertained us to lunch in the board-room. After lunch we went to the brewery, which occupied about fifty acres. It was like a small town in itself: the site was criss-crossed by twelve miles of roadway. Since we could not have visited the whole brewery on foot in half a day, a railway wagon had been carpeted and provided with seats to convey us along tracks inside the premises. After a quick tour of the different parts of the brewery, we were shown, briefly, the brewing process. Below ground level were the cellars, where there were a total of 10,000 casks. We were told that these would all be dispatched in the coming month, and that some of them would even find their way to Japan.

As the people of a country become more enlightened and more prosperous, so they develop a taste for ever finer beverages. There is a theory, therefore, that the volume of beverages consumed indicates the level of civilisation of a country, a view which would seem to be supported by the fact that at present the consumption of beverages in Europe is indeed extremely high. There are various kinds of beverages: tea, coffee, beer, wine and spirits. These, together with tobacco and sugar, are called 'trade goods' and are all heavily taxed. The fact that the consumption of beverages increases as the wealth and the level of enlightenment of a country rise is a natural law. Fermented beverages made from grain are called 'beer'; those made from the juices of fruits are called 'wine'. Both are drunk as everyday accompaniments to meals. When these are subjected to distillation, they are converted to ardent spirits. These are drunk only in small quantities before meals except by those with a constant craving for alcohol. It is only on excessive drinking, and on the habitual drinking of spirits, that Westerners place restrictions. Japanese *sake* is also a kind of beer. However, *sake* does not as yet appeal to the palates of Westerners. The appreciation of beverages is something which advances with civilisation, and it is a universal human propensity to appreciate exotic flavours. If in the future, therefore, we refine our methods of brewing *sake* and are able to build up a trade in it, there is no doubt that it could become one of our export goods. Soya sauce is a brewed condiment. The Dutch sent it to Europe and it is appreciated in the Germanic lands. The British also enjoy it. *Mirin*, which is a kind of sweet *sake*, is also beneficial as a flavouring for food. The art of brewing is thus one in which Japan is highly skilled. The European countries which brew the largest amounts of beer are Britain, Germany, Austria and Belgium. All of them devote much effort to this industry, and the size of this brewery alone is enough to demonstrate how huge an industry it is. Therefore, we ought to examine carefully the particulars of the consumption of beverages and give attention to Japan's exports of such products.

We caught a train at half past five and arrived at the station in Birmingham at ten past seven. The mayor was at the station to welcome us. We took rooms at the Queen's Hotel.

November 2nd. Fine in the morning; rain in the evening.
We caught a train at half past nine to travel fifteen miles to Coventry, the county town of Warwickshire. We went first to Cash's textile works. The only textiles manufactured here were laces made from cotton yarn, which are used for decorative purposes. Lace woven in narrow bands is sewn as a form of ornamentation onto the collars, cuffs and pleats of ladies' dresses in the same way as braid.

We then went to Mr. Stevens's silk-weaving factory. This factory wove narrow figured silks, some for use as ribbons for ladies' hats and some cut into short lengths for use as book-marks, on stationery for formal occasions, on envelopes for love letters, and on advertising material for companies. It also made fine silk ribbons for binding books and for tying parcels. Mr. Stevens was good enough to tell the ambassadors that it was a cause of considerable chagrin and much regret to him that while the fine quality of Japanese silk was unrivalled, it was so crudely spun that it could not be used in the best figured silks. It was hoped that efforts would be made to improve the quality of Japanese yarn. If this were done, not only would his company derive greater profits from the yarn, but the profits to Japan would also be considerable.

We were guests at a lunch in the townhall given by the citizens. More than forty people sat down to the meal, after which there were the usual speeches. Coventry is an ancient and famous city. Parts of this townhall had been built more than six hundred years ago, and in it was a chair in which King Henry VI had sat. The mayor greeted us on this day in civic state, accompanied by attendants bearing maces. This was a mark of great respect and the first time that we had seen these ancient usages. The attendants walked behind the mayor carrying the two maces, which were large and cylindrical, with silver-plated surfaces covered with carving. The mace-bearers wore long, sweeping robes of an antique style which were most picturesque. These robes would correspond, perhaps, to the coats bearing their lord's crest worn by the samurai. Paraphernalia such as the judges' robes and wigs which we had seen at the High Court in Edinburgh and the mayoral maces we saw here all appeared to be ceremonial objects handed down from the past. East and West alike have various insignia used in ceremonies. Westerners daily strive after new things but also keep ancient things constantly in mind and love what is old, preserving it and not discarding it. This is truly a civilised usage.

Afterwards we went by train to Warwick, which is also in Warwickshire. This is another famous city, originally the property of the earls of Warwick, whose imposing castle still survives. There are many old houses in the town and the smaller among them have low eaves, thatched roofs and wooden frames. Many had begun to lean and had been buttressed with brick. There are also many famous old churches.

We were invited to dine at the house of the mayor. His whole family joined us. The mayor, who was a doctor, was very wealthy. A room on the top floor of the house was filled with a collection of animal specimens, minerals and ancient artefacts. After dinner, the little daughter of the house urged us to inspect this museum. Her invitation was so warm that we went upstairs to look. In the West it is not only those who are professionally engaged in scientific work who carry out practical research: every man of wealth and education collects objects of interest and ancient artefacts in this way for the purpose of preserving and explicating them. House after house contains collections of such things as the products of different places, or sometimes stamps or foreign coins, which on social occasions the owners invite their guests to inspect. The fact that even a child pursued such diversions rather than playing with toys must be acknowledged to be the influence of civilisation.

It rained very heavily during the evening. We left the mayor's house in mid-evening and returned by train to Birmingham and our hotel.

CHAPTER 38

# *A Record of Birmingham*

November 3rd, 1872. Cloudy.
Today being Sunday, we rested. Birmingham has become the fifth-largest city in the country. It is known throughout Britain for its multitude of factories. There are iron-founders, goldsmiths, silversmiths, coppersmiths, glass-founders and a hundred more, but as we had already had the opportunity to make detailed inspections of factories of all kinds, we passed over most of them and there were a great many places which we did not see.

November 4th. Cloudy; rain in the evening.
We went to the Chance Brothers' works, where glass apparatuses for lighthouses were manufactured. In the shop where the lighthouse lenses were assembled, Mr. Chance himself explained the principle behind the operation, but his explanation went so deeply into the science of optics that even the interpreters could barely understand it.

In Japan, the science of chemistry had its origins in the practice of medicine. As a result, the object of chemistry has been wrongly understood by people in general to be the careful mixing of medicinal compounds in small quantities. This has been a great obstacle to the progress of industry. The Japanese people have experience of, and benefit personally from, one small corner of the science of chemistry, but none knows anything about the foundations on which it rests. The importance of chemistry to industrial progress is like that of water to a man dying of thirst. In particular, several basic substances produced by chemical processes are in great demand in the manufacture of a wide range of products. The most important of them are five in number: first, sulphuric acid; second, soda; third, chloride of lime; fourth, acetic acid; and fifth, nitric acid. These are manufactured on a huge scale in Britain so as to be available in large quantities at low prices. This should enable the reader to see how essential chemistry is to manufacturing in general, and that it is not confined merely to the dispensing of medicines.

We then visited Messrs. Hinks and Wells's steel pen factory. This company obtains rolled sheet steel from Sheffield, tempers it and manufactures pen-nibs with it. These are small objects, but a great deal of technological ingenuity is devoted to their manufacture.

First, the steel sheet is rolled to remove the scale. It is not at this point subjected to heat. Next, it is cut into long strips by means of cutters mounted on a pair of rollers. The pen-nib blanks are then punched from these strips by machine, which are of two types, one worked by hand and the other by steam. The faster of them can stamp out 141 blanks a minute. The blanks are sorted and any imperfect ones discarded, and holes are punched individually in the sound ones by a machine. Next, the point of each nib is slit in a press. The nib is then passed through another press which imparts to it a semi-cylindrical shape, after which the maker's name is stamped on it. There is a separate room for each process. The work is done by women.

When these processes have been completed, the nibs have attained their final form and they are collected and put into a vessel resembling a *sake* flask. Oil is poured into this and it is put into a kiln to be heated to a high temperature. As the oil evaporates the steel is hardened. The nibs are again put into a revolving metal cylinder over a stove providing a low heat to further toughen them and impart the desired elasticity. Finally, they are put into a box and a molten substance called 'naphtha', which resembles lacquer, is poured over them, the purpose being to cover the surface of the nibs with a brown coating. This is the final process. We were told that during the manufacturing process the nibs pass through a total of forty machines. We omitted to ask what kind of oil was poured into the container when the nibs were heated and toughened. It was our impression that the technique of imparting elasticity to the nib was the real secret of this manufacturing process. In every factory there were one or two important secrets in the processes we observed which were not shown to us. We asked about many things without receiving an answer. Sometimes, however, a process which was kept secret at one factory was shown to us quite openly at another.

November 5th. Cloudy.

At nine o'clock we went by carriage to Messrs. Cornforth's nail factory. The steel used for the nails was again obtained from Sheffield in the form of steel rods. This nail-making machine was simple but very ingenious. When a steel rod was fed into the front of the machine the mechanism inside cut and pressed it, and in one closing and opening action the nail was shaped and fell out from the other side. When we picked one up and examined it carefully, we found that a head had been formed at one end and it had been cut to a triangular point at the other. The machine produced about thirty nails a minute.

We also went to the factory of Elkington Brothers, gold- and silver-smiths. The white metal used at this factory was 'German silver', an alloy made by melting nickel, zinc and copper together. It is among the highest of the white metals in quality. Gold- and silver-plating, and the manu-facture of copper articles by the galvanic process, were also carried on here.

The firm had acquired numerous examples of Japanese copperware, inlaid work and cloisonné and had expended much effort in copying them. In the copper workshop there was a bronze Japanese charcoal brazier decorated with an engraved picture of Lady Murasaki Shikibu visiting Ishiyama Temple. Alongside it stood copies made with both gutta-percha moulds and plaster of Paris moulds. They were indistin-guishable from the genuine article. In the West, to make a copy of an object is proof that the original is greatly admired. The people in the firm wondered what sorts of techniques were used to make Japanese inlaid work. They said they had tried to copy it in the factory using all kinds of techniques, but without success. They would dearly have loved to learn the secret. Again, in the shop where they copied the cloisonné they placed a copy and an original side by side and challenged us to tell them apart. When we looked at them, it was obvious at a glance which was which, because a pair of phoenixes among paulownia leaves had been copied as though the artist were simply imitating an ordinary flower design. They were deeply disappointed that the resemblance was so poor. They then brought out a picture of Kakimoto Hitomaro and asked who and what he was. They were delighted when we were able to tell them that he was a famous poet of some twelve centuries ago. This information was written down on a label and attached to the picture.

We also went to the mint. This is a company operating under gov-ernment licence which contracts with both the British and foreign gov-ernments to strike various countries' coinages. The British coins are for the most part those used in Britain's overseas territories. The company manufactures, among other currencies, the mohur [the chief gold coin of British India] and the Hong Kong dollar. It also makes British shillings, but it is mainly contracted to produce copper coins.

November 6th. Cloudy.
At eight in the morning we left by train to travel twenty-five miles to Worcester. When we arrived at Shrub Hill Station we were met with

carriages by Mr. [Henry] Allsopp (the head of the brewery which we had visited in Burton-on-Trent) and driven four miles to Cotheridge Court. The house, that of a distinguished family, had beautifully laid-out gardens. Here the Worcestershire Hunt was meeting. It comprised sixty riders, led by a master. There were, in addition, four men dressed in scarlet coats and white breeches, whose job it was to find the quarry. These riders were going on a fox-hunt. A pack of more than fifty hounds was led to the spot where the chase was to start and then set off in pursuit of a fox, the members of the hunt following on horseback at a headlong gallop, jumping over any obstacles.

The point of the hunt was very like that of the Japanese sport of *inu-ou-mono* [dog-hunting]. Its fundamental object is to allow riders to practise horsemanship and to provide them with sport. It does not matter whether the fox is caught or not. The riders cross streams and jump over ditches, and the chase sometimes goes on for dozens of miles. To flush out the foxes, the exits from their earths are first stopped up with stones, then hounds are sent in to chase the foxes out. The whole field then gallops after the hounds. On this day, the hunt found one fox and pursued it for some distance, but in the end it escaped. We were told that sometimes a fox was indeed killed. The costumes and the chase were a marvellous spectacle.

Ladies also sometimes take part in the hunt. Today no ladies rode to hounds, but a dozen or so, including Mr. Allsopp's daughter, followed the hunt on horseback as spectators. Mr. Allsopp dearly loved hunting. He told us that he was sometimes in the hunting field four or five days a week.

When we left, we travelled four miles to the Royal Worcester Porcelain Works. This factory had been established ninety-five years before. Most of the china it made was for everyday use, and pieces of fine quality were few.

We then returned to our hotel in Birmingham, packed our bags and at five o'clock caught a train to travel north-west to Beeston Castle in Cheshire.

CHAPTER 39

# A Record of Cheshire

Beeston Castle is the name of a small railway station in the county of
Cheshire. Nearby are gently rolling hills, outliers of the Welsh mountains. Here are found the remains of a fort built in Roman times: on the
summit of a lofty crag are extensive remnants of stone footings and
ruined walls. This is Beeston Castle. Facing the crag on which these ruins
are is a ridge of folded hills, on one of which a new castle [Peckforton
Castle] has been built as a residence by Mr. [John] Tollemache. The
Tollemaches are an old and illustrious English family, a distinguished
house (although not a titled one) renowned throughout Cheshire. Mr.
Tollemache himself was a man of very high standing in the county. He
had been returned to Parliament at no fewer than six general elections in
succession, and had sat for thirty-one years. His reputation also stood
high in Parliament, where he was, we were told, renowned as an orator
whose like had not been seen in the history of the country. At the time of
our visit he was over seventy years of age [actually, sixty-six], but as
vigorous as a man in his fifties. It was because we had earlier received a
kind invitation from this gentleman that we had made a special detour to
come to stay at this splendid house. The sun had gone down while we
were still travelling and it was evening when we arrived, so, having been
greeted by the whole household, we were shown immediately to our
rooms, where we tidied our clothes before going down to the dining-
room to join the family for dinner. Mr. and Mrs. Tollemache and their
family all treated us most cordially, as though we were old friends.

November 7th, 1872. Fine.
At seven o'clock in the morning Mr. Tollemache's son and daughter led
us to the top of the hill, from where we could see in the distance both the
mountains of Wales and the city of Liverpool.
  After breakfast, at nine o'clock, Mr. Tollemache's carriages were
waiting for us. Mr. Tollemache himself took the reins of one of them, a

four-in-hand. Driving a four-in-hand is a skill which is only likely to be mastered by someone whose family keeps a stable of horses, so it is a branch of the art of handling horses which young gentlemen take a particular pride in. Today, accompanied by Mr. Tollemache's wife and daughter and one of his sons, we took a train from Beeston Castle Station to travel fifty-six miles eastwards to Stoke-on-Trent, arriving at half past eleven.

There were many different kinds of factories in and around Stoke, but we had the impression that those manufacturing earthenware and porcelain were particularly numerous. We saw tall kilns all around, a haze of black smoke and lines of chimneys advancing out into the open countryside.

Messrs. Minton's porcelain and earthenware works produces the most highly prized china in Britain, its reputation rivalling that of Paris. In the West, objects of porcelain are prized as the most exquisite of all domestic artefacts. The labour devoted to their production is highly skilled, and many pieces require months – sometimes half a year – to be completed. They are very much more expensive than glassware. This is the precise reverse of what is true in Japan. However, basins, jugs, cups and plates for everyday use are mostly of inferior quality. They are made by pressing the clay into moulds and are decorated by applying copperplate engravings or simple patterns, then firing them at a low heat. Pieces such as this are called 'faience'. They are cheap, but because they are perfectly regular in shape and decorated in bright colours, those who do not know much about pottery admire them extravagantly. The reason why Japanese and Chinese porcelain is valued in the West, even when it is not especially beautiful, is that it is extremely hard and fine, and both the shapes of the pieces and the decoration have a certain antique elegance about them.

Flower designs are printed onto objects for household use, such as table-ware, wash-basins and jugs, by the following method. First, pigment is spread onto an engraved copperplate and the design is printed onto a piece of paper. Once the pot has been glazed and fired, the paper is pasted onto its surface. The paper is then moistened with water and peeled off, leaving only the pigment on the surface of the pot, which is then put into an oven and baked. Pots decorated in this way are inferior goods and sundries, and this work is generally done by women. Valuable pieces are hand-painted by artists and go into the oven as many as five or six times. Of all the workers in this factory, the artists received the highest wages. Many of them were French.

We were shown copies which had been made of two Japanese flower vases: one with a carved dragon coiled around it and one decorated with a picture of cranes among pine, bamboo and plum. We were told that the most painstaking craftsmanship had been devoted to their execution and were asked for our opinion of them. This in itself is an indication of how highly regarded Japanese pottery is in the West.

In the West, Japanese pictures are held in higher esteem than Chinese pictures, their elegance and refinement being particularly admired. There were in this factory two scroll-paintings from Japan which had been used as specimens for the study of Japanese draughtsmanship. The Westerner's style of painting is imbued with the techniques of oil-painting, and the artists had fallen into the error of adding too much detail and had succumbed to the habit of rendering light and shade. Thus, although they had done their best to imitate Japanese technique, these ingrained habits could not be concealed. Similarly, when Japanese study Western painting techniques, they usually fail to get light and shade and perspective right.

We caught a train at three o'clock and arrived at Beeston Castle Station at five. The evening sun, screened by the autumn woods, was on the point of sinking behind the hills. People walking along the paths across the fields below the old Roman castle were so small as to look like figures in a painting. We strolled back to Mr. Tollemache's house and had dinner with the family. After dinner we played billiards and engaged in pleasant conversation, and it was after eleven o'clock when we went to bed.

November 8th. Thin cloud.
At nine o'clock in the morning we left in Mr. Tollemache's carriages, one driven by Mr. Tollemache himself, to catch a train to Northwich to visit a salt-mine, but when we arrived at the station the train had already left. We therefore returned to the carriages and drove off to the south. The horses were swift ones and we made good speed, covering the sixteen miles of country roads in less than two hours.

At twenty to twelve we reached West Northwich. All the houses along the main street had hung out flags and the church bells were being rung in welcome. Today the mayor and members of the company which owned the mine, having had word that our party was coming, had all gathered at the station to await us. They had been extremely disappointed when the train passed through without anyone getting off, and when we arrived by carriage everyone was astonished at the speed with which our horses had covered the ground.

The chairman of the mining company conducted us to the mine. A hundred years previously, when an exploratory shaft had been sunk here in the hope of finding coal, crystallised rock-salt had been found, so the venture had turned out to be very profitable after all. The mine was 360 feet deep. Soil impregnated with brine extended to a depth of 150 feet below the earth's surface. Underneath that was a thick layer of rock, and the rock-salt had been reached after drilling through this. The layer of rock-salt contained not a drop of moisture and had therefore retained its crystalline form well. The salt layer was 26 feet thick.

The entrance to the mine was huge. A cage had been installed to carry men up and down. Compared to the coal-mine at Newcastle, this mine was both dry and clean. We boarded the cage at the entrance to the mine. At the bottom of the shaft, which we reached after a descent of about two and a half minutes, broad galleries with dry, clean floors opened up before us. It was like entering a vast mansion built of salt. On this day, 70,000 candles had been lit to illuminate the interior. It was like walking through the streets of a city at night. Or, to put it another way, it was just like a festival day, when the streets are lined with lanterns. The lights inside the tunnels receded into the far distance, growing ever fainter, like an apparition of some great glittering city underground. We were told that this was only the second time since the opening of the mine that such a magnificent display had been put on.

The interior of the mine being dry, the crystals of salt were bright and clean. The temperature of the air remained at a constant 56°, summer and winter. Because the air had passed through the salt it was also good for the health. Air was circulated by means of a steam-driven pump. As we walked along the galleries, there was a gentle breeze which produced a pleasant sensation on the skin. The mine could best be described as a fairy grotto. On this day, the company's staff, men and women, had all come down the mine to decorate the interior so magnificently.

We were given lunch inside the mine itself. Over a hundred men and women were present, and after lunch there were speeches. We left at three o'clock.

November 9th. Fine.
After breakfast Mr. Tollemache showed us round his house. It was as large and as grand as Lord Blantyre's house in Scotland. Mr. Tollemache also had another house on a different estate. He told us that he spent most of his time there, leaving Peckforton Castle in the care of an agent. Peckforton Castle was modelled on a mediaeval castle. Its stone-built gateway, clad in ivy, gave it an appropriately ancient and melancholy appearance. It was a rambling house with lofty turrets and was built entirely of hard stone. A machine had been installed at the foot of the hill

to provide a water-supply to the castle at the top. This machine was a recent invention, and a very remarkable one. The mechanism used air pressure and the force of flowing water in opposition to cause the water to rise up a pipe to a higher point, where it spurted out vigorously.

We then went to Beeston Castle Station, where Mr. Tollemache's son and daughter, who had come this far to see us off, took their leave in a most cordial fashion. Mr. Tollemache himself came with us on the train to Chester, where we alighted to see the town.

There is an ancient church in the city [Chester Cathedral], built 772 years before. We went inside to inspect the architecture, and before leaving we signed the visitors' book. At the station we caught a fast mail-train, travelling at sixty miles an hour. We left at two in the afternoon and were back in London by dusk.

Since this day was both the prince of Wales's birthday and the day on which the new Lord Mayor took office, the city was illuminated by gas flares. The commotion throughout London was indescribable. We had spent several months touring the country and had visited many famous cities in turn, but when we came back to London we found its bustle and vigour extraordinary. On this day of celebration, in particular, it was like entering a nightless city.

# CHAPTER 40

# A Record of London, 4

November 15th, 1872. Cloudy; rain.

As we were travelling, we had been unable to celebrate Emperor Meiji's birthday last month, so this evening we held a celebratory dinner at our hotel. We invited Sir Harry Parkes, General Alexander and Mr. Stewart of the Oriental Bank. Japanese government officials and other Japanese of importance all attended. After dinner there were speeches.

November 20th. Fine.

At six o'clock in the evening we attended a dinner given by the London Goldsmith's Company. We returned to our hotel at half past ten.

November 25th. Cloudy in the morning; in the afternoon it began to rain.

At twenty to ten in the morning we left our hotel for Paddington Station, in the north of the city. We boarded a special train and departed at ten o'clock for the town of Reading, which we reached at eleven o'clock after a journey of thirty-five miles. It is known for the manufacture of biscuits and the production of seeds. There are many biscuit manufacturers in Britain, but it is recognised that the Reading firm leads the field.

The Reading factory belongs to the family firm of Huntley and Palmers. Thirty years ago, the Huntleys had been a local family in humble circumstances, whose entire wealth would not have amounted to much. They scraped a living baking biscuits, employing only three or four workers. Through this trade they made their fortune and eventually built a large factory and began to export to the whole world, until now they had become a noted family of great wealth. The number of people employed daily at the factory was between 2,200 and 2,300, and the amount paid out in wages each week was £1,700.

The factory, which occupied land on two sides of a river, comprised a number of three- and four-storeyed buildings packed along the length and breadth of the site as closely as the scales of a fish. A number of tall chimneys rose from among the buildings. The size of this factory was truly beyond anything we had expected. When we went inside it, the pounding of the steam-engines and the rumbling of the driving wheels and rollers were such that it was just like going round an ironworks. Machines were used to knead the dough and mix in the sugar.

The two basic ingredients of biscuits are flour and molasses, but various other ingredients may be included. Butter is added to produce a softer mixture. One kind of cake, which resembles the *castella* eaten in Japan, always has butter added. '*Castella*' is a Spanish [Portuguese] word. In Britain it is called 'sponge-cake'. Some mixtures have coconut added, some egg yolks, some lemon or orange. Cinnamon may be sprinkled in, or raisins or cherries added. Sometimes egg-white is added to the mixture before kneading. When ready, the dough is cut into appropriate shapes, which are dropped into boiling water, then retrieved and refreshed in cold water before being baked. The result is that the consistency of the biscuits is porous, like that of wheaten bread. All told, 120 varieties of biscuit and cake were made at this factory.

The firm of seedsmen [Sutton and Sons, Royal Berkshire Seed Establishment] stocked seeds of all kinds for the use of farmers and gardeners. It sold them throughout the world, and also provided education in methods of cultivation. People would buy seeds from the firm, sow them, and when they had harvested their crops of grain or vegetables, pick out the finest specimens and send them to the firm to be exhibited.

Such an exhibition was being held on the day of our visit. Among the produce sent from all over the country to be entered in this show and compete for pre-eminence were some sugar-beet which had yielded forty-six tons an acre and three artichokes which together weighed eighteen pounds. There were a great many other exhibits to rival these. There were even some potatoes grown by the queen and the prince and princess of Wales at Windsor Castle. Plaster of Paris facsimiles were made of the most remarkable specimens, to be kept in one of the upstairs rooms. Gold, silver and bronze cups and medals were displayed in the exhibition hall. After being examined, the exhibits were placed in classes, and the trophies were awarded as prizes to the exhibitors.

Agricultural shows, together with agricultural improvement societies, serve to stimulate this industry and encourage progress in it. These societies are very important and are to be found in all the countries of Europe. The mode of organisation adopted, however, differs according to the circumstances prevailing in each country. In Britain, all agricultural land is owned by the aristocracy or by wealthy families, and tenant farmers rent the land and employ labourers to do the work of cultivation. As a result, methods of promoting agriculture also fall within the purview of the aristocracy and the land-owning families. Societies for agricultural improvement are therefore extremely large, and the journals they publish are very highly valued. In France, on the other hand, land is, broadly speaking, evenly distributed among small landowners, so that small-scale local societies are established in each region. Agricultural exhibitions are arranged annually in each *département*, and shows are also held at which produce from a single *département* is exhibited. In Britain, too, there are county shows. The quality of the produce shown at such exhibitions is judged and prizes are awarded. We were told that all of these serve in no small way to advance the nation's interests.

December 2nd. Fine.

At nine o'clock in the morning, accompanied by Sir Harry Parkes and General Alexander, we travelled by train down the Thames to the gas-works at Beckton, a newly built town about a mile from Greenwich. London is so large that it burns 50,000,000 cubic feet of gas each day. It has more than forty gas companies, large and small, but this company is the largest of them all and it produces 16,000,000 cubic feet of gas a day. The works is on the river-bank, and coal is hoisted from barges to an elevated railway, on which it is transported to the four buildings in which the gas is manufactured. Hundreds of iron pipes leading from the sides of the furnaces convey the gas to another part of the works, where it is refrigerated, filtered and measured. The purified gas is then stored in a gas holder, from which it is distributed through pipes to the whole city.

We returned upriver by steamer to Greenwich. The Naval Hospital at Greenwich, being a former royal palace, was the property of, and used by grace and favour of, the monarch. The palace was turned into a naval hospital in the reign of King William III and Queen Mary. It is very famous and comprises a long range of buildings, all constructed of white stone. Inside the hospital framed paintings of British naval victories and desperate sea fights hang on the walls. There are flags seized at the Battle of Canton, in China, and objects looted from various other places. The death of Admiral Nelson, struck down at the moment of victory over the French and Spanish fleets at the Battle of Trafalgar, is one of the British navy's glorious episodes, and the uniform coat and waistcoat which he was wearing at the time are displayed in a glass case. They still bear copious bloodstains.

December 5th. Fine.
At one o'clock in the afternoon we were received by Queen Victoria at
Windsor Castle.

December 9th. Cloudy; rain.
At seven o'clock in the morning we left by train for Sandringham, where
the prince of Wales entertained us to luncheon.

December 11th. Fine.
At nine o'clock in the morning we went to the Agricultural Hall, in the
City of London. All kinds of agricultural implements, large and small,
were exhibited here: hoes, ploughs, harrows, and machines for cutting hay,
reaping grain, threshing, and binding straw. There were too many to list.

December 15th. Rain.
As we were to leave for France very early the next morning, we invited Sir
Harry Parkes, General Alexander and Mr. Aston to dinner in order to
take our leave of them.

Britain is a land of commerce. The minds of its people are devoted as
one to world-wide trade. They therefore send their ships to sail the five
oceans and buy the natural produce of different lands to carry back to
their own country. There they exploit the power of iron and coal to turn
them into manufactured goods, which they export again to other countries for sale. This is how these thirty million souls earn their livelihoods.
Those in the countries of the West who wish to engage in industrial
production are obliged to come to the British market to seek the raw
materials for their manufactures. And those who are engaged in agriculture must send their harvests to sell on the British market. Thus, the
world's market is held in this one city, London, and as the world's
production and trade have grown ever larger in scale, this city's prosperity
has grown ever greater, until it has reached its present great state as a city
of almost three and a half million people. If we take into account temporary residents from the four quarters of the world – travellers coming
and going, ships arriving and departing – then more than four million
souls dwell in this small place. Their businesses and occupations are
multifarious. The buildings towering into the clouds, the chimneys filling
the sky with smoke, the noisy crush of carriages and carts, the throngs of
people coming and going – all make every part of London parched and
hot. By far the busiest area extends from the Port of London to the City
of London.

We have now, in this volume, set down briefly some glimpses of what we saw on our tour, but we have in fact recorded no more than one or two things out of every thousand. The main purpose of this volume is to give a true account of the wealth and power of Britain and the conditions of the lives of all classes of its people as we observed them during our tour, and to present this account to the Japanese people for their consideration. Since we have recorded in detail everything which came to our eyes and ears concerning the circumstances of the nobility, of the farmers and of those engaged in industry, and have at the same time given some description of the landscape and scenery, we may claim to have offered a glimpse of the country. But with regard to London, although we wanted to explain the state of its trade, we found that it was not possible to give a full account simply on the basis of what we had seen and heard. We must therefore lay down our pen at this point.

VOLUME III

*Continental Europe, 1*

CHAPTER 41

# A Survey of France

Situated in the heart of the most developed part of the continent, France is the focal point for all kinds of merchandise and the core of the glittering culture of Europe. Approximately square in shape, the country faces the Atlantic Ocean to the west and north, and is separated from England by a narrow sea channel.

Although France has an overall area of 209,426 square miles and a population of 38,192,094, the terms of settlement made in the spring of the previous year [1871, ending the Franco-Prussian War], following the defeat by Germany, provided for the cession of an area of about 3,800 square miles with 2,000,000 inhabitants around Metz and Strasbourg. This treaty was imposed against the will of the people there, and it remains to be decided where they are to settle hereafter.

France possesses a number of colonies, including Indochina in Asia, Algeria, Senegal and various islands in Africa, as well as Guiana and Guadeloupe in America. These territories extend over a total area of 351,000 square miles inhabited by 3,633,000 people. Algeria, in particular, is like an administrative extension of France, with an area of 150,000 square miles on the opposite coast of the Mediterranean. A constant flow of traffic crosses the intervening waters, and produce from tropical Algeria supplies the raw materials needed for manufacturing.

In France the rise of royal authority reached a height during the time of Cardinal Richelieu some 230 years ago and culminated in the autocratic rule of Louis XIV. However, while France continued to become increasingly culturally enlightened, the common people found their suppression unbearable and in 1789 an extremist movement rose in revolt, attacking Louis XVI and establishing a constitutional government. This overthrew the 'ancien régime' by abolishing the aristocracy and confiscating the ecclesiastical estates. Louis XVI himself was executed in 1793 and the entire country fell apart. Then there emerged a man of humble origins by the name of Napoleon Bonaparte. Riding the tide of events, he persuaded the republican government to take advantage of the spread of liberal ideas in Germany and use military force to crush the surrounding feudal states. Eventually he became so popular that in 1804 he assumed the title of 'Emperor of France', and for a short time his resplendent power extended over almost the whole continent of Europe.

Following the defeat of Napoleon in 1815, France reverted to a monarchy, which lasted for the next thirty-three years until, in 1848, there were more uprisings clamouring for popular rights, which sent waves of unrest across neighbouring lands. Subsequently, the Italian states, too, were unified, and Austria, where the vision of feudalism still persisted, made sweeping reforms in 1867 to introduce a constitutional system. With this second French revolution, France was indeed the moving force in shaping the fortunes of Europe as we see it today.

By temperament the French find it difficult to maintain a co-operative spirit for long, and the system of government has been changed six times over a period of eighty years. Although a popular government was again established last year, the public is divided among a number of factions – the monarchists, Bonapartists, republicans, and red republicans known as 'communards' – all of whom are obdurate so that conditions remain volatile and unsettled.

With the revolution of eighty years ago, the remaining feudal powers surviving from ancient times were finally broken, and the entire country was brought under the jurisdiction of a uniform administrative system. This divided the land into 89 *départements* (like provinces), 373 *arrondissements* (like counties), 941 *cantons* (like districts) and 37,548 *communes* (like municipalities).

When the system of *départements* was introduced, Napoleon I gathered together a number of scholars to make improvements to civil law, and the resulting provisions to protect people's property and maintain their legal rights have been extolled in other lands and used as a model for reform. Changing circumstances since then have resulted in a tendency to regulate these still further, with numerous embellishments added, particularly during the reign of Napoleon III. These provisions have served to make France the wealthiest and most populous country in Europe.

In France the number of people living in the cities amounts to no more than 40 per cent of the total population, and wealth is obtained from agriculture as well as industry and commerce. Apart from Paris, there are three particularly large metropolitan centres: Lyons, Marseilles and Bordeaux.

France has the mildest and most genial climate to be found anywhere in Europe. Nonetheless, there are regional variations, for the country stretches over more than eight degrees in latitude, with mountains, plains and valleys inland. Moreover, much of the coastline faces the open sea, exposing it to either frigid air from the north or searing winds from the south. It is difficult to describe the climate on the strength of a short visit, but during our Embassy's sojourn in Paris in the depths of winter the frequent falls of sleet and snow which we did experience promptly melted away, and it was never bitterly cold. Neither was the heat very intense when we later passed through Lyons and Marseilles at the height of summer, and it generally felt much like the climate in south-west Japan. In the south, though, the luxuriant growth of trees laden with ripening fruit bore testimony to a sustained period of hot weather.

France ranks foremost in Europe in manufacturing, as the technical ingenuity and refined elegance of its products closely accord with consumer tastes, which is why this country is invariably the source of the most fashionable items anywhere on the continent. The most beautiful of all these manufactures are the woven pictorial tapestries known as 'Gobelins' and Sèvres porcelain, both of which are subsidised by the government in order to preserve their techniques. Silk fabrics and artificial flowers made of patterned silk from Lyons are also renowned across the world for their beauty. The spinning of wool is the country's most profitable industry and vies for supremacy with British textiles. French cloth does not have the thickness of British products, but the designs are very fashionable. The cloth here equals the best in Europe, with 320,000,000 pounds of wool woven each year, and although this industry has lost some of its prestige through the cession of Alsace to Germany, it remains unrivalled in technique. The spinning of flax is concentrated mainly in the north-west of the country, and the lace of Calais also has a high reputation. Other delicate crafts are becoming ever more sophisticated as new techniques emerge in gold, silver and bronze metalwork, the cutting of gemstones, clocks (many of them decorative standing clocks), mirrors, cosmetics, perfumes and scientific instruments.

France rivals Italy in sculpture and oil-painting, and competes with Britain in large-scale engineering works such as steam-powered iron warships, cannon and rifles, and buildings and bridges. Whether on a large or small scale, the French are fully accomplished in their crafts and technology. While industry in Britain depends on machinery, in France it is balanced between human skills and machines. Accordingly, the French ridicule the British for lacking sensitivity in their fingertips and relying on generated power for all their crafts. While products made in Britain excel in durability, those in France are supreme in their delicacy, so that the two countries are constantly competing against each other. Moreover, the French disparage the crafts of Germany and dismiss their fondness for extravagant decoration as being unsophisticated. As craftsmen, the Italians may possess varied gifts and their artefacts are quite superb, but even these are surpassed in splendour and originality by the products of France. With a total of 10,960,000 men and women earning their livelihood from manufacturing, or 30 out of every 100 people in the entire population, France may indeed be called 'the hive of industry' in Europe.

As far as inland trade on the continent is concerned, France's thriving commerce has made it the greatest market-place in all Europe. Since 1858, in particular, its maritime trade from far-off shores has also increased tremendously although it is still not remotely comparable with that of Britain, as the small number of merchant ships serves to testify. Nevertheless, in terms of both inland and coastal trade with neighbouring countries, France indeed holds a central position as Europe's emporium for merchandise. Once goods are imported into Paris from all over Europe and America, their market value rises, which leads to higher profits. As a result, there is not a single well-known firm in any country which does not have a retail shop in Paris. In commercial dealings, the courteous conduct and polite speech of the French win them favour among customers and secure their patronage. The gorgeous array of goods and the skill in displaying merchandise, moreover, prove irresistible to passers-by, and there is a saying that a man from the country will squander his entire fortune just by walking past the shops in Paris.

Due to the efforts of Napoleon I, the people's rights under French civil law are set out most comprehensively. As a result, the principle of protecting property is now widespread, so that numbers of households have sizeable fortunes and private savings are on a scale exceeding that in any other country. There were claims that the wealth of Britain outstripped that of France four times over, but the British have since been astounded by the French achievement of paying off the war indemnity of $950,000,000, promised to Germany under the treaty of 1871, in less than two years. This financial burden resultéd, moreover, in only a marginal depreciation in the value of its paper currency, while profits from trade have not suffered at all and there have been no signs of economic depression.

The government may have been impoverished, but the people themselves are rich, and daily business has carried on as before. Thus, the French say that the wealth of a country does not lie in filling the government's coffers but rests in the people's assets. They say that even while the German government is taking and stockpiling French gold, the German people are all so poor that, once this wealth reaches them, it will promptly come flowing back into France. Therefore, the French regard the huge war indemnity delivered by the French government to Germany as nothing but a loan from the French people, which will be paid back in full within seven years. In its reserves of wealth and numbers of brilliant individuals, France may indeed be called the quintessential glory of Europe.

Physically, the French are not noticeably tall or stout, yet they are bold in spirit and have a vivacious nature and an animated style of speech. In temperament they are akin to the Japanese and excel in their ingenuity, but they are quite the opposite of the British and Germans in their tendency towards recklessness and their lack of diligence or perseverance. They have a keen eye for enterprise initially, but in the final analysis they are imprudent since they often transgress accepted rules of conduct and find self-restraint hard. When a general of military genius emerges to spur them on, they become so invincible that they cast ravenous eyes over the whole of Europe, but the moment this leadership slackens their sense of unity shatters beyond repair. Their bloody defeat at the hands of the Germans [in the Franco-Prussian War], too, was not the result of weakness on the part of the soldiers but was due to the inferiority of the generals. The Germans bear grudges against Denmark, Austria and France, but Denmark is too small and Austria too weak to be taken seriously, so it is their fear of France alone which makes them maintain such a state of vigilance. Both countries view each other with the utmost hostility, and all the French harbour a burning sense of indignation and never lose their thirst for revenge.

The weights and measures used in France were revised by Napoleon I in 1799 to follow the metric system of 'natural measurement'. This has won wide acclaim in Europe, and on April 22nd of the previous year Germany proclaimed that it would adopt the system as well, so now a number of countries covering the greater part of the continent all follow the French system.

# CHAPTER 42

# A Record of Paris, 1

December 16th, 1872. Fine.

At half past six in the morning we packed our bags and left the Buckingham Palace Hotel for Victoria Station at a quarter past seven. At this time of year the sun rises at eight o'clock, and on days when light cloud fills the morning sky the waning light of the moon can still be seen filtering through the haze at daybreak, while gaslights in the streets glow dimly in the gloom. This scene of sad city streets bereft of traffic was to be our parting image of London as we left to catch the train.

As usual, a train had been especially arranged for us by the British government, and General Alexander and Mr. Aston travelled with us as far as Dover to see us off. From Dover to the port of Calais, in France, is a distance of twenty-one miles, and although Britain is often misty and the sky overcast, on clear days the coast on the other side of the Channel can be seen. As soon as ships reach the open sea a thick mist may obscure the land and the waves can be high, for this strait is normally rough and it is a notoriously difficult crossing for navigators.

Today, however, the sea was calmer than usual. Our mail-boat was a most beautiful vessel, about two hundred feet in length. There were no cabins on the main deck but there were two or three large saloons on the deck below. These were divided by railings and had red carpets for the passengers' comfort. At twelve o'clock we arrived at Calais. The port had white stone walls rising to a great height and solidly built wharves. General Appert and [Commandant Charles Sulpice Jules] Chanoine had been dispatched by the French government to accompany us, and they came out to greet our party, together with Minister Plenipotentiary of Japan Sameshima [Naonobu]. On the quay a line of soldiers presented arms as we were conducted to an hotel next to the station.

Calais is the most northerly port in France and an important terminal for people travelling to and from Britain, so the railway station is bustling with activity. We were served lunch in the hotel here. Although Britain and France are separated by the narrowest of straits, it is quite extraordinary how very different their languages sound. Whereas the British talk in subdued tones, when the French speak their voices take on an impassioned note. The two languages have separate origins and are completely different; the food, too, suddenly changes in flavour. Although the peoples have had constant contact and have invaded each other's countries for thousands of years, they remain divided by this narrow stretch of water and maintain their own cultural traditions. This shows that, in defining a country's boundaries, the inhabitants' ancient customs are as inalterable as the natural frontiers of mountains and rivers.

At one o'clock we finished our lunch and boarded the train heading south. We reached the Gare de l'Est Station in Paris at six o'clock and rode by carriage through the city streets. Tall buildings with gleaming white walls rose on either side of boulevards which were paved with stone. These were lined with trees and lit by gaslight, and as the moon rose clear in the sky above, this celebrated city pleased the eye in all its elegance. Beautiful dresses and fine clothing were displayed in every shop, revellers crowded together in restaurants, and the Parisians had an air about them which, again, was quite a contrast to the mood in London. Before long we were driving along the Champs-Elysées, and soon our carriages drew up before a mansion in front of the Arc de Triomphe.

This mansion had originally been leased to the Turkish Legation, but with the Embassy's arrival the French government had loaned it to us as our diplomatic residence for the duration of our stay and had also engaged a steward to attend to all our needs. The house looks out upon the north-west side of the Arc de Triomphe, although the main entrance is in Rue de Presbourg. It has three floors and is built of white stone. The back of the house overlooks a circular garden with a fine view of the Champs-Elysées. All the furnishings and utensils were supplied by the French government, although the Embassy had to provide its own food and drink.

December 17th. Rain.
In Britain during the autumn and winter, the days were invariably shrouded in gloomy mist and half-veiled in darkness. Emerging from this weather to arrive in Paris, the sky seemed to stretch in a vast expanse above us. Moreover, as our lodgings were right in front of the grand intersection where the Arc de Triomphe stands, a site known in Paris for its imposing majesty, cloud and fog were swept even farther from our minds and our spirits lifted. Today there was some rain, which made it

unsuitable for any excursions, but even so the sky was not dark and we still had splendid views from the upper storeys of our mansion.

The Arc de Triomphe is French for 'Triumphal Arch'. The surviving arches in the city of Rome are so pure in style that they have inspired architectural principles and served as models for buildings which enhance the beauty of cities all over Europe. The Arc de Triomphe is one of them.

When the Prussian army besieged Paris two years previously, the soldiers were under orders not to fire on this arch and it received not so much as a single scratch throughout the siege. Afterwards, however, a revolt against the government flared up in the form of the Paris Commune and brought chaos to the city. When defending themselves, the communards used this arch as a platform for a battery of guns. They fired south-west in the direction of Versailles and Mont Valérien, so the government troops had no choice but to return fire to drive them out. During the fighting the south-west face was damaged, and when we were there it was in the process of being repaired.

In 1800 the population of the city was 550,000, but this rose to 720,000 over the next twenty years and reached 1,825,274 in 1870. It is the greatest metropolis on the continent of Europe, and no city in the world, with the exception of London, can compare with Paris in size. In terms of splendour it attains heights unequalled anywhere else on earth.

Rows of soaring white stone edifices have been built along the twelve wide new avenues which radiate in all directions from the focal point of the Arc de Triomphe. One of these is the Champs-Elysées, a grand boulevard more than 120 metres in width leading from beneath the central arch in a straight line as far as the Place de la Concorde and the gates of the Palais des Tuileries. Trees have been planted along both sides so that people can stroll beneath them and enjoy the refreshing shade of their leaves. At night, the gas-lamps shine like strings of pearls and light up the paving stones of the boulevard below, glowing dimly when the weather is overcast.

All the road surfaces in this area are covered with small stones embedded in the ground, with fine sand strewn on top, as white as though it has been washed. Paving stones have also been laid in the middle of the footpaths between the trees, although on closer inspection one finds that they are not of stone at all but are made with a new cementing technique. Gravel is heated with a kind of tar, which when cooled sets as hard as stone to form a seamless road surface. All the streets around here are paved in this way, and the wheels of the carriages pass silently. In London the clattering of carriage wheels was so deafening that the horses could not be heard at all. In the streets of Paris the noise of carriage wheels is muted, and all one hears is the sound of hooves.

Directly in the line of sight from the Arc de Triomphe to the Obelisk in the Place de la Concorde is the front gate of the Palais des Tuileries, which encloses a beautiful courtyard. Looking out from inside the palace is a scene so delightful as to defy description, with the Obelisk bisecting the Arc de Triomphe far off in the distance. Originally built by Catherine de Médicis in 1563, the Palais des Tuileries was extended during the reign of Henry IV and its beauty further enhanced under Louis XIV, since when rulers have made it their residence, right up to the time of Napoleon III. The main façade is thirty-three metres across and the sides of the building are three hundred metres long, but these were badly damaged during the Paris Commune uprising last year and are also in the process of being restored.

Immediately behind the Palais des Tuileries is the Palais du Louvre, which was built in the reign of Louis XIV and extended by Napoleon III so that the two palaces were joined together. The Louvre survived the recent fighting unscathed. Inside it, bequests by Napoleon I of famous paintings, ancient vessels, models and machines formed a veritable treasure-house. A towering edifice itself, it is a magnificent palace with a wonderful array of sculpture and paintings.

Wherever one goes in Paris there are bars, restaurants, and tea- and coffee-houses. Chairs are placed under shady trees and customers sit and drink at tables, enjoying the cool air in mid-summer and watching the moon on clear nights. Here and there are theatres and music halls, awash with the atmosphere conveyed in the saying, 'Song and dance all through the day and no time left for sorrow'.

The Seine is not as wide as the Thames in London, and the water is clear and fast-flowing. Twenty-eight bridges span the river: sixteen are built of stone; seven are suspension bridges; three are of stone reinforced with an iron framework; and the other two are in the surrounding countryside and are made of wood. On both sides of the river are embankments of stone similar in appearance to the paving stones used on the roads. Stone steps lead up from the river-bank like stairs inside a house, and these are used by people alighting from their boats. On some boats people earn a living by washing clothes in the river. In the middle reaches of the Seine, the river divides to embrace two islands before converging again. These islands are called the Ile Saint-Louis and the Ile de la Cité. There, the elegant and imposing façades of government buildings and churches rise skyward with rugged grandeur, floating like apparitions in the setting sun.

In London there were railway lines underneath the streets, roads at ground level and railway lines running over one's head, and people rush around on three different levels as they go about their daily business. Smoke from coal fires pervaded the sunlight, and even the rain, too, seemed black. This is not the case in Paris, however, for the citizens all live in the midst of parkland, and everywhere there are famous places for the public's recreation. Neither are the people in the streets in any hurry as they walk, and the fresh air around them contains little smoke since they burn fire-wood rather than coal. While London makes people diligent, Paris fills them with delight.

In all there are as many as seventy squares and parks in Paris. These include the Place de la Concorde next to the Jardins des Tuileries in the heart of the city. In the suburbs to the east is the Parc des Buttes-Chaumont, and in the north-west is the Bois de Boulogne, the largest park in Paris. On Sunday evenings the nobility all ride here in their carriages, which vie with one another in splendour while the horses compete in speed, and the passengers dressed in their finery present a dazzling show of urbane elegance. Inside the Bois de Boulogne one can behold the grandeur of Paris, as wheel-hubs clash together and horses and carriages take the strain. To look at these scenes is to see the truth in the saying that one succumbs to the food in London and to the clothes in Paris.

France is a Roman Catholic country and falls under the jurisdiction and protection of the pope. There are many magnificent churches in Paris as Catholic priests have collected money from the faithful to build colossal religious monuments at enormous cost, for the Church once possessed extraordinary wealth and power. The clergy exploited the innocence of the masses and earned the hatred of the people, but the riches accumulated in the process are reflected in the splendour of these churches. Wherever we went in Catholic countries we saw lofty towers piercing the heavens and vast cathedrals soaring above the city streets, and in the shops there were more figurines of Mary and pictures of the crucifixion than one could ever count. Protestantism is quite the opposite, for the churches are undecorated and devoid of all pictures or statues as these are held to infringe the Ten Commandments. On arriving in any city, therefore, it becomes immediately apparent from these differences whether the religion there is Protestant or Catholic.

On Sundays in Britain and America, the people shut their doors and attend church from morning till night, and when we visited a park in Manchester one Sunday, we saw only two or three people. In Paris, however, Sunday is the true holiday of the week, and every park is filled with the clatter of horses and carriages, and crowds of men and women gathered there to make music and dance or drink tea and wine. When we left America and went to Britain, the intensity of religious observance dropped a degree, but when we moved from Britain to France, it dropped one or two degrees more. Indeed, nowhere on the continent of Europe did we see anything to compare with the strength of religious practice in America and Britain.

Paris manufactures every product imaginable, and all these articles excel in the sophistication and delicacy of their craftsmanship. This city is the centre of European elegance and taste, and in aristocratic circles across the continent the language as well as the fashion and hair-styles of the ladies all emanate from here. From household goods to toys, gold, silver and bronze articles, jewellery, porcelain, watches, hats, buttons and decorations, everything is finely made and low in price.

Throughout Europe and wherever in the world one finds Europeans, Paris is revered as the pinnacle of urbane refinement. Even proud British ladies imitate the latest Parisian fashions, and in the vast country of Russia the French are looked upon as cosmopolitan gentlemen. France has always been held in respect throughout Europe, with Paris as the hub of civilisation.

During the reign of Louis XIV, all the German princes made their way to Paris, where they became besotted by the power and glory of the king of France and the beauty of the royal palaces and government buildings. They took as their model the French language, French etiquette and French customs, and introduced them into the government of their own lands, together with the principle of absolute royal power. They considered this an excellent strategy to free themselves from the constraints of representative assemblies and used this empty sham to suppress their subjects whenever there were disputes or matters of contention. As a result, German aristocrats no longer counted for anything unless they spoke French, wore French clothes and imitated French customs, and they sent their children to study in Paris, where they all became accustomed to French ways. Even rich, flourishing cities which had once produced eminent scholars declined and weakened, and as it became more profitable for commerce and industry to copy French innovations, their own native skills were discarded. In the end German products lost their value, and there was no choice but to ignore any feelings of shame and imitate French goods. They lost their desire to study and could no longer invent anything themselves; ultimately, they were putting goods on the market which they had copied from French products down to the last detail, even in the labels.

London, Paris and New York are known as the three great trading cities of the world, but each has its own distinct features. The aim of trade in America has always been different from that in Europe. In London the main objective is to import raw materials from around the world and process them using Britain's manufacturing prowess before exporting them again. Thus, London can be called the market-place for the world's raw materials. Paris, on the other hand, is the centre of arts and crafts in Europe and the source of fashion, so it can be called the market-place for the world's manufactured goods. For Japan in the future, it will be essential to pay attention to these features when opening up export markets in Europe and America. When a wealthy French merchant by the name of Shwartz met the ambassador, he told him that Japanese goods in Paris are handled only by merchants of a middling level. Merchants of a higher standing, he said, are not disinclined to join this trade, but many have given up the idea because prices are unstable, the volume of exports from Japan is insufficient and the shipments are irregular. Consequently, there are now more merchants in London dealing in Japanese goods than in Paris.

Another merchant who met the ambassador recommended that Japan should export more Japanese tree wax, which is in short supply in Europe. This wax is an essential ingredient in a number of manufacturing processes (such as for soap, candles and the finishing of silk cloth). Due to the low supply, manufacturers have been forced to stop using it, and now it is employed only for making wax matches in Paris. Saying this, he took some matches out of his pocket to show us (the same as the ones we see in Japan). Japanese tree wax, he told us, is an essential ingredient in producing these. When we were in Britain, too, we met manufacturers in London and Edinburgh who expressed hopes for the export of Japanese tree wax. They told us that in the West they use wax extracted from bone or coal, which is soft and sticky. Tree wax, however, is hard and better, but the amount supplied is low and fluctuates from year to year. Without the assurance of a regular quantity, they said it would be difficult for them to make any manufacturing plans, so they were hoping that some dependable solution could be arranged. It is this malady which is always to blame for the small quantity of raw materials exported from Japan.

Japanese artefacts are already appreciated on the Parisian market, and some of them are greatly prized, such as bronze vessels, cloisonné ware and porcelain, which are copied in French and English workshops. In each country there is a particular kind of beauty in the appearance of its pottery and the charm of its pictorial style, and it is this which we call 'art'. The main purpose in promoting technical skills is to foster innovations and advances which exhibit this beauty and achieve new heights of elegance and refinement. To copy other countries is to masquerade under the reputation of others and to yield to common taste. This is shameful (although it is a different matter to copy other countries if this is to show that one's own skill is a match for theirs). The most important concern for suppliers who employ these skills, however, is to ensure that their goods always cater to their customers' tastes. I heard that in Paris there is a place where cotton is woven for export to Japan. Samples of the crested designs which are so sought after by the Japanese have been collected and are catalogued according to preferences in different cities – some for Edo and others for Kyūshū and the Kinai region – and these are generally woven into cloth with double-sided stripes or patterns. This shows just how much attention is paid in the West to craftsmanship with a view to increasing demand and expanding trade.

CHAPTER 43

# A Record of Paris, 2

December 20th, 1872. Fine.
Today we went for a tour of the city. There are so many places to see in
Paris that it is difficult to enumerate them all, but there is one sight in
particular which visitors arriving for the first time marvel at. This is an
exhibition hall of oil-paintings known as the 'Panorama'. Located on the
western side of the Champs-Elysées near the Arc de Triomphe, it is a low,
circular construction set among superb multi-storey buildings. On paying
a fee of one franc and entering, we saw a street before us which resembled
one of the boulevards. When we looked more carefully, we noticed that this
was a battlefield, with projectiles flying in all directions, soldiers running
about, an old man with blood pouring from a wound in his forehead, and
weeping ladies and terrified housemaids making their escape on carts laden
with household goods. To our amazement, it was not until we noticed that
this was a depiction of the scene of the Prussian army's siege two years
previously that we realised it was actually one of the paintings on display.

December 22nd. Cloudy.
Today we were told by the British chargé d'affaires that a telegraph had
arrived informing us of the adoption of a new calendar in Japan and
reforms in dress regulations.

December 26th. Cloudy.
At two o'clock this afternoon Mr. Conches and Mr. Mallard, the officials
who had been charged with welcoming the Embassy, arrived to meet our
party, while Captain de Noailles appeared at the head of two platoons of
cavalry, together with carriages provided by the government. On our
journey we were protected from all possible danger by this escort of
mounted guards in front and behind, and travelling in stately procession
we arrived at the presidential residence [Palais de l'Elysée] for our audience with President Thiers.

Louis-Adolphe Thiers is a celebrated scholar of political science. In the spring of the previous year, not only had he negotiated peace with the Prussians and the withdrawal of their troops by arranging an indemnity, but he also rendered service to the nation in its hour of distress by suppressing the subsequent rebellion in Paris and convening the National Assembly at Versailles. Now the foremost concerns preoccupying this elder statesman were how to formulate a constitution and raise the enormous indemnity payments while avoiding recession and conserving the nation's vitality so as not to lose any opportunities for future growth. Although he is held in great esteem by scholars, in France there are numerous parties with differing views, and with the military in its present state of indignation he has no shortage of critics. Arriving at what was indeed France's hour of deepest misfortune, Mr. Thiers was now an old man of seventy-five years, short in stature, brimming with cordiality, and with a genial manner of speech.

January 1st, 1873. Cloudy.
To celebrate the arrival of the new year, we travelled to Versailles, a city of more than 100,000 people to the south-west of Paris, an hour's journey away by train. Here in all its stupendous scale and beauty is Louis XIV's palace, situated in an imposing location on a hill looking beyond the batteries of Mont Valérien towards Paris. During the Prussian siege the other year [1870–71], the king of Prussia established his headquarters at Versailles while the French government took refuge in the city of Bordeaux in the south-west. It was in this palace in January 1871 that all the princes of the German Confederation voiced their support in proclaiming King Wilhelm of Prussia the new Kaiser of Germany.

Once peace had been concluded and the Prussian forces had withdrawn, the current president, Mr. Thiers, was returned to power, a republican government was formed and there was some discussion on re-establishing the government in Paris. It was just at this time that the 'red republicans' (a volatile republican party known as the 'Commune') incited a rebellion in the city, and riots continued thereafter. The government in Bordeaux, far away in the south-west, had too weak a power base to direct the affairs of the country as a whole, so more than two years ago Mr. Thiers decided to set up France's ruling body in Versailles instead, using the Opera House here as the assembly chamber. Meanwhile, the disturbances caused in Paris by the red republicans continued for two months, and they directed their forces to the west of Paris with the intention of attacking the government in Versailles. The government retaliated by severing railway lines, blocking roads and shoring up its defences on Mont Valérien to keep the rebels at bay. It was Mr. Thiers's own plan to gather all the government troops for an ambush in which the rebel forces were subsequently annihilated.

January 2nd. Cloudy.
Today the ambassador went to the Ministry of Foreign Affairs to convey his new year felicitations, while the vice-ambassadors visited Notre-Dame with Mr. [Frederic] Marshall as their guide. Famed as the pre-eminent church in Paris, this magnificent cathedral on an island in the Seine has a façade with two tall towers. The sculpture and ornamentation on the external walls are the height of accomplishment and style, while the immense interior and exquisite decorative designs delight the visitor with a feast of colours. Although work on the tops of the towers is yet to be finished, it deserves to be called 'a structure of superlative beauty'.

January 6th. Fine.
In the afternoon we went by carriage to a large library [the Bibliothèque Nationale], situated on a street near the Palais-Royal. Here three million volumes are stored on five levels, arranged in different sections and shelves by reference numbers according to subject. The library is maintained with government tax revenue, and it does not charge any fees from those wishing to inspect books from its collection. The spacious hall inside has enough chairs and tables to seat four or five hundred people. Attendants deliver the books upon request, although it is forbidden to take them out of the library.

At the far end of the building was a corridor with books from various countries, including China, India, Burma, Arabia and Persia. There was also a shelf of Japanese books, one of which was a Christian (that is, Catholic) work translated in the Keichō era [1596–1615]. This was written in a popular and comprehensible style and consisted of several volumes. As such books have long been banned in Japan, none of us knew that these curious works even existed.

Ever since news of the great progress made by the West reached Japan, impetuous individuals have tripped over themselves in a headlong rush to throw out the old and bring in the new. These so-called innovations, however, are not always beneficial and may lead to the loss of many old ways which are actually worth preserving. How can this be called progress?

Manuscripts such as books and records are treasures which enable us to follow the rise and fall of a nation through the ages, and every effort must be made to collect and preserve old papers and discarded letters. Whenever we visited a library or museum in the West, we saw that even items from far-away countries in the East were collected and catalogued in a comprehensive way, no matter at what cost or effort. As a result, we were frequently shown astonishing rarities of which we were unaware, and it was often we who ended up listening to explanations of the subtlest details about our own country.

At the root of the march of progress in the West is a profound love of antiquity. Look, for example, at the grandeur of the Arc de Triomphe, which draws its inspiration from the ancient triumphal gates in Rome, or at the bridges spanning the Seine, which derive in shape and style from those crossing the Tiber. It is the accumulation of knowledge over hundreds and thousands of years which fosters the enlightenment of civilisation.

Afterwards we visited the Conservatoire [des Arts et Métiers], a permanent exhibition hall filled with all kinds of agricultural and manufacturing equipment. We found everything here, from the most complicated devices to the simplest and from the most minute to the largest. In one room, for example, there was a collection of hundreds of weighing scales, the finest of them calibrated to infinitesimal degrees. In a room filled with musical instruments there was one curious device. The figure of a lady less than a foot high and wearing a gorgeous dress was seated on a piano stool in an attractive pose. When a key was wound, she glanced gently to left and right and her hands struck the keys lightly to produce a melody. She looked so lifelike to us as we watched from the side that we could not bear it when the piece came to an end, so we wound the mechanism up two or three more times before moving on.

On the upper floor were the tools used in manufacturing textiles, ceramics and glass, including examples of the remarkable craftsmanship involved in weaving fine glass threads into brocade. While the Conservatoire may be said to fulfil the same function as the South Kensington Museum in London, it has a style all its own.

January 7th. Fine.
This afternoon we visited the Hôtel de la Monnaie, the national mint, situated on the south-west bank of the Seine. All the new coins currently in circulation in Japan are already represented here, and almost all the old currency is featured as well. In addition to the Western specie, it has the largest collection of coins from the East.

From there we went to the central *mont-de-piété*, the warehouse for pawned goods. In Paris the government operates a system of lending money to the poor in return for personal possessions. These items are collected at twenty different pawnshops around the city and brought here for safe-keeping. According to this system, a loan is made for a one-year term with an interest rate of 9 per cent payable by the redemption date. After that, as long as this sum is paid by the end of each year, the article may be held for decades. The amount of interest charged is reduced pro rata if early payment is made during the course of the year, and it is also possible to borrow money one day and redeem the article the next. If the interest charged has not been received by the end of the year, six months' notice will be given before the article is sold. If the sum received for the item exceeds the loan and the interest and handling charges, the surplus will be sent to the original owner.

France has extremely well-regulated arrangements in financial affairs and the relief of the poor. Just as there are merchants skilled at commerce, so numerous experts are emerging in the burgeoning field of economics who manage fiscal matters with great prudence and skill. The fact that the French have managed to raise the funds to pay Germany a reparation so vast that the public was in a state of dismay, without affecting the vitality of the domestic economy in the process, has astonished even the British. Chancellor [Otto von] Bismarck of Germany, too, has lamented this as the biggest strategic mistake of his career. At the time of the issue of the new government bonds there were so many people at home and abroad clamouring to buy them that they promptly sold out, to the disappointment of many who applied too late. It is truly astonishing how France manages to command such a high degree of credit in all countries.

National bonds also create a source of funds for the government. The resulting interest payments and reduced taxes generate greater wealth overall and lead in turn to higher tax receipts for the government every year. Interest on these bonds ranges from 3 to 4.5 per cent, and at present the rate for most of them is 3 per cent (which in itself is proof of the government's credit). This practice was introduced in 1854 during the reign of Napoleon III, and proved remarkably successful, and national bonds were subsequently issued on six different occasions. Since 1871 this type of bond has again been issued both at home and overseas to help meet France's reparation payments to Germany, and together with the funds from taxes and an increase in the issue of paper currency, a large portion of the indemnity has now been accounted for. Prior to the war, interest payments on national bonds amounted to $1,030,000,000, so this must have swollen to a much higher figure by now. As these payments are distributed to people all over the country, this arrangement is also to the national benefit, for it stimulates the growth of private fortunes and leads to higher levels of public spending, which automatically increases revenue without taxes having to be raised.

The warehouse for pawned goods is a four-storey stone building, divided into separate rooms for each category of article kept. At present there are 1,500,000 items here, and all of them are stored with reverential care. Items of gold and silver are put in individual cardboard boxes and wrapped in paper and sealed; the boxes are tied with string with a docket attached, and the numbers are recorded before they are placed side by side on shelves. Articles with a value of over two hundred francs are put inside locked cabinets. There are more goods in this category than in any other, but the rooms in which they are stored are not large since they do not require a lot of space. Items of clothing are also wrapped and packed inside large cardboard boxes and tied in the same way, while bulky objects are simply wrapped in paper. When an interest payment is made to extend the loan for another year, an additional docket is attached. There was one article with twenty such dockets: interest had been paid on it for the last two decades without it ever being reclaimed. Looking at the docket on a parasol resting against a post, we noticed that the price marked was about two-fifths of the market value.

At the entrance to the warehouse is an office where the items are accepted and loans given out. By the time we reached this to see the system in operation, three hundred articles had already come and gone, and hardly any customers were left. Only seven staff are assigned to this office. In one of the rooms sits a senior official who is chosen with care and commands a high wage. It is his task to inspect and fix a price on each article. He is assisted by four clerks. In the adjoining room are two clerks, one to keep records and the other to check the cash and make payments. In the wall dividing these two rooms is a hatch five or six inches square with wire netting above, which allows documents to be passed from one side to the other.

On the front wall of the first room at about head-height is a window with a counter, which is where people come to pledge their possessions. Today two people, both of them women, had come to pawn some articles. When the first lady arrived, she rang a bell on the counter, whereupon an assistant on the other side stood up, took a ticket with a number written on it and gave it to her when she produced and handed over a gold watch and chain. This was taken to the inspector, who first removed the chain and laid it on a pair of scales before announcing its weight. Next he held it up to the light and inspected it closely. Then he weighed the watch, examined both lids with great care and looked at the inner mechanism before deciding on a price and handing it back. As he announced a figure of 150 francs, the assistant rose to inform the lady, who accepted the valuation, and the item was labelled accordingly.

On being informed of the transaction a clerk recorded the agreed price on two dockets, passing one through the hatch to the adjoining room and enclosing the other inside the watch. When this was done, another clerk wrapped the watch in leather and placed it in a basket for storage. Once the lady had agreed to the value, she went into the second room and handed over her ticket. One clerk entered in a ledger the details of the docket which had just been passed through from next door, while the other recorded the reference number and the amount before delivering the cash. The second lady who came today produced a ring inlaid with diamonds. Once it had been weighed, the inspector held it up to the light and examined the jewels for a long time. Diamonds are most difficult to inspect as they are exceedingly expensive, and not only is there a wide range in quality but there are numerous imitations.

CHAPTER 44

# *A Record of Paris, 3*

January 9th, 1873. Fine.
Today Napoleon III died in England after suffering from bladder stones.

January 10th. Fine.
This afternoon we visited a cemetery (we forgot to ask its name), which occupies a forty-acre site on a low hill in the eastern outskirts of Paris [the Père-Lachaise Cemetery]. Inside it there is hardly any room to spare apart from a single wide road for carriages and lanes between the grave-plots. The graves of the poor are marked with wooden crosses painted either black or white, while the middle classes erect headstones and memorials for their dead. Wealthy people construct family vaults of stone about twenty square yards in size with rectangular niches like shelves to store the coffins.

Today there was a funeral for what seemed to be a family of lowly means. A single hearse appeared accompanied by relatives, all on foot, and the wooden coffin was lowered into a grave about six feet deep. To conclude the service, the priest looked down at the coffin and scattered a handful of earth on top. The party was mourning the loss of a young woman, and all eyes were filled with tears, but not one person gave voice to their grief. From our observation of both sexes in the West – from high to low and old to young, even to babes in arms – we found them to be rather placid in temperament. Among the infants in the parks, we have not heard a single one crying nor noticed any defying the adults in charge of them. Labourers let no cries of exertion escape their lips as they carry heavy loads on their backs. The lack of loud wailing at funerals must be rooted either in custom or in racial character.

During the rebellion two years ago, this cemetery had been occupied and used as a base by the communards, and a fierce clash took place here when government troops encircled it and attacked. More than three hundred men lost their lives among the graves, and blood flowed down the wide sloping road from a mountain of corpses. It makes people shudder when they hear of this incident, which was the last stand of the Paris Commune.

Afterwards we visited the park of Buttes-Chaumont, which is situated near the cemetery. There are factories all over this eastern side of Paris, but education in the area is rather inadequate. Recently, a scholar who plans to set up schooling facilities here said that even if he were to begin today, it would take at least eighty years for the common people of Paris to have equal educational opportunities.

During the rule of Napoleon III, production in Paris increased and industry flourished, and 800,000 francs of the profits accruing from this growth were used to build this park and provide a place of recreation for the workers. The poor are said to revere Napoleon III even now, for many of them benefited from his efforts to improve the lot of the middle classes and below.

As we wandered around Buttes-Chaumont and looked out from the top of the man-made hill across the streets of south-east Paris, plumes of black smoke from a forest of chimneys were rising above roofs laid with tiles resembling fish-scales. The smoke formed clouds, but these carried no rain and the sky was blue. The setting sun shining over the city's red roof-tiles and brick walls turned the evening haze a shade of yellow. As this is an industrial quarter, the people in the park were labourers who live and work in the area: people who eat potatoes and corn, wear grimy clothes and rough shoes, run about in the soot and smoke and live on wages received from factory-owners. Every Sunday, as the magnificent carriages run wheel-to-wheel in the Bois de Boulogne, in this park married couples stroll arm-in-arm and old people promenade side-by-side. The setting of the two parks may not be the same, but in colour and gaiety they are as one.

The inspirational figure behind this scene was Napoleon III, with his expertise in economics. In 1848 France experienced extraordinary scenes of agitation, and a doctrine on the right of workers to work was for-mulated. It claimed that the government had a duty to give incentives to and support workers and that it must devise methods to provide employment so everyone could make a living. When planning a com-mercial or industrial venture, the West shows great prudence, and factory-owners regard the protection of their work-force as something honourable. Accordingly, the government also has a responsibility to implement means to look after the welfare of factory workers and the lower classes. While this is linked with the country's wealth and honour, the main intention is to give each worker incentives and support.

The doctrine of labour rights does not claim that the government has an obligation to provide employment and a livelihood for every worker in accordance with his capabilities, but it does maintain that it is responsible for those who are unemployed. This, however, is an extremely foolhardy premise. It is proposed by affluent gentlemen ignorant of basic economics who exhort people to seek justice and who adhere single-mindedly to benevolent ideals. This stirs up unrest in society, teaches the common people indolence and leads to their dreams of impossible riches. The advanced countries of the West are not spared from this trend, and when this argument is presented passionately, it leads to unrest throughout the country. This malady has been the cause of many instances of internal upheaval in France.

Napoleon III was elected president at such a time, and during the following twenty-two years of his peaceful rule, manufacturing and commerce flourished. If we were to imagine what the view from Buttes-Chaumont, with its rows of red roofs and walls, used to look like, it must have been similar to the empty fields of Vincennes and Saint-Cloud. At that time the land here was inexpensive, and it was a rural scene of scattered homesteads, so it was just the sort of large area sought by Parisian manufacturers to develop.

In general, this system works in the following way. An unused area on the city outskirts where land is cheap is first chosen as suitable for the construction of a factory. Encouragement is given to firms or manufacturers hoping to win honour by helping their workers. Streets are laid out, with provision made for their maintenance and repair, and rows of low-cost houses are built to rent to the workers. In designing these houses, consideration is given to the residents' means and tastes. There are higher-range homes with cellars and medium-range ones without; some have two storeys and others one; so all the workers are accommodated according to their social status.

In addition to paying rent regularly, the workers will be encouraged to save a little of their wages each week or month until they have accumulated a large enough sum to buy the property several years later. When the site is first developed, the sight of the few houses beside newly laid roads may make one feel one is in the middle of undeveloped countryside. Nevertheless, gaslights are eventually placed along the roads to obviate the need to carry lanterns, water-pumps are installed, and the roads are paved so no one needs walk through mud when it rains. Parks are also provided for relaxation, the Church will build houses of worship for holy day services, and the employers will build schools for the education of the children. Bakers, butchers, restaurants, bathhouses, barbers, laundries, tailors, shops for table-ware and other household goods, and even libraries will appear and flourish. A few years later, the lives of people here will be pleasanter than being packed together in the densely populated heart of the city.

The experience of walking in the dust thrown up by carriages in the Bois de Boulogne is inferior to the pleasure of strolling through the park of Buttes-Chaumont. Thus, what was initially a cheap area will rise in value every year. The land-owners will automatically become richer, and by the time the residents themselves own their houses, what were once cheap tenements will command high rents and they will have become owners of valuable real estate. This is why there are vast profits to be made from the work-force by setting up quarters for labourers and offering them encouragement and help.

January 11th. Fine.

At ten o'clock in the morning we set out by carriage for the porcelain factory at Sèvres. The town lies beyond a hill to the south of Saint-Cloud. The famous porcelain factory here was established by the government, together with an adjoining school, and it produces the ceramic ware known as Sèvres, which is highly prized in Europe and America and recognised as the world's foremost porcelain.

The factory is an extremely large four-storey building. Inside are spacious hallways around the kilns, which soar upwards through the second and third floors, with chimneys protruding through the tiled roofs. The complex is surrounded by a high wall, with gardens and a front entrance like an aristocrat's mansion. There is a shop where the porcelain ware is arranged in rows and can be purchased. The manager and his assistants showed us around several rooms filled with displays of ceramics, many of them fine articles worth several thousand francs or even as much as ten thousand. Some of them looked as if oil-paintings had been glazed onto their surface. The pictures had a deep, limpid quality which was even more beautiful than the actual works themselves.

Chinese and Japanese ceramics are outstanding for the natural beauty of their porcelain, and these have already acquired a high reputation in spite of the fact that they lag far behind in technology. At this factory strenuous efforts are being made to reproduce the Chinese and Japanese styles. The preferred motifs are flower-and-bird designs and decorative floral patterns; figures of people or animals are avoided.

CHAPTER 45

# A Record of Paris, 4

January 15th, 1873. Light cloud.

Escorted by Commandant Chanoine, we left by train at ten o'clock this morning and travelled to Versailles, where we toured a military college called the Ecole Saint-Cyr. This was built as a school for girls by Madame de Maintenon during the reign of Louis XIV, but was later extended and converted into a military academy during the time of Napoleon I. Accordingly, there is a chapel in the college grounds with an altar and a crucifix, and the tomb of Madame de Maintenon herself is to one side. It is the only military college we ever saw furnished with a chapel.

At the college we visited a platform for fencing, where instruction was being given in the art of combat with swords. In the recent war with Prussia, whenever the two armies engaged at a distance, the French troops would always lose on account of their inferior cannon. And they also suffered defeat at close quarters because so few of them were proficient with their swords, which is perhaps why efforts are now being made to train them in this skill.

The invention of fire-arms revolutionised the art of deployment on the battlefield, and the rapid advances in iron manufacturing ever since have likewise transformed the use of infantry, artillery and cavalry. Faced with powerful enemies on their borders, European countries increasingly vie to improve their military preparedness.

The reputation of the French for their powerful army dates from the turn of the century, when Napoleon I first deployed troops in honeycomb formations in his Italian campaign. He organised his infantry to increase their firing range and rapidity, which allowed them to disable powerful enemy guns. Thereafter, other countries in Europe made improvements to their armaments and encouraged military training until they could face the French on equal terms. The honeycomb deployment, however, had the weakness that as soldiers rushed forward they became separated from their officers and would fall out of line and be unable to regroup. This has some bearing on the belief that, in spite of the bravery of their soldiers, the French lost the recent war due to their inferior commanders, while the Prussians won because of the methodical organisation of their officers. When the two armies engaged at close quarters, bayonets proved extremely effective. At the fierce battle of Metz there were countless casualties on both sides, and these weapons apparently accounted for the large numbers of Prussian soldiers killed. This is why sword training is now being emphasised in Europe, for it appears too soon to abandon combat at close quarters.

Next we went to see physical instruction at an assault course. There a tall platform had been constructed with three tall steps. The cadets climbed up and jumped down from the top before running back and climbing up again. They also demonstrated swinging on ropes across a distance of more than ten paces, as if across a river, as well as other skills such as climbing up ropes and vaulting over horses. On the parade-ground, new recruits were being drilled in the use of bayonets. They all wore blue coats with red breeches (what we call 'momohiki'), and were shouldering leather packs of supplies.

After this we went to the stables, which had rows of stalls. The horses were very healthy and strong. Raising horses is a skill highly developed among Western people, who excel above all in training racehorses. The stables here, however, were inferior to those on private estates. There were no less than a hundred horses, and each had been given a name, just as in Japan. In the first stable there was a training arena twenty metres across and as much as sixty metres in length. The floor was of packed earth and the ceiling was high. Although the structure was not beautiful, the training taking place inside was beyond anything we could imagine in Japan.

Two rows of cavalry cadets in white uniforms faced each other on horseback on opposite sides of the arena. The horses walked, trotted and cantered in turn, exchanging places before finishing with a dozen or so circuits. After that, three horses were led out. There were two wooden posts in the arena padded on top with soft leather, and between these a horse which had been trained to throw its rider was tethered. As each cadet mounted the horse, it would immediately try to shake him off, but the cadets had been taught to avoid falling by riding high in the saddle. Today not one of them was unseated. The other two horses were on long ropes held by grooms who made them run in circles around the arena. The cadets would take turns to run after one of the horses and perform various feats such as suddenly mounting, lying down on or across the horse's back, or dismounting and leaping on again from the front or from behind. Before leaving we toured the entire college, even inspecting the bedding in the cadets' dormitories.

On our way back we looked around the château of Versailles which, as was explained earlier, became the seat of government at the time of the Paris Commune. In olden times it was a hunting lodge used by the kings of France. The château sits atop slightly higher ground which rose before us as we emerged from Versailles Station on our arrival from Paris. From here we had a view down a wide boulevard stretching in a straight line for more than 1,000 yards, with trees on either side. At the end of the boulevard is a gate opening onto a large courtyard paved with what looked like whetstones. This rises in successively higher levels and is flanked by wings on either side. An equestrian statue of Louis XIV stands at the courtyard's highest point, with rows of statues of Richelieu, Louvois and other illustrious ministers and generals on both sides.

There are so many rooms inside the palace that two days would not suffice to see them all. The deceased king's bedroom is lent greater solemnity by the original furnishings, which are kept just as they were in his time. No effort has been spared in its decoration, with ornate sculptures and a dazzling array of gold and jewels. In the upper storey the walls of a wide corridor are adorned with paintings of French military exploits. An imposing flight of stone stairs leads to the floor below, where there are rows of statues representing generations of the royal family, their retainers, wise ministers, brave generals and erudite scholars.

January 16th. Light cloud.
This afternoon we went to see the city's sewers, one of the most awe-inspiring sights of Paris. The sewers run eight metres below the ground and constitute a network of large, medium-sized and small tunnels into which narrow pipes carry waste from the streets above. The medium-sized sewers are one and a half metres across and four feet deep, with walkways on both sides. The walls on both sides are coated with cement and curve upwards in a vaulted ceiling to form tunnels one and a half times a man's height. Pipes running along the ceilings carry clean water and telegraph cables throughout the network.

The sewage flows swiftly away through the large tunnels, which are eleven feet across and the same depth as the medium-sized ones. A workforce of 520 people continually clear away the sludge on the bottom to prevent the channels from becoming clogged. All the tunnels are equipped with machinery; in the small and medium-sized sewers there are vehicles with a board with holes in it across the front. When this is lowered to the bottom of a channel, the water gushes through the holes while the sludge is trapped behind the board, and two men use iron hooks to churn up the sewage, working back and forth to dislodge the sediment and allow it to flow away. In the large tunnels, the sludge is dislodged by boats constructed on much the same principle.

The walkways on either side of the sewers are paved in stone, with rails laid on them for hand-pulled trolleys. Today our party travelled in two such trolleys as we were taken first through some medium-sized tunnels and next through some small ones. After reaching a large main tunnel, we climbed into a boat which carried us about a hundred paces before it emerged into the open air. Although the sewage itself does not smell of excrement, with so much filth collected in one place the air was quite foul, making it difficult to remain inside the tunnels for long. When we emerged, our cheeks were drained of colour.

This sewage network was constructed at the instigation of Napoleon III in 1855 at a cost of 75,000,000 francs. Every day a total of 100,000,000 cubic metres of dirty water containing various kinds of waste from all over the city is collected in these drains. It flows to a village called Asnières seven miles outside the city, where it is used as fertiliser for the surrounding farmlands; the surplus waste runs into the Seine and flows away downstream.

January 17th. Fine.
At eleven o'clock in the morning we travelled by carriage to the western outskirts of Paris to see the Mont Valérien batteries, which dominate a prominent hilltop about two miles west of the Arc de Triomphe.

When Prussian troops laid siege to Paris the other year, some of the shells in the exchange of gunfire reached the full distance of nine thousand metres between Mont Valérien and the Prussian headquarters at Versailles. Although these batteries had little effect on that occasion, after peace was concluded and the French government moved to Versailles, they won distinction as the bastion of the government's defences during the subsequent Paris Commune. The Seine flows between this hill and the suburbs of Paris, and when the rebel forces crossed the river and reached a crossroads on the near bank, troops were dispatched from the fort to intercept them on their march to Versailles. Pointing to the site of the fierce engagement which ensued at the foot of the hill, the general in charge here related how his men had harassed the rebels that day.

On the north face of the fort were some cannon with new American gun-barrels with breech-loading mechanisms. These had been fitted on their arrival in France and are proving extremely effective.

It goes without saying that artillery complements the infantry, each employing its respective strengths to unleash a concerted attack on the enemy. We had supposed that the copper and bronze field guns used by the artillery in Western countries had already become obsolete and had been superseded by iron breech-loading weapons, but this was not the case. In Newcastle, Mr. Armstrong himself explained to us that Parliament had not yet granted permission for breech-loading mechanisms to be used on larger weapons, and here in the armoury at Mont Valérien we saw numerous copper and bronze cannon. (Afterwards, in Russia, we would see numbers of new small cannon cast in bronze.)

We were told that bronze cannon are as effective as iron ones in power and range, and are inferior only in terms of durability. Moreover, they are easy to cast, and three bronze cannon can be finished in the time it takes to produce just one of iron. With France's current need for rapid re-armament, these old cannon are now being re-cast in order to supply two-thirds of the artillery's fire-power with bronze cannon. The country's arsenals are also seeking to emulate Krupp's guns in Prussia by concentrating on the latest design and manufacture of iron cannon. This is perhaps why, after their recent military campaigns, the Prussians are more inclined to mend their ways and live in peace.

The barracks on Mont Valérien are extremely crude, consisting in the main of low wooden huts. The soldier's daily fare is also simple – vegetables boiled with meat and fat, served in tin-plate bowls and eaten with bread. There is also a large bakery here which not only provides bread for the soldiers in the fort but also supplies the civilian population in Paris.

Ever since our voyage to America we had been eating bread every day, but only here did we see it being made. Bread is the staple food of rich and poor alike, and there are numerous methods of baking it. From America and Britain to France and Germany, every country has its own specialities. In Britain and America it is customary for bread to be sliced and passed around at meal-times, and the bread we saw baked at the fort was of this type. At the tables of the wealthy in France, fist-sized white rolls five or six inches long are served, while in Germany the wealthy are served round buns like Japanese *manjū* buns, sprinkled with such ingredients as sesame seeds. These are both products of the highest quality (as are the breads in Russia, Sweden, Denmark and Austria).

In the fort today we saw some soldiers firing at targets a hundred metres away. Few shots hit the mark, and, newly drafted recruits that they were, they frequently closed their eyes as they fired or pointed their muzzles downwards, so altogether it was an unremarkable display. The unusual feature of the target mounds here is that deep trenches in front enable observers to lie concealed. When a bullet is fired, they raise their heads just a fraction above the rim and indicate with a flag which area of the target has been struck. It appeared to be quite dangerous but was actually perfectly safe.

January 18th. Cloudy.
At ten o'clock this morning we travelled by carriage to the eastern outskirts of the city to see the barracks at the château of Vincennes. It is the most strategically important stronghold on the eastern side of Paris, but the other year, when the Prussian army laid siege to the city, they did not attack Vincennes at all as they concentrated their fire on other positions on the hills to the west, which is why it is the one place to have survived completely unscathed.

Inside the château was an armoury holding 45,000 rifles and 5,000 or 6,000 pistols, together with some Remington rifles covertly purchased from America at the time of the war with Prussia. Numerous pieces of cannon are stored here, and we saw many examples superior to the ones at Mont Valérien.

In the course of diplomacy in Western countries, while ostensibly amity and justice are displayed, deceit and envy invariably reign beneath. Whenever some incident occurs, even a declaration of complete neutrality is intended only for show. Once, in the Senate in Washington, we heard a debate on the issue of compensation in the Shimonoseki affair [in 1864, the Chōshū domain had attacked foreign ships passing through the Straits of Shimonoseki, and reparations were being claimed]. The senator of one state enumerated instances of how, at the time of the American Civil War, the European powers had covertly incited the South and even plotted to tear the union apart. One example he gave was the suspicion still hanging over the British ship *Alabama*. Here at the château of Vincennes, we saw weapons purchased from America by the French to use in their war against the Prussians, so it is patently clear that no one can be trusted to remain neutral. At the Siege of Sebastopol in Russia, although France and Britain were allies, in reality the French occupied the middle ground, outwardly co-operating with the British while secretly aiding the Russians.

The scheming in Europe in orchestrating military campaigns is riddled with deceit. At present France, Germany, Russia and Austria have each introduced national conscription and deployed troops in force along every stretch of border to guard against possible attack. Meanwhile, smaller powers like Belgium, Holland, Denmark and Switzerland fortify their defences like hedgehogs with spines bristling on their backs. They adhere to international law and maintain the peace, but, even if equal in strength, they dare not relax their vigilance. Is this not why countries puff themselves up and vie with one another to develop wealth and power?

In the open space here a garrison of twelve thousand troops has been established in makeshift wooden huts. Some officers told us that if we wanted lunch we were welcome to eat with them. They demonstrated a heartening resilience of spirit and were delightful company. Coming from the lofty sculptured halls of Paris to sit in this rustic hut, it made one weep to think of how bitter defeat must have been for the French; yet without this to spur them on, how can they hope to preserve the France they cherish?

CHAPTER 46

# A Record of Paris, 5

January 19th, 1873. Cloudy; rain falling from evening and a strong wind. At nine o'clock this morning we travelled by train to visit the château of Fontainebleau. Along the way the landscape was entirely flat, and villagers were going about their tasks, tilling and sowing the fields. This area is said to have the richest soil in the whole of France, and the farming we have seen in the fields around Paris seems more intensive than in Britain. There were fields of wheat and plots with rows of vegetables being grown in ridges. The trees between the fields had had their branches cut for fire-wood and tall shoots were sprouting from their stumps. Willow-trees growing along the river-banks provide charcoal for the manufacture of gunpowder. In the fields the ploughs are drawn by oxen, and the vege-tables are covered with glass domes to protect them from the wind and trap the heat without blocking out the sunlight. The glass itself is made from sundry odds and ends and is tinged a faint green. Soil enriched with manure is used for fertiliser, and we did not see any liquid manure used.

The royal palace of Fontainebleau is an old building, originally built by François I on the plans of a master-craftsman, since when it has been enlarged and embellished by generations of French monarchs. Napoleon I was extremely fond of this château and often stayed here, and it was to Fontainebleau that he came to surrender his imperial title and take leave of his officers and men following his defeat at Waterloo. It is thus cele-brated for both its old and recent history, as well as for being an essential destination for those interested in scenic views.

The château stands in extensive grounds surrounded by an outer wall. Passing through the gate, we entered an enclosed garden with lawns and stone-paved roads. Flights of white stone steps led up to the entrance in a curious fashion, curving around to form two bows. Stained with rain and dew, the stone surfaces were streaked with black moss, which is the feature most admired by scholars.

Walking into the palace from these gloomy ancient surroundings, the rooms dazzled us with their glittering decoration. There were columns entirely covered with ornate carving, stone statues, and intricate moulding all over the beams, ceilings, pillars and walls. Each room was in a different style, with the colour and decoration changing from one room to the next, and even the corridors displayed great beauty. We visited numerous royal palaces both before and afterwards, but in colour and embellishment Fontainebleau may be said to reign supreme. Notable features included Napoleon I's reception room, the council chamber and his private bedroom. One room was decorated with precious bowls and dishes from other countries, and there was an ancient lacquer vessel from Japan as well. In the empress's bedroom, tapestries received as a wedding gift from some monarch hung on the walls, and the brocade and embroidered cushions had been preserved just as they were in her day. In her dressing-room, mirrors were fitted on all the walls and across the ceiling, creating the impression of being bathed in a pool of light. This room led directly to Napoleon's office, which contained the small desk at which he sat to write his letter of abdication.

This evening we took dinner in the hotel in front of the château before boarding our train. It was now pouring with rain, the trees tossed wildly in the raging storm, and from time to time we heard peals of thunder. Outside it was pitch-black, and the rain came lashing down in rope-like torrents, but such was the comfort of our train that we slept peacefully as we sped through the darkness. During all our travels in Europe, on no other occasion did we encounter such a heavy rainfall as this.

January 20th. Fine.

At eleven in the morning we rode by carriage to the college of architecture [Ecole des Ponts et Chaussées] and then to the college of mining [Ecole des Mines]. On our way back we looked at the Palais du Luxembourg.

The college of architecture stands on the west bank of the Seine. One can imagine the flourishing state of this college from the fact that the construction of bridges and canals ranks among the technical strengths of the French. It is a public institution which provides training in building structures such as bridges and railways, lock-gates, docks and lighthouses. In addition to paying the staff's wages, the government provides 400,000 francs of funding a year, while donations and rents from bequeathed lands also serve to meet the college's needs. Seventy-four students are enrolled here on orders from the government, together with sixty privately funded students. The publicly funded students are forbidden to change their field of study.

Nine lecturers are engaged to teach such subjects as mechanics, physical science, surveying, chemistry, geology, hydrology and mineralogy, each of them essential disciplines in construction. Today, these gentlemen were all turned out trimly in formal dress to escort our party, and they had the courteous bearing of true scholars.

Plans and models of structures built according to the college's prescriptions, such as bridges, lock-gates and lighthouses, are kept here together with diagrams of newly invented construction machinery. It is through the accumulation of such diverse objects and research into the principles of construction that impressive achievements are appearing every year in the field of engineering.

The college of mining is even grander in scale than the college of architecture and was also established by the government. Even the walls of the rooms were decorated with different patterns of rock strata, and on the second and third floors sixteen or seventeen large rooms were filled with collections of minerals, marine rocks and fossils, all displayed on shelves inside cabinets. There were no fewer than fifty or sixty thousand kinds of rock, and just glancing at them as we passed was exhausting. We saw numerous rock and mineral specimens both before and after this visit, but nowhere was there anything to compare with the range here.

At the front of the lecture hall was a map of France, which was so large that it was fitted with springs so that it unrolled when a cord was pulled. The map indicated with colour the results of geological surveys in every province and district of France, together with the agricultural produce of each kind of soil. Even though this is such a large country, everything became perfectly clear to us just by looking at this map. No other country in Europe has produced national maps with such intricate detail as this.

January 21st. Light cloud; rain in the afternoon.
We left by carriage at ten o'clock to visit the Banque de France, the country's national bank. When a deposit is placed here, the bank makes no undertaking to pay any interest since it offers security and spares people from worrying about the safety of their money. Two identical documents are first drawn up, the original handed to the owner and the duplicate retained as the deposit certificate. At the same time the owner receives another bond which can be divided into several smaller vouchers, with subdivisions of the total sum recorded on each voucher in accordance with his wishes. Once again there is an original and a duplicate,

which is kept here. Later, when the owner needs to conduct a transaction with a third party, he may tear off and hand over some of his vouchers representing part of the sum he has deposited. If the third party brings these vouchers to the bank, he can then collect the money. The sums recorded can also be converted into the currency of other countries.

The paper currency in circulation in France, that is, bank-notes, is manufactured inside this building, just as notes in Britain are produced at the Bank of England, and in both countries the bank holds the rights over paper money. The system created by the banks is most reliable, making the circulation of bank-notes extremely smooth, and in Britain they can even be worth more than specie.

British bank-notes are produced on white paper decorated with letters and patterns, and the sum, names and symbols are printed on the surface. Although the patterns appear extremely simple in design, they are difficult to reproduce as a number of ingenious devices are employed in the manufacture of the paper. The smallest note has a value of five pounds. Bank-notes in France are produced in much the same way as in other countries; they pass through dozens of machines so that the most delicate lettering and patterns are created. In this process the essential element is a design visible only because one part of the paper is thinner than the rest; it is as if the image of a lion has been printed on the face of the note. To achieve this, the depiction of a lion is engraved in fine detail on two iron plates, one concave and the other convex, which fit into each other. A note is placed over the concave plate and covered with a sheet of fine copper studded with tiny raised conical points on its surface, which press out indentations around the edges of the lion image. As a result, when the convex plate is pressed down on top, only the area of paper trapped between these points is stretched and becomes thinner. This device is indeed the height of precision.

There is also an office for expired notes. Securities, bonds and exchange bills which are no longer valid have two round holes punched in each edge, and they are brought here so that they can be counted before being torn up and discarded. In order to count the notes, each clerk has his own cubicle with a locked wire-mesh door. From here we made our way to the cashier's office.

Last of all, we were shown around the vaults, which were close to the street. After passing through one or two offices we came to a corridor with a locked iron door set in one of the walls. It was six feet high and not quite wide enough to admit two people at a time. On entering we came to another door, and after passing a total of three doors we reached a vault filled with silver ingots and piled high with sacks of silver coins. It was dark inside at first, but then the chamber was illuminated with lamplight. Another door opened onto a staircase leading to more floors above and below. We climbed upstairs to another vault containing silver coins and sacks of gold coins. Behind a further door gold ingots were stacked on shelves.

CHAPTER 47

# A Record of Paris, 6

January 21st (continued).

The Gobelin factory lies on the south bank of the river Seine. 'Gobelin' is the name given to a colourful patterned textile woven from woollen yarn which is similar to the figured brocade of Kyoto. Gobelin designs are copied from oil-paintings and look as if they themselves have been painted; from a distance of several yards one cannot tell that they have been woven. In their supreme beauty and intricate workmanship, these tapestries are the most exquisite of fabrics and command exceedingly high prices. Small pieces are framed as pictures and larger ones used as wall-hangings. In the grand houses of royalty and aristocrats, it is considered the height of luxury to hang Gobelins on the walls, and we often saw them in palaces in every country. Other nations have studied and imitated the techniques, but none can match the beauty of the tapestries made in France.

While the pictorial, patterning and weaving skills in this factory are all extremely refined, there is no deep secret behind the design principles, but the technique of dyeing the thread is of critical importance. Threads are steeped in dye for successively shorter periods until they absorb virtually no pigment at all, thus creating more than ten shades of the same colour, from the deepest to the lightest. When these threads are laid next to each other, the colour becomes progressively fainter. Without this process, it would be hard to create the effects of light and shade. The wealthy houses of Europe and America part with sums of $100,000 or $200,000 to purchase Gobelins. France excels in this particular art, but because Gobelins are so intricate and expensive, a private company could not hope to make a profit from their manufacture. Thus, the French government built this factory to preserve the art for the sake of national pride, and profit and loss varies from year to year. As society develops and industries yield higher profits, the manufacture of such artefacts may decrease and disappear. The French are to be applauded for the fact that, despite their country's prosperity, these skills are still being preserved.

Next we visited a factory which makes chocolate, another noted product of France. Chocolate is made from the beans of cacao trees, which grow in the tropics and are cultivated in abundance in such colonies as Martinique and Guadeloupe. The confections here are the best to be found and are wrapped in tin foil and decorated with a lithograph picture pasted on top. These sweets provide nourishment to the blood and soothe the nerves. There are a number of chocolate factories in France, but this one is the largest. One hundred and fifty workers are employed here, and there is a steam-engine of more than twenty horse-power. The fact that large factories distribute such tiny confectioneries all over Europe gives one an idea of the profusion of commodities circulating throughout the continent.

With the advance of European civilisation, standards of food, clothing and housing have all risen, and spending is increasing continuously. It is the Europeans who manufacture and consume the products, but the raw materials are all imported from the fertile lands of Asia, Africa, America and Australia. When some natural commodity is discovered and becomes sought after, it can only be procured in a few places at first and thus commands an exceptionally high price. This leads everyone to compete for a share in the profits, and in ten years or so production will expand and consumption increase so much that prices will fall steadily.

The foremost objective of trade should not be to provide limited quantities of expensive goods but to supply large amounts at low prices. The reason the British and the French promote production of commodities in their colonies is that it is extremely cheap there. This enables private companies to monopolise profits from both the cost price and the retail price, so that by the time the market value levels off they have made huge gains, and continuing returns are guaranteed even at the lowest selling price. This is why Britain and France restrict trade from their colonies and prevent commodities from being exported anywhere other than to their own lands.

January 22nd. Rain in the morning; fine in the afternoon.
This afternoon we travelled south by carriage for fifteen minutes to reach the Observatoire, that is, the Paris Observatory. Four officials showed us around inside. The telescope here is the same size as the one at Greenwich, in England, and altogether 106 new stars have been discovered here in the last thirty years.

The making of fine mirrors for astronomy, medicine and chemistry is always entrusted to Parisian craftsmen. France has great expertise in the fields of astronomy and meteorology, and in the precision sciences it is unsurpassed. The country has many great scholars of astronomy, who look upwards at the heavens, and scholars of geology and mineralogy, who look down into the earth. To pursue research which probes the heights of the heavens and plumbs the depths of the earth, fearing nothing except failure, is the most edifying quality of civilisation.

What distinction can be drawn between the relative merits of wisdom in the East and the West? It is diligence and sloth, respectively, which cause the rise and fall of civilisations. Men dwell in the air amid the skies, so knowledge of astronomy is vital, and they live off the fruits of the earth, so they must know geology. How can neglecting astronomy on the grounds that it is not as profitable as mineralogy be called civilised?

We then visited the Cour d'Assizes [in the Palais de Justice], the supreme court of justice in France. Situated on an island [Ile de la Cité] in the Seine, this building presents its concave-shaped façade to the street. At the front is a broad flight of stone steps leading to a chapel [Sainte-Chapelle]. Built during the heyday of the Roman Catholic Church to glorify the wealth and power of France, words cannot describe the splendour of the architecture, and the sculpture and colours throughout the chapel are magnificent. Its structure consists of intricately carved vaulted Roman arches (semi-circular arches supported by pillars), and the utmost care has been taken with the stained-glass windows. These depict the cruel punishments inflicted on criminals since ancient times. One picture shows a man being forced to carry a tree-trunk so thick that he is crushed under its weight. Others show condemned men being beheaded, roasted or burnt to death and hanged, drawn and quartered. These were created as warnings to those administering punishments to be conscientious in their duty. Using the main hall of a law-court as a chapel is common in Europe and America. Perhaps it derives from the custom of taking oaths before Heaven whenever judgement is passed on a case. This chapel is also where all the members of the National Assembly are sworn in once a year.

We made our way to the court-room, where the trial of a woman accused of killing her husband was in progress. Five magistrates sat in a line at the front, with the public prosecutor seated on the left. The witnesses, jury members and defence lawyers were seated in separate sections before the magistrates, while the offender was led in from the right by a police escort. The seating arrangements only differed slightly from those in an English court. The woman was English by birth but had been married to a Frenchman. In Europe, there are many instances of a wife murdering her husband so that she can claim his fortune and marry another man. These are thus quite different from such cases in Japan, which are the result of adulterous lust.

In criminal trials in the West, barristers speak on the defendant's behalf to ensure that no false evidence is given. No mistaken accusations can be made as there is a jury which listens and adjudicates, and, after being given permission, arrives at a verdict. Witnesses all have to swear an oath to tell the truth, so it is difficult for them to exaggerate and show prejudice in their testimony. As several magistrates are always present, there is no fear of the hearing being biased. This may be regarded as a comprehensive system, but difficulties would arise if one tried to introduce it into Japan. In our country no one is sufficiently familiar with the law to appear in court as a qualified lawyer. If a jury were nominated, all the members would be intimidated by those in authority and would merely acquiesce to whatever they said. Even if outspoken people were selected, they would have no knowledge of the law and would create endless complications with moralistic arguments, constantly quarrelling among themselves and wasting their breath on irrelevancies. As regards the witnesses, none would speak the truth, for if the punishment were light, they would only earn the animosity of those concerned, but if it were severe, they would secure everlasting resentment in the land of the dead.

Just as we Japanese have the Five Cardinal Moral Principles, people in the West have the Ten Commandments, and one of these holds that a man shall not bear false witness. Thus, to step before a magistrate and swear to tell the truth is to obey one of the commandments, which everyone respects as this custom has been practised for two thousand years. In Japan, however, those who speak eloquently on matters of principle may gain the public's admiration, but since it is not considered a virtue to reveal other people's affairs, the disclosure of information is regarded with distaste. This attitude is the prevalent one, and it is often considered a duty and point of principle to conceal a crime, so who will dare to speak out? This is one of numerous examples in which customs in the East and West are diametrically opposed. The introduction of Western laws and regulations to the East would frequently be like trying to fit a square peg in a round hole.

# CHAPTER 48

# A Record of Paris, 7

January 23rd, 1873. Fine.

At eleven o'clock in the morning we went by carriage to the Christofle gold, silver, and bronzeware factory. Situated in a street near the Conservatoire, it is marked by a large bronze statue which was cast in these works. The factory has an unrivalled reputation on the continent of Europe and even bears comparison with the Elkington works in Birmingham.

This factory makes all kinds of household goods with such metals as silver, copper, nickel and brass, and uses galvanising devices to coat surfaces with gold and silver. It also produces bayonets. The bayonets in France are unlike those produced in Britain and America and different, too, from German ones. All countries compete in their industries, and rather than shamefully stooping to use a rival's goods they always turn to domestic products to supply their needs. The free peoples of Europe nurture their spirit of independence, which fills them with a righteous sense of pride.

In the record of Birmingham we saw the reputation which Japanese damascene and cloisonné work enjoys in the West, and these are frequently imitated in Europe. Inside the factory items of cloisonné enamel from China and Japan are displayed to serve as samples. Our hosts complimented the Japanese ware as being even more beautiful than the Chinese. (In our country we praise the cloisonné enamel of China as it was a technique introduced from there, and the Chinese ware thus commands much higher prices than our own, whereas in the West this evaluation is reversed.) With regard to damascene work, from a Japanese perspective the imitations made in France seem even more beautiful than the genuine articles.

The school for the deaf is located south-west of the Palais de Justice. It was built in 1734 by the Portuguese-born Jacob Pereira, who pioneered research on the education of the deaf and travelled from country to country promoting such schools. As he had no children of his own, he devoted his life to helping deaf children around the world.

The school is in a large, five-storeyed building and has five hundred students. Deaf children from wealthy homes are sent here to be educated, and tuition costs one thousand francs a year; fees are waived for students from poor families. Lessons consist of sign language, with instruction in writing and dictation. Thereafter, the students are taught to chop wood and till the soil. They also learn how to cultivate trees and carve wood. There are separate areas for teaching different handicrafts, such as masonry, engraving printing-plates, book-binding, copying pictures and making artificial flowers. The students are paid wages, half of which goes to the government and the other half they receive as a lump sum on leaving to help them set up on their own. They attend the school for a period of three years, and leave after their course when they reach the age of seventeen or eighteen.

January 25th. Fine.

At two o'clock this afternoon we visited the school for the blind, which is situated in a street near the tomb of Napoleon I [Les Invalides]. In France, it was long the custom to treat the blind with contempt, inviting them to banquets in order to subject them to pranks for the amusement of the guests. One Frenchman named Valentin Haüy, however, deplored this state of affairs and made exhaustive research to find a method of educating blind people. After several years he developed a system of raised letters, and with the help of a private company he built this school in 1784. The school preserves all the maps which were made using his technique to teach blind people about geography, with mountains, rivers and national boundaries moulded in relief. His achievements were highly praised by the people, and in 1791 his school was brought under government administration. It was temporarily amalgamated with the institute for the deaf, but not long after it separated again and became the school it is today.

Some students performed for us in the music room. The boys played instruments and the girls sang, and to us their clear, ethereal voices were extremely soothing. This quality is appreciated in the West as well, and blind people are said to have such a keen sense of hearing that it is as if Heaven has ordained that they should find their vocation in music.

People who are blind at birth may initially require a great deal of attention to be educated, but thereafter they are by no means inferior to anyone else in their studies. Statistics show that on average one person in every two thousand in France is blind.

February 10th. Cloudy.

This afternoon we went to visit the 'Queen Bee' firm's perfume factory [Maison Violet]. Located on the south-eastern outskirts of Paris (with a shop at 317 Rue St. Denis), this factory is conspicuous for the painted sign of a bee outside. The perfume and soap produced here in one year are said to cost up to two million francs.

About forty varieties of plant are used to make perfume. Once the aromatic oil is in liquid form, it is poured into large glass bottles which are stoppered and stored in a room on the top floor of the factory. Even though the bottles are tightly sealed, there is a fragrance in the air discernible on entering the room. Nothing compares with musk in the intensity of its scent, but it is so powerful that it is difficult to use in isolation and serves only as an ingredient for blending purposes. The most captivating fragrances come from the essence of flowers, with Indian flowers the most aromatic of all. Large quantities of raw materials for perfume are imported through the port of Marseilles.

The manufacture of soap in Europe dates to before the time of Christ, and it is used by everyone, whether rich or poor. There are different types of soap for washing clothes, bathing and medicinal purposes. With improvements in hygiene accompanying civilisation's progress, consumption has grown to such an extent that a country's level of development may be measured by the quantity of soap it produces. Although Japan is the most hygienic nation in the East, soap was never developed there, and while it is now being used, the manufacturing process is still unknown. Such disparities in one country's characteristics compared to another's are curious indeed.

Stored in the factory cellars was tallow made from beef and pork fat, together with ingredients for perfume-making and ten or so large barrels of alcohol. On the top floor of the building there were stocks of paper, including many rolls of *ganpi* [rice paper or thin paper made of *Wikstroemia ganpi*] paper, *usuha* [thin leaf] paper and Mino paper, all from Japan. We were told that up to fifty thousand francs' worth of paper is used each year.

Paper was originally introduced to Japan from Korea and is now used widely there, but its manufacture is unlike that of paper in China, and the paper is nothing like that in Europe. It is so fine in quality that some Japanese paper was awarded first prize at the recent exhibition in Paris, in spite of the fact that it was made with lacquer oil and was inferior even to ordinary paper used in Japan. Since then we have frequently heard Western people praising Japanese paper, and we learnt, for example, that in London there is even a merchant house for Japanese paper. We also heard that paper from *ganpi* bark was once made in the West, but so much bark was used that all the bushes were cut down and the species became extinct, which is why the *ganpi* paper of Japan has won such acclaim as a new source of supply of this type of paper.

In Japan, alas, we do not know the technique of bleaching early in the manufacturing process, and we lack the skill to reduce cloth to minute fibres. Moreover, despite its quality, our paper is too narrow to appeal to Europeans. The lack of sizeable exports is due to insufficient raw materials, and the paper does not command a high market-price. Some Western people believe that the *kōzo* (paper mulberry) bark used in Japan to make paper might be suitable as a raw material for textiles, and the French scholar of economics Professor [Maurice] Block, too, often suggested trying this to us. This fibre, however, becomes weak on exposure to water, and it would probably not be suitable for textiles.

February 13th. Cloudy.
This afternoon we went to the town of Saint-Cloud to visit a cartridge factory, which occupies a vast site on the west banks of the Seine. It employs 1,500 workers and uses 100-horsepower steam-engines to manufacture 131 varieties of '*patrons*' [cartridges]. These are charges wrapped in paper and packed in brass and copper tubes, which are shaped by feeding metal sheets through sets of rollers and cutting them to make all kinds of projectiles, from pistol and rifle bullets for military and hunting purposes to missiles, cannonballs, shells and grenades. They are not used exclusively by French soldiers but are sold all over the world. We were treated to a demonstration of a newly invented incendiary device which punched a hole through a sheet of iron and pierced a hundred or so sheets of paper before finally exploding.

February 16th. Cloudy in the morning; fine in the evening.
This evening we were entertained at a banquet hosted by President Thiers.

CHAPTER 49

# *A Survey of Belgium*

In the previous volumes we have described America as the land of European resettlement, Britain as the trading centre of the world and France as Europe's market-place. The extent of their world-wide commercial power is apparent just by looking at the accounts of these three countries with their large areas and populations. Japan is not far behind in terms of area, population and staple products, but in my view it is in our commercial weakness – born of the people's lack of vision or sense of unity and perseverance – that our strength clearly pales in comparison. Now that we have completed our tour of these three great countries, we will present a profile of two small countries, namely, Belgium and Holland. Their territory consists of unproductive wetlands; yet squeezed as they are among larger powers they manage to preserve their spirit of independence. If anything, their commercial power is superior, for they not only hold interests in Europe but exert an influence on world trade as well. This is due entirely to the diligence and co-operative character of the people. As we shall endeavour to describe, they possess features which we found more striking than anything in the three large powers. Although Belgium is one of the smallest independent countries on the continent, the density of its population is the highest in Europe, more even than that of Saxony in Germany.

The limited constitutional monarchy of this country is very different in style from that of other empires and monarchies, and it is, if anything, superior to any republic as far as its independence of spirit. Notwithstanding differences in politics, religion and custom, Belgium with its elected monarch, Switzerland with its republican government and Saxony with its erstwhile monarchy are the most flourishing and affluent states in Europe and have attained the highest levels of civilisation. Thus, the rise or fall of a country is not solely influenced by the political system, for politics is merely the embodiment of people's co-operative spirit. The saying, 'Government is the reflection of the people,' is well said indeed.

The constitution promulgated in the reign of Leopold I in 1831 includes representative government. The royal title is passed down through the line of legitimate male heirs from the ducal house of Saxe-Coburg. If there is no male heir, a successor will be elected by the parliament. When a king dies, the parliament will immediately assemble without needing a convocation order, and will govern the country in the name of the people in consultation with the executive until the oath of accession is formally concluded between the heir and the administration. If the successor is under eighteen years of age, a regent will be publicly elected to join him in attending the parliament and supervising legislation and government. The law also dictates that the successor may not assume office until he has made a pledge to protect the land of Belgium and the liberty of its people. The king is designated as a sacred figure, but it is the prime minister who is responsible for conducting all political affairs, and the king cannot enact any measure without it first being signed by the prime minister.

Belgium is a land of continuous plains. In the south-west there is a line of hills called the Ardennes, which slope gently north, and along the coast are sand-dunes fifty to sixty feet high, which save the land from being deluged with sea-water (as is also the case in Holland). Apart from this, the terrain consists entirely of broad, level fields; rolling hills may be visible on the distant skyline but never any mountains. Both the Meuse and Schelde rivers have embankments along their lower reaches to prevent flooding, and their waters are diverted into canals stretching in all directions. The longest of the canals from these two great rivers and their tributaries extends from the city of Bruges to Ghent, before flowing into the estuary of the Schelde. In all, there are some three hundred miles of canals. The roads are kept in an excellent state of repair.

The thriving state of railway construction ranks foremost among the countries of Europe. This is due to an abundance of iron and coal, as well as Belgium's location on a plain at the heart of a network of traffic arteries. There are three different approaches to railway construction in America and Europe. The first is for the government to build and operate the railways, the second is for private firms to do this, and the third is for the government to build the tracks and for private firms to operate them. The first approach predominates in Belgium, the second in Britain, France and the United States, and all three methods are used simultaneously in other countries. In Britain there has recently been a call for the government to buy up all the railways, but this has not yet been put into effect.

In the second approach, the disadvantage of entrusting the railways to a private enterprise is that if a line is potentially unprofitable, it will not agree to construct it without government subsidies. A company operating such a line will economise on labour and will have an insidious tendency to concentrate on the value of the company's shares rather than the long-term benefit of the whole country. Even if a private firm builds a railway, the government will have to buy the line up if the company sustains irrecoverable losses. On the other hand, should the firm make a large profit, it may become so rich that it will defy government directives about the railway. In America the power of the railway companies surpasses that of the government, and in Britain, too, their influence is so strong that it has led to abuse: they frequently raise passenger fares and assert their independence in various ways. Moreover, some of the capital of private firms is always in the form of foreign investment. (Huge sums spent on railways in America are received from British investors, and this is true in other countries as well.) In the event of war, a railway company will look only to its own profits without considering the needs of the government. Regarding this to be the greatest evil of all, the Belgian government's policy is to ensure that it retains absolute control of the railways along the country's lines of defence.

Belgium's wealth is founded on its efforts in farming and the extension of these to manufacturing. In spite of poor natural conditions, whatever advantages the land possesses have been utilised and the people have been encouraged to be industrious, so hardly any of the country's resources are left untapped. In recent years significant progress has been made in agriculture by employing sophisticated machinery. At the same time, due to this country's strategic location for commerce, the prices of home-made commodities have been steadily decreasing and now only the most astute farmers can return a profit. Half of the people in the country are engaged in agriculture, a quarter are in trade, manufacturing or mining, and the remainder comprise the non-productive sector of the population. As more and more people flock to the cities each year, the population in rural areas is gradually declining (this is true all over Europe). This is why Belgium, with its dense population, is the leader in the improvement of living standards.

The provinces of Antwerp, Brabant, the two Flanders, Limburg and Luxembourg all have plentiful supplies of water, and there are numerous water-mills for grinding both domestic and imported wheat. The flour produced is more than enough to meet Belgium's own needs, so the surplus is exported at a vast profit to France, Germany, Holland,

Denmark, Russia and America. Hops are cultivated since the fermentation of grain for beer is also a thriving concern. On one occasion during a
train journey to the city of Liège, we saw stacks of short wooden poles at
intervals in the fields, and when we asked about their purpose we were
told that they were used to support the hop plants.

Forestry regulations have recently come under increasing scrutiny in
Europe, even if in countries such as Britain the system of conservation has
not yet developed sufficiently for plantations of trees to be noticeable. In
our travels from France through Belgium and Holland we saw great
efforts being made to plant trees, and all the roads and boundaries
between fields were lined with broad-leaf trees whose branches are cut for
fire-wood. Few houses rely exclusively on coal for fuel, and it is only the
British and Americans who make it a habit to consume more coal than
necessary.

Extensive mineral deposits are found all over Belgium, including
abundant reserves of valuable iron and coal. In Belgium the most
flourishing industry lies in the ten or more iron-smelting works and
foundries in Liège, which make all kinds of iron products. Next in
prosperity is the textile industry, with cotton and linen produced in the
two provinces of Flanders. Lace made in the province of Brabant (the area
near the capital) has won a reputation for its quality. Porcelain is produced in Tournai, and in recent years glass-making has emerged to
become a prosperous industry. Commodities from Brussels include
porcelain, lace, rolling-stock, swords, iron and lumber, all of which have
acquired fame in Europe.

When Belgium seceded from Holland [in 1839] to become independent, Belgian goods were denied access to the sea as the coastline
downriver from its major port of Antwerp lay within Dutch territory.
Thereafter, attention was concentrated on inland transportation through
the maintenance of canals and the promotion of railways. Shortly afterwards, however, a European accord reformed international law to provide
for open ports, and since then Antwerp has managed to recover its former
prosperity.

The description in *Chiri zenshi* [a Chinese translation of *Universal
Geography* by William Muirhead] of the Belgian people as 'hardworking
in their daily livelihood, volatile in temper, hasty in making promises and
weak in faith' does indeed sum up their temperament. Nevertheless,
weakness of religious conviction is hardly a trait confined to this country
alone, for is this not the same among the lower classes everywhere? The
people are high-spirited and have an unfortunate tendency to make

reckless promises, only to break them afterwards, particularly in the region bordering France. Although the fortunes of the Belgians and the Dutch have always been inextricably entwined, they themselves confess that they are different in temperament. While the Dutch are closer to the Germans, the Belgians are closer to the French, yet they carry a certain Germanic trait in their limitless capacity for hard work.

CHAPTER 50

# A Record of Belgium, 1

February 17th, 1873. Clear skies.

We left the house in the Rue de Presbourg at two o'clock in the afternoon and boarded a chartered train at the Gare du Nord to embark on our journey towards the north-east.

Located near the Belgian border, Mons is a populous town. At the station a general in full military attire was waiting for us at the head of a guard of honour. The men were dressed in the Belgian uniform of black with gold buttons and pointed hats. Crowds of men and women walled in the guards on either side, and a band struck up an air as we alighted from the train. Inside the station building we exchanged courtesies with the general and speeches were made before we boarded our train and set off once more. We reached Brussels, the capital of Belgium, at half past eleven at night. The government had provided our Embassy with the use of the Hotel Bellevue, which is situated to one side of the Palais-Royal, and bore the expense of our rooms, so that we only had to pay for our food and drink.

February 18th.

At one o'clock this afternoon two carriages from the royal household arrived, manned by footmen in scarlet and gold livery. With them was a troop of guards and a steward who came to escort us to the royal palace, where we were granted an audience with King Leopold II.

Many of the buildings in Brussels are constructed of white stone or have their outer walls rendered in white plaster to present bright, gleaming façades wherever one goes. In style, the buildings resemble the architecture in France, and the citizens all speak French; they are vivacious in manner, and are devoted to the arts and crafts. Throughout the city there are wide, tree-lined boulevards, with benches in the shade for people to rest on. In one part of the bustling district of the old quarter called the Galeries Saint-Hubert, the thoroughfare has been covered with glass forming a long roof. This is a most prosperous market, and the rows of shops on either side display a range of goods and sell glittering ornaments of gold and precious stones and gorgeous inlaid carvings. The sparkling gaslights at night and the constant clamour in the streets recalled scenes we had witnessed in Paris, and when people describe Brussels as 'a little Paris', they do not stray far from the truth.

February 19th. Cloudy.
Accompanied by our escorts, [Lieutenant-Colonel Baron] Jolly and Mr. de Groote, we set out at ten o'clock this morning in the king's train and travelled north-west for twenty-five miles to arrive in the city of Ghent at half past eleven. From there we rode by carriage to Mr. de Hemptinne's cotton mill. We were told that up to three thousand bolts of cloth are produced here each week.

Ghent lies close to the English Channel, and from here one can travel to England in six hours, so the citizens have constant dealings with the British, and many speak both English and French. Much of the raw cotton at the mill arrives first at the port of Liverpool before it is imported here.

After this we strolled around a botanical garden. It featured a number of rare trees, although they were not particularly beautiful to look at. Seven or eight green-houses were filled with noted tropical and temperate trees such as palms, cycads and camellias, including different varieties of the same genus, all kept in a scented climate of perpetual spring. Fragrant camellias are made into garlands for ladies to wear around their necks, and these command very high prices. There was also a kind of selaginella, with moss growing about ten feet tall; it was said to have taken a hundred years to reach this height. Outside the green-houses were vines trained on trellises, and in one corner of the grounds was a steam-boiler which blew humid air into the green-houses, while an electrical device pumped water throughout. These gardens are solely for growing flowers rather than as a park for the recreation of workers. Ghent is celebrated as a centre of plant cultivation; a horticultural journal is produced here, and rare and wonderful trees and flowers are on sale everywhere.

Afterwards the mayor hosted a luncheon for us in the townhall with 256 guests, and no effort had been spared in the quality of the meal served. Following lunch we went to the La Lys plant, which is said to be the largest linen mill in Europe. Equipped with three steam-engines generating a combined output of 1,650 horsepower, the mill consists of five or six brick buildings, each five or seven storeys high, with chimneys rising to the clouds.

We left Ghent at four o'clock and arrived back at our hotel by five and changed for a soirée in the evening, which was hosted by the king in the Palais-Royal. This took the form of a party where liquor and confectioneries were served. Afterwards there was a ball attended by a hundred officials, and altogether three hundred men and women in formal dress were gathered there. With candlelight illuminating the palace and all the arrangements made with consummate skill, the occasion was a splendid affair.

February 20th. Cloudy.

At twenty past nine this morning we and our escorts travelled north for a distance of fifty-two kilometres, again by train. After stopping at a station where the mayor was waiting to greet us, we climbed into other carriages and continued three kilometres until we reached the batteries at Boech-out. The surrounding area is a barren wasteland, quite unfit for cultivation, and the only growth to be seen was a few scattered dwarf pines. Constructed fifteen years ago, this fort is garrisoned by two hundred artillerymen (with twenty-five officers), and the plain around has been transformed into a training ground. We were given a demonstration of the techniques used in firing cannon. Today the light was dim, for gusts of wind were blowing sleet everywhere. A blanket of mist had fallen and the freezing air felt cold enough to cut right through our skin.

First of all there was some target practice with field guns. Three initial shots were fired, and by watching where the shells fell it was calculated that they had a range of 1,500 metres. After that came thirteen more shots; eleven of them hit their targets, one struck the side and only a single shell missed completely.

The Belgian people are physically robust and are capable fighters. Living in a small country caught between the great powers, they have established their nation by making it a priority to protect their land themselves. At conferences of the assembled European powers in recent years, promises have been made not to march through Belgian territory in the event of a military advance. Even so, in the heat of war, when hostile troops are in a belligerent mood, how can the Belgians preserve their neutrality unless their entire territory bristles with defences? All the men in Belgium undergo training as soldiers and are summoned for target practice, so they are competent in the use of fire-arms. Those undergoing military service possess an heroic fortitude and a mastery of technique which is beyond anything found in the great powers.

When the target practice was over, lunch was served for us in the officers' mess. Then we returned to the station and travelled back by train.

February 21st.

This morning we travelled as usual by train on a course marginally south of due east. It was cold at daybreak, and a layer of snow covered the ground as we set out. Telegraph lines and tree branches sagged under the weight of the crystalline ice and snow, and everywhere shrubs and trees had burst into silvery bloom to create a world of ethereal beauty beyond our carriage windows.

After fifty-four miles we arrived at Liège Station at half past ten. We boarded carriages at the station and travelled back along the river before crossing a long bridge. After five miles we reached the village of Seraing. On the way we noticed what a thriving manufacturing area this is, with mountains of coal in several places and columns of smoke billowing skywards from factory chimneys.

In Seraing we saw the Val-Saint-Lambert glassworks, which employs 1,700 workers every day to manufacture glass objects – cups, glasses, bottles, medical flasks and every kind of household table-ware. There are in all eleven round brick furnaces.

Lunch was served here, and afterwards we rode by carriage around the factories of Liège. The ironworks of the Société Anonyme John Cockerill is located on the banks of the Meuse on the city outskirts. Iron-ore is found in this district and the coal is mined on site. This is the largest of the twelve ironworks in Liège, and it was founded by Mr. Cockerill, an Englishman, in 1807, when the area was still Dutch territory. After Belgium's secession from Holland, the government has devoted every effort to iron manufacturing, enabling it to grow into the vast works we see today.

People in the West say that a country's wealth lies in the production of iron and the mining of coal. Generally speaking, a single raw material is not enough to supply a country's diverse needs. For every advantage a material has, there is also a flaw – stone is hard but shatters easily, wood is thick but easily bent, and leather is supple but soft. Metals vary from malleable to brittle, but it is only iron which includes the whole range. And it is coal which brings out the properties of iron, and iron which reveals the utility of coal. In Europe, iron and coal have strengthened industry and increased commercial capacity immensely. It is in the relentless march of progress that the true value of iron has emerged, and rapid advances in knowledge have allowed manual labour to be replaced by mechanical power.

The purpose of industry is not to promote wasteful extravagance but to augment a people's commercial strength by raising national output and satisfying the demands of consumers. The ability of a cart to carry a greater load than a man or a horse is due to the use of machinery and is an advantage gained through industry. Is this not evidence enough for the great importance of iron? Fortunately, Japan has the most advanced iron production in the East, and we also have highly skilled craftsmen and abundant staple products. In these times of progress, if we were to develop the advantages of both iron and coal, we could produce all our blades, axes, drills, axles and screws domestically, which would bring enormous benefits to people in many occupations. If we strove to satisfy the demands of farming, spinning, construction, household goods and transportation, would this not result in an increase in our national output, leading to profits which could match those of America and Europe? Even if this did not happen, it would be a great mistake to say that the future of industry in Japan lies in tinkering with our traditional crafts to export just a small quantity of porcelain, copper work and lacquerware. It is because the factories recorded throughout this volume depend on the benefits of mining that we have stated our case strongly here.

CHAPTER 51

# A Record of Belgium, 2

February 22nd, 1873. Cloudy.

Leaving at nine o'clock in the morning, by train as usual, we headed south and passed through the city of Braine[-l'Alleud] before reaching the village of Courcelles, where we stopped to look at the manufacture of sheet-glass. This factory was planned five years ago, and it took three years to raise the necessary funds for construction, yet although it has been in operation for only two years, its rapid progress has defied all expectations.

Whenever plans for a new enterprise are drawn up, the people in the West are just the opposite of the Japanese in the degree of forethought and attention to detail they bring to the task. After they have carefully weighed the idea and consider the project to be feasible, they start by preparing models and charts, writing prospectuses, raising subscriptions and accumulating the necessary capital. Then they obtain a permit, put up a temporary workshop, install the machinery and gradually build up the enterprise over the course of two or three years. They will plan for the future, setting aside part of the profit for improvements in buildings and equipment, and it will take at least ten years of sustained effort before they can finally display their achievements to the world at large. People in Japan, however, assume profits will come easily even before they have made any money at all. They rush into plans for new firms and expand the business in such haste that within the space of a year, even as the fine premises they have built are still impressing people, their profits will be starting to dwindle. This may be attributed to their impulsive, carefree spirit, but the truth of the matter is that, as yet, they simply do not have an understanding of the fundamental nature of profit.

After travelling about two miles from here, we arrived at the Providence ironworks in a village with many low-roofed houses by the name of Marchienne[-au-Landelies]. Along the way we saw some collieries, and we were told that there are deposits of iron-ore here as well. This is one of three ironworks in the area, and between them they employ three

thousand workers. Eight hundred of the men are engaged here in producing mainly iron girders for construction. We all sat down to lunch in
the factory in the company of a party which included the governor.

The technique of manufacturing glass has not yet reached the East, so
everyone there considers it to be a valuable luxury. In the West, by
contrast, growing prosperity and recent improvements in glass-making
have reduced production costs, so that glass is no longer thought
expensive. There can be no doubt that in Japan more glass will be
appearing each year in the form of bowls and dishes and window-panes.
Depending entirely on imports is not in the interests of the economy and
causes substantial inconvenience, so sooner or later we must develop
glass-manufacturing ourselves. Furthermore, one cannot say that Japan is
a country unsuited to glass-making. Take, for example, the geology of our
land, with its exposed strata of hard granite and sand as white as snow on
river-beds and mountains. Ceramic clays like kaolin and feldspar are also
quarried, and there is no scarcity of chalk or lime. As glass is a compound
of silicate, lime, potash, soda and chalk, therefore, all the materials for its
manufacture are available in our country. Moreover, glass production
does not require any large machinery.

As representations had been made to our Embassy by so many factories
in Brussels, today we drew lots and separated into two groups, and the
party under Vice-Ambassador Kido toured the city.

First they went to a tin-plate factory. People in the West have a strong
aversion to the use of bronze for table-ware as it tends to oxidise easily,
producing a highly toxic liquid. In Japan we must endeavour to convert
to tin-plate and iron vessels as well. From here Kido's party moved to a
parquet-floor factory. Parquetry is very fashionable on the European
continent, and in the grander houses of France entire floors are covered
with squares of wood instead of tiles. These are polished to such a shine
that the surface becomes very slippery. Carpeted floors are also found in
the houses of the middle class and above.

After this they proceeded to a factory where sewing needles are
manufactured using very fast precision machinery. To give an outline of
the process, steel wire purchased from an ironworks first has its surface
rust removed with a roller in the same way as in the manufacture of nails.
The wire is cut into lengths equal to that of two needles. As pressure is
applied, drills bore through the wire and a blade falls to slice the steel in
half. By the time the wire has been cut into two, the eye in each needle
has already been pierced.

In order to sharpen the tips, each needle is inserted into a hole in a small steel rod, which has lines of files on either side to grind the metal. The faces of the files converge to meet at the top so that as each needle rotates and rubs against them, they shave the end to a fine point. To polish the needles, they are tied tightly together with a rubber band to make a bundle like a rolled-up scroll and polishing powder is scattered on top. When this bundle is placed on the edge of a roller and pressed with some force, the needles grind against each other so that in an instant they are gleaming and bright. Because needles are produced using machinery such as this, they are both fine in quality and low in price. The production of needles in Japan, however, involves the most intricate handiwork just to obtain the smallest numbers, since a craftsman holds each needle in turn in the process of forging, filing and drilling a hole. This is so dreadfully inconvenient that we had hoped to find a simpler and faster alternative in the West, and to watch the process here felt like a dream come true.

February 23rd. Snow.
We left by carriage at nine o'clock this morning and headed south for twelve miles to arrive at the village of Waterloo [Mont Saint-Jean]. This is the site of the famous battle where, on June 18th, 1815, the duke of Wellington, the British general, defeated Emperor Napoleon I of France. The topography affords a sweeping view over a rolling landscape of low-lying fields, with some wooded villages dotted here and there. The village lies beside a road and consists of several hundred houses, all built in a simple style, with a large church in which Wellington set up his headquarters.

On the way we stopped to rest at an hotel on the edge of the village. Heading south from here along a wide road, we turned right into a lane and continued west until we came to a ruined house surrounded by a brick wall. This was originally the country home of a wealthy family, but it was used by British soldiers on the day of the battle to hold out against the onslaught of the French. We could still see the openings made in the walls for firing field guns at the advancing enemy. The bullet marks left by the French were scattered over the walls like drops of water after a shower of rain. At the time of the battle there was a wood in front of the gate, and the bark of the surviving trees was still riddled with bullet holes, although these had partly disappeared during the course of their growth.

Leaving this building and heading east we came to a sloping ridge where we could clearly see the lay-out of the field of battle, such as where the British troops had drawn their lines and the positions of the Scots Guards. In a field five or six or seven hundred yards to the east is a high mound [the Butte du Lion], which was built in 1818 to mark the spot where the two generals had been engaged in their battle for supremacy. It was the scene of the heaviest casualties, and the bodies of the fallen were piled high. On top of the mound is an eight-foot-tall square stone pedestal, on which sits the bronze statue of a lion with its paw on a cannonball, glaring in the direction of Paris to the south.

On the morning of June 18th Napoleon was rousing his best troops, calling on them to trample the enemy soldiers underfoot and scatter the motley host from Britain and Germany. As he sat astride his white horse and looked out across his lines at daybreak, however, rain began to fall, which hampered his preparations and the deployment of his army. At last the standard was raised and, with a thunderous roll of drums, the French launched a direct assault on Wellington's lines. Knowing that Napoleon possessed the ferocity of a starving tiger and would have the advantage in a short-lived battle, Wellington courageously kept his ranks steadfast and immobile as the two armies clashed in these fields, and thus he withstood a French onslaught as powerful as the charge of ten thousand horses.

Looking out from the summit of the mound, it was as though we could see the scenes on the battlefield unfolding before our very eyes. Beyond a field to the south of this road lies a village in the middle of a wood, and it was from here that, as twilight approached, the Prussian army advanced to attack the French on the eastern flank. With nightfall so near, the instant the standard of the Prussian army came into view Napoleon knew his cause was lost. Abandoning his carriage, he rode with all speed towards France. The French troops, unaware of Napoleon's flight, continued to fight well into the night, but the British, reinforced by Prussian forces attacking the French flank, took fresh heart and battled on. With thousands of galloping horses and bullets falling like rain, the outcome of this tumultuous struggle did not become apparent until nine o'clock that night. The area immediately in front of this mound is where the two armies were locked in combat, as the dead piled up around them during twelve intense hours of fierce fighting.

The Butte du Lion is 225 steps high from the ground to the top. The bronze lion weighs 46,000 pounds and was cast by Cockerill, the English industrialist in Liège. It wears an expression of indomitable courage as it gazes defiantly towards Paris. The French are still indignant over their defeat at Waterloo and detest this lion. When the Belgians later severed relations with Holland, they were assisted in their struggle by French reinforcements, and after their victory over the Dutch there was a campaign to have the lion destroyed. Although it was once in danger when a charge of gunpowder was placed under it, the Belgians have protected it, and the French never come to visit here even now. In contrast, a never-ending stream of men and women from Germany and Britain arrive daily to pay their respects.

From here we made our way back on foot along the wide road, passing a building on the right which the French troops had used as their field hospital. Snow had fallen today and the fields were covered with patches of slush, and with an overcast sky and dampness in the air, the whole scene felt wretchedly bleak.

February 24th. Cloudy.

We left Brussels at nine o'clock this morning, and all our escorts accompanied us to see us off. After a journey of twenty-seven miles, the governor and leading citizens of Antwerp were at the station to meet our train, and from there we made the journey by carriage as far as the city's batteries.

Although Belgium has only a short stretch of coastline, Antwerp boasts a safe natural harbour unequalled in the region. With merchant ships arriving from London, from Holland and Germany to the east and from France and Spain to the west, it is the most strategic port in the North Sea. This is why Emperor Napoleon paid it so much attention, and the reason Antwerp is thriving today. The batteries built by Napoleon Bonaparte consist of vast ramparts encircling the entire city in the form of a star-shaped military fortress.

We visited the Royal Exchange and the townhall. Re-built in 1859, the exchange is housed in a grand new structure in white stone, and in both sets of assembly halls there were numerous old paintings from two or three centuries ago.

In the museum we saw a large collection of old paintings. The Belgians possess fine artistic technique and there were works by the celebrated Rubens, as well as a number of masterpieces from other lands. Among the many people studying the paintings and copying them was one man about forty years of age who comes from a wealthy family but who was born without any hands. Nevertheless, he manages to use his feet for all his daily needs by bending his legs with such dexterity that he can even shave himself with a razor. Moreover, he is a skilful artist, and he was making copies of paintings in the gallery by holding the brush with his foot to apply colours no differently from anyone painting by hand. Later we took a painting he had copied back with us and presented it to the imperial household. This city has a high reputation as a centre for the study of painting.

We were entertained to luncheon in the governor's residence, and at twenty minutes to four we reached the station, where we took leave of our escorts as our train set off for Holland. Beyond the window the fields finally gave way to low-lying woods of pine-trees stretching for several miles, with the wind soughing through their branches. They were all rather young trees, and the entire forest looked as if it must have been planted about ten years ago. With advances in agriculture in Europe, techniques in the cultivation of forests have progressed accordingly. In sandy areas, easily propagating grasses are sown increasingly in order to alter the nature of the soil before trees are planted. Pine-trees grow easily, so pine saplings are planted on land like this.

In areas with plentiful supplies of cheap timber, people use wood indiscriminately so that forests are soon depleted. Owners of private woodlands are always seeking profits by planting large numbers of deciduous trees and later felling them. Another unfortunate practice is for people to clear forested land for gains from crops and pasture. Before the advance of industry in Europe, in an age when people did not know that iron could be used in place of timber, vast tracts of woodland were cut down and forests decimated in Greece, Spain, France and Britain. It was in light of this that forestry was subsequently promoted so that nowadays, while liberal politics are spreading in Europe, in forestry laws the former freedoms are being curtailed. This has led to a restrictive system, but one that is intended for the long-term benefit of the people.

# CHAPTER 52

# A Survey of Holland

Holland also goes by the name of The Netherlands, and to us in Japan
the country is known as 'Oranda'. Today it is one of the smaller nations
in Europe. Three hundred years ago the Dutch sailed overseas, establishing colonies in various parts of the world, and Holland's power was
unchecked. This was followed by a period of decline and disorder as
many of these territories were taken over by Britain, but Holland still
holds colonies in the East and West Indies and Africa. Among these, Java
serves as the administrative capital of the Dutch East Indies, and it was
from here that, over the last two centuries, a single merchant ship was
dispatched each year to Japan. As our country had rejected diplomatic ties
during this period and Holland was the only nation allowed to send
vessels to our shores, the Dutch made vast profits through their control of
all Japanese products reaching Europe.

Spread over the earth is an array of nations inhabited by peoples with
diverse customs and lifestyles who present as magnificent a display as a
hundred flowers in bloom. While countries in Europe resemble one
another in their shared political roots, it is in their ways of life that the
differences between them lie. We had already seen how the Belgians
struggle to gain independence in a land of plains comparable in size with
the island of Tsukushi [an archaic name for Kyūshū]. Now, on our arrival
in Holland, we were once again impressed at how a country with the
same number of people as the four Kyūshū provinces of Chikuzen,
Chikugo, Hizen and Higo has contrived to build a wealthy and populous
nation from a land wallowing in mud. Could it be Heaven's way of
achieving a balance, with men blessed with a rich environment idle while
those without are diligent?

Holland has a fraction of the area of Japan in a cold northern climate
with clayey soils useless as paddy-fields, where sugar-cane and cotton do
not grow and there are no minerals, masonry stone or forests, yet the
diligence and thrift of the people have transformed the land into one of

the world's richest nations. Holland is low-lying and damp to an unimaginable extent, and one may say that the majority of the population lives below sea-level. Dikes are built along the coast, windmills are set up inland to prevent flooding, and the rivers flow several feet above the ground. Canals intersect the fields like the lines on a *go* board to form parcels of farmland where cattle and sheep roam and graze, calling out to each other across the watery divides. There is higher land along the border with Germany, but the population and centres of commerce are concentrated in the western half of the country, from the border with Belgium as far as the provinces of North and South Holland. It is here that the major cities such as Amsterdam, Rotterdam, The Hague and Leiden are located, whereas in the north-eastern parts of the country the soil is poor and the population sparse.

With its low-lying marshes and coastline along the North Sea, it is not an agreeable climate for visitors, but the winds which blow continually across the country drive away the humid air and prevent any ill-effects to one's health. Advantage is also taken of this natural resource as windmills are used day and night to pump away water and prevent the land from being flooded. Each year, however, strong winds from the west and south-west cause extensive damage to plants and dikes.

Cow's milk is used to make butter and cheese, and breeding cattle is profitable through the export of live animals to Britain and Germany. Although butter is produced all over Europe, Dutch butter is in a class of its own. The superb cheese is also greatly appreciated by visitors to Holland when it is served in their hotels.

Holland benefits from fishing off the North Sea coast, with sardines the particular speciality of these waters. Dutch fishermen are always setting off in small boats to Belgium, France and Britain to sell freshly caught fish, just as the people of Bōsō Peninsula bring their fish to Nihonbashi in Tokyo.

Another speciality is diamond-polishing, and Holland is also famous for its inexpensive cloth woven from cotton imported from the colonies. From weaving wool, spinning flax, tanning leather and making paper to ceramics and brewing, there are no crafts to which the Dutch do not turn their hand. Shipbuilding is another strength.

The Dutch may be called the foremost in Europe in their commerce, and river-boats and canals within the country allow trade to flourish, so people pay meticulous attention to water-transport facilities. The Amsterdam–Den Helder Canal stretches over a distance of fifty-one miles. It is never less than 113 feet wide and as much as 22 feet deep, which is ample for two frigates to sail side by side. This is the largest of several canals converging on Amsterdam.

The Dutch are of Teutonic extraction, and although they have their own language they are grouped in the Germanic race. They are serious in character and handsome in appearance, and the ladies are particularly beautiful. They possess a tranquil disposition to work, so they may be somewhat tardy, in contrast to the sprightly Belgians, and this distinction is immediately apparent on crossing the border. Nevertheless, they are methodical, modest, industrious and thrifty, with a capacity for endless endurance. With their eye for fine detail they excel in scholarship and are masters of commerce. Looking at the famous cities of Europe and America, we find that many of them were originally developed by the Dutch. It was the arrival of immigrants from Holland which led even to the prosperity of London, and it was the Dutch who first colonised New York. What superlative entrepreneurs would be born from a union of the Dutch and the British!

Only Holland and Britain have shown the indomitable perseverance necessary to take advantage of improvements in navigation and traverse the globe in pursuit of trade. Not only have the Dutch managed to conduct trade with Japan, but there is no port to be found in the East or West where they have not left their mark. As a people they have a liking for neatness, and all their houses are elegantly designed. Every day they sweep their doorsteps and gardens and wipe their windows, and the shops and streets are always immaculate, without a speck of dust. The Dutch have a reputation for being the most fastidious of the people in Europe. In their everyday lives they take thrift to an extreme and manage without luxuries. When we first arrived in England from America, the daily life of the British appeared unfailingly frugal, but after we reached Holland English households appeared riddled with unnecessary expenses and positively extravagant.

February 24th (continued from Belgium).
At ten past three this afternoon we set off from Antwerp Station and reached the border with Holland at Roosendaal at twenty minutes to five. Mr. [Dirk de Craeff van] Polsbroek, the former Dutch minister to Japan, and Mr. [Martinns Willem] Van der Tak, the former consul, had been sent to welcome us as our official escorts, and we exchanged greetings in the station building. A single railway track runs between both countries, so there was no need to change lines at the border. In the station building the passengers' luggage underwent an inspection by customs officials, and once this was finished the train moved off again.

Presently our train crossed the Maas, a river 1,200 metres across – as broad as a sea. It is spanned by an immense bridge with a railway track, which is a celebrated example of engineering. Hollow columns of brick descending to a depth of twelve metres below the river-bed admit light from above so that people may climb down inside, and balustrades on either side of the bridge are supported by a mesh of iron rods. It would require ten minutes at least to walk all the way to the other bank, and trains slow down as they approach, taking three minutes to complete the crossing. When our train reached the midway point, the land on either bank lay beyond the horizon and all we could see was endless water around us, so for a whole minute we felt as though we were flying over the ocean. The Dutch take great pride in this bridge, which they call 'the pre-eminent bridge on earth', and it is indeed a sight to behold. Although this river is known as the Maas, it is actually the mouth of the Rhine, and at no time before or after did we see such a vast expanse of water.

Alighting at the train terminal we boarded a boat which ferried us across the river to Rotterdam on the far bank. From the jetty we took carriages through the city to the railway station. The streets along the way were intersected by canals, with buildings hemmed in between stretches of water, very much like the Honjo and Fukagawa districts of Tokyo.

Afterwards we took another train before we finally arrived at our lodgings at the Hotel Halle in The Hague at half past eight in the evening. Our accommodation here was being paid for by the Dutch government, with the Embassy only having to provide for its food and drink.

# CHAPTER 53

# A Record of The Hague, Rotterdam and Leiden

February 25th, 1873. Still no end to the snow.

Den Haag, also known as The Hague, is the capital city and royal seat of Holland. The city is girdled by canals of calm water, the banks lined with rows of luxuriant trees. Dutch people are fastidiously clean by nature, and the city has a neat and tidy appearance, with no dead branches on the trees, no rubbish floating in the water and not a speck of dust in the streets. There are very few carriages and horses, and throughout the day no loud voices are to be heard. The houses are built of red brick with large windows all over the façades; few of them are of stone, but nevertheless there are a great number of beautiful residences.

At the end of some streets are open squares with stone and bronze statues around which trees are planted. Wide avenues are lined with trees, and sand is strewn below them to form long strips of parkland. The people are greatly attached to trees since there are so few of them in Holland, and many trees in the city have aged trunks and gnarled branches.

At four o'clock the steward of the royal household arrived with carriages and a cavalry escort to take us to the royal palace, where we had an audience with King Willem III.

February 26th. Rain in the morning; fine in the evening.

With the arrival of dawn the chill in the air rapidly faded, and we left our hotel at nine o'clock for the journey by train to Rotterdam. This took us through a landscape of muddy fields criss-crossed by canals. As we passed villages here and there, we saw windmills rising above the treetops, their sails flapping in the breeze, and water flowing in channels along the tops of the embankments. This is what people mean when they say that the land in Holland lies below the level of the sea.

Rotterdam lies along a tributary of the Maas and is a gateway for incoming and outgoing merchandise. Today a steamboat was moored at the river-bank waiting for us, all rigged out and flying the Japanese flag. We embarked and travelled downstream for about a mile to a shipyard. The river here was five or six hundred feet wide, and we saw a railway bridge in the process of construction, with the tracks being laid across a row of foundation pillars.

The shipyard of the Maatschappij company employs 1,000 labourers each day, although there is no fixed work-force as such and, depending on circumstances, this figure may rise to 1,500 men on occasion. No foreign workers are employed in this shipyard, as they have the reputation of being volatile and quick to protest.

All the countries in Europe abide by international law. They observe diplomatic courtesies and maintain cordial relations, but when we examine the underlying reality we find that they are locked in bitter struggles for power, and some often fail to preserve their independence. In relations between peoples of different lands, those in the great powers inevitably take pride in their strength and look down on those in small countries. Moreover, they may be opposites by nature, as the British and the Dutch, with one as vigorous as the other is plodding. When it comes to pitting one nation against another, however, neither is ever content to concede defeat, so conflicts are likely to break out at any time. The governments of the West are siblings, and their peoples all belong to the same race, yet they are different in national character, and when they mingle confusion naturally ensues. It is hardly surprising, then, that relations between countries of the East and West are far from being entirely amicable.

There were currently two ships under construction at this yard. An order had been placed by the government of Java for four ships, two of which were to be made in Amsterdam and the other two were being built here. Nine-tenths of the work had already been completed on one of the ships.

Java is an island in the Malay Archipelago in the seas to the south of Asia. (Nowadays it is also said to belong to the continent of Oceania, that is, Australia.) It is the most important of Holland's overseas colonies. In 1824, the Nederlandsche Handel-Maatschappij [Netherlands Trading Society] was established in Amsterdam under the auspices of King Willem I, who became a partner in the firm himself. This trading company took charge of Java's commercial affairs, with dividend payments of 4.5 per cent guaranteed by the king from the royal treasury to supplement any initial shortfall before the venture began to flourish. As a result, an agricultural system was promoted in Java, intended to meet the food requirements of the native population as well as to cultivate produce for the European market. Since then the company has grown into an increasingly prosperous enterprise. This agricultural system now forms the basis of administration in Java, attending to even the smallest details of production, so that any land which is not owned by Dutch residents is usually under government ownership. The officials in each area employ a system of forced cultivation, making local chieftains grow sugar, coffee, tobacco, pepper, indigo and tea, which the company buys at fixed prices and ships to Amsterdam.

After leaving the shipyard we boarded a British mail-boat and sat down to lunch. Speeches were made and candied fruits from Java were served.

February 27th. Fine.
This afternoon we went to the Admiralty Office, which is situated on the other side of the parkland in front of our hotel. In the days of republican rule long ago, Dutch naval power was unsurpassed in Europe. The Dutch frequently defeated the British and the Spanish, and made full use of their seafaring skills to venture far and wide. Some mechanical equipment captured from British warships during the celebrated sea battle in the Thames estuary [in 1667] is kept here, together with models of vessels of the time. There were five or six other rooms filled with model lighthouses, cannon, small-arms, swords, flags and captured naval weapons.

February 28th. Very fine.
At nine o'clock in the morning we left for Leiden by carriage with Dr. Pompe [van Meerdervoort] as our guide. Dr. Pompe once spent eight years in Nagasaki, where he taught medicine, and by the time he returned to Holland in 1862 he had become a prominent figure in the development of medical practice in Japan. Now over sixty years old, he seemed like a man in the prime of life.

The road to Leiden led eastwards from The Hague forest. Situated on the lower reaches of the Rhine, Leiden is the fifth-largest city in Holland. Long ago, in the seventeenth century, the valiant troops of Leiden resisted the invading Spanish army and fought so fiercely that they eventually repulsed the enemy. The government did not know how to reward them for this achievement, and when it enquired of the citizens what they wished for most, the people all asked for a college to be created for the benefit of future generations. A university was thus established, and academic studies have flourished here ever since, producing scholars of renown through the ages to maintain Leiden's prestige up to the present day.

All over the world, religious beliefs are so ingrained in people's hearts that they are practically invincible in spirit, and this has a great bearing on human relations, politics and military affairs. Those brought up on the political morality of East Asia cannot imagine the influence which religion exerts, but it is due to this that a European never fails to ascertain another man's religious beliefs whenever they discuss their affairs.

Looking at wars fought in Europe, it is invariably religion which unites the hearts of the people, and in wars involving religion their fury is as terrifying as that of raging lions and tigers. In the case of Holland, the people are restrained and amiable by nature, they excel at letters and do not have the robust physique of the Belgians. Back in the days when it was said that the sun never set on the Spanish empire, it was the power of religion which thwarted the might of King Philip II of Spain when he invaded the million or so people of this tiny land. Philip was tyrannical in his efforts to convert Protestant Holland to his Roman Catholic faith, but, as Confucius said, a great army 'failed to rob a common man of his soul'.

The streets of Leiden are not wide but they are immaculately kept, with boulevards on either side of canals in which clear, calm water flows. Trees line the river-banks and the roads are paved with bricks. Cities in Holland have a special street lay-out in which canals serve as thoroughfares and pedestrians walk along paths on the banks. This avoids the clamour of horses and carts, since men and women make their way on foot. The streets are also exceedingly clean, for they are swept every day and any dust is washed away, and when an occasional carriage does appear, the jingling of its equipage can be heard far and wide. The fact that Leiden is not a thriving commercial metropolis also enables it to be kept so clean, making it an ideal centre of learning.

The museum attached to the university in Leiden is famous throughout Europe for its rich collection, and today we first spent some time looking around it. In the hall of animals were some gigantic rare specimens, either placed in the middle of the room or suspended from the ceiling. Groups of smaller beasts were arranged in glass cases at the sides. Among the dozens of giant beasts, the most impressive were the largest elephant, which was fourteen feet high, and a rhinoceros over nine feet tall. The skin of each was preserved by a special method of curing. There was also a collection of countless horns and antlers of all shapes, including a brightly coloured and translucent one which was said to belong to an animal found in Cape Colony known as an 'antelope'. In the museums we visited abroad, there were rarely any animals from Japan, but here we saw a species of monkey with a red face and no tail and, on enquiring, we were told it had been sent from Japan by [Philipp von] Siebold. Most breeds of monkey inhabit tropical zones, and not all of them are the same as the ones found in Japan. Here we saw many Japanese monkeys, and there were also some Japanese cormorants in the bird collection. We were told that training cormorants to catch fish originated in China.

There is also an ethnology museum housing artefacts from the southern and eastern oceans [Rijksmuseum voor Volkenkunde], where pride of place is given to several rooms devoted to the objects collected by Siebold in Japan. Those which had already been here for a decade or more had changed so greatly in colour and become so disfigured that they did not bear inspection. There were many clumsily executed paintings, and one rather beautiful votive picture of a horse on a golden screen which had been painted by a member of the Kanō school. Western people value this painting as a rare prize, claiming that it can only be the work of a master. A great quantity of Japanese coinage has been amassed here, although regrettably some coins from China were mixed in as well, but this stems from the fact that Western people are not familiar with the history of China and Japan. There was also a Dutch–Japanese dictionary compiled by a certain Minamoto in 1806. In the process of assembling the collection in this museum, Siebold endured a great deal through the severity of Japan's exclusion laws, and we were filled with admiration for his enthusiasm. The exhibits from the South Sea islands were coarse, rustic objects, with nothing worth looking at.

CHAPTER 54

# *A Record of Amsterdam*

March 2nd, 1873. Cloudy.

At a quarter past ten we boarded our train with our escorts and set out for Amsterdam. The landscape on the way was entirely flat and intersected by canals with dikes on either side planted with willow-trees. These trees grow easily, so they are planted in copses of short trees and pollarded each year, providing an indispensable product for military purposes since the charcoal made from their branches is ideal for the manufacture of gunpowder.

Situated on the shores of the Zuider Zee, Amsterdam is the capital of North Holland province and the pre-eminent city in the country. There was a time when it was also the royal capital, but now it serves as a crucial centre of commerce within Europe. Trade in this port is such that invariably a hundred ships will come in with each tide, and on occasion up to double that, and there is never a day when one finds fewer than six hundred ships moored in the harbour. The oysters cultivated in the sea here are the best in all Europe and command a high price. Europeans have a passion for oysters, which has proved very beneficial to the Dutch, and these shellfish can also be found in abundance along the coast off New York. It was due to their experience in turning a profit from this trade that the Dutch used to come to Nagasaki to purchase and export oysters from Hizen.

The water from the harbour flows into the city through a complex network of canals, which are wider than those we saw in Rotterdam. In the whole of Amsterdam there are nearly a thousand canals, spanned by more than three hundred bridges which link the streets. By and large the bridges are built entirely of wood, with beams balanced above to allow the drawbridge to be raised and lowered when boats pass. This style of bridge is common to cities in Holland.

The average house in the city is narrow but has large windows, and is as much as five storeys high. The way they stand shoulder to shoulder at

varying heights overlooking the canals is just like the view of the warehouses along the river-bank from Edobashi, in Tokyo. In terms of
grandeur three great canals – Herengracht, Keizersgracht and Prinsen-
gracht – rank with the most celebrated boulevards in all Europe. Even
though less than a foot separates the ground from the surface of the water,
the buildings always have cellars beneath them. The walls are sealed with
brick and stone to prevent water seeping in, and, as elsewhere in the
West, the cellars are used to store belongings or as rooms.

We visited the Koninklijk Paleis [royal palace] in Amsterdam. It was
originally the townhall until its conversion into a palace, and the council
chamber from those days is still preserved here. The interior decoration
dates back two hundred years, to the time it was constructed, but there is
no dazzling gold – only pure white stone, with light streaming in through
the windows to wash over the rooms inside; yet it seemed all the more
beautiful for its simplicity. There were rooms decorated with paintings,
and some had silken tapestries hung across the walls. The largest room
was the dining-hall. It is directly beneath the tower and has a domed
ceiling ninety feet high. Suspended from the exact centre was a long
golden chain, with the branches of a crystal chandelier suspended from
the end of it. The floor was completely covered with parquet, which was
so smooth that it was difficult to keep one's footing. In times past, before
The Hague became the capital, this was the official royal residence, and
since then it has been maintained as a second royal palace.

We also visited the Rijksmuseum, a two-storey building with high
ceilings which houses famous old paintings. This was established for the
study of the arts, so painters living in the city could always come here to
copy the works and learn the different styles. There was nothing else of
note.

We had lunch at the Amstel Hotel, a large five-storey building situated
in front of three inlets in the harbour and one of the finest hotels in
Amsterdam. This is a prime location for observing the scenery, with light
streaming through the windows and the water reflecting the clouds. From
here we could see the 'hall of glass' rising high before us, and weeping
willows and attractive lawns, with ships trailing clouds of smoke and
causing gentle ripples as they passed back and forth.

The diamond-polishing works of Amsterdam is the most famous place
in the city. Diamond jewellery is immensely fashionable throughout
Europe, but it is only here that diamonds can be polished satisfactorily into
flawless gems. This factory was originally founded by a Mr. Coster forty
years ago, when he became the French consul. Now, a thirty-six-horsepower

steam-engine has been installed, and 315 workers are employed every day. The largest diamonds to be polished here since the factory was founded are three stones, each measuring an inch or so across, which have been added to the crown jewels in Britain, France and Russia. Cut into individual shapes, these superb gems are unequalled anywhere in the world and are valued at more than 2,000,000 francs. Replicas made of glass are kept on the shelves.

From here we turned our carriages about and made for the house of our guide, Mr. Van der Tak, where we were entertained to dinner that evening. Boarding our train at half past nine, we arrived back at our hotel at eleven o'clock.

March 4th. Light cloud.
Today we were received at the Ministry of Foreign Affairs. Late in the afternoon we looked around the royal palace, and in the evening we dined at the house of Mr. Polsbroek, the former Dutch minister to Japan.

March 5th. Thick fog, followed by light cloud in the afternoon.
Today we went to view the coastal scenery to the north of The Hague, while Vice-Ambassador Kido travelled by train to visit a village in the vicinity of Amsterdam and see a new canal being constructed for twenty-five kilometres from the North Sea to Amsterdam. When finished, it will enable ships in north European waters to sail directly to Amsterdam without having to go all the way around and into the Zuider Zee.

Along the North Sea coastline, which we visited, breakwaters projected into the sea from the headlands [at Ijmuiden] and dunes formed a continuous sandy shore. The sand is used to produce blocks of concrete, which become harder the longer they are left in water. Six or seven kilometres inland is a plant for manufacturing these, and it is linked to the coast by railway. The blocks are produced by mixing the sand with imported volcanic rock and adding water so that, when compressed in wooden moulds, it becomes as hard as rock in a matter of minutes. Holland may not possess any rock or stone, but this technique has for-tuitously transformed all the sand along its coast into a raw material for masonry blocks. What wondrous possibilities there are to be found by exploring the mysteries of nature!

From the harbour a canal 1,200 yards long with stone embankments channelled the water as far as a stone-walled lock, which was just wide enough to allow one large ship to enter at a time. Today the lock-keeper was delighted by our visit and took the trouble to show us around himself, treating us to some excellent wine when we stopped to rest. This area is in the middle of the Dutch countryside, with just the occasional village. With light cloud in the sky and a chilly wind, it was bleak and desolate but had a rustic charm all of its own. We walked for over a mile along a path through the fields before reaching the railway station, and we were back at our hotel by five o'clock in the afternoon. This evening we were invited to dine at the country residence of Prince Frederick.

March 6th. Cloudy.

Today Vice-Ambassador Kido went to Amsterdam to see the [Artis] zoo, which has a reputation for being the best in Europe. It is constructed on level ground, and although there are no landscaped hills, it has ponds encircled by trees for people to stroll under. Other noteworthy features are the variety of animals and the expertise of the staff in caring for wildlife.

Tropical plants and animals are raised in a long building with tightly fitting panes of glass and iron pipes supplying steam. We saw several gigantic snakes, the largest measuring one and a half feet around the middle, which were quite loathsome. Some apes were also kept here, and there was one room for raising newly hatched fish. Holland has long reaped the benefits of fishing, and in recent years Germany and Russia have also paid increasing attention to this industry, with fish farming developing into a branch of study within the field of agriculture.

Using innovation and labour to breed stocks of fish, and engaging officials for their protection, may be likened to the work of rangers in the field of forestry. The raising of fish is like the cultivation of trees. First, the right type of soil is prepared and a pond built with the exposure to sunlight calculated to ensure suitable temperatures. Water-plants are grown and trees planted to provide shade, and healthy male and female fish are released into the water to breed and spawn. When the eggs hatch, the fry are removed to a separate pond to grow into fish, so it is all very much like sowing seeds to cultivate plants. The fry are safe from predatory fish and other water creatures and protected from marauding birds for three years until they are fully developed, whereupon they are released into other ponds. This is briefly how fish farming is practised in many places.

A technique recently developed in Germany accelerates the process by cutting open the adult fish and removing the eggs and sperm. These are kept warm inside folds of fish-flesh before mixing them underwater to induce fertilisation. The fry we saw in this zoo had all been hatched using this procedure. Although premature, they already had the fish shape. On hatching they had heads larger than their bodies, with a protective membrane around their bellies. We saw unhatched fry inside eggs which looked like large beans tinted an orange colour. They were loosely spread over a mat of wire netting which was being gently shaken by a constant flow of fresh water. Once they hatch, the fry fall through the holes in the mesh into the basin below, whereupon they immediately begin swimming vigorously. In general, fish lay their eggs close to water-plants, and after receiving sufficient sunlight they hatch within sixteen or seventeen days. Although the fish farmer earnestly explained these techniques to us, we could not absorb all the details, so this description amounts to as much as we could remember. The temperature inside the tanks was 60° Fahrenheit.

It is customary in the West to eat the flesh of animals, and the level of meat consumption is comparable with the quantity of rice eaten in Japan. If anything, poultry is somewhat more expensive and may be compared in price with fish in our country. Fish is the most appreciated food of all and has become increasingly common in recent years. By and large, huge amounts of salted fish are consumed in all these countries, and it is also enjoyed by the upper classes. Fresh fish is also popular among them and large quantities of salmon, trout, halibut and cod are served at their tables, since these are the most common varieties found in the rivers and seas around Europe. Although there is little fishing in northern waters beyond Scandinavia, rich fishing grounds lie in the Baltic Sea and along the North Sea coast, and also in the Black Sea and the Mediterranean. The British and French have turned to imports, and vast quantities of salted fish are supplied by America and Canada. Fish caught in distant waters cannot be eaten fresh, so regulations have been instituted on the European continent for fish farming in rivers and ponds, and restrictions have been placed on inshore fishing. With the growing consumption of fish in recent years, these regulations have become stricter to prevent too many nets being cast in a particular stretch of water.

This evening we were entertained at a banquet held by a member of the royal family, Duke Hendrik, at his country residence.

March 7th. Light cloud.
We left The Hague at eight o'clock this morning and headed for Germany.

# CHAPTER 55

# A Survey of Prussia

The great central European plain inhabited by the German race stretches over a vast tract of territory in which emperors, kings, princes and dukes have risen and fallen since ancient times, and the marriage alliances they have forged with other rulers have spread their connections throughout the continent to make Germany an important part of Europe. Even now this region is divided among a number of aristocratic houses into several dozen principalities and duchies. To the south is the Austrian Empire, while across the centre to the French borders lie the lands of the former Confederation of the Rhine, known as southern Germany, and in the north are the territories called northern Germany, among which the largest is the kingdom of Prussia. Its power has grown prodigiously in recent years, and both north and south have been united under Prussian rule since 1871, when the king was elevated to the title of 'Kaiser' [emperor] of Germany and a federal assembly of the states was established in his capital at Berlin. While the country thus passes under the name of Germany in its relations with foreign powers, political authority is still divided internally among a number of states, just as before.

The land of Prussia resembles a silk patchwork. The separate fragments have been stitched together in the course of political manoeuvring by successive generations of lords and vassals, and the formation of this large country over the last two hundred years is inextricably bound up with the history of the Prussian royal family.

Friedrich II, who came to the throne in 1740, was the outstanding figure of his generation and an heroic ruler with a passion for achievement. He reacted against his father's extravagance by training himself to a life of frugality. It was through his strong rule that the culture and military organisation of Prussia emerged, for in an effort to strengthen the nation he reinforced armaments, developed political strategy, reformed the administration and recruited foreign experts for official posts and schools. From the time of his accession he devised schemes to invade neighbouring territories, Silesia among others.

Although the country's fortunes were at a low ebb during the reign of Friedrich's effete successor, Friedrich Wilhelm II, Prussia still managed to absorb the margravates of Ansbach and Bayreuth and, in concert with Austria and Russia, destroyed Poland altogether. This, however, coincided with the rise of Napoleon Bonaparte, and Prussia suffered such an onslaught by the French armies that the kingdom temporarily lost half its land. Nevertheless, even though Napoleon's troops entered Potsdam and imposed a humiliating surrender, both king and subjects remained resolute in their resistance. The final defeat of Napoleon at Waterloo in 1815 was a military triumph for the British and Prussian armies, so when all the countries convened at the Congress of Vienna, not only were Prussia's former territories restored to her but more possessions were added, including the whole of Swedish Pomerania (that is, the present-day province of Pomerania), together with lands along the western borders in the provinces of Westphalia and the Rhineland. The kingdom was now a great power in the north of Germany, consisting of two strips of territory known today as the old heartland of Prussia.

The current emperor of Germany, Wilhelm I, came to the throne in 1861, but shortly afterwards, in 1864, a dispute broke out because the family line of Holstein had died out in Denmark. Prussia joined forces with Austria against Denmark to reclaim the former German duchies of Schleswig, Holstein and Rowenburg, and eventually successfully restored these lands to Germany. However, relations with Austria deteriorated, and in 1866, in collaboration with Italy, Prussia defeated Austria at the Battle of Sadowa, expelling it from the German Confederation and assuming the leadership in its place. It was at this time that Prussia dissolved the kingdom of Hanover, the three principalities of Hesse-Cassel, Hesse-Homburg and Nassau, and also the free city of Frankfurt, adding them to its own territory to unite the country from east to west in the form it takes today.

As a consequence of the Franco-Prussian War of 1870–71, the two provinces of Alsace and Lorraine became part of the Confederation of Southern Germany rather than part of Prussia. It was at this time that a council of German princes bestowed on King Wilhelm the title of 'Kaiser', and a united German government was established in Berlin.

The climate of Germany is bitterly cold during the long winters as its great plains lie to the north, exposing them to winds from the Baltic, North and Arctic seas. The rivers are covered with such thick ice that even heavy carriages can cross them, and much of the land is buried under snow for three or four months of the year. Our party stayed in Berlin in the middle of March, and the first few days were bitingly cold. The fields we walked in were white with frost and we encountered deep banks of snow. Soon, however, after several days of rain and snow the temperature began to rise and it became mild enough to change into spring clothes. It was similar to our subsequent arrival in the north of Russia, which coincided with the onset of spring. In spite of the severe winters, it is fiercely hot in mid-summer, and these extremes of heat and cold make for a less than agreeable climate.

Seven-ninths of the population in Prussia are of Germanic stock. The people are honest and sincere by nature, and although slow in their work they are diligent, resilient and tenacious. They are not vivacious by temperament, but they follow rules and procedure methodically, which saves them from careless errors. The accent of those living in the highlands is somewhat softer and they are also more carefree in character. Prussia is a land of marshes with the poorest soil in the whole of Germany, and these harsh conditions have drawn out the strengths of its inhabitants, and they are accomplished at both the literary and the military arts. Their systematic approach and industriousness enables them to cultivate the study of letters, and their tireless research opens up a wealth of knowledge; consequently, Prussia leads Europe in producing great scholars of literature. The discipline and diligence of the Prussians have fostered their martial skills and they make well-trained soldiers, resilient in adversity, valiant in battle and steadfast in victory or defeat, with the result that their power has expanded until their military fame now resounds across the continent.

The standard of education in Prussia is among the highest in Europe, and it is an area of particular concern for the government. The construction of elementary schools is always paid for with taxes collected from the residents in each town and district. School maintenance is a mandatory responsibility of local officials, and sending their children to school is compulsory for parents. Every year 2 per cent of government income is used for the education of children from poor backgrounds at public expense. One in six of all children of school age in Prussia regularly attend classes, and it is rare to come across anyone who cannot write.

The religion in Prussia is Protestant; that is, Lutheranism is the national faith. Two-thirds of the population are Lutheran, one-tenth is Catholic, and there are 315,000 Jews as well as some who belong to the Greek Orthodox Church and other smaller sects too insignificant to mention. People's faith is not as deep here as it is in America and Britain.

One of the many customs which differs greatly from America and Britain is the scant respect shown to women. In Berlin, even the ladies themselves scoff at American and British men for their servile behaviour in front of their womenfolk, which they dismiss as a curious habit. Wherever we went in continental Europe, we found numerous customs which were at variance with those we saw in America and Britain.

CHAPTER 56

# The Journey by Rail Through Western Prussia

March 7th, 1873. Cloudy.

We had sent a telegraph to the German legation to announce that our Embassy would be leaving The Netherlands today, so an official from the German imperial household called Mr. Kanzki was dispatched by the emperor to meet us. He arrived in The Hague yesterday and rode with us in our railway-carriage this morning. When we reached the German border at Bentheim Station, we found Colonel von Wright, [Lieutenant-] Colonel Roerdansz and Mr. Kniffler, the former consul in Japan, waiting for us in the station building in full dress uniform. After alighting and exchanging greetings, we boarded together and the train pulled out, while people in the station crowded round to watch.

The next stretch of our journey took us through the borders of the province of Westphalia. The terrain here was generally flat, with gentle undulations, and the fields were planted with wheat and bordered by trees, interspersed with occasional thick woods of broad-leaf trees or conifers.

Advances in agriculture have led to the discovery of the principle of crop rotation, a system in which the crop is changed from one year to the next. Wheat might be sown in the first year, for example, and some variety of pulse (peas or broad beans) the year afterwards. In the third year hay may be planted, and the stubble left after mowing will be burnt. Sugar-beet or potatoes may be sown in the fourth year, and barley the year after that.

It is common for farmers to undertake livestock and arable farming in tandem. Fertiliser for crops is made by using hay and animal manure to make compost, and if this is insufficient, more is purchased from outside. There are traders who sell bone-meal, guano and all kinds of special fertilisers, and recently in Germany deposits of lime phosphate have been discovered, which have also been of great benefit. Various fraudulent tricks occur in the fertiliser trade, however, so agricultural societies have set up organisations licensed by regional authorities to inspect fertiliser and prevent such abuses.

In this region, all the wheat is sown in rows. As in Britain, the farmer ploughs with a team of two horses, which is a more sophisticated method of cultivation than that employed in the huge fields of America, where the farmers sow their seed by scattering it. On the whole, soil on the continent is rather soft and loose, reminiscent of the fields in the eight provinces of the Kantō plain in Japan. The soil in Germany is poor, with small stones mixed in, and nothing like the fertile earth along our coasts. This soil is found throughout the central European plain, which explains why farmers here use six or seven times as much fertiliser as farmers in Japan.

After travelling south for about two hours, we passed through a city where the sign in the station read 'Münster', informing us that we had taken a detour through the centre of the province of Westphalia. Here we changed to another railway line and travelled along the eastern border of the Rhineland. The Rhineland is such a thriving region that it is easy to see why it has been fought over by the French and Germans, for not only is the soil fertile but the land is also rich in coal deposits. On our journey west from Münster, therefore, we saw heaps of coal in the station-yards, long lines of goods wagons on the tracks, and black smoke gushing from chimneys.

At half past five in the afternoon we arrived in Essen, the city where the renowned Krupp guns are produced. Mr. [Alfred] Krupp sent carriages to meet us, and after travelling nearly a mile we reached our lodgings in a guest-house inside the Krupp factory. Meanwhile, company officials took several secretaries in our party and accommodated them separately at the Hotel Essen in the city, and Mr. Krupp himself took care of the arrangements for our entertainment.

March 8th. Fine.
Essen is a large city in the province of the Rhineland and has reserves of both iron and coal. This is why Alfred Krupp built his ironworks here when he embarked on the manufacture of fire-arms, and in the last ten years it has expanded into the largest industrial plant in the world. Iron production may be a thriving industry in Britain, but there is nowhere like this enormous factory. Shops in the city are few and far between, but there are up to three thousand workers' houses, all of them built by Mr. Krupp. After breakfast, we paid a visit to the factory.

The plant covers an area of 400 hectares, and it is here that the cannon are cast, while small-arms are manufactured at another site. Between them they employ a daily work-force of 20,000 men, of whom 12,000 are engaged here. Since there are more than 10,000 workers at this one factory, Mr. Krupp was granted a special licence by the government to maintain armed guards to keep order. The factory mainly produces cannon, gun-carriages and platforms, cannonballs and iron rails. Rails were being manufactured in several workshops, and we were told that one thousand rails are produced every twenty-four hours. The spectacular scale of it all was extraordinary.

We visited the site where cannon are forged. There was a fifty-ton hammer, ten feet long and so heavy that it would take the strength of eight hundred men to lift it even slightly. After being raised, it crashed down onto an iron platform below to hammer out the barrel of the cannon. The steam power used for this hammer is said to be 800 tons, whereas the largest hammer we had seen since our visit to Britain was 30 tons. That one was a fine specimen and large enough to dominate the entire workshop there, but it was like an infant compared to the gigantic hammer here.

Until forty years ago, Mr. Krupp had no family fortune and was in the iron trade, employing six workers to produce iron goods which he marketed himself. At some stage he went to Britain and worked there for several decades, gaining a wealth of practical experience in the process. Eventually he established his own factory here, and in the twenty-five years since then it has grown into the thriving place we see today.

It goes without saying that Prussia's spectacular ongoing military success is founded on the political legacy of Friedrich II. The appointment of men such as Chancellor Bismarck and the brilliant Field-Marshal [Helmuth von] Moltke has restored harmony between ruler and subject and enabled the exercise of shrewd government. The production of weapons of unparalleled power to equip the infantry, cavalry and artillery, however, has been achieved through the extraordinary technical skill of this manufacturer, Mr. Krupp. By establishing this bustling hive of activity with more than 20,000 workers in the countryside of western Germany, his name will be linked forever with the military prowess of Prussia.

The rifle used by the Prussian infantry was changed to the needle-gun in advance of the war of 1866, and its ensuing success in defeating the Austrians has led to the whole of Europe adopting breech-loading rifles, with the British making the Snider and the French the Chassepot. During the Franco-Prussian War in 1870–71, however, the Chassepot rifles proved superior in range to the needle-guns, and the Prussians were unable to approach within a thousand paces of the French riflemen. As a result, the Mauser rifle was developed in Prussia, and the existing needle-guns were reconditioned. It was decided to equip the regular troops with the new rifles and to supply the regular national guards with the refitted needle-guns. The cannon now used by the army are Krupp's latest model, and their performance is unrivalled by any other cannon.

To meet the specifications for Krupp's steel, a particular kind of iron-ore from Spain is mined and blended to make a metal which is hard but flexible and peerless as a material for cannon. Other countries cannot match this feature. Following their recent defeat, the French, too, have been paying more attention to cannon-manufacture and have begun making Krupp-style steel cannon in their own factories. To produce cannon from steel, however, requires much labour and cannot be accomplished quickly, so to conserve resources the French are manufacturing a new version of the same model using steel for the breech and bronze for the rest. This is not as hard or as durable, but in terms of fire-power the guns are by no means inferior. Bronze field guns are also used in Russia, and orders for some of these have been placed with Mr. Krupp. Although the British, with their advanced steel industry, are not in awe of him, all the small countries are following Mr. Krupp's example as they strive to raise their prestige, so his products have considerable influence on affairs of state and wield tremendous power.

Afterwards we were invited for dinner at Mr. Krupp's house. It is located more than 1,000 yards from the factory in open ground on top of a hill by a river. It is still in the process of being constructed, however, so although grand in scale, we were unable to see it in its completed form.

At half past seven we took our leave and boarded our train at Essen Station at half past eight. It departed at nine o'clock and took us as far as the next station, where we changed to a train heading east, on the route between France and Germany. This was an express train travelling at thirty miles per hour, which gave us a thrilling sensation of speed. From Westphalia we crossed the provincial border into Hanover, but by now it was the middle of the night and there was nothing to be seen.

For the most part, the Prussians make their living by cultivating crops and raising livestock, and 12,000,000 people, or half the entire population, are employed in farming. As Prussia's trade with Britain reveals, agricultural produce is sufficient for the surplus to be exported. The profit from this forms the basis of their economy, and at the same time the people work at mining and manufacturing, trading with foreign lands and sailing far and wide. They are not, however, like the British or the French, who enrich their country by profiting as brokers in maritime commerce through processing raw materials imported from far-off lands and exporting them again. Consequently, Prussia is known in distant countries only for its military prowess; yet in terms of the determining features of national policy, it actually bears a close resemblance to Japan, and there is more to be gained from studying the politics and customs of this country than those of Britain and France.

# CHAPTER 57

# A Survey of Berlin

March 9th, 1873. Fine.

When dawn broke, the train was already travelling through the province of Brandenburg, across a still broader plain with the occasional stretch of marshland. We were now in the county of Potsdam, to the west of Berlin, an area of picturesque lakes and marshes. The fields this morning were covered in white frost, and there was a biting chill in the air. At seven o'clock we reached Berlin to find the minister plenipotentiary [Sameshima Naonobu], the secretaries from the legation and a party of Japanese students all waiting at the station to meet us. People in Germany are punctilious in showing respect to their emperor and obeying the government, so when they heard of the arrival of our Embassy, the professors of the Japanese students allowed them to absent themselves from classes in order to call on us at our official residence. Even those lodging in outlying districts gathered in the city for the occasion. If the students had failed to come on the grounds that our visit was unrelated to their studies, the professors would have criticised them for neglecting their duty. In Britain and America, on the contrary, people had found the efforts of Japanese students to welcome and see us off amusing, so sentiments vary from one country to the next.

We were accommodated at the Hotel de Rome on the Unter den Linden. The imperial household took care of all arrangements, from our rooms to our meals, and separate dining-rooms were provided for the Embassy officials and the delegation staff. Several guards manned sentry posts at the hotel gates and in the corridors, to be on hand to protect us and attend to our every need. The level of care taken over our reception surpassed that in the other countries we visited.

Berlin is the capital of Prussia and now the capital of the German Empire. Although the fourth-largest city in Europe, it is actually a new metropolis with a history dating back no more than 120 or 130 years. The city is divided into five districts. The first is central Berlin, which has churches, schools, an armoury, hospitals and orphanages. The second, Kölln an der Spree, is where the palace and the imperial family's church are located. In the third district, Friedrichswerder, is the emperor's second palace, the medical college, the tax office and the mint. The fourth district, Dorotheenstadt, is also known as the 'New City', and the imperial family's school, the observatory and the mortuary are here. Also located here is the Brandenburg Gate, which is the finest sight in the whole city. The fifth district is Friedrichstadt, where goldsmiths' and silversmiths' workshops and the great court of law are found. The fourth and fifth districts have been developed more recently, so their broad streets are particularly splendid. Leading from the Brandenburg Gate is an avenue called the Unter den Linden, the grandest boulevard in Berlin. It has a middle lane which is used for light carriages, and trees are planted on either side forming two long gardens for people to stroll in. On either side of all this are lanes for heavy carts, with space to unload goods, and pavements for pedestrians next to rows of shops. Lined with numerous grand buildings and prosperous stores, it is the most perfectly appointed of boulevards. The hotel in which our party stayed is situated halfway down this avenue.

Proceeding to the very end of the Unter den Linden and crossing over a canal, one enters the second district, and from here onwards there are continuous rows of shops in what is the most flourishing quarter of Berlin. Throughout the first and third districts the houses are crowded together, and in many places the roads are narrow and haphazard, with canals flowing in all directions. A number of canals branch out from the river Spree, providing the benefits of water transport, and these are spanned by more than forty bridges. The scenery in Berlin is unlike that in Dutch cities, and it is also unlike cities in Britain or France. Just as in London and Paris, tall stone buildings soar skywards, and although they are not decorated with much colour or ornate carving, a great many are substantial edifices nonetheless. In Berlin the people are skilled at firing bricks, which are used to cover the walls with ornamental floral patterns. They are also adept at sculpture, and the upper colonnades of many buildings are decorated with statues. By and large the roads are all paved, but the paving stones are often uneven.

As Berlin is a newly emerging capital, its citizens are simple in their ways and not as frivolous as people in other great cities. However, as the city has prospered, they have become more decadent and have degenerated noticeably over the last few years. Moreover, with the recent spate of military campaigns on all fronts, the people have become volatile and wild in their behaviour.

In the many parks found all over the city there is always a café, and the men and women of Berlin come here to pass the time, sitting and sipping beer together at small tables in the gardens. Even inside the theatres, men and women do not refrain from drinking beer. It was all very different from the customs we observed in Britain and France. This is the leading country in Europe in terms of alcohol consumption, for each Prussian drinks an average of four hectolitres of beer a year, while people in Saxony drink an average of six hectolitres.

The reason for the coarser manners of the people in Berlin lies principally in the domineering attitude of soldiers and students. While this may be natural in soldiers after the recent wars, the students, too, are highly excitable and even the police do not have much control over them. This is perhaps due to the spread of liberal ideas to Germany in the wake of the French Revolution, together with the introduction of constitutional government in Prussia. Although this has not led to unrest as in some countries, the students and society in general exerted considerable pressure on the government, with the result that the universities have now become tremendously influential. Students drink heavily in the parks, and in their stupor roar out drunken songs or urinate by the roadside. On every holiday soldiers in uniform roam through the parks, casting amorous glances at the coquettish ladies who pass by; indeed, they behave like actors.

Prostitution has been growing steadily, and it has become of such concern to politicians that they have looked overseas for effective methods of curbing this problem. They have great admiration for the Yoshiwara quarter set up in Edo during the Kan'ei era [1624–44], and there was once some debate about creating a similar system. On one occasion, when we went to a photographer's studio in the Unter den Linden, the shopkeeper was drunk and was openly trying to sell indecent photographs. Throughout our travels in Europe, only in Berlin did we ever encounter somebody blatantly dealing in pornographic pictures.

At the time of our stay, Germany had largely recovered from its old wounds and people rejoiced in peace, only for a dormant problem to re-surface in the shape of an ongoing dispute with the Roman Catholic Church. Ever since the emergence of Protestantism four hundred years ago, the Catholic Church has regarded the Protestant states as enemies and conspired with Austria, France and Spain to force them to follow Rome's will. Recently, in the wars against Austria and France, the Church embarked on a secret campaign against Prussia, but Chancellor Bismarck uncovered the plot after the triumph over France, and in May 1872, in a daring manoeuvre to remove the source of this threat, he announced the expulsion of the Jesuit Order from Germany. The vociferous denials and intrigue which this provoked, however, reached such proportions that the chancellor has been forced to back down. Even now there is no end to the dispute in sight, and the Catholic side continues to plan new attacks on Bismarck.

The citizens of Berlin lack any depth of religious feeling, and on one occasion, when civil register figures were inspected, it was discovered that only fifteen in every hundred people had been married by a priest. A three-point law passed in 1868 made it possible to marry by applying to the municipal office without having to go to church. It also imposed restrictions on the role of the Church in schools and instituted legislation concerning religious sects. The Church's involvement in education is viewed as a harmful influence on the hearts and minds of the people.

The first time that we in Japan heard the name of this country was probably when a Prussian warship arrived in Nagasaki [in 1860]. When a treaty of amity and trade was concluded in the first month of 1861, all that people in our country knew about Prussia was that it had a reputation in Europe as a strong nation. Then in 1866 news arrived of the defeat of Austria, with accounts of Prussia's ascendancy in Europe, but it was not until three years before our visit, with the defeat of France, that the might of Prussia truly reverberated around the world, signalling its emergence as a great nation on a par with Britain and France.

In Japan, the name of Prussia conjures up its political skills, its flourishing literature and its successful military system, whereas commercial relations, which are the whole point of the treaty of amity and trade, are just a vague afterthought. In our opinion, though, Japan's trade with Prussia cannot be viewed as of less importance than our thriving commerce with America, Britain, France and Holland. Prussia's trade with the East is flourishing to such an extent that it ranks second to America and above France, and this despite the fact that the direct sea-routes from Hamburg and Bremen on the North Sea coast are more circuitous than the route from Holland. Three years ago, however, the marvellous construction work on the canal in the Isthmus of Suez was finally completed, opening up a direct route between Europe and Asia through the Adriatic Sea. As a result, both Austria and Italy have begun to place greater emphasis on commerce with the East, so the signs are that the volume of trade reaching Prussia by this route will grow sharply in future years.

With the recent removal of the last traces of feudalism in Europe and the relaxation of constraints on industry and commerce, enterprises now

compete to satisfy consumer demand by developing machinery to produce useful tools and high-quality goods, with the result that the level of
indulgence in luxuries is galloping out of control like a runaway horse.
Prosperity in cities and towns has followed this, and on arriving in Berlin
after London and Paris, although the city may outwardly still appear to
emphasise frugality, with its increasing extravagance it is a pale reflection
of its former self.

The political culture in Prussia seems to be founded on the legacy of
Friedrich II, a monarch who despised outward showy displays. It is even
said that at the time of his death he had no new clothes he could be
dressed in. As a result, ministers and others in authority even now cherish
the memory of his life-style, yet the ordinary Prussian whose virtues used
to be thrift and hard work is now prone to ostentation. Friedrich II once
said that Prussians are not frugal by nature, and that those with even the
smallest sums to spare will dress themselves up in fine clothing complete
with tall hats, long boots and walking-sticks. Evidence for his words can
be found in the German aristocracy's admiration of French culture, and
the way Austrian noblemen wallow in a life of gilded splendour, all of
which reveals the true character of the German people. It is in the nature
of man that a convenience once employed can never be foregone, while a
taste once acquired cannot be forgotten.

Prussia is poised to compete for the thriving trade between Europe and
Japan, which has hitherto been limited to the Dutch and recently opened
up by Britain and France. The opportunity is fast approaching for all
European countries to develop markets in the East as they endeavour to
make up for the shortfall in raw materials at home. In other words, the
attention we have hitherto devoted to London and Paris must now be
shared with Berlin and Vienna.

March 10th. Fine.
At twelve o'clock we were taken by Colonel von Wright and some other
escorts to the zoological garden, which is located in the western quarter of
Berlin and may be reached by the road leading from the Brandenburg
Gate. This gate is constructed in stone in the style of Ancient Rome, and
it is surmounted by a plinth crowned with a forty-two-foot-high bronze
statue of a goddess driving a four-horse chariot. Beyond this magnificent
gateway, surpassed only by the Arc de Triomphe in Paris, stretches a wide
avenue.

Beyond the Brandenburg Gate lies the Tiergarten Park, the largest park
in Berlin. The zoo is in one part of the park grounds. In its scale, in the

skilful design of its landscape and in the sheer number of its animals, this surpasses the zoo in Amsterdam. As one enters the park, the smooth road is lined with full-grown trees whose branches offer shade during the day, and at night a line of gaslights flows into the distance in a river of light. Carriages with iron wheels pass along the bustling thoroughfare, and the boulevard eventually divides into two roads which curve left and right. In addition to ponds and squares with statues and standing columns, there are mature trees throughout the grounds. Fallen leaves are swept away and the lawns are mown regularly, resulting in quite sublime surroundings. It is a grand and luxuriant park, reminiscent of the Bois de Boulogne in Paris.

March 11th. Fine.
At one o'clock today the steward of the imperial household came to meet us with carriages, two pulled by six horses and four pulled by twelve, with coachmen in splendid livery and a cavalry escort. We were granted an audience with Emperor Wilhelm I at the Königspalais, and in the evening we went to the imperial theatre.

# CHAPTER 58

# A Record of Berlin, 1

March 12th, 1873. Fine in the morning; rain in the afternoon, clearing by evening.

At one o'clock in the afternoon we went in ceremonial dress to the Königspalais, also known as the Opera Palace, the main residence of the king of Prussia where official functions are held. Today a hundred civil and military officials were gathered in the chapel, and after observing the service for a while we took a look around inside.

Once the service was over, the doors of the assembly hall were opened, and diplomatic representatives of all nations gathered inside in formal dress. The emperor himself was seated on a high dais, and Bismarck, the chancellor of the German Empire, was in attendance, together with a hundred civil and military officials and representatives from the various German states. There was first a speech given by the emperor, and the remaining time was taken up with addresses summing up the political situation.

After 1806 the title of 'Kaiser' of Germany remained unused for sixty-four years until December 1870, when all of the states both north and south agreed to place Wilhelm, king of Prussia, on the imperial throne. Accordingly, a central government was set up in Berlin, with representatives from all the states sent to attend the Bundesrat, the federal assembly there, and deputies were elected by public ballot, forming a popular assembly known as the Reichstag. Between them these bodies constitute the legislature, and administrative power is vested in the emperor and the chancellor, the post now conferred on Bismarck. The emperor conducts diplomatic relations and holds the right to use the armed forces on behalf of the German Empire, but this is only exercised with the consent of the Bundesrat and Reichstag unless the country is under immediate threat.

Within the legislative body there are eight different departments in the Bundesrat (the upper house), which are in charge of the army and navy, taxation, trade, finance, law (civil and criminal) and diplomacy, together with the railways, and telegraphs and postal services. We may infer from this the extent of the jurisdiction held by the central government of Germany.

The government of Prussia, which is quite distinct from that of Germany, also resides in Berlin (perhaps in the Königspalais as well?). Under the constitutional monarchy here, the crown passes from one generation to the next through the male line of the Hohenzollern family to heirs over eighteen years of age, ranked in order of birth. No queens are allowed on the throne. The king has complete authority over the administration and appoints the prime minister and cabinet ministers to preside over state affairs, and he also has some power over legislation. Established in 1849 during the reign of Friedrich Wilhelm IV, this system fully observes the provisions of constitutional government.

At four o'clock this afternoon we were given an audience with the crown prince [Friedrich Wilhelm] and princess [Victoria Adelaide Mary Louise], who treated us with great courtesy. Afterwards we were entertained to a banquet in the royal palace. The empress [Augusta] and crown prince and princess were all present, and the heads of each ministry and Field-Marshal Moltke were among the 150 people who sat down together for a feast which lasted until half past six, when everyone dispersed.

In the evening the rain cleared and the moon appeared a pale blue behind the clouds. Crown Prince Friedrich Wilhelm has been convalescing after a recent illness, but yesterday he returned to his palace in Berlin, so the streets were full of people waving flags in celebration. In the rejoicing tonight, professors and officials came in horse-drawn carriages, while the students held torches aloft and marched in procession down the Unter den Linden towards the Kronprinzen-Palais [crown prince's palace]. The band music and people's cheers filled the streets with a carnival of sound.

March 13th. Fine.
This afternoon we had an audience with the king's younger brother, Prince Karlus (formerly field-marshal of the Prussian artillery), his nephew Prince Albert and his younger cousins Prince Alexander and Prince George.

March 14th. Snow.
At half past ten this morning our escorts took us to Mr. Siemens's factory, which produces electrical machinery. This plant is equipped with a

steam-driven wheel of fifty horsepower and employs eight hundred workers every day. All the machines manufactured here are electrical, and the majority of them are telegraphic devices.

There are various kinds of telegraph machines, and each country has invented a different design, with its own strengths and weaknesses; some draw lines or punch out holes, and others print letters of the alphabet or rotate a needle to point to letters on a dial. There is a standard code for the telegraph signals on railway lines which employs the simplest instrument of all, and accidents rarely occur when this is used. We were given a demonstration of a machine of this type which had been fitted with a new device invented just this year.

From there we went to a large hospital [the Charité]. Established in 1770 during the reign of Friedrich II, the Great, this is situated in a secluded part of central Berlin in the midst of parkland, far from the bustling thoroughfares of the built-up city districts. It was a splendid sight, constructed in brick on three floors, with the walls painted so that it resembled a building of white stone. It has recently been extended and renovated to ensure the flow of fresh air from outside, in accordance with an architectural principle developed in America which has lately become widely adopted in hospital design. The reason hospitals have gradually been converting to this design may be due to recent experiments which have found fresh air to be so efficacious in the cure of ailments and the restoration of health that it far outweighs the benefits of medicine.

In all there are seven hundred rooms in the hospital, with enough beds for more than 2,000 people. At the time, 1,600 patients were here. There are also eleven laundry rooms for clothes and bedding. The hospital costs $400,000 a year to operate. The government pays $80,000 of this, and the rest is provided by income from the hospital's assets. No fees are collected from the patients themselves, and there are no religious restrictions regarding admission. The nurses are paid about $80 a year.

In the kitchen there was a row of six huge cauldrons, the largest of which was seven feet wide, and even the smallest one measured six feet across. Enough soup can be cooked in these to serve 1,500 people. As bread is the staple, all a Western kitchen does is boil broth and stew meat, for, as we saw here, the cooking facilities are simple but cater for large numbers. The smoke from the cooking stoves is channelled through a tunnel to a chimney half a mile away, where it escapes. This is to prevent carbon dioxide from contaminating the air in the hospital

Air is the single most effective element in preserving our health, and it has more power to cure illness than any medicine. Air, just like food and drink, works constantly to sustain our bodies day and night, but people are not aware of this because it is invisible. Therefore, hospitals should ensure an ample supply of fresh air by choosing locations with abundant vegetation far removed from the fires and smoke of built-up areas. They should also avoid the toxic effects of carbon by keeping chimneys at a distance and installing ventilation systems in the sick-rooms.

The new [Augusta] hospital was built by the empress, and today she had provided a special escort to give our Embassy a guided tour. Inside, there was a chapel and a mortuary in which patients who die are laid out. Everything from the kitchen to the cellars was immaculately kept and fully equipped with the most comprehensive range of table-ware and supplies. In the laundry room, five or six women were washing everything by hand as no washing machines had been installed. Many of the women employed here are young widows from aristocratic and wealthy families who offer their services as charity. To escort our party around the hospital, we were accompanied by more than forty ladies, who were most elegant and refined in their deportment. These women, we were told, were the wives of members of the nobility.

The empress herself paid a visit to the wards this morning, but she had already left by the time we arrived. She makes a point of going to see all the patients three or four times a month to enquire after their health. We all signed our names in a visitors' book on our way out. At the time we left there was a blizzard, so we were unable to look around the grounds.

In the afternoon we went to the Royal Museum. This is also famous and is built on a scale that even surpasses the British Museum.

March 15th. Snow, clearing with light cloud.
At a quarter past ten this morning our escorts took us to visit the Royal Porcelain Manufactory. This is situated on the river-bank outside the Tiergarten Park. It was moved to this site seven years ago from its original location within the city of Berlin. Constructed only recently, it was built under the auspices of the government, so it is even larger than the Sèvres porcelain factory in France.

The Academy of Fine Arts in front of the royal palace (the king's private palace) is an imposing work of architecture and one of the notable sights of Berlin. Built on three floors, the galleries hold collections of sculptures and paintings, and in general the pictures on display are famous works of the present day. Here men and women are paid to pose without their clothes on – standing, lying down or crouching – to enable artists to depict the human body accurately and to allow sculptors to make models of them in clay. Today a beautiful woman was lying naked on a bed, and she lay perfectly still so that artists could sketch her; she was allowed to relax only once every one and a half hours. It is like this every day, with models posing for a whole day, or sometimes for as long as a week. Copying the human form requires the utmost care on the part of the artist, but, even so, it seems odd that the pursuit of perfection should involve such a disgraceful practice.

This evening we had an invitation to dinner with the minister of foreign affairs, Prince Bismarck. Born in Berlin on April 1st, 1815, he studied law at Göttingen, where he also mastered several languages and learnt about international diplomacy. At the age of thirty-three he became a member of the Prussian Diet, and was made ambassador to France when he was thirty-six. He was transferred to Russia as ambassador at the age of forty-four, but on the accession of the present emperor, Wilhelm I, in 1861, Bismarck resumed his former posting in France. During the two months he served in Paris, shuttling between Prussia and France, he was already directing the country's affairs behind the scenes and devising various political schemes. In September 1862, he concurrently held the offices of minister of foreign affairs and prime minister, and worked tirelessly to help the emperor realise his ambitions. In 1864 Denmark was defeated and two duchies [Schleswig and Holstein] were returned to Germany, and in 1866 Austria was overcome and removed from the German Confederation. Then, in 1871, France was defeated and the lands of Alsace and Lorraine were annexed by Germany, so that now the fame of this prince reverberates around the world.

During the dinner this evening the prince referred to the time when he was young, saying: 'Nations these days all appear to conduct relations with amity and courtesy, but this is entirely superficial, for behind this façade lurks mutual contempt and a struggle for supremacy. As you gentlemen know, when I was a young boy Prussia was weak and poor. The state of this small nation at that time fills me with such intense indignation that I cannot dispel the image from my mind. First, so-called international law, which was supposed to protect the rights of all nations, afforded us no security at all. When there was a dispute, the great powers would invoke international law and stand their ground if they stood to benefit; but if they stood to lose, they would simply change direction and resort to military force, which was never limited to self-defence alone. However, small nations like ours would assiduously stick to the letter of the law and abide by universal principles, not daring to transgress these. Consequently, in the face of manoeuvring with flattery and contempt by the great powers, we invariably failed to protect our right of independence, no matter how hard we tried.

'Incensed by this deplorable state of affairs, we gathered our strength as a nation and strove to cultivate our patriotic spirit in order to become a country worthy of respect in diplomatic affairs. In the decades since then up to the present, all we have ever set out to achieve is simply to uphold the autonomous rights of every nation. Nevertheless, we hear constant expressions of horror from other countries at the way Prussia has used force, and they censure us for rejoicing in our military prowess and for depriving people of their sovereign rights. This, however, is entirely contrary to our intention, for we are motivated solely by respect for every nation's rights, and it is our hope that each nation may be independent and conduct diplomatic relations on equal terms, living within its rightful territories without its borders being violated. Fortunately, the learned men of the world realise that, in past campaigns, too, we have been left with no choice but to use force to protect Germany's sovereign rights.

'We hear of the distress caused to nations by the way Britain and France abuse their power, coveting overseas colonies and exploiting their resources. So the day has not yet come when we can trust amicable relations in Europe. Neither must you gentlemen relax your vigilance, for having been born in a small nation myself and knowing its state of affairs intimately, this is a point I understand most deeply. It is also precisely why I am determined not to let public debate divert me from my quest to win full sovereign rights for our nation. So while Japan may now have amicable diplomatic relations with a number of countries, its friendship with Germany should be the closest of all because of the true respect in which we hold the right of self-government.'

For the envoys listening during the banquet, these were significant words indeed, and we appreciated a chance to learn from the prince's eloquence, knowing full well what a master tactician he is in the world of politics.

# CHAPTER 59

# A Record of Berlin, 2

March 16th, 1873. Cloudy.

At twelve o'clock we travelled by carriage to the Arsenal. This is a square building enclosing a quadrangle, and on entering through the gates we saw in the middle a giant brass statue of a lion standing over ten feet high. Originally this was made by the Danes to commemorate a victory over Prussia long ago, and it had been cast by melting weapons and set up in the Danish capital. After Prussia defeated Denmark in 1864, however, it was taken down and brought to Berlin and kept here in the Arsenal [it was later returned to Denmark].

The individual nations of the West are fiercely competitive and possess a strong spirit of independence based on their inhabitants' love of country. This is so intense that the nations never miss an opportunity to avenge a slight to their honour, even after hundreds of years. Western people seem to possess a more passionate sense of patriotism than people in the East. Thus, British people do not care to enter the United States' Capitol because of a painting inside which depicts an American victory over the British army. Yet there is a constant stream of British visitors to Belgium who come to pay their respects at the site of the Battle of Waterloo, whereas the French avoid the area completely.

On another occasion, when the French defeated the Prussians, the bronze statue on top of the Brandenburg Gate was taken down and set up in front of the Palais-Royal in Paris, but after the Prussian victory of 1815 it was brought back and restored to its original place. When the Prussian army entered Paris recently, it carried away a bronze statue from the city gates of the French capital. Victors exult in their prizes, while the vanquished are consumed with resentment, and the enmity between the two sides over possession of a single bronze statue endures forever. Would taking these trophies down and removing the source of resentment not be a better way to preserve peace? The political systems in Western countries are based on listening to the people, but if the people reach such a pitch of excitement after each bloodthirsty triumph that they cannot celebrate with good grace, would it not be better to restrain their martial spirit?

The armouries in each European capital are laid out as military museums, with weapons old and new displayed inside them as exhibits bearing testimony to past campaigns. Separate arsenals are kept by the army and navy for weapons currently in use, such as at Springfield in America and Vincennes in France. The Tower of London, Warwick Castle and this armoury in Berlin are maintained as records of past exploits rather than as arsenals of modern arms. Afterwards we saw similar armouries in Austria and at Geneva in Switzerland. The finest spirit of our forebears is remembered through their words and deeds, to say nothing of the weapons they once used. It would be an act of barbarism if these old pieces of equipment in the armouries were to be thrown out or burnt and destroyed.

Monbijou Castle was built by the first king of Prussia, Friedrich I, as a garrison rather than a palace. Inside it were relief maps of cities such as Jerusalem and Sebastopol, and statuary, porcelain and furniture, including a substantial collection of pottery from China and Japan. Farther inside were portraits and a waxwork figure of Friedrich II. This bust of his head and shoulders resting on its stand looked most lifelike, with its eyes open and its gaze fixed on passers-by. There were also a dozen or so wax models of members of the royal family. The Germans are most adept at paintings and sculpture, and these models are so skilfully crafted that they surpass the famous waxworks in Baker Street in London [Madame Tussaud's].

March 17th. Light cloud.
At nine o'clock this morning we went by carriage to a soda-water factory, one of three factories in the city owned by the Soltmann company. Together they produce 1,000,000 bottles of soda-water (called '*Seltzerwasser*' in German) every year, and this is drunk by everybody, including the emperor, the crown prince and all the government ministers.

The Royal Printing Office has been newly built by the government on a grand scale over four floors, and it is here that national bonds, bank-notes, various bills and securities, and postage-stamps are printed. To make an envelope the paper is first cut into the shape of a diamond, and two lines of lettering are printed on the surface in faint black ink. This is both to prevent forgeries and to indicate the area on the envelope for the stamp. Next the stamp is printed in alignment with these letters and the paper is put in a machine where it is folded into the shape of an envelope.

This machine places the paper in the middle of an iron plate over a large square hole. When a square iron block of exactly the same dimensions is pressed into the hole from above, the four triangular corners of the paper rise up as the centre of the sheet is pushed down. When the block is raised and lowered a second time, the corners of the four triangles will have folded over far enough for them to be pressed flat, and the edges overlap and are joined underneath to make an envelope. The finished envelope is then ejected diagonally from the machine.

Postcards with printed messages are produced because written communication is so frequent in everyday relations in Europe. These range from dinner invitations to polite enquiries after people's health in extremely hot or cold weather. First the message is printed, together with the stamp. Once two or three words have been added by the sender and the name and address written, this may be put into a post-box.

The techniques used in printing bank-notes vary from one country to the next so as to preclude any risk of their being copied abroad. In France a technique is used in which an image on the note becomes visible when the note is held up to the light. The bank-notes in Prussia are almost the same as those in France, although the ones being printed now incorporate a method of super-imposing printed silhouettes of a person's profile. These shadow portraits consist of two facing images of the same individual, with three or four more images super-imposed on both sides, just as shadows overlap when lit up by several lanterns at once. The image in front is the largest and those behind are progressively smaller, but they are all identical in shape.

March 18th. Light cloud.
At half past eight this morning we went by carriage to the Franz Barracks in the south-west of the city. This consists of several beautiful new brick buildings five storeys high which are sufficient to accommodate seven thousand men. It is the largest and finest among the numerous barracks in and around Berlin.

The first four floors of the barracks were the soldiers' sleeping quarters, while the top floor was equipped with everyday facilities such as washrooms, stores for uniforms, and a place to repair boots. The soldiers sleep on bunk-beds with iron frames, which were far superior to the ones we had seen in the French barracks at Vincennes. In the basement was a bar supervised by non-commissioned officers which serves drinks to the men. All the soldiers probably receive the same rations of food and drink. They are not allowed to go out as they please, and if they want any more, they have to buy it here with their wages.

We then paid a visit to the Dragoons' Barracks in Belle-Alliance Street. At the front were the stables in two-storeyed rows, with the horses kept on the ground floor and hay stored above. An area between the stable buildings is used as a training paddock, and there the horses are drilled, galloping in a straight line or in a circular fashion. In the middle of this paddock a course has been laid out enclosed by a hedge, with mounds of earth over three feet high for practising jumping.

More than six hundred horses are kept in the stables. Novice cavalrymen are first taught on wooden horses, and inside each stable is an arena with an earthen floor which is used for training the horses. Here again troops were going through some foot drills, for on occasion cavalrymen, too, may abandon their horses and fight on foot.

Since 1814 it has been the military system in Prussia for all men capable of bearing arms to receive full-time training for a minimum of one year in the regular army, so every male in the country has some experience of serving as a soldier. Following Prussia's victory over Austria in 1866, all the states of the North German Confederation were compelled to adopt the Prussian system, with the size of the army in each state designated as one soldier for every hundred people in the population. This resulted in a standing army of 319,824 regular soldiers led by 13,804 officers, with 73,307 horses. This number could be increased to 700,000 men in wartime.

In February 1874 [less than six months after the Embassy's return to Japan], Field-Marshal Moltke made proposals to the Diet in which he recommended strengthening the German army to a force of 401,000 regular troops. The reasons he gave for this vast military expansion need to be outlined here, for they throw light on the situation in Europe today:

'The principles of law, justice and freedom serve to protect the country domestically, but only military power can protect it abroad. International law, too, is concerned only with a country's strength or weakness, for it is the small nations which remain neutral and are protected solely by this law, whereas great powers must use their strength to claim their rights.

'Some now begrudge military expenditure and yearn for a life of peace, but if war were to break out, would this not promptly squander the wealth we have worked so hard to accumulate all these years? To disband our regular army in response to encouraging signs of peace is a dream for future generations, not something which can be accomplished at present. On all sides our neighbours fear and detest our power, as if the devil himself were glaring down at them from pictures hung on their walls. We can see evidence of this in the way many people in Belgium today are siding with France.

'Does not the situation beyond the Vosges Mountains indicate that the French are solely intent on avenging the national humiliation they suffered [in 1870–71]? What I wish for now is not simply to keep the peace, but to control the peace and make all nations say that it is Prussia, situated in the heart of Europe, which is preserving peace throughout the continent. This can only be achieved by exercising military force.'

CHAPTER 60

# A Record of Berlin, 3; with a
# Supplement on Potsdam

March 21st, 1873. Cloudy.

At three o'clock in the afternoon we went by carriage to visit the [Moabit] prison, located a thousand yards or so north-west of the Brandenburg Gate. This prison has long had a good reputation for its extensive facilities. At present there are 490 convicts and a total of 49 officials including the guards; the prison for female offenders is in a separate part of the city. It costs $93 a year to keep a single criminal in custody, half of which is funded by the government and the other half is recovered in profits from the sale of goods produced by the prisoners, for they are forced to engage in regular work during the time they are held, just as in other countries.

Each prisoner has his own cell, in which he is free to keep personal possessions. The cell doors were opened so we could see the living conditions, and in every one there was a mattress and some utensils. Daylight was shining in through a glass window, and gas-lamps were provided for use at night. Many of the men also find diversion by keeping caged birds as pets. One prisoner who had been here for eleven years was serving a twelve-year sentence for setting fire to someone's house. In general there is a great disparity between the East and the West in the laws concerning arson. In the West the punishment for burning down a person's house is to pay the value of the property lost, which frequently amounts to a vast sum of money. Unless the offender delivers this sum, he is made to pay through a term in prison.

Adjoining the prison cells were an assembly hall and a chapel, in which two different styles of seating arrangements had been installed for the inmates. Minor offenders can sit in the rows of chairs, just as in a lecture hall, while those convicted of serious crimes occupy individual cubicles separated by partitions. This is because the criminals are prohibited from mixing freely in order to prevent bad habits spreading. A convict may ask for permission to walk around inside the prison, but on leaving his cell

313

the guards place a hood over his head so that no one can see who he is. Instructors from each general field of study are brought in to deliver lectures in the assembly hall. In the chapel there hung a picture of the cross, some musical instruments had been provided, and, just as in the assembly hall, cubicles for serious offenders had been fitted here as well.

March 22nd [23rd]. Cloudy.
Today was the emperor's birthday. A banquet was held at the palace. Everyone in the city streets was waving flags, and in all the shop-windows tonight gas-lamps were arranged in floral patterns and the shapes of letters, or shone with different colours. In the streets crowds cheered and sang the emperor's praises, and the illuminations were so brilliant that it was as bright as daytime.

March 25th. Fine.
We went to the fishery companies' exhibition [Grosse Fischerei-Ausstellung]. As it was the opening day, the emperor himself was to make an appearance, so our escorts ensured that we arrived in time to see him. When we reached the hall, a large crowd of men and women was already gathered there. After a while, the emperor arrived with some ladies from the imperial family, all of them dressed in everyday clothes. They appeared without undue ceremony at the main entrance, protected only by three or four attendants, so they were at the mercy of the crowds since the public had not been moved out of the hall. The people inside the hall simply parted to either side, opening up a passage for them and bowing politely. This harmonious intimacy between sovereign and subjects was a delightful sight. When the members of our Embassy paid our respects in the same manner, the emperor turned to the ambassador and made some cordial enquiries.

Inside the hall all kinds of fish were on show, either fresh or dried, together with exhibits of fishing boats and tackle, and models of coastlines and equipment used in the South Seas and the East as well as in nearby countries. Among these was a truly impressive display with the models of Japanese sailing and fishing boats, and of a fisherman's hut and a seaside inn.

In the basement were some stone tanks in which fresh fish were kept packed in ice. It is not easy to obtain fresh fish here as it takes several days for boats from the coast to reach Berlin, so in Germany and Austria large numbers of freshwater fish are cultivated in ponds. Some of the tanks had fish eggs which were incubated by being stirred in clean water, in the same way as we had previously seen in Amsterdam. In the last few years, fishery regulations and techniques have become increasingly refined in Europe. Severe restrictions have been imposed on fishing in the North Sea and the Baltic Sea to prevent depletions in stock, and studies are being made on trawling and fish farming, both fields in which Prussia and Russia are particularly advanced. This is an example of the careful attention civilised countries pay to detail in order to maintain their livelihood, not only through commerce but also by exploring every area of research in the interests of the people's welfare.

March 27th. Fine.
At half past eleven we left the station in the south-west and travelled in the emperor's own train some twenty miles to the city of Potsdam. All we saw en route was low-lying undulating land, with mostly sandy soil and numerous wooded hills covered with pine-trees.

Potsdam is the capital of Potsdam county and the provincial capital of Brandenburg. The Palace of Shells and Jewels here was built by Friedrich II over a seven-year period between 1763 and 1769. It is the largest of all the palaces in the area. The pillars and walls in the front hall are all adorned with shells which have been inlaid with jewels. These are said to be most beautiful at night when illuminated, as light reflects off the shells. There was a six-foot-high porcelain vase here which had been sent from Russia twenty years ago and, just as in other royal palaces, fine ornaments were set out in all the rooms. In one of these, the bedroom of Friedrich Wilhelm I, there were many fine paintings. This king was passionate about dogs, and there was a couch bearing a dog's teeth marks, left just as it was in his lifetime.

To the north are some dense woods featuring a broad avenue which veers eastwards towards a long slope crowned by Friedrich Wilhelm II's palace, named the Orangerie. Adjoining the Orangerie is another palace called Sans Souci, which was built as a residence for Friedrich II, and it was here that he died on August 17th, 1786. The king had lived most frugally all his life, and at the time of his death he had no new shirts of his own, so one of his courtier's shirts had to be borrowed for the funeral. The chair in which he was sitting when he died has been kept as it was, with the faded stains on the left of the silk upholstery made by the blood he coughed up. The clock has also not been wound since then. All the furniture was crudely made and did not seem fitting for a king. On the eastern side was Friedrich's study, and this, too, has been kept as it was when he lived. Also here was the bed in which Friedrich Wilhelm IV was laid out when he died, complete with hanging wreaths and surrounding screens, calling to mind his passing and filling people with sadness. People in the West mourn their dead with great sincerity and depth.

To the west of this palace stands a windmill. When Friedrich Wilhelm IV's palace was restored [by Friedrich II], the windmill was bought by a local landlord who told the miller to demolish the building as it spoiled the view from the palace grounds. When he heard this, the miller simply replied, 'Surely there must be at least one expert in law in Berlin,' and he boldly refused to tear it down. The issue was eventually debated by the government, whereupon it was decided that even a king had no right to make his subjects lose their livelihood. In the end, the building was left intact, and this episode has now passed into folklore. The windmill has been handed down to the miller's descendants and stands out clearly against the skyline to this day.

Babelsberg Castle was built by the present emperor as a country retreat. Situated at the foot of a hill overlooking the lake, it is constructed in the Gothic style, with brick walls and a timber interior. Although extremely simple, it is richly endowed in surrounding scenery. In the bedrooms were wooden beds with cloth hangings, and not a single piece of gold brocade was to be seen, nor any sculptures or paintings. Berliners extol the virtues of this palace, enquiring of visitors who have paid a visit to Potsdam if they saw the present emperor's palace and noticed how exceedingly frugal it is.

The crown prince's bedroom was filled with weapons and maps of battles. A cannonball from the war against Austria in 1866 was used as the base for a candle-stand, so he would appear to like military affairs. There was also a ball-room with an adjoining dining-room, both of which were built entirely of wood. In the palace there were some beer tankards, the largest ones as tall as a man. Berliners become very animated when they drink beer, and there are stories of how after heated debates duels are fought in the emperor's presence to decide the winner of the dispute. The indications are that these tales are not without foundation.

March 28th. Cloudy.
At eight o'clock in the morning Vice-Ambassador Ōkubo left for Frankfurt-on-the-Main to start his journey back to Japan, and at half past eleven tonight we left Berlin ourselves. Arriving at the Ostbahnhof Station at five minutes past eleven, we boarded a train with two carriages which had been especially arranged for us. Our escorts – Messrs. Wright, Roerdansz and Kanzki – also travelled with us to see our party on its way.

March 29th. Fine.
It was already light by five o'clock this morning as our train continued on its journey across an open expanse of flat fields. We crossed a wide river [the Vistula], then passed over the bridge [across the Nogat] at Marienburg before reaching the town of Elbing. Around here there was a great deal of wild marshland to be seen, and at half past ten the bay of Königsberg came into view. This is called Frisches Haff and is the most important harbour in Prussia. It was in the palace here in 1701 that Friedrich I was crowned king of Prussia. We stopped to take some lunch in the station.

At half past four we reached Eydtkuhnen Station, the last station in Prussia. We were invited to dinner in the station by our three escorts, and we made our farewells with a parting toast.

VOLUME IV

*Continental Europe, 2*

CHAPTER 61

# A Survey of Russia

It was in Russia that we ventured into the remotest regions in the course of our peregrinations around America and Europe. As we travelled steadily eastwards after leaving Paris, signs of civilisation became ever more sparse. Along the Baltic coast and the northern parts of Poland we saw dense forests and empty plains stretching away endlessly. In the midst of them were some miserable and humble dwellings which reminded us of the American plains, and when we opened our maps to investigate the matter, we discovered that most of the continent of Europe presents just such a prospect as this. For all the talk about civilisation and development, when the whole world is taken into consideration these notions amount to no more than the light of a star on the ground in one corner of the world. Fully 90 per cent of all dry land is still desolate.

In terms of territory Russia occupies two-thirds of Europe and almost one-half of Asia. One-seventh of the land of the entire world comes under the sway of the Russian empire. If one excludes Britain and all the territories which belong to it, Russia covers the largest area in the world. As for the population of Russia, its Asian territories consist mostly of nothing but dense forests or desolate land over which savage peoples and wild beasts roam, and its European territories are more populous than the rest of the country. In the north the average population is less than twelve people per square mile over an area of 700,000 square miles; in the steppes to the south it is no more than eighteen people per square mile over an area of 400,000 square miles; the average for the whole of European Russia, on the other hand, is thirty-two people per square mile. In marshy areas by the sea, people till their fields in snowy and icy conditions. In other parts the plains are covered with forests. The natives live in thinly scattered hamlets, and their livelihoods are similar to those found in our Hokkaidō.

Until two hundred years ago Russia had no presence in Europe. As a result of Tsar Peter's energetic efforts, however, it became for the first time a great country within Europe. Ever since then its strength has grown, and it gained a reputation for having a strong army during the disturbances of early this century [such as the Napoleonic invasion of 1812]. Cultural progress has been conspicuous over the last twenty years. Nevertheless, the government remains subject to pressure from the autocratic ruler, change is retarded by the old religion of Russia, wealth is concentrated in the hands of the powerful, and the progress of the ordinary people cannot rise above a mediocre level.

The name of the present imperial family is Romanov. Peter the Great came to the throne in 1682. His bold vision turned north-western Russia into a strong country for the first time. At that time Sweden was at the height of its formidable powers in the central plains of Europe. Peter built up a navy in the Baltic and went to war with King Charles XII of Sweden. Then, in 1704, he moved his capital to the present city of St. Petersburg and launched a weak two-pronged attack on Sweden. Thus, he brought the Duchy of Finland under his control and incorporated the whole of the eastern maritime provinces of the Baltic within the territory of Russia. Thereafter, as time passed, Russia's achievements became more impressive and its political power grew. At the end of the eighteenth century, when Empress Catherine II was on the throne, Russia destroyed Poland and absorbed it, and thus Russia's lands became what they are now.

When Russia was extending her territories, she took over other countries and brought them under her thumb. Provided that they did not vigorously resist Russian rule, they were allowed to follow their old customs and were not forced to change their ways. Accordingly, the governance and customs of each general government are different. Poland and Finland, in particular, still seem like sovereign countries, although they remain under the rule of the Russian emperor.

Russia is a vast country, and for the purposes of the long-distance transportation of domestic produce the gently flowing rivers are convenient, so canals have been dug and roads built to provide connections to them. The inhabitants are thinly scattered over the whole country, so there are no great works of construction. However, since Moscow was long the centre and the seat of government, canals were dug to connect the city with the rivers Volga and Don, and thus it is in communication with the important cities of the south. After the foundation of St. Petersburg, another route was opened as far as Lake Ladoga.

Ever since the coming of the railway, great efforts have been made to construct railway lines in Russia, for they offer a convenient solution to the difficulties of overland transportation. Since the lands over which these railways have been built are so vast, the railway lines can at present do no more than simply connect the main parts of the country with one another. Moreover, the track-laying is somewhat rough and ready. When we entered Russian territory after having passed through other European countries, the violent motion of the train on the tracks was most irritating. We heard that the route from St. Petersburg to Moscow, being the line commonly used by royalty, the aristocracy and others of quality, is kept in the best state of repair and is equipped with luxurious and comfortable carriages. On this occasion our party had the use of a carriage reserved for the imperial family; it was very well appointed and comfortable, but we were still shaken about tiresomely and we could imagine the discomfort of travelling in the ordinary carriages.

The Russian lands enjoy several different climates. Moscow is in the centre of the country, but in the south, on the shores of the Black Sea, the climate is almost tropical and natural produce is abundant. In the north the climate is generally severe, so there is little agricultural produce and extensive forests cover the plains. In the winter everything is frozen and the temperature drops to 22°C below zero. In St. Petersburg all the houses are sealed with two sets of glazed doors, and around the edges of the doors moss is planted, so the atmosphere indoors is damp and wet. Still farther north, even mercury freezes. In the summer the heat is extreme, too, usually around 90°F.

Nine-tenths of the arable land and the forests of this country consist of private estates belonging to the emperor, the aristocracy and the wealthy. There are very few independent farmers. Most of the peasants of Russia were called 'serfs', and they cultivated land granted to them by the landowners. Ten years ago [in 1861], however, serfdom was abolished; the serfs have now to pay 20 per cent of their total earnings to the landowners, while the government has issued bonds with interest and has used them to compensate the former owners of the serfs. For forty-nine years the peasants have to pay a land-tax of 6 per cent to pay back this debt. Thus, most of the people in the country are little different from slaves and hardly any have gained their liberty. The gulf between the rich and the poor is truly vast. In the country, people live in hovels, and we have seen here and there places which were like cave dwellings or animal sheds, while the big cities are full of towering mansions and their splendour gives Russia a superficial brilliance.

In the famous capital of St. Petersburg, manufacturing is making rapid progress. This is because the city's many aristocrats and men of wealth compete with each other in the ostentatious display of their riches and because, when one compares the state of affairs in the capital with the lives of the ordinary population, a huge quantity of manufactured goods is consumed there. It is for this reason, too, that trade with Germany, Britain and France is flourishing. Exports to foreign countries consist of goods manufactured by artisans from the produce of arable and livestock farming and forestry. The most important of these in overall export earnings are distilled spirits and other alcoholic drinks. The Germans control the profits derived from internal commerce and from imports to Russia, while maritime commerce is in the hands of the British. It is as if Russia were a storehouse for the West.

In the capital there are as many medical schools and hospitals as in Germany. In addition, there are six universities, where agriculture, chemistry, mineralogy, geology and other subjects are studied. Some women enter the universities, too. We actually saw women following a course of study in the department of anatomy at the Medical Academy.

There are as many as 219 newspaper companies in the whole of Russia. All these newspapers are published under government censorship, and freedom of expression is limited.

The national religion is the Greek religion [Russian Orthodoxy]. Since the time of Peter the Great it has been established that the emperor himself is the head of the Church. Thus, in court he is the tsar (in other words, emperor), and in church he is the pope (head of the Church). The Greek religion is a branch of Catholicism, rather like the relationship of the Ōbaku sect to Zen Buddhism. This Church is even worse than the Western [Catholic] Church, for the people are much misled and are taught a great deal which stands in the way of progress in knowledge and skills. There are people in Russia who talk of apparitions and see ghosts. Also, in some districts there are clergy who pursue their own lust. The folly of the people can thus be easily apprehended. On account of this, the emperor has unlimited power and the army has unprecedented strength, and Russia has been able to extend its power to control regions which are only partially developed. When we saw Russians worshipping their God and reciting their sacred scriptures, the way in which they prostrated themselves on the ground, offered up candles, put their hands together and recited aloud seemed very similar to Buddhist practices. In [Western] Christianity, when they make the sign of the cross and recite a prayer they start on the right [as seen by an observer], while in the Greek Church they start on the left. Everybody in Russia proper follows this religion; foreigners are permitted freedom of worship for the first generation, but their children are required to subscribe to the national religion.

The people of Poland are Catholic, and those of Finland Lutheran. In the Caucasus more than half of the population is Mohammedan, and so are 40 per cent of the population of Siberia. There are also followers of the Jewish religion in all regions, some 2,300,000 of them, and small numbers of Armenian Christians and followers of 'heathen' religions.

CHAPTER 62

# A Survey of Russian Railways and St. Petersburg

March 29th, 1873. Fine.

Today, at four o'clock in the afternoon, we enjoyed a farewell meal at Eydtkuhnen Station [now Chernyshevskoie] with the three Germans who had been in attendance on us. We reached Russian territory after our train had travelled two miles. The signs displayed on the walls of the station buildings were all in Russian script, and everything around us looked dramatically different. The station was called Wierzbolów [now Virbalis in Lithuania]. The German railway comes to an end here, and on the other side are the Russian railway tracks.

Everywhere our party went in Europe we found custom-houses on the borders between the countries we passed through. There, luggage is inspected and duties are charged, but we did not experience this ourselves. Wherever there is a custom-house on a border, the train stops for a long time. In the station building there is usually a large room and the passengers all disembark. Inside is a long counter, serpentine in shape like ancient calligraphy. The passengers take out their keys, have the porters bring their luggage and place it on the counter, and then sit down beside it to wait for a customs official to arrive. There are several customs officials and they take the keys from the passengers one by one, open their luggage and perhaps ask them about the goods they are carrying. In dubious cases they sometimes open sealed items. There is apparently a secret method [bribery?] used at such times by experienced travellers, who request the customs officials to curtail their inspection. During the inspection, all the other rooms are closed off and nobody may enter them; this is to prevent people evading customs dues. The actual manner in which the inspection is carried out varies in thoroughness from person to person. It is true of all countries that the most junior officials behave unkindly, but at this particular station the inspection was more thorough than anywhere else. The Russian government had appointed Mr. Verski, a member of the Asiatic Department of the Ministry of Foreign Affairs, to escort us, and he came to meet us in a special train consisting of three carriages. Two of them were luxury coaches for the use of the imperial family; the interiors were divided into rooms, fitted with long sofas and equipped with stoves and wash-basins. After hesitantly greeting Mr. Verski, we boarded the train and it soon departed.

Not long after we had begun our journey the sun set and darkness fell. We then reached Vilna Station, where we drank some tea. It is 180 miles from the border.

March 30th. Fine.

At dawn we were crossing an empty plain covered by a disorderly assortment of twisted pines and various bushes and trees. Here and there on the ground were patches of lingering snow, and water from the melting snow had accumulated, turning some areas into marshy land. The view was truly hideous. The farther north we went, the more snow there was on the ground; streams were iced over, fields were covered in slush, and in forests of denuded trees we saw some which were frozen. We glimpsed only the occasional village on the plain. The crude houses were made of logs, with planks nailed on to make walls and with one or two round windows, so that they looked like dove-cotes. There were no trees or fences around the houses, and the scene was of a hundred – or as many as five or six hundred – houses, some dilapidated, leaning unsteadily against one another. They made us wonder if the houses of the natives in Hokkaidō are like this.

Earlier we had travelled across the plains of America for three days and three nights, but this region felt more desolate. The circumstances of the people settled on these plains must be little different from the lives of the Eskimos. Education is not yet widely available in Russia, there is no system of provincial assemblies and widespread illiteracy and ignorance prevail, so perhaps it is unavoidable that the people have to submit to the only absolutist government left in Europe.

The great forests in this region consist mostly of straight-standing pines. Even the largest are not so big that one cannot put one's arms around them, whilst the smallest are no thicker than an arm or a leg. There is one tree which resembles a cryptomeria or a cypress. There are also stunted trees, which are probably black alders, chestnuts, elms and maples. Since the Russian climate is intensely cold, a tree only becomes useful thirty or forty years after having been planted. Although the country is a vast one and has many trees, there is a ban on felling them. Indiscriminate logging is not permitted. Before this ban, there used to be a number of factories on the banks of the Volga in the Urals which would cut down trees and turn them into fire-wood. After a few years, all that was left was bare, red soil, and even water sources dried up. Accordingly, so we were told, the provincial governments have instituted laws to prevent indiscriminate felling.

Today the temperature outside the windows of the train was 45° F, while inside, thanks to the stove, it was a steady 68°. The sky was clear and the view over the fields was a pleasant one. At eleven o'clock we had breakfast at Pskov Station, 392 miles from the border.

At four o'clock we had our evening meal at Luga Station. There were few houses there. Because there are no towns where meals can be taken on the railway between Pskov and the capital, the station here has been made especially large to allow passengers to rest and to take victuals. After leaving this station, we crossed the river Luga, which is more than two hundred feet wide. It was icy and there was snow on the ground, so the whole plain looked white. In parts we could see tracks made by the sledges which are used by the locals to travel around. After that, as far as the eye could see, there was nothing but the monotony of dreary forests and open plains.

At twenty to seven we watched the sun sink below the horizon and saw for the first time a village with proper houses. The land around seemed to have been neglected and abandoned. We noticed a magnificent white mansion standing on a hill of red earth. Upon asking, we were told that it was the St. Petersburg Observatory, and thus we learnt that we were now not far from the capital. Before long, the train pulled into St. Petersburg [Warsaw] Station. In the midst of a desolate plain there is just this single fine city with its beautiful domes and towering palaces. This is sufficient to show how different people's energy is in this country compared with other countries.

In the station guest-room we were greeted by General [Fyodor Fyodorovich] Trepov and Lieutenant-Colonel Katarski [?], appointed by the government to attend us, and by Mr. Merinikov [?] and Mr. Frosse [?] from the Ministry of Foreign Affairs. The station was fitted with stoves and the air was pleasantly fragrant. It is a Russian custom to perfume the air when waiting for guests: apparently, they pour perfume on a heated piece of iron and the particles of scent are dispersed in the steam. It was the night when the new moon makes its appearance, and we could see its slender shape in the winter sky. The blue sky seemed to wash over us, and the cold invaded our carriages, making us wonder if the tips of the crescent moon were making ice fly through the air. When one sees a new moon at a latitude of 60° N, it is impossible not to feel that one is at the ends of the earth. We rode in carriages to the Hotel de France, next to the palace, where we were to lodge. Our accommodation at this hotel was provided for us by the government, which also gave us all our meals.

St. Petersburg is the capital of Russia and it lies in the remote northeast corner of Europe. The port is ice-bound and closed for half the year. More than twenty miles upstream from the city is a large lake called Lake Ladoga. The great river which flows out of it is called the Neva. Seven miles from the city it pours into the sea, into a stretch of water called the Gulf of Finland. Eighteen miles from the city is an island in the sea called Kronstadt, on which a great fortress was constructed. By occupying this stronghold, Russia provided a defence for the city. In the past, during the Crimean War, British and French warships did not dare to enter the port for fear of this imposing fortress. Apart from three or four months in the summer, however, the port is difficult for vessels to use.

The streets of St. Petersburg are wide and orderly. The architecture is probably the most splendid in the continent of Europe. Most of the streets are covered with pieces of timber laid end to end in something like a tortoise-shell design, and only a few streets are paved with stone. It is said that this method is used because every year there is a great deal of snow and ice which enters the gaps between paving-stones, making them rise up during the spring thaw; it would be very inconvenient to have to re-lay the stones every year.

The palaces, the government buildings and the residences of the aristocracy are mostly built of granite, and the scale is grander than in any other country. There were originally many wooden houses, but now more than half are made of brick and they look splendid on the wide avenues. Here and there areas have been set aside for leisure, with gardens for walking in. Since both the ground and the air are cold, plants and trees do not flourish here, so the scenery in these recreational parks is rather desolate. The lay-out of the city is refreshing, but it seems it was modelled on that of Dutch cities; its appearance – criss-crossed by canals and with empty spaces planted with trees – is very similar. Tsar Peter [the Great] went to Holland and became a shipwright, and that is probably why it was based on Dutch cities.

The principal thoroughfare is called Konnogvardeyski [Horse-guards] Boulevard. It is a broad avenue with a road for vehicles in the centre and rows of trees on either side, along which run bridle-paths for horse-riders. It is a beautiful street.

The city seems busier than Berlin. The carriages are driven hub to hub along the countless wide avenues. Carriages found in other countries differ from those made in this city. The upper part is the body of the carriage, with iron rails on three sides, and it is fitted with cushions to sit on. The uniform of the grooms is also strange. They wear long garments with tight sleeves, rather like a morning coat, and leather belts. Russian horses are small in stature and have short necks, but they are exceptionally sturdy. In the streets the grooms race their horses, which seems exceedingly dangerous. Indeed, we were told that many people are injured every year.

The principal products of St. Petersburg are linen, followed by leather goods and sail-cloth. The manufacture of woollen cloth began to develop at the beginning of the nineteenth century. The reputation of Russian cigarettes has spread across the continent of Europe, so that wherever one goes one finds cigarettes on sale with St. Petersburg trade-marks. The government pays the greatest attention to armaments, and there can truly be few places in Europe to rival the enormous naval and military manufactories here where cannons are cast, warships built and ammunition produced.

The development of the railways has made the transportation of raw materials from the south more convenient, and now fresh fruit and fish travel thousands of miles to satisfy the palates of the residents of St. Petersburg. Fruit is scarce in the city, but fresh fish is in plentiful supply. The price of fish is low because, as a result of the abundant snow and ice, underground storage places can be utilised to keep raw fish in ice all the year round. However, the flavour of frozen fish is far inferior to that of freshly caught fish. Owing to the convenience of ice storage, in St. Petersburg it is even possible to obtain products from the tropics.

The members of the aristocracy have their mansions along the streets of the city, and the wealthy and the great families have their residences side by side. I dare say it is the equal of Paris or London in being a haven for those with money and for the nobility. Among the people of the lower classes are many who are poor and foolish, but those of high rank from the upper strata of society tend to congregate together and live in luxury, and in consequence the city shops are thriving and trade is booming. This is true of trade with the East, too, as is evident from the fact that expensive teas are consumed here at a more prodigious rate than anywhere else.

It used to be argued that in Britain, France, Belgium and Holland there were more wealthy people among the commoners than among the nobility, and that for precisely this reason the population in each country was flourishing and popular rights were well developed. In Germany (including Austria) and Italy, the wealth of the nobility exceeds that of the common people, and therefore those countries cannot escape being poor in the visible levels of civilisation, and the rights of the rulers are greater than those of the people. In Russia, by contrast, it is only the nobility who are at all advanced and the common people are like slaves. Consequently, Russian trade does not flourish and the profits are in the hands of foreigners. The grand shops worth looking at in St. Petersburg are all run by Germans (some are run by British or French people, but I am speaking here of the majority). The Germans hold the Russians in the greatest contempt and hardly have anything to do with them. In recent years, now that they have acquired a measure of freedom and have developed somewhat, the Russians have come to resent the arrogant treatment they receive from the Germans and desire to be rid of them. That these two peoples, in one and the same city, should treat each other with mutual animosity is a very disharmonious state of affairs. The French, on the other hand, are respected by the inhabitants of St. Petersburg. It was in Russia that the power of French civilisation in Europe was first recognised (after the recent [Franco-Prussian] war, the whole of Germany strongly rejected French civilisation). Britain is held in great awe. Even compared with what may be seen in London and Paris, the architecture of St. Petersburg offers not a few truly outstanding sights, and if one praises them in such terms to Russians, their delight shows that such praise surpasses their expectations.

The principal goods imported into the city are cotton cloth, woollens, silks, sugar, coal, iron-ore and luxury goods, which come mainly from Germany but also from Britain and France. Since the river Neva enjoys deep water and wide banks, large ships have no difficulty navigating it, and the city's location at the head of the Gulf of Finland in the Baltic Sea has allowed it to engage in maritime trade with all the countries of Europe. Yet in the months of September and October, when the snow and ice take over, the river-mouth is frozen as far as seven or eight miles out from the shore and so thickly that carriages can be driven over it. Consequently, river traffic is enclosed by the ice, and the frozen waters are indistinguishable from the dry land. In April of the following year the ice melts and drift-ice floats down to the river-mouth. This makes the sea even more dangerous. By May the ice has all gone and foreign ships can enter the harbour to load and unload goods of all sorts.

Although the cold in St. Petersburg is severe, the heat can be considerable, too. At the height of summer, the noble and wealthy families travel to Baden-Baden or Wiesbaden in Germany, or the mountains of

Switzerland and Saxony, to escape the heat. Usually, at the beginning of April, the coming of spring raises the temperatures; the days are gloomy and dark, and rain falls instead of snow. One can no longer cross the river on foot and waves begin to lap the shores. At this time, all the dirt frozen during the winter is released by the rising temperatures, and a foetid stench pervades the air. This often causes epidemics. It was precisely at this time that our party visited the city.

CHAPTER 63

# A Record of St. Petersburg, 1

April 1st, 1873. Fine.
We went to the Ministry of Foreign Affairs, which is located inside the
Russian government offices, and there met Mr. [Alexander] Gorchakov,
the minister. He has filled this office for seventeen years and enjoys great
fame as a shrewd statesman.

The governance of Russia is completely different in nature from that of
other European countries, for it is characterised by imperial absolutism.
The government consists of four institutions. The Council of Zemstvo
consists of members of the national deliberative assembly, half of whom
are appointed by the emperor. There are also the Directing Senate and
the Holy Synod. These, together with the heads of the eleven cabinet
ministries, form the government. All are under the control of the
emperor, and the emperor's wishes are, in effect, law. The main duty of
the forty-two members of the national deliberative assembly is to
supervise the work of administrative officials throughout the country and,
in collaboration with the cabinet, to enquire into various matters and to
determine whether laws are appropriate or not. Both the assembly and the
cabinet are located within the imperial government buildings. The senate
is a body which combines executive and administrative functions, and it is
located in a separate building. The senators have the right to admonish
the emperor.

April 2nd. Fine.
At ten o'clock we boarded carriages and went to the Agricultural
Museum, which stands to the east of the palace. This consists of one
building with a straight frontage; it is not large, but it contains all sorts of
equipment and covers the essentials, and we considered it worth looking
over. The wooden gate of a farmhouse was on display to show how it was
constructed. There was another type of gate which opens and closes by
itself. When a carriage approaches and the gate opens, the fencing of the

333

gate rolls upwards to form a shape like a tree-trunk, and when the carriage departs, it comes down automatically to form a door to close the gate. All these mechanisms are worked by springs and were invented by an American.

The next room showed animals and plants and their structure. In this room there was a great deal which was agriculturally useful. First, the demonstration of the constituents of the human body and of various food-stuffs was valuable not only for showing how nourishing the latter might or might not be, but also in connection with giving fertiliser to various kinds of crops and with crop-rotation systems. Similarly, it was also of great benefit to see how various insects are transformed. Seeing how a cutworm changes to become a flying insect, one can kill the insects and prevent them from laying eggs. Similarly, if one is cultivating and extending a forest, there are certain beasts, birds and insects which protect plants and others which hinder their growth. Every cultivator should investigate such matters, and for this purpose he would find it beneficial to examine the displays in this room.

Next there was a collection of tools from various countries, such as ploughs, spades, hoes and scythes. There were machines to plough the soil, to remove rocks, to extract sand and pebbles, and to remove tree roots. There were vehicles which cut grass and barley and then separate them, and machines which compress hay into hard bales. All sorts of other machines of various sizes were on display.

Because the countries of the West have flourishing iron industries, tools and machines of all sizes are cheap to purchase and easily repaired. Accordingly, hundreds of types of ordinary spades, ploughs, hoes, scythes and the like are produced, each having its own advantages. In general, equipment which is useful and serves the public good is widely diffused and in time gives rise to the invention of new machines of greater size and power. First, the principles are established, then pictures are produced, and in this way people in the Russian countryside learn how to use these devices, despite not understanding the principles. However, if one showed such tools to the Japanese, they would undoubtedly reject these unfamiliar devices. This is not because the West is clever and the East stupid. Rather, it is because the directions in which the minds of the people tend to move are different. It is truly an urgent political task for us to develop an iron industry and to derive the benefits from hundreds of kinds of tools.

We then saw the Treasury in the palace buildings. To mention a few of the particularly noteworthy items, there were water basins and vases of enormous size entirely encased in malachite. This is a beautiful green-coloured stone with a mottled pattern which is found in the Urals. The largest pieces weigh hundreds of pounds, but they often contain other substances and it is exceedingly difficult to find pure pieces. St. Petersburg is famous for its malachite, which decorates goods of all sorts. Even small buttons made of it cost at least one or two dollars. The huge items decorated with malachite kept here must be worth extraordinary amounts of money.

The gallery of the Treasury contains many statues and portraits of Peter the Great, and statues of Catherine I and Catherine II [the Great], and of all the successive tsars. There are also various items said to have been made by Peter the Great with his own hands. He travelled around Europe and was a man endowed with practical skills, so in addition to making ships he produced some beautiful ivory carvings. The skin of the horse he always used to ride was supposedly removed and cured, and a stuffed statue made out of it; this stands beside a statue of Peter himself. The horse looks just as if it were alive. It is fitted with the harness and saddle Peter used at the Battle of Moscow, and beside it stand his two favourite dogs, also cured and stuffed. At his side are his staff and his carriage. Seeing all this gives one the impression of being alongside Peter himself two hundred years ago.

The most astonishing item in the gallery is a great clock [the Peacock Clock] which was especially made in England in the time of Catherine the Great. It stands eight feet high and is made of gilt bronze. It shows the trunk of a maple-tree with abundant branches and leaves, and at an opening in the trunk stands a peacock. On a branch to the left there is a cock and to the right an owl; at the foot there is a fox. There are bells hung around, and about the roots of the tree is a circular garden of flowers with frogs, lizards and grasshoppers, which is bordered with coloured glass beads. The diameter is twelve or thirteen feet. The workmanship is exceptionally fine. From a distance it looks like a miniature model of a garden, and one does not realise that it is a clock. I first suspected it was a clock when I saw numerals moving around amongst the grass at the front. A clockmaker came and set the mechanism working for us. Immediately the peacock opened its wings, lifted its head, opened its beak and spread out its tail-feathers, turning round on the maple trunk as it did so; it was just as if it were alive. The cock stretched out its wings, raised its head and crowed thrice, signifying that it was three o'clock. Then the owl began to turn and the bells at the side to tinkle, while the grasshopper at the front had opened its wings and was turning at one revolution per minute, thus standing for the clock's second hand. After every revolution the number displayed in the grass changed.

In the evening we were invited to a circus. It was on a scale similar to that in Berlin.

April 3rd. Light cloud.

At eleven o'clock the chief of the imperial household came for us with a six-horse carriage and four four-horse carriages, with grooms wearing splendid scarlet livery decorated with gold braid. We were taken to the imperial palace, where we had an audience with His Majesty Alexander II.

The emperor of Russia enjoys the greatest income of any of the sovereigns of Europe. The private lands of the imperial family amount to one-third of all the arable land and forests in the empire; he owns goldmines in Siberia and all sorts of other mines, and the annual income of 4,000,000 roubles derived from them is entirely his own.

Although the ordinary people of Russia have at least escaped serfdom, in their poverty they cannot support themselves. Similarly, the government's financial policy is constantly in difficulties, with a heavy national debt and high inflation, and it no longer enjoys the people's confidence. Meanwhile, the wealth of the imperial family and its relatives grows year by year. Their grand and lofty residences rise above the great cities of St. Petersburg and Moscow, which they have built on the desolate Russian plains. Their horses fill the streets with their neighing, and the glitter of their gold and their jewels is bedazzling. Wealth overflows from the coffers of the urban aristocracy and all is bustling prosperity. For that reason the abundant treasures collected in the imperial palace are famed throughout the world; the magnificent and beautiful palaces, too, for the most part have no equal.

The Eastern races are less inclined to greed; they submit themselves to moral governance; their sovereigns are conscientious and frugal and thus have raised their people to great heights. Even so, the wealth they have accumulated is found astonishing by foreigners. The Western races, by contrast, are given to rampant greed and are slow to correct their conduct; as for their rulers, it would not be a calumny to say that they tax the people on their lands heavily and make themselves wealthy by keeping the revenue for themselves, and that they are all but tireless in their cupidity and rapacity. This explains why the notion of freedom has sprung forth among the peoples of Europe and why Europe is seething with the views of those who would wipe out the rights of sovereigns and establish the rights of the people. The peoples of the East and the West are different in character; they are almost opposites.

April 5th. Fine.

At ten o'clock in the morning we walked across a temporary bridge over the frozen waters of the Neva to the Peter-Paul Fortress. I had heard that during the severe winters of northern Europe water freezes so thick that carriages can be driven across it, but this was the only time during our travels that we walked across ice. The river is usually frozen by October, and the fifteen or sixteen miles separating the city from the harbour at the estuary become brilliant white tracts of land. The ice is more than three feet thick. The local people stick wooden signposts in it to mark the way, and they race about on horse-drawn sleighs. The muddy ruts left by the runners gradually make a mess of the ice, and the various routes across look as if they are made out of mud, but the parts where the sleighs do not go look like a silvery world as far as the eye can see. There are some places where the ice is so clear that one can see to the bottom of the water, and one wonders if the ice may not be melting, but this effect is caused by melted snow freezing again. Even when the surface appears to be very thin, we were told it is several feet thick. Our sojourn here coincided with the time when there was warmth in the air, although the ice remained as solidly frozen as before. Yesterday, however, the fourth of April, horse-drawn sleighs were banned from driving over the frozen river. By the time of our departure, waves were rippling across the water.

The Peter-Paul Fortress occupies a sand-bank in the middle of the Neva and rises up opposite the imperial [Winter] palace. The ramparts with their artillery emplacements are constructed in the shape of a star, with openings in the stone walls on the outside for cannons to fire from. It was built on a grand scale, but is of no practical value today. In the middle of it stands the family church of the emperors.

The powerful authority which the Church exercises over the Russian people could not be conceived of in an Eastern country, where the state is governed by civil ethics, and it weighs most heavily on those people at the lowest levels of society. They worship images and seek to appease unicorns or suchlike beasts. The religions – the Mohammedanism of Turkey, the Greek religion [Orthodoxy] of Russia, the Catholicism of Austria and France, and the Protestantism of America and Britain – are all the same in that religion has engrained itself so deeply in the people that, no matter whether the sovereign is conducting the business of government, or commanding his armies, or promoting commerce and industry, or developing new agricultural lands, the Church always has a great deal of influence when the people need to be deployed to some purpose. The upper classes of European society appear outwardly to treat the Church with the greatest devotion, but when one looks into their real feelings, it seems rather as if they are treating it as a tool to make the people follow them and their laws and thus are using it for their own ends. King Friedrich II of Prussia has said that the Church's influence has no effect other than to dull the intellect. Although this apt but extreme view came only from the lips of Friedrich, when one observes how sovereigns and ministers everywhere govern their countries and engage in diplomacy, pursuing their strategic ends with wiles and deceit in a hundred different ways, one sees that the Church is no more than a tool they play with and that they use the mask of piety to control the foolish masses.

Peter the Great's cabin lies several hundred yards to the east of the entrance to the fortress. It is a plain, single-storey wooden dwelling just six yards long and fourteen yards wide. The interior is divided into four rooms. To the left, there is a sitting-room, three yards square, with hand-made chairs and so on. To the right is a dining-room, forty square yards in area. This is where Peter lived after he had seized this land from Sweden when he was founding the city, building the fortress and a palace, having warships and merchant vessels built, and supervising all these activities. This small, humble dwelling is evidence of the tight rein he kept upon himself and the arduous labours he undertook from the time he went to Holland until the time he defeated the king of Sweden and was acclaimed the tsar of Russia.

In the study there is now a Christian icon which Peter had faith in, and before it a table on which ordinary men and women who have come to worship place lighted candles; they recite prayers for the repose of his soul. Next to that is the bedroom, just six square yards in size, which has been made into a place for a priest to rest. At the entrance to the cabin a lot of women were selling candles, collecting donations or begging. It is perfectly true that the believers of both the Roman [Catholic] and Greek [Russian Orthodox] Churches willingly practise beggary. This old cabin has been repaired and has lost its original appearance since another building has been built all around it. There is a veranda to protect it, and outside is a small garden. Such a cramped dwelling is a rare sight indeed in the West.

As we walked along the veranda we encountered a priest and some believers who had just begun a memorial service. The sound of their voices was similar to that of such services in our country. The men and women who had come to worship were all kneeling on the ground and making the sign of the cross with their hands, and this, too, seemed much like the magical practices of Buddhist monks in Japan. Whenever the tsar-emperor proceeds through the city, men and women prostrate themselves on the ground and worship him with their hands held together, just as the followers of the Shinshū sect in Japan behave when worshipping at the Honganji [in Kyoto]. We had never seen anything like this before in Europe.

April 6th. Cold and overcast; temperature outside dropped to 40°F.
At twelve o'clock, we went in full dress to a military training-ground where we watched soldiers at their drill.

# CHAPTER 64

# A Record of St. Petersburg, 2

April 7th, 1873. Cold and overcast; temperature fell to 38°F; flurries of snow.

We went to the Ministry of Foreign Affairs, where there was a reception.

At half past one we went to the bank-note printing works, which is larger than that of any other country. The paper manufactured in the printing works is a different colour on each side and contains watermarks. The design, made of copper (in other words, a mesh made of copper wire), is placed on the wooden frame which holds the paper-making screen and then pressure is applied to the screen to make one side of the paper. Then, after removing the mesh, they pour in paper pulp of a different colour; as a result, paper of a different colour is formed in those parts where the screen was covered, leaving the design clearly visible on the reverse. Once the paper is formed, the screen is placed on a flat piece of flannel to deposit the paper; thus, a pile is gradually built up, and steam-power is used to apply pressure to the paper and the flannel and thereby expel the water. The paper is then dried by steam, and after the sheets of paper have been removed the process is completed (by rolling them between two sheets of copper to give them a sheen, and so on). The paper thus produced is pliant and of excellent quality, but it involves a great deal of labour and is therefore costly.

To insert simple patterns in paper they use a mechanical paper-making machine. The paper pulp is mixed with water and poured onto a cotton cloth resting on a copper mesh. After the cloth has been rolled up and removed from the mesh, it is taken to rollers to which copper mesh with the desired design has been attached. The rollers revolve, gripping the soft, wet paper between them; when the paper emerges, the shape into which the mesh was formed has been transferred onto the paper by virtue of making the surface of the paper thinner in places to form the pattern. It then passes over revolving drums filled with steam in order to be dried. Then it is sized. The actual printing of the bank-notes and the engraving of the copperplates is more or less the same as that which we had already seen in other countries.

No limits have been placed on the production of paper currency, so the Russian people have lost confidence in paper money to a higher degree than in any other country in Europe. Although the government has issued a coercive decree with regard to bank-notes, which strictly requires gold coins to circulate at a value of 5 roubles 15 kopecks in paper money, the value of paper currency is discounted by comparison with gold and silver currency and actually loses between 10 and 22 per cent of its face value in transactions. Coinage such as that of Britain is valued at extraordinarily high levels, and prices in St. Petersburg have become highly inflated. The loss of trading profits brought about by this state of affairs is apparent from the very great difference we Japanese experienced when spending the same amounts of money in St. Petersburg as we had in Britain and finding that we could purchase far more in Britain.

We next visited the library [now the National Library of Russia]. This grand library is famed throughout the world and is housed in a lofty two-storey building as tall as a five-storey block. It contains approximately one million books. In recent years, at a cost of 100,000 roubles, the library has acquired some Egyptian documents two thousand years old and an old Turkish book [a famous Koran]. In the latter, the script is very large, the letters being the height of one's little finger; it is read from right to left. This book was kept at the ruler's right hand in ancient times, and once, when he was reading it, he was stabbed to death by an assassin, and traces of blood are still visible where it seeped into the paper. It is one of the most prized items in the library. The library also has books from Arabia, India and China.

In the West, oil-painting started in the fifteenth century, but the library also has books containing pictures from earlier times. In them the techniques of chiaroscuro are used to depict shade in the same manner as today. The only difference lies in the use of colour pigments. Some manuscript books dating from before the invention of movable metal type were on display, together with a contemporary desk and bookstand to show how books were read in those times. Until then there had been no books apart from manuscripts, and because they were of great value and easy to steal, each book had a chain attaching it to a desk. They were jealously guarded, and borrowing them was not permitted. Seeing them now, one cannot but be struck by the great inconveniences occasioned by the crude ways of the past. Yet this was no more than five hundred years ago. The library has a collection of translations of the Old and New

Testaments into many different languages and they fill 120 boxes. There
was no translation in Japanese script amongst them, for the Bible has not
been translated into Japanese. Those who wish to read the books in the
library have to read them there and are not required to pay a deposit. The
reading room is divided into sections for men and for women. The actual
number of readers these days ranges from four hundred to, at most, seven
hundred.

On our return, we passed an office building on a street which ran along
the bank of one of the canals and observed many people gathered there.
On enquiring, we were informed that this was a place where serfs used to
be bought and sold. Ten years had elapsed since the abolition of serfdom,
and the terminology had changed so that one now spoke of 'hiring men'.

April 8th. Snow settling on the ground; colder.
At half past one we took carriages to Moscow Station and boarded a train
for Kolpino, a town lying fifteen miles to the south-east. Since it is a
resort, the buildings in the town are rather fine; yet it is merely considered
one of the more attractive towns in Russia and nothing else. Most of the
townspeople wear leather clothing and fur hats. Their carriages are crude
and their horses filthy, and the wheels are soon made dirty by the muddy
roads. It cannot be compared with towns in the principal countries of
Europe.

The ironworks at Kolpino mostly makes materials used for the construction of naval vessels. The armour-plating produced here is six inches
thick, sometimes as much as fifteen inches thick. The production techniques are the same as those we witnessed at Sheffield. However, it was
our impression that the din at Kolpino was greater as the workers, more
than forty of them, pulled the trolleys, seized the chains and made haste
to put the iron into the rollers. Furthermore, it seemed that in quality the
iron plates were inferior to those in Sheffield.

Very many difficulties stand in the way of developing an iron industry
in Russia. First, the extreme cold reduces the temperature of the furnaces,
so measures have to be taken to prevent air infiltrating through the many
chimney apertures. Second, it is not possible either to build tall structures
or to install glass roofs to make it light inside. Third, supplies of iron-ore
and coal have to be transported over long distances, and it is difficult to
meet needs. Fourth, in order to make use of water-power, it is necessary
to draw water from the bottom of the river when it is frozen, for
otherwise the water supply would be inadequate. However, because the
land around is completely flat, there are very few undulations [to allow

water-power to be used]. These four difficulties have to be overcome, and it must be said that great efforts have been made.

There are said to be four or five major ironworks in St. Petersburg. This factory falls under the Admiralty and it is administered by several resident naval officers. On this day we took luncheon at the home of a certain naval officer. His wife, who was also present, greeted us warmly and ate with us at table. She was exceedingly kind and gracious. When it was time for us to return to the city, all the officers came to the station to see us off. We arrived back at our hotel at ten past six.

It is one of the legacies of Peter the Great that ever since his reign the Russian government has devoted its energies to the navy and has paid great attention to the production of warships. Even in Europe, of the great powers only Britain and France have naval forces which surpass those of Russia. The rest all fall short. In order to raise a navy, Peter travelled to Holland to acquire knowledge of shipbuilding. When he returned, he made use of Dutch techniques to establish a navy on the Baltic. These techniques were the same as those used in England. However, the structure of the navy and its personnel was based on the French system, with some variations.

In naval matters, Britain proudly goes its own way. Hitherto, Russian military equipment has either been built by British workmen or been dependent on French skills, so naturally the Russians have been considered to be rather child-like in this respect. However, the news has reached Britain that Russia is manufacturing the mastless, turreted warships, and that in some respects they are superior to the warship now being completed at Portsmouth. When we were in Britain last year, the British were urging their shipbuilders to greater efforts as soon as they heard the news, and they said that Russian manufacturing had improved to the point where the Russians, too, could construct sturdy iron-clads. They also warned the public, saying that the future now looked threatening, so Britain could not fail to answer this competitive challenge. At present, these British and Russian iron-clads are the most powerful naval vessels in the world.

April 9th. Cloudy.

In the afternoon we had an audience with the tsarevich, Grand Duke Alexander. We then went by carriage to the Foundling Hospital. A foundling hospital is a place where the children of poor people who are unable to raise their children themselves are looked after. Similar institutions have been established in all countries, including America, Britain and France. Some are founded by the government, some by members of religious orders as a form of charitable work and some by members of the public. Many of them are run by Roman Catholics. A considerable number of such children raised by members of religious orders take religious vows themselves later. This is, of course, one method of spreading the faith and preventing it from dying out. The largest institutions established by governments are to be found in Russia, but those in France and Austria are comparable in size. Governments in Protestant countries prefer not to establish such institutions.

When it comes to the question of increasing the population, politicians in Russia are of two minds. While it would be irresponsible to make an increase in the population the main goal, both Russia and America have small populations and therefore they find it difficult to accept European opinions on this question. Could this be the explanation for establishing such large foundling hospitals?

The hospital itself is a four-storey building built of brick, wood and a little stone. It is an impressive white structure, and the windows were wide open to allow for good circulation of fresh air. It is very clean. At the entrance there is a room where people deposit the infants they have brought. Sometimes they are carried in by their parents, sometimes by relatives. No enquiries are made; they are simply asked whether the child has been baptised or not and then allowed to depart. Thereafter, the children have no contact with their parents. The child is placed in a small perambulator, its sex is determined and the details are written down on a record card, blue ones for boys and yellow ones for girls. The exact date is noted to facilitate record-keeping, and the child is then sent to the next room with its record card. A perambulator is a vehicle with a soft, warm blanket inside which gently rocks when moved. They are widely used in the West for small children.

In the next room there is a white marble bathtub full of warm water. The temperature of the water is checked and the child is bathed. Next, the child is weighed on scales mounted on a stone platform beside the bath; it is laid on the scales so that its weight is indicated; this, too, is recorded. The child is then put in a cot in the same room for four hours. Checking the child's weight is essential in order to ascertain how many years and months have passed since birth, and determining its age is essential for raising the child properly. On the day we visited there were four boys and seven girls at rest in this room. Once four hours have passed, the children are taken upstairs where they are given wet-nurses.

Once they have entered the hospital, the infants are raised for six weeks on the milk of their wet-nurses. Then they are sent to the countryside where they are taken in by ordinary families and raised on cow's milk. The wet-nurses are paid nine roubles monthly, excluding food and clothing. The country families who take the children in and raise them are paid two and a half roubles per month; this is reduced to two roubles once the child is five years old, and one and a half roubles when the child is ten years old. After the age of fifteen, no payments are made. Until they reach the age of twenty they work in their homes without wages in order to repay the costs of their upbringing. After that they are legally independent. Children with some academic ability are, upon investigation, taken back into the hospital, where they are educated.

In each ward in the hospital there is a place where the wet-nurses gather to be instructed in methods of child-rearing. The children are vaccinated whilst they are in the hospital, and on the second floor there is a ward where sick children are cared for. Premature babies are kept warm by placing them in cots under which hot water is kept circulating. Children with eye diseases stay in darkened rooms from which sunlight is excluded. Children with pulmonary difficulties are assigned to rooms where the air is filled with fumigants. When a child dies, a post-mortem examination is performed twenty-four hours afterwards. On the topmost floor there is a chapel for the wet-nurses, as well as school-rooms for the older children who are receiving an education, with different rooms for different subjects; the sexes are segregated.

The School for the Deaf is also very large. Dumb children are born deaf, as the root of their illness lies in their ears, but their ability to produce sounds is not impaired in the slightest. However, since they are unable to hear others speaking, they simply fail to learn how to speak. On the day of our visit, boys and girls of around ten years of age were being made to voice letters to which their teachers were pointing. The sounds they produced were all different, but they did approximate the sounds represented by the letters. Amongst them was an extremely pretty girl aged eleven or twelve who could articulate well. When we encouraged her to talk by gesturing to her, she said in Russian that she was too embarrassed. One of our party who has a good knowledge of Russian could understand her clearly.

CHAPTER 65

# A Record of St. Petersburg, 3

April 10th, 1873. Snow fell during the night; cold rain in the morning. At twelve o'clock we had an audience with Grand Duke Nicholas. He is the emperor's younger brother and a general in the army.

At twenty past two we took carriages to a military clothing factory which supplies uniforms and footwear for all the regular soldiers in Russia. It is under the supervision of army officers and employs poor men and women from the city, although women are few. The uniform worn by Russian soldiers consists of a black tunic with grey breeches; since the country is a cold one, there is also a greatcoat, which is made from a rough kind of woollen cloth. On their feet they wear boots, and everything is made here. The tunic and breeches are changed every two years, the greatcoat every three years and the boots usually twice a year. For the welfare of the soldiers it was essential to establish this factory.

We then went to the Museum of Mining, which is located on the north bank of the Neva. The four leading countries in Europe in terms of mineral resources are Britain, Belgium, Prussia and Russia. Russia has the largest territory in the world, much of it consisting of cold, desolate, barren steppes, but it has substantial mineral resources. On account of transportation difficulties, however, these resources have yet to bring much profit. From the Urals come iron, copper, silver and platinum; sulphur comes from there, too. The eastern foothills are rich in metals; the western foothills produce coal, marl and gypsum (both used as fertilisers), and sulphur and copper.

On our way home we crossed the Nikolai Bridge, a stone bridge across the Neva. It is five hundred yards long and cost three million roubles to build. It is the finest bridge in the city. In that area there are rows of magnificent buildings along both banks of the Neva; the river itself is broad and the roads wide, and the view of St. Isaac's Cathedral is extraordinarily beautiful.

April 11th. Snow falling and settling.

On this day we were to have travelled by train for twenty miles in a south-westerly direction to the emperor's summer palace and to have had a view of the famous fortress at Kronstadt, but on account of the blizzard we abandoned the trip. At two o'clock we boarded carriages and went to the School of Anatomy attached to the Medical Academy. Each year between six hundred and seven hundred full autopsies are conducted here; the number of partial autopsies exploring one diseased part is unknown. The corpses are all of people who have died of disease. When we asked if the corpses of criminals were also dissected, we were informed that they were not. It has been decided that the bodies of all paupers who receive treatment free of charge at the hospital under charitable assistance provided by the government and who subsequently die are to undergo an autopsy. Once the autopsy has been completed, the body is sewn up to restore it to its former shape and it is then buried by the government. In some cases lime is used to desiccate the corpse and the skeleton is preserved; these must be the corpses of homeless paupers.

On the day of our visit full autopsies were being performed on five or six corpses, and partial autopsies on another six. The school also has a department of veterinary pathology, where autopsies are performed on cows, horses, sheep and dogs. In the various rooms were large quantities of desiccated bones, internal organs preserved in spirit, and wax models. There was a petrified corpse, which had been desiccated using lime eight years earlier, and tens of thousands of skulls filling a number of rooms and piled up in the corridors.

Among the pupils at the academy were some Mongolians and Manchus, as well as women students. In Russia, some women pursue their studies at university; this does not happen in other countries. They mostly study medicine. In the School of Pathology we saw twenty-eight charming women; one was sitting at a desk drawing some internal organs preserved in alcohol and comparing them with a book, the better to study them, while another was examining an amputated arm. We found this astonishing. In Europe the only countries in which women attend university are Russia and Switzerland.

April 12th. Fine.

At eight o'clock we took carriages to the ironworks belonging to Mr. Obukhov's company. These were formerly located beside an iron-ore mine in the Urals, but in 1864 they were moved here. With government assistance the company manufactures naval machinery and casts cannon.

Russia's territories being so enormous, many barracks have been built for the large numbers of soldiers sent to guard the borders. Since the government now desires to expand to the south in the direction of Turkey, Persia and the independent parts of Turkey, and to secure a sea-route to India as quickly as possible, arms are at present being manufactured on a vast scale.

The items manufactured here are larger than anything we saw in Britain, and there is probably not a factory which can compete with it, apart from that of Mr. Krupp.

April 13th. Cloudy; flurries of snow.
Snow had now been falling for several days in succession, but the ice-bound river was gradually melting and waves were reappearing. During the thaw, we were informed, the air loses its warmth and so the ground actually gets colder, hence the snowfalls.

At twelve o'clock we went in our finery to the drill hall, where we saw two hundred new recruits doing marching and horseback drills. At one o'clock the emperor made an inspection on horseback. Each squadron made one circuit of the hall at a slow pace to finish the session. The emperor himself came up to our party for a moment to give us his views. Then twenty cavalrymen performed a drill; they were all Cossacks. They are agile and accomplished horsemen and are famous throughout Europe for their valour. They all carried a sword, a lance and a rifle; a target was placed on the ground and each man raced his horse towards it, hung down from his saddle to pierce the target with his lance, then straightened up in his saddle and galloped on. Their nimbleness was astonishing.

The Cossacks have always been a free people, with all their villages belonging to their own kind and no taxes whatsoever levied upon their land; each enjoyed his own rights over cultivation, livestock farming and even fisheries and hunting grounds. These rights are received only in return for their service in the armed forces of Russia. The Cossacks are not included in the regular army of Russia; rather, they constitute an essential emergency force which is deployed when there are disturbances on the borders.

After the drills were over, the emperor dismounted, bade us farewell and returned to his palace.

April 14th. Fine.
At eleven o'clock we left our hotel, and at twelve o'clock we departed from St. Petersburg by train. Mr. Verski rode with us to see us off; our route was the same as that by which we had come. The snow had settled

and was adorning the bare fields, rendering the forests and the trees extraordinarily beautiful. We felt a freshness in the scenery. Again we dined at Luga Station, and in the early evening took tea at Pskov. That night the moon was pale and illuminated the broad plains, inducing a feeling of solitude in us.

April 15th. Fine.

At eight o'clock we reached Vilna. From this point on we saw many hills covered with pine-trees. After travelling for a further four hours, we came to the frontier. We had lunch and then bade Mr. Verski farewell. We thereupon changed trains and entered German territory.

Our journey to and from Russia was in total about one thousand miles. We were furnished by the emperor with a special train which was very comfortable. This was the first time we had travelled on such a well-appointed train since the sleeping-cars we had used in America. However, there were no beds on the train so we were unable to sleep. The ordinary sort of railway-carriage in Europe is equipped only with the means of stretching out one's legs at night. They have neither wash-basins nor lavatories, and three people, or six, have to take their rest on the upholstered seats. When travelling day and night, one finds the discomfort unbearable. In general, the trains stop for five minutes at each station, and in the larger stations they stop for fifteen or even twenty-five minutes, allowing one to take a meal. If one hesitates and delays, one has nothing to eat for the whole day.

I suppose that the most powerful countries in Europe are the five monarchies of Britain, France, Germany, Austria and Russia. It is on account of the strength of these five nations acting in concert to preserve the balance of power that the countries of Europe, irrespective of strength or size, are able to maintain their independence. The most influential are Britain and France, while the most backward of them is Russia. People in the West cannot help seeing Russia as a country which has risen one notch above Turkey. The Russians cannot help feeling inferior to Britain and France. The efforts the Russians are making to advance are inspired simply by the desire to bestow upon their country a lustre similar to that of the leading countries. This is the nature of Russia's reaction to Europe. The impression held by people in the East is rather different.

Hitherto, the Japanese have feared Russia more than Britain or France. In the popular mind Britain and France seem to be trading countries like Holland, while Germany and Austria seem to be countries struggling for power in Europe. Meanwhile, Russia, the largest and most powerful country, seems to be perpetually stalking the land in a rapacious mood and nursing ambitions of conquering the world. This is what people say among themselves, and they admit of no doubts. If we consider why it is that such a delusion has implanted itself inside the minds of the Japanese, there has to be a reason.

In ancient times, after warring came to an end in the Genna era [1615–24], Japanese contacts with England, Spain and Portugal declined, Christianity was strictly prohibited, and all opportunities to glimpse foreign countries were brought to an end. In this way the country was kept securely at peace for more than two hundred years. Suddenly, however, in the ninth month of the first year of the Bunka era [1804], a man-of-war carrying the Russian legate, Mr. Rezanov, entered Nagasaki harbour at Kaminoshima, and from the moment it fired its cannon in salute, the peaceful dreams of the entire country were brought to a startled end. From this point on there were furious debates about revering the emperor and expelling the barbarians, and about the policy of seclusion. Between the Bunka era and the Kaei [1848–54] and Ansei [1854–60] eras, those concerned with the seclusion policy turned to the study of foreign countries, and their first feelings were of apprehension towards Russia.

The cannon salute in 1804, which woke the Japanese up from their isolationist dreams, has induced people to fear Russia and has produced deeply regrettable delusions in the friendly relations between our two countries. If so-called amity between nations, whereby nations understand one another and the strong and weak protect one another, is considered to be superficial, just a mask, then surely it is not Russia alone which we ought to be suspicious of. How can one say that it is only Russia which desires to conquer all the continents of the world? The expansion of their territorial possessions by Britain and France offers us a true example of countries which control the continents of the world. On the other hand, the sale of Alaska by Russia represents the abandonment of one of the three continents covered by its territory. Germany is not yet powerful overseas, but how can one say that this means that it does not have ambitions? If one suspects foreign countries of being wolves, what country is beyond suspicion of being a wolf? Since the countries of Europe deal with each other on amicable terms, they are all brothers. When it comes to determining strategic policy, we should have a clear grasp of the true situation in the world and ponder accurately whether we should be most friendly to Britain and France, to Russia, or to the states of Germany and Austria. It is to be hoped that men of good sense will vigorously reject the delusions and falsehoods of hitherto and clear their minds.

CHAPTER 66

# A Record of Northern Germany, First Part

Yesterday afternoon we took our leave of Mr. Verski at the Russian border and once again entered the province of East Prussia. We travelled along the north-east coast and at seven o'clock reached Königsberg [Kaliningrad] Station. We arrived at Kreuz Station [now Krzyż in Poland] early in the morning, at half past two. Vice-Ambassador Kido changed trains here and headed for Berlin via the province of Posen [now Poznań in Poland] on his way back to Japan. The main party of the mission travelled along the Baltic coast, through Pomerania and Mecklenburg, to Hamburg, in order to make the arrangements for our passage to Denmark. During the night, while the train was stopped [at Kreuz], we hurriedly said our farewells and then the train started again in a moment. The route we followed today has been described in the account of our outward journey, so I shall omit any mention of it here. Our travels took us onwards, out of the territory of Prussia and into that of northern Germany.

April 16th, 1873. Fine.
Through the train windows we could see that day had already broken, and when we turned our heads we could see that the plains stretched away endlessly without so much as a hill in any direction. Only the occasional village could be seen, and the view from the train was dispiriting. This area is part of the province of Pomerania (also called Pommern), and it borders the Baltic.

At eight o'clock we passed through Stettin [Szczecin] Station. The flat, monotonous plains continued beyond Stettin, and the only sights to meet our eyes were villages and trees. There was nothing worth recording. After another hour in the train we reached the town of Neustrelitz, on the shores of the Zierker See. The view was quite pleasing although the surrounding land was flat. This was the capital of the grand duchy of Mecklenburg-Strelitz.

From here we crossed the border into Mecklenburg-Schwerin, which also consists of miserable plains; we sometimes caught sight of marshes. There were few signs of human habitation, and we even saw some meadows which were uncultivated. There is no attractive scenery whatever.

The people of the two Mecklenburg states are no better than slaves living on the property of their dukes and the nobility. Their income is sucked out of them by their superiors, and many of them leave to settle in other countries, so the population is declining year by year. Most of the land is unproductive, and neither forestry nor livestock farming is promising as a source of wealth. It must be the most backward of the German states.

We passed out of the territories of Schwerin and Strelitz and at half past eleven reached the station in the city of Lübeck, where we had lunch before proceeding. After a further seventeen miles, we arrived at one o'clock at the city of Hamburg, where we took rooms in the Hotel de l'Europe.

April 17th. Beautiful weather.
The free city of Hamburg lies at the mouth of the river Elbe. It has its own government, which is independent and republican. Its revenue comes mostly from direct taxation; on top of that there is income tax, the full amount of which is left to the discretion of the tax-payers themselves. Then there are stamp-duties and emoluments, to which must be added interest on loans and the fees for renting state-owned property. In all it amounts to around four million dollars, half of which goes towards construction costs, for Hamburg shoulders the burden of maintaining the Elbe and protecting shipping, and a quarter covers the costs of education, welfare, police and the legal system.

The Hotel de l'Europe is in the centre of the city beside Lake Alster, which is square in shape and surrounded on three sides by broad avenues and on the fourth by a bridge which carries a main-line railway and encloses Lake Alster. It is a very attractive area, with rows of shops selling all sorts of articles and trees planted along the embankment to make a park. Pleasure-boats ply the lake and trains cross the bridge, under which a canal leads into the city.

It was a day with clear skies and fresh air. The white-painted walls shone brightly, and the many-storeyed houses lining the lake and continuing up into the hills made a charming sight. On reflection, just three days earlier we had still been in Russia, where our visit had coincided with the beginning of the thaw and where we had trodden in snow before making our departure. We had then passed across muddy, desolate plains, and on the following day travelled from the eastern end of the Baltic to the state of East Prussia and beyond, where barley was shooting up but there were as yet few leaves on the trees. Sea-breezes from the Baltic chilled our bones, for it was still the time of the spring equinox. The day before our arrival in Hamburg we had crossed the plains of Pomerania and Mecklenburg, and there the barley was already green and standing high in the fields, the trees were clothed in a soft green and there was a scattering of houses; spring was more advanced there. Now we had arrived in Hamburg, where a gentle breeze was blowing through the greenery, the fragrant scent of flowers hovered around the houses, and we saw green fields veiled in mist. In three days we had experienced three different springs. The pleasures of travelling by train are unsurpassed.

Hamburg is an important North Sea port for Germany, and its trade with Britain and France used to be particularly flourishing. In terms of tonnage, the merchantmen here are almost double those of Belgium and Denmark combined. Two-thirds of Hamburg's trade is with Germany and Britain; mail-boats also voyage to the United States carrying emigrants, but Bremen is the busiest port in that respect. Going around the city, one finds that, away from Lake Alster, the streets are often narrow and irregular, the water in the canals is dirty and the banks are uncared for.

The brothel quarter is in the north-west; the prostitutes are licensed and there are three categories of brothel, each on a different street. The brothels in the best street are in fine buildings divided into rooms, each with its own courtesans. At night they sit in their rooms in soft candlelight behind lattices, and they look like beautiful women as they wait for their customers. The brothels of medium and poor quality are in small buildings with poorly furnished rooms, we were informed. In the West there is no town without some women selling their bodies, and as the economy grows, not a day goes by without their numbers increasing further. They usually just stroll around the streets trying to lure customers, but it was in Hamburg that we saw for the first time a brothel quarter operating openly. Those responsible for the administration of every town endeavour to rid themselves of this evil custom, some by licensing it, others by banning it; yet no matter what measures they take, removing one source of evil merely leads to another taking its place. Here they have publicly licensed brothels, but could this, I wonder, be a good means of control?

In the afternoon we toured the zoological gardens, which are situated on the northern bank of Lake Alster, beyond its embankment. They cover a vast area; the land undulates somewhat and has been made to resemble hills and plains. At the highest spot rocks have been carefully placed to suggest a ruined castle, and inside it kites are kept. (In the West, this bird is considered to be of ill-omen and is often used to give the impression of a deserted place or an abandoned building.) There is so much which is attractive about the way the gardens are laid out that we had no thoughts of fatigue as we walked round.

Next we toured the city, and from another spot on the bank boarded a boat which took us along the river, affording us a view of both banks of the Elbe and the ships there. Docks have been constructed all along the river-banks, and ships using the port are moored along both banks, resting there at anchor. The flow of the river is gentle, but the banks are not kept in good order. The water is muddy, and the river-bed is silted up and filthy. The river is so unclean that it gives off a vile smell, so we could not stay on the boat for long. We quickly reached the river-bank and disembarked onto a pier.

Downstream on the northern bank of the river Elbe, piers have been built out from the banks, facilitating access to the ships. Running along the bank is a wide road paved with stone, with clean sand scattered over it. It is a good road and causes no damage to the wheels of the vehicles which use it. The other side of the road is hilly, and on the top of one hill is an old castle which has been restored and is now a park called the 'Bank of the Elbe'. If one looks to the south-west, there is a panorama of the lower reaches of the wide-flowing Elbe, with ships at anchor and a forest of masts. Here and there on the mirror-like surface ships were on the move, puffing smoke or with sails spread out. The view was wonderful. There was a six-sail windmill on the hill where barley is ground to make flour. (From our stay in Holland we were used to three-sail windmills, although sometimes they have four sails. This was the first time we had seen a six-sail one.)

At nine o'clock in the evening we left our hotel, and at ten we boarded a train at a station in the north-east. After travelling in a northerly direction through the former state of Holstein for fifty-eight miles, we reached Kiel at midnight.

Kiel is the most important port in Holstein. From here run regular mail-boats to Korsør in Denmark. We descended from our train and boarded a ship. Having embarked in the middle of the night, we fell asleep immediately.

CHAPTER 67

# A Record of Denmark

As one moves north, the German lands gradually slope downwards to form a huge plain which spreads along both the Baltic and North seas and finally ends in the peninsula which constitutes Denmark [Jutland]. The border between Denmark and Germany is not marked by any mountains, nor are they separated by a river; rather, their territories are simply divided by drawing a line across the plain. However, the difference between the two peoples is obvious even after a thousand years, and it is as if the boundary were a natural one.

Heaven created all the peoples of the world and made them racially distinct according to where they lived, in the same way that birds and beasts and plants and trees came into being. Languages and customs, demarcated perhaps by mountains or rivers, become matters of habit; they formed the character of the people and gave them a feeling of solidarity, and in this sense the tribal differences between native peoples are mostly Heaven's doing. Germany and Denmark share the same continuous plain, and although their borders may move as a result of human agency, the fact that the difference between the two races is still clear after thousands of years must surely be attributed to Heaven. Believers in Christianity say that in the beginning all people were one and shared the same language, and that the differences came later. How is it possible to believe that?

The people of Denmark are of the Scandinavian race, as are the peoples of Sweden and Norway. They are sturdy and skilled in the art of sea-faring. Until a thousand years ago, the various states bordering the North Sea and the Baltic Sea did not exist, and the Danes sailed abroad, practising brigandage and wielding their superior force far and wide, to the point that they even captured England for a time. They were cunning and evil in their habits then, and were constantly fighting amongst themselves. They trod the lands of the present countries of Denmark, Sweden and Norway until they were bathed in blood, demonically

355

slaughtering the people. Their ways were truly savage. Thus it was that, in olden times, the word 'Danes' had a very powerful effect on northern Europe. As the world progressed, however, the Danes abandoned their wickedness and became a people which steadfastly respects the law. Those who were wild in their evil ways have become vigorous in their good ways, and now, with the passage of time, they stand among the great powers and preserve their independence, although they are numerically inferior even to the inhabitants of Paris. All this is due to their character, which is solid, industrious, patriotic and unwavering.

Although Denmark has the shape of a peninsula jutting into the sea, the entire country is flat and no hills or mountains are evident, just a few hillocks rising some five hundred feet. When viewed from the sea, the tree-tops and pointed roofs seem to float in the middle of the sea like a mirage. For the most part the land rises only a few feet above sea-level.

As for the climate, the severity of the winter is said to exceed that of Britain. Although it was already thirty days past the spring equinox when our party reached Copenhagen, snow was still flying through the air and plants had yet to put out shoots. Further, as a marshy country, it often has mists and fogs. Storms on the North Sea break out unexpectedly, sometimes eroding or destroying coastal areas.

The soil to be found both in peninsular Denmark and on its several islands is fertile and contains soft sand. It is, therefore, suitable for the cultivation of cereals. Accordingly, the principal occupation is farming, and on the larger farms many hired labourers work on the land. Under Danish law, it is forbidden for small farms to amalgamate into larger ones, and the land is divided into many small plots so as to allow people to possess their own land. On account of the various laws which have been enacted in order to parcel out the land belonging to the farming population, every year the number of small holdings increases while that of large farms decreases.

The areas which are marshy and damp are suitable for grazing cattle, and there used to be a substantial export trade in live animals, although this has fallen off somewhat in recent years. Twenty-six million kilograms of cheese are produced, a considerable proportion of which is exported. Danish horses also enjoy a good reputation and are excellent as draught animals.

April 18th. Fine.
At seven o'clock in the morning our mail-boat reached the quay at Korsør in Denmark. Korsør is an important port; it is on the Danish island of

Zealand and faces the Baltic Sea. Since it is a thriving and busy centre in the south-east of the country, it plays an essential part in trade with Germany. A train was waiting for us at the station, so we boarded it and then departed to the north-east. All was flat along our route, with only some undulations here and there and a few marshy areas and ponds. The peasants were in the fields, working hard at their spring ploughing. They had two horses to pull each plough and were tilling the level fields, making the soil as soft and fine as ashes. After having prepared the fields with furrows, they were planting them with barley. Some new shoots were already poking up through the soil. To divide up the fields they use dikes rather than surround them with hedges or fences as they do in America. Sometimes they dig a ditch and use that as the boundary, or plant some trees to mark the limits.

At eleven o'clock we arrived at the city of Copenhagen, which is sixty-three miles from Korsør. Through the hospitality of the government we stayed at the Hotel de Royal.

Copenhagen is on the east side of the island of Zealand and faces Sweden across a narrow strip of water. It is approximately two miles in diameter and six miles in circumference, but the circle it traces is irregular. Around the city there are moats into which flow the waters of the Baltic. Offshore lies a fort with a battery, and on the land earthen walls have been built for defensive purposes. The harbour is large and could accommodate one thousand ships and still have room to spare, but the entrance is very narrow, just enough for two ships to pass each other. The water is apparently very deep, so it is possible for even the largest ships to enter the harbour. The city is divided into three districts, which are called the 'Old City', the 'New City', and 'Christianshavn'. The Old City is a thriving place densely packed with shops. In the New City there are many mansions belonging to the royal family and the aristocracy. It is one of the most attractive cities in northern Europe.

At one o'clock we boarded carriages and went to the Ministry of Foreign Affairs. On our return we saw a fort on the coast [the Kastellet, or Citadel]. After that we went to the barracks of the royal guardsmen and watched them drilling. Danish soldiers are men of great physical strength. After they had finished marching, the men in one platoon did some exercises and then drew their swords and showed us how they could cut through pieces of wood the thickness of a man's arm, such was the soldiers' strength. It seems that the smaller countries of Europe which have managed to establish their independence maintain strong armies. This is true of Belgium as well as of Denmark.

Next we went to the royal palace [Rosenborg Palace]. This was built two hundred years ago when Denmark was a strong power in the Baltic. Although it is not large, the beauty of the interior is second only to the palace in Potsdam. Its grandeur is astonishing, and since generations of the kings of Denmark used to live here, it is full of their possessions.

April 19th. Fine.

At half past one a chamberlain came from the palace for us with three carriages, each drawn by two horses and with liveried grooms aboard, and conducted us to the [Christiansborg] palace, where we had an audience with King Christian IX. We then had an audience with Queen Louise. She is the niece of the previous king, Christian VIII.

At six o'clock we were once again in the palace, where we had the honour of having dinner with King Christian and Queen Louise. The food was exquisite, and a drink was served which was 317 years old. At banquets in Western countries one is generally given several fine wines and spirits which one drinks in succession. Some of these cost as much as a couple of dozen gold coins. Wealthy people keep some wines and spirits to savour which are hundreds of years old. Apparently, some cost as much as one hundred dollars a bottle. They are a mark of the greatest hospitality. During the meal the king rose and made a speech in honour of our Emperor Meiji, to which Ambassador Iwakura replied. Afterwards, we repaired to another room where we had the pleasure of conversing with Their Majesties, which was most enjoyable. After half an hour we withdrew. We were invited to the theatre on our way home.

April 20th. Fine again.

At half past one we walked to a museum. The exhibits included objects gathered from Iceland and Greenland in the European part of the North Atlantic, from the East and West Indies and from native communities in the islands of the South Seas. It is called the Ethnographic Museum. The museum in Berlin includes a similar section, but Copenhagen is the only city with a museum solely devoted to this subject, and for this reason it is well known in Europe.

Throughout the world there are many different peoples, and they have severally marked off their territories and made nations for themselves. Just as plants differ from region to region, people take many different forms in appearance, and their levels of development are not all the same. Even in Europe, where civilisation is advancing, there are some people who are buried in their own customs and unable to show their true worth; at the same time, in regions which are backward and simple there are some people who are outstandingly gifted. The point of learning is to develop natural advantages and to gather together the knowledge of all peoples. The results sought from it are the expansion of trade and industry and the enrichment of the population. When one travels from Japan to Europe, one finds that all things are flourishing there, and we cannot but be ashamed of our backwardness, but Europeans find their own brashness distasteful and have found, so it is said, much sincerity in things from the East. A visit to the Ethnographic Museum is indeed very beneficial and instructive.

We then took carriages and went to the western district of the city to tour the Frederiksberg Have gardens. Since these occupy a lofty eminence, from here the whole city is laid out before one's eyes. It is a pleasant place.

At six o'clock we went to the Danish Great Northern Telegraph Company. This company has a contract with Japan and has laid the submarine cable between Shanghai and Nagasaki, which is some indication of its prominence.

April 21st. Fine; fresh wind blowing dust everywhere.
At nine o'clock we boarded carriages and proceeded to the naval dockyards. The most solid armour-plated warships in the Danish navy are monitors. The Danish navy has long been famous, and when Denmark fought Prussia some years ago, the navy pressed Prussia hard and achieved a comfortable victory.

We then went to the department of naval plans, where we saw a model of a small ship which was made by Christian IV. In this way the monarch himself took the lead in encouraging people to devote their energies to shipbuilding. There was also a model ship which was made over a period of three years by three artisans who had been dispatched to Spain for the purpose. The cost of that one model was as much as twenty thousand dollars. To make good ships, huge amounts of money have to be expended, even on models, before construction can commence.

In the afternoon we went to the Ministry of Foreign Affairs, where we had an interview. In the evening we were invited to dine with the foreign minister, and afterwards he accompanied us to a ball given by the king. The evening stretched late into the night, so we left before the king, who stayed until three o'clock and doubtless enjoyed all the entertainment.

April 22nd. Snowstorm in the morning; blizzard conditions.

We had no visits arranged this day and simply wandered around the city. The capital of Denmark is a quiet and peaceful place. There are few fine views, but many of the buildings are worth examining for their architecture.

In 1801, Copenhagen was attacked by the English admiral Nelson leading a fleet of thirty-six men-of-war, and there was a fierce fight off-shore. Nelson was sorely pressed, but the city could not stand up to his superior force and much of it was burnt down. Danish soldiers are strong, but the country is a small one and is often oppressed by larger countries.

The spirit of the people is confident and they do not give in. Denmark excels in the arts of both war and peace. The people are simple in their way of life, do not neglect their occupations, are trustworthy in their dealings and are modest in their tastes. Consequently, although the shops in the city may be prospering, they have few luxury goods. On the other hand, there are many objects which are the product of knowledge and skill.

April 23rd. A beautifully clear and warm day.

At eleven o'clock we left the Hotel de Royal and went to the pier in the north-eastern part of the city, where we boarded a mail-boat for Malmö in Sweden. Our companion, Mr. [Julius Frederick] Sick, and others came to the ship to see us off and say farewell, and at a quarter past twelve we set sail. It was a perfect day for wind and sunshine, and we had a fine view of the harbour entrance. We sped on for less than an hour. The smooth water seemed endless and steeped in the colour of the sky. Only a few tall buildings protruded above sea-level. Then the hilly landscape of Sweden came more clearly into view, and the azure colours of the hills drew closer. In two hours we sailed twenty-four miles and at a quarter past two we reached the quay at Malmö in Sweden. The sea was calm this day; there was a sea-breeze blowing in our faces and so it felt a little cold.

CHAPTER 68

# *A Record of Sweden, 1*

Sweden is united with Norway, and they are ruled by a single monarch. Together they form a peninsula resembling a hollyhock-shaped fan. The backbone of the peninsula is the Scandinavian range, an endless chain of rolling mountains extending 1,150 miles. The region to the east of the mountains is Sweden, and that to the west is Norway. In the south it faces Denmark, and in the east it is separated from Russian Finland by the Baltic Sea.

Although Sweden and Norway cover large areas and have small populations, because the people are engaged in pastoral agriculture and are widely dispersed, there are no areas of land which are uninhabited for dozens of miles. The Swedes and Norwegians, along with the Danes, are called 'Scandinavians' by race. In ancient times they were fierce people, ever ready to kill, and they lived by piracy and brigandage. Even now they are tough and pertinacious by temperament, and they are famed for their sturdy soldiers.

There are two kinds of national amalgamation. One is called 'personal union', and this refers to cases where a union is formed by reason of family relationships between the ruling houses. Examples include the position of Luxembourg within Holland and the former union of Holstein and Denmark. Should the royal line change, then the union disintegrates. The other kind is known as 'real union'. As in the case of Sweden and Norway and that of Austria and Hungary, this is based on an agreement between the two countries, which are then ruled by a single monarch. In such cases, even if the royal line should change there is no change to the agreement. The agreement of Sweden and Norway to their union is contained in a document called the 'Riksakt' [Act of Union, 1815], and unless there are dire circumstances the agreement cannot be abrogated, nor can the countries part company. However, they retain their own separate governments, constitutions and laws. After the conclusion of this agreement, the king of Sweden was accepted in Norway, too, and became the king of Norway.

In terms of size, there is no country in Europe apart from Russia which is the equal of Sweden and Norway. Our party passed through no more than 450 miles in the south, so we barely set foot on one-quarter of Swedish territory, and this is inadequate for learning about the geography of the country as a whole. It is only in the south that Sweden can be said to be flat, for here the Scandinavian mountains come to a ragged end. The latitudes are high, but the soil is better than elsewhere in Sweden, so this is the region which is densely populated.

The Scandinavians are skilled at navigation and their shipping industry surpasses that of all other nations. Just as the small country of Denmark is a match for Russia in numbers of merchant vessels, so Sweden, too, has an abundance of cargo ships. Norway is also well provided with ships, so much so that it has the highest ratio of ships to inhabitants in Europe. It is, one must admit, a flourishing state of affairs. In 1871, Sweden had 1,463 ships, and the principal port is Gothenburg, followed by Stockholm. Norway had 6,993 ships, and as many as 49,337 men work as sailors. Most ships are small coastal vessels, but there is also a sufficiency of large, ocean-going steamships, which ply the routes to America.

As for the national character, the Norwegians are sturdy folk who are fond of sailing the seas, whereas the Swedes are lively, intelligent and extremely fond of learning and the arts. They are all self-reliant, and in times of war produce strong and energetic soldiers. It is because the people are such accomplished sailors that when America was opened up they had already settled one part of it. Even after American independence, strapping young men emigrated to America in such numbers that at one point there were far more women than men in Sweden.

As for other matters, political life in Sweden, Norway and Denmark is entirely different from that in Russia or Prussia. Schools and education are advanced in both Sweden and Norway. Even among the peasants who work the land, it is seldom that one encounters a person who cannot read.

As in Denmark, the religion of almost the entire population is Lutheranism, which is a branch of Protestantism. They are like the British and the Americans in their fervent belief. They are very stubborn when it comes to religion and have no wish for liberal laws providing for freedom of worship, since they consider that if other sects were to spread their faiths, this would promote discord. It is a country with a strict ban on other religious activity.

April 23rd, 1873. Fine.
At fifteen minutes past two in the afternoon we docked at Malmö. Escorts appointed by the government came to the pier to meet us, and they took

us by carriage to an hotel in the city where we were invited to take luncheon. Crowds of men and women from the town formed a long line on the bank to watch us. On account of its northerly latitude, it is rare for visitors from foreign countries, especially Japan, to visit Sweden. Earlier a travelling entertainer had visited and performed here, but this was the first time that Swedes had seen Japanese gentlemen.

Malmö is an important Baltic port and the area around it is one of the most densely populated in Sweden, as well as the region with the richest soil. The government had provided a special train consisting of three carriages, which we boarded at half past three before heading off in a north-easterly direction. The coastal lands offered a pleasant prospect, but soon a hill obstructed our view and we lost sight of the sea.

The farther we proceeded the hillier it became. The railway was enclosed by pine forests, which continued without a gap for more than ten minutes at a time. Because there is a plentiful supply of trees, the locals use them to build their houses, placing logs one on top of the other. The prettier dwellings are roofed with shingles, the plain ones thatched with grass. Even the smallest windows are at least a foot square. They keep their fields tidy, and one sees none of the slovenly houses we saw in Russia; nor do they have to cultivate barren fields as the Russians do.

The tracks our train ran along through the night were bumpy and the carriages shook terribly, just as they do on the Russian railways.


April 24th. Fine.
At dawn we found that we were running through a forest of pine- and maple-trees, here and there encroached upon by lakes. The farther east we went the steeper it became. We went through two or three tunnels and then suddenly found ourselves amidst rows of houses and lofty buildings. The banks of a lake were bathed in reflected light and we saw a multitude of masts. This was our approach to the capital of Sweden.

Pulling out of a tunnel, we crossed a bridge to reach Stockholm Station; it was twenty minutes to eleven in the morning. Our two escorts came here to receive us. There was a packed crowd of onlookers, bigger than anything we had experienced since Bradford. We boarded carriages and went to the Rydberg Hotel, where we were to stay.

The city of Stockholm stands on the Baltic at the end of Lake Mälaren, which is vast. The lake divides into a number of streams at the end, and there are nine islands surrounded by fresh water leading to a narrow strait. The banks are covered with rocky hills of no great height. Much of the land on the islands has been levelled and houses built, so many people live there; the islands are connected by stone bridges. Sweden is a stony country, which is convenient for building stone houses, and they are all beautiful. Stone is used to pave the streets and line the river-banks. The entire city is built upon granite and surrounded by clear water. Pine-trees add a touch of green, and the tall, blue-grey granite houses are reflected in the azure waters. Stockholm has an air of exceptional purity which no other city in Europe can match.

At two o'clock we paid a visit to the foreign minister, Mr. [Oscar de] Björnstjerna, and explained the purpose of our mission.

April 25th. Snow settling on the ground.
At ten o'clock our escorts took us to a museum [the Royal Swedish Academy of Sciences]. At the entrance there was a large rock which had fallen from the heavens. It was a ferrous rock and lay inside a huge basin full of sea-water. According to a scholar of antiquities, in ancient times when smelting was poorly developed, meteorites were used to make iron utensils and were accordingly highly valued. Seeing them here one can appreciate the truth of this. These ferrous rocks spoil if they are exposed to the air, even in a sealed glass container, so they are steeped in brine instead. They are yellowish in colour, being covered all over with rust. We had seen meteorites before in various cities in Britain and America, but those were all dry. This one seemed no more remarkable for being large and steeped in brine.

In the afternoon it was snowing heavily. At half past one, three carriages came for us from the palace with liveried grooms, and at the palace we had an audience with King Oskar II.

From five o'clock onwards there was a banquet for us at the palace. In the evening we attended a royal ball and returned at eleven o'clock.

CHAPTER 69

# A Record of Sweden, 2

April 26th, 1873. Fine.

At ten o'clock we were taken to the naval dockyards at the express wish of the king. The dockyards are on the coast in the east, and we went first to the docks themselves, which are on the seashore and very basic in construction, for the ships are simply moored directly to the bank. Here we were shown three iron-clads with turrets.

Next we went to the training facilities, where we watched a company of the royal Norwegian guards, more than one hundred men, being drilled. There is only one company of these Norwegian royal guards, and they are apparently accommodated here. The king himself was already present; he took Ambassador Iwakura by the hand, and they observed the proceedings together. Soon after the king's departure we boarded our carriages and returned along the route taken by His Majesty, following on the heels of his carriage, so we saw his military escort. His coach was protected by two platoons of guardsmen at the front and back, and his roofed one-man vehicle was surrounded by guns and helmets moving in a dignified manner. It is a great mistake to suppose that European monarchs are but lightly protected and do not travel in ceremonial procession.

At two o'clock in the afternoon we went to the museum of antiquities [now the National Museum]. The collection of old bronze artefacts from three thousand years ago includes a kind of sword in use at that time which had been found in excavations at various sites in Sweden, Norway and Denmark. They are all identical in shape and nothing similar has been found in any other country. This proves that long ago the lands belonging to these three countries were inhabited by one and the same race.

In the evening the minister of foreign affairs entertained us to dinner.

April 27th. Cloudy; mixed rain and snow.

At the wish of the king, a river steamer was prepared for us, and at twelve o'clock we left our hotel and went upstream through the lake to the

365

palace at Drottningholm. It is a lofty structure of three storeys; inside it
glitters with gilt stucco ornamentation. There is no pictorial decoration,
for it is a palace designed to give an impression of freshness. The walls are
hung with tapestries and there are also several old pictures. Some of the
rooms contain collections of beautiful paintings, and there is a group of
busts of kings and queens of many countries from all ages. There are also
pictures of Swedish battles against Russia and Austria, battles which are
famous in Sweden. There are stone statues and porcelain, too, but in
small quantities.

Carriages took us at a trot back to Stockholm over two very long
wooden bridges; the lower part of the bridges lay in the water, and with
the shaking as our carriages passed, water splashed up through the gaps
between the boards.

We passed a hospital and came to a military academy, where we
climbed a hill in the precincts to enjoy a view of the lake. It was a
magnificent scene. In front of us, on the other side of the lake, was a
village and within it a prison, built there deliberately so that the clean air
could be enjoyed. Less than two miles farther on we reached Stockholm.
In the evening we were invited to the theatre.


April 28th. Fine.
At ten o'clock we went southwards by carriage a distance of two miles to a
factory where woollen cloth is manufactured. The factory was built by a
company but then received government assistance, for prisoners are made
to work there. They are all under sentence of imprisonment and wear
prison clothing, and guards stand at the gate. The prison is near the
factory, so at night the prisoners are transferred there and locked in.

Next we visited the shipyards of the Bergsunds company, where many
iron ships are built, as well as some wooden ships. These shipyards do not
include a dry dock; rather, workshops are constructed on the shores of the
lake where the ground slopes down to the water. Iron chains are used to
hold the framework of the ship at the top of the slope, and pieces of
timber are laid underneath the frame. When the construction has been
completed, the pillars on both sides supporting the body of the ship
underneath are removed by being hammered away, and once the angle of
incline becomes steeper, the ship slides of its own accord down into the
waters of the lake. Most dockyards follow this method. Three ships were
currently under construction when we visited, and an armour-plated
warship had been finished and was already on the bank at the edge of the
water. We saw it launched and then returned to our hotel.

At three o'clock in the afternoon we rode in carriages to a woodwork factory. Sweden is one of the two most fortunate countries in Europe in terms of its endowment of timber. Here, a large variety of goods are made, including tables, window-frames, doors, cupboards, scrubbing-boards and picture-frames. Since there is little coal in Sweden but abundant wood, wood is used as the fuel to produce steam. In this factory, scraps of wood left over after sawing, plane-shavings, and saw-dust are burnt, as well as tree branches.

The match manufactory was built only last year. The wood of a tree called the 'aspen' is used for match-making. This tree is native to Sweden and is the most suitable for the production of matches; it is similar in quality to the '*maki*' [Chinese black pine] of Japan. The factory includes a place where matchboxes are made and a room where the igniting substance for the match-heads is prepared. The composition of the igniting compound is kept secret; one senior person makes it in that room by himself, and nobody else knows the secret. The whole factory produces sixty thousand boxes of matches per day. One hundred and fifty workers are employed there, both men and women.

Swedish matches seem to be considered the best; they are slow to ignite, strong, the wood catches fire effectively and they never go out at that stage. Matches made elsewhere seldom combine all these good features. In the whole of Sweden there are twenty-four companies producing matches. Upon our return to Tokyo we were astonished to see Swedish matches everywhere in shops selling imported goods and to realise that they are exported so widely.

April 29th. Snow.
At half past ten we went by carriage to an elementary school. It is a large school, and one of the best-known in Stockholm. Pupils, both boys and girls, are admitted from the ages of five or six and stay until they are fourteen or fifteen. Most of them are the sons and daughters of poor people; they are taught the standard subjects and upon leaving school follow their family occupations. All expenses are covered by the school and their families have nothing to pay, for the fees are met by contributions from the citizenry. The teachers include both men and women; inexperienced teachers are assigned twenty-five children, but later the number reaches anywhere between forty-five and fifty, or even sixty.

American educational methods are used, and the pupils are taught the etiquette of sitting in class and of deportment. It is rather like the teaching of manners in Japanese schools. In brief, the pupils line up in two rows and enter in step, proceeding to their desks in order, sitting in their places all at the same time, just like a troop of people marching. It seems that Western deportment concerns itself with standing and walking, while Japanese deportment concerns itself with squatting and kneeling. Small guns are made for the use of children, and each child is made to hold one when taught rifle drill, and in this no discrimination is made between boys and girls. While they are at school, their teachers are required to make them work hard at their studies. The subjects taught to the children of ordinary people are kept deliberately simple in order to avoid any feelings of boredom or weariness forming in the children's minds. When elements of higher learning are taught, it is difficult to make the children understand and learn. If such subjects were a compulsory part of the curriculum, they would induce a dislike of learning in young children, which would damage them for the rest of their lives and prevent the development of a love of learning. The professor himself told us that this concern lies at the heart of ordinary education.

At half past four we left our hotel, boarded our train and departed from Stockholm. We were escorted as on the outward journey. Before nine o'clock we reached Hallsberg, where we had tea. At this time of year Scandinavia retains the light of day; night only falls at ten o'clock, with dawn following at two o'clock.

April 30th. Fine.
At half past nine we reached Malmö Station, where we took breakfast and said farewell to our escorts. At half past ten we boarded a packet-boat from Lübeck, reaching Copenhagen in Denmark at half past twelve. Since the wind was up and the sea was rough, some of us disembarked and returned to our earlier lodgings. The secretaries remained on board and went directly to Lübeck in Germany.

CHAPTER 70

# *A Record of Northern Germany, Second Part, 1*

We boarded the packet for Lübeck yesterday morning at Malmö. Half the members of our party disembarked at Copenhagen and went on by train, but the wind then abated, the waves died down and the green seas around Denmark became as smooth as the surface of a tray. Islands were scattered as far as the horizon.

May 1st, 1873. Fine.
By four o'clock in the morning we had already sped past the lighthouse on the promontory at Lübeck. From here we went up the river channel, where there was a gentle swell as the waves flowed past. On both sides the land was little more than a foot above sea-level, and the river was wide enough for even the biggest ships to pass one another. For the most part there were no embankments, but here and there we saw humble fishing villages with fires alight for breakfast. There were a few undulations but no sign of any hills. The green grass of spring carpeted the ground and leaves were coming out on the trees; it seemed a different world from Sweden. At half past five we reached the port of Lübeck. Lübeck is situated at the base of the peninsula of Jutland, facing the Baltic Sea. It is one of the three free cities of Germany, and its political system is similar to that of Hamburg, with a republican constitution and a government consisting of a Senate and a house of the citizenry.

As we passed through Germany and Denmark, we observed that even now the various races are quite separate and retain their different customs, and this is a sure sign of the important connections between race and government. Earlier, when we sailed from Hamburg to Korsør in Denmark, we had noticed that the station-master had a strong facial resemblance to Moltke, the famous Prussian general. Similarly, travelling to and fro in the area around Hamburg we often observed at one station after another how similar the people were, with their deep-set eyes and rotund cheeks, to the people of Britain; and when we enquired about the roots of the Anglo-Saxons, we discovered that they are a mixed race of people from Schleswig and Saxony and that their roots are in this very area. It is true, indeed, that there can be no dissimulation where race is concerned. If those who travel here in the future pay close attention, they will surely find that my account is not a fabrication.

May 2nd. Fine.
We spent the day in Hamburg. We had been to this city before, on our way to Denmark, but then there were still few signs of spring in northern Germany. Now we returned to Hamburg to find spring at its most colourful and the leaves on the trees beginning to cast shadows.

In the area around Hamburg, women bedeck themselves rather oddly, and even their clothes seem to have been sewn in an unusual way. The hats which sit on their heads are particularly strange; also, on the back of their heads they wear a piece of starched black cloth (or possibly paper) which passes through their large topknots and hangs down to the waist. These are farming women from the villages, and they wander through the city selling vegetables or flowers. Once we saw two such women standing on either side of the white columns of a wealthy household; they looked, at a glance, like part of a sculpture and we wondered if they were statues representing women from the distant past.

All over the continent of Europe, the various peoples and races living in their own villages do not seek to improve their habitual ways. Not only is it very upsetting suddenly to discard the old and replace it with the new, but there is also a strong desire not to abandon old customs and to preserve the ways of the past. People prefer to restrict the size of their country and to retain those characteristics which make them distinct, and even at the level of districts and villages there is no desire to amalgamate with others simply for the sake of it. That is why these people make steady progress, all preserving their own customs, stimulating one another and competing for prosperity.

Near Hamburg the lands of seven or eight states jostle one another, and if one were to make a picture of their disposition it would look like a pattern on a piece of printed cotton. Although Prussia is increasing in strength, it has not sought to incorporate these states or to unify them; rather, it has followed the old ways in its treatment of these states, simply because there is little advantage to be had from forcing people to abandon their habits, and considerable danger of damaging their stability and making them insecure.

It is almost impossible to convey how much customs vary from village to village in the West. During our travels, we mostly passed through cities and rarely stayed in villages, so we had very few opportunities to observe local customs. Nevertheless, there are several which could be mentioned here. The uniform of Scottish soldiers is completely different from what is customary in England. They wear a strange and ancient type of garment which hangs down their legs, long socks like puttees, and leather shoes, thus leaving six or seven inches around their knees completely bare. In the Scottish highlands we saw a man who had been hunting dressed in similar fashion. He said that this was the traditional dress of the Celtic people of Scotland. Now since Scotland is not far from the Arctic circle, it must be harmful to the health to expose one's knees like this. Yet, even in these enlightened times, they stubbornly cling to this practice simply because this is their custom. Again, when ordinary European women are in their finery, their bodies are naked above the breasts, but this is simply their custom. Similarly, ear-piercing and constriction of the waist are simply customs, as also is the practice of wearing shoes which squeeze the foot simply because small feet are considered more attractive. None of these practices is healthy. The women of the state of Zeeland in Holland wear brass helmets. At the exhibition in Paris a few years ago [1867], there was apparently a proud-looking woman wearing one of these helmets and serving tea and cakes at a tea-stall. Russian people wear leather; Swedes, too, wear strange clothing, but things are different in Norway. Danish women wear white cloth caps like nuns. Austrian village women wear white clothing with a sleeveless black tunic on top, gathered at the waist; they look like Japanese nuns. In Hungary, clothing of a completely different kind is worn. Italian women wear a folded veil on their heads. In Berne, we saw women wearing strange clothing with long silver or nickel chains across their chests and asked why, whereupon we were told that this was the local custom and that women's accessories are different in each of the twenty-two cantons of Switzerland. The president presented a photograph of them to Ambassador Iwakura.

At a dinner party we attended in Holland, there were a number of ladies of quality present. One of them, seeing that all the men in our party had black hair, black pupils and a similar bone structure, asked the Japanese minister plenipotentiary in Holland in puzzlement if all men in Japan had the same bone structure as we had. On being informed that throughout Japan people were like us, she expressed astonishment and wondered if it was rather unusual for a country with a population ten times that of Holland to consist of entirely the same race. He replied that continents usually contained a mix of races and that in neighbouring China, too, the customs and language were different in each province.

It is a vulgar notion, born of a narrow-minded outlook, to suppose that other people, because of some minor difference in bone structure or customs, are not our equals, and a notion to which educated people pay no heed. What is it that politics should be about, that education should be inculcating? Surely not such trivial matters as these. Rather, let the focus of politics and education be on these two words: 'wealth' and 'strength'. The goal for which we should be striving is that all the people in the land work hard at their occupations, achieve independence, be courteous in their dealings with others and be trustworthy, and that we exploit the benefits of all the goods which are desired. Thus will our national pride not be affronted abroad and we will be able to live in good public order at home and progress towards a state of peace.

Although the strength of the nations in the West has gradually grown, the nobility remains powerful and the wealthy have some share in power, too, but in some instances government has even been subordinated to the will of the people. With brilliance unparalleled in history, Kaiser Wilhelm of Germany and Chancellor Bismarck have created a unified Germany; this may seem to be a simple thing, but their deep subtlety is evident from the fact that they rule in accordance with local customs. In Berlin I once asked why it was that Bismarck and the Prussian crown prince were not always in agreement. 'In dealing with the Confederation,' I was told, 'Bismarck sometimes tries to make reforms, but the crown prince says that, because Bismarck is proud and ambitious and covetous of a meritorious reputation, he goes too far in reforming the Confederation and does not think of the future.' Bismarck is a wise and skilled minister of long experience, while the crown prince is but a youth, and yet he is of a decisive mind. Men who govern civilised countries can be as resolute as this, but it is almost the opposite of what one finds in Japan.

Hamburg and Bremen are the two most important ports in the whole of Germany in terms of imports and exports. They handle four-fifths of all exports and two-thirds of all imports. Bremen stands on the lower reaches of the river Weser and is one of the three independent city-states of Germany.

In the last few years, Bremen has become the busiest port for people emigrating from Germany to the United States. The Norddeutscher Lloyd steamship company had a fleet of luxurious steamers constructed on the Clyde which sail to various ports in the United States and Central America, carrying emigrants and export goods; it is a thriving business. From America, cotton, tobacco, linen, tea and sugar are imported and sold at a huge market in Bremen; most of these goods are dispatched to factories in the Rhineland and southern Germany.

May 3rd. Fine.

At half past six in the morning we set out from our hotel in Hamburg and headed southwards on a train which started at a quarter past seven. As we left the city we crossed a bridge over the river Elbe. This unusual bridge is famous in Germany, for it is constructed from iron in a wavy-line shape and has separate sections for trains and for pedestrians. At twelve o'clock we arrived at Hanover Station.

Hanover was once a kingdom and one of the largest countries in southern Germany. George I of England was simultaneously elector of Hanover; following his accession to the English throne [in 1714], the royal family was called the House of Hanover, and this is a result of the connections between England and Hanover.

From Hanover we took the southerly line in the direction of the city of Frankfurt-on-the-Main.

It is characteristic of Europeans that, in general, they have a strong desire to possess wealth. Subjects high and low compete with one another keenly to achieve this. Even now, kings, dukes and nobles who own land pay a portion of the rents they receive to the government for miscellaneous expenses, but they keep all the rest for themselves, even though they are the rulers. When they provide money for the purpose of bringing some benefit to their lands, this is considered a public debt, and they help themselves to the public purse for the annual interest. Thus, while European governments may claim that the people derive benefits from the public debt, what is certain is that their rulers profit enormously from it.

As a race, the Germans are said to be particularly attached to their right to own land and to have a burning determination to protect their own kind and keep others at a distance. Feudalism in Europe spread from the lands of the Germans, and although modern civilisation has recently made feudalism extinct, in Germany all the small states still retain these passionate attitudes. Perhaps this shows that even a thousand years are not sufficient to change the ways of a people.

At half past nine we reached Frankfurt, where we stayed at the Hotel d'Angleterre. From Hamburg we had travelled 350 miles.

# CHAPTER 71

# A Record of Northern Germany, Second Part, 2

May 4th, 1873. Fine.

The famous city of Frankfurt was for many years the political seat of the assembled body of German states, just as the thirty-seven republican states of the United States of America sited their Congress in Washington. To the south and east of Frankfurt lie the fragmented states of southern Germany, to the north and east the fragmented states of northern Germany. On our journey here from Hamburg yesterday, we passed through five or six states, but there are many other small states in the mountains and plains to the north and in Saxony, which adjoins Frankfurt to the east, and then Bavaria lies over the mountains to the south.

Frankfurt-on-the-Main is so called to distinguish it from Frankfurt-on-the-Oder in Prussia. Since it is a fine old city, the various quarters are built in the old style, with narrow streets which do not run straight. It is full of old buildings, although they do not have the beauty of white façades. In the centre there is a wide avenue, and all around there are ramparts in the shape of a star, with long, narrow flower-beds here and there. A wide road runs along the top of the ramparts. From the banks of the Main one has a view of the wide expanses on the opposite bank and of the distant mountains, while the clear river flows by under a long bridge. What a charming scene it is!

At noon today we boarded carriages and went to the Palmengarten in the north-west corner of the city. On the way we saw flowers and trees in full bloom, and the green leaves were so pleasant that we felt as if they were going to moisten our clothes with the fresh mountain air. The gardens cover a huge area. In the centre was a glass pavilion; in front of it was a tea-room to rest in; on the other three sides the pavilion was heated with steam and all sorts of flowers were growing there. At the time of our visit, the azaleas were at their best and we were enveloped in their fragrance. To the north-west the plain opens up, and we had a superb view of the distant mountains of Bavaria to the south.

The wide avenue passing in front of the gardens had tracks laid in the middle for trams, just as in American cities, and it was lined on both sides with horse-chestnuts. These trees are much admired in Europe. Their flowers are small and not worth looking at, but when the branches are bursting with leaves, they provide pleasant shade. In winter they shed their leaves and let the warm sun pour down. Such are the delights afforded by these trees.

The former German assembly building [the Römer], which is in the middle of the city, is a three-storey edifice of very small dimensions, and rather old. On the top floor is a tall chamber with a row of portraits of the forty-one men who were installed as German emperors from the tenth century to 1806.

To the south-west there is a town called Wiesbaden, which is fifty miles away by train. Hot-springs abound in this area; there are many of them in Germany and the most famous are Wiesbaden and Baden Baden. A few years ago, during the Franco-Prussian War, the French president [Marshal Patrice de] Mac-Mahon [who succeeded Thiers] was imprisoned at Wiesbaden. Some members of our party visited the hot-spring there today.

May 5th. Fine.
At nine o'clock we rode by carriage to the Naumann company and toured the factory where bank-notes are printed for use in Japan. It is a five-storey building with yellow brick walls and not very attractive. On the ground floor is an office where incomings and outgoings are recorded. Those who work here are carefully examined by an inspector once they have finished work before they pass to the next room. The locks on all the rooms are very secure, and security is extremely strict. In the West, this amount of care is commonly given to a building where a large number of workers are employed. It is economically important to prevent misdemeanours, to eliminate waste of money, to keep an eye on diligence and laziness, and to allow work to proceed smoothly. This is not just the case for factories where bank-notes are printed. Four men and women do the engraving of the printing plates. Apparently, it takes three years to complete a copperplate. The Germans are good at this kind of work, for they are persistent and diligent by nature.

# CHAPTER 72

# A Record of Southern Germany

Southern Germany also used to be called the Confederation of the Rhine. With northern Germany and Austria, it is one of the three regions which constitute Germany; yet it is different from both in its customs and its politics.

The Rhine nobility always featured in the centre of French, German and Italian feudalism, having provided its foundation; they regarded intrepid rulers as an instrument to throw Germany into disorder and adapted their policies to suit the needs of the time. It was in this way that the states of southern Germany came to exert so much influence on the preservation of peace throughout Germany. Later, when the wealth and power of Louis XIV of France were at their height, the German states had sunk so low that their noble rulers, led by those of the Rhine states, took themselves to Paris and besought the friendship of the king and followed his cultural example. In 1701, when France and Austria mobilised their armies [in the War of the Spanish Succession], the Rhine states sided with France. As a result they were later treated cruelly by Austria, which gave them cause for resentment.

Meanwhile, in northern Germany Prussia was on the rise and was encroaching upon the territory of the various German states, to the point that Austria and Prussia finally came to war. Within a short time revolution had broken out in France, and Napoleon I, ambitious to become emperor of Europe, first created the Confederation of the Rhine and then eroded German power by defeating Prussia, seizing the Austrian imperial throne and proclaiming himself emperor. At this time, the rulers of Bavaria and Württemberg began calling themselves 'kings'. Thus, there were now three forces engaged in a balance of power, namely, northern Germany, Austrian Germany and the Confederation of the Rhine, and they were unable to unite.

As a result of the Congress of Vienna of 1815, the great powers withdrew, the imperial throne at Frankfurt was abolished and Austria was made the leader of the [German] Confederation. However, during the Austro-Prussian War [1866] the Confederation of the Rhine re-formed and remained neutral; thereafter, this confederation was led by the king of Bavaria. After Prussia's victory, Bavaria returned to the allied Prussian confederation. During the Franco-Prussian War of 1870–71, Bavaria rendered great assistance to Prussia, and so in the following year, at the palace of Versailles, the king of Bavaria proposed that the king of Prussia [Wilhelm I] become the German Kaiser.

May 5th, 1873. Fine.
At half past ten we left our hotel in Frankfurt and went to the southern station, where we waited for our train for half an hour before heading southwards. Frankfurt is surrounded by the states of Hesse; first, there is the state of Hesse-Cassel, and to the south the state of Hesse-Darmstadt. Our journey today took us into the latter.

After an hour we reached Aschaffenburg Station. The terrain here was still flat. The lights in the carriages had been lit because there were tunnels ahead. From here, the land gradually became more uneven and we passed a succession of hills. At one o'clock we reached Lohr Station. The village is pleasantly situated in a valley by a river. These are the upper reaches of the river Main, but it must still be more than 300 feet wide here. We followed the river, which shrank to half its previous width, and we saw mountain folk riding down the river on rafts which they had made out of logs farther upstream.

We passed Gemünden Station and at half past two we reached Würzburg, where we took lunch. This is on the Bavarian border. In this region we saw many large churches in every town and village, with pointed spires soaring to the sky, a prospect quite different from what we had been seeing hitherto.

Most of the states in southern Germany still have a majority of Roman Catholics. In the sixteenth century, after Dr. Martin Luther had denounced the Catholic Church and founded the Protestant Church, Protestantism spread from northern Germany; it was adopted in the north and percolated to the north-west. Extremists destroyed Catholic churches and often there was nothing left, with the result that large churches are a rarity in Protestant states. Bavaria once had a considerable aristocracy, and as soon as they were deprived of the right to maintain armies they joined forces with the priests, oppressed the people and contrived to secure their wealth. The priests, in turn, sought to strengthen their authority and repulse Protestantism. So the nobility duped the

people into making contributions to the Jesuit Order, set about constructing churches and carried their extravagance to an extreme. Thereafter, thanks to their support of this order, the spread of Protestantism to
Bavaria and the countries to the south – Austria, most of Switzerland,
France, Spain, Belgium and Italy – was halted. Without even asking, as
we passed through this area we were able to conclude from the scale of the
churches that it lay on the border between the two religions.

Hereafter the terrain became flat again. At six o'clock we reached
Nuremberg, which is the second-largest city in Bavaria. Here there is
what is considered to be the main hop market in Europe. Bavarian hops
are the best; those produced in Bohemia in Austria are also of optimal
quality, but their quantity is barely half that of Bavaria. The hops are the
reason for the fine quality of German beer.

Less than an hour after we left Nuremberg the terrain began to rise
again. Half an hour later, we encountered a south-flowing river for the
first time. Our journey through the mountains came to an end here as the
plains reappeared. At dusk we crossed the upper reaches of the Danube.
Night came and we could see nothing more. At half past nine we reached
Munich, where we stayed at the Hotel Vier Jahreszeiten.

May 6th. Fine.
We toured around the city of Munich. The palace of the king of Bavaria,
which is called the Palais Royal, dominates the central square [Max-
Joseph-Platz]. It is a magnificent three-storeyed structure, newly built and
brilliant white, and the many windows in the walls give it a spacious look.
The part at the back is architecturally older, and to the east are the king's
family church and the theatre. At the gates soldiers on guard wear tall
bearskin helmets and a dark costume with silver buttons. They look
different from Prussian soldiers. (This morning we saw a troop of cavalry
passing by and they were similarly dressed.) Behind the palace are some
enclosed gardens [Hofgarten], where the trees afford refreshing shade over
rows of benches and where wine and tea are sold. This all lies within the
palace grounds.

If one goes south, there is a large open piece of high ground with a
museum containing stone statuary [the Ruhmeshalle]. The square before
it is used for military training. To the right is a ring of mountains, and the
houses of the city fill the space in front of them. The view is splendid. A
colossal bronze statue stands here, which took ten years from 1833 to cast.
It stands fifty-eight feet high and the width of the body is eight feet. It is a
representation of a goddess, the protective deity of Bavaria. In her left

hand she holds a grass wreath which she is raising to her head, and in her right hand she has a sword. She is leaning over a lion. The statue rests on a stone plinth more than thirty feet high and weighs eighty tons. It is hollow and inside there is a spiral staircase leading up from the plinth to enable visitors to reach the top. At the entrance a guard hands out a candle as one begins the ascent. After sixty-five stairs one is at the top of the plinth, and after another sixty at the base of the neck of the statue. On both sides of the face, that is to say, inside both sides of the jaw, benches jut out with enough room for six or more people to sit. The mouth is so big that even the tallest people do not need to bend. Light is admitted through the pupils of the eyes and the mouth. From there one has a fine view of the city. This statue is unrivalled in Europe.

The people of Bavaria are Roman Catholics. There are many large churches in the city and lesser ones of various sizes scattered about. On street corners one sometimes finds part of the wall cut away to make a small arched niche containing a painted picture of Mary holding Jesus and pious offerings of incense and candles. One does not see such things in France or Belgium.

May 7th. Showers.
At half past ten at night we left our hotel and boarded our train, which departed at eleven o'clock for the south. The moon was shining brightly, illuminating the plains around Munich. For much of the night the way was monotonously flat. Leaving Bavarian territory, we passed through the Austrian province of Tyrol and so made our way to Italy.

CHAPTER 73

## *A Survey of Italy*

May 8th, 1873. Light cloud in the morning.

After departing from Munich, there was nothing to see until we passed Innsbruck in Austria, for we were travelling at night.

After Innsbruck we were startled when the carriage windows suddenly became dark and then light again; when we raised our heads we perceived that the train had run through a tunnel. On both sides the mountains rose sheer, with their rocky ribs exposed; streams ran down between them and pine-trees were growing wherever they could. These are the mountains of the Tyrol, an eastern branch of the Alps. Wherever the mountains close in, tunnels have been dug; the longer ones take five or six minutes, the shorter ones only a minute before the train emerges. The track follows many rises and descents, and the speed of the train is consequently reduced.

At five o'clock in the morning, when we reached Brenner Station, the mountains were becoming even more impressive and the way more perilous. The massed peaks folded into each other and there were still patches of snow amongst the pines. As the snow melted, it trickled down in tiny streams, collecting in pools beneath the rocks with a sound like that of falling pearls. The water forms waterfalls in the valleys, the highest cascading a thousand feet, and even the smallest falling around thirty feet; they look like bolts of white silk tumbling down.

At seven o'clock the train stopped at Franzenfeste [Fortezza]. The morning air was refreshing and everybody left the train, washed away the sleep and breathed in the pure mountain air. The mountain vista, combined with the clear sound of flowing water, was delightful. We took refreshments at this station: the coffee was bitter and the tea tasted astringent, but the mountain folk stubbornly pressed for high prices. Their manners were uncouth, so sometimes they incurred the anger of the passengers. Strolling up and down alongside the train and admiring the scenery was far better than resting in the station building. It was here that

380

we encountered south-flowing rivers for the first time and realised that we had now passed the highest peaks of the mountain range. At eight o'clock we passed Brixen [Bressanone] Station. The mountains were ever-changing, as when one peels the leaves off a bamboo shoot. At the foot of the mountains were fields where the villagers cultivated the land and had planted vines.

After passing through a long tunnel, at ten past nine we reached Bozen [Bolzano] Station. The valley is encircled by mountains which vie with one another in height. A thriving town fills the valley, and all around are vines growing on supporting frames, with peach, pear, apricot and cherry trees planted amongst them. Here we saw poplar trees for the first time; this is the Italian name of the tree we call '*hakoyanagi*'. It has long branches which reach upwards, and leaves which are small and plentiful. It looks rather like our ginkgo tree. Europeans think highly of this tree and often plant it in their gardens or along the sides of roads. At ten o'clock we reached the town of Trient [Trento]. In every house in all the towns and villages around here they ferment grapes to make wine, and at each station there is newly made wine for sale, but it is sour in taste and quite undrinkable.

The train ran on and the valleys changed. The river frequently fell in cascades: there were as many as thirty-one of them. Although not large waterfalls, they are delightful to see as the water threads its way down. At eleven o'clock we reached the town of Rovereto, which lies in another valley enclosed by peaks. There are many old castles in this area. On leaving this station we came to the end of the territory of Austria.

At eleven o'clock we reached the station at Ala, where there is an Italian customs post. We had lunch in the station: rough country wine with vegetables to accompany it, there being no good food available. From here on we descended along the course of the river Adige. It was already quite a substantial river, flowing thick and fast and with a constant roar. The mountainous landscape gradually opened out. It is in this valley that we first saw mulberry trees, planted around the edges of fields of wheat. Their leaves were soft and yellowish.

The train ran on from Ala Station for one hour, and the mountains gave way to plains. The Adige twists and turns on its way to Verona, and alongside it runs a wide road. Ten years ago, before the railway through the mountains was constructed, people travelled across this narrow pass through the mountains in horse-drawn vehicles. Along the road fragrant flowers were in bloom, amongst them poppies, enchanting with their red blossoms. The springtime scenery was like a colourful brocade. In

Europe, once one crosses the Alps and comes south, the flora is more colourful and the flowering plants are captivating in their beauty. It is like the scenery in our country of Japan.

Verona is one of the biggest cities in Italy. Within it are the remains of ancient Roman buildings such as the theatre and the old walls of the citadel. It is a place which travellers interested in antiquities must be sure to visit, but since we had to press on, we did not have time to look around. At this station the line from the city of Milan in the west joins the one on which we were travelling, and so it is extremely busy. We alighted here and waited for a train from the west. While we were waiting, it suddenly grew dark as the sky clouded over, there was a loud peal of thunder and rain came down in bucketfuls. This was right at the moment of our departure, and as we left we saw the rain streaming down from the eaves of the carriages, as if ropes had been attached to guide the water down.

At four o'clock we reached Padua Station. Here we took dinner and then headed south on our train, which had now joined with another train from Venice. At three o'clock in the morning we reached Florence and lodged at the Hotel de la Paix.

A Survey of Italy

The country of Italy is a peninsula which juts out into the Mediterranean Sea in a south-easterly direction. Its northern boundary is the great mountain range of the Alps, where it borders the three countries of France, Switzerland and Austria; to the west the island of Sardinia and the French island of Corsica face each other across a strait, and the mainland peninsula lies across the Tyrrhenian Sea. To the south, across a strip of water called the Etna Strait [Straits of Messina], is the triangular jewel-shaped island of Sicily. To the east the Adriatic Sea thrusts its way up, and across its waters are Austria and Turkey.

After the French Revolution the countries north of the Alps protected the rights of their peoples and reformed themselves by adopting constitutional governments, but Austria and Italy, considering the Alps to be their Great Wall of China, resisted the idea of liberty. Nevertheless, they were unable to hold back the changing mood of the times, and before five years had passed popular rights supporters were all over southern Italy. The king borrowed Austrian troops to overcome them and treated them with savage cruelty. Thereafter, Italy was in uproar as people became increasingly divided. Finally, in 1848, the idea of liberty stirred up trouble in Austria and even the troops garrisoned in Milan (the capital of

Lombardy) absconded from their barracks. The king of Sardinia took advantage of this opportunity and raised an army to protect the rights of the people, while the famous and heroic leader Garibaldi led his band of republicans to Rome. The two armies united and resisted the Austrian army, but the strength of the country was temporarily exhausted and they were finally defeated; even the king of Sardinia had to abandon his throne in flight.

The present emperor of Italy ascended his throne at that point. He accepted the principle of constitutional politics, won the confidence of the people, joined with Emperor Louis Napoleon of France to defeat the Austrian army and regained the territory of Lombardy. The various states in the north drove out their rulers and attached themselves to him. In 1860 the heroic leader Garibaldi was named general: he fought and vanquished the kingdom of Naples and thereby Naples ceased to be a country. Thus, Italy was unified for the first time barely twelve years ago. The king of Sardinia, by a vote of the assembly of his kingdom, became king of a united Italy. He established constitutional government and moved the capital to Florence.

At this time plans were being made to bring the territories of the pope in Rome under the jurisdiction of the united government as well, but those territories consisted of lands which had been donated piece by piece ever since the time of King Pepin, the founder of France. France, acting as the pope's protector, did not consent to the union of those lands with Italy, and so it overran Italy with a large army. Peace was eventually agreed, but in 1866 France formed an alliance with Prussia, defeated Austria and restored Venice to the jurisdiction of Italy. Then, in 1870, Italy took advantage of the opportunity provided by the Franco-Prussian War to bring the territories of the pope under its jurisdiction and thus restored unity to the whole country. In the same year the capital was transferred from Florence to Rome and the country was ruled from there. This was just two and a half years ago.

As for the climate of Italy, considering its latitude the summer heat is very strong. Probably this is because across the Mediterranean Sea are the deserts of Africa, which send over their dry, burning heat. Yet because the land is enclosed by the sea on three sides there are refreshing sea-breezes and pleasant currents of air, and so the climate is a healthy one. As our party reached Italy at the beginning of the summer, the warm temperatures made our spring clothing seem too heavy.

It says in an ancient text that 'rich soil makes people lazy', and it has to be said that this holds true throughout the world. Once one has crossed the Alps and entered the confines of Italy one notices an immediate change. The mountains are lofty and the water pure, the air is clean and the soil fertile; plants and trees flourish and wild flowers enchant the eye. And yet the weeds which grow in profusion beside the roads are not cleared away, nor is the refuse in the city streets swept up. Farming people sprawl in their fields for a midday nap, while at street corners people sit on the ground passing the time. Coach-drivers sleep in their wagons, leaving their horses to find the way. In the towns people sit around in their everyday clothes just drinking wine or twiddling their thumbs, or the whole family gathers together to eat and drink. In their working lives there is little sign of industriousness and one is aware immediately that customs here are different from those in more northerly countries.

Since the staple crop in Europe is wheat, we had not seen any paddy-fields before, but here, in marshy areas to the west of Padua, we occasionally saw rice growing in paddy-fields. Even in Europe, then, they practise wet-rice agriculture, at least in the southern countries. However, in Europe rice is a food for the lower classes, or it is used in the production of processed foods. Given the amounts harvested, the profits are low. Moreover, just as in Japan, little profit comes from beans or wheat, so fields once cultivated are no longer and many of these marshy places in Italy have been abandoned. In recent years good-quality rice has started to appear on the tables of the well-to-do.

It was the beginning of summer as we travelled around the agricultural areas of Italy, so we saw the ears of wheat swelling with grain. In Europe and America most of the wheat is sown in November or December of the previous year, and it generally ripens in July and August. This is just a little earlier than the time we harvest our rice. It is for this reason that European fields, at least in Italy, resemble fields in the East.

The Italians have a natural aptitude for manufacturing and produce work which is refined in taste and technically proficient. In this way they differ from people who use machinery to produce quantities of cruder wares. The areas which are most industrially productive are in the north, Lombardy and Venice being particularly advanced. Their most famous product is silk, and they export it to the value of more than $50,000,000, mostly to France. Special products of Italy include Venetian glass and mirrors, and mosaic work from Florence and Rome. Cotton and linen goods are also quite highly esteemed on account of their lightness and softness. In oil-painting and stone sculpture, Italy has reached the highest levels. Straw is also bleached and used to make summer hats, which are another famous product. Italian porcelain has been renowned since

Roman times, and the techniques have been passed down to the present day. Naples is known for its coral work, and Venice for items made out of shells. In addition to these there are innumerable other crafts of exquisite beauty and subtle workmanship.

The Italians are the descendants of the Romans and there is a huge variety of racial types. Since ancient times people of every race have settled here, so it is unclear what the original race was. Subsequently, Greeks, Gauls, Goths, Germans and Arabians also migrated here. The wealthier people are elegant and refined in appearance, but the poor are copper-skinned and wear old and coarse clothing. In general they delight in the pleasures of life and are skilful with their hands. They are good musicians, too, and in theatres everywhere, whether in town or country, they entertain audiences with delightful music. They even perform in the streets, making passers-by stop to listen. In Venice, musicians play on boats as they cruise around the canals. The entire country loves music.

# CHAPTER 74

# A Record of Florence

May 9th, 1873. Fine.

The Italian government had appointed Count [Alessandro] Fé d'Ostiani, one-time minister at the Italian legation in Japan, to accompany us and he came to meet us in Florence, extending to us a courteous welcome.

In terms of prosperity, Florence ranks sixth among the cities of Italy, but in terms of its beauty and its bountiful countryside it surpasses even the city of Milan. The clear waters of the river Arno tumble through the centre of the city, while serried ranks of roof-tiles climb the hills. The valley is ringed with hills, and smoke from kitchen fires gathers there. The valley floor is broad and the river-waters clean and fast-flowing. In places weirs have been made to stem the current, and water splashes down over the edges of them. The hotel where our party stayed was right beside one of the weirs. All night long we could hear the sound of the wind soughing through the pine-trees, a sound pleasant to our ears both in the daytime and in the evening. Five bridges have been built across the river, and here and there lofty palaces and magnificent towers rise above the city. On the summits of the hills are some old forts and fortifications. Great churches soar above the roofs of the city, and even the smaller ones thrust tall towers above their surroundings. There are, it is said, 250 churches in the city. The Roman Catholic Church has constructed large numbers of imposing churches here, and their sumptuous decoration is utterly astonishing. To protect the city from attack, a fortified wall runs all around it, with eight gates through it.

At eleven o'clock we boarded a carriage and went to the church of Santa Maria del Fiore [the Duomo], founded when the Roman Catholic Church was at its height, having spread all over Europe and appropriated the wealth of the people. The building itself faces south; on the left there is the great dome and on the right a tall square tower. In between and adjoining both is a tall structure, the entire interior of which is taken up by a large hall [the nave], which leads to the lower part of the dome. The main altar is located beneath the dome. The height of the dome is 460 feet: it rises majestically into the sky, and a circular gallery on top lets light into the nave below. Above the gallery, in turn, is a gold-plated sphere, which is hollow and large enough to hold six people. If one goes to the main altar beneath the dome and looks up into that vast spherical space, it makes one dizzy. Even a tall person standing at the side of the nave looks as insignificant as a cicada on some patriarch of a tree. From beneath the dome through the area adjoining it, the entire floor consists of nothing but square stone tiles of black and white laid alternately, each polished to a shine. It is easy to lose one's footing when walking on them. The altar is surrounded by a metal railing. This is more than three yards in height; from afar it appears to be minuscule, but from close up it is necessary to raise one's eyes to see the top of it. The nave in front of the dome is one hundred and forty feet in width and is dominated by two rows of giant columns.

Across the street from the dome there is an octagonal structure [the baptistery]. This, too, is enormous by comparison with ordinary buildings, but it looks diminutive beside the dome. Each of its sides must be forty-five feet long, and they all have bronze doors with scenes from the Old Testament in relief. The exquisite workmanship attracts carvers from all over Europe, who come to make copies and to learn the techniques.

The museum [Uffizi Gallery] is situated on the northern bank of the Arno beside the second bridge. It is a superb four-storeyed structure with a pleasing air. At the opening on the south side there is a loggia formed of pillars of white stone linked together in the style which uses cruciform arches [to make a vault]. Inside are three large old stone statues, together with ten or more other stone statues, and a bronze one of a male god decapitating a female demon [Benvenuto Cellini's *Perseus and Medusa*]. They are all old pieces sculpted with great sensitivity and are from Ancient Greece. We had previously visited museums in various countries and in each we had seen copies of these statues, but seeing the originals for the first time we had a particularly strong sense of their admirable qualities. Italy is the true fountain-head of art, and the ancient stone statues and paintings which survive to this day are the magnificent treasures of this country.

In the upper storey of the left-hand part of the Uffizi there is a long corridor where stone statues are displayed in a row. In the area behind this are separate rooms, each full of famous paintings old and new. Painters from every country in the West come here thinking nothing of the distance in order to copy the works and improve their technique.

Moreover, artists from all countries engage the skills they have learnt to paint their best pictures to send here, hoping to make their names known and to have them preserved here forever. Artists gather here every day, both men and women, to gaze and to copy, and they fill every room. It is one of the most famous art galleries in the world. We looked at most of the displays and then departed.

From the rooftop a raised walkway becomes a passage inside the bridge over the Arno, eventually leading to the streets on the south side of the river. This passageway runs over the streets and through gardens, but one is not aware of that. When we passed over the river, all of a sudden we saw from the windows the ripples breaking up the sunlight on the surface of the water, and we had the extraordinary feeling that we were at the end of a rainbow.

May 10th. Fair skies and warm temperatures like those in Japan in the fourth and fifth months of the lunar calendar.
At eleven o'clock Mr. Fé d'Ostiani took us on foot to a workshop in the city where they do mosaic work. To do this, the craftsmen have to collect all sorts of patterned stones, sort them according to colour, cut them to shape, and set them in a stone surface to make a design. It is good for both human figures and flowers, and the works are so finely executed that one is deceived into thinking they are paintings. The technique is one which has been handed down since the time of Ancient Rome three thousand years ago.

Another product for which Florence is famous is its marble-work. Tuscany has numerous marble quarries and has excelled in the art of stone-carving since antiquity. If somebody goes to one of the workshops to request a likeness, the craftsman asks for a photograph and compares it closely with the person's face, carefully noting its characteristics. After fifteen or sixteen days, or seven or eight days, the carving is done and an exact likeness in marble will be delivered. In Europe, stone-carving is practised to the same extent as painting and people have the highest regard for it. Its reputation is quite different from that of our stone-work in Japan. It is considered one of the fine arts and is studied in all countries, but Italy is said to produce the most accomplished sculptors.

We went to a shop selling Japanese goods. Most countries have shops selling Japanese products, but these are usually vulgar trinkets. This particular shop, however, had a number of finely made items, from lacquerware, pottery, bronze metalwork, inlays, cloisonné, fans and ivory carvings to woodblock prints. None of the articles in the shop made us feel ashamed. The Italians resemble the Japanese in their intricate craftsmanship, and although their work is excellent the prices are low.

On this day we drove through the countryside outside Florence, and as we looked around us the spring colours were at their finest, the sun was shining brightly and our spring garments felt burdensome. At noon the heat was oppressive. The country roads were not in good condition: here and there the mud walls beside them had collapsed, and our carriage trailed clouds of yellow dust behind. Alongside the roads we saw rows of mulberry trees. It was precisely the time of the third sleep in sericulture, and labourers were pulling down the branches, collecting the leaves and filling baskets with them.

We were given a general account of sericulture in Italy. Cleanliness is highly valued in the rooms in which the silkworms are raised, and attention needs to be paid to the sunlight and the moisture in the air. They therefore daub the walls of the room and all the equipment with a mixture of white lead powder and a calcium chloride solution. In addition, they boil up a mixture of vitriol and calcium chloride, open the doors and leave them ajar for a day and a night to remove all the bad smells and vapours in the room and to purify the rooms. Chlorine gas, being a strong agent for removing colours and odours, is used in Europe as a bleach and as a substance for deodorising and purifying the air. In farmhouses they raise silkworms on shelves which are suspended from the ceiling, and all the men and women of the household sleep in that one room. If they take great care to keep it clean and if they are skilled at raising the worms, they obtain silk thread of good quality and make a considerable profit.

When the silkworm eggs are hatching in the spring while the mulberry leaves are being gathered, the leaves are chopped up and spread out on clean sheets of paper which have previously been perforated with innumerable small holes. They place this paper over the sheet of paper on which the eggs are hatching. The more vigorous silkworms, in their eagerness to eat the leaves, climb through the holes and are placed and raised in baskets. Those which fail to make their way through are constitutionally more feeble and are raised in separate baskets. Thereafter, from the first sleep through to the fourth, the technique of raising silkworms is largely the same as in our country. The room temperature is maintained between 15°C and 16.5°C, and for this purpose the rooms are without fail equipped with stoves. In these they mostly burn the branches of mulberry trees, probably for reasons of economy. In rainy weather the heat is used to remove the humidity and freshen the air. Blankets are used to screen off the stoves so as to protect the silkworms from direct heat, and white fabric is always hung over the windows to keep out the rays of the sun. In rainy weather paper screens are used to preserve the warmth, and on sunny days they hang bamboo screens to keep the sunlight out.

From time to time they use a convex mirror to illuminate the silk-worms and inspect them for any signs of illness. After the fourth sleep there are various methods in use for settling the silkworms down so that they spin cocoons. Sometimes bundles of straw and grass are used, or the silkworms may be placed on the branches of bushes, or on sawdust spread on pieces of finely cut wood tied together; alternatively, they may be settled on twigs laid over mulberry branches. Depending on the type of silkworm, they are either allowed to climb up vertically placed branches and settle there, or to settle on branches laid horizontally. Whatever the case, when settling the silkworms a temperature of 17°C to 18°C is necessary.

At half past eight in the evening we left our hotel and headed for Rome. It was a clear and pleasant night, the moon was bright, and the sight of the mountains and the rivers was very refreshing.

CHAPTER 75

# A Record of Rome, 1

In all the leading countries of Europe, the arts and sciences are flourishing; at the same time, no piece of land is left untouched by the hoe and no hill is without its wheel-ruts. There is no shortage of money, and wealth and luxury are at unprecedented levels so that city life is magnificent. Everything is at its finest in Britain, France and as far as the mountains and plains of Germany. However, when one crosses the Alps and enters Italy, one finds the soil rich but the people lazy. The present king [Victor Emmanuel II], through his courage and genius, has aroused the nation's energy, but throughout the land the people seem too degenerate to be able to respond. This may well be because his administration is still young. It has to be said, nevertheless, that a nation which has flourished in the past cannot easily be revived once it has fallen on hard times. Look at Italy as it is today and think back to the days of old: how wonderfully vigorous it was then!

Rome contains many remains dating back two thousand years, and gazing at them one cannot but feel wonder. At that time London and Paris were areas where barbarians lived, where brambles and weeds grew unchecked in marshy areas and wild beasts wandered at will. A place such as Germany, for example, was mostly made up of forests or plains where the winters were harsh. When people came to settle there, the beasts fled and the birds flew away. Some people painted their bodies or tattooed themselves, others wore animal skins, and they roamed freely, ignorant as they were. When they took local produce in tribute to Rome and saw the splendour of Roman civilisation and the magnificence of the city, they voluntarily reformed themselves and joyously exchanged their habit of idleness for better ways. What finally brought Germany to its present prosperous state was precisely the elements which the people had derived from the culture of Ancient Rome.

Our party had recently visited the capitals of Britain and France, and now, coming to Rome, we found dust and rubbish blowing around and

391

considerable numbers of street urchins. Thus have the wild thorny bushes of ancient times become the civilisation of today, and the prosperity of yesteryear become the degeneration of today. It seems to me that the vigour of European civilisation has natural limits, as if one part must be in decline when another part is thriving. If Britain, France and Germany are flourishing now, it is because their progress has depended on elements which originated in Rome. This became abundantly clear when I saw the city for myself. It is said that people who talk about European civilisation have all had to come here once to ponder its history for themselves. How true it is that the achievements of any civilisation are not simply a matter of a day and a night! Rather, they are conceived thousands of years earlier and only much later emerge in all their brilliance.

This thought prompts other considerations. East and West lie so far apart that they were beyond each other's reach even had they wished to meet. Feelings and customs differ in the East and the West, and generally they are at variance due to their very different origins. As we travelled around western Europe, we did indeed feel that all men are brothers no matter where they come from. Yet if one casts one's mind back four hundred years, nobody then could have imagined for a moment that the lands of Europe would become full and that there might be other lands lying to the east of India.

May 11th, 1873. Beautifully clear; in the afternoon hailstones as large as soya beans fell.

It was already light outside the carriage windows as our train continued its journey around verdant hills and through fields thick with green grass. From here onwards we followed the left bank of the river Tiber. The scenery was wonderful, with beautiful flowers amidst the lush grass; hills and mountains towered up, and there were countless trees. When we reached the station at the city of Rome at half past five, Consul-General Nakayama [Jōji] and other Japanese government officials posted here came to meet us. We boarded coaches and took rooms at the Hotel de Constantin [Albergo Constanzi].

The city of Rome is located sixteen miles upstream from the mouth of the Tiber, where its waters pour into the sea. The area around the city is a flat plain, but seventy Italian miles (that is, kilometres) away to the south the Alban Hills rise out of the plain, their impressive peaks making a delightful view from Rome. The streets of the city are for the most part narrow and irregular, and they are not kept clean. Dust swirls in the air and makes it difficult to see. In outlying areas, weeds are rampant, the houses dingy and the streets unkempt. Ruins from two thousand years ago lie scattered around, sometimes dug out of the ground, and they make one lament for the splendour of the city which once was.

For well over a thousand years this city has been a state under the jurisdiction of the Catholic Church. Consequently, there are so many churches that the whole city seems to consist of nothing but churches. Night and day, when the hands of the clocks point to the hours, bells peal out everywhere, their clangour filling the city; the din is beyond description.

The people here are the most skilled in Europe in the arts of painting, sculpture, music, weaving and architecture, and many people come from afar to study the techniques. There are also a lot of child beggars, and whenever one enters or comes out of a church, nuns or old women approach and press one to buy candles; sometimes boys do this, too. Apparently, some of these children come from homes which are not necessarily poor. The hideous old custom which all religions have of encouraging people to assume the appearance of beggars is not confined to Buddhism.

It is almost impossible for people from the East to imagine the extent of the connection between the Catholic Church and political change in Europe. Because of the authority it has acquired, the Catholic Church has had a large part to play in the rise and fall of governments in all Western countries. (If Buddhism, too, had had a headquarters and for centuries had held authority over the monks of China, Korea, Annam and Siam in matters of precepts and doctrine, then it might well be exercising that power in the East now.) When Europe was a feudal world, kings and nobles owned both the land and the people on it. It depended entirely on the sovereign whether he chose to win the people's hearts and make the country strong and prosperous, or to tax them heavily to enrich himself, and so the Church, standing between the ruler and his people, became an implement for accomplishing his will. From that time on, the authority of the sovereign and the power of the clergy worked together and caused untold suffering to the people. Resentment grew as a result, and in the early sixteenth century the famous priest of Saxony, Doctor [Martin] Luther, and others established the Protestant Church.

'Protestant' signifies opposition, and it was with the intention of opposing the Roman Church that Luther proclaimed ninety-five theses concerning the sins of the established Church. The Protestants spread their message from central north Germany to other countries, and people everywhere inclined to it, smashing churches and destroying images. This enraged the adherents of the Church of Rome, who seized them and threw them into water or fire. In every part of Europe blood flowed and was trodden underfoot. It was an extraordinary upheaval, but the fervour of the adherents of the new faith grew ever greater and the pope's authority was dangerously weakened. Around 1540, therefore, Spaniards founded the Jesuit Order with the aim of halting the spread of the new Church. From this time on, the two religions were in conflict in Europe, and much blood was cruelly shed until the new religion finally prevailed in the northern parts of Germany, and in Sweden, Norway, Denmark, Holland and England. The leading countries at that time – Austria, France, Spain and Italy – remained with the old religion.

Republican ideas were the enemy of monarchical rights, and the ideas of the new religion were the enemy of the pope. Constitutional polities have now been established in many countries, but this is a measure to keep republicanism out. The power of the pope is gradually being eroded, and since the Italian government has already taken jurisdiction over Rome, Protestants are openly proselytising in the city, which arouses the anger of the clergy. What, one wonders, will be the consequences? It is impossible to predict.

May 12th. Fair sky; temperature warm.
In the afternoon we boarded carriages and saw the principal sights and antiquities of the city.

The basilica of St. Peter is attached to the pope's residence, and it is in fact the principal church of Roman Catholicism. It stands on a hill in the western part of the city and faces east. On the two sides of the façade, columns of white stone form a semicircular colonnade enclosing a vast paved courtyard which slopes gently upwards; to the left and the right are ponds with fountains, and in the centre there is a square pillar, tall and pointed at the top. On the roof of the colonnade there is a row of stone statues. A church had stood on this spot for a very long time, but it was re-built in 1586. Kept inside is a fragment of the bodily remains of St. Peter, Jesus' foremost disciple long ago; some say that it is a fingernail. That is how St. Peter's acquired its name. For sheer size, beauty and dignity, it is without peer among all the churches of Europe. It is a huge structure with an overall area of 222,321 square feet. Although St. Paul's in London is large, it is no more than half the size.

To the north of the basilica is the Vatican, the pope's palace. Situated on a hill, it soars up storey upon storey, with rooms for 17,000 clergy. When the Roman Catholic Church was spread over the whole of Europe four hundred years ago, it imposed its authority everywhere and collected riches so that this church could be made impressive, with the result that the luxury and ornamentation reached the extraordinary level seen here.

The ancient Castel Sant'Angelo is 650 yards to the east of St. Peter's. It stands imposingly to the north of the Tiber. A stone bridge crosses the Tiber in front of the Castel Sant'Angelo. This has now been completely repaired and is used for traffic. It was constructed in A.D. 135 by a Roman emperor [Hadrian]. At that time the imperial graveyard was inside the castle, so this bridge made it easier to go to and fro. After the passage of two thousand years, this magnificent structure survives proudly and its exquisite beauty has never been matched in later ages. Even now architects come here to learn how this famous bridge was made. It consists of a succession of curved arches and on the parapets stand stone statues of Christian figures, so they must have been carved and placed there later.

The Pantheon is the oldest church in the city. Although the precise date of its construction is not known, it was before the Christian era. The ground in Rome has risen over the ages, and the ancient city is now some six or seven feet below ground. In the year 609, when Boniface IV was pope, the Pantheon was, with the permission of the Roman emperor, turned into a Christian church, so it has remained complete to this day. In front of it is an open space with a square stone tower in it, apparently another relic of the past.

To the south of the city are the foundations of the Forum, which was built in Roman times. From 30 B.C. to A.D. 476, Roman citizens used to gather here, and it was here, too, that Caesar was assassinated. Afterwards it gradually fell into ruin and now all that remains are the foundations and a few columns.

The theatre for fights with beasts (in other words, the Colosseum, also called 'the amphitheatre') was built around the beginning of the Christian era by the Roman emperor Vespasian after he had conquered Judaea and enjoyed a triumphal parade. The walls are made of brick and form an oval five storeys high. The highest levels are open to the sky and are 179 feet above ground level. One feels dizzy just looking down at the ground from there.

In ancient times the Romans used to hold courageous men in high esteem and enjoyed watching them face wild beasts in combat. Lions, tigers and other wild animals were released into the arena and men were made to fight them. Crowds of men and women gathered to watch from the spectators' area, just as though they were watching a play. The stands were large enough to accommodate between 80,000 and 120,000 people.

It was built most cleverly, with entrances on both sides to prevent congestion when tens of thousands of people were leaving at the same time. When Emperor Titus ascended the throne, as many as 5,000 wild beasts and 10,000 domestic animals were slaughtered there. Criminals were also brought here and made to fight, and those who won were sometimes pardoned. Such things continued up to the sixth century. It is not difficult to imagine the savagery of these occasions. Even now, watching men fight wild beasts is apparently still popular in Spain.

# CHAPTER 76

# A Record of Rome, 2

May 13th, 1873. Fine; the air felt hot.

At ten o'clock, officials from the Italian royal household arrived with four carriages, equipped with two horses apiece and grooms in splendid livery, to collect us and take us to the palace. There we had an audience with King Victor Emmanuel II. In the evening, we toured a park and went on as far as the Chamber of Deputies before returning home.

May 14th. Beautifully clear; we felt the heat.

At one o'clock, we boarded carriages and went to the museums at St. Peter's. They are spacious buildings with sculpted interiors and painted throughout with white lead, so they seem clean and fresh. The floor is paved with stone and richly ornamented with decorative inlays. Everything is thoroughly in the ancient style, so there are no annoyingly elaborate details. Displayed in the museums are prodigious numbers of sculptures in white stone, of exceptional quality. It would be no exaggeration to say that the art collection of any other European museum would barely amount to a fraction of what is displayed here.

Since Rome is naturally the fountain-head when it comes to the sculpture and antiquities of Ancient Rome, the items on display were of such exquisite beauty that we rubbed our eyes in disbelief. In the entrance hall there was a huge porphyry sarcophagus: it was eight feet high, nine feet wide and twelve or thirteen feet long, and all made from one piece of stone with no sign of any joins. Most of it was covered with carvings and the detailed stonework was extraordinarily graceful and translucent.

We then entered the pope's treasury, in other words, the Vatican Palace itself. It is so extensive that one or two days would be inadequate to see everything there. This palace adjoins the Vatican Museums, and as we entered the rooms the richly coloured paintings dazzled us with their detail. Corridors branch off to the left and the right, almost too long to

see to their ends; we felt as if we were looking through the wrong end of a
pair of binoculars.

At six o'clock we had the honour of attending a banquet given by the
king and queen at the palace.

May 15th. Pleasantly sunny; 19°C.

At nine o'clock we boarded carriages and once again drove past the
Forum and the Colosseum in the southern part of the city.

Proceeding farther, we reached Emperor Caracalla's baths. The
remaining walls of the bathhouse are vast and second only to the Colosseum in size. The baths cover an area of 14,000 square yards. There was
a bathhouse here from about 25 B.C., but in A.D. 212 Emperor Caracalla
re-built and extended it. The people of Rome at that time used to gather
here to bathe together and afterwards to meet in a great hall to converse
and amuse themselves. Those who had demonstrated their courage in
dispatching wild beasts in the Colosseum had special favours extended to
them by the emperors: after bathing they were offered seats in the hall
and given special consideration, and they enjoyed fame among the
populace.

To the south of the baths are the catacombs, which are a graveyard
from Roman times. A low hill was dug to a depth of more than eight
yards and tunnels were excavated horizontally, forking sometimes like
roads. On both sides of these tunnels there were niches, and there were
also burial chambers. Inside the passages it was so dark that we could
barely see to walk, so the guide gave us each a candle and we all proceeded
through this land of the dead with lighted candles in our hands. There
were junctions here and there, and it was easy to lose one's way. In order
to penetrate to the farthest parts it is apparently necessary to walk as many
as fourteen Italian miles (equivalent to French kilometres). We just followed in our guide's footsteps and had a general look round. The old
coffins in the graves have been removed by later generations and very few
of them are now left. There are also some human remains to be seen, and
a stone coffin with the word 'Alexander' inscribed on its surface; this is
presumably the name of the person buried inside. The corpses of a
husband and wife were perfectly preserved.

When the city was at the height of its prosperity, Jesus Christ was
crucified in Judaea. Christianity was strictly prohibited in Rome, too, and
Peter, the leading disciple of Jesus, was crucified. The religion was treated
more harshly than an enemy, but nevertheless people turned to it in ever
greater numbers. So dank and gloomy are these underground passages

that a visit of just an hour was enough to induce unpleasant feelings. Accordingly, it inspires horror to think of the sufferings of those who spent their lives here keeping their faith alive. The reason for the spread of Christianity is that, ever since the time of Jesus' disciples, people have preserved the teachings, steadfast and fearless of death, ready to withstand savage treatment, and the religion has proved resistant. The people who follow it, therefore, are bold in spirit and unyielding whether in good or bad, and their determination to achieve what they aspire to do is strong. Buddhism, being a feeble and idle religion, does not stand up to comparison.

Italy is a country which is on the rise. The first stage was when it joined the ranks of more important countries; then it recovered the territories it had lost to Austria, and now it has made further progress by absorbing the lands of Rome. Mr. Thiers, the president of France, said in praise of the present king of Italy that he is second only to the German emperor and that those who say his strength derives only from his aides-de-camp are much mistaken.

We visited a military hospital. There were at the time one hundred and fifty patients. Eleven doctors were assigned to treat them, and there were nuns to nurse them. What was noteworthy about this hospital were the bathing facilities. There were many ordinary bathtubs, but in addition there was a room with various devices for curative hot-water treatment. In the middle was a bench on which the patients were made to sit; when a wire was pulled, hot water spouted out of holes in something shaped like the seed-pod of a lotus flower. If a different wire was pulled, hot water gushed out in all directions from pipes placed around a chair at the side of the room. There were other pipes which directed water at the shoulders or the ears or the eyes. We never saw such an arrangement in any other country.

May 16th. Fine.
At half past nine we went to the Capitoline Museum, which is on a hill [Campidoglio] west of the remains of the Forum. The old stone statues gathered here are beautiful and the most famous in antiquity. So great is the visual beauty of European statuary that when we came here we simply rubbed our eyes and bestowed the highest praise on what we saw. It is truly a remarkable treasure-house.

Behind the museum is a prison dating from Roman times. It was as dark and gloomy as the catacombs. St. Peter was imprisoned here. An iron chain was fastened to his feet which has survived to this day, and worshippers place lighted candles in front of it. St. Peter had been found guilty of propagating a heretical religion and kept chained here and closely guarded. Nevertheless, he continued, calmly and persuasively, to preach the religion of Jesus, even to the warders, and they actually repented. The government, therefore, had to change the warders frequently. St. Peter then decided that he wished to die and tried to break his head against the wall, which became pitted with dents although his skull was unharmed. An iron frame has been fitted over a slight depression in the bricks at the top of the stairs leading down to the cavern, and this has been made into a shrine. This seemed very strange, for although it is said to be a mark made by his head, it merely resembles such a mark.

On reaching Italy after passing through Bavaria, we were filled with disgust whenever we discerned the magnificent remains of churches which had been built by falsely propagating the teachings of the Roman Catholic Church and tricking the people out of their money. When we reached Rome, however, it gave us a feeling of profound sadness whenever we imagined the followers of Jesus welcoming persecution, relishing the hardships and pain and trying to preserve the way which had been handed down to them.

May 19th. Fine.

At nine o'clock in the evening we left Rome to go to the city of Naples.

As we had been travelling around the old ruins of Rome, we came to understand that the source of the so-called progress of the West lies here and that its roots are ancient. This shows that the knowledge held by any nation, once it has established itself, lies deep; it stretches far and wide and does not die; even when it becomes blocked, it can break forth again.

When people in the East hear about Westerners talking of hydraulic engineering, they cannot help but be astounded. Since antiquity there have always been pools with fountains in Rome, for the Romans are very fond of fountains. Three thousand years ago, they constructed an aqueduct extending more than twenty-four miles, and that was the beginning of the water-pipes now found in every city in the West. These, then, are the origins of hydraulic engineering.

When building, the Romans carefully chose stones which would not be damaged by water or crumble when exposed to the air. That is why bridges built two thousand years ago are still in use. The beautiful old walls, columns, statues and coffins which have survived to the present day represent the origins of mineralogy.

The Romans were good at baking bricks and laying them one on top of another to make walls and houses; they used arches as supports, and pillars to support roof beams, and these have lasted until the present. These are the origins of structural engineering.

When they painted pictures, they took great care to show light and shade distinctly and to portray reality, and when they carved a statue in stone they endeavoured to make it resemble real flesh. It is said that their consummate skill with the knife and chisel could by no means be equalled today. These are the origins of fine art.

In the East, the theatres are square, so the lines of sight and hearing do not come together and the corners are always useless. In Rome, on the other hand, the theatres are round, so the lines of sight and hearing come together at one point, thus eliminating the difference between being close and being far away. And again, houses were so well constructed that they lasted for a long time without collapsing, and they remain solid even after a long time has passed. These are the origins of architectural science.

Since ancient times, our country has made few discoveries or inventions but has been skilled in acquiring the knowledge of others. Architecture, iron-smelting, porcelain and embroidery were all derived from Korea and China, but now we have surpassed them in all these. Although there are many old countries in the East, the only one which has made progress in its development is Japan. If we somehow manage to consolidate that progress, develop its good qualities and extend them to areas where they are needed, then even what is not now worth looking at will one day present a different aspect.

CHAPTER 77

# A Record of Naples

May 20th, 1873. Cloudy; rain in the evening.

At five o'clock in the morning we arrived at the town of Caserta, twenty miles short of Naples, where the king has a palace [Reggia di Caserta]. Today we were entertained there by royal household officers and palace officials at the express desire of His Majesty. Accordingly, when we descended from our train at the station, palace guards were there to meet us with horse-drawn carriages. We followed a road which ran directly from the station and the palace was at the end of it. They furnished each of us with a separate room for washing and gargling. After tea, we boarded carriages and toured the gardens.

We walked along a path among the trees where the shady foliage hid the sky from view. One path descended into a hollow, and the air there was refreshing. At the end of the path was a pavilion and a pond. Before us stood Mt. Vesuvius, the volcano, conspicuously thrusting its smoking peak into the sky. There, this side of the Bay of Naples, were the houses and bustling streets of the city. Before our eyes we beheld a view which is famous throughout Europe, and how spectacular it was! Then we returned to the palace, where luncheon was provided for us. After lunch we toured the palace itself, where countless excellent paintings and other fine things were on display.

At four o'clock we boarded our train, and before six we had reached the station at Naples. There we took carriages and after twenty minutes reached the Hotel d'Angleterre, where we were to be accommodated.

The hotel faces the Mediterranean Sea and the azure waves in the distance were delightful. A straight road runs along the coast and a long park has been created where there had been some vacant land by the shore; there are many trees and it is an ideal spot for relaxation. It is one of the places in the city which affords a superb view. Along the shore fishermen were putting out in their boats to fish. The fish is fresh and wonderfully plump. They eat sea-bream here; after leaving Japan it was only in Italy that we ate this fish. In Europe it is customary to eat meat, and the meat of domestic animals is as common as our daily bowl of rice in tea. By contrast fish is highly valued, and its price is twice that of meat. The fish served in Britain, France and Germany is mostly plaice, cod or salmon, but we were even given pickled herrings to eat, which were disgusting. Yet the delicious sea-bream is not eaten. The official accompanying us, Count Fé d'Ostiani, knew that people in our country appreciate sea-bream and so had had it especially prepared for us. Neither in the United States nor in any of the countries of Europe is it eaten; nor did we see it being reared in aquaria, probably because it is somewhat uncommon.

May 21st. Rain.

The city of Naples is the biggest city in Italy. It was the capital of the former kingdom of Naples, which was the most important state in southern Italy.

The streets in the city are very narrow and do not run straight. As a whole, Naples describes an arc facing the sea. A ring of hills skirts the bay, with only a narrow belt of land between the hills and the sea. The streets looking down upon the harbour fill all the flat land available and crowd around the foothills, so they are quite without order. Also, it is an old city, and for that reason, too, the streets are not straight. The paving in the streets is as in Rome, with huge stone slabs roughly aligned. For the most part pedestrians and vehicular traffic are not kept apart. The houses and shops stand side by side, six or seven storeys high, so in many streets one feels as if one is walking through a tunnel.

Most of the inhabitants are uneducated and indolent. They do not clear the rubbish from the streets, which are an utter confusion of carriages and horses. Moreover, coarse people stand at the sides of the streets bawling out their wares from makeshift stalls. Destitute children chase after passing carriages, urging passengers to buy their flowers. The streets along the waterfront are thronged with child beggars. The destitute lie sprawled on the ground, sleeping with wicker boxes for pillows. Others collect cigarette ends and try to sell them. On sunny days the dust blows into one's eyes and hideous smells assault one's nose.

The people follow the Roman Catholic faith; in the streets, pictures are to be seen everywhere of the crucifixion or of Mary holding the infant Jesus in her arms, which they worship. Wealthy people consider it a good deed to give alms to the poor and do not consider begging to be shameful. There are many poor people in Italy. Rome is worse than

Florence in this respect, and Naples worse than Rome. In our tour of Europe and North America we visited cities in twelve countries, but in no other city was there so little cleanliness, so much indolence and so many destitute children. One may say that Shanghai and Naples are very similar in appearance.

There is an Italian proverb which says, 'See Naples and die.' From this it is obvious that Naples is a city of scenic beauty. There are three famous sights, of which the first is the volcano Mt. Vesuvius. There are not a large number of volcanoes in Europe. This one rises up from the shore on a bay which is shaped like a bow, and its peak thrusts impressively into the sky. It has a beauty which cannot be captured in a picture. Smoke belches forth from the summit, making one think of seething white clouds. At night it spews out a fiery glow, which sometimes seems to scorch half the sky. Below it, the sea is imbued with the blue colour of the sky. White-washed walls line the bay and behind them snakes a group of hills clothed in green. The climate is warm and the skies generally clear, so as one looks around in wonder it strikes one as a place of sublime beauty. It is lavishly praised in Europe; it is sketched and painted, and its image is found everywhere, rather as the image of Mt. Fuji is in our country.

The second famous sight, in the village of Pompeii, is the excavated remains of a city buried around the beginning of the Christian era. This will be described in detail in the entry for the next day.

This morning we took carriages and went to the museum [now the Museo Nazionale]. It is filled with old artefacts, pictures and fine sculptures in exceedingly great numbers. Amongst the items on display are mosaics found at Pompeii dating to the year A.D. 50, and frescoes and pictures which have survived on the walls; some have beautiful patterns or depict people and contemporary palace rooms. There are also everyday articles used at the time. When one enters the museum one has the feeling of being born into the world of 1,800 years ago.

On the upper storey is a library with a collection of old books. The whole building is made of stone, and on the paved floor of the library there is a mosaic design with a symbolic representation of the twelve signs of the zodiac, with a north–south line running through it diagonally. In the south wall an aperture lets in the moonlight, so constructed that every month when the moon resumes its path, it is possible to observe its passage across the symbols by the light admitted through the aperture. Everywhere in the West there are sundials for determining noon, when the sun is at its zenith, but hardly anywhere is there a device for showing the phases of the moon. In my opinion, measuring the phases of the moon is probably a custom followed in those countries which used the lunar calendar. Now I have seen such a device here. The path of the moon depends on how dark or light the night sky is. In our country many people these days have fixed their eyes on the West; they think their task to be a simple matter of discarding existing practices, which are actually quite advanced, and thus consider themselves to be civilised, without realising that this runs counter to civilisation.

The third sight worth seeing is the coral work of Naples, which is one of its most notable products. In the streets there are rows of awnings where articles made of coral are sold. The larger pieces are like jewels, the smaller ones like flowers, and coral is also sold in the form of branches or beads.

May 22nd. Alternately cloudy and sunny, with many sudden changes.
At eight o'clock in the morning we set out in carriages in a southerly direction and after twelve miles reached the village of Pompeii, which is at the foot of Mt. Vesuvius. In ancient times there was a fortified town here, a flourishing city with a population of forty to fifty thousand people. In A.D. 79, however, Vesuvius erupted and hurled vast amounts of mud and ashes into the air. In the space of one night the whole town was buried and became an empty plain. Until the eighteenth century it lay beneath meadows and fields of barley. There were few historical records of how things had been in the past, and nobody knew for sure that this was where the town was buried. In the 1740s, quite by chance, an old building was dug out of the ground; this was thought to be peculiar, and more excavation was carried out, with the result that remains were found everywhere. Antiquarians realised that this had to be the town which had been buried in antiquity and dispatched men there to excavate. Now one-third of it has been uncovered. Naturally, nobody who heard that an ancient town – all but two thousand years old – had suddenly been brought to light could fail to be astonished. From every corner of Europe people have been coming to see Pompeii for themselves, and the streams of people are unending.

Upon entering the gate one finds a museum to one side. This is where the ancient artefacts recovered from the ground are kept. There are a few bodies of people who collapsed and died in the mud and ash, laid out on stands just as they were, together with the ash in which they lay. One is the body of an adult male lying supine; another is prone and seems to be a woman. Then there is what seems to be the body of their daughter, who died with a head-covering over her eyes; she may have collapsed in tears, or possibly been buried by ash. She has a gold ring on her finger. It is a pitiful sight.

Proceeding farther, we entered the old town itself. The streets are wide enough for a carriage to negotiate with room to spare, and some are wide enough for two carriages to pass each other. There are raised pavements on both sides of the streets for pedestrians, and these are paved with stone to prevent them from deteriorating. Most of the streets are two or three feet below the pavements. At crossroads, flat stepping stones have been placed to enable people to cross, while carriages can pass with their wheels running on either side of the stones. The surfaces of the streets are paved with stone, using pieces which are naturally flat, so some unevenness is inevitable. There are wheel-ruts in the surface of the stones, so deeply scored that they show how much traffic there once was. From this it is apparent that it has been the custom in the West since antiquity for roads to be built with separate parts for people and for horses, for them to be paved, and for vehicles to be used.

In front of some of the shops we saw copper pipes buried in the ground and the tops of [Archimedes] screws used to draw up water. The houses are erected on flat pieces of land, with no sign of any cellars beneath. In some cases the columns and walls are plastered and decorated with either floral designs inscribed in the plaster or paintings of people and animals. The windows are small, the walls very thick and the size of the houses no different from houses today. Since not one of the roofs has survived, there is no way to see how the upper parts were constructed. The floors are paved with stone and many of them include mosaics.

By consulting ancient histories, scholars have been able to draw up a plan of the city as it was and, by examining the streets, they have, to a considerable extent, been able to establish that here, for example, are the remains of a bank, there the remains of the court-house, and this a school. There is a bathhouse which is far from small. One area was a pleasure-quarter, with houses divided into small rooms, each with an earthen bed with a raised part where the pillow would be. In some cases, pictures have survived above the doorways, mostly lewd ones. In one large brothel there is a hall with well-preserved erotic pictures no different in style from those of today. There are the remains of a theatre, a large one quite the equal of the Colosseum in Rome. Underneath the hills and fields on either side lies more of the city, the streets buried to a depth of about six yards. From this it was clear to us what a truly extraordinary disaster this had been. In turn, this explains why the remains which have come to light are so remarkable. It is, it has to be said, one of the most impressive sights in Europe.

May 23rd. Fine.

At ten to one we boarded a train and left Naples. We travelled around the foothills of Vesuvius and passed Caserta. The volcano towers up amidst the plain, and we could see it smoking. There were many fine views as we went in and out of the folds of the mountains. In Rome we spent the night in the hotel we had used before.

May 25th. Fine.

Today we went to the royal palace for a farewell audience with the king.

May 26th. Fine.

In the morning, the empress [Maria] of Russia entered Rome in the course of her visit to Italy. The route from the station to our hotel was guarded by soldiers. In attendance were ladies-in-waiting and court attendants riding in dozens of carriages, which passed in a line along the streets, all uncovered.

We left Rome at a quarter to ten at night.

# CHAPTER 78

# A Record of Lombardy and Venice

May 27th, 1873. Fine.

After leaving the station in Rome yesterday evening, we saw nothing whatsoever during the night. At dawn we emerged from a tunnel on a curve and travelled on through mountains and valleys. We were still en route from Rome to Florence, in other words, in an area which we had passed through on our way down, albeit at night. This region has some deep valleys, and we heard the roar of water cascading down the hills. We could see villages straddling the hills, steep mountainsides soaring to great heights, and exposed rocks and trees drenched in spray. Everything imparted a cool and refreshing feeling. Fifteen minutes later the train emerged onto the plain, and at half past six we reached Florence Station.

To the north of Florence the mountains are especially steep, and since the taller sort of railway carriages are too dangerous for this part of the line, they are exchanged for shorter ones at Florence Station. There was a stop of half an hour for this purpose, so we all sauntered around in the vicinity of the station, drank some tea and awaited our departure. Our train left at seven o'clock. For the first thirty-four miles, until we reached the town of Pistoia, the terrain was not particularly uneven. Nevertheless, the view of the mountains racing to meet us offered a delightful prospect from the train. We travelled eighty-four miles from Florence before the steep mountains came to an end and we were greeted by plains again. Here lies the town of Bologna.

Bologna is the largest city in this region. We took lunch here and then departed. From this point onwards the flat plains were continuous, with many fields of barley and plantations of mulberry trees. We crossed a bridge over the river Po, which is the longest river in Italy. The land on both sides of the river is quite flat, and the soil is amongst the best in Italy. This area is called the Lombardy Plain. The part of Italy which extends northwards from the former country of Tuscany is quite different from the rest, for it is here that Italy reveals itself to be well developed. In particular, Milan, Venice and Genoa have long been distinguished for their culture and their craft industries.

From this point on we saw some hills with castles atop them. Around the foothills were some villages, sparkling white. There were marshes in this area, and we saw rice growing in paddy-fields. Coming out of a tunnel, we caught sight of a hot-spring in the hills to our left. Steam was billowing out of one of the buildings. A short while later we reached Padua Station.

Padua lies at the meeting point of four roads in the north of Italy. It is an important northern town, with trains coming and going. It is full of activity and the schools are particularly impressive. Recently, the government built a school of sericulture here, which was apparently completed this year.

From here the land became increasingly flat. There were many marshy areas in the fields, and in some places the land was lying under more than a foot of water. No hills or mountains were to be seen in any direction; it was like crossing Holland. At ten o'clock in the evening we crossed a long bridge over a lake and so came to the station at the entrance to the islands of Venice. Our consul-general, Nakayama, and a consulate official were there to greet us. We took a boat along the canals to the New York Hotel, where we stayed.

Venice is a maritime city in the north-eastern part of Italy and consists of a group of islands jutting out of the water at the end of the Adriatic Sea. The Grand Canal runs through the islands, tracing the shape of a whirl. From it other canals of various sizes branch off, criss-crossing this way and that; they connect with small islands in the vicinity, and thus it all constitutes one city. Every corner of the island is covered with fine towers and palaces. Rivers take the place of roads, and boats the place of carriages. It is a remarkable place, one which offers a prospect altogether different from that of any other city in Europe. It is called 'the city of the islands'.

Venice is an old centre of European trade, and it flourished from around A.D. 300. It occupied neighbouring territories and became an independent country with a republican system of government. Goods from the eastern part of Europe, Asia Minor, Arabia and India were transported here from across the Mediterranean Sea and dispersed throughout Europe. With the reins of trade firmly in its hands, it flourished for a thousand years until the Portuguese opened up the African sea-routes, rounded the Cape of Good Hope and began trading with Arabia and India. Then the livelihood of the city shrank.

Nevertheless, it continued to occupy a pivotal position in the Mediterranean and had unhindered access to profits from the East. The city lost its independence [in 1797] after the disturbances brought about by Napoleon, and it was absorbed and administered by the Austrian Empire. As a result of the war of 1866, however, it was restored to Italy. Subsequently, the British moved the terminus of their mail steamer lines running to the Red Sea and the Indian Ocean from Marseilles to Venice. Accordingly, Italy constructed a railway from Venice to Austria, thus facilitating European trade. Thereafter, Venice once again became an important European port.

On this day, we immediately boarded a gondola after emerging from the station. The construction of the boat is very curious. The stern and the prow are curved upwards and the keel is rounded. The stern area has a roof and is fitted with comfortable cushioned seats, and the boat is propelled with a gentle, floating motion by a pole being pushed. It felt as if we had placed ourselves in a picture of a pellucid river. The houses and shops jostling together were reflected in the water, the air was clean, the sunlight pleasant and the water, suffused with an azure tint, was marked by gentle ripples. The boat glided through the dim and misty air, and it felt as if one was being wafted into the sky. The local people are fond of music and delight in song; they make up a party and idle away their time in a boat, relaxing in midstream. The water and the music are in harmony and ring out so melodiously that the sea and the clouds seem to come to a stop. It is said that travellers who come here and share in these pleasures are usually too enraptured to think of going home. When we reached our hotel, music was being played on the water in front of the lounge to celebrate our arrival in this city.

May 28th. Fine; very pleasant.
In the afternoon, we visited the assembly hall of the former united provinces [Palazzo Ducale]. It was here that republican government was practised, and from here that trade with the south-east was controlled continuously from the fourth century to the nineteenth.

The Basilica of San Marco is the largest church in Venice and is adjacent to the Palazzo Ducale. Construction began around the year 1100 and it cost $7,000,000 to build, but it is still incomplete. The walls and pillars inside are made of marble, and the ceiling consists of a mosaic made with gold-coloured pieces of glass. It has ancient bronze doors rich in sculptural detail. In front of the basilica stands the Campanile, which is one hundred metres high. It was built on a square plan, and a twisting stairway inside leads to the bells after thirty-seven flights of steps. It was a bright, clear day, and when we climbed up and gazed around we had a magnificent view of the Adriatic Sea ringed by the Alps and of the many islands of Venice floating amidst the waves.

In front of the basilica is an open space enclosed on three sides by fine buildings. People walk under the arcades, where there are shops selling all manner of goods. In Venice, people use boats instead of carriages, so the streets are only wide enough for people to pass on foot. There are many narrow alleys, and in some places there is insufficient room for two people to walk side by side. All the streets are paved, but they are similar to the alleys of Tokyo in that there are few shops. The only place where goods are available is in the piazza in front of the Basilica of San Marco, which is the most commercially lively part of the city. The whole piazza is paved with stone, but since there are no carriages in Venice one does not hear the grating noise of wheels. There are always men and women strolling in pairs past the shops. At night, gas-lamps are lit, and it is like daylight right up to midnight. It is a place of pleasure and delight.

May 29th. Fine; a sudden shower in the evening.
At half past nine we boarded a boat and went to the library in the city archives [Biblioteca del Reale Archivio di Stato], which contains books and documents dating as far back as the eighth century. In all, it contains 1,300,000 volumes.

The books and ledgers of towns and cities are the origins of commercial and civil law, and the peace and good order of any country depend upon such documents and are probably the result of the importance placed on them. The official documents of the courts are precious, and if they are treated lightly, in the end the laws of that country will ultimately lose all effect. This is the natural course. In the West, there are museums where the most insignificant objects are kept and libraries where even discarded scraps of paper are stored. This has to be regarded as the essence of civilised behaviour.

The library contains two letters sent by Ōtomo [Sōrin] of our country and delivered by his legate. We expressed a desire to see these relics, so they were taken out of a folder and shown to us. Both were written in Latin on Western paper, and at the end they bore holograph signatures, written in pen. Ambassador Iwakura bade me make copies of them.

We next went to the church of Santa Maria della Salute, a large church in front of our hotel. On the interior wall of the church is a plaque in memory of the Japanese mission. The plaque is made of white stone and is set into the wall; the text gives the names of all the members of the mission and the date: 1630. There are also many other stone plaques commemorating missions from other countries.

May 30th. Fine.
At nine o'clock we boarded a boat and went to visit the glassworks, which is on one of the islands [Murano] north of the city. Glass-making in Venice has a very long history. Glass has been made here continuously since the fifteenth century, and many samples are on display in the museum. We went around the museum, following the chronological order of manufacture and observing the progress which had been made, and saw that great benefit is to be gained from a careful study of these matters. The glass made on this island is expertly coloured and many skills are employed to achieve different effects. The techniques used to produce very fine threads of glass and to weave them to make various objects are unique to Venice and famed throughout Europe.

June 2nd. Fine.
At half past ten in the evening we left Venice. Two attendants came with us on the train to see us off. We slept that night on the train. To the south we could see the jagged coastline of the Adriatic, and to the west the Alps, with layer upon layer of snow-capped mountains reaching to the sky. Between the mountains and the sea the plain is quite flat; the grass was growing luxuriantly, the barley was thriving, the mulberry trees were spreading their leaves and charming flowers were in bloom beside the track. Shortly after passing through a tunnel we reached Nabrežina [Aurisina] Station on the Austrian border.

CHAPTER 79

# *A Survey of Austria*

Austria consists of eleven German provinces and two others, each with its own provincial Diet, and a central Diet under the emperor; thus, there is a duplication of debate on political and legislative matters, just as in Germany. Originally, Austria was part of the German Confederation, but later it withdrew and formed the Austrian Confederation.

The Austro-Hungarian lands are more or less rectangular in shape. While Austria is one area of Germany, Hungary is a part of the land of the Huns, so in race and customs they are quite distinct. The topography of Austria-Hungary, put most simply, consists of mountains and valleys in Austria and plains in Hungary.

Because Austria is such a mountainous country, there is no possibility of river transportation. Furthermore, the terrain is rather steep and difficult for constructing railways, but by 1860 more than 4,800 miles of track had been laid. By 1873 this had already been substantially increased to 9,158 miles. The principal cities, such as Vienna, Pest [Budapest], Prague and Trieste, are all well connected. The Austrian and Prussian governments resolved by law to construct the main lines connecting their countries themselves and to leave branch lines to private companies, but at one time the Austrian government, suffering from financial difficulties, abrogated this law and thereafter all new lines were left to private companies to construct, and even sections due to be constructed by the government were entrusted to them. There are a considerable number of British men involved in the railway companies of both Italy and Austria, and the machinery is mostly brought from Britain. The benefits of railways have spread from Britain all over the world, not only to South and East Asia but also to Europe, where, as this example shows, they are flourishing.

With regard to the climate, when our party was in Vienna in the early part of May it was much less hot than in Italy, but the weather was very unstable and changed constantly every day, so it did not seem to be very good for the health. Nevertheless, considering the latitude, Austria is generally a warm country.

Since the soil is rich and the climate mild, the forests and fields alike are abundantly productive. Austria is one of the most agriculturally rich countries in Europe. In mountainous areas the people are mainly employed in manufacturing, and in the three provinces of Lower Austria, Bohemia and Mähren [Moravia], in particular, they tend to converge around factories and the agricultural population is less than half. Hungary, being flat, is called 'the farm of Europe'.

Austria is regarded in Europe as a multi-racial country, and truly a great mixture of peoples lives there. In countries such as Prussia and Russia, one race is far more numerous than the others and so racial rights are in equilibrium, but in Austria there is not even one province inhabited by a single ethnic group. This renders governance considerably more difficult.

The educational system falls short of that in Prussia, but it has made rapid progress in recent years. The German areas in particular are well provided with elementary and secondary schools, and education has reached the populace at large. The medical schools are especially renowned. In the south-eastern provinces, because of the great ethnic mix, people speak various languages, and sometimes three or four different languages have to be used in one and the same school. This has hampered progress, but recently the people have hastily bestirred themselves and made efforts in education to achieve literacy. By a national law and provincial laws passed in 1869, an education system has been established and boys and girls are now required to attend school between the ages of six and twelve. Their parents or guardians are punished if they neglect to send them to school; if they work in factories and find it difficult to attend school, the proprietors are bound to establish a school in the factory.

By religion Austria is a Roman Catholic country, and this is one reason why it is at odds with other German countries. However, a mixture of various religions is found here, just like the ethnic mixture.

# CHAPTER 80

# Travels by Rail in Austria, and a Survey of Vienna

June 3rd, 1873. Fine.

At six o'clock in the morning we passed out of Italian territory and arrived at Nabrežina [Aurisina] Station. This is on the border between Venice in Italy and the Austrian maritime territories. It is on the Adriatic coast and here the rugged Alps reach down close to the sea, so the countryside is far from flat. Eight miles south of Nabrezina the railway reaches the port of Trieste.

The Austrian government had ordered its former minister in Japan, Mr. [Heinrich von] Calicé, to accompany us. He, together with our Mr. Sano [Tsunetami], had been waiting for our party to arrive at the port of Trieste, but on receipt of a telegraph announcing that we were to arrive overland, he had come to meet us at Nabrezina Station. We were welcomed at the station and took breakfast there, too. We then boarded a train kindly furnished for us by the Austrian government and departed at half past seven.

Upon leaving the station, the train followed a route into the mountains, where boulders were strewn on both sides of the track, hemming it in. The mountains stretched ahead layer after layer, and the track wound its way through them. At nine o'clock we passed the village of Saint Peter [Pivka], and all the way to the station at Laibach [Ljubljana] the scenery through the mountains was unchanging. Our route from here ran downstream alongside the Sau, which is the largest river in southern Austria and has its source in the eastern Tyrol. At twelve o'clock we reached Steinbrück [Zidani Most] Station, where the train halted for a while. This is where the river Sann cascades into the Sau. From here the train ran alongside the Sann through an oppressively narrow gorge as before, and the track twisted and turned.

We rounded a mountain, crossed a bridge and so arrived at Marburg [Maribor] Station at one o'clock. At four o'clock we crossed a river called the Mur and thus came to the station at Graz. From Graz we travelled on to Bruck. As the evening sun dipped low on the horizon, it was an exceptionally fine scene.

At seven o'clock we traversed the Semmering Mountains. Ever since we had entered Austria our route had taken us through steep mountain country and there had been very many fine views of rivers and peaks, but those at Semmering were particularly impressive. Since the railway engineering was so magnificent, the views from the train this day were the best. In this region the landscape consists of ranges of mountains formed of rocks vast in size and strange in shape which surround strips of plain in the valleys, so just to look down from the tops of the mountains is exhilarating.

Occasionally, when the train is travelling one thousand feet up, one sees the highway down below, just a thread-like line, with tiny figures of men and horses. As the train rushes on, a succession of magnificent views greets one's eyes, but there is no time to appreciate them. After spending an hour in this way, the mountains came to an end. Mt. Semmering straddles the border between Lower Austria and Steiermark, and thereafter the mountains gradually fall away and we came onto a plain, although some spurs straggled on. By the time we reached Payerbach Station it was already half past seven.

At ten o'clock we arrived at the southern station of Vienna. Vienna resembles Munich in that it lies in the middle of an open plain and is encircled by mountains in the distance. It resembles Paris in that the surrounding terrain is uneven and undulating. Through the courtesy of the Austrian government we were accommodated at the Hotel Austria [Österreichischer Hof], but we provided for our meals.

Vienna is a bustling city like Berlin, and second only to Paris in beauty. The city is so big that it apparently stretches five miles in all directions. It is divided into nine large districts, distinguished by their inner or outer locations. In its physical setting there are hills to the north, and to the north-east the great Danube is divided by sand-banks. The western branch flows through the centre of the city, and on its west bank a fortress mound was built in the shape of a pentagon. The part within the walls of that fortress constitutes the old capital city of Vienna dating to Roman times, and the imperial palace lies in its western part. It is a tall, grand structure with a large park in front of it; behind it, in the centre, stands the cathedral, which is called St. Stephen's. It is the family church of the emperors; its tall spire soars 445 feet, the third-tallest church tower in Europe. To the south, east and north the streets are crammed together with few changes in ground level. They are irregular and narrow, and the squares no more than fourteen or sixteen yards across. The closely packed houses are five or six storeys high and all the streets are paved with stone. No city surpasses it for the din made by pedestrians and carriages.

The fortress mound in the shape of a pentagon used to separate the inner city from the outer city, but as this proved disruptive, in 1857 the emperor, following the example of the Boulevard des Italiens in Paris, ordered it to be levelled and the empty moat filled in. This created a thoroughfare fifty-seven metres wide called the Ringstrasse, which is still in the process of construction. This is the most important street in Vienna, and the buildings on both sides are grand and most elegant in appearance.

The inner parts of the city are the busiest and are paved with pieces of granite, which are either brick-shaped or cut square and come in various sizes. In general, large square pieces are used when the streets are paved so that replacements can easily be inserted if there is damage from the hooves and wheels of the horse-drawn carriages. Cracked ones are apparently broken up and used for other roads.

Manufacturing thrives in Vienna. They make silk cloth, embroidered brocades and silk twills, as well as linen and fine lace, gold- or silver-flecked shawls (to cover ladies' shoulders), woollen cloth, blankets and cotton goods, all with exquisite decoration. Porcelain, glassware, paper, decorated papers, maps, colour pictures, cosmetics, objects with precious stones, and all sorts of domestic goods are made, too, again of high quality. There are also scientific and artistic goods, such as portraits, sculptures, axles for carriages and so on; they display the finest workmanship to satisfy the desire for luxury among the aristocracy and the wealthy, and even Berlin could not match them.

It has been argued that both the Austrians and the Prussians are German in the sense that they are circumspect and slow, but they deserve praise for their natural aptitude for intricate craftsmanship. Because they spend their lives on the cold, bare plains of the north, the Prussians nurtured their spirit in poverty, practised perseverance and elevated their morale; thus, they excel at war and often indulge in harsh practices. Of late they have been victorious in war against four of their neighbours and the mood in Berlin is fierce. Austria, by contrast, enjoys good soil and a milder climate and has long been used to the civilised ways of its famous capital city; it has learnt to live with riches and has steeped itself in urban elegance; the people are discriminating and fond of the arts. The two seem to be opposites; yet they both share the phlegmatic character of the German people. At present Prussia is on the rise and Austria in decline, and everybody lauds the military culture of the Prussians. Military skills are not one of Austria's strengths, but its literary arts are truly amongst the finest in Europe. It is a leader in politics, law, science and engineering, and in medicine it is virtually without equal. In their temperament, the people may lack inventiveness, but they are receptive to innovation; they are most adept at learning new ways.

Austria has a large aristocracy which takes great pride in their flourishing and noble nation. Therefore the freedoms of the ordinary people are poorly developed. In 1789, as a result of the first French Revolution, the notion of liberty stirred the whole of Europe and the German countries threw off the vestiges of feudalism. However, Mr. Metternich, the Austrian prime minister, considered the Alps and the Erzgebirge Mountains to be the 'Great Wall' of Austria and so rejected any theories emanating from abroad. He emphasised monarchical absolutism, and for more than forty years Austria preserved its political system. Up to the present this has acted as a brake on the nation's progress and is to blame for the lack of industrial and commercial development. While a host of other countries were suffering the turmoil of adopting constitutional systems, in Austria alone officials reigned supreme and the clergy continued to exercise power. Freedom of opinion was harshly suppressed, and trade and industry were subject to restricting controls. The lower orders laboured under heavy taxes while the aristocracy continued their feudal dreams, so the backbone of the country weakened and Austria lived in a different world from the countries to the north-west.

During the second French Revolution of 1848, the waves of discontent at last affected Austria and split the country. Various factions were astir, each with separate opinions, and riots broke out in the two capitals of Vienna and Pest. Although the previous emperor, Ferdinand I, promised to introduce constitutional politics, from the outset the aristocracy was opposed to the idea so it was impossible to put it into practice. Ferdinand finally abdicated in favour of the present emperor [Franz Joseph]. The imperial household and the aristocracy wished to retain absolutist rule, while the artisans, merchants and other citizens sought extended freedoms. The Hungarians were plotting their independence and the clergy were wielding power as of old. The whole country was split and divided, and its difficulties grew year by year.

Thus, when revolution broke out in Italy and war ensued, all the classes were thrown into confusion. Prussia spotted a strategic opportunity and took its enemy from the rear, with the result that the Austrian armies were in a critical situation. In the war with Prussia that followed in 1866, it was distasteful to the Austrians to fight people of the same race as themselves. Moreover, they had been forced into war and were militarily unprepared, and the exchequer was in a dire state. At its heel, Italy was allied with Prussia. When Hungary secretly lent its support to Italy and there was unrest in Bohemia and war in Venice, how could Austria maintain itself? In the south Venice was restored to Italy, in the north Austria lost its position as leader of the German Confederation, and in the east it granted Hungary independence. These events were the beginning of constitutional politics in Austria. Since they occurred only six years ago, and since a spirit of freedom had not flourished there before, Austria could not escape being forty years behind the countries to its north-west. It is inevitable that conditions in Austria should be different and still rather unpropitious.

In 1867 Austria and Hungary agreed to unite as two separate countries. Austria is called the Cisleithanian empire and Hungary the Transleithanian kingdom. They have their own parliaments, governments and political leaders and their own hereditary sovereigns. The Hungarian emperor is now the king of Hungary. Only in matters diplomatic and military do the two countries act as one. For these purposes they each elect sixty representatives to take part in national deliberations and they entrust legislation to them. When important matters are being debated, the representatives of both countries assemble and pass resolutions. State business is transacted by three bureaux headed by the ministers of foreign affairs, war and finance, and they are responsible to the Diet for the execution of their duties.

June 4th. Fine.

At eight o'clock we went to watch an exercise of the massed ranks of the army on an open field. Since the Universal Exposition had opened in Vienna, a succession of members of the ruling and aristocratic families of all countries were coming to see it, including the emperor of Russia, who was then in the middle of his visit, so the emperor of Austria had arranged for a military display to entertain him. Only members of the nobility were permitted into the enclosure. Entrance was by ticket, so ordinary people had no option but to stand outside. In those parts of Europe from Germany to the east, remnants of feudalism still exist, and in Austria, in particular, the old habits of the aristocracy persist. Thus, the different treatment accorded to people depending on their rank in society is the same as the practice in our country before Emperor Meiji. The families of the nobility were riding in decorated carriages, couples in some, women alone in others. At the place where we stopped to view the proceedings there was a press of carriages all around, so we were able to observe the dignified Austrian aristocracy for ourselves. Outside, men and women were crowded together and looking into the enclosure; they were in their thousands and there was no room to stand anywhere.

June 6th. Changeable; poor weather.
In the afternoon we boarded carriages and went to the Prater Park in the north-west and looked around the Universal Exposition.

CHAPTER 81

# *A Record of Vienna*

June 7th, 1873. Cloudy; rain in the afternoon.

At nine o'clock we boarded carriages and proceeded to the Arsenal, which is located in the southern district of the city and covers a vast area. In the centre stands the Arsenal itself, a huge building with a round tower in the middle; attached to it by arches are enormous, elegant, two-storey structures extending in all four directions. Inside they are brilliantly decorated with gold-leaf and festooned with paintings showing Austrian soldiers in wars with neighbouring countries. The decor was magnificent.

Austria's military prowess has never been remarkable, and it was on account of marriage connections and inheritance that Austria was able to exercise imperial domination over the German Confederation, to absorb Holland, Belgium, Switzerland and even at one time Spain, and to exert its power over all Europe. If Charles I was able to bask in military glory, it was because he used Spanish troops. That is the reason there is merely a small amount of booty in the Arsenal. From the time of the religious wars of the sixteenth and seventeenth centuries up to the country's recent defeat of 1866, it is rather Austrian arms which have been captured by other countries and placed in quantity in their arsenals.

All countries currently manufacture cannon by casting refined iron, and they have made some wonderful discoveries. When one sees manufacturing at Woolwich in England, at the Krupp works in Germany or at the St. Petersburg works in Russia, one finds extraordinary precision, with robust pieces being produced. I had thought that making iron and milled brass cannon had already ended in Europe, and it was most unexpected to see it here with my own eyes. In my astonishment, I asked for an explanation and was informed that the military experts, remembering their own experiences, felt that an army is not properly equipped for battle without cannon, which provide an extra striking force when needed. I was unable to comprehend the reasoning for this since detailed explanations were not offered, but the Austrian armaments we saw did

421

give the impression of being forty years behind the times, the same as its constitutional arrangements.

June 8th. Fine.
At one o'clock palace officials in three splendid royal carriages came with liveried grooms and mounted guards to take us to the palace, where we had an audience with Emperor Franz Joseph and his empress.

June 9th. Fine; rather cold, with some rain; unsettled weather.
On this day we went to the Universal Exposition and closely examined the exhibits in the main galleries.

June 10th. Cloudy; rain in the evening.
In the afternoon we took carriages to the Treasure House, which is in the vicinity of the palace. It was built on a grand scale and contains astounding items. Several cases were filled with quartz, including three or four pieces which were one foot thick and eight or nine inches in length and height. Bejewelled crowns belonging to the emperor and empress were displayed inside glass cases. The diamond on the emperor's crown was a huge stone with a faintly yellowish tinge worth 800,000 florins; smaller diamonds like beads were used for decoration. We were told that the total value of all the jewels on display was 13,000,000 florins. There was a white silk robe embroidered with gold pieces which belonged to the Roman emperors, and a sword with scabbard used by a king of Persia eight hundred years ago; the sword was similar to a Japanese sword. There was a small carriage made for one of the children of Emperor Napoleon I when he was at the height of his power, so he used it to pretend that he would make his child the emperor of Austria. Austria is an important country with a long history and glorious rulers, so naturally it should have a great many antiquities.

   We went to the imperial stables, where five hundred horses are kept when not in use by the emperor and empress or by officials. More than seventy carriages are stored on the upper floor, fourteen of them made two hundred years ago, twenty one hundred years ago, and approximately thirty of them more recently; ten are for children and two are for funerals. In one corner is a device which lowers and raises a section of the floor to move the carriages between the upper floor and the ground. A room on the second floor holds a large collection of saddlery from all ages. Another room held a collection of guns. These were ordinary hunting pieces and had inlays of gold, silver and ivory. Since Europeans in general, including women, are accustomed to using guns on horseback and take their pleasure in hunting, a large variety of guns is available for them. Even the cheaper ones cost one or two hundred dollars apiece, but one thousand pieces of gold would not be enough to acquire one of the more beautiful ones. In the willingness of royalty and the aristocracy to spend tens of thousands on a single gun, they are like our samurai who spare no expense on their swords. Infantry rifles and the like are considered to be inferior, being mere 'soldiers' guns', again rather like the swords and armour used by guards in our country in the past.

June 11th. Cloudy.
We had audiences with several princes.

June 12th. Cloudy.
In the morning the emperor himself was to conduct a celebration [the Corpus Christi procession] and to proceed to a church with princes, members of the aristocracy, and all the civil officials and priests in attendance, so we went to a part of the palace to observe the ceremony. The order of procession was briefly as follows. A band of sixteen players marched by, followed by four infantry platoons, comprising some five hundred men; then came more than ten flags carried in procession, four groups of orphans, amounting to two hundred children, and some priests with a band in their midst. Following them were priests from fifty-one churches, some of them carrying two or three banners – those with two banners were accompanied by four priests, those with three banners were accompanied by six priests. Some carried one or more baskets of flowers, depending on the status of the church. Next came priests carrying more banners and baskets of flowers; these were the most important members of the clergy in the country. After them came one hundred priests followed by sixteen attendants wearing dress-coats, with others in the same dress carrying candles – columns of soldiers marched on both sides of them, so they were probably government officials. Then there were seven or eight people carrying big drums; sixteen children; an official of the church surrounded by thirty officials in uniforms decorated with gold-braid, so he must have been high-ranking; six men carrying big drums; thirty-four officers, probably of high rank, wearing scarlet; four hundred members of the aristocracy wearing formal costume with gold braid; and the archbishop under a canopy with ten acolytes. The emperor and leading members of the imperial family followed on foot, with cavalry and infantry parading behind them. There was a seamless flow of people

proceeding to the church. In a square they halted and a ceremony was conducted. The ordinary people all knelt down on the ground. The emperor rose and, with a candle in his hands, followed the archbishop into the church and disappeared from view. This ceremony, we were informed, happens once a year.

Earlier, in March, there had been a ceremony at which the emperor and the empress had washed the feet of poor people. For this purpose twelve men and women, the oldest paupers in the country, were chosen and taken to a church. There the emperor washed the feet of the men and the empress the feet of the women, drying their feet with towels. Then the paupers were seated in a hall and served a sumptuous meal by the emperor and empress in person. Afterwards they were apparently each given one hundred florins in gold. Austria is a thoroughly Roman Catholic country and these are all Catholic ceremonies, remnants of old religious practices.

In the afternoon we had an audience with an imperial prince.

June 13th. Cloudy.
We were received at the Ministry of Foreign Affairs.

June 14th. Fine.
We visited the Exposition.

June 15th. Fine, warm.
We had undertaken to visit Pest, the capital of Hungary, on this day, but we cancelled our visit on receipt of a telegraph from Pest stating that there was some obstacle to our visit. Pest lies on the shores of the Danube and there is constant river traffic between Pest and Vienna.

Hungary has connections with the Mongolians and is the country of the Huns. Its land area is approximately the same as that of Japan, although the population is less than half. It lies on the eastern periphery of Europe, and its customs and ways are quite different from those of Europeans. The people wear strangely old-fashioned clothing, and their physiognomy is rustic. It cannot be denied that they are but semi-civilised. Domestic production consists mostly of natural produce, and Hungary makes few industrial products worthy of notice. Over the last seven years it has awoken from the dreams sustained by old habits and has developed a desire to advance towards civilisation. Hungary's situation, therefore, seems to resemble that of Japan in recent years.

Dr. Moreshī [István Mórocz?] of Austria has written of the recent situation in Hungary, and his work contains much which is worth paying attention to in advancing civilisation in our own country, so I shall append a summary of his views. Hungary was one of the most agrarian countries in Europe; most of the people worked with their hands and made little use of machines. Roads were few and transportation undeveloped. Although there were mineral deposits, no effort was made to exploit them or to derive profits from them. The aristocracy was arrogant and the people were downtrodden. Learning and the arts did not flourish. Wages rose to absurd levels and the country was very backward. However, in 1867, the people achieved their long-cherished goal of gaining their independence. Both high and low were gladdened and suddenly set about developing their land, inspired by a desire to make their country powerful. The government took the lead, devoting more than half its tax revenue to launching grand enterprises. Soldiers were conscripted, the numbers of officials increased, funds were raised and attempts made to expand education. Efforts were undertaken to construct railways, and in the space of two years eight hundred miles of track were completed. Large amounts of steam-powered machinery were purchased, too. Although huge sums of money were spent, no investigation was made into the factors which nurture the process of civilisation, and in many ways energy and financial resources were simply wasted to create an attractive façade.

June 16th. Fine.
June 17th. Fine.
On these two days we looked around the Exposition.

June 18th. Fine.
We packed our luggage and left our hotel at five o'clock; the two officials who had been in attendance upon us and various diplomats came to escort us to the border. At a quarter past six our train set off in a westward direction.

Night had already fallen when we entered the province of Upper Austria. We passed Linz and entered Salzburg province, reaching the city of Salzburg at eleven o'clock. This is at the limit of Austrian territory, so here our escorts partook of a light meal with us and then took their leave. We boarded our train and went to bed as our train headed towards Bavaria.

# Continental Europe, 3; and the Voyage Home

# CHAPTER 82

# The Vienna Universal Exposition, 1

Less than eighty years have passed since, as a consequence of the French Revolution, the principle of liberty was disseminated among the peoples of Europe and the countries of Europe adopted constitutional forms of government. Of these countries, Austria retained its emperor but twenty years ago adopted a constitutional system, and for the past ten years even the autocratic tsar of Russia has sought to grant his people some kinds of freedom. European civilisation derives from such reforms, some of them superficial, others profound. Its finest fruits have been the products of the industrial arts, and profits have poured forth constantly from those sources. As we travelled through America, Britain and France, and through the rest of the European continent, we observed, in the great towns and cities, such competition in manufacturing and such effort in promoting trade that all day long we heard the rumble of machines and at night we saw the heavens scorched by flames. In each city we visited, thanks to the generosity of manufacturing companies, we were allowed to observe the processes first-hand. However, we saw no more than one or two out of hundreds and thousands, and those which we saw were always the largest and most flourishing enterprises in each country. How could these have sufficed to give a complete picture of manufacturing in the continent as a whole? Fortunately, we happened to be in Europe when the Universal Exposition was held in Austria, and a visit to it allowed us both to re-consider what we had already seen and to study various products and processes we had not seen before. This was a great help to us in completing the account of our journey.

The countries of Europe are divided into large and small. On the one hand, there are the large nations – Britain, France, Russia, Prussia and Austria – and, on the other hand, there are the small countries – Belgium, Holland, Saxony, Sweden and Denmark. So far as each people's earning an independent livelihood is concerned, however, the larger countries are not to be feared and the smaller ones are not to be despised. In both

Britain and France, for example, civilisation flourishes and industry and commerce prosper together. However, when one looks at the products of Belgium and Switzerland, the achievements of their peoples in attaining independence and accumulating wealth would impress even the largest nation. Prussia is a large country and Saxony a small one, but the latter is by no means inferior to the former in the industrial arts. Conversely, Russia is a large country, but it cannot stand alongside these nations.

A public display of manufactured articles is called an 'exhibition'. Products from various countries are brought together to be exhibited within a single large exhibition hall, where they are viewed by considerable numbers of people, who are thus made familiar with the ways of life, the agricultural products, the industrial arts, and the tastes and customs of the peoples of the world. On the one hand, those who bring their products for the public to see regard this as an opportunity to enhance the reputation of their businesses, which serves the purpose of generating long-term profits. And, on the other hand, by examining the products displayed by others, they are able to see where they themselves fall short and can try to increase their own business opportunities by considering what new inventions are needed to cater to diverse tastes. It is, at the same time, an opportunity to seek the views of experts and to take note of their criticisms, and so it provides guidance which makes further progress possible. Exhibitions are, therefore, an all-important means of expanding trade, encouraging manufacturing and spreading knowledge among the general populace, thus helping to promote peace and order and to increase the wealth and power of the host nation.

International exhibitions make one aware that Western industrial development does not, in fact, have a long history. The first gathering of this kind in Europe was an exhibition held in Paris by Louis XIV at the beginning of the eighteenth century, and so far there have still only been five truly comprehensive exhibitions. The first took place twenty-three years ago, in 1851, when, at the instigation of Prince Albert of Coburg, the consort of the present British queen, the Crystal Palace was erected in Hyde Park in London. This exhibition began on May 1st and continued for 141 days. Over six million visitors came from Britain and abroad to see it. Until then, British manufacturing techniques had relied entirely on machines and British products lacked elegance. However, this exhibition made the British aware for the first time how unrefined their products were. They learnt the importance of elegance and of aesthetic beauty and understood the need to accommodate the tastes of other countries. As a result, they have made astonishing advances since then. Moreover, because the exhibition's effectiveness came as a revelation to other countries, it was decided to preserve the Crystal Palace and also to establish a permanent exhibition in South Kensington.

Four years later, in 1855, an exhibition was held in Paris for 200 days. At the time French manufacturers looked down on those from other European countries, but British industrial arts had freed themselves from imitation of the French style and many British products attracted attention. Thus, the people of France, too, came to realise that they must make further efforts. Another exhibition was held in London in 1862. In 1867, an exhibition was held in Paris which lasted 217 days. This was the largest of these events. More than eight million visitors attended. Both the former shogunate and the Kagoshima and Saga clans sent articles from Japan to be displayed. Until the second Paris exhibition, the battle for supremacy at these exhibitions had been between France and Britain. Britain sought to show what progress it had made; France strove to prevent its reputation from declining. As British industrial production was increasing annually and that of France was falling, the French roused themselves to action. They established museums of technology and technical schools to promote education. Examples of the results are on display in the permanent exhibition in the gardens near the Place de la Concorde and at the museum of machinery in the Conservatoire. Thereafter, all countries embarked on the same course and began to set up similar museums and schools. Consequently, European industrial arts and commerce now inspire all people to make their best efforts and have flourished, but this has only happened in the last fifteen or twenty years.

It was at the time of the second Paris exhibition that a constitutional system was first established in Austria, providing the people with the opportunity to develop, to some extent, a spirit of freedom and to turn their minds to economic matters. They therefore followed the lead of the British and French and planned an exhibition. This delighted the Austrian emperor [Franz Joseph], and he offered considerable support. In May 1870, the government granted permission to proceed. Baron Schwarz[-Senborn] was selected as director-general of the exhibition. Not only the European nations but also countries in Asia, Africa and the Americas were invited to send artefacts for display. Even before the departure of our Embassy, exhibits were being prepared in Japan. On May 1st of this year, the emperor performed the opening ceremony. Each country had its own pavilion. By the time of our visit in June, the displays were almost complete.

The exhibition hall, a large circular building [the Rotunda] with long galleries on either side, was built in a park called the Prater in the north-east of Vienna. The Prater is on an island in the river Danube, a flat expanse more than five square miles in area. To the right and left of the Rotunda stretched two rows of galleries connected to one another by long promenades. The solid floors of the galleries were raised above ground level, and their roofs were lofty. In front were large gardens surrounded by long galleries. Access at six points allowed people to enter and leave. Carpets of fine grass extended right and left, and there were expanses of fine sand as white as snow. From the centre of two stone basins in which waterfowl sported freely a jet of water spurted to a height of fifty or sixty feet. At the rear, to right and left, were various buildings erected to supplement the galleries. In the centre was a pleasure-garden with taverns and tea pavilions, each in the architectural style of a particular country. Here, the customs and ways of life of each country were on display; one felt as though the whole world was represented in miniature within this one garden.

The enormous size of the Rotunda in the centre was enough to astound the visitor. The dome of this structure was 250 feet in diameter and 370 feet in height. An iron frame supported the dome itself, and the apex was so high that one could not see it clearly. The doors and windows were glazed. At the top of the Rotunda there was a replica of the jewelled crown of Austria. Above this flew the country's flag. Seen from a distance, it seemed to rise into the very clouds. Around the perimeter of the Rotunda flew the flags of the participating countries. Every section was filled with treasures; at each step one discovered marvels. If one walked without stopping, taking in something new at every step, at the end of a day one would still have seen only a fraction of the exhibition.

Entry to the exhibition required the purchase of an admission ticket. This ticket was then checked at the entrance to each exhibition hall or gallery. There were two kinds of ticket. A ticket for the duration of the exhibition cost 100 florins; women paid half that much. For a one-day ticket, the charge was 5 florins for either sex. Those who left the grounds and then returned on the same day paid another florin at the gate. On Sundays the charge was half a florin.

The exhibits from the various countries were beyond enumeration. Merely to look at them was tiring enough; to study them carefully would have been completely exhausting. One was taken aback by the sheer size of some exhibits, and stunned by the astonishing ingenuity of others. The most amazing ideas have been applied to the humblest of products. In other words, the most wonderful and resplendent objects have been assembled here, embodying the spirit of the peoples of the world. An area of about 200,000 square yards was filled to capacity, but the best that we could achieve was to see one or two out of every hundred articles. Other Japanese officials sent to the exhibition will no doubt write more about it at some future time. Here we will simply give a general account of one or two things which were particularly striking.

A problem had arisen with the American exhibits with the result that they were in some disorder. There was a display of small-arms by Mr. Remington of New York, but they could hardly be called 'new'.

Exhibits from Brazil were generally modelled on those of Europe, but the Brazilians' technical skills are not yet as advanced and their exhibits betray an under-developed quality. In one section were samples of several hundred varieties of wood. A vast stretch of forest extends across the tropical and temperate zones in the centre of this country. It is said to be impossible to determine the limits of these forests, so Brazil could be described as 'the guardian of the world's forests'.

Exhibits from Britain were surprisingly few. Many were the products of the companies we had seen earlier on our tour of British cities, so we felt as if we were encountering old acquaintances. Particularly outstanding were iron and steel products. Among the latter from Sheffield was an enormous circular saw-blade which must have been fourteen or fifteen feet in diameter.

French industry was formerly dominant in Europe, and the refinement and elegance of France represented the quintessence of the whole exhibition, even amid the present competition among European countries. The technologies of porcelain manufacture and of tapestry-weaving grow ever more refined in France, and French cast-bronze objects manifest exquisite skill. The artificial flowers used to adorn women's hats were set with gold, silver, pearls and precious stones, introducing an opulent note and giving the exhibition a spring-like air. French woven fabrics, such as woollens and linens, are light and delicate, qualities unmatched by any other country. In silk-weaving the French are rivalled only by Italy.

The various German states had, ultimately, to concede the winning place to France. However, tobacco pipes are made from meerschaum, false teeth and artificial eyes from porcelain, and these would all deceive nature itself. The varieties of imitation gems produced by makers of artificial jewellery in Paris would, again, almost deceive nature. Among them was a diamond about three inches across which took visitors' breath away. French utensils of gold- and silver-plate are of very fine quality. The French also produce first-rate imitations of Chinese cloisonné and

Japanese damascene work. Among glass manufacturers, French mirrors are particularly renowned for their craftsmanship. The intricate execution of French marquetry was also masterly. Various luxury items such as fans, personal adornments and perfumes, as well as surgical instruments and trinkets for amusement, made people rub their eyes and look again. Because visitors to the French shops at the exhibition were treated with attentive courtesy, sales were particularly high and were very profitable. In general, French products make a different impression from British ones. British products sell because of their quality; although expensive, they are extremely durable. French products sell because of their craftsmanship. They are inexpensive, but their elaborate design and decoration give them a luxurious feel.

The displays of Spanish and Portuguese exhibits were not yet ready so we have no detailed information about them.

Switzerland is the land of industrial arts par excellence. From the cities of Geneva and Berne came extensive displays of clocks and watches, products for which Switzerland is celebrated. Indeed, the scale of the demand for timepieces in all European countries is truly surprising. London, Paris and all other major cities, without exception, manufacture clocks. The desire of the thrifty Dutch to save time may be inferred from the fact that they have a clock in every room. However, the timepieces in all those countries are cheap and crudely made wall- and table-clocks which sell in large numbers. Well-crafted watches have become the monopoly of Switzerland, and the quality of its workmanship has advanced steadily, outstripping the factories of other countries. The Swiss craft next in importance after watch-making is the manufacture of musical instruments. There was a golden cage on display with a tiny bird inside. By means of a spring mechanism this bird flapped its wings, opened and closed its beak and warbled in clear, bell-like tones. Its singing, appearance and movements were all equally lifelike. This was a sort of musical box, so cleverly made as to pass for a real bird.

The craftsmanship of the Italians is such that even the French would probably concede that it is a step ahead of their own. The crafts of the two countries reflect their different tastes. In general, the French esteem flamboyance and elegance and take pleasure in the novel and the unfamiliar. The Italians, on the other hand, are fond of unaffected beauty, their products are quiet and restrained, and they have high regard for what is natural. Italian china is not translucent but derives its attractiveness from its forthright style, recalling the noble simplicity of ancient times. Even the craft of laying mosaics is a legacy of this country's antiquity. Italian silk fabrics such as taffetas, satins, velvets and figured silks rival those of France in artistry, as do Italian cottons, woollens and lace. There were abundant products from Milan on display. Such fine crafts as the coral work of Naples and the glassware of Venice are unique. Objects made from shells are produced along the Mediterranean coast, and the skill of the Italians in these matches that of the French. Sculpture in stone represents the supreme accomplishment of this country's craftsmen. The display of statues in the Art Hall had not yet been completed, but what was on show in the main hall invariably stopped visitors in their tracks. There were statues of a child at play carrying a fish, of a child standing on a sack of wheat, of a child staring intently at a half-finished sculpture, pondering how to improve it, of a bespectacled figure making a model of a train, and a figure of a small girl in tears looking after a baby. These were all full of life and vitality, and attained the very summit of the sculptor's craft.

Among the items from Belgium on display were a stratigraphic map of the whole country, as well as mining machinery, maps of mine interiors and a new type of safety lamp. There were samples of iron and coal and a huge block of alum. Various craft works using hemp and flax and other vegetable fibres were exhibited. The most highly praised of these were the samples of cotton lace, which exhibited supreme skill in weaving. Belgian cotton yarn, cotton textiles, crystal and china were all superb. Belgium also showed various iron products, objects of cast-copper, raffia work, tobacco, fine leatherwork and a variety of woollens. Because these exhibits are practical rather than showy, they may not have appeared beautiful to the visitors, but the high level of this nation's skills impresses even the larger, more advanced nations.

Holland has numerous specialised skills. In diamond-polishing, the bleaching of cotton and linen fabrics, and the purification of waxes, it has no rival among other countries. However, these skills were not on show at the exhibition. Great quantities of bottled mineral water and beer had been sent, which could not be judged from their external appearance. The porcelain was inferior. What caught the public's attention was that country's lacquerware. Japanese screens and *maki-e* reliefs were also on display.

# CHAPTER 83

# *The Vienna Universal Exposition, 2*

Exhibits from the twenty-five German states filled two galleries and overflowed into the Rotunda itself. There were so many as to exhaust the visitor. German craftsmanship was epitomised by exhibits from the great city of Berlin. A considerable proportion of the silk fabrics on display were velvet tapestries with gorgeous colours and beautiful designs. This cloth is woven by a different method from that in France and Italy, and in the final analysis it is not the equal of French and Italian tapestries. There were very many cotton fabrics manufactured by the Tannenburg Company, but it was the textiles from Alsace, displayed in the Rotunda, which gained the highest reputation in Europe. These, however, could hardly be counted to Germany's credit as Alsace had only recently been annexed from France [after the 1870–71 Franco-Prussian War]. The artificial silk flowers were very beautiful. French silk flowers are unrivalled for their craftsmanship, while those made in Germany are unmatched for their faithfulness to nature. The Germans have also invented a process of drying fresh flowers by soaking them in a chemical solution, which preserves the vividness of the colours.

In the garden in front of the domed hall a small brick building had been erected. The eaves and walls were decorated with patterns in different-coloured tiles and with tiles with relief mouldings. Tiles are also used to adorn balustrades, the edges of pools, household fixtures and stoves. Every country in Europe and America seeks to achieve high quality in the manufacture of bricks and tiles, but those made in Berlin are the finest.

Since this was an Austrian exhibition, displays of articles from that country filled several galleries. More than half of the Rotunda, for example, was taken up with Austrian exhibits. In politics, Prussia and Austria are brothers, and the manufacturing styles of the two countries are identical: both place emphasis on colourful and lavish decoration. Berlin is the equal of Vienna, and Bohemia is comparable to Saxony, as Moravia is to Silesia. However, the Austrian preference for elegance and opulence appears to be greater, so its products are particularly ornate. The reason for this is that Austria was once a powerful country, long steeped in the extravagant tastes of a large aristocracy. France and Italy are alike in the skill of their people; yet one country is wealthy and the other poor. Similarly, Prussia and Austria are alike in their industrial arts; yet one is strong and the other weak. Thus, a nation's wealth and strength depend on the spirit of its people, and the excellence or inferiority of its industrial arts is determined by its people's tastes.

Among the numerous products from Russia, many were related to government, scholarship, agriculture and mining, and in general the luxury goods which were exhibited did not match the elegance and beauty of those produced in France, Italy, Prussia and Austria. Although Russia clearly still depends very largely on agriculture, many of the exhibits revealed advances in science and learning. Some of the items were related to medicine, such as anatomical drawings of the human body and anatomical models made of wax or plaster of Paris.

The very small number of exhibits from Denmark offered nothing noteworthy. However, the large slabs of stone, such as marble from Greenland, were very impressive.

Sweden and Norway, too, had few exhibits, among them examples of their celebrated iron and steel products, for the quality of Swedish iron and steel is unrivalled in Europe. Sweden has discovered a new chemical formula for the manufacture of matches, and since the wood used in this is a particular resource of the country, match production brings considerable revenue from overseas.

Exhibits from Greece consisted principally of ancient sculptures. Minerals and various kinds of stone were also displayed, as well as different kinds of wood. Manufactured goods were few.

Nothing of much interest was offered by Egypt and Romania. A great many Persian rugs were on display. The Chinese exhibits fell far short of the country's highest standards of elegance and beauty.

The exhibits from Japan at the exhibition won particular acclaim from visitors. One reason was that the Japanese exhibits were different from European ones in taste and design, so to European eyes they had the charm of exoticism. A second reason was that there were few notable exhibits from countries neighbouring Japan. A third reason was the growing admiration for Japan among Europeans in recent years. The reputation of Japanese porcelain is high, due only to its hardness and strength and because some enormous pieces are made. The careful study of firing temperatures, of the mixture of pigments, and of decorative techniques has hardly begun in Japan. Our silk fabrics are beautiful only because of the quality of the yarn, as Japanese weaving itself is often uneven. Since Japanese dyeing techniques employ vegetable dyes which are not fast, the colours of our textiles lack the rich lustre of European fabrics. Lacquerware, a particularly Japanese craft, is highly esteemed, and although our craftsmanship in copper lacks refinement, our cloisonné and damascene workmanship drew great attention.

Japanese styles of painting differ from those of the West. The elegance and tastefulness of our bird-and-flower pictures were much admired, but the clumsiness of our portraits and pictures of actors in make-up were frankly embarrassing. Our marquetry was also praised, although the joins were less than perfect because they depended solely on the bonding strength of lacquer. Having seen how these crafts are practised in Europe, we concluded that if we were to improve our techniques, these could become valuable exports for Japan in the future. Although our straw and raffia work has a good reputation, such articles are cheap and crudely made and quickly wear out. Our dyed leather products, on the other hand, were much praised, perhaps because they demonstrated secret techniques as yet unknown to Europeans. Our paper and linen astonished visitors. Both the materials and techniques used in Japanese paper-making were markedly different from those of other countries. The whiteness of Echigo linen was dazzling, and we heard one Westerner exclaim that he would consider using it as imitation silk. Our hand-crafted papers, made from the paper mulberry tree, were also highly regarded, but our oil-paintings were beneath the standard of even European children. Paintings in true Japanese traditional styles received high acclaim.

This completed our tour of the main buildings of the exhibition. We will now provide a brief account of the Art Hall. This housed an exhibition of painting and sculpture. The enthusiastic pursuit of these arts by gentlemen of the upper classes resembles the study of literature, painting and seal-engravings by educated people in Japan. The Art Hall was built of brick and lay to the east of the main buildings. Its interior was extremely clean. Gardens to its right and left were planted with shrubs and contained fountains in tiled pools. Altogether it made for a very attractive scene, and devotees of landscape-painting came here to sketch. There are five techniques in Western picture-making: drawing in pencil, drawing in pen and ink, lithography, etching and painting in oils. The last is the most highly esteemed. There is truth in the power of the pen, and a painter's ability can be judged by his sketches. Consequently, some drawings made by a painter of the first rank are highly regarded.

The essential characteristic of European painting is that it seeks above all to reproduce reality, depicting actual scenes. It thus models itself on nature. In painting a landscape, the natural features are never rearranged to create a false picture. The actual scenery is always observed on the spot, and a careful study made of the changing effects of clouds, mist, shadow, sunlight, rain, snow, the time of day and the season. Choosing a favourable view, the artist expresses in his painting what he grasps with his mind. Thus, the spirit of the artist is stimulated, and both the landscape as it is seen from the chosen vantage-point and the atmosphere of the place as it is captured by the artist appear in the finished work. In depictions of the human figure or of animals, the anatomy, character, disposition, spirit and situation of the subject must be rendered accurately. This is the most exacting trial even for a great artist. For a fine oil-painting, therefore, even a price of tens of thousands of dollars for a single canvas is not considered expensive, while an inferior work showing the same scene, painted with the same colours and of the same size, will not fetch a hundred dollars.

As a result, it is extremely difficult to judge Western oil-paintings, and because of our superficial knowledge we found it hard to assess the paintings in the Art Hall. When we looked at pictures of mountains, gardens or forests, it was obvious that these were scenes of particular places in particular countries, and we were able to see that we were looking at a landscape at dawn or after a shower. Only when the painter has rendered with perfect accuracy the mountains, rivers, lakes and vegetation (whether lush or sere) of the landscape, or the different emotions of his human subjects (joy or anger, tranquillity or impatience), or the colours of the clouds and the mood of the weather, and achieved all this with vigour and boldness in his brushwork, does he regard his picture as finished. This is not the case in Japan, where an artist may be praised for the quality of his brushwork even if he paints Japanese mountains using techniques developed in China for depicting Chinese mountains, or puts Cantonese riders on the backs of Satsuma horses.

To the north of the Art Hall was a hall in which machinery was displayed. In front of this, floating on the Danube, was a model of a steamship. In the easternmost section of this hall were the exhibits from Russia. Agricultural machines and windmill and water-wheel machinery were particularly numerous. In the next section was an extensive display of products from Hungary, but these were mixed with those of Austria, making it difficult to distinguish between them.

The next section was devoted to Austrian exhibits, which were the most numerous. There were spinning machines and looms for weaving broad webs of lace. There were also locomotives and carriages. Most astonishing of all was a printing machine of great ingenuity. It first set the type, then performed all the necessary operations in the proper sequence, before finally ejecting a complete newspaper properly folded. We were shown it in operation.

Next were the German exhibits, among them a great many agricultural machines. Krupp of Essen displayed the largest artillery piece in the exhibition. It weighed a thousand pounds and was housed in a special structure built outside the hall. The biggest items from France were textile and wood-working machines.

As we went around the hall, we saw exhibits ranging from those small enough to fit in one's hand to machines dozens of feet long. Every one of them was both useful and cleverly designed. Some machines possessed the strength of thousands of men; others could distribute the force applied by one finger to perform hundreds of operations. When the machines were not in operation, it was difficult to appreciate their intricacy and ingenuity. We only had time to look briefly at each exhibit before passing on. This made us feel rather like coming down from a holy mountain empty-handed.

We will now give a brief description of the gardens in the exhibition grounds. The garden to the south of the main building was well tended. The lawns were soft and there were many trees. In the leafy shade of the trees were restaurants and tea-rooms in the styles of the different countries. Men and women in national dress served those who came for refreshments. There were many elegant touches. We passed Eskimo dwellings (but not made of ice) from the Arctic zone in the north of Sweden. The Eskimos wore traditional costumes. In a wood to the east of the South Gate was a large tent representing a black people's dwelling from America. Being served with tea and wine by black people gave the illusion of visiting the tropics, although it was not so hot. In the garden in front of the Art Hall were booths from Persia, Egypt and Japan. The Egyptian section had a reproduction of a royal palace built in the ancient style of that country. Behind this a reproduction of a Japanese Shintō shrine had been erected, together with a Japanese garden complete with a pond, a stone bridge and stone lanterns. In front of the Japanese garden was an administrative building of Japanese cedar wood, with a roof in the style of the ancient capital. This was a shop selling various small items, which were very well regarded. Even the Austrian emperor lauded the skill and craftsmanship of Japanese carpenters. This was the first time Japanese cedar wood had been seen in Europe, and all praised it for its fragrance. Many people asked for cedar-wood shavings to take home with them. Every day people flocked to the shop; it was constantly crowded. The merchandise included swatches of silk, round fans, folding fans, lacquerware, earthenware and copper objects. Silks and folding fans sold best.

Persia had also erected a large pavilion in the national architectural style. It was an unusual building with large ornamental glass windows, but the walls between the windows were not sturdily constructed, giving the impression that much effort had been wasted on the superficial decoration. When one walked past the building, one felt that the glass might break at any moment and fall on passers-by and injure them. Inside, Persian goods were on display and people in national costumes were in attendance. The shops of Persia, Egypt and Japan were called the 'three wonders of the exhibition'.

CHAPTER 84

# *A Record of Switzerland*

The country inhabited by the Swiss is called Switzerland. In Germany it is called 'Schweiz'. It occupies mountainous terrain, interspersed with lowland areas, and is bordered by three countries: France, Italy and Germany. It has a federal system of government. The original twenty-two cantons of Switzerland have now, as a result of subdivision, become twenty-five. They are grouped into three regions. German is spoken in the north-east, French in the north-west and Italian in the south. Under an agreement of 1848, the central government is located in the city of Berne. The office of president is held by one of the seven members of the executive government. The president in the year of our visit was [Paul] Cérésole.

All Switzerland's national policies are determined by three objectives: to safeguard the country's rights; to refrain from interfering with the rights of other countries; and to prevent other countries from interfering with Switzerland's rights. In order to strengthen Switzerland's autonomy, education is encouraged and flourishes particularly in the German-speaking region. Because education is so widespread, the people of this country are reputed to be the most civil, the best-informed and the most diligent at their occupations. An unending stream of students come to study at Swiss universities rather than going to those of larger, better-known countries.

Switzerland also fosters its military strength. Should there be any upheaval in a neighbouring country, Switzerland follows a policy of strict neutrality and does not permit a single foreign soldier to come within its borders. If an enemy invades, he is driven back. And since Switzerland also respects the rights of other countries, once a retreating enemy has crossed the Swiss frontier he is pursued no farther. The Swiss would never send troops into another's territory.

The entire people would willingly fight to the death to defend the country from foreign invasion, as though fighting a fire. Every household provides a soldier with a rifle and uniform. The Swiss are particularly well trained in mountain warfare: they are able to put up a fierce fight against any enemy on steep mountainsides and among rocky peaks, and are expert skirmishers. If a neighbouring country threatens invasion, all the people become soldiers. The young men are called on first, but those more advanced in years will also be called to arms if they are sound in body. Women would serve in the commissariat or nurse the wounded. The people would risk death rather than suffer the shame of yielding their rights to others. Despite its small size, therefore, the country's military strength is regarded with the highest respect among the great powers, and no other country would dare to try and conquer it.

Switzerland lies on the mountainous spine of Europe, among the interlocking ranges of the great Alpine chain. The glistening cones of mountain peaks are ranged side-by-side, with summits above 9,000 feet cloaked in gleaming white snow throughout the year. The rivers and streams are pure; the lakes deep. In Switzerland the water is unusually green, the colour being even richer in deep rivers and lakes. There are, in addition, many snow-capped peaks among the mountains, so that everywhere one looks one sees pinnacles like polished sword-tips, emerald-green waters, thick woods and deep forests, and range upon range of lofty mountains. Rushing torrents roar; cataracts plunge from on high. There are mountains all around, then a valley opens up before the eyes, while here and there villages nestle amidst the lovely scenery. Europeans laud the beauty of this country, and in summer they come – bringing their wives and children, or accompanied by friends – to seek out the country's scenic splendours and to escape the heat and dust. The Swiss derive not a little profit from this. In many mountain hamlets and lakeside villages the most beautiful hotels and inns have been built for visitors.

Swiss manufacturing is esteemed throughout the world for its crafts-manship and refinement, and Switzerland has come to be regarded as an industrial nation. This is probably the result of its remote and moun-tainous location: because it has inadequate agricultural resources and transport is difficult, it has had no alternative but to concentrate on developing advanced skills and producing articles demanding great pre-cision. Everyone knows that Swiss watches are the most highly regarded in the world. The Swiss are also expert jewellers.

The people of Switzerland comprise three races: German, French and Italian. The Germans are most numerous, there being three Germans to every person of the French race. The Italians, who are ethnically Roman, number one-quarter as many as the French. The three languages are spoken in the same proportions. The systems of government established in the cantons are simple. The usual apparatus of a state is largely dispensed with; government is conducted through the collective power of the assembled people. As a result, there is an even distribution of wealth among the citizens of this country, and there are very few poor households. It may be said that it is because the people are educated in the spirit of a pure republic that harmony reigns throughout the country and the Swiss treat the peoples of other countries with such generosity. The Swiss are open and unaffected in their manners, straightforward and good-humoured.

June 19th, 1873. Fine; cloudy in the afternoon, light rain in the evening. Last night our train crossed the Austrian border and at two in the morning we arrived at a large station which was probably in the city of Munich. After spending an hour here the train departed, and we travelled through the Bavarian countryside. At a quarter past twelve we arrived on the quay at Lindau, a harbour looking out on the Bodensee.

A ferry service was provided by a small steamboat. We boarded it and travelled sixteen miles diagonally across the lake to Romanshorn, in Switzerland. On arrival, we found that the departure time of our train had passed and it had already left. We had no choice but to wait at the station for another train and so spent several hours resting here.

At half past five we boarded the regular train for Zürich and departed. We had the impression that agriculture here was more flourishing than in southern Germany. The farmhouses are built with broad eaves projecting on both sides to protect the walls, just like Japanese houses. The walls themselves are covered with wooden shingles, overlapping like the scales of a fish. Every house has a lightning-rod, because lightning is common in this western region of Switzerland. Square red tiles with raised edges on two sides are used on the roofs. These tiles are unlike those manufactured in Germany and are different in shape. All the roads are well maintained. White sand is strewn on their surfaces to keep down the dust, and the roads are clean and so bright that we could barely open our eyes. At six in the evening we passed through Weinfelden and crossed the Thur: this river eventually empties into the Rhine. After another half hour's travel we arrived at Frauenfeld Station. Here we entered the canton of Zürich.

From this point on, the land began to rise before us. To right and left were mountains, not particularly steep but thickly forested, with scattered houses and an occasional village. Sometimes we would see a stream tumbling down a valley on its way to join the head-waters of the Rhine. After passing Oerlikon Station, the train entered a tunnel. When we emerged we saw a river flowing from left to right below us. This, we were told, was the river Limmat, which emerges from the Lake of Zürich and also eventually empties into the Rhine. Along the river-banks were streets of houses, and mountain ranges opened out to right and left like two folding fans. The scene was very attractive. Between the two ranges of mountains lay a strip of flat land on which stood the city of Zürich. We went by carriage from the station to the Baur en Ville Hotel in the city, where we took rooms.

June 20th.
Zürich is the principal centre of textile-manufacturing in Switzerland: cotton yarn is spun here, and cotton and silk fabrics woven. Geneva, in the west, and Zürich, in the east, are known as the busiest manufacturing towns.

At twenty to two we left Zürich by train to travel to the east. A private carriage was provided for us. Mr. [Hegner] Siber, the former Swiss minister to Japan who was to act as the official representative of the government, had come to meet us. After following the Limmat for some twenty minutes we came to a bend where a village overlooked the river. Here the river became a roaring flood, cascading to the foot of a gorge scores of feet deep and flowing along its bottom. The mountain terrain gradually began to press in on us. The outline of the mountains in front of us was humped like the backbone of an ox. The scenery became more and more beautiful. The mountains then suddenly opened out, leaving broad areas of flat land on either side of the river. Here the Limmat, flowing north-west from Zürich, emptied into the broad river Aare, flowing from the west.

From here the railway ran upstream along the right bank of the Aare to Aarau Station. We passed through a tunnel under a mountain, and on emerging saw for the first time jagged peaks, clad in glistening snow, to the south. We arrived at Olten, a populous village. We rested here for half an hour, and it was a quarter to four when we set off again. At half past five we came to a place where hilly terrain enclosed a strip of flat land. A river meandered along the valley floor. The snow-capped peaks to the south took a hundred picturesque forms. The air was pure and cold. Suddenly we seemed to have forgotten the sultry heat. When we arrived at Berne Station, carriages were waiting to convey us to the Bernerhof Hotel, where we stayed.

Berne, the largest of the Swiss cantons, is surrounded on all four sides by mountains, and those to the south are the most striking. Far off, beyond the plain, one can see crowded peaks shining like white gems and gleaming like polished sword-tips, with ridges as jagged as the worn teeth of a saw. The highest peaks rise to 14,000 feet. The windows of the hotel all faced the mountains: the views were magnificent.

In the morning we had an audience with the president at his palace. In the evening we drove round the city in carriages. The streets were clean and well maintained and were all paved with flagstones. In front of the shops on both sides of the broad streets are covered arcades which provide shelter for people on foot. This is convenient when walking on rainy days. The same price seemed to be charged for the same goods throughout the city. While Berne's manufacturing must, perhaps, yield pride of place to Zürich and Geneva, it exhibits craftsmanship of a high order. The musical instruments made here are, we were told, of particularly good quality.

CHAPTER 85

# Switzerland's Mountain Scenery

Two-thirds of the European continent is flat; the remaining one-third is mountainous. The south consists for the most part of range upon range of mountains. Switzerland lies on the spine of this great mountain chain and the splendour of its scenery is renowned throughout the world. After our party had arrived at Berne and had been received by the president, we were told by our official host, Mr. Siber, that as the federal government did its best to avoid any expenditure which was not essential, it was unable to match the lavish hospitality which the Embassy had enjoyed in other countries. All that Switzerland had to offer visitors for their diversion was its beautiful scenery. A new mountain railway had just been built to the south of Berne, and the people there hoped that the Embassy would be able to join them to celebrate its completion. It would give them great pleasure, he said, if we were able to spare two days for such an excursion.

June 22nd, 1873. Fine.
At nine o'clock we left Berne Station by train. After half an hour's journey to the south-east we stopped at the station in Münsingen, a village of several dozen dwellings. We saw that flags were fluttering from all the houses, a tent had been erected beside the station to sell tea and fruit, and large crowds had gathered. We were told that a wrestling tournament was to be held here. The bouts are conducted in much the same way as our own sumō. The wrestlers compete either naked or clad only in undershirt and drawers. In countries which are militarily strong, the people usually enjoy the entertainment of feats of strength. The Belgians and the Swiss take pleasure in wrestling and shooting. As a result, their soldiers look extremely robust.

From here we travelled for another twenty minutes, skirting the foot of a mountain and crossing a river. Soon we arrived at the station at Thun. After travelling another mile, we arrived at a landing-stage at the Lake of

447

Thun. When the train pulled in at the quayside, the packet-boat which plies the lake had already arrived and was waiting. We alighted from the train and boarded the boat. Looking around, we saw that green mountainsides and snowy peaks encircled us, and the mirror-like lake spread out before us. It was a beautiful day, and we all exclaimed in astonishment at the upside-down reflection of the blue sky, the brilliant sun and the pure white clouds as the boat cast off and pulled away from the bank. The source of Switzerland's water is melting snow. The lake is remarkably green in colour, so the white peaks and blue mountaintops reflected in it have a particular crystal-clear beauty. Mountain peaks towered above the lake, each more precipitous and more impressive in form than the last. Those close by were high and steep; those far off were even loftier. The highest of these snow-capped peaks is the Jungfrau, which rises to 13,000 feet.

As the steamer moved away from the shore and the lake opened up before us, the mountains changed their positions and new vistas presented themselves. By the time we were halfway across the lake, the snow-capped peaks were all hidden behind the nearer mountains. The mountains along the shore spread out like a folding screen of fantastically shaped rocks. After an hour we reached the landing-stage at Därligen.

Därligen is on the southern shore of the lake. A new railway station had just been built here. The carriages of the trains had been especially designed to carry tourists. Unlike ordinary railway-carriages, the passengers are carried on two decks, like London omnibuses. The lower deck was completely enclosed with glazed windows and had warmly upholstered seats. Passengers of the upper class and ladies were seated here. Travellers who liked fresh air and wished to see the striking scenery, and regarded even a single pane of glass as an obstacle to their enjoyment, climbed to the upper deck, which was roofless and surrounded only by a railing. It was from here that the finest view was obtained. We boarded the train and it set off along the lake-shore. We came to a vast outcrop of rock which lay in our way, but the train plunged undaunted into its very heart. We emerged from the darkness to find ourselves on a suspension-bridge which soared across an arm of the lake. On the right bank loomed a sheer rock wall, rising vertically as though it had been deliberately cut away. With a blast of its whistle, the train crossed the bridge; it was as though it had sprouted wings and was flying over the water. After five miles or so we reached the village of Interlaken, and the beautiful scenery of the Lake of Thun lay behind us. We were given lunch at a pretty inn set among lawns and shady trees and rested there for an hour and a half. Earlier in the day the heat of Berne had drenched our clothes in sweat.

But when the damp air of this cool place penetrated our garments, we felt a chill.

On leaving the inn, we went by carriage to Unterseen, near the Lake of Brienz, where we again boarded a boat. At this point the river which flows from the Lake of Brienz into the Lake of Thun is narrow, so its current is swift and its green water turbulent. As we rounded the foot of Mt. Graggen, the beautiful scenery of the Lake of Brienz came into view.

This lake is oval in shape, eight miles long and two and a quarter miles wide, and extends in a direction slightly north of east. There are no islands in it, nor any large promontories, and there are no towering snow-clad peaks among the mountains to right and left. High folded hills line the shore on either side, and the green trees reaching skywards among the rocky crags seem like a circle of countless folding screens with trees painted in kingfisher green. At the head of the lake, on the right, are two waterfalls side-by-side. These are the famous Giesehof [or Giessbach] Falls. The stream tumbles through jagged rocks to pour from a height of more than 200 feet into the lake below. For the passengers' benefit, the captain took the boat close in under the falls and slowed the engine. A swirling mist drenched the craft; the trees on the cliffs dripped with water. Spray from the falls flew out to a distance of dozens of paces, so although we were in bright sunlight we felt as cold as though we were in the middle of a storm. When the boat turned away from these falls and proceeded on its way, another waterfall came into sight, cascading down a valley from a snow-field on one of the high peaks [the Scharzhorn] to the long ridge at the very foot of the mountain. It looked exactly like white yarn being reeled onto a spindle. We had not seen all the waterfalls there were before we reached the landing-stage at Tracht. It was now three o'clock.

The village of Tracht consisted of no more than ten houses or so. Here we hired carriages to travel through the narrow valleys to the north-east. The road passed through a narrow gorge, below looming cliffs composed of layer on layer of rock. The drivers began to shout at the horses, urging them up the steep mountain road. On our left rose the mountainside; on our right was a deep valley. The narrow road twisted and turned. Now and then we passed a house: two, three, four or five together would constitute a village. Their walls were of logs placed one on top of another; their roofs consisted of branches laid parallel to one another and weighted down with stones. The walls were decorated with ornamental shingles, like fish-scales, and they had upper storeys and broad eaves.

At Brünig, about five miles from Tracht, there was nothing but a small inn, where we watered the horses. Here we were once again surrounded by rank upon rank of mountain peaks, like the waves of a turbulent sea. The lake was now hidden by a ridge. There were also many waterfalls in sight, and, looking to right and left, we counted eight or nine tumbling down from the high peaks. We were told that it is possible to see as many as twenty waterfalls from here.

As we descended the mountain from Brünig, the snowy peaks behind us were lost to sight, but suddenly another lofty snow-capped pinnacle was revealed before us. This was the Schärhorn in the canton of Uri. Its fantastic peak looked as though it had been chiselled into shape, and half of it seemed about to fall. Its rocky ridge resembled a knife-blade thrusting up towards the blue sky. The wind at the summit raised flurries of snow which reflected the evening sun. The sight gave us gooseflesh.

The road continued on its downward path among scattered pine-trees. The sound of the bells on the horses' collars was like tinkling jewels, and, together with the soughing of the wind through the pines, it relieved the silence of the mountains. Farther down the mountain we came to a small lake called the Lake of Lungern. At the head of this lake lay the village of Lungern, where we stopped for tea at the inn. It was half past five.

We then drove along the bank of the Lake of Lungern. By then the picturesqueness of these mountain lakes was beginning to pall somewhat. Our carriages arrived at the village of Sarnen at the foot of the lake, where we took rooms at an inn called the Obwaldner-Hof. The time was half past seven.

A banquet was held at the inn that evening, and the villagers saluted the Embassy by playing music outside the windows. Lighted lanterns – some spherical, some cylindrical – were hung in the windows of the inn. Just like Japanese lanterns, they consisted of a frame of thin strips of wood onto which a paper covering had been glued. Naphtha flares were lit and placed in the street. The villagers gathered around them and raised a cheer. All this was done to express courtesy and respect towards honoured guests from afar. So great is the warmth with which Europeans welcome visitors from distant countries that it was manifested even in this remotest of mountain villages.

June 23rd. Fine; cloudy in the afternoon.
At dawn the bells of the village church were rung in our party's honour. At half past five it was still barely light. We had tea, and at seven o'clock boarded our carriages and left. After travelling five miles we came to a bay, an arm of the Lake of Lucerne called the Lake of Alpnach. We left the lake behind us and in less than an hour reached the city of Lucerne.

Lucerne, capital of the canton of that name, lies at the foot of Lake Vierwaldstätter [or the Lake of Lucerne]. The houses and shops are all clean, with whitewashed walls gleaming like snow. The lofty conical roofs are reflected on the shining surface of the lake. The strikingly scenic mountains which surround the lake are reflected upside-down in the water, and the scene is reminiscent of a painted landscape.

On this day, we rested at the Schweizerhof Hotel on the quay and had breakfast there. President Paul Cérésole, together with the head of the finance department and the other members of the federal council, had already arrived. They accompanied us aboard a packet-boat which plies the lake. The time was ten minutes past ten. There were musicians on board to play for us and a five-gun salute was fired in our honour. The wife of the president, who was also aboard, welcomed us most cordially. The boat moved off across the lake to the accompaniment of charming music. The lake was broad and the mountains steep. Occasionally we passed through a fine shower. Behind us the lake was still bathed in sunlight, and the mountain peaks around were wreathed in drifting mist and flying snow. We did not have a clear view into the far distance, but the constantly changing shapes of the clouds created interesting effects on the lake. We continued to gaze right and left for a long time. We were still doing so when the boat reached Vitznau, on the left bank. Another five-gun salute was fired as we disembarked.

Beside the landing-stage at Vitznau were a few dozen houses and a church with a tall steeple; together they made a pretty picture. Close by was the station for the Rigi Railway. Both the track and the locomotives were of a kind recently invented in Switzerland, designed to enable trains to ascend and descend steep mountainsides. This day marked the completion of the railway.

The project had been started three years earlier. Funds were raised, and the construction of the line was completed in one year. Seven kilometres of track were laid from the lakeside to the summit of the mountain [the Rigi-Kulm], 5,500 feet above. The track consists of the usual pair of rails, with a third rail laid between them. This central rail is a toothed rack. The locomotive which travels above it is lower at the front and higher at the back and has two toothed wheels at the front and one such wheel at the rear. When the train is set in motion, the teeth of these wheels engage with those of the rack. In this way, the power of the wheels on the two outer rails is augmented. The train is thus capable of moving up and down a gradient as steep as thirty degrees. When ascending, the locomotive pulls the train forward, and when descending, it holds it back. It covers the seven kilometres in one and a half hours. The fare is seven francs.

The scenery here is unsurpassed for beauty in the whole country, and the purpose of building this railway was to carry visitors from all parts up this high peak to enable them to enjoy the views below. The carriages therefore have glass on all four sides so that passengers may enjoy the scenery. We boarded the train, and as it made its ascent up the mountains the lake fell away below us. When we were about halfway up we passed through a tunnel, emerging onto an iron bridge which spanned a ravine [the Schnurtobel] a hundred feet deep. A wall of rock had been cut into the mountainside, and a few solitary trees were growing out of it. Ahead was a tumbling cascade; below was a rushing torrent. The scenery was majestic.

We continued up the mountain and eventually, after passing Kalt Bad, reached the summit. We took rooms at one of the hotels there.

When we looked down from the summit, the high peaks were like an angry sea and the lower mountains like breaking waves. On a clear day, when it is possible to see even farther, fifteen lakes are visible, but on that day the sky was filled with scudding clouds and visibility was poor. From moment to moment the far peaks would be hidden by drifting clouds; only our view of the closer mountains remained unobscured. Consequently, at two o'clock, having seen as much as we could, we returned to the hotel.

A banquet to celebrate the completion of the railway was held in the dining-room. More than a hundred men and women sat down to the meal, which was extremely lavish. During the banquet speeches were made. Everyone praised the astounding achievement of the engineers and a gold cup was presented to them. The banquet ended at four o'clock. We stayed the night here.

June 24th. Fine, partly cloudy; fine in the afternoon.
At six o'clock we took the train back down to the lake. Today the mountain was enveloped in thick cloud, and as the train descended through this the scenery was completely obscured from view. We sailed back across the lake to Lucerne and returned to the Schweizerhof Hotel. The president and those accompanying him then returned to Berne, but our party remained at the hotel in order to go sightseeing in the city.

At ten to five we boarded a train at Lucerne Station and departed. We returned to our hotel in Berne at twenty minutes past eight.

CHAPTER 86

# *A Record of Berne and Geneva*

June 25th, 1873. Cloudy.
In the evening the president gave a banquet for us at a nearby hotel. All the members of the diplomatic corps attended. The food was sumptuous and music was played throughout the meal. Afterwards, we all went outside to converse in the pleasant coolness of the garden, which was decorated with Swiss lanterns. The hospitality offered us was extremely lavish.

June 27th. Fine.
At nine o'clock we were taken by Professor Schachter [?] to visit one of the city's elementary schools, which was housed in a large four-storey building. Some infants as young as four or five attended the school and were taught the rudiments of subjects such as writing and arithmetic, but most of the pupils were aged between seven or eight and thirteen or fourteen. The eight subjects taught here were reading, French language, writing, drawing, mathematics, history, geography and physics. They were also taught singing. The only history taught was that of Switzerland.

All eight of these subjects are indispensable to the people if they are to play their part as citizens fully. In addition, singing nurtures the people's poetic feelings and makes their dispositions gentler. Birds naturally sing – simply, it seems, for their own enjoyment – and there is no species with a voice which does not do the same. There is nowhere in any of the countries of Europe or in America where singing is not taught in the schools. Because music has the effect of instilling docility and grace in the hearts of women, this is the subject to which most attention is devoted in the curriculum. Its role in education is far from negligible. The importance attached to ritual and music in the East in ancient times was equally great, which goes to show that human feelings differ hardly at all between East and West.

Elementary education must be given to all, regardless of sex, social position, wealth or occupation, for it provides people with essential and appropriate skills, which they require in order to function as citizens.

453

In Switzerland the view is that although education is not compulsory, everyone desires it. Simple and useful subjects are chosen for the curriculum, and people fear the consequences of not having an education. This may be said to be the secret of universal education. Education in the East, it seems to us, is founded on the [Confucian] view that the basis of government is moral authority and so the whole curriculum is subsumed under one subject: moral training. Pure science and fine literature are treated merely as amusements, while practical matters of daily life have been considered rudimentary and coarse and therefore beneath consideration. The foundation of what the West regards as education, on the other hand, is imparting such knowledge as will ensure that the people may all acquire wealth or make a living without difficulty, and that none is deficient in performing the duties required of a citizen. Applied sciences are taught and instruction is given in practical book-keeping. The inculcation of moral principles, therefore, is left to the clergy. Even though literacy is widespread throughout a country, people still look for happiness in the next world. Nevertheless, in the course of receiving a thorough grounding in the practical skills necessary for making a living, the people acquire an understanding of the rules of proper behaviour and come to forsake uncivilised conduct. This is why education in the East and West tend in different directions.

June 29th. Fine.
At twenty to eleven in the morning we left Berne Station by train and travelled west. We reached Freiburg at half past eleven. Of the towns in this region, Freiburg is second only to Berne in the beauty of its setting. At ten past one we reached the mountain station of Vevey. We then passed through a curving tunnel, and when we emerged the broad expanse of Lac Léman (also called the Lake of Geneva) lay before us, with gleaming white houses of the town of Vevey lining the shore. The train ran along the mountainside. The mountains before and behind, mirrored in the lake, were wreathed in mist. Each one was beautiful in shape; the scene was truly magnificent. The land beside the lake was all planted with vines.

At ten minutes to two we reached Lausanne Station. There we took carriages to the Hotel Ouchy, where we rested and had lunch. At five past five we boarded a packet-boat from Lausanne and departed for the city of Geneva. This is the widest part of the lake, where the banks are more than seven miles apart. On the shore opposite Lausanne is a town called Evian-les-Bains, which is in France and where we were told there was a hot-spring. We made a stop on this bank and then sailed rapidly along the shore to the quay at Thonon-les-Bains, which is also on French soil. The broad expanse of the lake reflected the light; the surface was smooth, with a shimmering haze on it. A thin mountain mist caught the evening sun. We now re-crossed the lake, and at five past seven reached the northern bank at Nyon. To the south, a snow-clad peak revealed itself, glistening white, as lustrous as a jewel and as sharp as a sword. This was Mont Blanc, the highest peak in the Alps. Its foothills spread into three countries – France, Italy and Switzerland. It rises to 15,900 feet, more than 1,500 feet higher than Mt. Fuji.

We reached Geneva at eight o'clock and we took rooms at the Hotel des Bergues.

June 30th. Cloudy.

Geneva's setting is majestic. Before it lies the lake; to right and left of it rise range upon range of mountains; through it flows the great river; and above the lake towers Mont Blanc, with its dazzling mantle of snow. The buildings are imposing, and the streets are well maintained and clean. The citizens, we were told, receive visitors with such cordiality and are so punctilious in their business dealings that foreigners forget to return home.

In the morning, we went by carriage to the Cathedral of St. Pierre. It is an ancient church, famous for the fact that when Luther's new religion made its appearance, John Calvin came here to preach and propagate its teachings.

On our way back to the hotel, we inspected the city's waterworks. The water-wheels which raise the water are installed in a large building erected in the middle of the river at the point where it emerges from the end of Lac Léman. Originally, the water was raised by means of two water-wheels, but they were not powerful enough, so a horizontal wheel of a recently-invented type has been installed. The pressure is so great that the water would spout to a height of 800 feet. The earlier water-wheels have been retained and are used to augment the power of the larger wheel. The efficiency of this machinery manifests great technological ingenuity. It is immense in size. Projects such as this show that in the West no effort is begrudged and no expense spared in devising the best ways of meeting the daily requirements for food and water.

July 1st.

At ten o'clock we went to Patek Philippe's watch factory. Mr. Philippe is a Russian immigrant, and his workshops are located on the southern shore of the Lake of Geneva, at the end of a long bridge. Every day he employs 3,000 people in the manufacture of watches, both in the factory and outside. (The outside workers make parts in their own homes and bring them to the factory.)

The manufacture of watch movements is divided into many separate tasks. The craftsmen who make the wheels make only wheels, and the craft of making wheels is itself subdivided according to the type of wheel. Thus, each person is employed in making a single piece of the mechanism. The delicacy of craftsmanship required in watch-making is such that if there is the slightest imperfection in the machinery making the parts, they are useless. Consequently, the greatest care is taken to guarantee the quality and precision of the machinery.

With seasonal changes in temperature, the wheels expand and contract, causing the watch to run fast or slow. In order to prevent this, the wheels are made of two metals, brass and iron. Consequently, each wheel is composed of an outer rim of iron into which is fitted an inner brass ring, so that expansion and contraction do not take place when the temperature fluctuates.

When the watches have been completed, those priced at more than about 700 francs are tested to confirm that they are not affected by changes of temperature. This is done by packing them in ice for twenty-four hours, then placing them in a box maintained at a temperature of 120° for twenty-four hours. If they show no variation under either set of conditions, they are considered truly finished.

July 2nd. Fine; light haze.
In the afternoon we went to visit some of the villages on the southern shore of the lake.

July 3rd. Fine.
We climbed a nearby mountain and enjoyed the views.

July 5th. Fine.
In the afternoon, after driving through the southern suburbs of the city, we visited the house of a learned gentleman who had spent many years studying the construction of prisons. During the past few years he had collected plans of prisons in many countries and had written a book which discussed their various advantages and disadvantages. He presented us with a copy. Afterwards, he accompanied us to the city's prison. This had been built in the early nineteenth century and was very solidly

constructed. But since it was no longer adequate, plans had recently been drawn up for it to be re-built. There were 300 cells in the prison. Of the seventy-six convicts incarcerated there at the time of our visit, almost all, we were told, were foreign residents, Frenchmen being particularly numerous.

July 8th. Fine.

On this day we visited the offices of the various administrative departments which are under the direction of the members of the State Council, as well as the Council Chamber and the Legislative Chamber. The appointment of officials in the various departments is simple in the extreme. At very busy times, when there are not enough clerks for the work on hand, passers-by are sometimes asked to help in such tasks as copying documents. This obviates the need to employ superfluous officials, which would lead to a reduction in the amount of work done by each. One lazy official with nothing to do, we were told, would infect the others with his idleness.

In the offices of the department of internal affairs is a room for the public solemnisation of marriages. At the front of the room is a large table, on which are laid a copy of the laws and regulations relating to marriage and a register to be signed by the couple being married. In front of this table, to left and right, are placed three or four chairs facing each other. The two people to be married, accompanied by their parents and relatives who will act as witnesses, present themselves here and formally declare their intention to marry. An official of the department of internal affairs explains to them the duties of husband and wife and ensures that they read, understand and consent to the regulations in the book on the table. He then asks them to sign the register. The marriage is now officially recognised, and the couple have acquired rights which will be protected by the government.

It was in a room in this building that the *Alabama* dispute between America and Britain had been heard in the autumn of the previous year [1872]. During the American Civil War, Britain, which was clandestinely aiding the South, had sent warships, including the *Alabama*, to destroy American vessels on the high seas. After the conclusion of peace, this matter was thoroughly investigated, and the then-president of the United States [Ulysses S. Grant] sought an indemnity of $45,500,000 from Britain. Britain thought the amount unjust, and no agreement could be reached. When our party was in America, the dispute was at its height. For a time it rose to such a pitch that the two countries were on the verge of war. Eventually, however, in order to resolve the affair, delegates from Italy, Brazil and Switzerland were sent to deliberate with delegates from Britain and America in this building and to act as an arbitration tribunal. The chairs occupied by the American and British delegates were set out in the middle of the room, while one of the delegates from the other three countries, acting temporarily as investigator, took the principal chair to hear what they had to say. The other delegates sat in chairs on either side, listening carefully to the questions and answers, cutting off digressions, rejecting unproven assertions, and making the greatest efforts to clarify the fundamental issues. Finally, they decided that the amount of the indemnity claimed should be reduced by $30,000,000, and that Britain should pay $15,000,000, thus restoring good relations between the two countries. The tribunal had completed its work on August 13th of the previous year, but the tables and chairs remained just as they had been at the time.

July 9th. Fine.
A telegraph arrived from the Japanese government informing us that we should return to Japan immediately, so we abandoned plans to visit Portugal and began to make preparations to go home.

July 10th. Fine.
We were invited by the government to go on a steamer cruise on the lake, during which music would be played. We departed from the quay in front of the hotel and steamed out onto the lake. Thirty or forty officials and leading merchants of the city accompanied us. Some had joined the party because they were accomplished musicians. The principal passengers all sat on chairs set about the deck, enjoying the lovely views. Conversation flowed and amusing stories were told. We were all free to do as we pleased. In the saloon, tea and wine were provided for us and there was fruit to eat.

   From the stern of the boat, the musicians' charming melodies drifted across the lake on the breeze, so light and airy as to put one in mind of Taoist immortals taking wing to rise to Heaven. The snow and ice of Mont Blanc glittered, and by the town of Nyon mist shrouded the lake and the summer mountains were a hazy green. We sailed beneath the walls of an ancient castle [Château de Chillon] near Vevey and finally arrived at the head of the lake. Just to the south of this point, the river Rhône debouches into Lac Léman. The Rhône is a great river, rising in the canton of Uri in central Switzerland and gathering to itself streams from many valleys before pouring into the lake at this point, then flowing out again from the foot of the lake and on to Lyons, in France, where it turns south to the Mediterranean.

A little way up the mountainside was an hotel called the Hotel Byron, where we were entertained to lunch by the gentlemen from Geneva. The food was sumptuous, and the wine was clear and cool. At the end of the meal there were speeches. When the meal was over we sat outside in the garden enjoying the cool air. The feelings of the Swiss, brought up as they are under a republican government, are brotherly and benevolent. They are straightforward, humorous and open-hearted. Those who sat down at table with us on this day were for the most part wealthy men, prominent in the city, whose names were known throughout Europe. Sometimes the conversation touched on politics; at other times it turned to economics. Nothing could have been more enjoyable. At sunset we left the hotel and went down to the shore of the lake, where one of the leading inhabitants of the village cordially invited us into his house, desiring to show us how he made his own wine. Accordingly, we went into his cellar.

When we boarded the boat again, the evening sun was about to set at the western end of the lake. The boat set off on the return journey. By the time we reached Vevey, the sun had already disappeared. As we passed Lausanne, the lights of the city banished the darkness falling over the lake; at Nyon, the moon rose; and when we reached Geneva the city mounted a display of fireworks to greet our return. On this evening there was bright moonlight, and water and sky were all one colour. The music from our boat drifted through the night sky; the multi-coloured fireworks on the shore made it seem as though the stars had slipped from their positions. The cheers of welcome from the great crowds of citizens who had gathered on the two sides of the river went on and on. We felt that of the many occasions when we had been entertained, before and after, this excursion had been particularly delightful.

July 12th. Rain.
We had been invited to a banquet in the city of Lausanne, and so travelled there by train. At the end of the meal there were speeches. We returned to Geneva after a thoroughly enjoyable evening.

July 14th. Cloudy; rain in the evening.
In the evening we entertained a dozen or so officials and wealthy merchants from the cantons of Geneva, Vaud and Neuchâtel to dinner at our hotel. Music was played during the meal and afterwards there was a

fireworks display on an island in the lake in front of the hotel. The proceedings lasted until midnight.

July 15th. Fine.
At twenty minutes past four we left Geneva. Mr. [Aimé] Humbert, from the canton of Neuchâtel, who had served as ambassador to Japan, had been in Berne and acted as our official host since our arrival in Switzerland. He had been among those present at the dinner on the previous evening. In the end he had stayed the night, and on this day he accompanied us in our carriages to the station to see us off. We greatly valued the genuineness of his friendship, his profound courtesy and the warmth of his feelings.

On leaving Geneva, the railway began to descend, following the valley of the Rhône. On emerging from the tunnel, we arrived at a station called La Plaine, where there was a French customs post.

# CHAPTER 87

# A Record of Lyons and Marseilles

July 15th, 1873. Fine.
We left the city of Geneva and travelled to the station of Bellegarde in France, arriving there at half past five. We rested briefly while waiting for the customs inspection to be completed, then departed. At seven o'clock the mountains on either side fell back and level land opened before us. By now it was growing dark, and night fell before we arrived at Lyons. We stayed at the Grand Hotel de Lyon.

July 16th.
Lyons is renowned for silk-weaving. The city stands at the confluence of the Saône and the Rhône. All the streets are paved with flagstones, and there are many spacious gardens. Trees are planted everywhere, as luxuriant as any forest, and their leafy shade provided relief from the summer heat. In the early evening the people of the city take leisurely strolls beneath the trees. When night falls, gas-lamps are lit and glitter like stars.

Sericulture began in Europe during Roman times. Mulberry trees do not survive in cold climates but thrive in the warm southern parts of Europe. As a result, all the countries which had such southerly regions subsequently developed sericulture. It was the silk yarn of Italy and France, however, which achieved the highest reputation. In the 1550s, when civil strife in Italy drove people from their homes, Francis I of France took advantage of the situation to acquire the secrets of silk-weaving by inviting master weavers from the Italian city of Genoa to come to France. The subsequent establishment of the silk-weaving industry on a large scale in Lyons laid the foundations for this region's prosperity.

The spread of the 'pebrine' disease throughout Europe some years ago brought about a considerable decline in the silk industry and led to the enormous rise in the price of silks. The Europeans dealt with this decline by buying, at exceptionally high prices, raw silk from Huchou [in China] and silkworm eggs from Japan. The disease has now been eradicated, however, and French production of cocoons is so vigorous that it seems likely not only to return to its former level but even to exceed it. The price of raw silk and silkworm eggs from China and Japan is therefore bound not merely to level off but actually to fall.

At four o'clock we went by carriage to an office where the raw silk imported from various places is inspected before being distributed throughout the city. First, the sacks of raw silk are weighed: the weight of a standard sack is fifty kilograms. Ten hanks are then removed from each sack and sent to an assay room on the floor above. Here, each hank is weighed again. The scales stand inside an apparatus consisting of a set of pipes through which steam is circulated so that when the silk is placed on the scales the heat of the steam rids it of moisture. The amount of weight lost is ascertained and the proportion by which the original weight has decreased is recorded. The silk is then sent to another department where the length of the thread is checked. This is done by winding the hank of thread onto a frame of fixed dimensions mounted on a reeling machine. A single thread of raw silk consists of a number of filaments twisted together, and there is a machine which determines how many filaments each thread contains.

We then visited a silk-weaving workshop. These workshops are numerous throughout Lyons, and the sound of flying shuttles issues from many of the houses. At the one we visited, figured velvet was being woven. Beneath the loom were 1,400 bobbins, lined up in rows. The weft threads passed between the warp threads according to the order in which they had been arranged, thus producing a pattern in the fabric. The weaving was done by hand.

The warp threads are controlled by means of a Jacquard apparatus, which was invented in about 1800 by a Mr. [Joseph-Marie] Jacquard of Lyons. This method is now used for producing patterns in textiles of all kinds, and has been adopted in other countries.

July 17th. Fine.
At eleven o'clock at night we left Lyons to travel to Marseilles by train. The railway followed the river Rhône southwards. The land was level, but as it was night we did not see anything.

July 18th. Fine.
At six o'clock in the morning we reached Marseilles and took rooms at the Grand Hotel de la Ville. This city is the principal conduit for trade going from the Mediterranean to the South Seas and the East, and vice versa.

Its buildings are not as handsome as those of Lyons and its streets are not as well maintained, but the city is reminiscent of Paris. The splendid boulevards are flanked by six- or seven-storeyed buildings, their large windows furnished with decorative balustrades of delicately wrought iron. The big houses and the large public buildings enclose square paved courtyards, to which access is gained by means of passageways leading from the front of the buildings. The shops set out their goods behind display-windows of crystal-clear glass. The streets are mostly cobbled, and vehicles pass along them with a clatter. Pavements are provided on either side of the street for those on foot. Some are flagged and some are of asphalt, and both are very firm.

Our hotel stood near the principal intersection of the city, on a broad avenue lined with imposing buildings and bustling with people. Along it runs a wide pavement lined with trees whose verdant shade keeps off the glare of the sun. Here traders set up stalls in the open-air to sell second-hand clothes and curios. The prices of goods in the shops of Marseilles are not notably high, but few of the articles offered are of very high quality. People travelling home [through Marseilles] after visiting Europe are bound to feel somewhat disappointed, but those arriving from Asia are invariably astonished by the opulence of the shops. A comparison of the populations, and of the number of ships arriving and departing, reveals that Marseilles is first among the ports of Europe. Even Hamburg, in Germany, cannot match it. However, the existence of the great city of Paris means that all the goods which arrive here are destined simply to be packed for onward shipment there, and because of that the shops of Marseilles would probably have to yield pride of place to those of Hamburg.

July 19th. Fine, but a wind arose and blew yellow dust into our eyes.
We toured the port of Marseilles. The ships of the Messageries Maritimes de France sail from this port for Hong Kong and Shanghai in China. One ship departs every two weeks, taking forty-nine days to reach its destination. Passengers bound for Yokohama disembark at Hong Kong and transfer to another vessel. First-class passengers pay 2,700 francs per person to share a two-passenger cabin. Second-class passengers pay 1,700 francs per person for a berth in a four-passenger cabin. The boat leaving on this occasion was called the *Ava*.

CHAPTER 88

## *Spain and Portugal*

Earlier in the year, after the ambassadors had completed their diplomatic mission to France, the matter of where the Embassy should then proceed had been discussed. It was decided that since it was the middle of winter the ambassadors should next carry out their mission to Spain and Portugal, warm countries of the south, and afterwards proceed to Belgium and Holland. On February 11th, however, King Amadeus of Spain abdicated and the Spanish people proclaimed a republic. In view of a number of reports received, including the information that even France would not recognise the new government immediately, we eventually decided to proceed eastwards to Belgium. As a result of these unavoidable circumstances, we would be unable to tour Spain to observe the lives of its people first-hand. It was further decided that on our homeward journey we would travel back through France to Bordeaux in order to sail to Portugal from there. However, while we were in Switzerland we received a telegraph from Japan, requiring us to set out on the homeward voyage immediately. Consequently, we were unable to tour Portugal, either.

# CHAPTER 89

# Political Practices and Customs in Europe

That Europe and the eastern part of Asia have been separate regions since ancient times with hardly any communication between them may be inferred from the customs embodied in the cultures of their races. Customs are the fundamental elements which distinguish one country from another, and it is customs which have given rise to differences in systems of government. In the West, the chief concern of government is the protection of people and their property; in the East, it is the inculcation of morality. When we observe Western nations in the light of our own system of government, therefore, we see that even when circumstances appear to be the same, distinct basic ideas shape peoples' temperaments differently.

There are two reasons for the division of the earth's surface into countries: the fact that geographical regions are determined by mountains and seas, and the fact that peoples differ from one another. The role played by mountains and seas is evident if one looks at the topography of countries: a strait forms the boundary between Britain and France, for example, and France and Spain are divided by a mountain range.

Europeans offer the following explanation for the fact that China has remained one country. The mountain ranges in China are scattered and discontinuous so the natural tendency of people to intermingle has meant that although China has at times been divided into separate states, these have in time always come together again. The countries, both large and small, lying on China's periphery, however, being isolated by natural barriers, have not been able to become powerful enough to counterbalance China. Consequently, these countries have all been content to bend the knee to China. Europe, on the contrary, is criss-crossed by mountain ranges and has a convoluted coastline. There, the different peoples have delineated their separate territories, within which they flourish and multiply. Strong countries and weak always keep one another in check through shifting alliances. It is precisely because they are independent and have developed a vigorous competitive spirit that they have managed to achieve their present level of power. Nevertheless, even these natural frontiers may change as a result of human action. This is why race plays such an important part in the formation of states.

According to European theory, the race which inhabits East Asia (that is, China and Japan) is superior to the Huns (who inhabit Turkey and neighbouring areas). They are remarkably civilised, and their rulers exercise benevolent and compassionate government. However, the principles of law and those of morality became confused at some stage, and so the rules governing relationships within the family came to be the model for relations between ruler and subject. The idea of a right to be independent has never arisen among them because they lack 'a sense of shame'. While the upper classes in China (and Japan) strive towards the noblest moral ideals, the lower classes, being poor and weak, simply depend on the upper classes, making a livelihood as though by pilfering, without finding any shame in doing so; thus, a spirit of independence is generally lacking.

The idea which dominates Europeans of all classes, on the other hand, is the pursuit of one's own desires in order to live a happy life. Thus, they claim the right to independence above all and are avaricious in their wish for property and profit. From our Asian point of view, many aspects of their desire for wealth and their great reluctance to part with it lay them open to the charge that it is they, in fact, who lack a sense of shame. Government in the West is based on the rule of law and respects most of all racial integrity, marriage taboos, religious beliefs and differences in language and customs. Avoiding constraints on these is regarded as benevolent government and a basic principle of liberty. In contrast, the assumption in the East is that when a new regime comes to power it will make people abandon their old customs and adopt those of their new rulers. In Western eyes, this represents a lack of principles and results in confusion.

The right of the different races to propagate and maintain their customs is called 'people's rights'. These are regarded as a precious element in the principle of freedom in European politics. Three distinct rights have arisen: those of marriage, language and religion. All are vitally important in government.

Much weight is given to the rights of ethnic groups in Europe, so it is natural that marriage rights should also be taken seriously. The fact that marriage can influence relationships between countries can be seen from the way in which these have resulted in countries joining together or separating. It was through the marriage of King Ferdinand of Aragón and Queen Isabella of Castile that three of the four Spanish kingdoms were united. And Philip II of Spain subsequently, through his line of succession, united Portugal with Spain. Through marriage, Charles V of Germany acquired Spain and Hungary, and Britain and Holland were united by the marriage of the Dutch king William and the British queen Mary. Marriage rights can even affect a country's system of government.

The part played by language in uniting or separating ethnic groups is also considerable. In times past, oppressive laws on language, which were considered tyrannical in the extreme, were enacted in both Rome and Germany. Later, it became common practice among European governments to treat all people using the same language as one, to allow every group the freedom to use its own language, and to regard as inadmissible any attempt to prevent this by government edict or law. It is invariably the case, however, that a single language is designated in matters concerning the country as a whole. Switzerland is the only country where three languages are used on an equal basis.

The creation of a new people by splitting off from a common race is not caused solely by their living in a different place or speaking a different language. Religion also exerts a strong influence on this. History abounds with examples of new peoples emerging as a result of religious beliefs, and the phenomenon has not entirely disappeared even now. Consequently, the right to practise one's own religion is as important as the right to use one's own language.

Western peoples hold that human nature is innately bad. As people are subject to powerful passions, so their desire to pursue happiness is also strong. The main aim of their religion is to curb these passions and desires. This thinking runs entirely contrary not only to the Confucian belief that human nature is essentially good, but also to the Buddha's teaching of the obligation to perform charitable deeds.

Once the Westerner believes in his religion, he will observe its tenets as tenaciously and as fervently as he guards his wealth and profit. He also tends to reject and scorn the beliefs of others, just as he tries to extend the area under his control. For these reasons, religion strengthens the feeling of solidarity in ethnic groups and promotes co-operation in religious bodies, creating invisible frontiers even within the same country or province.

Race is involved with the formation of nations, language differs according to race, and religion differs according to language. These are all reasons why political cultures differ.

The French scholar Professor [Maurice] Block told us that systems of government vary one from another in the same way that countries do. So long as a country's government and religion are one, it is certain that it will not split apart. The prevailing view among politicians is that, if we take only the most fundamental differences into account, there are no more than two types of polity: a monarchy and a republic. Those who propound theoretical forms of government probably include another, to make three – a monarchy, an aristocracy and a republic – or else distinguish between several types: despotic, absolute, constitutional, union, federation, confederation, democracy, and so on. Examples of all these systems emerge with great frequency and flourish. The difference between despotism and absolutism lies in the temperament of the monarch; a federal union and a confederation are distinguished only by details of their legislative processes. Ultimately, all such differences spring from differences in the origins and customs of the peoples.

Government in Europe, taken as a whole, is completely different in character from government in the East. Embedded deep in the European character is the disposition to form corporate bodies, something which the Eastern races lack completely. Consequently, if we examine the political customs and practices of Europe closely, we find that every unit of government – from the largest (the polity of a country, through the states, provinces or counties into which that polity is divided) to the smallest (the towns, and the villages into which the towns are in turn divided) – is without exception organised in the form of a corporation. The forming of corporations is a trait inherent in Europeans of all classes. The republican form of government arises by appointing the head of state through public election; the monarchical government adopts the practice of selection through hereditary succession. Superficially, these differ immensely, but in fact neither is very different in character from a body corporate.

The people of Europe make their livelihoods through competition with one another, at the same time seeking to satisfy their desire for profit. The character of their political culture may be reduced to four elements: the pursuit of personal goals, perseverance, obstinacy and self-centredness. The 'principle of independence' consists of nothing more than the right to pursue one's personal goals in the quest for profit. Having determined one's goals, one applies oneself to an occupation in order to attain them. The more obstinate one is in this and the firmer one's resolve, the greater the admiration with which one is regarded. So the establishment of a parliament, the formation of a company, the creation and the governance of a country – such enterprises are simply these four elements brought to fruition. The customs and traditions of the East are quite the opposite. The linchpins of European government are invariably given as 'justice' and 'society'. By 'justice' is meant the clarification of rights and duties; 'society' refers to the warm relations which exist within a community. These words might be regarded as the equivalents of the Confucian 'righteousness' and 'benevolence'. However, these latter concepts are based on morality, while 'justice' and 'society' are ideas derived from the protection of property. In meaning they are therefore diametrically opposed. When considering the political culture of Europe, it is of the utmost importance never to lose sight of this fundamental point.

# CHAPTER 90

# European Geography and Transportation

Topographically, we were told, Europe holds an advantage over the North American continent in as much as it has a larger proportion of lowland terrain and a smaller proportion of mountainous land. When we travelled across America, however, we passed through few of its mountainous regions, so our subjective impression was that it was Europe which had more high peaks.

To have a great deal of low-lying land is not invariably an advantage to a country; nor is an abundance of mountainous terrain necessarily the reverse. Most of the Russian plain is uncultivated; Holland has productive wet pastureland but suffers from a lack of timber; and there is little activity on the great North German plain. Conversely, countries such as Saxony, Bohemia and Switzerland, although situated among mountains, surpass others in wealth. A country like France has mountains and coasts, fields and forests, but when we passed through it we saw that the plains along the northern coast were infertile and the lowlands on the southern coast were also barren.

There are no limits to the uses that human intelligence may make of the benefits offered by land and water. With sufficient numbers of people nature can be conquered. Thus, provided the people work hard, a country will grow rich even if its soil is poor; but if its people are idle, the country will be impoverished even if its soil is fertile. People who live along the coasts devote themselves to commerce; people who live in the mountains put their effort into manufacturing. Both depend upon nature's resources.

If we consider how topography influences human enterprise, we find that the products on which coastal regions concentrate are those which are profitable to trade by sea. These are also sent inland up rivers and canals or by overland routes. The products on which mountain regions concentrate are those which are profitable to trade overland. These are transported down rivers to markets, then sent on to sea-ports. Factories in coastal regions often produce bulky, heavy articles of low value, such as coarse cotton cloth, articles made of iron, or ships. Factories in mountainous regions produce lightweight articles of high value, such as embroidery, jewellery, clocks and watches, and pigments.

In general, high ground is always located in the centre of a continent. Mountain ranges form the backbone, and the sides of the mountains slope down to foothills and plateaux. Below these are the plains and wetlands suitable for arable and livestock farming. The earth produces enough for the surplus to be transported and marketed, thus ensuring that all enjoy nature's benefits. Consider this: A steep mountainside is hard to ascend, but the effort required to bring a heavy weight down is reduced. At the same time, a slope offers the mechanical advantage of an inclined plane, allowing objects to be raised by a circuitous route. Cataracts become streams which seek the lowest level and thus enrich the soil. Water collects in rivers and lakes and offers the advantage of water transport. Everything can be useful provided that nature's blessings are utilised.

The civilisation of Europe is the cumulative result of competition among countries and the encouragement of activities to further the people's interests. During our tour we were often astonished at what was achieved by exploiting the natural benefits of land and water. In any account of European trade, the main distinction is that between transport by land and transport by sea. However, the two are interrelated and interdependent; they are as inseparable as an object and its shadow.

All European countries seek to promote manufacturing internally and expand trade externally. Carts on land and boats on rivers bring goods to the ports, there to be loaded onto ships which sail west to America and east to Asia in search of profit. Even though Japan is far from Europe, its products can reach European markets in a few weeks. If asked to name the principal ports, one would naturally mention London, Marseilles, Amsterdam and Hamburg, but there are many more whose names are heard less frequently. These ports are no more than temporary way-stations from which goods are distributed to the centres of overland trade. This, then, is how the world's products circulate. Raw materials are carried across the sea and unloaded at ports. There they are sent overland to factories and the goods manufactured are sent to the principal inland hubs of commerce and thence back to the ports. It is like the flow of blood from the heart through the arteries. These goods flood out of the ports and are dispatched to countries all over the world. This is like the flow of blood back along the veins.

The essential purpose of roads and waterways is not simply to enable people to move. It is to facilitate the transportation of all the goods produced to places where their value is higher. The Europeans never carry loads on their shoulders, and horses in Europe do not carry goods on their backs, yet the volume of freight transported by road in Europe is a thousand times greater than elsewhere. It is imperative to understand the reason for this. Europeans put the effort which they would otherwise use to carry goods themselves into the upkeep of their roads, and instead of using horses as pack-animals they exploit the power of the wheel. By using a wheeled vehicle on a smooth level road, the same amount of energy can move a weight ten times greater.

Our circulatory system keeps us in good health by carrying nutrition to every part of the body. The slightest blockage at any point will inevitably cause sickness, and will eventually impair the well-being of the whole. Consequently, all the countries of Europe devote great effort to the construction and maintenance of their roads and waterways. Countries which have done so have gradually attained wealth and power. We found that as we travelled through a particular country the condition of its roads would reveal to us immediately whether its government was vigorous or in decline and whether its industry and commerce were active or sluggish.

The use of horses to pull carts and the use of wind and water power for boats are the first steps in the process of utilising physical forces to economise on human effort. The next step is when inventions are made which exploit the power of steam and electricity. However, even when economies of time and effort are achieved with steam and electric power, costs may not necessarily be reduced. Each of the different ways of utilising physical forces has its own advantages. Thus, horse-drawn carts and boats are still in use alongside the steam-locomotive, and even though the steam-engine has been invented, wind- and water-power continue to be widely used. Steamships ply the oceans, but the number of sailing-ships is still increasing.

# CHAPTER 91

# The Climate and Agriculture of Europe

Considering its latitude, the climate of the European continent is much milder than that of other continents. A number of factors account for climatic differences in various parts of the world. The first is latitude – that is to say, distance from the equator. This is regarded as a sound guide in general, but if it is the only one considered, it will lead to serious error.

The second factor is the location of the region – in other words, whether it is adjacent to a large body of water. If it lies next to the open sea, winds from the tropics will sweep across the water's surface, lose heat and pick up sea-water, before blowing across the land. Such winds always have a moderating effect on climate. This phenomenon causes temperatures to be comparatively low in such places as the South Sea islands despite the fact that they lie in the tropics. Europe faces the Atlantic to the south-west, and prevailing winds from the south and south-west always pass over this ocean, so the continental land mass is warmed by them.

Ocean currents are the third factor. The main current in the Atlantic is called the 'Gulf Stream'. As a result of the influence of this warm current, Britain enjoys a mild climate. Although the islands of Great Britain are on exactly the same latitude as the island of Karafuto [Sakhalin], north of Hokkaidō, their climates are very different. This is because a cold current from the Arctic Ocean passes close to Hokkaidō, the precise opposite of what happens in Britain.

The fourth factor is the proximity of a region to any area with a distinctly different climate. Because the southern plains of Russia are bordered by the deserts of Arabia, hot desert air flows unobstructed into Russia, and in summer this great heat even reaches regions lying north of latitude 60°.

The fifth factor is the proximity of the region to a large mountain range. A country like Austria has mountains to its south which shield it from the heat of Africa; and because the Alps extend through southern Germany and Switzerland, the heat of Arabia and Africa has little influence on the German climate, even though that same heat flows up into the interior of Russia.

The sixth factor is the height of the area above sea-level. On mountain-tops the air is thin; at sea-level it is thick. Because Switzerland consists of mountains interspersed with high plateaux, it has the coolest climate in Europe.

The seventh factor is the direction in which the land slopes. Variations in climate resulting from this are quite remarkable. When the Russian snows melt, the warmth in Prussia is suddenly dissipated and snow starts to fall. When the ice melts in the seas around Russia, the volume of cold air over Sweden abruptly increases.

Thus, one cannot discuss climate with reference to a single factor alone. Variations in climate between regions are innumerable. It is of the greatest importance economically that geographers study each region with the greatest care.

In European economic theory, human economic activities may be divided into three categories: those bringing about 'change of substance', 'change of form' and 'change of location'.

'Change of substance' means exploiting the power to change the natural forms of Creation. The qualities inherent in soil and manure transform seeds into blossom and fruit; fodder fed to cattle and sheep is converted into milk, meat and wool; fruit juices and grains undergo fermentation to become wine and beer. This is the business of agriculture.

'Change of form' means the conversion, through manufacturing, of materials produced by 'change of substance'. Examples are the trans-formation of iron and steel ingots into machines, and of vegetable and animal fibres into cloth and yarn. This is the business of crafts and manufacturing.

'Change of location' means transporting goods produced by 'change of substance' and 'change of form' from where there is a supply to where there is a demand, so that the best price will be obtained. For example, raw cotton from Brazil is shipped to the ports of Britain, where it is sent to the mills of Manchester. There it undergoes a 'change of form' to become cotton yarn, which is then sent to the weaving-sheds of Holland, where it is turned into cloth. Finally, the cloth is made into clothing for the Javanese. This is the business of trade and commerce.

Produce obtained from land through a 'change of substance' is not, of course, limited to cereals. So much importance has been placed on grain in Japan that even the wealth of a feudal domain is assessed solely by its yield of grain. This is because manufacturing and commerce are still undeveloped in Japan, and other ways of making a livelihood are unknown.

Since European agriculture aims to exploit the benefits of the soil in every possible way, it is not grain alone which is cultivated. What is grown is whatever is most profitable; no single class of agricultural produce will suffice. This must be discussed first in any account of European agriculture.

Cereals are usually thought of as the staple food of Europeans, but they also play a part in trade as one of the raw materials of manufacturing. Even when used as food by people or animals, they can be regarded as being raw materials to produce the capacity to work. This is in no way different from burning coal to produce power in the form of steam. In addition, cereals are not merely food-stuffs: starch is necessary for the textile industry, and brewing begins with an infusion made from grain. It is thus appropriate to regard cereals as raw materials for manufacturing.

The benefits derived from the three industries of arable farming, arboriculture and livestock farming are interdependent. The European farmer keeps animals beside his house, tills his fields and plants trees along the boundaries of his fields. Villages where such careful husbandry is exercised are always in countries where agriculture is advanced (such as France, Germany and Belgium). In former times Europeans only used animal manure to fertilise the land, but with the development of agriculture as an industry night-soil has in recent years come to be used in many countries. The case of Japan is just the reverse: night-soil, fish refuse and seaweed have been generally employed, with little use made of dung-heaps, bone-meal and manufactured fertilisers. The land now under cultivation in Japan amounts to no more than one-tenth of the total land area. One important way to improve our agricultural efficiency and to convert uncultivated land into productive land would be to try to meet the need for fertiliser.

Improvements in agricultural efficiency in Europe in recent years have been basically due to the assistance and encouragement of agricultural societies, which first started a hundred years or so ago. Farmers and small landowners formed co-operative associations, and these disseminated the benefits of, for example, good methods of tilling and raising animals, the exchange of seeds, and improvements in machinery; they also rewarded diligent farm workers. The results were remarkable, and these associations spread to many countries.

Germany is pre-eminent in Europe in its promotion of agriculture, with agricultural improvement societies widespread in its states and counties. Their zealous and unceasing efforts have brought about striking progress, and their numbers have increased steadily over the past seventy years. At the same time the number of agricultural schools has also increased. Such schools and societies are very closely linked. Agricultural improvement societies are also numerous in France.

In Europe, agriculture was long regarded as a menial occupation, and gentlemen gave it little thought. In feudal times the aristocracy all owned land and had labourers supply them with grain and fruit and raise animals. The landowners left the working of the land to humble people while they themselves lived off the profits. This in no way differs from the situation in Japan. In Europe, commerce is regarded as being of primary importance, and inevitably less attention is paid to agriculture. Thus, agriculture has lagged behind, and it is only in the last twenty years, we were told, that it has shown any noteworthy progress.

Agricultural exhibitions have proved extremely effective in encouraging and guiding such progress. In France these are called '*concours*'. The first was held in 1849, and the benefits from it exceeded all expectations. As a result, the country was divided into fifteen '*régions*' (one *région* comprising about five provinces), in each of which an annual exhibition is held. Since this exhibition is held in the provinces in turn, each province holds one every five years. When the time comes, experienced farmers are selected to inspect other farmers' land and livestock and to look over their books, comparing the written record with the actual results. If anyone is judged to have made an outstanding contribution to agriculture, the governor of the province will request the department of agriculture and commerce to confer an award on him. Usually these awards are for the invention of new farm equipment or new kinds of fertiliser, or for increasing yields, or for obtaining plants or seeds from overseas and cultivating them successfully. Prizes are also awarded to farm workers in charge of stock and to general labourers, both men and women, who have worked exceptionally well. Sometimes a national exposition is held; or the farmers of a whole region gather to display their produce; or such shows are put on by the agricultural society of a single province. Agricultural exhibitions like these are held in every European country.

CHAPTER 92

# *European Industry*

The soil of the European continent is not naturally fertile, so people do not depend on farming alone. Although they supplement crops by raising livestock, they are still not able to make a sufficient livelihood. They have therefore become an acquisitive race, searching for what lies under the earth and mining it. Of all the minerals, the one with the richest benefits is coal. Huge deposits of coal lie in the earth, and there is no country in Europe, large or small, which does not produce at least a small amount. (Holland and Denmark produced extremely small quantities.) It is a cheap fuel and generates three times as much heat as wood.

The mineral second to coal in its benefits and used in conjunction with it is iron-ore. So great is its usefulness that in Europe the amount of iron-ore consumed came to be a measure of a country's level of development. Every type of manufacturing depends upon iron, and in Europe machinery is used on a huge scale. The country which dominates the iron industry is Britain. America ranks second in production, and Germany is the main producer in continental Europe.

The contribution of coal and iron in increasing a country's productive capacity and assisting manufacturing is immense. Of such industries, spinning and weaving are the most important. In terms of value, silk fabrics command the highest prices, but in terms of the quantity produced cotton comes first. More profit is derived from articles for which there is a greater demand than from articles with a high unit price.

Human beings have three basic needs: clothing, food and shelter. First, as regards clothing, the middle and lower classes in Europe buy ready-made clothing in shops, and so factories produce this in large quantities. They buy their shoes ready-made, so there are large shoe factories. There is also a demand for galoshes and dance shoes. Hats are required by all, both men and women, rich and poor. As a result, there are factories making hats. The manufacture of leather gloves is similar. The quantity of clothing manufactured determines the number of buttons produced.

477

These are all parts of a vast industry whose factories and workshops are to be found in every city of every country.

Among products answering the need for food and drink – that is to say, the processing of agricultural produce – are wheat flour, bread, beer and wine, spirits, dairy produce, dried meat, tobacco and sugar. The provision of housing is also a vast industry embracing the manufacture of doors and windows, tiles and bricks, patterned wallpaper, paint and tar.

However, even when the three basic needs for clothing, food and shelter are satisfied, everyone, high and low alike, requires several other categories of articles. The first is household furniture and furnishings – beds, chairs, tables, chests of drawers, shelves, stoves, candlesticks, lamps and clocks. The second comprises utensils for eating, drinking and cooking – everything used at the table or in the kitchen, such as knives, spoons, forks, glasses, cups, plates, bowls, water-jugs, dishes for serving meat, and tin-plated iron utensils. The third category consists of objects used for one's toilet and grooming – wash-bowls, hairdressing implements, items of personal adornment, wigs and hair-pieces, and brushes. In the fourth category are materials used in writing and printing. Paper is the foremost of these, for the uses of paper are boundless. There are also type fonts, printing and bookbinding machinery, ink, pencils, steel pens, account books, ledgers, and various items used in schools. As the world becomes more civilised, will not all these be indispensable to every person and every family? Besides these, there is another category of everyday items which includes matches, candles, soap, oil, fat and perfumes.

There is no state or province which does not manufacture some necessities. This is why the number of factory hands is second only to that of agricultural workers. People even take on manufacturing work in their own homes to do in their free time. The vast scale of the consumption of such necessities is revealed by the fact that a few years ago America paid off the nation's deficit by imposing a tax on matches. Whenever people need fire they use matches. They carry boxes of them in their pockets in the same way that the Japanese always carry paper on their person to use as handkerchiefs. Despite the invention of gas-lighting, the huge demand for candles seems undiminished. Soap is said to be one of the articles which attest to the level of a nation's civilisation. All this shows that the supply of these necessities increases with time.

Another important factor which increases a nation's productivity and helps it become rich is transport. The ports and harbours of the West are filled with forests of masts; the streets of the cities are thronged with elegant carriages. Every one of these is a product of industry. The art of shipbuilding has developed into one of the leading scientific disciplines; bridge-building has become a principal branch of architecture. The ever-increasing number of travellers and goods transported bring ever-greater profits.

Industry not only furnishes people with items that are useful; its products constitute their wealth as well. It is natural that the quality of workmanship in articles which are available should reflect the level of people's taste. To an ever-increasing extent, wealthy households seek to outdo one another in acquiring items of the highest quality; as a result, the study of the industrial arts and of the fine arts both advance. This is not wasteful manufacturing; it is simply that people work harder in order to display their prosperity through the goods they own. Too often Easterners neglect manufacturing industries which provide people with their daily needs, regarding the purpose of manufacturing to be the creation of fine works of art. To do so is to lose sight of the distinction between what is essential and what is not.

If we consider manufactured goods for which the East has a high reputation, we find that in textiles it is greatly admired for its silks, and in ceramics for its fine porcelain, and that its beautiful copperware and lacquerware, embroidery and chased metalwork are all highly prized. But there is no large-scale manufacture of products requiring machines and skilled operators. The West manufactures on a huge scale but cannot match the East in the skill and taste of its craftsmen, or the delicacy and beauty of its workmanship. France and Italy are the most accomplished in European crafts, but neither derives much profit from them.

As the industrial arts have advanced in the West, so too has the study of the fine arts. Painting and sculpture are the noblest and most elevated of the arts, and admiration of them may be likened to the appreciation of calligraphy, painting and seal-engraving among cultured gentlemen in the East. Since aesthetic refinement is determined by a person's character and capacities, it takes a unique form in each country and in each individual and cannot be imitated. This is what we mean when we speak of the 'industrial arts' of a particular country. The novelty of French design; the austere restraint of Italian work; the German fondness for decoration; the durability of British products – all these characteristics give the products their reputations. It is these qualities which enable a country to continue to derive profits from its industrial arts. The arts do not profit a nation directly, but indirectly they lay the foundation on which national profit is built.

There are two categories of people whose object is to secure profits through manufacturing. Those who set up enterprises, furnish the raw materials, cause the work to be done, and find markets for the goods are called 'entrepreneurs'. Those who receive the materials, do the actual work of manufacturing, and are paid wages, are called 'workers'. A manufacturing industry can only be established when entrepreneurs and workers come together. The main objective in encouraging manufacturing is to ensure that these two categories of people first enter into a contract and then carry out all their obligations while maintaining amicable relations, so that profits are not adversely affected.

In order to become a factory-owning entrepreneur, one must first risk one's wealth by buying a factory, machines and the necessary raw materials. Turning these materials into goods is entirely dependent on the labour of the workers. (This differs from agricultural labour, which assists the forces of nature.) If an entrepreneur is unable to find workers, or the workers demand excessive wages, the machinery, instead of making his fortune, will become the means by which his family is bankrupted. Or if he is unable to obtain suitable raw materials, he will not be able to operate the machinery and give employment to the workers, and his enterprise is again bound to fail. Only when he has succeeded in avoiding these two eventualities and has devoted every effort to finding a market for his goods can he expect to receive profit. Chambers of industry should deliberate carefully on these matters and, by means of the protection afforded by the law, enable factories to increase in size and number year by year.

It is impossible for a worker to be an entrepreneur at the same time. The worker hopes to be given employment by the entrepreneur and to receive an appropriate wage. Consequently, entrepreneurs and workers wish to maintain good relations. When these good relations are ruptured, the cause is always a dispute over the price of labour. This is the nub of the protection of industry, for there are strict regulations in the West concerning employees' working hours and increases or cuts in their wages, and entrepreneurs cannot determine these themselves. When we were in London and the Gas Light and Coke Company's workers demanded a wage increase, a dispute boiled up and they stopped work. That evening all the gas-lamps in the streets suddenly went out. In the end the matter was taken to the industrial court. In considering the case, this court inquired into the wages of workers in all the industries connected with coal, such as miners and iron and steel workers. One may infer from this what great care must be exercised in industrial affairs.

The maintenance of good relations between entrepreneur and workers has given rise to an admirable custom: it is considered a matter of honour in the West for an entrepreneur to improve the lot of his workers and to offer them protection and support. Workers are the same in every country: for the most part they are ignorant and unintelligent, capable only of devoting themselves to a single craft. They waste their wages on eating and drinking, or on sexual gratification or games of chance. But their lifetime of labour ends by destroying them body and soul. Once they become old and ill and can no longer work, they think they have a right to demand that their employers acknowledge an obligation to help them. Consequently, employers devise in advance ways to protect and help them, and the government encourages this. The most important ways of helping workers are these: employers keep them in good physical health (by not imposing unreasonable and cruel drudgery on them); they spread education among them; they improve their morals; and they inculcate the idea of thrift in them. The growth of industry is followed by the rise of charitable corporations; the setting-up of schools in factories; the provision of workers' housing; and the establishment of savings organisations, mutual-aid societies, almshouses and funds for old age. Sometimes there are company stores which lay in stocks of consumer goods to be sold to the workers, so they can obtain goods of high quality at low prices. Sometimes co-operative companies are established in which workers pool the profits derived from their own labour and thus become collective entrepreneurs. Sometimes finance companies are set up to provide capital to small merchants and artisans.

Industry advances as a result of both improved technical skills and new inventions. Technical skills, on the one hand, are acquired in the process of making profit. Inventions, on the other hand, are the foundation on which the making of profit rests. Consequently, some method is required to ensure that inventors are able to gain financially from their inventions as a reward for their investment of money and labour, and thus there will be no decline in the spirit of enterprise. This is why, in the West, exclusive sales licences are granted, which are called 'patents'. The people to whom such licences are awarded are classed as inventors, discoverers or improvers.

CHAPTER 93

# *European Commercial Enterprise*

Individually, Europeans fall far short of the Japanese in craftsmanship. Yet how the industrial arts flourish among them, and what vast gains in wealth and power they have made! Because they are no more able to depend on their native ingenuity than on their infertile soil, they make every effort to conquer nature by thoroughly investigating its mechanisms, by unremitting labour, and by close co-operation with one another. Their capacity for investigation leads to advances in knowledge, their capacity for hard work leads to the invention of machines, and their capacity for co-operation brings prosperity in trade. It is the combination of these qualities which has produced the flourishing civilisation we see today. An examination of the situation in Europe shows that while people in the East have developed agriculture and manufacturing through 'practical' experience, people in the West have developed agriculture and manufacturing through 'theoretical' study. Thus, their technology cannot escape a dependence on machines. We should not, therefore, be overawed by their engineering feats. What should give us the greatest cause to fear arises from their capacity for co-operation and their untiring attention to the minutiae of trade. They always obtain the best possible prices for the goods which their nations produce, and their commerce is like an army on the march. They cannot rely on nature, so they make human co-operation their chief principle. It is in commerce that Europe can best serve as an example to the world.

European economists define commerce as the occupation of re-locating goods, bringing them away from where there is a supply to where there is a demand, from where prices are low to where prices are high. Unless goods are moved, they will not command a good price.

Each European country has its strengths and weaknesses in commerce, but the people there all wish for commerce to thrive just as people in the East wish for an abundant harvest. The invitations which our Embassy received were prompted by nothing other than this: a desire to promote

482

friendly relations and thereby increase trade with Japan. When we had audiences with emperors, kings and queens or were received by foreign ministers, the theme of their addresses was invariably 'trade'. As we travelled around the cities, commercial and manufacturing firms competed to welcome us. They entertained us at lavish banquets, where the conversation always turned to 'trade'. When we visited townhalls, chambers of commerce and commercial exchanges, the speakers would unfailingly express a hope for 'friendly relations and increased trade' with Japan. When they did so, all present would wave their hats in the air, stamp their feet and cheer. A high regard for commerce permeates the innermost hearts of all Europeans.

Profits from commerce derive from two sources: one is the price charged for transporting goods; the other is the price charged by an intermediary. The merchant performs the function of an intermediary, receiving goods from a vendor and conveying them to where there is a demand for them. He sells them at the local market-price and transmits the money to the vendor.

The volume of goods exported and imported gives a clear indication of productive capacity. Information on the trade volume of a country comes from customs inspectors' reports; information on the trade volume of individual towns and cities comes from the reports of presidents of chambers of commerce. These reports are vital in assessing commercial activity in each region. The most important basic principle of commerce is to increase the yearly circulation of goods, thereby increasing the wealth of the people. A large volume of imports is not necessarily to be regretted, and a large volume of exports is not always a blessing. In general, exports and imports should be more or less in balance.

A nation's profit can be clearly inferred from its level of imports and exports. In Europe, commercial goods are divided into three types: 'non-manufactured goods', 'semi-manufactured goods' and 'manufactured goods'. As a rule, the value of an article always increases each time it undergoes a manufacturing process. Produce such as grain does not necessarily need manufacturing, but when German barley becomes Danish flour, or Russian and American barley is turned into British beer, value is added. All the products of nature, therefore, are best described as non-manufactured goods. Cotton and wool spun into yarn and iron rolled into wire are semi-manufactured goods.

If a country has a surplus, even of non-manufactured goods, this is exported, or if it suffers a shortage, even of manufactured goods, the country will allow unrestricted imports. When many people have made fortunes from their industriousness, the country will import costly manufactured goods to satisfy their desire for a pleasant life. The value of Britain's exports of manufactured goods to France never exceeds one-third of the value of those imported by Britain. This shows the high standard of living attained by the British.

With regard to the net inflow or outflow of money, it is generally true that the purchase of non-manufactured and semi-manufactured goods results in an outflow of money, and the sale of manufactured goods results in an inflow of money. Countries with a large maritime trade and colonies adopt the 'mercantile system' and enact laws to increase imports. These harsh laws are strictly enforced and give the country the exclusive right to buy the natural produce of the colony and to suppress industry and commerce there. They permit their merchants to obtain produce from the colony equivalent in value to the goods sent there, and this produce is then sent back to the home country. The Dutch, for example, force the Javanese to work as slave labourers growing coffee, tobacco, sugar and indigo. All of these products fall under the monopoly of trading companies in Amsterdam and are brought back to Holland. In British India and French Indo-China – indeed, in all territories under foreign rule – trade conditions are like this.

As public opinion has become more enlightened in recent years, such evil practices have been checked. However, the result is that many colonies have found themselves with expenditure but no income. If trade is so unregulated that produce is unable to fetch a reasonable price when exported, even independent countries find themselves in the same position as if they were subject to mercantilist laws.

Places where goods are brought together for sale and purchase are called 'markets'. These are held every other day or on certain fixed days each week so that perishable goods may be sold. They are licensed by a regional authority (such as the prefectural governor or local magistrate) and are under the supervision of the mayor of the city or town. There are also smaller markets than these. Morning markets, evening markets and open-air markets are extremely important in the lives of the common people, so local officials encourage them and help them flourish by enacting regulations and supervising them strictly.

When transport facilities are undeveloped, the transporter cannot promise delivery by a given day or even guarantee that the goods will be handed over or accepted when they arrive. However, when there are well-maintained roads, ships and vehicles, and solidly built warehouses, the owner of the goods can go about his business with peace of mind and simply await the arrival of a telegram or letter on the promised date of delivery. If the ships, vehicles and warehouses are well constructed, he may rest easy about storms at sea, fires, and other such eventualities. There are also insurance companies, which allow one to regard the destinations of ships or vehicles carrying one's goods as as safe as though they were rooms in one's own house. When a Japanese person, having travelled far across the ocean, arrives in a city in a civilised country and buys something, he will be asked whether it should be sent to the hotel or to Japan. If it is to be sent to Japan, the customer's name and address will be asked, as well as the port where the goods are to be delivered. The delivery date will then be determined and the article dispatched either to Yokohama or to Nagasaki. In the same way, some institution is necessary so that the owner of goods may be entirely confident that when the goods arrive at their destination the sales transaction in the market there will be completed reliably. That is the reason for the establishment of exchanges.

This meeting place for merchants is called the 'Royal Exchange' in Britain, and the 'Bourse' in France. In brief, it is where market-prices are determined, for commodity prices are of the utmost importance to commerce. Commodities have three prices: the 'real' price, the cost price and the market-price. The real price is the value of the commodity to human beings. The cost price is the price of the article at the place where it is produced. Based upon its real price, human labour is applied to it and manufacturing is carried out; thus, the cost price is arrived at by adding the cost of labour, the cost of manufacturing, and a profit. By adding transport costs to this, one arrives at the market-price, that is to say, the wholesale price. The market-price depends on the level of competition and on consumer wishes. Since the market-price is influenced by supply and demand, it is sometimes higher and sometimes lower than the cost price, and a dealer enjoys the resulting gains or suffers the losses. The real price, however, never changes. Consequently, the real price of goods which are useful and beneficial is high. The market-price does not always reflect the real price; the two are as different as fire and water.

In every town and city, merchants and those wishing to buy or sell meet at a particular place at fixed times on fixed days. There they may confer with the commercial agent, talk to dealers, hear the latest news of business conditions and learn the financial standing of brokers without wasting time or exertion. That is the purpose of these exchanges. The opening and closing times are set according to local conditions. The exchange is open several times a week, and when open the commercial agent attends. That day's market-prices are determined by bidding and are guaranteed by the seal of the commercial agent. Anyone may go into the exchange and offer bids. No town where commerce is conducted on any sort of scale will lack an exchange.

The business of a merchant is generally the buying of merchandise for the purpose of re-selling it at a profit, in some cases displaying it in a shop and in other cases finishing semi-finished products before offering them for sale. But there are other areas of commerce. Those who guarantee market-prices are called 'commercial agents'; those who act as intermediaries in sales transactions are called 'brokers'. There are banks; there are insurance companies; there are people who issue bills of exchange, ship-repair contractors, those who rent out warehouses, operators of transport companies, those who rent out ships, and those who make loans with cargoes counted as surety. All these are important activities in commerce.

The business of merchants is protected by laws, and public institutions are established called 'chambers of commerce'. The members are elected from among the leading merchants. Some cities also have a separate chamber of industry, but the two are usually combined. Anyone who is active in commerce or manufacturing and lives within the chamber's designated district is eligible for election. The president, who is chosen from among the members, will convey to the government opinions on regulations and policy relating to industrial and commercial matters. Because of this, European cities where commerce is conducted on a large scale are most republican in spirit. With trade increasing daily, the establishment of such public bodies is an important means of planning for a region's prosperity. Well-informed people should consider this carefully.

# CHAPTER 94

# The Voyage Through the Mediterranean

July 20th, 1873. Fine.

We left the hotel at eight in the morning and boarded the mail-boat *Ava*, which sailed from Marseilles at ten o'clock. This port lies in a bay opening out to the south-west. To our right was a headland, on which stood a lighthouse. To the left of the tip of the headland was a short stretch of shore; to its right was a long sweep of coastline. Soon the Maritime Alps on the south coast of France came into view, curving away to the east. The hills along the coast were red in colour and almost bare, with little vegetation. The soil was uniformly reddish, and from a distance showed no evidence of being fertile. The town of Marseilles lies in the north-east of the bay. Spurs of hills extend into the sea to form promontories, and islands of brownish-red rock jut out of the water. Docks have been built along the shore, providing shelter from wind and high waves at all times. The valleys among the coastal hills are rocky and barren, but as the city prospered houses were built there, which then spread to the coast. On top of one hill stood a Roman Catholic church, crowned by a gilded statue of the Virgin Mary, which glittered in the sun. In the middle of the bay were two or three fortified islands guarding the city's southern approach.

As we sailed away from the port, the peaks of the Alps gradually receded into the distance until by evening they were no longer visible and sea and sky merged into one.

July 21st. Fine; little wind and calm sea.

In the morning we sailed through the strait separating the islands of Corsica and Sardinia. The island of Corsica belongs to France. The strait is only a little over one nautical mile wide, and is defended on the French side by a fort with a garrison. There are no more than 3,000 residents and no commercial docks. The island's capital [Ajaccio] lies on the west coast; it was there that Napoleon I was born.

The island of Sardinia belongs to Italy. Its northern tip lies on the south side of the strait, and it spreads out southwards in a roughly oblong shape. It is three times larger than Corsica. The most famous product of this island is sardines in oil, which are sold in hermetically sealed boxes made of tin plate. In European countries, preserved fish and fresh vegetables are eaten before a meal to stimulate the palate. Sardines are served as an appetiser and are considered a delicacy. Considerable profit is made from them.

There was an island [Caprera] off the coast of Sardinia where we saw a white-walled residence which is the home of the Italian advocate of people's rights [Giuseppe] Garibaldi. Garibaldi rose to prominence during the upheavals of Italian unification, and his heroic deeds made him a celebrity. After a constitutional government was set up to bring about unified rule, he continued to advocate the establishment of a republic. He had supported the movement for people's rights in Europe and had taken upon himself the task of dethroning kings and emperors and removing the power of the Church. During the time of the American Civil War, Garibaldi had said, 'The cause of the North is just.' Later, when France was defeated by Prussia and a republican government was installed, Garibaldi went to Lyons and gathered a group of Frenchmen to fight furiously [against the Prussians]. He is still in good health and lives here, swimming and fishing and enjoying the scenery. He also admires the landscape and people of Switzerland and sometimes stays there.

July 22nd. Sky again clear, with little wind.
We reached the port of Naples and dropped anchor at four o'clock in the morning. We stayed in this city for two days, but did not see it in its normal state because it was raining on the day we arrived, and the next day there was a festival so the streets were crowded. When we dropped anchor, boatloads of Neapolitans swarmed about us like ants, competing greedily for the fare to take us ashore. The price was one lira each. Once we had landed, we found the quay milling with poor, grimy-faced children as well as adults, all in dirty clothing. They buzzed around us like flies, demanding coins. The roads on which we passed over in the city were paved with large stone flags, but the streets were narrow and there was no separation between the part used by vehicles and that used by pedestrians. Rubbish was strewn everywhere. It gave us the impression that the city was in decline and had seen better days. This was the last port in Europe where we could go ashore, so all passengers wrote letters and posted them here.

Today the weather was fine. The summit of the volcano called Mt. Vesuvius was emitting a column of smoke, which looked like a cloud rising straight up into the sky. No matter how long we gazed at this harbour, we could not get enough of the view. At nine o'clock we went back on board. The Neapolitans had set out displays of coral ornaments, walking sticks made from grapevine wood, paintings and buttons, and were making a great commotion trying to sell these to the passengers.

At twelve o'clock we weighed anchor and at one o'clock we rounded the headland called [Punta] Campanella, which lies at the southern end of the Bay of Naples. The hills of the headland were of purplish-red rock, extending right down to the sea. There were scattered patches of green trees, like bristles on a hog's back. A little distance from the cape lay an island called Capri. It had steep cliffs, with some flat land above. We never tired of leaning on the ship's railing and looking at the view. After we had rounded the cape, we saw the mountains of southern Italy curving away to the south and obscured by cloud in the distance. However, as the ship sailed on we lost sight of the distant mountains, and sky and sea became one.

At midnight sky and sea were dark, with only the Milky Way shining brightly, but we could just discern a range of mountains to the south-west. Suddenly, fire shot up from one of the summits like flames out of a fanned stove, creating a glow rivalling that of a setting sun before subsiding abruptly. A few minutes later the flames shot up again. These were eruptions of Mt. Etna, a volcano on the island of Sicily. In Japan there are many volcanoes, but even though we had seen smoke rising from Asama, Aso, Unzen and Sakurajima, we had never seen flames as spectacular as these. We had imagined that all the world's volcanoes would be similar to those of Japan and had no idea there could be a volcano that constantly belched forth this terrifying fire. At times the eruptions were so colossal that they are unnerving even in recollection. The people of Europe admire the scenery of Mt. Vesuvius and Mt. Etna, just as we Japanese marvel at Mt. Fuji and Mt. Tsukuba.

July 23rd. Sky clear, sea calm.
At three in the morning we sailed along the strait between Sicily and the Italian mainland and hove to for a while in the Bay of Messina, where both sea and mountains were shrouded in darkness. Only the gas-lamps everywhere, shining like twinkling stars, enabled us to see that the city was a large one.

July 24th. Pleasantly fine, with a cool wind.
Passing the islands of Greece in the distance, we sailed past the Turkish island of Candia [Crete]. Seeing mountains or islands on a voyage is like meeting old acquaintances on the road: one cannot help greeting them warmly and with enthusiasm. As we progressed towards the east, leaving Cape Lithinon [on the southern coast of Crete] behind, the sun set. This was our last sight of European land.

July 25th. Fine.
We sailed across the Mediterranean and saw nothing of note the whole day.

July 26th. Fine.
At five in the morning we found ourselves off the coast of the part of Africa called Egypt. We passed in front of the lighthouse of Alexandria and at nine o'clock arrived at Port Said, where we dropped anchor. At four o'clock we weighed anchor and moved forward into the canal. We sailed another twenty nautical miles and dropped anchor in the middle of the canal.

   This morning we had passed along the northern coast of the continent of Africa and the plains of Egypt. From the sea not a single mountain was visible, only vast undulating plains. The city of Alexandria lies on the coast, on the western bank of Lake Maryut, which is surrounded by the deserts of the interior. It is the second-largest city in the country and an important port in trade between Egypt and Europe. Towards the end of 1850 a British company made a contract with the king of Egypt to build a railway [from Alexandria] to the docks at Suez by way of Cairo. Consequently, Alexandria became a port of call for passenger ships and merchant vessels plying the Mediterranean and the Red Sea. From then on, the city's prosperity increased year by year. Later, Egypt and France agreed that a canal should be built across the Isthmus of Suez, and both the railway and the canal prospered.

   Port Said, to the east of Alexandria, is also situated in Egypt, on the north-east shore of Lake Menzala. Beside the quays are the residences of foreigners, built in the European style but with wide, overhanging eaves added for the sake of coolness. These houses are not more than three storeys high. (All European houses in the tropical regions to the south are exactly the same.) The British and French also have consulates here. Broad avenues have been constructed in the city. The white sand which is everywhere becomes scorching under the hot sun, burning one's feet and making it impossible to walk for any length of time. Natives with donkeys urge people to ride. In the districts where the Europeans live, gardens have been cultivated beside the roads. Swampy areas have been filled in and trees and shrubs planted, so the air is clear and cool. It is very pleasant to stroll there. Fertile soil must have been brought from elsewhere by ship and laid on top of the sand. Because of the warmth, flowers and plants grow with great luxuriance. Vines and ivies are planted even in front of shops, climbing up buildings as far as the eaves and providing a refreshing coolness. The shops on two or three streets were scenes of great hustle and bustle, and their stock lacked nothing in the way of clothing and crockery. Coffee and tobacco are the leading local products here, and there is a variety of luscious fruits and vegetables.

Today we rode on donkeys in the city. Despite the saddles not being properly secured and the stirrups being of different lengths, we ventured out onto the sands on these animals. This was one of the most memorable experiences of our journey. The natives are copper-coloured and their black beards are long and curly. The way they speak is vehement, as if they are shouting angrily. Some of them understand English and French in a rough-and-ready sort of way. When we passed along streets on which the natives live, we found them to be poor and narrow. Some of the people lived in dwellings with roofs and walls made of woven rushes. There were also ramshackle structures roofed with wooden planks which were old and half-rotten. The men wear unlined jackets with tight-fitting sleeves over loose trousers; the women cover their faces with black veils and only their eyes are visible.

Finally, we were taken to a coffee-house whose interior was fairly pleasant. Here wine, beer, soda-water and lemonade were served. The prices were extremely high. The people were most hospitable towards guests, but their voices were loud and shrill, and when one of them said something one feared that he was about to use violence. In front of this coffee-house were three or four buildings which, we were told, were brothels. Inside were beds and tables, and long lace curtains. The women in these establishments were black or copper-coloured and sat behind the lace curtains. They wore gold rings and bracelets, and pure white cotton gowns with floral patterns printed in red. They also wore trousers and were not veiled. Some prostitutes belonging to an even lower class were outside, sleeping on the ground. Since Egypt is a hot, dry country, people do not mind sleeping like this. In houses of the common people earthen beds are customary.

At one o'clock, when we returned to the dock to board the ship, native boats swarmed about us, competing for passengers. The din was almost unbearable. On the ship fezzes of red felt, tobacco, pipes and pictures were laid out for sale. British and French currencies are accepted in this port, as well as Egyptian currency.

At four o'clock we weighed anchor and entered the Suez Canal. The speed at which ships may move in the canal is restricted, so we advanced slowly, at about five miles an hour. The entrance to the canal is in Lake Menzala. On the left bank there is an endless sweep of sand, and on the right are mounds of sand accumulated from the digging of the canal. These form a long narrow bank along which run telegraph poles. Beyond this causeway is an endless expanse of lake, whose far shore is not visible. At times all we could see showing above the water was the causeway. This section of the canal measures more than a hundred metres in width. Today we met a British mail-boat coming up the canal, and there was ample room for the two vessels to pass. After leaving Lake Menzala we anchored for the night. Travel by night is not permitted in the canal.

# CHAPTER 95

# The Voyage Through the Red Sea

July 27th, 1873. Beautifully clear; not a cloud in sight.

At half past four in the morning we weighed anchor and set sail. We passed through three [four] lakes: Lake Menzala, [Lake Ballah], Lake Timsah, and the Bitter Lakes. At half past four in the afternoon we reached the port of Suez, where we dropped anchor for a while. We had covered eighty miles. At eight o'clock we left the harbour and put out into the Gulf of Suez.

It is only four years since it became possible to travel by ship from Port Said to Suez through the Isthmus of Suez. For this we must thank the French engineer [Ferdinand] de Lesseps. The construction of a great canal through this neck of land a hundred miles wide was the fruit of long years of dedication on his part. It was an immense undertaking. This hundred-mile stretch of land blocked communications between the Mediterranean Sea and the Red Sea and hindered trade among the continents of Europe, Asia and Africa. For thousands of years people had either to brave the stormy seas off the Cape of Good Hope or cross the red desert and dusty yellow wastes of Egypt on foot. The plan to make communications more convenient by removing this obstacle severely tested human knowledge and endurance.

De Lesseps had previously been the French consul-general in Egypt, so he was already familiar with the country's topography. He had told Ismail, the khedive, that nothing would make Egypt richer and more powerful than the construction of a canal across the Isthmus of Suez. It would be a magnificent endeavour, he said, whose benefits would not be confined to one country, but which would be of boundless value to the whole world. The khedive was greatly impressed by his earnestness and finally agreed to the project.

De Lesseps maintained the necessity for the canal in the face of immense opposition. He continued to express his conviction that it would succeed, and his courage was admirable indeed. When he received word that opinion in the French Assembly was favourable, his resolve hardened and he decided to proceed with the construction. Egypt became the principal supporter of the project, and substantial aid was received from France, with some contributions made by other countries. The project was finally begun, and the clouds should have parted and welcome light shone through, but more problems arose during the actual excavation. Even after several years of digging, completion of the canal was nowhere in sight, and loud criticism of the inefficiency of the work was heard in every country. Accusations of the failure to complete the canal were as thick as a hedge-hog's spines. However, construction proceeded slowly regardless, and at one time as many as 20,000 labourers were employed in digging and removing sand and soil. Every task was carried out in the most laborious and time-consuming way because Egypt was an undeveloped country and there was not enough machinery. Moreover, the whole region was one vast stretch of red earth and sandy, sun-scorched desert. The Egyptians were a backward people, ignorant and unaccustomed to engineering work. Complaints by the workers about the harsh conditions increased as the sun grew hotter. Criticism and censure were as numerous as grains of sand. De Lesseps was attacked on all sides. Yet day after day he persevered.

At first the labourers removed the mud and sand by hand; their hands and feet became callused and they were exhausted. On top of this, disease spread among them. As the number of dead rose, de Lesseps tried to complete the project quickly. By day he supervised the work; by night he thought long and hard, assailed by all manner of worries. He ordered machinery from countries in Europe. On land he devised steam-driven machinery to carry off sand and mud; in the water he used floating dredgers to remove mud from the bottom. Thus, the work advanced one step at a time. Because years had elapsed since the project had begun, and the enormous investment was nearly exhausted, de Lesseps had to seek new funds, but no end was in sight and criticism in many countries grew ever stronger. The furore continued unabated and on one occasion the grand undertaking was almost halted. De Lesseps rejected all criticisms, raised the funds to cover the immediate shortfall, and bore almost insurmountable difficulties in digging and dredging amid the continually encroaching sand. Finally, to counter the slanders and misrepresentations he requested each country to send some reliable people to investigate the work-site, and each country duly did so. By this time the canal was more than half-finished. Subsequently, the unjust clamour subsided and eventually more funds were collected. After fifteen years of hard work since the construction project was first proposed to the khedive of Egypt, the canal was opened in 1870.

The overall length of the canal measures one hundred miles. It passes through four lakes, and the combined length of the stretches between the lakes is forty miles. It is seventy-two feet deep. For the first twenty miles the canal is a hundred metres wide, and for the next twenty miles it is sixty metres wide. It then enters a lake. The bottom of the lake was dredged and the banks raised to enable large ships to pass. There was no time to line the banks of the canal with either wood or stone, with the result that whenever a ship moves through the canal, the waves of its wash run along the banks. The water subsides when the ship has passed, but each time sand from the banks is washed down and settles on the bottom, so the task of dredging cannot cease for a single day. Because of this, maintenance expenses are said to be enormous.

The twenty-mile stretch from Port Said constitutes the widest part of the canal, and it was on this that we travelled yesterday evening. To the right lay an endless expanse of water which merged with the sky. To the left was a vast plain of sand stretching to the horizon. As one looked across the sweep of shifting sand, one's impression was that the lake water was retreating and exposing the sand. On this evening the stars were brilliant. No hills were to be seen in any direction. We were in the midst of dry land, but felt as though we were aboard a ship on the high seas. In the sky above the expanse of sand, streams of fire appeared, several times flowing a few hundred feet before fading away. This was the so-called heavenly fire [perhaps St. Elmo's fire] which is seen in south-west Japan.

This morning we weighed anchor and entered Lake Ballah. At the head of the lake by the shore were three or four wooden houses with thatched roofs. After this the earthen banks of the lake became too high for us to see what lay beyond them.

At nine o'clock we entered Lake Timsah, where we saw two or three half-naked natives walking beside the canal. On the west bank of the canal were hills of sand as white as snow; on the other side was a station on the railway line to Suez. At the top of the sloping sand-dunes stood two or three large houses with dazzling white walls, encircled by poplar trees. The whiteness of the sand made the trees seem all the greener. On the east bank there was a red wasteland, with sparse vegetation on which natives were grazing their camels. The desert, scorched by the blazing sun, was blinding to the eyes. The camels ambled along serenely with their necks stretched out. These animals are one of the wonders of the desert.

At noon we entered the [Great] Bitter Lake. Its water has a bitter taste and causes anyone who drinks it to vomit immediately. After another ten miles we had passed through the entire length of the canal and entered Suez, the port located at the northern end of the Red Sea.

Suez has white-walled houses both high and low, and some tall towers. Wisps of smoke curled over the city, and its bustling air gave it an impression of prosperity out of proportion to the size of its population. Yellow dust floated in the air, and even the light of the setting sun looked yellow. We were told that Cairo lay on the other side of this stretch of desert. The distance from Suez to Cairo is about a hundred miles.

The strait leading from Suez to the Red Sea proper is called the Gulf of Suez. From here to Aden is the hottest part of the sea route to the Indian Ocean.

July 28th. Again pleasantly clear and cloudless.
A thick mist over the water obstructed the view. The wind at our backs was pleasant. On the eastern bank was Arabia. A peninsula juts out between the Gulf of Suez and the Gulf of Aqaba, and along its spine rises a single mountain range, which was not visible through the distant haze.

Some say that the Red Sea was so named from ancient times for the beautiful coral found on the sea-bed. The water is very clear, which makes it easy to gather the coral. There are others who say that it took its name from the many rocky red peaks along its shores. In the morning we passed to the east of the island of Shadwan. There were three islands here of different sizes, all of dry red rock. In the evening we bade farewell to the dark, indistinct mountains of Egypt.

July 29th. Fine; thin mist.
Since leaving Suez the heat had increased each day, and it was usually at its most intense until about the middle of the night. By morning it was four or five degrees cooler, and because of this we were able to sleep soundly. A gentle breeze was also blowing, so in the daytime we could enjoy the cool air on deck, although the blazing sun was blinding.

July 30th. Fine; mist thickening.
Today was the hottest day of the whole voyage. Still, when a wind arose, it felt pleasant on the skin. Since morning the temperature had not fallen below 90°. The temperature in the cabins is said to have reached 100°. From now on the sun was to the north.

July 31st. Fine; still misty on the surface of the sea.
Today the wind died down and the sea was like oil. Fine sand from the desert covered the surface of the water, and this made the sea yellow. (After we entered the Red Sea, not a day passed without our seeing this

floating sand, but it was most evident on this day.) In the evening the wind and waves rose. We wondered whether a storm was approaching, but in the end there was no rain. The heat was stifling.

At nine o'clock we passed the lighthouse on [the British coaling station of] Perim Island. This small island belongs to Abyssinia in Africa. On the opposite bank was Cape Mandeb in the south-west of Arabia. This neck of the Red Sea is a strait less than three miles wide, with winding mountains on both banks. The British have leased the island from Abyssinia for ninety-nine years, and they maintain the lighthouse and have built a fort there. Every fifteen days the garrison is replaced from Aden. The heat here is the most extreme in the world, and there is neither vegetation nor potable water. Because this narrow strait lies on the sea-route to India, the British have fortified it and garrisoned soldiers here. They have spared no expense to command the strait, where ships of all nations pass under their guns. The British have made India and Australia their treasure-houses and have taken such measures as these in order to protect them. Without their spirited determination they could not wield such power. The rise and fall of nations depend on the spiritual strength of their people. Technology and wealth are of secondary importance.

# CHAPTER 96

# The Voyage Through the Arabian Sea

August 1st, 1873. Fine.

At half past six we reached the port of Aden, in Arabia, and dropped anchor. We ventured ashore to look around. After visiting the fort, we went into the town to see the reservoirs, then returned to the ship. We spent the night on board.

The town of Aden lies in a valley on the other side of the hills. The people are copper-skinned, at times almost black, and resemble Europeans in physical appearance. They speak Arabic, and some understand English. Their high-pitched speech grates on the ear. For the most part they go about naked to the waist, with a long piece of white cotton cloth wrapped around their lower body like a petticoat. Over this is worn a narrow-sleeved garment fastened with buttons. Such people belong to the upper classes; the poor wear no more than the length of white cloth around the waist. Their hair is frequently unkempt; some colour it with yellow earth or dye it. The usual head-covering is a white cloth tied around the head. Some wear amber necklaces on their chests. The women dress in similar fashion. Their bodily decorations are their only attractive feature; many wear a gold ring inserted in a hole pierced in the right nostril. When we saw native women at work, carrying heavy loads along the roads, they, too, were wearing nose-rings. This, we were told, is the custom in India as well. They have black, straight hair, which is coarse in texture and is worn tied up behind. When the mail-boat arrives, people living along the shore come out in their boats and compete to ferry passengers ashore. Children come in twos or threes in little wooden boats; they ask the ship's passengers to throw silver coins into the sea, then dive to the bottom to retrieve them. They do not miss one coin in ten. As long as the boat is anchored there they are in the water, begging the passengers to throw more coins. They look like frogs in a pond. When the passengers urge them to dive under the ship, from one side to the other, they happily comply, then ask for money. Their agility in the water is astonishing.

Today we disembarked and rested at an hotel on shore. It was far from elegant. We were offered fruit and vegetables, but they were not of good quality. Poor people swarmed around us, peddling goods and begging for coins. It was a disagreeable scene. They had ostrich feathers for sale, but were asking several times what they were worth.

The houses here have wooden doors and do not look clean inside. The large two- and three-storeyed white-walled buildings which occupy a sizeable section are the residences of the Europeans. The roads intersect in a grid-like pattern, and as the land is flat vehicles can move easily. There was nothing worth seeing in the town. Here and there were tumbledown shelters made of woven palm leaves, but the town still retains a European flavour. The poorer parts consist of clusters of wretched hovels resembling dove-cotes.

In the evening, when the sun was setting, we saw natives on the small boats in the harbour at their evening prayers. This is a Moslem ritual. They first prayed standing up, then knelt and prayed. The way they knelt when saying their prayers resembled the way we pray in our own country.

August 2nd. Cloudy.
At half past five in the morning we weighed anchor and put out into the Persian Gulf. Today we did not see a single mountain.

August 3rd. Fine; weak sunshine.
The wind was blowing across the sea from the south-west and the ship rolled violently.

August 4th. Weak sunshine.
We passed to the north of the island of Socotra, which sheltered the ship from the wind somewhat. Socotra is a large island in the Arabian sea, but there was a haze so we could not see the mountains. In the afternoon the wind was the strongest we had encountered on the voyage.

August 6th. Cloudy; wind and waves relatively calm.
On the surface of the sea in this area we saw some fish about seven or eight inches long. They had green backs and white bellies, and schools of ten or more would leap up in unison between the waves and fly with fins outstretched, covering sixty or eighty yards before falling back into the water. They resembled flights of plovers.

August 7th. Wind abating; those who have been suffering from seasickness left their bunks.

Although the weather was fine the boat pitched and rolled; there was little pleasure in looking out. Today, less than six hundred miles directly north of us, lay Bombay, the most important port on the west coast of India.

CHAPTER 97

# A Record of the Island of Ceylon

August 9th, 1873. Fine.

At three o'clock in the afternoon our ship reached the port of Point de Galle, in Ceylon, and dropped anchor. We immediately disembarked and took rooms at the Hotel Oriental. From there we went in carriages to see the Buddhist Atapattu Vihara Temple and the Bonavista Temple in the China Gardens. On our way back we drove around the town's outlying districts. In the evening we went for a stroll along the shore in the bright moonlight.

The harbour opens directly onto a vast expanse of ocean stretching all the way to the South Pole without a single island in between. The mouth of the bay is very wide, and even on windless days waves from the south sweep across the harbour and cause even the biggest ships to roll continuously. The surface of the sea is constantly white with foam, and the ceaseless booming of surf is heard. It is a magnificent scene. There are dense growths of coconut and other wild palms all over the promontory, and some of the trees are very tall. Their luxuriant leaves are green throughout the year. Houses are scattered among the trees, and we spied the occasional spire or tower above the treetops. This is the port of Galle.

This city lies in the tropics, so the trees are lush and their leaves a deep green, competing in luxuriance under the hot sun all year round. We had not seen such scenery anywhere in Europe, Africa or in the red deserts and barren hills of Arabia. In tropical countries the mountains are green and the waters blue; plants flourish, the earth is fertile and the air is pure. Seeing such natural beauty after Europe makes one feel that this is, indeed, a paradise for human beings.

When the ship dropped anchor, swarms of natives approached us in small boats. The people here hollow out large logs to use as boats. These canoes may look dangerous, but in fact they are extremely stable. Each canoe is paddled by two people. Primitive people living in tropical regions with palm-trees fashion such boats by hand, and they are simple

501

to use. The canoes carried us ashore, where we disembarked onto a jetty, with an awning of fresh palm leaves to provide shade from the evening sun. Perhaps because this was the time of the Buddhist festival of the dead, we saw that a structure resembling an altar for 'hungry ghosts' had been set up on the shore among the palm-trees. Since leaving Europe we had passed through Moslem countries, and here in Ceylon we observed several native customs and practices. We were struck again and again by how curious a place the world is.

Most of the Europeans in the city live in imposing mansions inside the fort. Here, too, are found the consulates of the various nations, the municipal offices, the courts, the Oriental Bank, the hotel and the exchange. There is also a handsome Anglican church, built in the Scottish style. The roads are not paved but are well maintained. The natives live in the area outside the fort, and some of the dwellings there are also very large. Here and there are markets selling vegetables, fruit and coconuts. There are theatres and a brothel quarter. There is also a Moslem mosque, but we saw no Buddhist temples even though more than half the people are Buddhists.

The China Gardens lie more than two miles north of the city. Beside the road, under the shade of palm-trees, are native villages. Some houses had bananas for sale hanging from the eaves; others were surrounded by low, roughly woven fences. Potatoes and bananas were cultivated in plots alongside the houses. The rice in the paddy-fields was ready for harvesting. Here and there were thick groves of palms, the most numerous being coconut- and hemp-palms from nine to twelve feet high, with spreading leaves. Shrubs and tall trees grow in profusion, and even the grass is lush. One's impression was of a tangled jungle of trees and plants.

We climbed three or four hundred yards to the top of a hill, where there was a Buddhist temple called Atapattu Vihara. This complex consisted of three or four small temples enclosed by a wall. Among them was a small temple with a tiled roof whose architecture showed great refinement. When the caretaker unlocked the door to show us the interior, we saw a statue of the seated Buddha with features carved in exactly the same style as similar figures in Japan. Seeing this, we realised that Buddhist carving has its own history. In front of the figure were statues of two disciples of the Buddha in white stone. Before this small temple was a round tower built in a European style. We were told that jewels, gold and silver were kept inside. Perhaps these were the 'bones of the Buddha'. Outside the compound were the monks' quarters. All the monks shaved their eyebrows, as well as their faces and heads, and wore lengths of yellow cotton cloth draped from the right shoulder down to the left armpit, where a knot was tied.

The Bonavista Temple was on a hilltop a little to the north. We climbed for about two hundred yards before coming to some stone steps. After going up a dozen or so flights, we reached the monastery. Here we found a temple roofed with tiles. Within it was an enormous statue of a reclining Buddha. This figure was more than twenty feet in length, and its face was the same as that of the figure in the previous temple. Its right shoulder was bare and its cheek was resting on its bent arm. The legs were stretched straight out.

Behind this temple was another, and beside that a bone of the Buddha (or, according to some, a fingernail) is said to be buried. The burial-place has been paved with stone, a terrace built on top, and a pipal tree planted there. Neither of these temples was completely dilapidated, but they were neglected and overgrown. The hilltop itself was covered with thick vegetation, and the road was not well maintained. One regrettable aspect of Buddhism is its neglect of its holy sites, whose significance to Buddhists is comparable to the significance of Jerusalem to Christians. On our visit here we were shown around by a priest who called the Japanese '*danna*' and the temple a '*garan*'. Both words are Sanskrit, and we were impressed by the fact that they had survived uncorrupted. Ceylon has many holy places associated with the Buddha as he underwent ascetic practices. The natives all follow the Buddhist religion and are content with little. How much less concerned with worldly things are the lives of the priests! Even the sacred places of the founder of the faith are overgrown and neglected. Buddhism stands aloof from the world, but such neglect must nevertheless be an indication of the state of the religion. In this region we saw only these two Buddhist temples, and within the city itself we saw no priests or nuns. Westerners always say that the ancient teachings of India were transmitted to Japan and China but are not handed down in the land of their origin, adding that many of the priests are illiterate. When we saw the state of affairs here, this seemed close to the truth.

August 10th. Fine; the morning temperature fell to 70°.
At ten o'clock in the morning we went by carriage to the Cinnamon Gardens, a famous arboretum of cinnamon trees somewhat more than three miles north of Galle.

When we reached the gardens we found an area of white sand full of cinnamon trees, tangled and untended, with a pavilion among them.

Behind was an irrigation channel, and beyond that we saw paddy-fields, open land, woods and hills. The trees on the hills were unkempt, and the scenery was not especially remarkable. The irrigation channel was half filled with mud, so the water flowed sluggishly. As crocodiles lived in the irrigation channel, swimming was of course forbidden.

The natives are content with little. They pick and eat bananas and coconuts, which are available in abundance all year round. Rice, too, is always ready for harvesting. They cook it in earthenware pots, pour a sauce over it and eat it by scooping it up with their fingers. This is the origin of the Western dish 'curry and rice'. Because life is so easy, people are indolent.

The scenery overall consisted of wooded hills and flourishing vegetation. The sight of rice growing abundantly in paddy-fields surrounded by dikes and irrigation ditches made us feel we had returned to Japan.

August 11th. Torrential rain in the morning cooled the air; temperature 80°. At four o'clock in the afternoon we went aboard the ship. Today 3,600 chests of opium were being transferred from the Calcutta mail-boat onto our vessel, and this prevented our departure that evening. We remained in the harbour. During the night there was a sudden downpour, accompanied by thunder and lightning.

Ceylon was originally known as Kandy. It has no connection with India and has been an independent country since ancient times. The houses are single-storeyed, and have neither chimneys nor flooring. Because the earth is always dry, people sleep on the ground. They build their houses beneath palm trees. They pick bananas and chew betel. They do not eat with chopsticks but use their fingers to scoop up rice mixed with chicken or fish sauce. Those who are well-off own houses, clothing and household utensils, but the habits of most are those of a completely primitive people. Nonetheless, they are usually good-natured and courteous in manner and are never violent. They are simply without a spirit of diligence and consequently lack any accomplishment in the useful industrial arts. The natives come to sell their goods in front of the hotel. They urge visitors to buy and try to make them offer a price. If one asks the price, it will leap to more than ten times what was mentioned before. Even if they had refused to reduce the price even by 10 per cent the previous day, when the visitor's departure is at hand they will reduce it by 20 per cent. They are not all habitual beggars, but seeing how rich visitors are the village children ask for money.

Most of the people are Buddhists. They speak the language of this area, and they also understand English. (When this was a Dutch colony they learnt Dutch, but it is no longer used.) There is another type of people called Tamils, who migrated from the Indian continent. Physically they resemble Europeans. These people are vigorous and energetic, work hard at their occupations and are comparatively intelligent. A third people, called Moors, are Mohammedans. They have shaved heads and wear fezzes. These people are energetic and industrious, and many of them are engaged in commerce. Deep in the mountains of the interior are a people called the Vedda, who choose to live hidden away. They build shelters in trees in the depths of the forest and gather fruit and hunt animals for food. These are the wildest and most primitive of the inhabitants.

# CHAPTER 98

# The Voyage Through the Bay of Bengal

August 12th, 1873. Fine.

At half past six in the morning we weighed anchor and left the harbour of Galle to sail along the southern coast of Ceylon.

This southern part is the most mountainous region of the island. From the ship we could see a mass of mountains with ridges coiling and writhing before sweeping down to the plains. The trees were a deep green. The grass, still wet with the rain which had fallen during the night, was a carpet of emerald. The mists of kingfisher blue around the mountain-tops seemed about to turn to rain; the air was crystal clear. Topographically, the whole of Ceylon consists of long chains of mountains interspersed with plains and gently sloping foothills. The entire island is made up of this kind of scenery. Nowhere is there landscape like this in the world, we were told. In every country mountains rise up and water flows down, but the colours and features of the landscape are different. The more we saw of the fantastic variations of Creation, the more astonished we were.

August 14th. Cloudy.

Today we were sailing across the middle of the Bay of Bengal. On the north coast of this bay lies Calcutta, one of India's most important ports.

The Japanese, having been inspired by Westerners to embark on voyages, now depart for Europe in droves, entirely ignoring India and the southern seas. They are completely unaware that if people work hard at trade and develop their industrial arts, an enormous amount of profit lies hidden halfway between Japan and Europe. Rosewood and ebony come from Siam and Sumatra, and ivory and rattan from Annam; thus, an abundance of natural products is available in nearby countries. Henceforth, the number of people travelling westwards to Singapore, Calcutta and Bombay will increase each year, and they will record the geography and the products of these regions. When books like this record are circulated, people will realise for the first time where Japan's riches and strength really lie. For this reason, we await someone to fire the gun to start the race.

August 15th. Fine.

In the afternoon we came within sight of the coast of Sumatra and entered the Gulf of Malacca.

Sumatra is one of the largest islands in the southern seas. Its northern tip lies at the eastern edge of the Bay of Bengal, and from there the island stretches diagonally to the south-east. At the north-western tip are two islands, one called Weh and the other Beras. They lie side-by-side, like an extension of the main island. Our ship passed between these islands and the Nicobar Islands, lying to the north. These islands, which are actually mountains rising out of the sea, resemble the rocky islands of Japan, with gnarled trees growing over their sides. The topography of the main island is a mixture of grass-covered hills and forested, craggy peaks. They are high but not steep. It is evident at first sight that this is a fertile country.

The city of Aceh lies three miles inland from the northern coast of the headland, on a low-lying section between areas of mountains. In the middle is a range of low, wooded hills running along the coast and embracing a broad plain. Opposite, a single peak rises abruptly called 'Gold Mountain' [Gunung Geureudong]. In shape it closely resembles Mt. Fuji, and its name is derived from the many seams of gold found in it. Aceh is the royal capital of an independent Sumatra. Trade at this port is said to have prospered greatly over the last few years.

The island of Sumatra straddles the equator diagonally. Its inhabitants are a mixture of indigenous races and Malays. Malay is the national language, and the people are followers of the Islamic faith. They have few works of literature since the country's history has been handed down orally instead of being written down. Not even the laws are written. A single sultan (or king) rules one-third of the island in its north-east sector. Aceh is his capital.

The land is fertile and has abundant water. Along the south-eastern coast are many plains and wide rivers whose water is drawn off into irrigation channels to produce plentiful grain harvests. The islanders live on fruit and on such crops as sago and yams. The fruits are unsurpassed in variety and flavour. The amount of coffee produced is second only to that of Ceylon. Horses, oxen and sheep are numerous, and there is an animal called a 'buffalo', which lives in the wild but can be domesticated and used in place of oxen and sheep. The island is also rich in mineral resources. Pure gold is mined on Gold Mountain, as well as copper, iron and tin. These are the country's main products. Coal and sulphur are also mined, and the highland areas contain a number of medicinal springs.

This country has natural wealth in abundance, but the people lack energy and initiative. Both crafts and trade are conducted in the old way and so no progress is made. There is one shameful custom: that of buying wives. When a man becomes bored with his wife, he sells her and takes another.

Holland has already made inroads into Sumatra from Java. For many years it has wished to seize the whole island, and in the spring of this year hostilities broke out with Aceh. When news of this reached Holland, a debate was held in the legislature and the decision was made to dispatch an army from Java and a fleet from the home country in order to attack the island and subdue it. The Dutch are now making their preparations. One of the passengers on our ship was General Vanswieten, who had been sent from Holland and was accompanied by his son and two or three officials. They travelled with us as far as Singapore. Two fleets – thirty-seven ships in all, carrying 10,000 soldiers – had been sent from Holland and Java. The soldiers from the home country to Aceh numbered 4,500. At Aceh we saw a warship blockading the harbour. Two warships had already been dispatched from Europe before our ship had left, but one had struck a reef in the Red Sea and the other had had its rudder damaged in a storm in the Arabian Sea. The soldiers had disembarked at Aden, so our ship, the *Ava*, had hurried there to pick them up and take them as far as Singapore. However, another mail-boat reached Aden before us, so when we arrived there were no soldiers left. We saw the ship which ran aground on the reef on our left when we were sailing through the Red Sea.

The attack on Aceh proved very costly for Holland. It is difficult to understand the precise origins of the confrontation, but we were told by General Vanswieten that when the Dutch went to complain to the people of Aceh about their acts of piracy, the Achinese fired on them. The Dutch then sent troops there. A London newspaper reported that, the previous May, according to a statement by a Sumatran mission which had been sent to Turkey to ask for assistance, Dutch warships had arrived at Aceh in February [1873] and demanded a positive response from the sultan on three points: first, the Achinese people were to submit to the flag of Holland; second, the slave trade must be abolished; third, the fort and all weapons must be surrendered. Because of the seriousness of the demands, the Sumatrans requested a month to deliberate. The Dutch mission insisted that they reply within twenty-four hours. Dutch soldiers then landed on the island and began to advance inland. They were fired on from the fort and thus war broke out. More troops were dispatched from Holland, but the Sumatrans fought fiercely and managed to split the Dutch force into two. Half the Dutch soldiers fled back to their ship while the other half panicked when their retreat was cut off. More than a hundred of them were captured alive and their weapons were seized. The government of Aceh then relayed the answer that it was impossible to agree to any of the three points. The Dutch warship requested the return of the captured soldiers and their weapons, and the Sumatrans replied that this would only happen if the Dutch agreed that the harbour fortifications would not be attacked and that friendly relations would be restored. The Dutch accepted these terms, but when written assurance was sought, they said it would be provided later as it could not be done at a moment's notice. When the prisoners and their weapons had been returned to the warship, the Dutch suddenly attacked the harbour fortifications again. The Sumatrans were furious and swore they would eat the flesh of the Dutchmen. They repelled the attack once more, and the Dutch warship lost the advantage and withdrew. Later, in June, a newspaper report stated that the Dutch fleet had attacked again, once again lost its advantage and withdrew after promising to pay an indemnity. Since all military matters are shrouded in secrecy and rumours and hearsay are rife, it is difficult to determine the precise facts.

Holland treats Java as its principal city overseas. If the Dutch had showed the slightest weakness in their response to the Achinese, people in the neighbouring colonies, who are always restive under the tyrannical Dutch, would all be encouraged and Dutch rule would probably collapse. This is why Holland decided to spare no expense and to send troops out to suppress the opposition by any means.

The strong feed on the flesh of the weak. Ever since the Europeans began to undertake long sea-voyages in search of trade, they have competed with one another to feed off the weak countries of the tropics and import their rich natural produce to their own countries. At first Spain, Portugal and Holland monopolised the profits of this trade, but as their treatment of the natives was arrogant and cruel, the latter constantly changed sides whenever it was to their advantage. As a result, the Europeans made gains, only to lose them again. The British, therefore, avoided this practice and made liberalness their guiding principle. They have attained the present size of their empire by educating the people and using conciliatory methods. Observing the European passengers on our ship, we were struck by the extreme affability of the British in their dealings with other races. The Spanish, Portuguese and Dutch are generally arrogant. This shows that the attitudes handed down from earlier times have become ingrained and persist to this day. One cannot imagine what sort of tyranny the natives of their colonies are forced to live under.

On boarding the mail-boat in Marseilles, we noticed that the passengers were all white-skinned and fair-haired. However, they were not like their countrymen in Europe. Their behaviour was coarse; their words were insulting; their laughter was raucous; they were over-familiar with women and flew into a rage over trivialities. Half of them were given to violent language. In their homeland this would be the behaviour of inferior people and would be regarded as shameful. Those among them who behaved in a half-decent manner, who in Europe would have been regarded as perfectly ordinary, gave the impression on board this ship of being models of gentlemanly conduct. Those who venture far from home to make a living at some risky business in the southern seas are probably among the more disreputable representatives of their countrymen. They have probably been driven out of their home towns or villages for acts of dishonesty and bad behaviour, or have been in prison and thus cannot return to society.

Many such people leave home with the intention of seeking their fortunes overseas. Those who seek wealth in the southern seas, therefore, are usually those who have been rejected by civilised societies. It would be a great mistake to assume they are civilised people because they have the same white skin and fair hair. They scramble to reach the colonies, where they despise and maltreat the natives. Even the most ignorant natives must find this unbearable. Spain and Portugal, in particular – because their people lack civilised and tolerant manners – produce many such villains. In their own country the Dutch are an industrious and orderly people, but in the southern seas they, too, behave with arrogance and brutality. Europeans boast of their civilisation and profess universal benevolence, but their deeds do not match their words. Japan does not have much experience of dealing with foreign countries and the Japanese are not yet familiar with the real state of affairs in Europe. They can only judge Europe's civilisation by what they see of Europeans who come to Japan. Thus, any Japanese who travels to the West should pay careful attention to his behaviour. If he is a gentleman, his conduct will be correct and amiable and will gain him the immediate respect of everyone he meets. Behaviour such as that described above is completely unacceptable.

August 16th. A fine, driving rain fell during the morning.

In the morning the sky was overcast to the north and clear to the south. The mountains of Sumatra rose and fell like a dragon's back, the peaks wreathed in white clouds like wisps of cotton wool. The prospect of this island from the sea was magnificent. In the afternoon the rain stopped, but drifting clouds hid the sun. Since sea-water evaporates quickly in the tropics, clouds form continually. Even on clear days, puffs of cloud are dotted across the sea and cap the mountains. The air is always humid. The climate is quite different from that of Europe and resembled Japan when May is giving way to June.

August 17th. Fine; wind still gentle.

At six o'clock we dropped anchor off the coast of Malacca. We left again at dawn, and before long we docked at Singapore.

   Today we set off early in the morning and sailed along the coast of Malacca. The Malacca Peninsula resembles neither Ceylon nor Sumatra. The coastal area has many plains, beyond which lie high mountains, all of them rounded in shape and thickly clad with trees. There were no precipitous or craggy peaks.

CHAPTER 99

# *The Voyage Through the China Sea*

August 18th, 1873. Light cloud; a gentle breeze.

At nine o'clock we reached Singapore. Because of a recent cholera epidemic we did not go ashore, and our ship was anchored at the harbour mouth.

The coastal region of the district of Malacca consists mostly of low hills with some scattered mountains. The people are Malays, descendants of migrants who came from Sumatra about the year 1200. They are followers of Islam, and in temperament and culture they are like the Sumatrans. Warlike and cruel by nature, they think nothing of killing. They are implacably vengeful and have no patience to bear wrongs. They have no fixed occupations, but often put out in boats to commit acts of piracy in nearby seas. In their arts and crafts they simply adhere to their customs and traditions and make no progress. In recent years they have started to engage more in trade. Foreigners who come here to trade find that once they have obtained their goodwill it is easy to establish friendly relations. But if anyone crosses them in the slightest way, they become enraged and will not forget the slight for a long time, and will invariably seek revenge. Because of this, all Europeans fear the people of the southern seas. They are as wary of them as of snakes or scorpions.

There is no overall government in the region. Chieftains called 'sultans' and 'rajahs' hold sway over the whole of the southern part of the peninsula, but their power is limited. The people are divided into several tribes, and each region is under the control of the chief of that tribe. Since each chief rules in accordance with his own prejudices, there is little co-operation in administration at the national level. Disputes turn bitter, and warfare is frequent. Moreover, the evils of religion are embraced, and many of the laws and regulations are intended to mislead and deceive the people. In general, their customs are perverse and far from civilised.

Singapore is the gateway for ships sailing between the Indian Ocean and the China Sea, and it is growing more prosperous each year. Its population has now reached 100,000. Of these most are Chinese: they number 58,000; Malays account for no more than 13,500. There are 12,700 Hindus, 6,500 'Asiatics' and only 6,000 Europeans (statistics for 1870). Singapore derives its wealth not from land but from its harbour. From there packet-boats depart westwards for India, eastwards for China and Luzon, and southwards for Java and Australia. It is a very important port for ships sailing in all directions.

At night, fires were lit in several places along the shore. Coal was being loaded onto ships, and the natives were chanting '*Ei-ya!*' as they worked. The chanting went on all night.

August 19th. Fine in the morning; temperature 85°; barometer 29 inches. At noon we weighed anchor and departed. We passed to the west of Bintan Island, which is governed by the Dutch.

August 21st. Fine.
This evening we stayed on board the ship, which was anchored at the mouth of the Saigon River.

August 22nd. Fine.
We sailed up the Saigon River to the city of Saigon. We slept on board. The Saigon River is second only to the Mekong. For thirty miles upstream there is nothing but swampland on either bank. These swamps are criss-crossed with waterways over a thousand feet wide, the same as the width of the river. No mountains or hills were to be seen in any direction, nor did we see any houses, although the sight of fishermen moving up and down in small boats suggested that there might be villages a few miles inside the swamps. Only when we had sailed thirty miles upriver did we see cultivated fields for the first time, and these were sunken paddies. The villages consisted of sparse settlements of a dozen or so houses. There were few trees and many rice-paddies. We reached the city of Saigon at one in the afternoon and dropped anchor.

Saigon is the capital of the province of Champa in Annam. Wide streets have been laid out, but they are not well maintained. There are trees growing in the streets, as well as grasses, so despite the streets being level it is not easy for vehicles to pass. The area where the foreigners live is beautifully maintained. It is surrounded by a stone wall, and the streets are paved with stone slabs. The houses are dazzlingly white three-storeyed buildings in the European style but with some Asian influence. The small dwellings on the river-banks are humble thatched huts, some of which are constructed entirely – roof, walls and doors – of interwoven palm leaves.

They were much more skilfully made than the houses we saw at Galle. The better houses have red tiled roofs; the method of tiling is the same as that used in Japan, which is more skilled than the European method. Most of the houses have earthen floors and very low roofs.

Along the riverside are dwellings jutting out over the water. Some people even live on boats. The small houses on land have gardens at front and rear, but they are neglected and untidy. Next to them are pens for ducks and pigs, and entire families dwell contentedly on ground churned up by the animals' hooves. The Chinese race will put up with dirt to an astonishing degree. When Westerners first saw Japan when they came to Nagasaki, they remarked that the Japanese had a desire for cleanliness which was positively morbid. But Nagasaki was not a city particularly clean in its habits, and thus the Japanese began to suspect that the West itself was not very clean. Indeed, they believe this even now. However, the Westerners were contrasting the Japanese with the Chinese when they said this. The love of cleanliness of the Japanese is in no way inferior to that of the Europeans.

The population of the whole city is 180,000. The Chinese are the most numerous, and they live together with the Malays, Siamese and Europeans. The people are of differing types. In their physique the natives resemble the Japanese, but they have smaller noses and flatter faces. Their hair is black and straight, and the men have sparse beards. Among the ordinary people both men and women chew betel leaves, and as a result their teeth are so black as to make one suspect they have applied *kane* or *o-haguro* [stain used for blackening teeth in Japan]. Among the lowest classes, the men and women dress alike, and it is difficult to distinguish between them. Their hair is combed and done up in a topknot, and they do not wear any headgear, except for a bamboo hat occasionally. Women of a slightly higher class plait their hair and arrange the braids in more elaborate coiffures. Their gowns have tight sleeves and collars, like those of Japanese raincoats. They are fastened, left over right, with three or four loops of cord on the left breast. These gowns reach to the feet. The skirt is split and swings to and fro. This is the men's attire. The women's gowns have wide sleeves which, like the split skirts, swing as they walk. On their heads they wear bamboo hats. There is not much nakedness, but many people go about barefoot. The Siamese have darker complexions and coarse skins. They have broad, flat noses, wide mouths with thick lips, and bright eyes. They are extremely robust. The Malays have shapely noses and bright eyes. Their lips are not thick. They are lean and have strong builds. They wrap lengths of cloth round their heads in place of hats. Both these races are brave, but they are quick to anger. Their voices become shrill, and they are hard to mollify. If they meet with even the slightest annoyance, they at once begin to grind their teeth in fury.

Many of those who make a living through trade in Saigon are Chinese. The sights worth seeing here are the temples. The buildings are not as lofty as European churches, but they have tiled roofs and courtyards paved with stone or tiles; some are decorated with carved dragons. There are also Roman Catholic (that is, Christian) churches. There are shipyards, hospitals and granaries, but these are not worth seeing. There is a botanical garden, which is large but not well-tended. Since this is the tropics, however, the trees are luxuriant and the flowers fragrant. The rare and exotic trees and shrubs found here are too many to enumerate. There are banyan trees with roots so large as to require ten people to encircle them with their arms; the leaves of the hemp-palm cast shade for ten paces all round; bamboo as thick as a man's thigh also grows here.

We drove about the area, coming eventually to the town of Sien Long, in the south. The Europeans call it Cholon. It is composed of several thousand households, but the mean, narrow streets hardly merit a glance. There is a temple called Sui-ch'eng Hall, dedicated to the Empress of Heaven; the God of War is enshrined on the left and the God of Wealth on the right. This structure was built by the Chinese and is a marvel of craftsmanship. The walls are of bricks, blue-black in colour and extremely hard. Even European bricks would probably have to yield pride of place to these. The roof is tiled in the same manner as in Japan. Ceramic dragons are mounted on the ridge-poles. The eaves are tiled, and the flat porcelain surfaces decorated with paintings.

At six o'clock we all returned to the hotel and had dinner. The food was so delicious and the service so good that we became nostalgic for Europe. We were served a fruit called 'mangosteen', which was excellent. It resembles a pomegranate with its dark brown rind. When the rind is cut open, one finds that the flesh of the sweet fruit is white. The five segments of the fruit fit together like the five petals of the plum blossom used as a Japanese family crest.

August 23rd. Cloudy.
At noon we weighed anchor. As we were sailing down the Saigon River there was a great downpour and the rain came down like ropes. Towards evening we sailed out into the China Sea.

August 24th. Cloudy; no wind.
We followed the coastline of the Gulf of Cochin. All along it, the mountains come down to the edge of the sea, and there are many harbours, large and small, as well as scattered islands.

August 26th. Cloudy.
At sea we saw nothing. We passed to the east of Hainan Island today, but caught no glimpse of it because of the fog. We had stayed close to the coasts of Malaya and Annam, rarely venturing into the open sea because we were near the equator and the intense heat can cause typhoons to spring up suddenly, and these sometimes destroy even large warships. We were told that these seas are very dangerous.

CHAPTER 100

# A Record of Hong Kong and Shanghai

August 27th, 1873. Fine.
At nine o'clock in the morning we berthed at Hong Kong. At ten we went ashore and took rooms at the Hotel de Hong Kong.

At daybreak we had found ourselves passing among a multitude of mountainous islands, large and small, scattered over the sea. The mountains were all covered in grass, but there were no trees. The shapes of the steep mountains on the mainland around Canton were very graceful. Among their folds were fallen rocks looking just like the brushed dots in a Chinese landscape painting. For the first time we could see where the Chinese style of painting had its origins.

China ceded Hong Kong to Britain in 1841. The British then built a harbour here, and the population has increased over the years to 126,051. Most of these are Chinese. The mountains here are all high and steep. There is no land fit for cultivation, and very few trees. There are no rivers, but a plentiful supply of clean water is piped to the city from reservoirs. Granite is quarried in the mountain valleys, and the buildings constructed by the British with this stone are beautifully white and clean. The British began building stone houses to rent to the Chinese some time ago because wooden houses so easily caught fire. As a result, the streets are clean even though most of the inhabitants of the city are Chinese. These buildings are three storeys high and have passageways along the front. They are European in style but with some Eastern influences. The shops in the streets have no glass in the windows and therefore do not look elegant. In each shop the owner displays a wide variety of goods, mostly lacquer and porcelain. The Chinese love the colour vermilion, and shelves, boxes, blinds and signs are all painted bright scarlet. We have previously said that when one enters a shop in Europe the glitter of gold and pearls catches the eye. When one enters a Chinese shop, it is the gleam of vermilion lacquer which one notices. The calligraphy of the characters on street signs, shop signs and posters shows great vigour.

517

The city maintains a public garden on a hillside overlooking a valley. It consists of several terraces, connected by flights of white stone steps. It has a magnificent display of rare trees and exotic plants. Opposite the park stands the governor's residence, an imposing granite mansion. There is also a barracks nearby housing the British garrison.

August 28th. Fine; temperature 91°.
In the evening we were invited to a dinner given by the Oriental Bank.

In former times Canton was the centre of China's trade with foreign merchants, with the result that even now those who engage in commerce with other countries are exclusively people from Canton and Fukien. Hong Kong's principal trade is in Chinese products exported through Canton. The population of Canton now exceeds 1,000,000, and it is the largest city in China after Peking, with many important merchants and businessmen. Earlier, the Chinese government often started quarrels with foreign countries, exacting money from businessmen to cover its military expenditure and generally obstructing trade. The big merchants therefore left Canton, with the result that now few wealthy families remain there. This caused a decline in Canton's trade, to the point where the profits are now monopolised by foreigners. Even the amount of raw silk exported by Canton is less than a quarter of that from Shanghai. Governments in the East do not simply ignore trade: they often actually impede it, thus bringing about a fall in their nations' fortunes.

August 29th. Fine; we weighed anchor at four o'clock in the afternoon; temperature 91°, falling to 81° at night.
In the morning we called on the governor, but he was out. At three o'clock we returned to the ship. The governor sent two boats to convey us to the ship. A guard of honour made up of soldiers from the garrison presented arms while a military band played. Several government officials and wealthy merchants came aboard to see us off, and we chatted pleasantly. As the time for departure approached they bade us farewell with great courtesy. After passing through the Hong Kong straits, we sailed along the coast of Huichou. The coast was lined with mountains, some of them most attractive.

August 30th. Fine; at noon latitude 22°35′ N, longitude 114°50′ E; distance sailed, 180 nautical miles.
Today we left behind Huichou, on the eastern border of Kwangtung province, and sailed along the coast of Fukien province. The coast was

indented with bays and inlets, and the mountain peaks were covered with grass without any trees. Trees are scarce in China, and timber is imported from Siam. During the day we passed the entrance to Amoy harbour. Amoy is an important port in southern Fukien and the principal port for vessels sailing between Taiwan and Manila (on Luzon Island).

August 31st. Light cloud.

Since the previous evening we had been sailing between Fukien province and the island of Taiwan. An examination of the sea-routes will show that Taiwan and Luzon are separated by a strait no wider than about 120 miles from north to south, and that Taiwan is separated from Fukien to the west and the Ryūkyū Islands to the north by no more than 120 or 150 miles in each case. The Ryūkyūs are scattered over the sea like stepping stones leading to the island of Yakujima, which is part of Satsuma in southern Kyūshū. It is therefore not difficult to follow these sea-routes. The benefits of maritime trade last a long time. In this age when coal is burnt and iron floats, going back and forth between Japan, China and Luzon is just like calling on neighbours. Yet we do not hear of coal from Taiwan being exported to Shanghai, or of indigo from Manila finding its way to Nagasaki. People talk of the benefits of commerce, but it does not occur to them to think of this fact. They look immediately to America and Europe, thousands of miles across the ocean. Indeed, 'The Way is near at hand, but they seek it far off.'

September 2nd. Fine.

In the morning we reached the mouth of the Yangtze. We sailed up the Huang-p'u River on a river lighter and at eleven o'clock reached Shanghai, where we took rooms at Astor House.

Where the Yangtze enters the sea, its mouth is so wide that one seems to be looking at the sea itself. The river churns up yellow mud so that the sea is also yellow, with silt up to some distance from the shore. Mud builds up on the river-bed and creates a bar stretching more than ten miles. Today we anchored in the southern channel, off the district of Pao-shan, at the point where the Huang-p'u River joins the Yangtze to drain into the sea. The great river is so immensely wide that it is indistinguishable from the sea.

Along some stretches of the Huang-p'u, embankments have been built to protect against flooding. The landscape resembles that along the Saigon River. Here and there we saw villages. We realised that the inhabitants of these clusters of houses lived partly by fishing and partly by farming: in the fields we saw thick stands of sugar-cane. On reaching Shanghai, we found that the areas beside the river were the foreign settlements, with well-kept streets and imposing houses. The masts of merchant ships in the river were as thick as trees in a forest. On land the gleaming white walls of houses were surrounded by trees. Flags of all countries fluttered in the wind, as befitted this great Eastern emporium. Farther away from the river were the streets and shops of the Chinese. At the centre was the old walled city.

September 3rd. Fine.

In the morning we visited the walled city, which, we were told, dates to the time of Sun Ch'üan of Wu [182–251]. The outer wall is made of bricks and is encircled by a narrow moat. Inside the wall are streets, shops and markets. The streets are so narrow that in many places only three people can walk side-by-side. Long rows of shops offer a variety of goods for sale, and the crowds milling around give the area the appearance of a bees' nest or an ant-hill. There are no sewers, and urine flows along the streets. Amid all this, the inhabitants seem quite unconcerned.

The bustle and gaiety of the Ch'eng-huang Temple was like that of the temple in Asakusa in Tokyo. There were all kinds of shops and many stalls selling bonsai. A love of flowers is customary among the Chinese. Flowers are regarded as the most luxurious adornment for a woman, and women may spend as much as five or ten yen on flowers for their hair. They take pride in wearing fresh flowers every day. Since courtesans of the highest class wear fresh flowers, the amount they spend on their personal adornment is very high. The Chinese word for 'courtesan' consists of two Chinese characters, one meaning 'singing' and the other 'dancing'. These are women whose occupation is to entertain guests at banquets by singing and dancing, after which they return to their brothels and share their beds. There were many houses of prostitution. There were also many shops selling antiques and paintings. The antiques were inferior and the paintings crude; both were of little worth. The shop-keepers are probably even craftier than those in Japan. It is said that famous paintings, calligraphic works and antiques can be found more easily in Japan. There were numbers of bookshops, mostly stocking superficial commentaries on the Confucian classics and historical works. There were also many works of fiction and humorous books.

In the past the Japanese have failed to inform themselves about foreign lands. They imagined the voyage across the narrow strip of water to Shanghai to be immense, and they regarded every Chinese to be a refined gentleman well versed in literature and the arts. Thus, the custom still persists of holding any curios, calligraphy, paintings, poetry or literature from China in high esteem. In recent years a constant stream of dealers from Kyoto and the adjacent Osaka–Kobe region have been travelling to China and bringing back inferior articles they have bought, turning a profit by hoodwinking literary gentlemen with a taste for antiquities and literature. This is especially deplorable. Under the Ch'ing dynasty [1644–1912], learning has long been stagnant in China, and even men who have gained fame are not always worthy of being revered for their artistic accomplishments. How much less should we value vulgar poetry and street curios! There is much here to reflect on for those who admire China and take the high reputation of its products at face value.

This evening Ch'en Fu-hsün, the governor of Shanghai, invited us to a banquet. The food was Chinese. Bird's nest soup was served, along with seventeen or eighteen other dishes, including dried *bêche-de-mer*, kelp, eggs, poultry and pork. We ate with bamboo chopsticks and porcelain spoons. It was neither Western nor Japanese in style, but had an altogether different flavour.

After the meal, on our way back to the hotel, we saw a theatrical performance. The musical instruments were extremely crude and the actors' make-up was clumsy. Some of the costumes, it is true, were more beautiful than those of Japan, but the actors, the stage, the properties and the stage machinery were all of an inferior level. The music consisted of ringing bells and hitting pieces of wood together, producing nothing but a discordant clamour, with hardly an elegant note in it.

September 4th. Rain.
We travelled three miles or so down the Shen River to visit a shipyard. We were welcomed by Feng Chün-kuang, the superintendent of the yard. He invited us into his house, where we chatted pleasantly for a while. He then showed us round the various sections, all equipped with the expected machinery. In its early days the yard had been run by twelve British men, as well as some Chinese who had been overseas to learn factory management. Over the years the Chinese had become more skilled, and now the entire management is in their hands. The government provided a subvention of $42,500 a month. Inside there was a school where British, American and German teachers were employed as instructors. This one yard was capable of carrying out any kind of work, from ship repair to ship construction. Most of the coal and iron was imported from Britain, and Japanese coal was also used.

September 5th. Rain at first; fine later.
At ten o'clock we set sail down the Huang-p'u River. At eleven we reached the mouth of the Yangtze. The tides along the coast are coloured yellow by the waters of the Huang-ho and the Yangtze, so it is not misleading to speak of the 'Yellow Sea'. Throughout the day, the sea we sailed on was indeed yellow; only at dusk did it become blue.

We saw nothing of note during the whole day. In the middle of the night we saw the mountains of the Gotō Islands.

September 6th. Fine.
We passed the islands of Iōjima and Kamishima, and at eight o'clock we reached Nagasaki. All the islands, large and small, at the entrance to the harbour have splendid mountains; all the peaks, near and far, are magnificent. As the ship proceeded it seemed as though it was the islands which were gliding past. At every moment a new scene revealed itself. The beauties of the harbour fully justify the epithet 'Jade Anchorage'. Even the islands off Singapore and Hong Kong fell far short of this. It is one of the finest landscapes in the world. We disembarked and, after resting a while at the Imperial Guesthouse, toured the city. In the evening we embarked and at one o'clock we set sail.

September 7th. Fine.
At dawn we passed the small harbour of Yobuko, near Karatsu; in the afternoon we passed through the Shimonoseki Channel. The sun set when we were off Suō [in Yamaguchi Prefecture].

September 8th. Fine.
The captain had the passengers woken at five in the morning because we were now passing through the most beautiful scenery in the world, the Geibi Strait. One or two of the American and British passengers, filled with admiration for the beauty of the scenery since Nagasaki, spent the whole day drawing and painting.

September 9th. Fine.
In the afternoon we reached Kobe, where we went ashore and took rooms at an inn.

September 10th. Fine.
We remained in Kobe all day.

September 11th. Fine.
In the afternoon we went on board and the ship sailed.

September 13th. Fine.
In the morning we arrived at Yokohama.

# Index